ASCENT®
CENTER FOR TECHNICAL KNOWLEDGE

Autodesk® Inventor® 2026 Introduction to Solid Modeling

Part 1

Learning Guide

Mixed Units - Edition 1.0

ASCENT - Center for Technical Knowledge®
Autodesk® Inventor® 2026
Introduction to Solid Modeling - Part 1
Mixed Units - Edition 1.0

Prepared and produced by:

ASCENT Center for Technical Knowledge
630 Peter Jefferson Parkway, Suite 175
Charlottesville, VA 22911

866-527-2368
www.ASCENTed.com

Lead Contributor: Jennifer MacMillan

ASCENT - Center for Technical Knowledge (a division of Rand Worldwide Inc.) is a leading developer of professional learning materials and knowledge products for engineering software applications. ASCENT specializes in designing targeted content that facilitates application-based learning with hands-on software experience. For over 25 years, ASCENT has helped users become more productive through tailored custom learning solutions.

We welcome any comments you may have regarding this guide, or any of our products. To contact us please email: feedback@ASCENTed.com.

AS-INV2601-ISM1MU-SG1 // IS-INV2601-ISM1MU-SG1

Contents

Preface

Autodesk® Inventor® 2026: Introduction to Solid Modeling (Part 1 and Part 2) provides you with an understanding of the parametric design philosophy through a hands-on, practice-intensive curriculum. You will learn the key skills and knowledge required to design models using Autodesk Inventor, starting with conceptual sketching, through to solid modeling, assembly design, and drawing production.

Topics Covered in Chapters 1 to 15 (Part 1)

- Understanding the Autodesk Inventor software interface
- Creating, constraining, and dimensioning 2D sketches
- Creating and editing the solid base 3D feature from a sketch
- Creating and editing secondary solid features that are sketched and placed
- Creating equations and working with parameters
- Manipulating the display of the model
- Resolving feature failures
- Duplicating geometry in the model

Topics Covered in Chapters 16 to 28 (Part 2)

- Placing and constraining/connecting parts in assemblies
- Manipulating the display of components in an assembly
- Obtaining model measurements and property information
- Creating presentation files (exploded views)
- Modifying and analyzing the components in an assembly
- Simulating motion in an assembly
- Creating parts and features in assemblies
- Creating and editing an assembly bill of materials
- Working with projects
- Creating and annotating drawings and views
- Customizing the Autodesk Inventor environment

Prerequisites

- Access to the 2026.0 version of the software, to ensure compatibility with this guide. Future software updates that are released by Autodesk may include changes that are not reflected in this guide. The practices and files included with this guide are not compatible with prior versions (e.g., 2025).
- As an introductory guide, *Autodesk Inventor 2026: Introduction to Solid Modeling* does not assume prior knowledge of any 3D modeling or CAD software. You need to be experienced with the Windows operating system, and having a background in drafting of 3D parts is recommended.

Note on Software Setup

This guide assumes a standard installation of the software using the default preferences during installation. Lectures and practices use the standard software templates and default options for the Content Libraries.

Note on Learning Guide Content

ASCENT's learning guides are intended to teach the technical aspects of using the software and do not focus on professional design principles and standards. The exercises aim to demonstrate the capabilities and flexibility of the software, rather than following specific design codes or standards, which can vary between regions.

Lead Contributor: Jennifer MacMillan

With a dedication for engineering and education, Jennifer has spent over 25 years at ASCENT managing courseware development for various CAD products. Trained in Instructional Design, Jennifer uses her skills to develop instructor-led and web-based training products as well as knowledge profiling tools.

Jennifer has achieved the Autodesk Certified Professional certification for Inventor and is also recognized as an Autodesk Certified Instructor (ACI). She enjoys teaching the training courses that she authors and is also very skilled in providing technical support to end-users.

Jennifer holds a Bachelor of Engineering Degree as well as a Bachelor of Science in Mathematics from Dalhousie University, Nova Scotia, Canada.

Jennifer MacMillan has been the Lead Contributor for *Autodesk Inventor: Introduction to Solid Modeling* since 2007.

In This Guide

The following highlights the key features of this guide.

Feature	Description
Practice Files	The Practice Files page includes a link to the practice files and instructions on how to download and install them. The practice files are required to complete the practices in this guide.
Chapters	A chapter consists of the following: Learning Objectives, Instructional Content, Practices, Chapter Review Questions, and Command Summary. • **Learning Objectives** define the skills you can acquire by learning the content provided in the chapter. • **Instructional Content**, which begins right after Learning Objectives, refers to the descriptive and procedural information related to various topics. Each main topic introduces a product feature, discusses various aspects of that feature, and provides step-by-step procedures on how to use that feature. Where relevant, examples, figures, helpful hints, and notes are provided. • **Practice** for a topic follows the instructional content. Practices enable you to use the software to perform a hands-on review of a topic. It is required that you download the practice files (using the link found on the Practice Files page) prior to starting the first practice. • **Chapter Review Questions**, located close to the end of a chapter, enable you to test your knowledge of the key concepts discussed in the chapter. • **Command Summary** concludes a chapter. It contains a list of the software commands that are used throughout the chapter and provides information on where the command can be found in the software.
Appendices	Appendices provide additional information to the main course content. It could be in the form of instructional content, practices, tables, projects, or skills assessment.

Practice Files

1. Type the URL *exactly as shown below* into the address bar of your Internet browser to access the Course File Download page.

   Note: If you are using the ebook, you do not have to type the URL. Instead, you can access the page by clicking the URL below.

   https://www.ascented.com/getfile/id/cardaminePF

2. On the Course File Download page, click the **DOWNLOAD NOW** button, as shown below, to download the .ZIP file that contains the practice files.

3. Once the download is complete, unzip the file and extract its contents.

   The recommended practice files folder location is:
   C:\Autodesk Inventor 2026 Intro Practice Files

   Note: It is recommended that you do not change the location of the practice files folder. Doing so may cause errors when completing the practices.

Stay Informed!

To receive information about upcoming events, promotional offers, and complimentary webcasts, visit:

www.ASCENTed.com/updates

Chapter 1

Introduction to Autodesk Inventor

Understanding how Autodesk® Inventor® models are built and how they react to change is fundamental when designing robust and intelligent models. In addition, learning the working environment is important. The environment consists of many different components, including toolbars, panels, and menus. Learning to interact with all of the components increases your modeling efficiency.

Learning Objectives

- Understand how the Part, Assembly, Presentation, and Drawing environments enable you to create and document a 3D digital prototype.
- Understand how the five key Inventor attributes contribute to creating robust parts and assemblies that can be easily documented.
- Load a project file.
- Open existing Autodesk Inventor files.
- Navigate the software interface to locate and execute commands.
- Use the model orientation commands to pan, zoom, rotate, and look at a model.
- Assign visual styles to your models.
- Use object selection techniques to efficiently select objects in your models.

1.1 Autodesk Inventor Introduction

The Autodesk Inventor software takes you beyond 3D to Digital Prototyping by providing a comprehensive set of tools for 3D mechanical design that enables you to design, visualize, and simulate products before they are built. Digital Prototyping helps you to minimize the need for physical prototypes, design better products, reduce development costs, and get to market faster.

There are a number of tools available to design models in the Autodesk Inventor software. To begin, you must start with a foundation in solid 3D part design. Then you progress to placing the models relative to one another in an assembly, followed by creating drawings that document the 3D parts and assembly models in a 2D format.

The following are the basic environments that are commonly used for 3D model design. Parts and assemblies are often referred to collectively as components, because of the similar manner in which they are treated. For example, a drawing file might reference either a part or another assembly file.

Environment (File Extension)	**Description**
Part (.IPT)	All part modeling, sketching, and complex design takes place on individual parts.
Assembly (.IAM)	Parts are added to assemblies to position and constrain them together to form a completed design. Parts are not stored in the assembly but their data is referenced from the original part model. The only modeling data stored in the assembly is the positional data that locates each part in the assembly.
Presentation (.IPN)	Used to document disassembled views in a drawing. Additionally, it can be used to animate tasks for visualization of component movement.
Drawing (.DWG & .IDW)	Used to communicate the 3D design in a 2D format. Views and annotations are used to document the design.

The part, assembly, and drawing files shown in Figure 1–1 illustrate how the original data created in the part model is passed to the assembly and finally used in a drawing to document a 3D design in a 2D format for manufacturing.

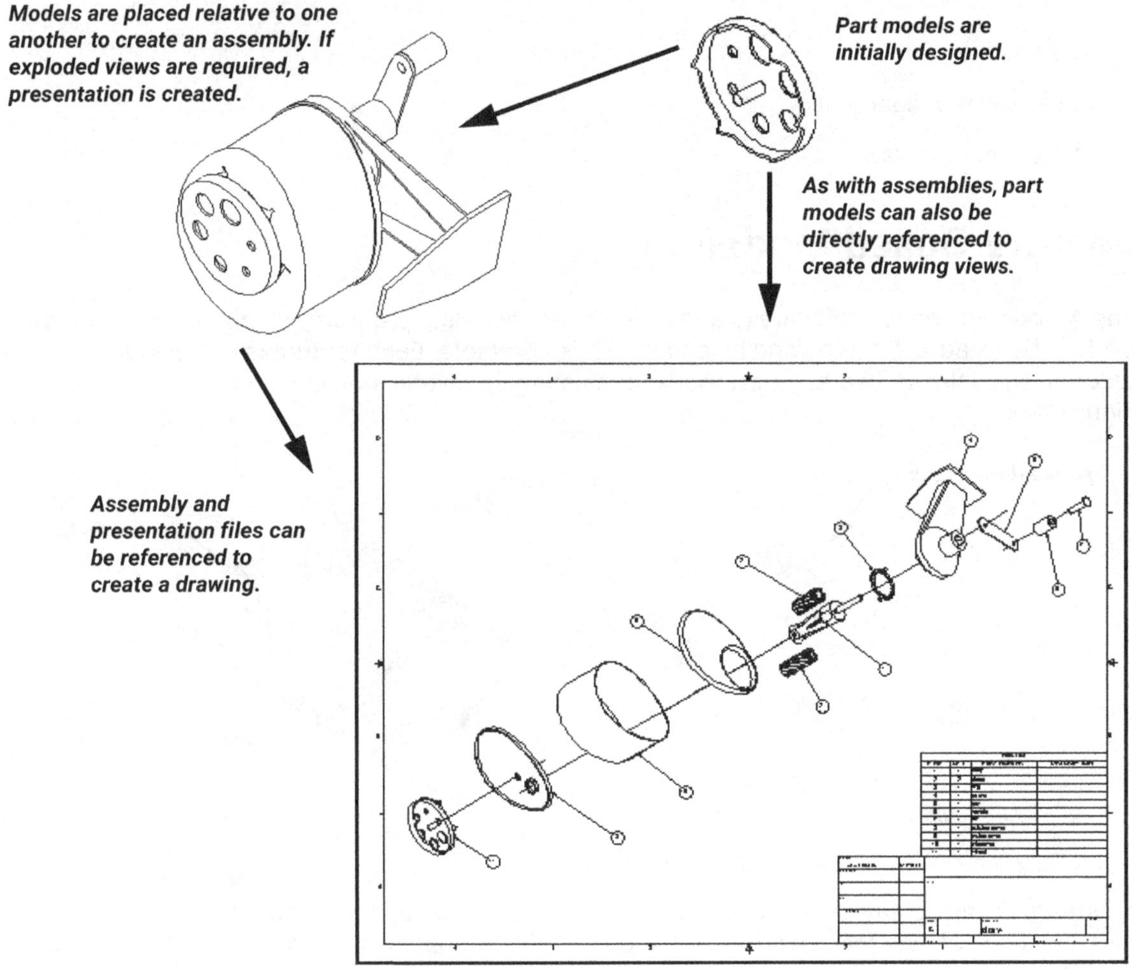

Figure 1–1

Hint: Autodesk Inventor and AutoCAD Interoperability

There are several ways to incorporate AutoCAD® DWG files in an Autodesk Inventor file. The method you use depends on your project requirements. You can open the file directly in the Autodesk Inventor software for review. You can also import and convert the AutoCAD DWG into an Inventor DWG file, where all links to the original AutoCAD DWG file are lost or you can use it as blocks in the Inventor drawing file. Alternatively, you can import and use an AutoCAD DWG as an associative underlay in an Autodesk Inventor file. These tools are discussed in detail in *Autodesk Inventor 2026: Advanced Part Modeling*.

The Autodesk Inventor software has the following five key attributes:

- Feature-Based Modeling
- Parametric Features
- Associative
- Assembly Management
- Model Documentation

Feature-Based Modeling

The Autodesk Inventor software is a feature-based modeling program, which means that a part evolves by creating features one by one until it is complete. Each feature is individually recognized by the software. A part model consisting of several individual features is shown in Figure 1–2.

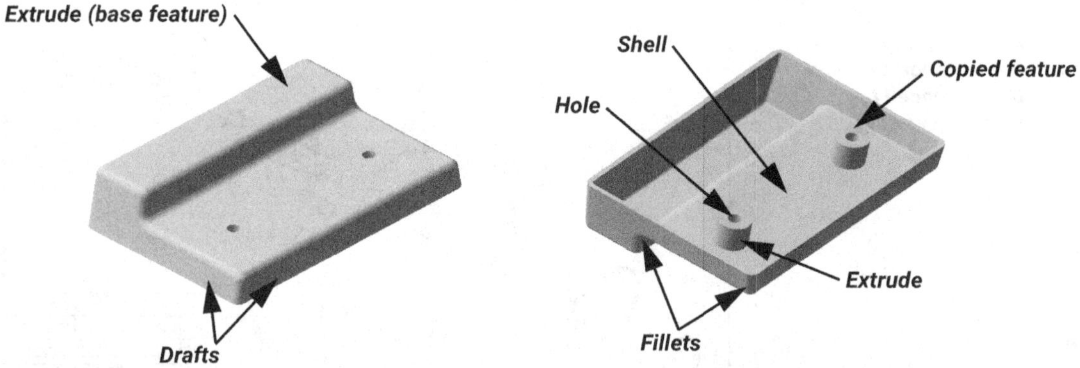

Figure 1–2

To start a design, create a simple extruded base feature that approximates the shape of the part. Continue adding features that add and remove material from the model until the part is complete, as shown in Figure 1–3.

1st (Base) Feature: Extrude

2nd Feature: Drafts

3rd Feature: Fillets

4th Feature: Shell

5th Feature: Extrude

6th Feature: Hole

7th Feature: Copy

Figure 1–3

Sketched Features

A sketched feature is created by sketching and constraining a 2D cross-section on a placement plane. Then, the profile is used to create solid geometry, similar to the extrusion shown in Figure 1–4. Sketched features can either add or remove material.

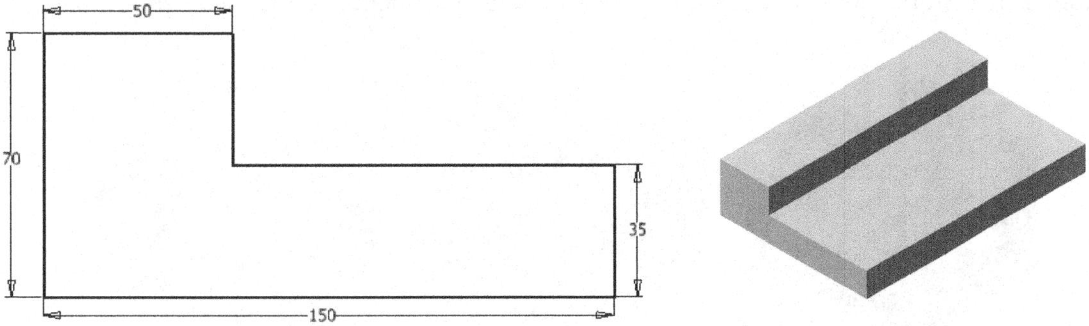

Figure 1–4

Pick and Place Features

A pick and place feature is a feature for which a shape has been predefined. For example, the cross-section of a Hole feature is a circle. To create a pick and place feature, you must define the location of the feature and the references required to locate it with respect to the existing geometry. An example of a pick and place Hole feature is shown in Figure 1–5.

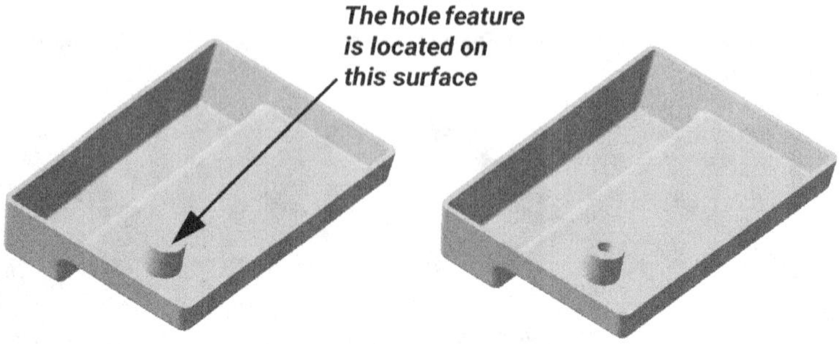

Figure 1–5

Feature Relationships

Feature-based modeling requires that features be added one by one. As a result, feature relationships are created as new features reference existing ones. For example, the hole shown above in Figure 1–5 cannot exist without the cylindrical extruded feature because the hole's placement references exist in the extrusion. Feature relationships are created with all features.

Parametric Features

Parametric features are features that are created using dimensional constraints to define the feature's shape. The dimensional constraints are considered parameters: changes can be made at any time, and the features automatically update.

For example, the dimensional value that positions the cut feature shown in Figure 1–6 is changed. Therefore, the position of the feature updates to reflect the design change.

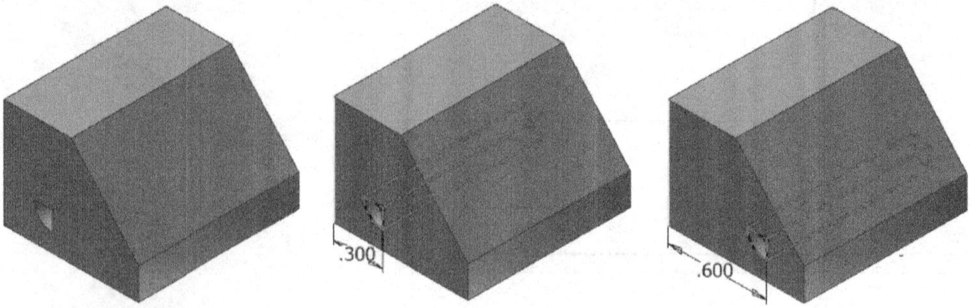

Figure 1–6

Dimensioning is an important step in the modeling process. When creating dimensions, use the following guidelines:

- Consider the dimensions that are going to be displayed in drawings and be aware of the resulting feature relationships.
- Consider changes that might need to be made to the model and how easily the dimensions facilitate these changes.
- Periodically modify dimensions to test *what if* scenarios. This is called *flexing the model* and ensures that the model behaves as expected.

Parameters and dimensions can be used in an equation to capture and control design intent. The ability to use equations in a model becomes extremely important in making a robust model.

Associative

The Autodesk Inventor software is fully associative, which means it operates in a concurrent engineering environment. You can work with the same model in different modes (e.g., Part, Assembly, or Drawing), and all modes are fully associative. Therefore, changes made to a model in any of the modes propagate to all other modes.

Assembly Management

Models built in Part mode can be used as components in an assembly. Assemblies are created by constraining components with respect to one another. The addition of constraints creates feature relationships between components and builds intelligent assemblies. Similar to features in Part mode, assembly constraints are assigned a unique internal identification number and can be used to establish relations between components.

Model Documentation

The tools available in the Drawing environment enable you to quickly create production-ready drawings for manufacturing. Drawings are created from part, assembly, or presentation models where their geometry and assembly specifications have already been defined. This information is used to create the required views in a drawing file. Adding details to your drawings enables you to communicate additional information about the design.

Drawing models are not actually contained in a drawing file. There is a link between the drawing file and the source model. If a change is made to the source model, all drawing views that reference it automatically update. The reverse, where a change made in the drawing also reflects in the model, can also be true if your workflow permits.

1.2 Getting Started with Inventor

Home Page

When you launch the Autodesk Inventor software, the *Home* page displays, as shown in Figure 1–7. This page enables you to activate a project file, create a new file, open files from the recently used list, or browse for a specific file and open it. Figure 1–7 displays the *Home* page with the default project active. Note that it does not show any previously opened files; as files are opened, they will appear in this list.

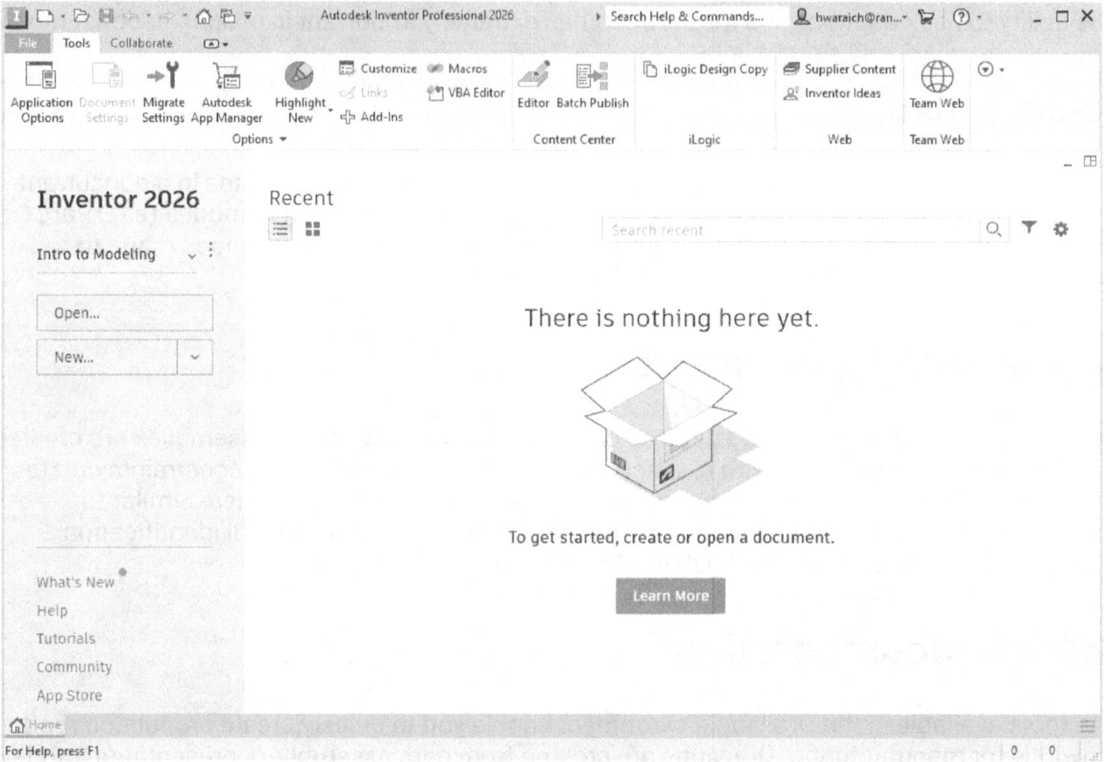

Figure 1–7

Hint: UI Theme

The **Dark** UI theme is now set as default for the software. This means that the background color of the interface and graphics window will be black or dark gray, and commands and tools will be lighter gray or white. This material uses the **Light** UI theme for printing clarity.

To change the UI theme to be as shown in Figure 1–7, click **Tools>** (Application Options), and on the *Colors* tab, change the *UI Theme* to **Light**. Also change the *In-canvas Color Scheme* to white by selecting the **Presentation** option, and change the *Background* to **1 Color**.

Opening Files

Files can be opened using a number of different methods in the Autodesk Inventor software. Use one of the following methods to open an existing file:

- On the *Home* page, select **Open**.
- Click (Open) in the Quick Access Toolbar at the top of the interface.
- In the **File** menu, select **Open>Open** or select a file from the *Recent* list.

For all but the recent document methods, the *Open* dialog box opens. Navigate to the required file, select it, and click **Open**. The (Find Files) button in the *Open* dialog box can also be used to find a file to be opened.

Hint: Home Tab

The *Home* tab is available even when files are open. To return to the *Home* page, select the *Home* tab at the bottom of the Inventor graphics window, as shown in Figure 1–8.

Figure 1–8

Recent List

The *Recent* area on the *Home* page lists previously opened files for the active project and enables you to open files directly from this list. List View ( ) displays the file names in a list format and Grid View ( ) displays the files as thumbnail images. Use any one of the following methods to open files in either view:

- Double-click on the files name or the thumbnail image.
- In List View, right-click on the file name and select **Open**. Alternatively, click adjacent to the Pinned column and select **Open**.
- In Grid View, hover over the thumbnail image, select , and select **Open**.

*Note: The **Open with options** option enables you to open specific model state or design view representations in the file. This will be discussed in a later section.*

Additional tools in the Recent list include:

- Sorting files by selecting column headers in the List View or selecting the **Sort by** option in the Grid View. These enable you to sort by **Name, Location**, or **Date Modified**.
- Clicking 📌 in the *Pinned* column in the List View or on the thumbnail image to add a recent document to the pinned list so that it is listed at the top of the list.
- If you are using the Autodesk Vault software, a file status column displays in the *Recent* area.

Hint: Controlling the number of Listed Recent Documents

By default, a maximum of 50 recent documents are listed in the *Recent* area of the *Home* page. To remove a file in List View, right-click on its file name and select **Remove from Recent**. Alternatively, in Grid View, hover over the thumbnail image, select ⋮, and select **Remove from Recent**. To change the default number of files, click **Tools>** (Application Options), and on the *General* tab, change the value for the **Maximum number of recent documents**.

Project Files

If you work as part of a design team, managing access to the shared Autodesk Inventor data is crucial. Incorporating project files enables you to organize and access the files that are used. A project file is a text file that has an .IPJ format. At a fundamental level, a project file specifies the locations of the files in the project and maintains all of the required links to the files. When you open a model, the paths specified in the active project are searched to find all of the referenced files. At a more advanced level, project files can specify library locations and set many options. Project files are discussed in more depth later in this guide.

How To: Load a Project File

1. Use one of the following methods to open the *Projects* dialog box to load a project:
   - On the *Home* page, select ⋮ (Projects and Settings)>**Settings**.
   - Click (Projects) in the Quick Access Toolbar at the top of the interface.
   - In the **File** menu, select **Manage>Projects**.
   - In the *New* or *Open* dialog boxes, click **Projects**.
2. Click **Browse** and navigate to the location of the project file. Select it and click **Open**. The *Projects* dialog box updates and a checkmark displays next to the new project name, indicating that it is the active project.
3. Click **Done** to close the *Projects* dialog box.

Once a project has been loaded it remains listed as an available project. A previously loaded project can be activated by:

- double-clicking on its name in the *Projects* dialog box, or
- expanding the *Projects* drop-down list (˅) on the *Home* page (as shown in Figure 1–9) and selecting the project name.

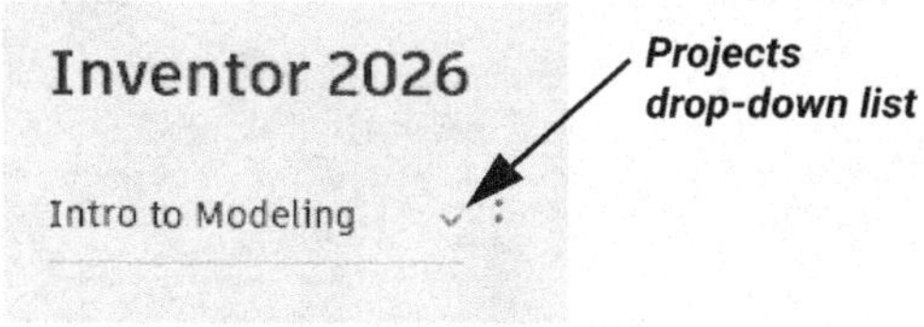

Figure 1–9

Additional options are available in the lower left corner of that *Home* page that enable you to review the What's New documentation for the latest software release, online Help and Tutorial documents, as well as links to the Inventor Community forum and App Store.

1.3 Autodesk Inventor Interface

Once a file has been opened, the interface updates to include additional elements. These are consistent among the various environments. The Part environment and many of the interface elements are shown in Figure 1–10.

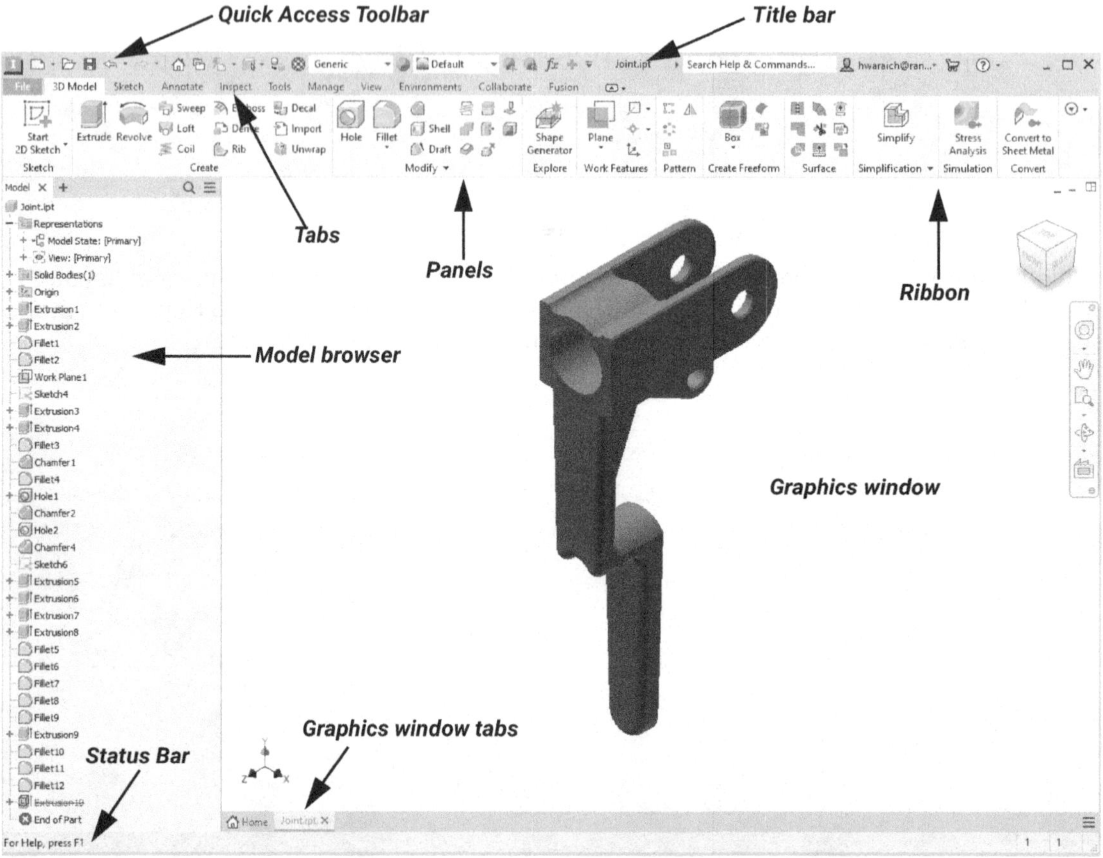

Figure 1–10

Interface

The following interface elements exist in the Part environment and the other Autodesk Inventor environments.

Title Bar

The title bar at the top of the interface displays the name of the current active file.

Ribbon/Tabs/Panels

The ribbon provides access to commands and settings. The ribbon is divided into tabs and they are further subdivided into panels. The tabs that are available vary depending on the mode that is currently active. All commands are listed in panels. Many commands can also be accessed by right-clicking on a feature in the model or in the Model browser. In Figure 1–11, the *3D Model* tab is active. *Sketch*, *Create*, and *Modify* are some of the panels in this tab.

Figure 1–11

- Commands can be hidden in either compressed panels or commands. To expand hidden commands, click ▾ on the panel or command name, as shown for the *Modify* panel and **Start 2D Sketch** command in Figure 1–12.

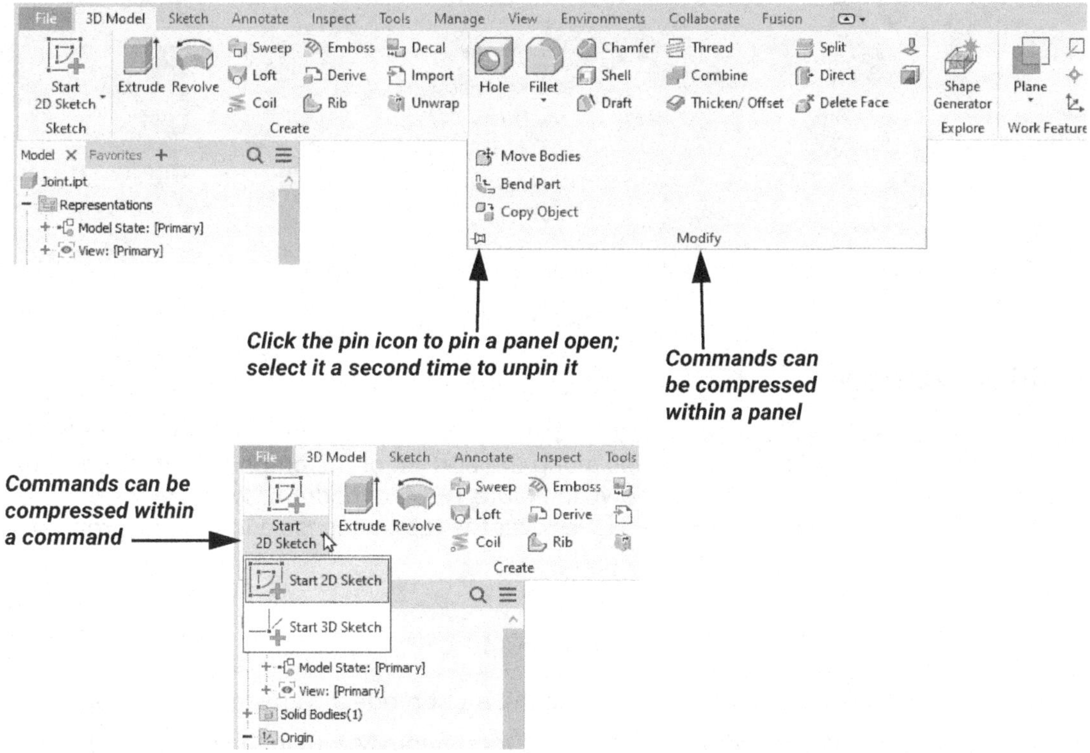

Figure 1–12

- Only commonly accessed panels display by default. To customize which panels display, expand (Show panels) at the end of each tab and select from the available list, as shown in Figure 1–13. Alternatively, you can right-click on the ribbon, expand **Show Panels**, and then select a panel.

Figure 1–13

Graphics Window

Open files are displayed and can be directly manipulated in the graphics window. As individual files are opened, they display listed as tabs along the bottom of the graphics window. Select a tab name to display it. In the example shown in Figure 1–14, a model, drawing, and *Home* tab are shown. The active model is **Joint.ipt**. Hover over the tab to access a thumbnail preview.

Figure 1–14

- Generally, maximizing each window provides the most modeling space. As required, you can minimize and resize windows, or click (Documents Menu) in the bottom right of the graphics window and use (Arrange), (Horizontal Tile), and (Vertical Tile) to customize your graphics window layout.

Quick Access Toolbar

Commonly accessed commands are available at the top of the software window in the Quick Access Toolbar, as shown in Figure 1–15.

Figure 1–15

- Click on the right of the Quick Access Toolbar to customize the toolbar. Alternatively, you can right-click on any command on the ribbon and select **Add to Quick Access Toolbar**.
- The selection filter in the Quick Access Toolbar enables you to filter entities, features, or components so that you can only select that type of object.
- The (*Undo*) and (*Redo*) drop-down lists provide you with a list of previously-completed actions that were performed on the model. To jump forward or back to a point in the model's history, select it in from the drop-down list.

Model Browser

The Model browser lists all of the features or components in your models, in order of creation. The Model browser is a powerful tool that can be used to complete any of the following actions:

- Select features.
- Access commonly used options (e.g., **Delete** or **Edit**).
- Search for features.
- Edit features.
- Display information on features.
- Change the order of features (click and drag).
- Open components in an assembly.
- Open drawings of components.
- Create drawings of parts and assemblies.
- Investigate relationships between features and components.

In the Model browser (shown in Figure 1–16), each feature is identified by its name and a symbol that identifies the feature type. Expandable nodes reveal additional information on the features.

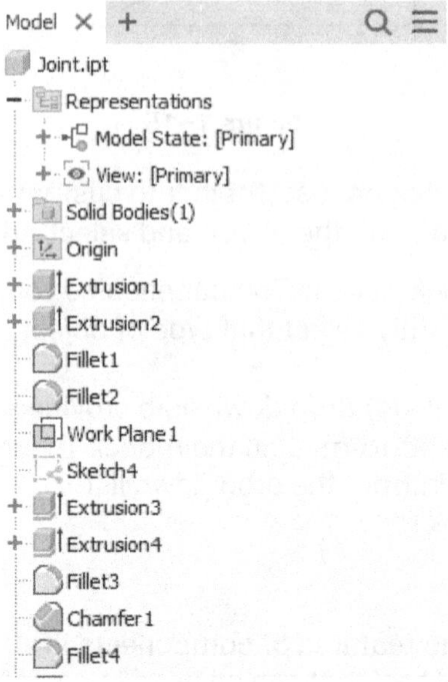

Figure 1–16

- The header of the Model browser indicates the active panel. Model is the panel that displays by default. Click + to expand the list of available panels.
    - For part models, you can activate the *iLogic* or *Favorites* panels.
    - For assemblies, you can activate the *iLogic*, *Favorites*, or *Representation* panels to help view model information.
    - For assemblies you can also toggle between an Assembly or Modeling view.
- Click the search icon in the Model browser header to access the quick search field. A search is conducted as you type in keywords. In an assembly model, the quick search also provides access to the two filter icons, which enable you to filter unresolved and out of date data respectively.
- Click the menu icon in the Model browser header to access options to expand and collapse the browser nodes, conduct an advanced search, disable the ability to edit values in the Model browser (assemblies only), set display preferences, or access help.

__Note:__ The Model browser can be displayed or removed from the interface. To control its display, enable or disable it in the User Interface drop-down list (View tab>Windows panel).

Status Bar

The Status Bar displays messages that are related to the active command. For example, in a sketch, the Status Bar can display information related to sketching, dimensioning, and constraining an entity.

Modeling Tools

The marking menu and feature creation controls are commonly used in the design process.

Marking Menu

The marking menu provides alternative access to commands. When you right-click in the graphics window, a radial marking menu and a vertical menu display. Both menus provide quick access to commonly used, context-sensitive commands.

- The marking menu consists of eight wedges that contain different commands. To activate a marking menu command, move the cursor in the direction of the command so that it is highlighted (as shown on the right in Figure 1–17) and select it.

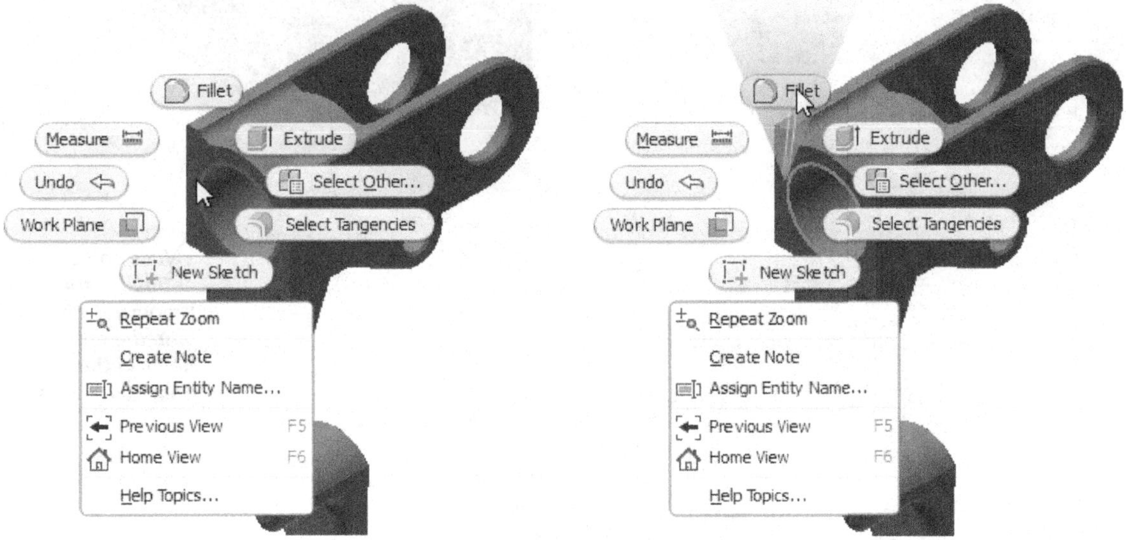

Figure 1–17

- As you become familiar with the marking menu commands, you can use gesturing behavior to initiate commands. To gesture, click and hold the right mouse button, immediately drag the cursor in the direction of the required marking menu wedge to create a trail, and release the mouse button. If these operations are completed in 250 milliseconds, the selected wedge is briefly displayed to confirm that the operation has been performed.

- To close the marking menu, you can start another command, select away from the marking menu, or press <Esc>.

*Note: The marking menu can be customized using the **Customize** option in the Tools tab. This is covered later in this guide.*

Feature Creation Controls

When you create a feature, you must define a variety of properties. Depending on the feature type being created, you can define these using the *Properties* panel, a feature dialog box, or the mini-toolbar.

- In the example shown in Figure 1–18, a Hole feature is being created and it uses the *Properties* panel to define all the hole properties. Dimensional values and references can also be defined directly on the model geometry.

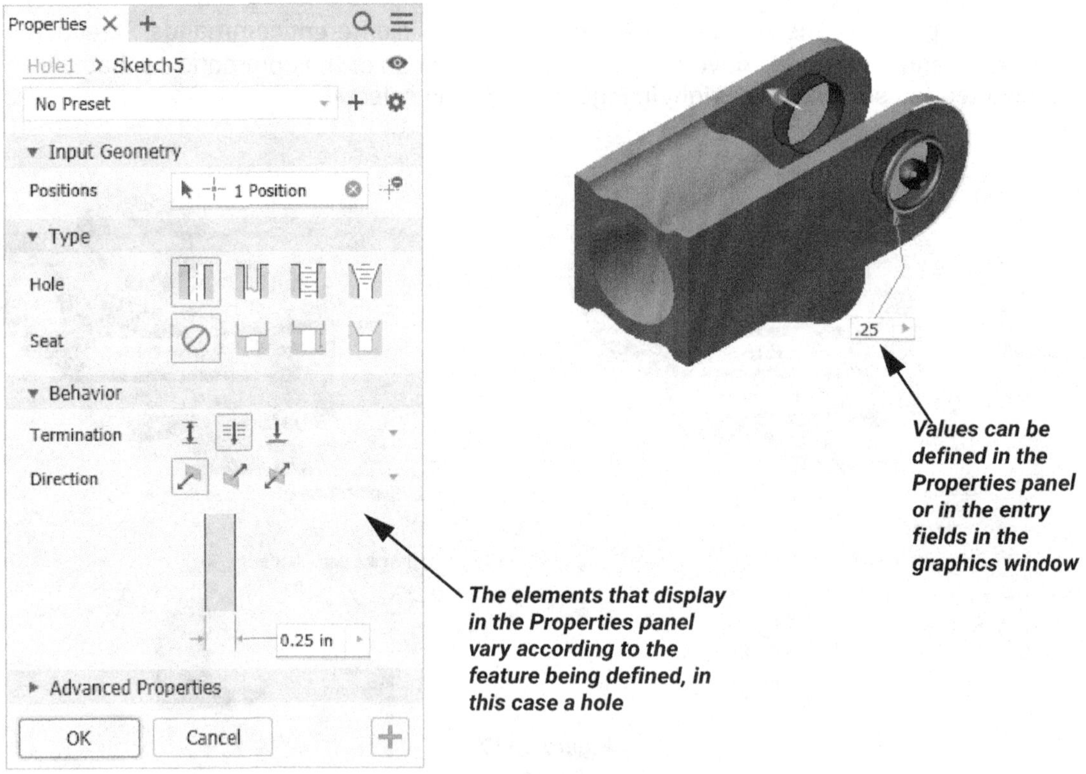

Figure 1–18

Note: Autodesk is slowly transitioning all feature creation controls to the Properties panel interface. As of the 2026 Inventor release, this has not yet been completed.

- In the example shown in Figure 1–19, a Chamfer feature is being created and the *Chamfer* dialog box and its mini-toolbar are displayed. Options can be selected in either location.

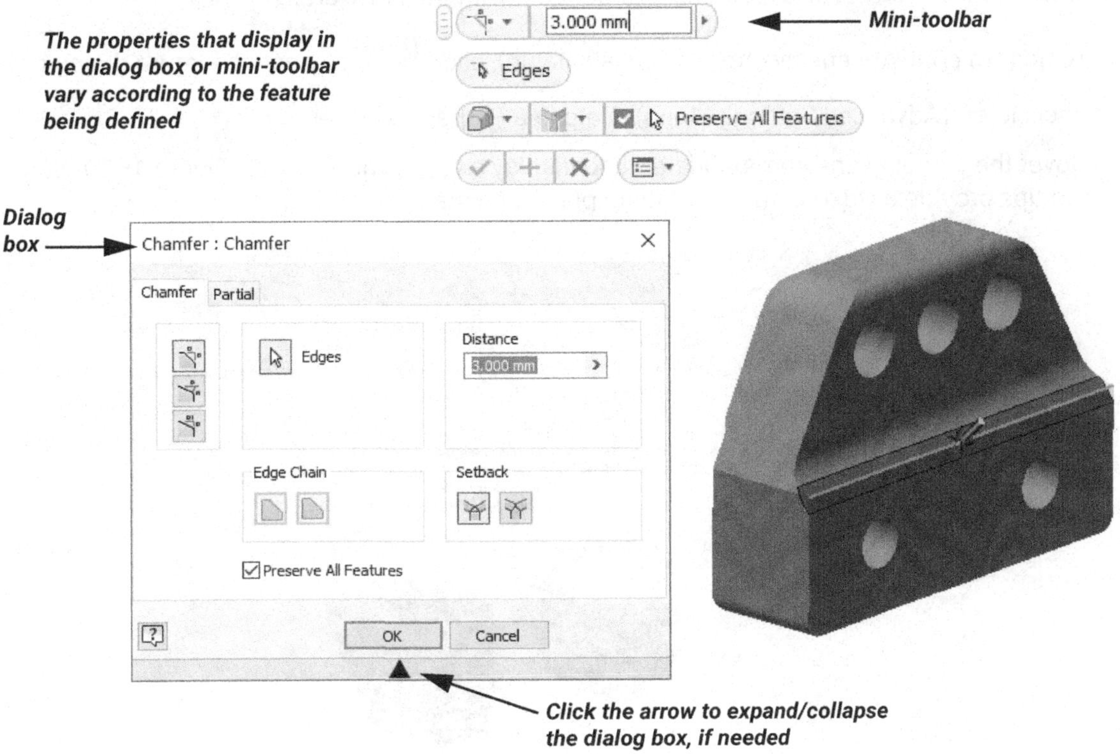

Figure 1–19

Hint: Mini-Toolbar Display

By default, the display of the mini-toolbar is toggled off. To toggle on its display, on the *View* tab, expand **User Interface** and enable the **Mini-Toolbar** option in the list of interface items. The use of the mini-toolbar is optional. In this guide, you will toggle it on and learn how to use it. The mini-toolbar is only available for features that use a feature dialog box. They are not available when creating features that use the *Properties* panel.

Accessing Help

A number of different tools are available to get help with the software:

- To access context-sensitive help (when available), click in any active feature dialog box or click (Advanced Settings Menu)>**Help** in a *Properties* panel.
- Hover the cursor over a command name to display a tooltip, as shown in Figure 1–20. Some tooltips provide a video demonstration in place of a static image.

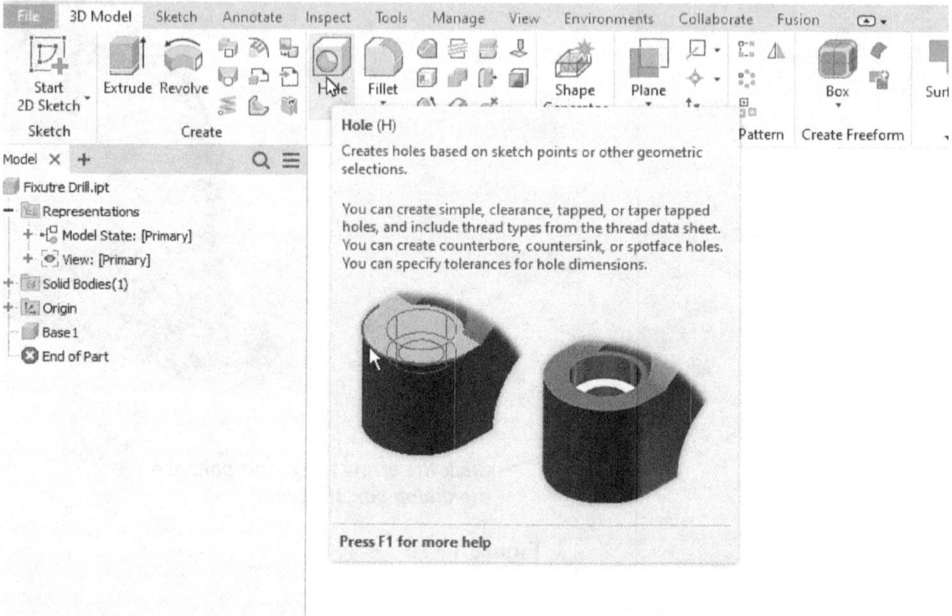

Figure 1–20

- If connected to the Internet, you can use Online Help. To access the Help documentation, click (Help) in the top-right corner of the interface, click **Help** on the *Home* page, or press <F1>. Use the *Search* tab to enter a topic to search for or browse the available topics in the Help window.
- The Help documents can be installed locally. This installation is done in the software load point to ensure that it located when required. Once installed, in the *Application Options* dialog box>*General* tab, enable **Installed Local help**. A link to download the files is included in this same location.
- Enter text in the *<Search Help & Commands>* field in the title bar to search for a keyword or phrase. The resulting list updates as you are typing and is divided based on the type of the result (e.g., commands, help articles, support articles, discussion groups, etc). If you press <Enter> after entering a keyword or phrase, the Help files are loaded.

1.4 Model Orientation

When working with Autodesk Inventor models, being able to manipulate their orientation and display style helps you to better visualize them. The interface elements that control this are shown in Figure 1–21.

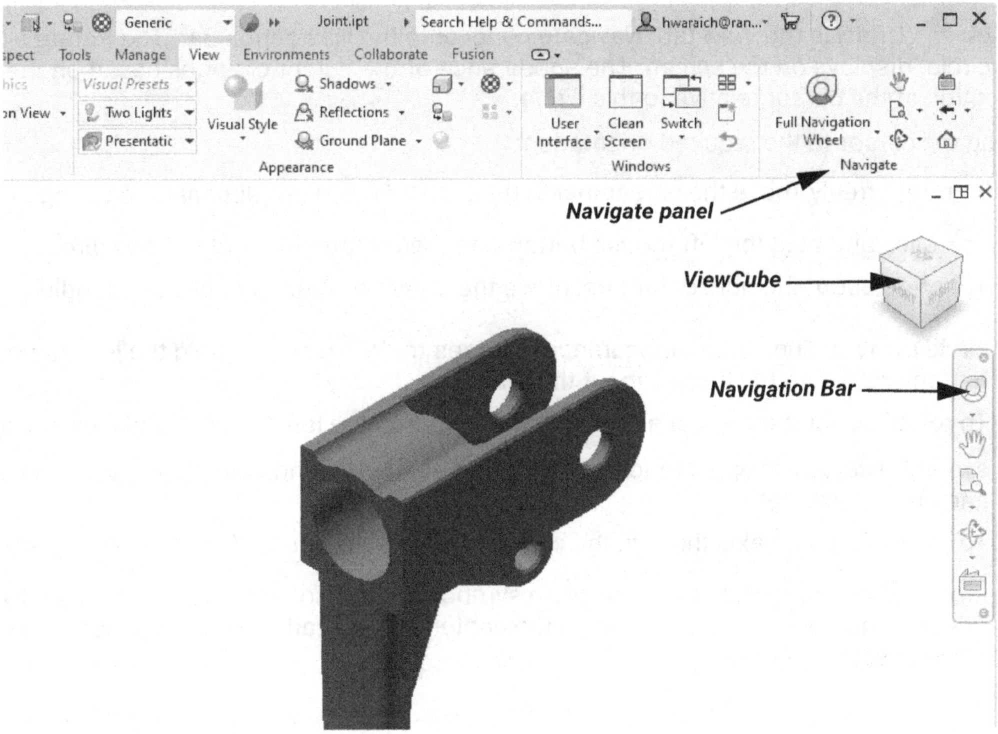

Figure 1–21

A model can be oriented using the software's pan, zoom, rotate and ViewCube controls.

Pan a Model

The **Pan** command moves a model in the graphics window in any direction planar to the screen.

How To: Pan a Model

1. Click  (Pan) in the *View* tab>*Navigate* panel or in the Navigation Bar.
2. Press and hold the left mouse button.
3. Move the mouse to drag the model.

Note: *You can also pan a model by pressing and holding the middle mouse button while dragging the mouse, or by holding <F2> and panning with the left mouse button.*

Rotate a Model

The **Orbit** command rotates a model around the center of the window, free in all directions, or around the X- or Y-axis.

How To: Rotate a Model

1. Click (Orbit) in the *View* tab>*Navigate* panel or in the Navigation Bar. The Rotate symbol (a circle) displays on the screen. The appearance of the cursor changes based on the location of the cursor relative to this circle.
2. Drag the cursor to the required orientation.
   - To rotate freely, move the cursor inside the circle. The cursor appearance changes to . Click and hold the left mouse button and then rotate the model in any direction.
   - To rotate about the horizontal axis, move the cursor to the top or bottom handle of the circle symbol. The cursor appearance changes to . Press and hold the left mouse button and rotate the model about the Y-axis.
   - To rotate about the vertical axis, move the cursor to the left or right handle of the circle symbol. The cursor appearance changes to . Press and hold the left mouse button and drag horizontally.
   - To rotate about an axis through the center of the circle symbol (normal to the screen), move the cursor to the rim of the circle symbol. The cursor appearance changes to . Drag the mouse to rotate. To change the center of the rotation, click inside or outside the circle to set the new center.
   - To stop rotating, click again to clear it. Alternatively, while still in the orbit circle, move the cursor away from the model until displays, and click in the graphics window.

   Note: *You can also press and hold <F4> to rotate using the rotate symbol.*

As an alternative to using the (Orbit) tool, you can press and hold <Shift> and use the middle mouse button to rotate the model. Using this method, the model is rotated about a pivot point that appears in the graphics window. Where the pivot point will appear on the model depends on the following:

- If the full model displays in the graphics window, the pivot point is the model geometry center.
- If the model is only partially displayed in the graphics window, the pivot point snaps to the nearest edge/face/vertex.
- If the model is fully panned outside the graphics window, the pivot point is at the cursor location.

Zoom a Model

The **Zoom** command zooms in and out on the model, on a specific entity, or on an area. The available zoom types are shown in Figure 1–22.

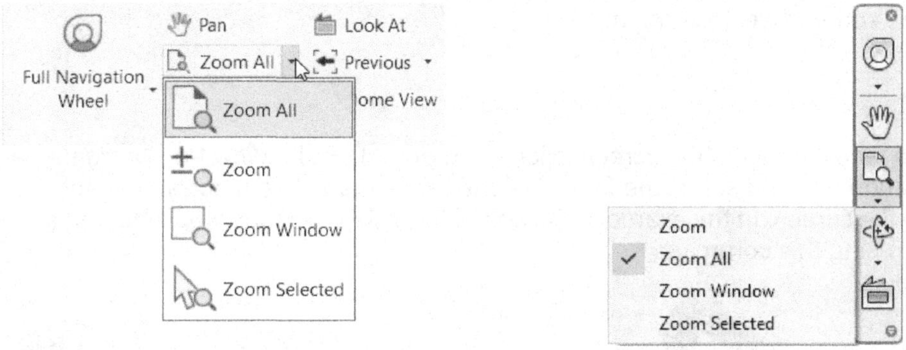

Figure 1–22

How To: Zoom in a Model

1. In the *View* tab>*Navigate* panel or the Navigation Bar, expand the zoom controls and click **Zoom**.
2. Press and hold the left mouse button.
3. Move the cursor down to zoom in, and up to zoom out.

Note: *You can also press and hold <F3> to zoom.*

How To: Zoom to a Specific Entity

1. In the *View* tab>*Navigate* panel or the Navigation Bar, expand the zoom controls and click **Zoom Selected**.
2. Select a location to zoom to on the model.

- Alternatively, to zoom to a specific entity or feature, select the item first directly in the graphics window or in the Model browser and then select **Zoom Selected**.

How To: Zoom to an Area

1. In the *View* tab>*Navigate* panel or the Navigation Bar, expand the zoom controls and click **Zoom Window**.
2. Select a location on the model using the left mouse button to define the corner of the bounding box zoom area.
3. Drag the mouse to draw a box over the area to zoom.
4. Press or release the left mouse button when the box has been drawn.

Refit the Model

In the *View* tab>*Navigate* panel or the Navigation Bar, expand the zoom controls and click **Zoom All**. The view returns to its default zoom level and the model is centered in the graphics window. As an alternative to using the **Zoom All** command in the Navigation Bar, you can also double-click on the scroll wheel to zoom all.

Look At

To orient a face parallel to the screen, click (Look At) in the *View* tab>*Navigate* panel or in the Navigation Bar, and select the face. The model reorients and displays the selected face parallel to the screen. In the example shown in Figure 1–23, a face was selected and was reoriented using this command.

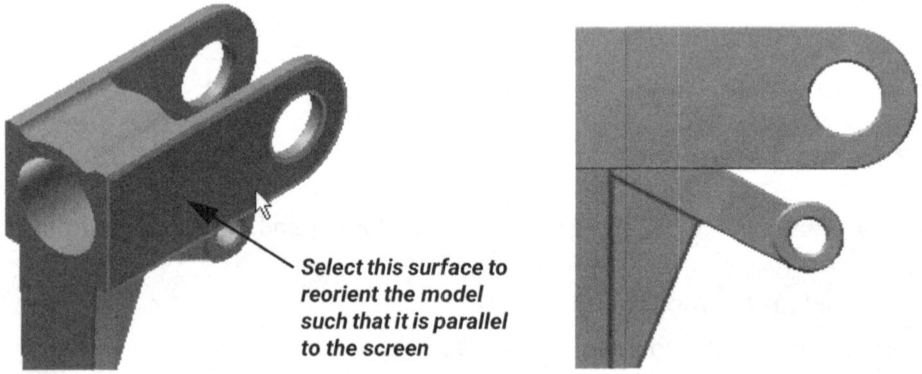

Figure 1–23

ViewCube

As an alternative to the **Look At** command, you can use ViewCube functionality to orient a model face parallel to the screen. By default, the ViewCube displays in the top-right corner of the graphics window, as shown on the left in Figure 1–24. When you hover your mouse over the ViewCube in its 2D or 3D orientation, you can return to the Home view or access additional orientation options.

Figure 1–24

The ViewCube enables the following:

- Select any of the sides of the cube to display the parallel view that is associated with it (**Front**, **Right**, **Bottom**, etc.). Edges can also be selected on the ViewCube to reorient the model.
- Set the type of view to **Orthographic**, **Perspective**, or **Perspective with Ortho Faces** by right-clicking on the ViewCube and selecting the required option.
- Return to a Home view by clicking , which displays at the top-left of the ViewCube when you hover the cursor over it. Initially the Home view is the default isometric orientation.
- Set a new Home view for your model by right-clicking on the ViewCube and selecting **Select Current View as Home**.
- Select and drag a surface on the ViewCube to rotate. If in a 2D orientation, select the rotation arrows that appear.

*Note: To display the ViewCube settings, right-click on it and select **Options**. The ViewCube Options dialog box enables you to control the location, size, default ViewCube orientation, etc. The orientation enables you to select two parallel origin planes to define the orientation.*

Full Navigation Wheel

The Full Navigation Wheel (shown in Figure 1–25) provides an alternative to the *View* tab and Navigation Bar commands for zooming, panning, and rotating. The **Rewind** command on the wheel enables you to navigate through previous views.

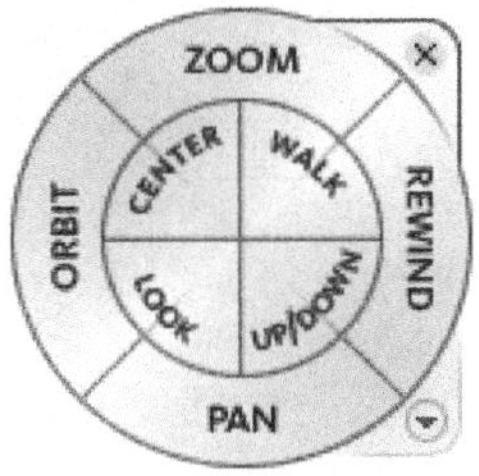

Figure 1–25

The Full Navigation Wheel moves with the cursor to provide access to the navigation tools.

How To: Use the Navigation Tool

1. Enable the tool by clicking (Full Navigation Wheel) in the *View* tab>*Navigate* panel or in the Navigation Bar. The Full Navigation Wheel displays attached to the mouse.
2. Press and hold the mouse on a command (e.g., **Zoom**).
3. Move the cursor to change the view as required.
4. Release the mouse button to end the navigation command.
5. Click or the **x** in the top-right corner of the tool to close the Full Navigation Wheel.

   Note: *In addition to the* ***Zoom****,* ***Orbit****,* ***Pan****, and* ***Rewind*** *commands, other more advanced tools are available on the inner ring of the Full Navigation Wheel that are not covered in this guide.*

1.5 Model Display

By default, new models created using the default templates display as **Shaded with Edges**. However, other visual styles can be assigned. All visual styles are available in the *View* tab> *Appearance* panel, as shown in Figure 1–26.

> **Note:** *The ability to use many of the styles depends on your computer's graphics hardware.*

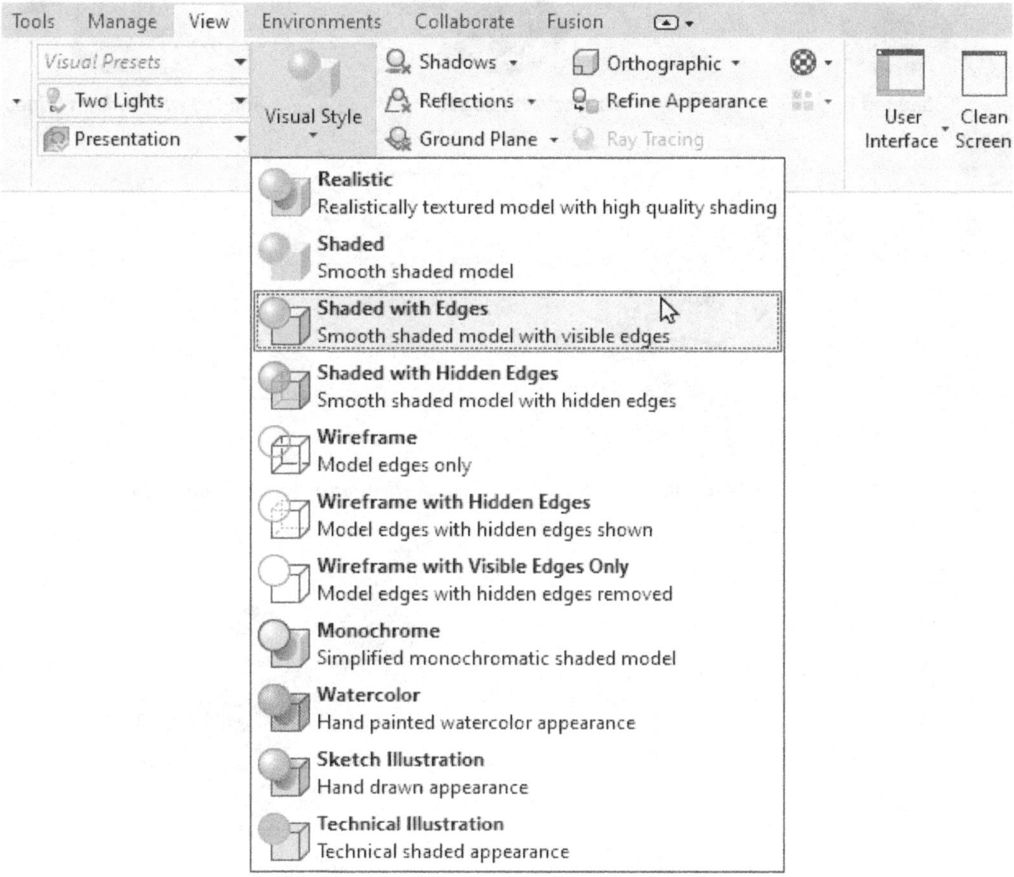

Figure 1–26

> **Note:** *The* **Realistic** *setting is dependent on the color and lighting settings that are applied in the model. When using this style you can also incorporate Ray Tracing to further enhance model display. Additionally, the watercolor and illustration settings provide artistic, hand-painted, and drawn representations of the model.*

Figure 1–27 shows some examples of the available visual styles.

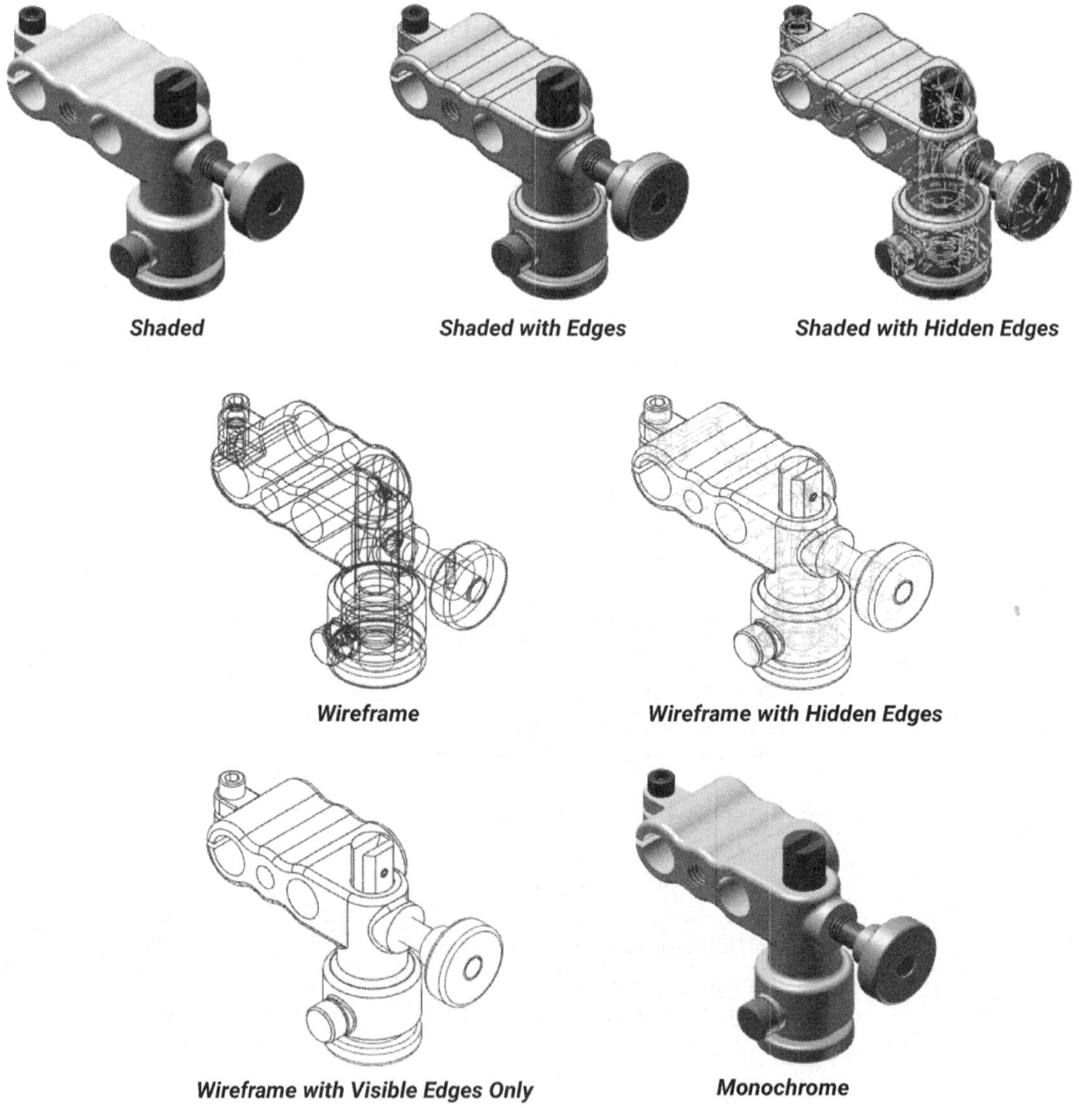

Shaded ***Shaded with Edges*** ***Shaded with Hidden Edges***

Wireframe ***Wireframe with Hidden Edges***

Wireframe with Visible Edges Only ***Monochrome***

Figure 1–27

1.6 Selection Techniques

Sketched Entity Selection

There are several ways to select sketched entities for editing. Consider using any of the following:

- To select an individual object in a sketch, select it using the left mouse button.
- To add additional objects to the selection set, hold <Ctrl> or <Shift> and left-click additional objects.
- Select and drag a boundary box from left to right around objects (as shown in Figure 1–28) to select them. Only objects that are entirely enclosed in the window are selected. This is called the Window Selection technique.

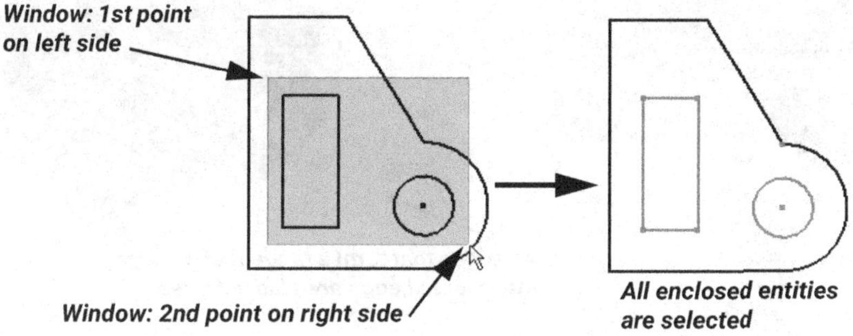

Figure 1–28

- Select and drag a boundary box from right to left around objects (as shown in Figure 1–29) to select them. Objects are selected if they are entirely enclosed in the window, or if any part of the object crosses the sketched border. This is called the Crossing Selection technique.

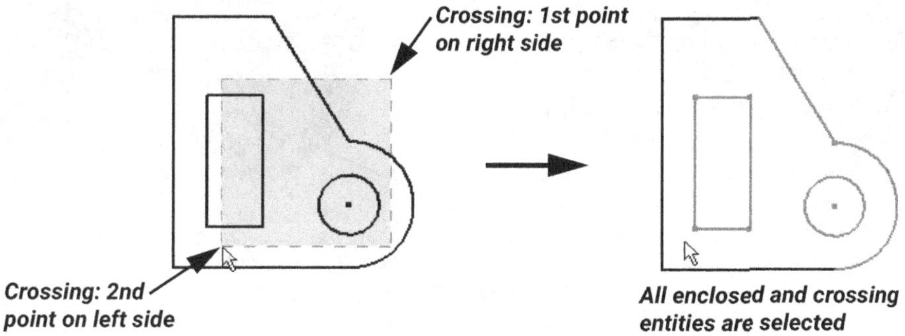

Figure 1–29

Note: *If you drag a boundary box in the wrong direction (i.e., start a window instead of a crossing), select a second point so that the sketched area is empty, and start again.*

- To clear objects, you can hold <Ctrl> or <Shift> and individually select entities, or use the window or crossing techniques to select entities. To clear all of the objects, click in a blank space in the graphics window.

Tangent Entity Selection

To select tangent entities (edges or faces) in a model, right-click on an entity and select **Select Tangencies**, as shown Figure 1–30. As an alternative to using the context menu to access the command, you can also double-click on the entity to quickly select all tangent entities.

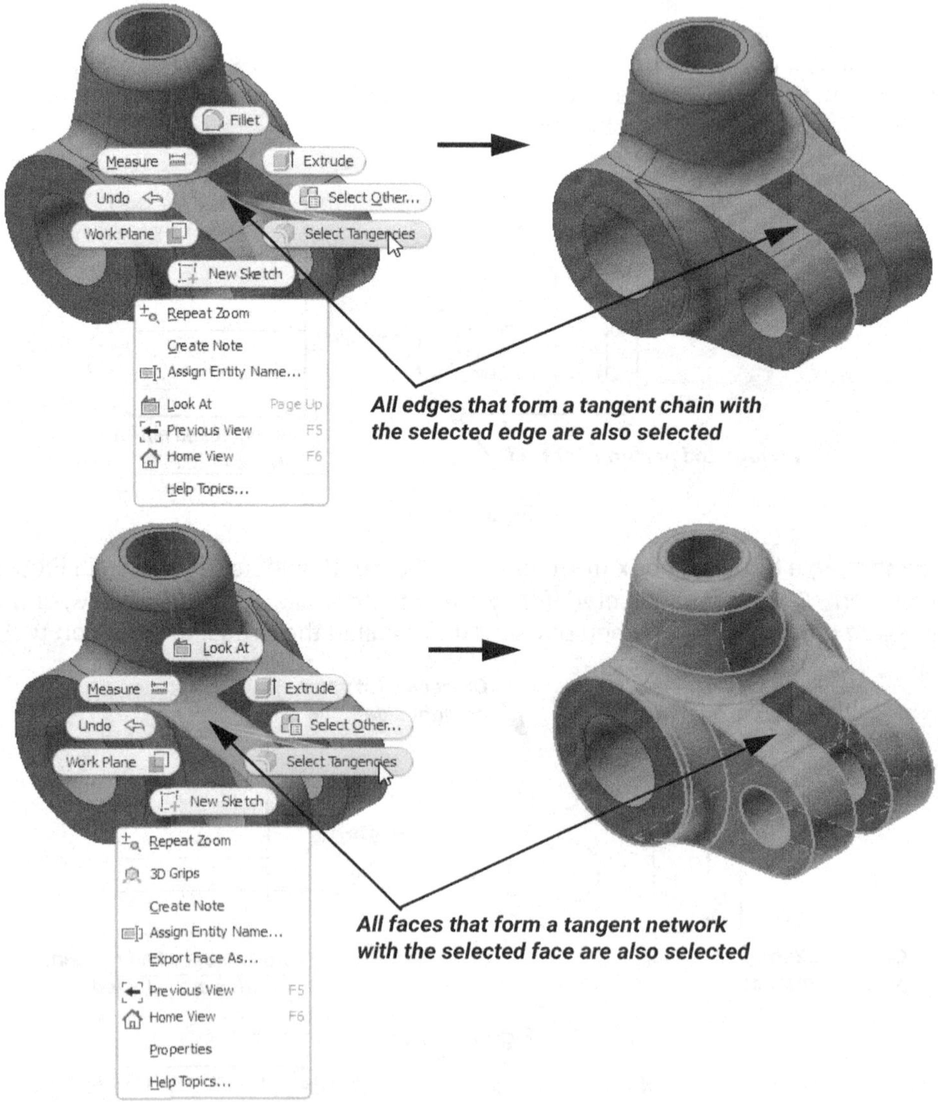

Figure 1–30

Selecting Hidden Entities or Features

To select hidden entities or features, hover the cursor over an object until a drop-down list displays, or right-click and select **Select Other** to open the drop-down list. The list displays all of the shown and hidden features and entities based on the current cursor location, as shown in Figure 1–31. Scroll through the drop-down list and select the required entity when it is highlighted. Alternatively, you can also use the middle mouse button to scroll through the shown and hidden features.

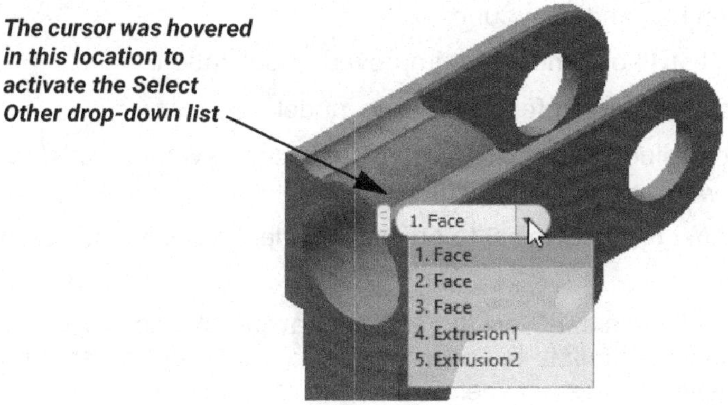

Figure 1–31

Selection Filter

The selection filter in the Quick Access Toolbar enables you to filter entities, features, or components so that you can only select that type of object. For example, if you select **Select Face and Edges**, you can only select the faces or edges on the model. The options that display in the drop-down list vary depending on the current mode. Part mode options display as shown in Figure 1–32. To quickly access the filter options without having to use the Quick Access Toolbar, press and hold <Shift> as you right-click in the main window.

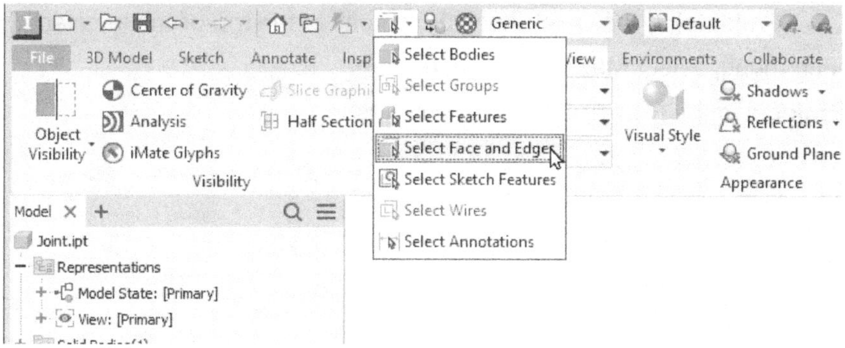

Figure 1–32

Practice 1a
Open and Manipulate a Part

Practice Objectives

- Open part and drawing files and navigate between them using the tabs at the bottom of the graphics window.
- Orient the model using the **Zoom**, **Pan**, **Rotate**, and **Look At** commands available in the ribbon, Navigation Bar, and ViewCube.
- Change the visual style of a model for improved visualization.
- Change the visibility status of features in the model.
- Modify dimension values and delete features associated with a model to verify associativity between a part and its drawing file.
- Use the *Select Other* drop-down list to efficiently select hidden features in a model.

In this practice, you will open and work in part and drawing files to learn the Autodesk Inventor interface. You will also manipulate the orientation of a model, delete, and modify features to learn about associativity of files between environments.

Task 1: Open a model.

1. If the Autodesk Inventor software is not already open, select **Start>All Programs>Autodesk Inventor 2026>Autodesk Inventor 2026**, or double-click on the **Autodesk Inventor 2026** icon on the desktop.
2. Project files identify the folders that contain the required models. Use one of the following methods to open the *Projects* dialog box to assign the project file:
   - On the *Home* page, select ⋮ (Projects and Settings)>**Settings**.
   - Click (Projects) in the Quick Access Toolbar at the top of the interface.
   - In the **File** menu, select **Manage>Projects**.
   - Click **Projects** in the *New* or *Open* dialog boxes.

3. Click **Browse**, navigate to *C:\Autodesk Inventor 2026 Intro Practice Files* (or the directory to which you extracted the practice files) and select **Intro to Modeling.ipj**. Click **Open**. The *Projects* dialog box updates and a checkmark displays next to the new project name, indicating that it is the active project. Click **Done**.
4. On the *Home* page, verify that the **Intro to Modeling** project is listed as the active project, as shown in Figure 1–33. Once a project has been loaded, you can use this drop-down list to activate an alternate (loaded) project file.

Figure 1–33

Hint: UI Theme

The **Dark** UI theme is now set as default for the software. This means that the background color of the interface and graphics window will be black or dark gray, and commands and tools will be lighter gray or white. This material uses the **Light** UI theme for printing clarity.

To change the UI theme to be as shown in this guide, click **Tools>** (Application Options), and on the *Colors* tab, change the *UI Theme* to **Light**. Also change the *In-canvas Color Scheme* to white by selecting the **Presentation** option, and change the *Background* to **1 Color**.

5. Use one of the following methods to open a new file:
   - On the *Home* page, click **Open**.
   - In the Quick Access Toolbar, click (Open).
   - In the **File** menu, select **Open>Open**.

   Note: *If the file extensions do not display, open File Explorer. Select* ***View>Options>Change Folder and search options****, select the View tab, and clear the* ***Hide extensions for known file types*** *option.*

6. Select **Joint.ipt** and click **Open**. The model geometry displays and the Model browser lists all of the features in the model, as shown in Figure 1–34.

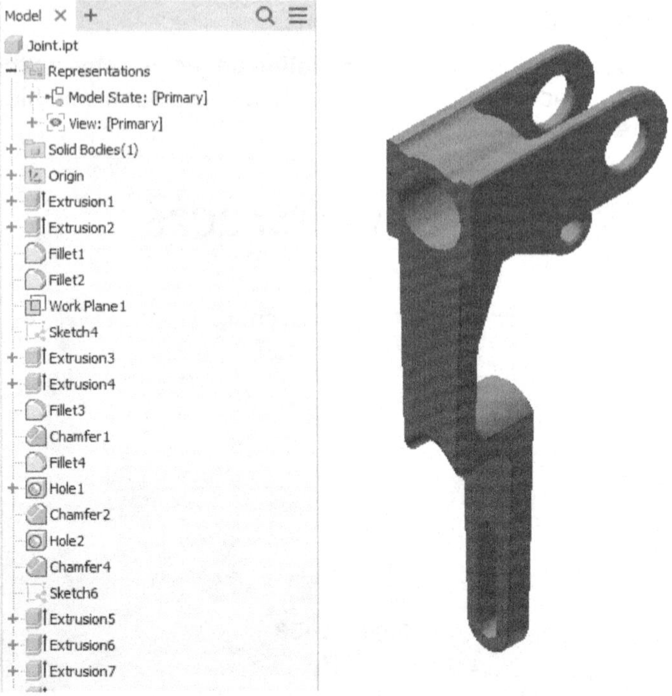

Figure 1–34

The model name displays in the header of the interface and at the top of the Model browser listing. Both names identify the model as a part (.IPT) file. The model consists of solid geometry and work features that were used as references in creating the solid geometry. In addition to the geometry and work features, there are nodes at the top of the Model browser that group the model's solid bodies, model states, and default origin features.

Task 2: Zoom in and out on the model using the Zoom command.

1. The *3D Model* tab is the active tab. Select the *View* tab at the top of the ribbon interface. The options in each tab are subdivided into panels to help you quickly find commands. Locate the *Navigate* panel. It contains all of the commands that you can use to manipulate the location and orientation of the model in the graphics window.

2. In the *Navigate* panel, click (Zoom), as shown in Figure 1–35. In some situations, similar commands are compressed in a panel and you must expand commands to access them.

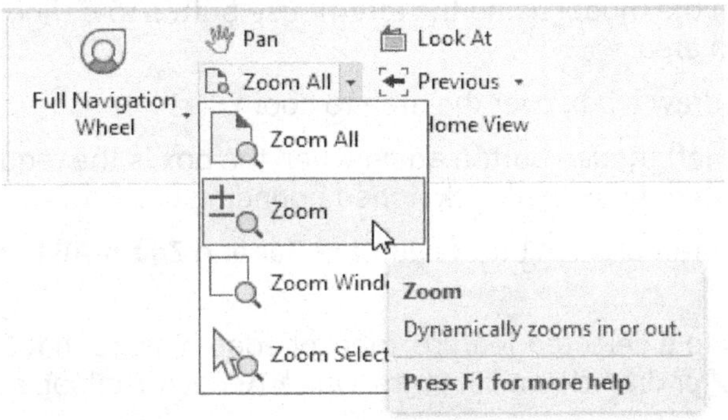

Figure 1–35

3. Move the cursor to the graphics window, click and hold the left mouse button, and move the mouse towards you to zoom in and away from you to zoom out.

4. Click (Zoom) again in the *Navigate* panel to toggle it off. You can also use the mouse scroll wheel to zoom in or out, when the Zoom option is not enabled.

5. As an alternative to the *View* tab>*Navigate* panel, you can manipulate the model display using the options in the Navigation Bar on the right side of the graphics window. Similar to the *Navigate* panel, you need to expand the zoom options. Expand the Zoom command grouping in the Navigation Bar and click **Zoom All**, as shown in Figure 1–36.

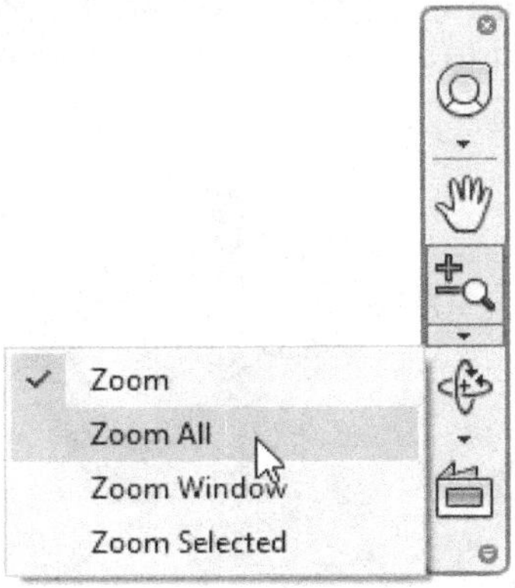

Figure 1–36

6. The model should refit to the center of the screen. If not, click (Zoom All) in the Navigation Bar.

Task 3: Zoom in on an area of the model and zoom out on the model.

1. Expand the zoom commands in the Navigation Bar and select **Zoom Window**.
2. Select a location on the model using the left mouse button to define a corner of the bounding box zoom area.
3. Drag the mouse to draw a box over the area to zoom.
4. Click or release the left mouse button again when the box is the required size. The model zooms in on the area defined by the sketched bounding box.
5. Expand the zoom commands in the Navigation Bar and **Zoom All** to refit the model in the center of the screen.
6. You can also zoom to a selected feature, face, or edge. Ensure that **Select Face and Edges** is selected in the *Filter* drop-down list in the Quick Access Toolbar, as shown in Figure 1–37.

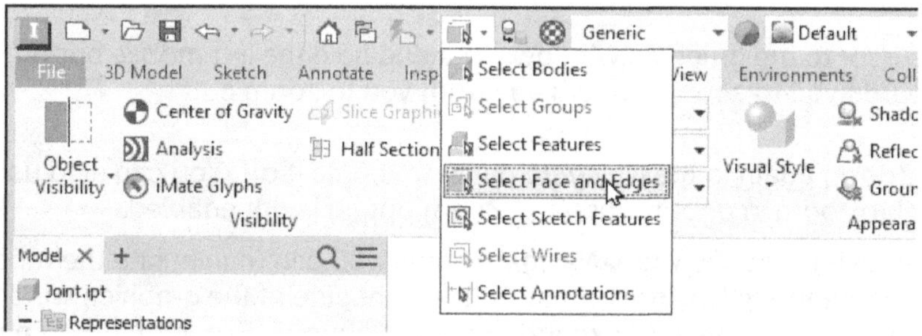

Figure 1–37

7. Select the face shown in Figure 1–38, then expand the zoom commands in the Navigation Bar and select **Zoom Selected** to zoom in on a selected element. The model is zoomed to the selected face.

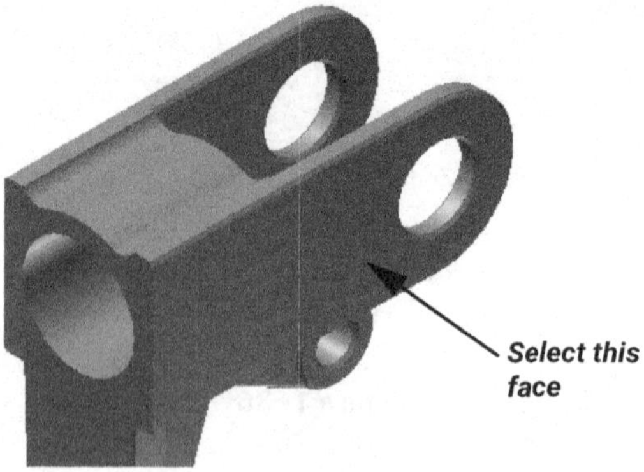

Figure 1–38

8. As an alternative to using the **Zoom All** command in the Navigation Bar, you can also double-click on the scroll wheel to zoom all.
9. Select away from the model to clear the selection of the face.
10. When using Zoom Selected, the order in which you select the entity and the command is important. With nothing selected on the model, expand the zoom commands in the Navigation Bar and select **Zoom Selected**. Hover your mouse over the model and note the yellow dot at the tip of the cursor. Select anywhere on the face shown in Figure 1–39. When selected in this order, the selection point on the face is positioned approximately in the center of the screen and the model is zoomed to this location.

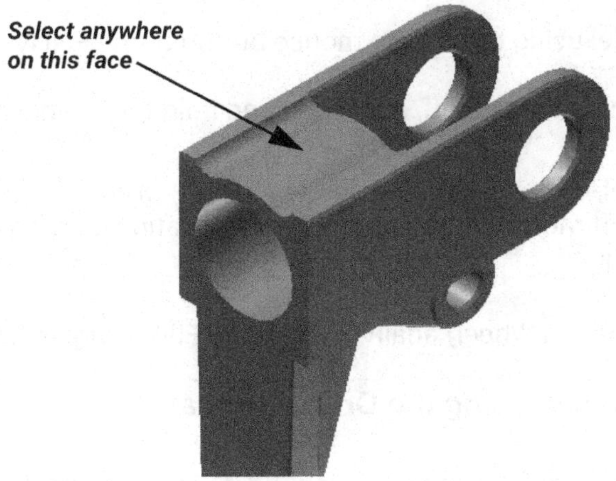

Figure 1–39

11. Use either of the **Zoom All** options to refit the model in the center of the screen.

Task 4: Zoom in and out on the model using the Navigation Wheel.

As an alternative to using **Zoom** (not **Zoom Selected**), you can also use the Full Navigation Wheel.

1. In the *Navigate* panel or Navigation Bar, click (Full Navigation Wheel).
2. Click and hold the left mouse button on the **Zoom** navigation command.
3. Drag the mouse to change the view as required.
4. Release the mouse button to end the navigation command.
5. Click (Full Navigation Wheel) in the *Navigate* panel or Navigation Bar to close the Full Navigation Wheel. Alternatively, click the **X** icon on the Full Navigation Wheel.
6. Refit the model in the center of the screen.

   Note: *Consider trying the various zooming alternatives so that you can decide which works best for you.*

Task 5: Pan the model using the Pan command.

1. In the *Navigate* panel or Navigation Bar, click (Pan).
2. Click and hold the left mouse button.
3. Move the mouse to drag the model.
4. Refit the model in the center of the screen.

Task 6: Pan the model using the Navigation Wheel.

You can also pan a model using the middle mouse button or the Full Navigation Wheel.

1. Ensure that (Pan) is toggled off, and press and hold the middle mouse button to drag the model.
2. In the *Navigate* panel, click (Full Navigation Wheel) to enable the Full Navigation Wheel. Click and hold the left mouse button on the **Pan** navigation command. Drag the mouse to pan the view as required.
3. Click (Full Navigation Wheel) again to close the Full Navigation Wheel.

Task 7: Rotate the model using the Orbit command.

1. In the *Navigate* panel or Navigation Bar, click (Orbit). A circle displays on the screen. The appearance of the cursor changes depending on its location relative to the circle.
2. Move the cursor inside the circle. The cursor appearance changes to .
3. Click and hold the left mouse button and rotate the model freely in any direction.
4. Release the mouse button and move the cursor just outside the circle. The cursor appearance changes to .
5. Click and hold the left mouse button to rotate about an axis through the center of the circle symbol (normal to the screen).

   Note: *To change the center of the rotation, double-click inside or outside the circle to set the new center location.*

6. Move the cursor to the line at the top of the circle. The cursor appearance changes to .
7. Click and hold the left mouse button and rotate the model about the horizontal axis.
8. Move the cursor to the line at the right or left side of the circle. The cursor appearance changes to .

9. Click and hold the left mouse button and rotate the model about the vertical axis.

   Note: *While you are still in the orbit circle, you can also disable the* ***Orbit*** *command by moving the cursor away from the model until* displays *and then clicking in the graphics window.*

10. Move the cursor over the ViewCube and click in the top-left corner of the ViewCube (as shown in Figure 1–40) to orient the model into its isometric Home view (3D). Alternatively, you can right-click and select **Home View** to orient the model in the same way. Note that (Zoom All) only refits the model in the center of the screen while maintaining the same orientation.

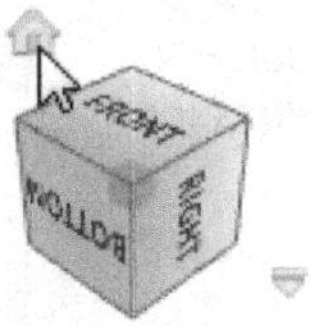

Figure 1–40

Task 8: Rotate the model using the ViewCube, keyboard, or Navigation Wheel.

As an alternative to using (Orbit), you can use the ViewCube, keyboard, or Full Navigation Wheel to rotate a model.

1. Ensure that (Orbit) is toggled off, click and hold the left mouse button anywhere on the ViewCube, and drag the mouse. Move the mouse away from the ViewCube to stop rotating.
2. Press and hold <F4>. By keeping <F4> depressed, the cursor behaves as it did when (Orbit) was active. Release <F4> to stop rotating.
3. Hold <Shift> and the middle mouse button and drag to rotate the model. Release <Shift> to stop rotating.
4. In the *Navigate* panel, click (Full Navigation Wheel) to enable the Full Navigation Wheel. Click and hold the left mouse button on the **Orbit** navigation command. Drag the mouse to rotate the view as required.
5. Click (Full Navigation Wheel) again to close the Full Navigation Wheel. The selection of the method to use to rotate the model is based on user preference.
6. Click in the ViewCube to orient the model into its isometric Home view, or right-click and select **Home View**.
7. Click the **X** icon in the top-right corner of the Navigation Bar to toggle off its display.
8. In the *View* tab>*Windows* panel, expand **User Interface**. Select the box next to **Navigation Bar** to return it to the display. The remaining options enable you to control the display of the Model browser (Model), ViewCube, Status Bar, Document Tabs, and other interface tools.

Task 9: Orient the model.

1. In the *Navigate* panel or Navigation Bar, click (Look At) to orient a model face parallel to the screen. Select the face as shown in Figure 1–41. The model orients into a 2D orientation.

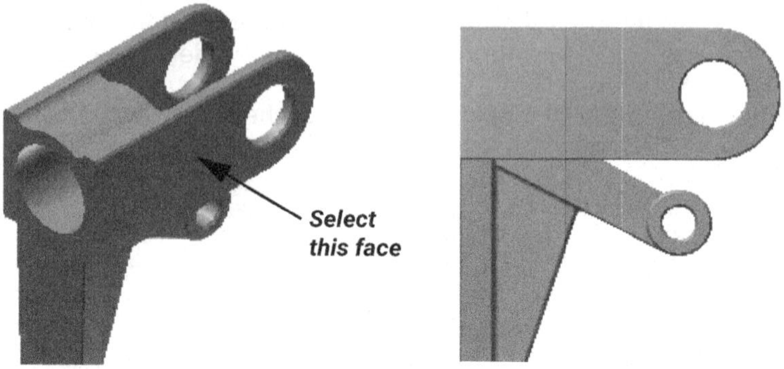

Figure 1–41

2. Note that the ViewCube has reoriented and **RIGHT** displays. Click to orient the model to its isometric Home view.

Note: The (Look At) command can help to orient faces that are not parallel with the origin planes. However, the ViewCube is a more efficient option for orienting into views that are parallel with the origin work planes.

3. Select the **RIGHT** face in the ViewCube as shown in Figure 1–42. The model orients as it did previously with one less step.

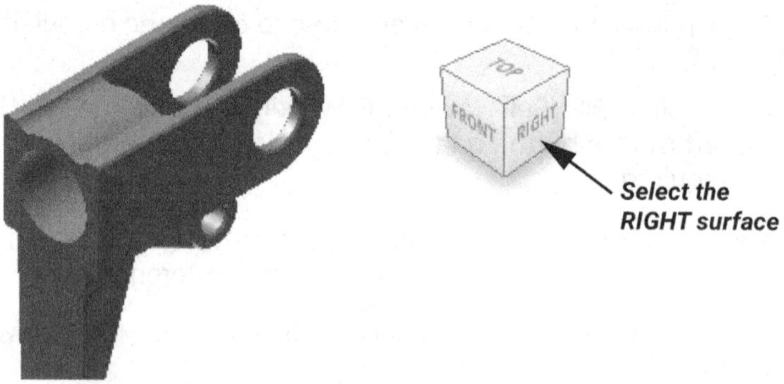

Figure 1–42

4. With the model still in a 2D orientation, move the mouse back over the ViewCube. It displays as shown in Figure 1–43. Select either of the rotating arrows to rotate the model while remaining in the RIGHT view.

Figure 1–43

5. Click any of the four triangular icons on the ViewCube to change to a different orientation.
6. Practice orienting the model into different orientations. You can also select edges of the ViewCube for orienting.
7. Click to orient the model into its isometric Home view.

Task 10: Manipulate the visual style of the model.

The default visual style for models that are started with a default template is **Shaded with Edges**. In this task, you will learn how to change the models' visual style. Note that the ability of Inventor to spin a shaded model and use all styles depends on your graphics hardware.

1. In the *View* tab>*Appearance* panel, expand **Visual Style**. Note that the model display is set to (Shaded) for this model, as shown in Figure 1–44.

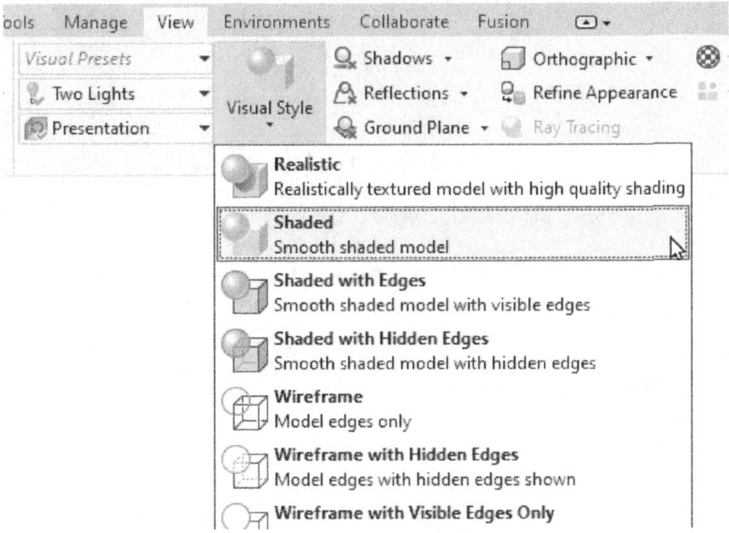

Figure 1–44

2. Click (Shaded with Hidden Edges) to set the view display so that it displays hidden edges while shaded.
3. Click + next to **Origin** to expand it in the Model browser.
4. Right-click on the **YZ Plane** in the Model browser and select **Visibility**, as shown in Figure 1–45. The YZ Plane displays.

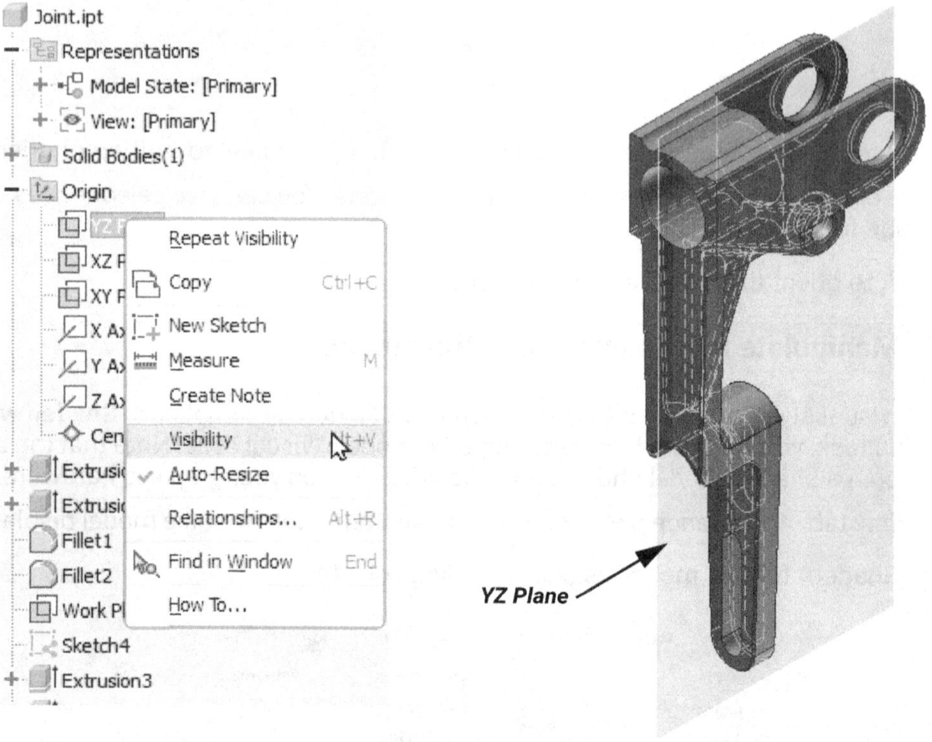

Figure 1–45

Note: To temporarily display an origin object, hover the cursor over the feature name.

5. Hold <Ctrl> and select the **XZ Plane** and **Y Axis** in the Model browser. Right-click and select **Visibility** to display both the XZ Plane and Y-axis in the model.

6. Return the model to the (Shaded) display. The model displays as shown in Figure 1–46.

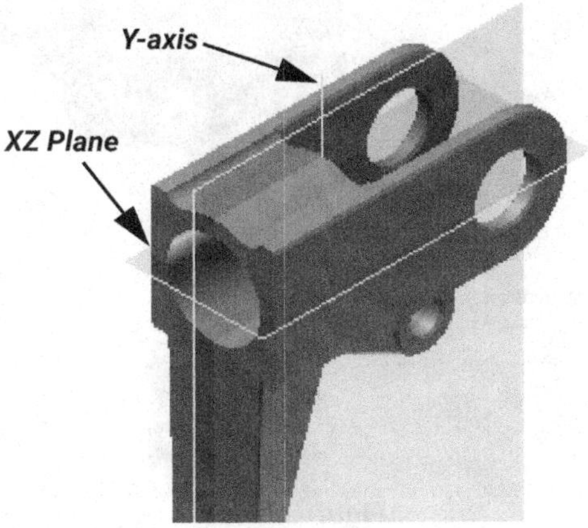

Figure 1–46

7. Toggle off the visibility for the three origin objects by selecting them again and disabling the **Visibility** option. Press and hold <Ctrl> while selecting to select all of the objects at once.

Task 11: Open a drawing of the model.

1. Use one of the following methods to open **Joint.idw**. The header in the graphics window displays the name of the drawing.
   - Select the *Home* tab and click **Open**.
   - Click (Open) in the Quick Access Toolbar at the top of the window.
   - In the **File** menu, select **Open>Open**.
   - In the Model browser, right-click on the filename (Joint.ipt) and select **Open Drawing**.
2. Note that there are now three tabs along the bottom of the graphics window. One tab is the *Home* page, one is the part model and one (currently active tab) is the drawing of that model.
3. Select the *Joint.ipt* tab to activate it.

Task 12: Edit feature dimensions on the model.

1. Right-click on **Fillet9** in the Model browser and select **Show Dimensions**.

   Note: *To select features directly on the model in the graphics window, you must have the selection filter in the Quick Access Toolbar set to (Select Features).*
2. Double-click on the .010 dimension in the graphics window.

3. Enter **0.05** as the new value, as shown in Figure 1–47, and press <Enter>.

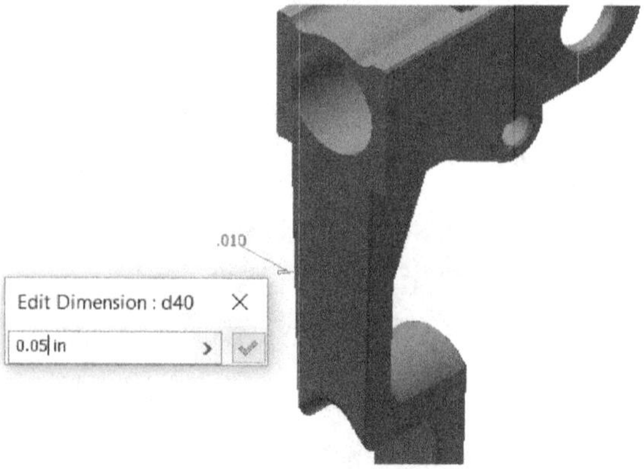

Figure 1–47

4. In the Quick Access Toolbar, click (Local Update). The radius of the fillet updates.

   Note: *(Local Update) recalculates the model geometry. The length of the update time depends on the complexity of the change and the model.*

5. Double-click on **Hole1** in the Model browser or graphics window to open the *Properties* panel that was used to create the hole.
6. Change the 0.25 diameter to **0.15** in either the *Properties* panel or the on-screen entry field. Click **OK** in the *Properties* panel to complete the feature change. The model displays as shown in Figure 1–48.

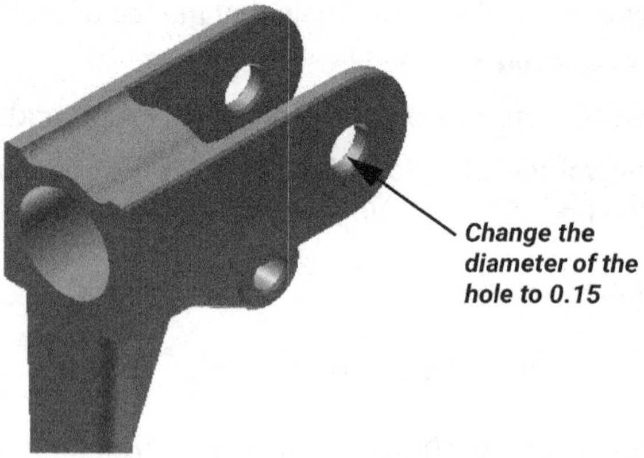

Figure 1–48

In the Hole diameter example, you edited the feature by opening the *Properties* panel. Alternatively, you can right-click on the feature and select **Show Dimension**. This is faster for editing multiple dimension values because the model is not updated until you explicitly click (Local Update). Using the *Properties* panel, the model is updated when you click **OK**. Therefore, each is updated individually. If you are making a lot of changes, the update can be more time-consuming.

7. Select the *Joint.idw* tab to activate the drawing. Note how the sizes of the fillet and hole update to reflect the changes that were made in the model.

Task 13: Delete a feature in the model.

1. Select the *Joint.ipt* tab to activate it.
2. In the Model browser, select **Extrusion11**. Right-click and select **Delete**. The *Delete Features* dialog box opens, as shown in Figure 1–49. It prompts you to determine whether the sketch that was used to create Extrusion11 should also be deleted. You might want to delete it or you might want to retain it for use in another feature.

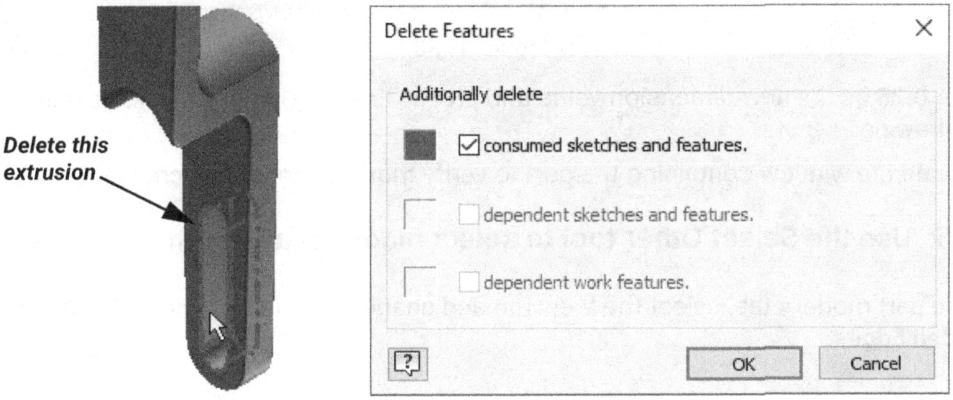

Figure 1–49

3. In this case, click **OK** to confirm the deletion of the sketches that were created as part of the extrusion (slot cut). To retain the sketch, clear the **consumed sketches and features** option.
4. Select the *Joint.idw* tab to activate the drawing. Note that the extrusion has been removed from all of the views in the drawing. If it does not update, click (Local Update).

Task 14: Edit a hole diameter in the drawing.

1. Right-click on the Ø.15 diameter dimension as shown in Figure 1–50 and select **Edit Model Dimension**.

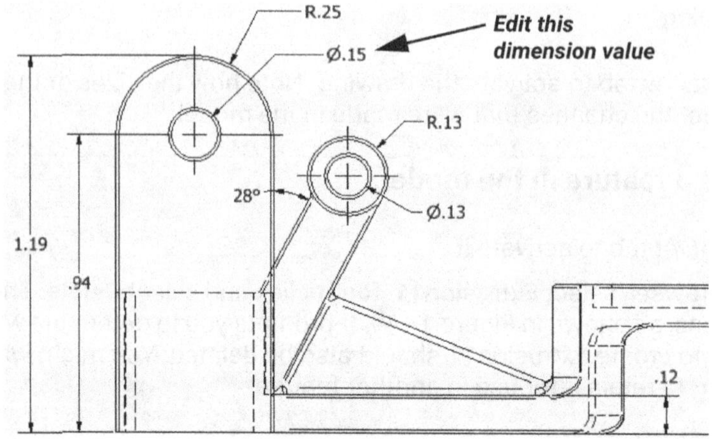

Figure 1–50

2. Enter **0.25** as the new dimension value and press <Enter>. The size of the hole updates in the drawing.
3. Activate the window containing the part to verify that the model has changed.

Task 15: Use the Select Other tool to select hidden features in the model.

1. In the part model's tab, select the *View* tab and change the visual style to **Shaded with Hidden Edges**.

2. Hover the cursor over the extruded cut, as shown in Figure 1–51. In this orientation, you cannot directly select the cut geometry that lies behind this face.

   Note: *The* ***Shaded with Hidden Edges*** *is only being used so you can see the hidden feature for the purpose of this practice. The Select Other tool does not require this visual setting to be used.*

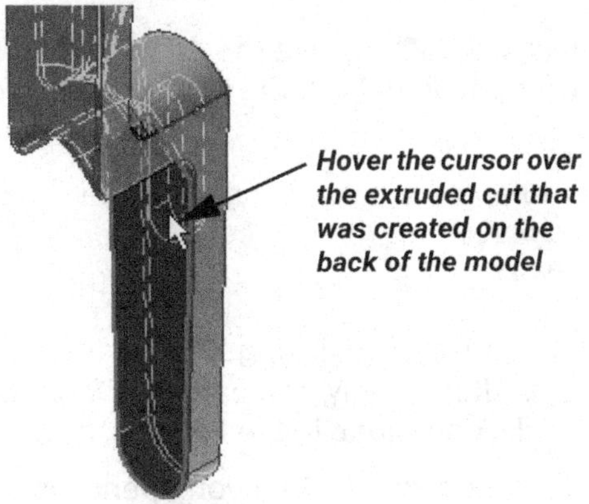

Figure 1–51

3. A drop-down list displays. Expand it as shown in Figure 1–52, and hover the cursor over each of the selections. When **Extrusion10** highlights, click to select it. The cut is highlighted in the Model browser. As an alternative to expanding the down-drop list to review the other options, use the middle mouse to scroll through the options.

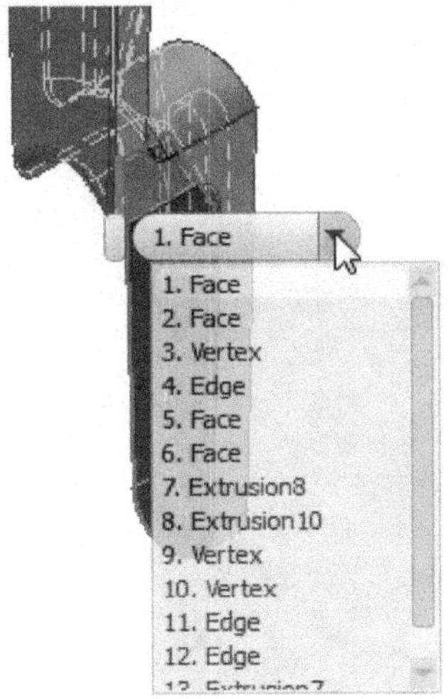

Figure 1–52

4. Right-click and select **Suppress Features**. Note that the Model browser displays **Extrusion10** in gray and is crossed out. Alternatively, you can select **Extrusion10** in the Model browser to suppress it. The previous method is more effective when you have a model with a large number of the features, and it is difficult to identify the features in the Model browser using only names.
5. Activate the window containing the drawing to verify that the drawing has changed.
6. In the Quick Access Toolbar, click to save the drawing. The *Save* dialog box opens indicating that changes were made to both the Model and the drawing. Click **OK** to save both files.

   Note: *The Save dialog box opens when you are saving drawings or assembly models. It indicates whether the associated files need to be saved and enables you to do so. This dialog box does not open when you are saving a part model.*

7. Close both the drawing and part file by clicking **X** in the top-right corner of the graphics window for both of the files. Alternatively, you can click **X** on the file's tab at the bottom of the graphics window or by clicking **Close** in the **File** menu.
8. On the *Home* page, note that the two files that you opened in this exercise are now displayed in the *Recent* list for the Intro to Modeling project.

End of practice

Chapter Review Questions

1. Match the numbers shown in Figure 1–53 with the interface components listed below.

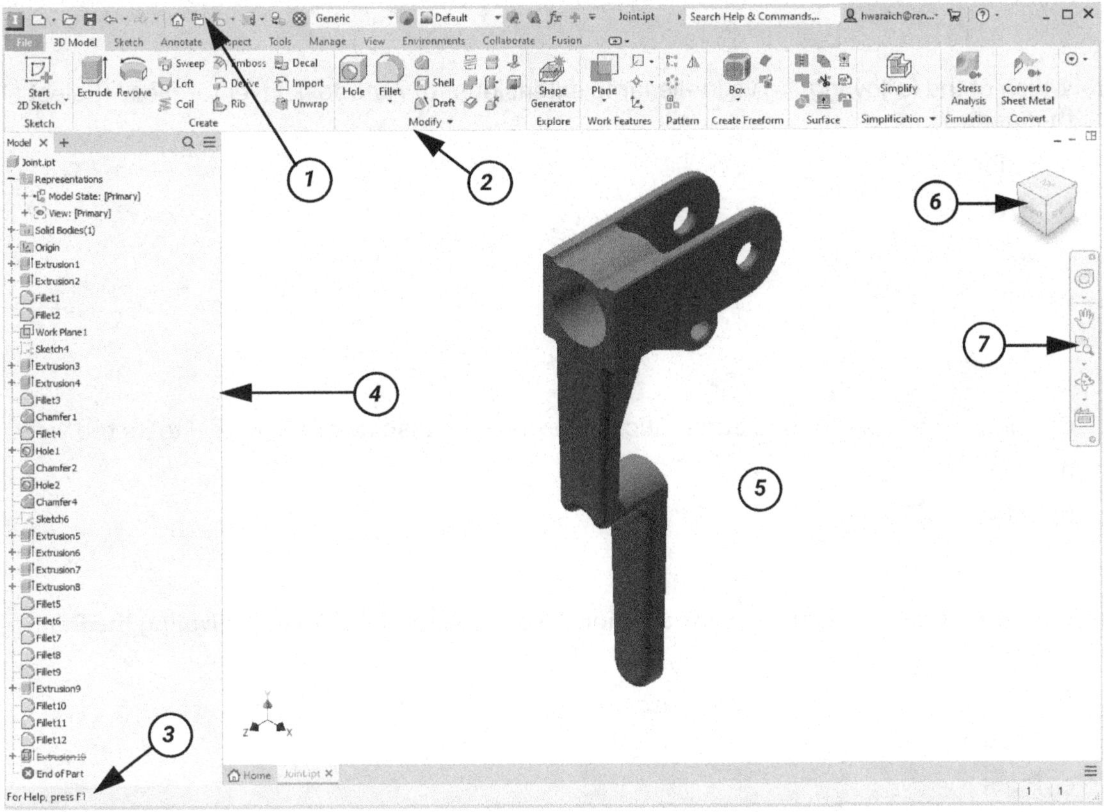

Figure 1–53

a. Navigation Bar	
b. Model Browser	
c. Status Bar	
d. Quick Access Toolbar	
e. Ribbon	
f. Graphics Window	
g. ViewCube	

2. After editing the dimensions of a part model, you must open all drawings referencing that part to make the same dimension changes.
    a. True
    b. False

3. Which of the following are valid filename extensions for Autodesk Inventor files? (Select all that apply.)
    a. .IPT
    b. .IDW
    c. .IAM
    d. .INV

4. Clicking  enables you to automatically reorient the display of the model to its top view.
    a. True
    b. False

5. Which mouse button do you click and hold to pan the model without activating the **Pan** command?
    a. Left
    b. Middle
    c. Right

6. Which combination of items do you select to quickly orient a model face parallel to the screen without spinning? (Select all that apply.)
    a. A surface and .
    b. A planar surface and .
    c. A surface and .
    d. A planar surface and .
    e. A face on the ViewCube.

7. You can open multiple windows in one session.

a. True

b. False

8. What is the purpose of the menu shown in Figure 1–54?

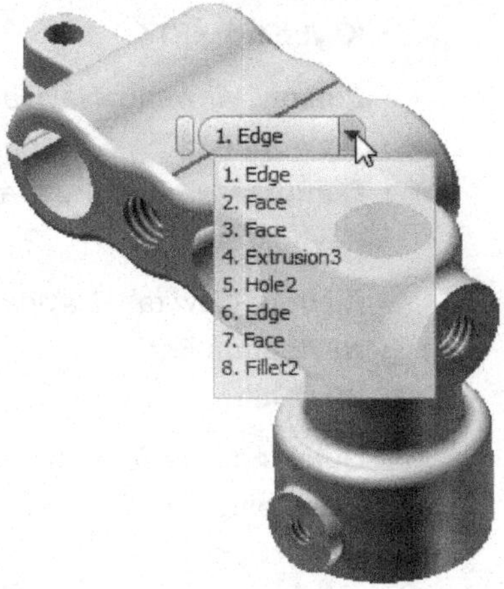

Figure 1–54

a. To switch back to a previous view or ahead to a current view.

b. To cycle through different objects for selection.

c. To pan the view left or right.

d. To zoom in or out on the selected object.

Command Summary

Button	Command	Location
	Full Navigation Wheel	• **Ribbon:** *View* tab>*Navigate* panel • **Navigation Bar**
	Help	• **Quick Access Toolbar** • **Keyboard:** <F1>
	Home View	• **Ribbon:** *View* tab>*Navigate* panel • **ViewCube** • **Context Menu: In the graphics window** • **Keyboard:** <F6>
	Look At	• **Ribbon:** *View* tab>*Navigate* panel • **Navigation Bar** • **ViewCube**
	Open	• **Quick Access Toolbar** • **File Menu** • **Home Page**
	Orbit (rotate)	• **Ribbon:** *View* tab>*Navigate* panel • **Navigation Bar** • **ViewCube**
	Pan	• **Ribbon:** *View* tab>*Navigate* panel • **Navigation Bar**
	Projects	• **Dialog Box:** *Open* or *New* • **Home Page:** Projects and Settings
	Save	• **Quick Access Toolbar** • **File Menu**
	Visual Style	• **Ribbon:** *View* tab>*Appearance* panel
	Zoom	• **Ribbon:** *View* tab>*Navigate* panel • **Navigation Bar** • **Full Navigation Wheel**
	Zoom All	• **Ribbon:** *View* tab>*Navigate* panel • **Navigation Bar**
	Zoom Selected	• **Ribbon:** *View* tab>*Navigate* panel • **Navigation Bar**
	Zoom Window	• **Ribbon:** *View* tab>*Navigate* panel • **Navigation Bar**

Chapter

2

Creating the Base Feature

A base feature is the first solid feature that you create in an Autodesk® Inventor® part file. It forms the foundation on which other features are added to the model. The general workflow for creating a base feature is to create a sketch and then use the feature creation controls to create solid geometry.

Learning Objectives

- Create a new part model using a predefined template.
- Create a sketch by appropriately selecting a sketch plane.
- Project references onto a sketch plane for use in locating entities.
- Create, dimension, and constrain 2D entities in a sketch.
- Create a 3D solid base feature.
- Make changes to a sketched feature.

2.1 Creating a New Part File

All part files are created using templates. Templates ensure the part is created with standard configurations and settings. Template files can contain features and settings, such as units, grid settings, origin planes, work features, sketches, geometry, parameters, and properties. By default, Autodesk provides template files that can be used by either selecting the template each time you start a new part or by assigning the template that should be used for all new parts.

Create a Part with a Selected Template

The following procedure explains how you can select a specific template for part creation.

How To: Create a New Part with a Selected Template

1. Select the **New** option in any one of the following locations. Once selected, the *Create New File* dialog box opens, as shown in Figure 2–1.
    - On the *Home* page, select **New**.
    - In the Quick Access Toolbar, select the (New) option.
    - In the **File** menu, select **New**.

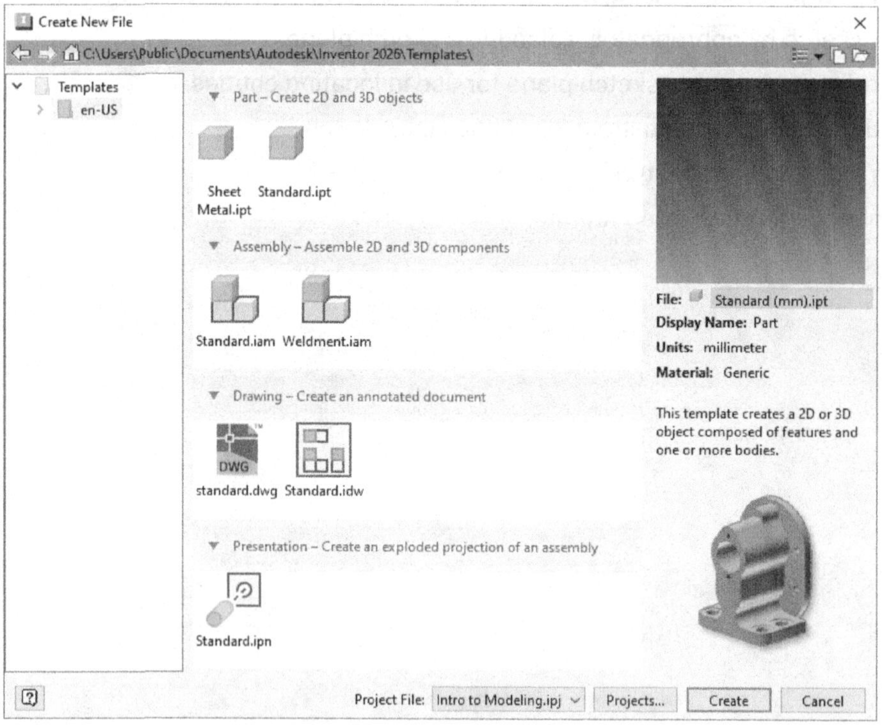

Figure 2–1

2. Expand the *Templates>en-US* folders in the left pane and select the required unit of measure (e.g., *English* or *Metric*). Note that the right pane updates to show that the *Units* for the new part file is as expected.
3. In the *Part – Create 2D and 3D objects* area of the dialog box, select the standard file that is to be used to create the new part file. Note the appended letters after the word "standard" to help ensure that the correct standard is selected. The (in) indicates an English standard and (mm) is a Metric standard.
4. Click **Create**. A new part file is created and the *3D Model* tab is active.

Create a Part Using the Default Template

Using the *Create New File* dialog box enables you to review and ensure that the correct template is being used to create a new part file. This approach is recommended until you are comfortable that you understand the template assignment. Otherwise, you can use the following techniques to start a new part file using the default template directly, without using the *Create New File* dialog box:

- On the *Home* page, select ⌄ to expand the **New** menu and select **Part (.ipt),** as shown in Figure 2–2.

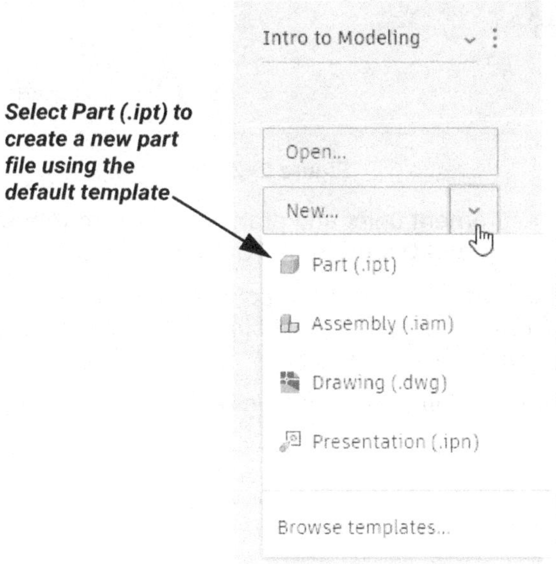

Figure 2–2

- In the Quick Access Toolbar, expand the (New) option and select **Part**. In the **File** menu, select **New>Part**.

Note: *If you select the (New) option directly in either the Quick Access Toolbar or the* ***File*** *menu, the Create New File dialog box opens, allowing you to select the template.*

By selecting any one of these individual options, the new part file is created and the *3D Model* tab is active. The default template that is used when creating a new part file can be customized by assigning the template in the Inventor **Application Options**.

How To: Set the Default Template for New Files

1. In the *Tools* tab, click  (Application Options). Select the *File* tab in the *Application Options* dialog box and click **Configure Default Template**. The *Configure Default Template* dialog box appears showing you the current units and standard for the currently assigned default template. For example, Figure 2–3 shows that the currently assigned default template is in **Inches** with the **ANSI** drawing standard.

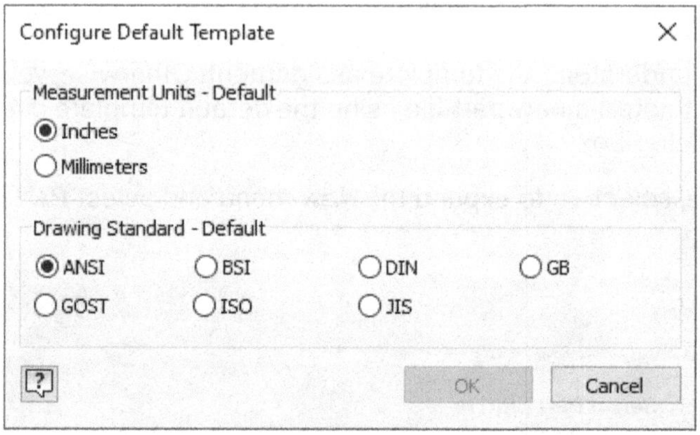

Figure 2–3

2. Select the required measurement units and drawing standard that should be used as default. Click **OK** and confirm to **Overwrite** the default template.
3. This sets the default template that is presented when you create a new part file; however, it does not prevent you from creating a model in inches by selecting **New** on the *Home* page, as was shown in the previous exercise.
4. Click **OK** to close the *Application Options* dialog box.

Origin Features

Origin planes are non-solid features that only exist in space. They do not have a thickness or mass.The default part templates contain the following origin features:

- Three orthogonal planes: YZ Plane, XZ Plane, and XY Plane.
- Three axes: X Axis, Y Axis, and Z Axis.
- A Center Point at the default (0,0,0) point.

These origin features can never be moved or deleted. Figure 2–4 shows the default origin features and how they are listed in the **Origin** node of the Model browser. When an origin plane is selected, it highlights in blue and its name appears in the graphics window to help identify it.

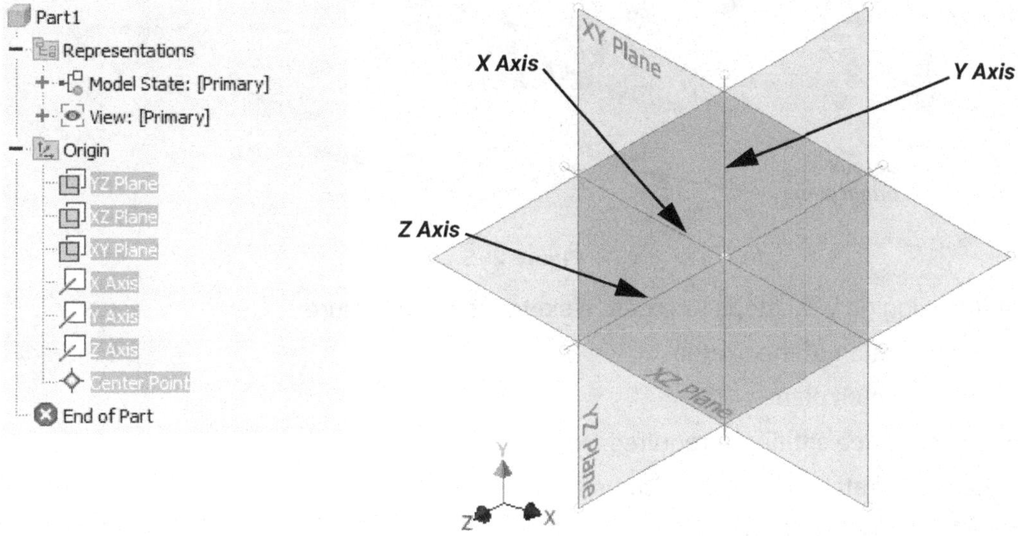

Figure 2–4

When you create a new part, the origin features are not displayed. They can be displayed in any of the following ways:

- To toggle on origin feature visibility, expand the **Origin** node in the Model browser, right-click on the feature (e.g., YZ Plane), and select **Visibility**. Alternatively, select the features in the Model browser and press <Alt>+<V> on your keyboard. This shortcut enables you to toggle an origin feature's visibility on and off.
- To temporarily display an origin feature, hover the cursor over the feature in the Model browser to display it in the graphics window.

2.2 Sketched Base Features

The base feature is the first solid feature in a new part. It is created by locating new geometry using references to the origin features. The base feature is often a solid extrusion with a sketched cross-section. This section discusses the workflow that creates and modifies a sketched base feature. An example of a base feature is shown in Figure 2–5.

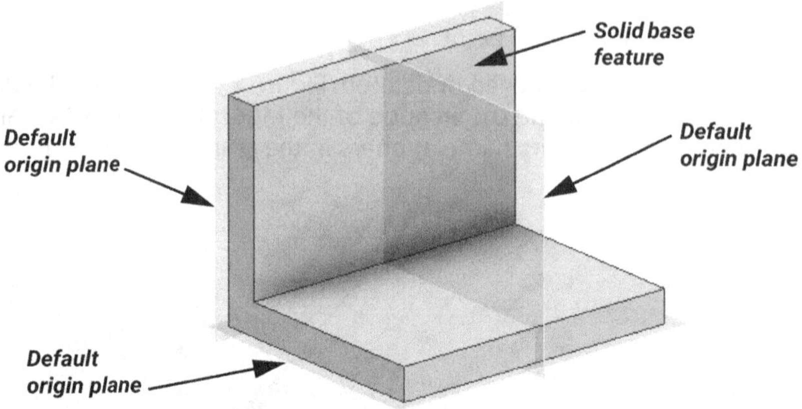

Figure 2–5

Use the following general steps to create a sketched base feature:

1. Start the creation of the sketch.
2. Define the sketch plane.
3. Project reference entities, if required.
4. Create a 2D sketch of the base feature.
5. Select the base feature type.
6. Define the depth and direction.
7. Complete the feature.

Step 1 - Start the creation of the sketch.

To create a sketched base feature, you must start with a sketch. A sketch is a 2D representation of the section that is used to create the solid geometry in the model. To start the creation of a sketch in the model, use one of the following methods:

- In the *3D Model* tab>*Sketch* panel, click (Start 2D Sketch).
- Right-click in the graphics window and select **New Sketch**.

Step 2 - Define the sketch plane.

Before sketching you must define the 2D plane on which to sketch the entities. During base feature creation, any one of the default origin planes (YZ, XZ, and XY) can be selected. Once the new sketch command has been initiated, the origin planes are temporarily displayed in the graphics window and can be selected, as shown in Figure 2–6. You can hover the cursor over any of the displayed planes to display the plane's name. Select any of the planes to define the plane on which the sketch is going to be created.

Alternatively, in the Model browser, next to the **Origin** node, click + to expand it and select any of the origin planes, as shown in Figure 2–6.

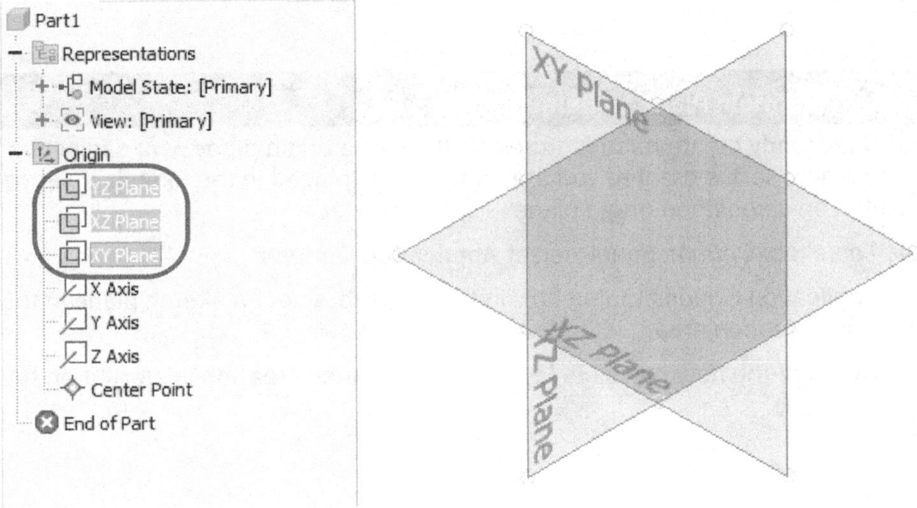

Figure 2–6

Note: *As you create geometry in your models, refer to the origin indicator ( ) in the bottom-left corner of the graphics window to ensure that you understand the X, Y, and Z orientations when selecting origin planes.*

Once the sketch plane has been selected, it is reoriented parallel to the screen. The origin (0,0,0) of the sketch is positioned at the center of the graphics window. You are now in the Sketch environment and the *Sketch* tab is active.

Hint: Creating the Sketch

As an alternative to initiating a new sketch command and then selecting the sketch plane, you can select the sketch plane first and then initiate the command, using any of the following methods:

- Right-click on the origin plane name in the Model browser and select **New Sketch**.
- Select the origin plane name in the Model browser, and in the *3D Model* tab>*Sketch* panel, click (Start 2D Sketch).
- Select the origin plane name in the Model browser and click (Create Sketch) in the graphics window.

Hint: Setting an Origin Plane as Default

When you consistently create base features on the same origin plane, you can set an option so that when a new part is created you are immediately placed in the Sketch environment, ready to sketch on a specified origin plane.

1. In the *Tools* tab>*Options* panel, select **Application Options**.
2. In the *Application Options* dialog box, in the *Part* tab, select a sketch plane in the *Sketch on new part creation* area.
3. Click **OK**. All of the new parts are launched and sketch creation is started on the specified plane.

Step 3 - Project reference entities, if required.

Sketched geometry should be located with respect to existing reference entities. Reference entities provide a reference for dimensioning and constraining sketched entities so that their location is fully defined in the model. While a part can be created without referencing origin features, using them is strongly recommended to create a robust model that is easy to modify.

For a base feature, the origin features that exist in the template can be used. By default, the origin center point is projected onto the sketch plane. You must explicitly project any of the origin planes (or axes) as further references. As you progress in a design, previously sketched or solid entities can also be selected and projected as reference entities for new sketches.

How To: Project a Reference Entity

1. In the *Create* panel, click (Project Geometry) or right-click and select **Project Geometry**.

2. Select any of the origin planes or axes to be projected onto the sketch plane. The references are represented as yellow lines on the sketch plane.
3. Right-click and select **OK** to complete the reference selection or press <Esc> to cancel the command.

Step 4 - Create a 2D sketch of the base feature.

Once the reference entities have been projected, you can begin to create the 2D sketched entities using the options in the *Create* panel of the *Sketch* tab. The *Sketch* tab is shown in Figure 2–7.

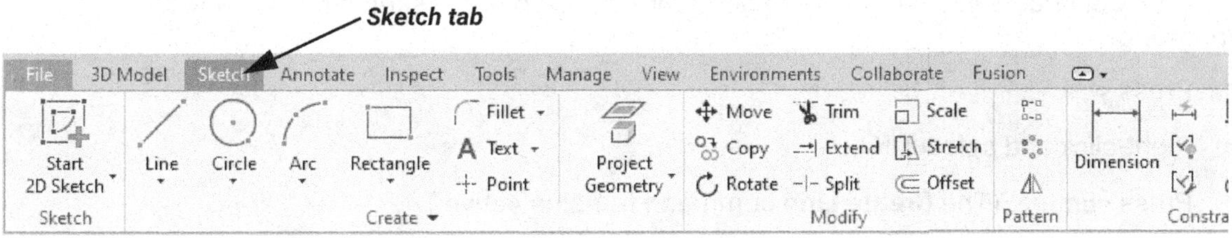

Figure 2–7

Grid and Axis Display

By default, grid lines are not displayed in a sketch. You can control the display of the grid lines in the *Sketch* tab in the *Application Options* dialog box (*Tools* tab>*Options* panel, click (Application Options)) using the options in the *Display* area, as shown in Figure 2–8. You can also toggle the coordinate system indicator on and off. To control grid snapping, which causes the cursor to move in increments, toggle on the **Snap to grid** option on the *Sketch* tab.

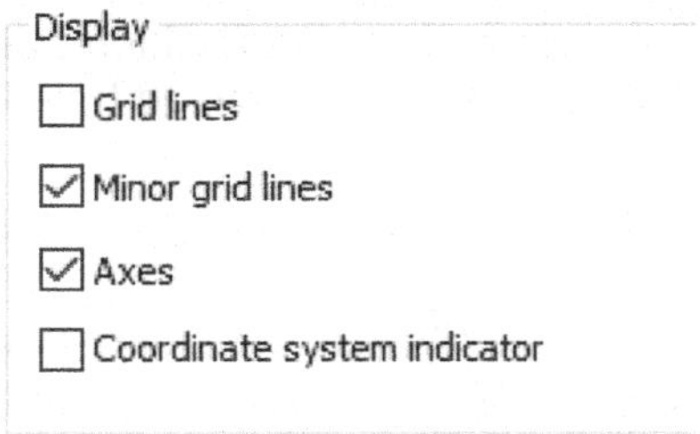

Figure 2–8

Note: *The Application options are global and affect all files that you open. For individual files, snap and grid spacing can be set in Document Settings.*

Sketch Entities

To create a solid base feature, the sketched entities must form a closed section. If the sketch's section is not closed, you can only create surface geometry. The available sketch entities are all located on the *Sketch* tab>*Create* panel. Only a sub-set of the available entity types are covered in this section. Additional types are covered later in this guide.

Line

In the *Create* panel, click (Line), or right-click and select **Create Line**, to sketch a geometry line. Move the crosshairs to the start point of the line and click the left mouse button (do not press and drag). Move the crosshairs to the end point and click the left mouse button to locate the line. Continue selecting points to add more lines. To finish sketching, use any one of the following:

- Press <Esc>.
- Right-click and select **OK**.
- Press <Enter>. (The **Create Line** command remains active.)
- Activate a new sketcher tool.

Line Close

After two or more line segments have been drawn consecutively, you can right-click and select **Close** to automatically add a final line segment between the first and last points entered.

Rectangle

In the *Create* panel, click (Rectangle) or right-click and select **Two Point Rectangle** to sketch a rectangle. Move the crosshairs to the point at which the rectangle begins and click the left mouse button. Move the crosshairs to the point at which the rectangle ends and click the left mouse button. Use any of the methods listed above to finish sketching.

Circle

In the *Create* panel, click (Circle) or right-click and select **Center Point Circle** to sketch a circle. Select the center point and a point on the outer extent of the circle.

Slot

In the *Create* panel, expand **Rectangle** and click (Slot Center to Center) to sketch a slot. The marking menu does not contain a **Slot** option. Move the crosshairs to the start point of the arc-center on one end of the slot and click the left mouse button. Move the crosshairs to locate the arc-center on the other end of the slot and click the left mouse button to locate the centerline. Move the cursor away from the centerline to the required size of the slot and click the left mouse button. Other **Slot** options are available in the drop-down list. The selections required to create each type vary slightly. Refer to the Status Bar for guidance with entity placement.

> ***Note:*** *When sketching, you will often need to delete and undo/redo. To delete a sketch entity, select the entity and press <Delete>. You can also right-click on the entity and select* ***Delete****. To undo or redo sketching actions, click and in the Quick Access Toolbar, respectively. The* ***Undo*** *command is also available in the marking menu.*

Sketching Revolved Sections

Only half of the cross-section of a revolved feature needs to be sketched. It is then revolved about the axis of revolution at a specified angle. The sketch of a revolved feature must:

- Contain a straight entity to define the axis of revolution if an existing axis in the model cannot be used (i.e., lines, projected edges, projected work planes, and construction lines).
- Have all entities on one side of the axis of revolution.

Examples of a sketch and its revolved features are as follows:

Sketch	Revolve Geometry	Description
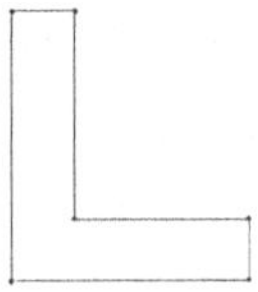	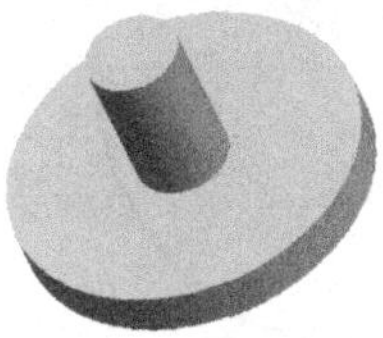	In this sketch, entities are revolved about the line that is part of the sketch.
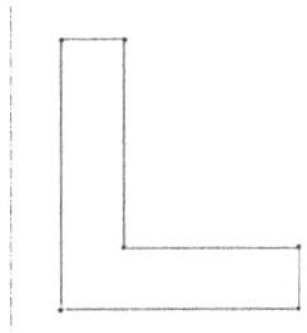	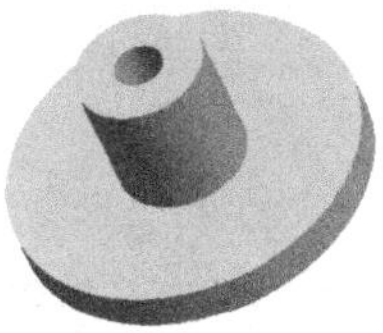	In this sketch, the centerline is offset from the section. The result is a hole in the revolve.
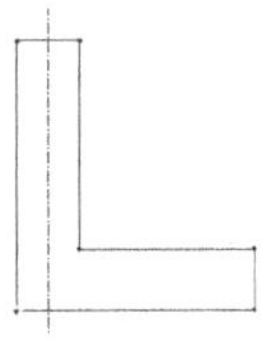	**Invalid**	This is a sketch with the centerline intersecting the section. A **Revolve** feature cannot have sketched geometry on both sides of the axis of rotation because the geometry would overlap.

Dimensioning

Dimensions define the size and locations of the objects in the sketch. A sketch does not need to be dimensioned or constrained to create 3D geometry. However, it is recommended to verify the correct design intent in your model. Once entities are added, the number of dimensions required to fully constrain the sketch displays in a field in the bottom-right corner of the main window.

How To: Create a Dimension

1. In the *Constrain* panel, click (Dimension) or right-click and select **General Dimension**.
2. Select the entity or entities with your left mouse button.
3. Move the cursor to the dimension's placement location and press the left mouse button to place the dimension.

The dimension type created depends on whether you select an entity or its endpoints. For example, selecting two non-parallel lines creates an angular dimension, while selecting two end points creates a linear dimension. A constrained sketch is shown in Figure 2–9.

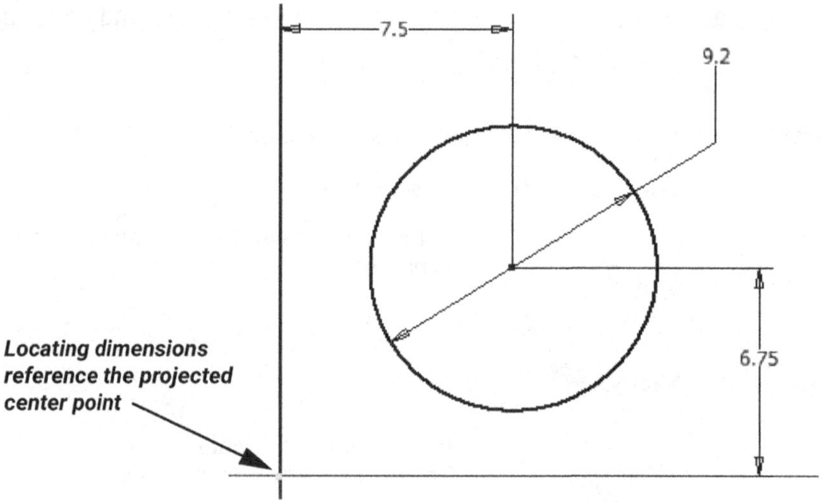

Figure 2–9

When dimensioning the cross-section of a revolved feature, you can create a diameter dimension. To dimension, select the center of the revolved cross-section, then select the geometry, right-click and select **Linear Diameter**, and place the dimension, as shown in Figure 2–10.

> ***Note:*** *This type of dimensioning scheme can also be used to dimension symmetrical entities.*

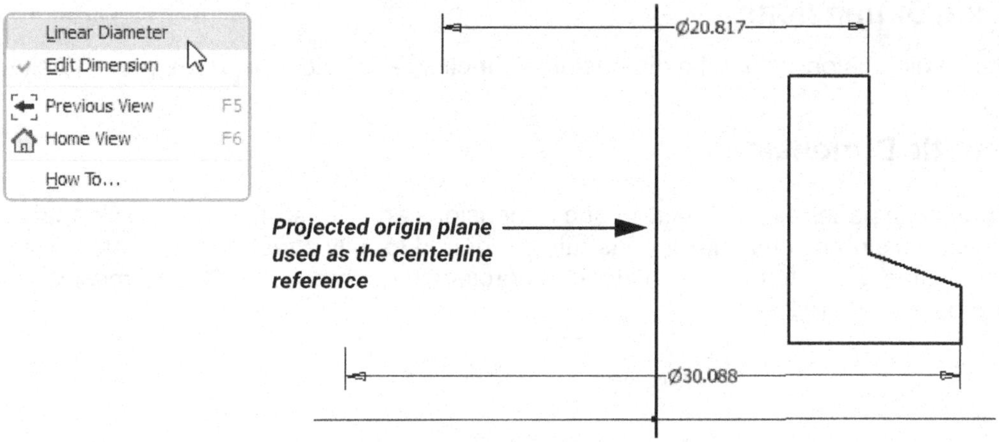

Figure 2–10

The first General dimension (not automatic) that is added to a sketch and then subsequently modified determines the sketch's scale. All of the other sketch entities scale to reflect the value used. As soon as a second dimension is added, automatic scaling is disabled.

Hint: Disabling Entity Scaling Based on Modification

To disable entity scaling, complete the following:

1. In the *Tools* tab>*Options* panel, select **Application Options**.
2. In the *Application Options* dialog box, in the *Sketch* tab, clear the **Auto-scale sketch geometries on initial dimension** option.
3. Click **OK**.

Modifying Dimensions

Sketch dimensions control the size of the geometry and therefore are parametric. By default, a dimension is immediately modifiable as soon as it is placed in the sketch. To disable this functionality so you can first place all of the dimensions and then modify them later, right-click in the graphics window and clear the **Edit Dimension** option before placing the dimension. Alternatively, in the Constraint Settings, clear the **Edit dimension when created** option.

How To: Edit a Value of a Dimension

1. Double-click on the dimension. If the **Dimension** command is already active, only a single-click is required.
2. Enter a new value in the *Edit Dimension* dialog box.
3. Click  or press <Enter>.

Deleting Dimensions

To delete a dimension, select the dimension, right-click, and select **Delete** or press <Delete>.

Automatic Dimensions

In the *Constrain* panel, click (Automatic Dimensions and Constraints) and click **Apply** to place all of the dimensions and/or constraints required to fully constrain the sketch. This command dimensions to existing sketched or projected geometry. The *Auto Dimension* dialog box is shown in Figure 2–11.

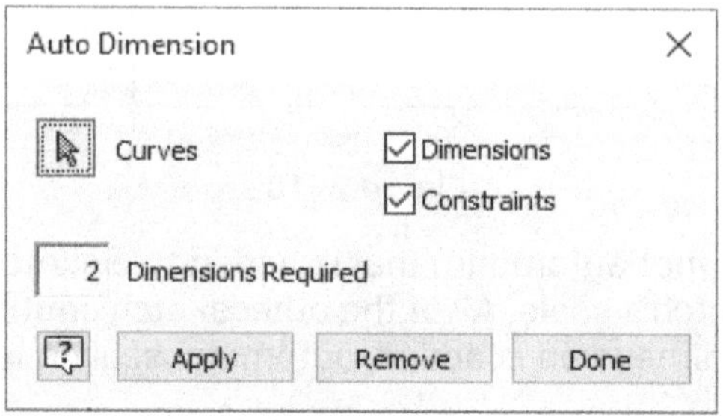

Figure 2–11

The **Automatic Dimensions and Constraints** command automatically assigns dimensions. However, it might not create them to suit your design intent. Consider using this option to determine how many additional dimensions and constraints are required and where. Once added, if they do not meet your design intent, consider using **Remove** to quickly remove dimensions and constraints from selected objects. The options in the *Auto Dimension* dialog box are as follows:

Curves	Enables you to select the objects to be dimensioned.
Dimensions Required	Lists the number of dimensions and constraints required to fully dimension the sketch.
Dimensions	Enables you to apply dimensions to the selected objects.
Constraints	Enables you to apply constraints to the selected objects.

Driven Dimensions

An error message opens when you try to add a dimension that over-constrains a sketch. You can cancel the command or place a driven dimension. A driven dimension (shown in brackets) is a dimension that changes as the result of a change to another dimension. The dimension shown in Figure 2–12 is a driven dimension and acts as a reference. A driven dimension cannot be modified, but updates if changes are made.

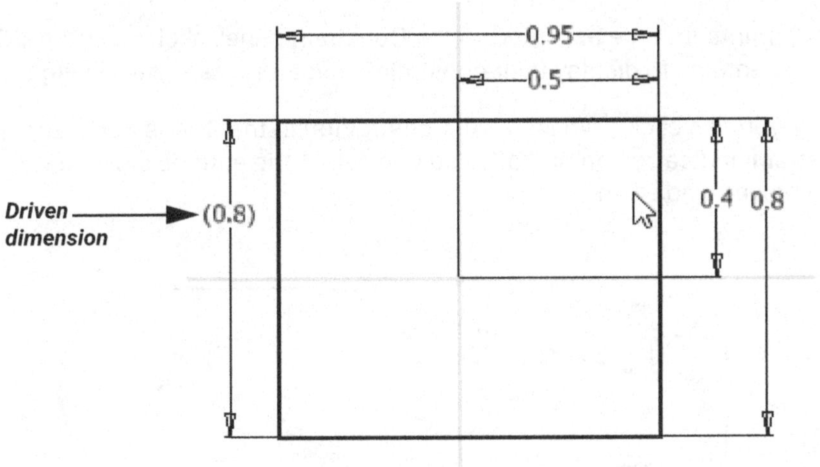

Figure 2–12

Constraining

Constraints are relationships between:

- two entities,
- an entity and the coordinate system, or
- an entity and projected reference entities.

Note: *A sketch does not need to be dimensioned or constrained to create 3D geometry. However, it is recommended that you ensure the correct design intent.*

Constraints can be implied in a sketch or they can be explicitly assigned. By default, the software automatically infers constraints as entities are sketched. For example, constraint indicators are displayed as you sketch an entity that is horizontal/vertical, or parallel/perpendicular with a reference. Once located, the constraint is applied.

Hint: Changing the Inferred Constraint Reference

The software automatically determines which existing reference and inferred constraint type is assigned to an entity as it is being sketched. If the inferred constraint is not as required, hover the cursor over a different entity in the sketch to infer a different constraint type and then place the entity.

To control which constraints are inferred while sketching, in the *Sketch* tab>*Constrain* panel, click (Constraint Settings). Select the *Inference* tab in the *Constraint Settings* dialog box and enable/disable the constraints that are to be inferred, as required.

- To view constraints that are assigned, in the Constrain panel, click (Show Constraints) and select the entities to display their constraint indicators, as shown in Figure 2–13.
- Alternatively, you can click (Show All Constraints) in the Status Bar to toggle the display of the constraint indicators on and off. You can select the entities individually or by drawing a bounding box around them.

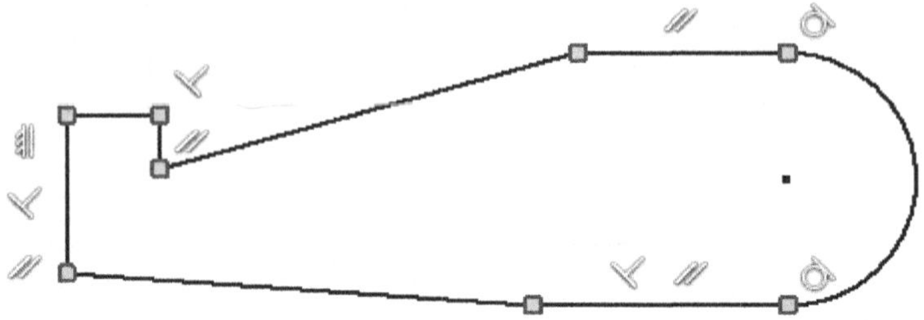

Figure 2–13

*Note: The **Show Constraints** and **Show All Constraints** settings remain active while sketching, or until they are disabled.*

The default sketched geometry colors (based on the default color scheme) are as follows. The sketched geometry colors depend on the assigned Color scheme, which is set in the *Colors* tab in the *Application Options* dialog box.

Green	Sketched geometry that is unconstrained.
Dark Blue	Sketched geometry that is fully constrained and dimensioned.
White	Sketched geometry (e.g., lines) is white when you hover the cursor over it.
Light Blue	Sketched geometry (e.g., lines) is light blue when selected.
Yellow	Projected geometry or origin features.

Although constraints are automatically assumed and created as you sketch, you can also apply your own constraints to further capture your design intent. Assigning constraints is discussed later in this guide. To ensure that the sketch is fully constrained, review its status in the lower-right corner of the graphics window, as shown in Figure 2–14.

Figure 2–14

Once the sketch is fully constrained, in the *Exit* panel, click (Finish Sketch) or right-click and select **Finish 2D Sketch**. To cancel sketch creation prior to finishing the sketch, expand the *Exit* panel and click (Cancel).

Step 5 - Select the base feature type.

Once the sketch has been drawn and constrained, the next step in creating a 3D object is to add thickness or depth to the sketch. The simplest options to add depth is to extrude the sketch so that it is perpendicular to the sketch plane or revolve the sketch about an axis, as shown in the following table. There are other feature form types that are discussed later in this guide (e.g., loft and sweep) that can also be used to create more complex solid base features.

Form	2D Cross-Section	3D Base Feature
Extrude	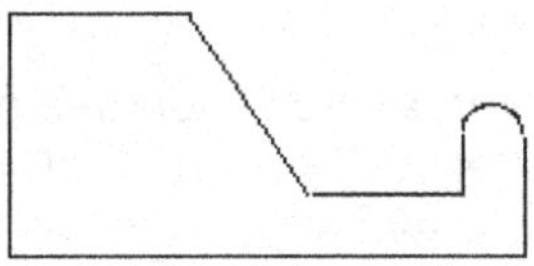	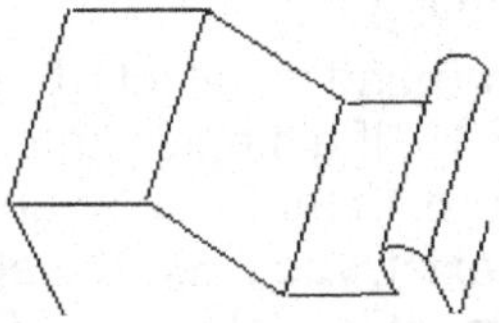
Revolve	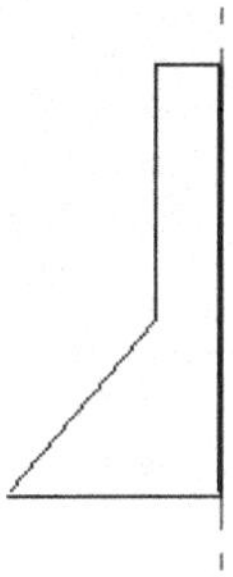	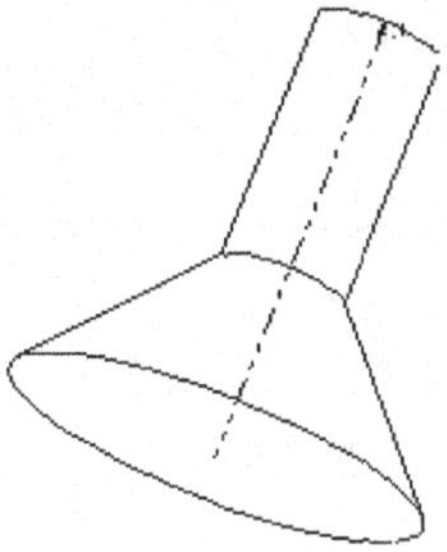
Loft	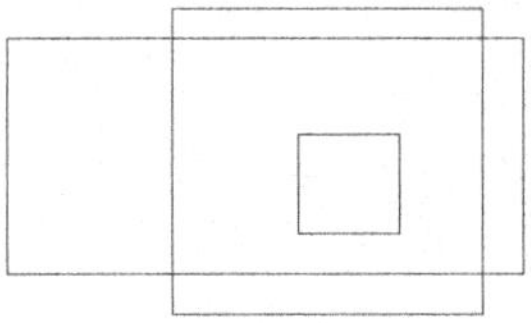	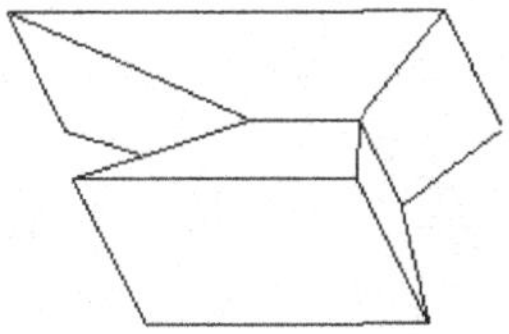
Sweep	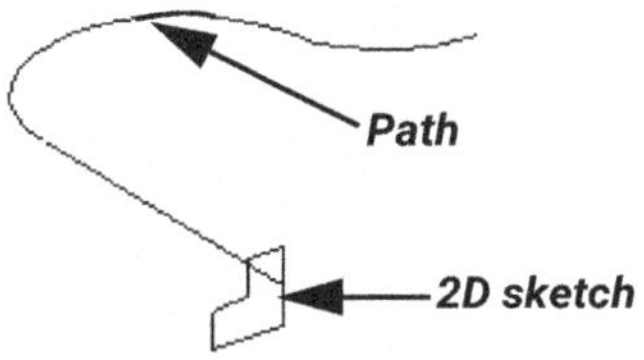	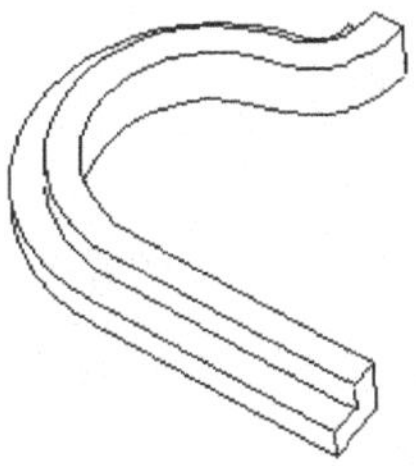

__Note:__ A solid base feature cannot be created without a sketched section. If initiated without a sketch, a dialog box opens indicating that you need to create a 2D sketch to proceed. Click __Create 2D Sketch__ to start a new sketch.

Use any of the following methods to create a solid base feature extruded from a sketch:

- In the *3D Model* tab>*Create* panel, click  (Extrude).
- Right-click in the graphics window and select **Extrude**.
- In the Model browser, left-click on the Sketch name and click  in the graphics window's Heads-up display.
- Press <E>.

The option to create a Revolve feature (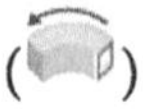) is found in the same locations as those listed above, or by pressing <R>.

Once a feature command is selected (e.g., **Extrude** or **Revolve**), its *Properties* panel opens, as shown in Figure 2–15. If a single sketch exists in the model, it is automatically selected as the profile for the feature. In the case of an Extrude feature, a preview of the model displays. If multiple sketches exist, you need to select the profile, and in the case of a Revolve feature, the axis of revolution must be selected before a preview displays.

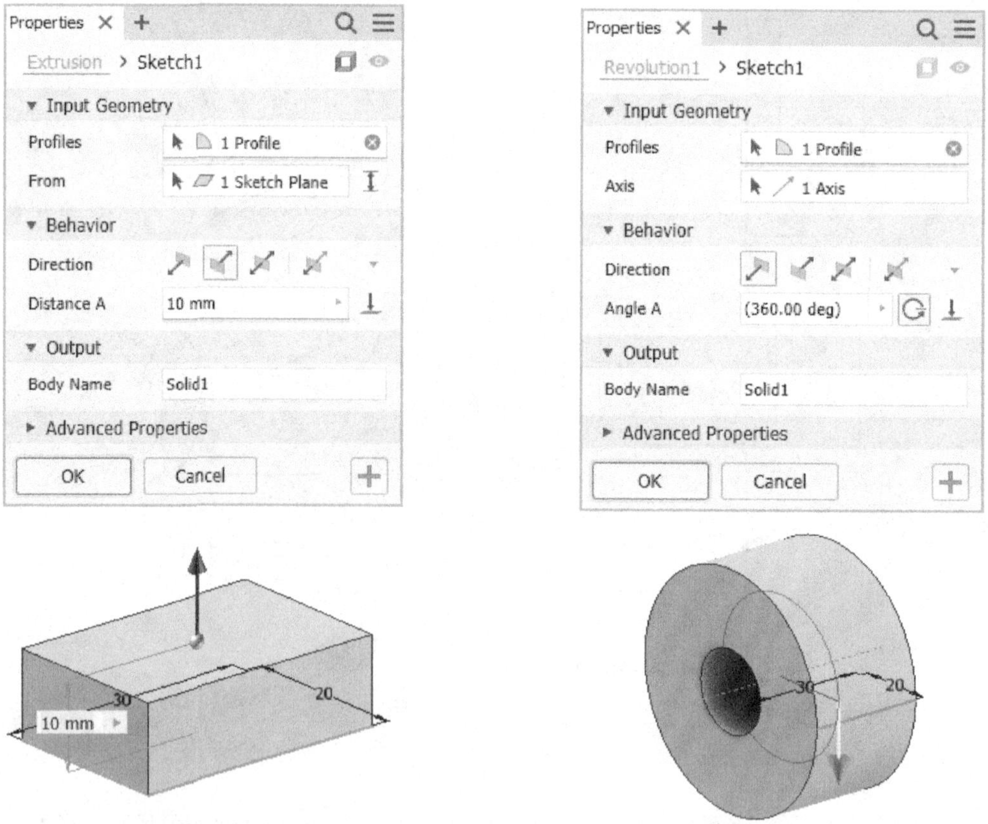

Figure 2–15

Step 6 - Define the depth and direction.

Distance (Depth)

There are two methods that can be used to define the distance (depth) of an extrude for base features. These include:

- Entering a value in the *Distance A* field. This extrudes the geometry from the sketch plane of the profile to the specified *Distance A* value.
- Enabling the (Between) option adjacent to the *From* field to customize a start and end plane for the geometry. This enables you to define the start plane as something other than the profile's sketch plane. For a base feature, it enables you to extrude between two work planes, as shown in Figure 2–16. When used, the *Distance A* field populates with a reference dimension shown in brackets (e.g., **(7.000 in)**).

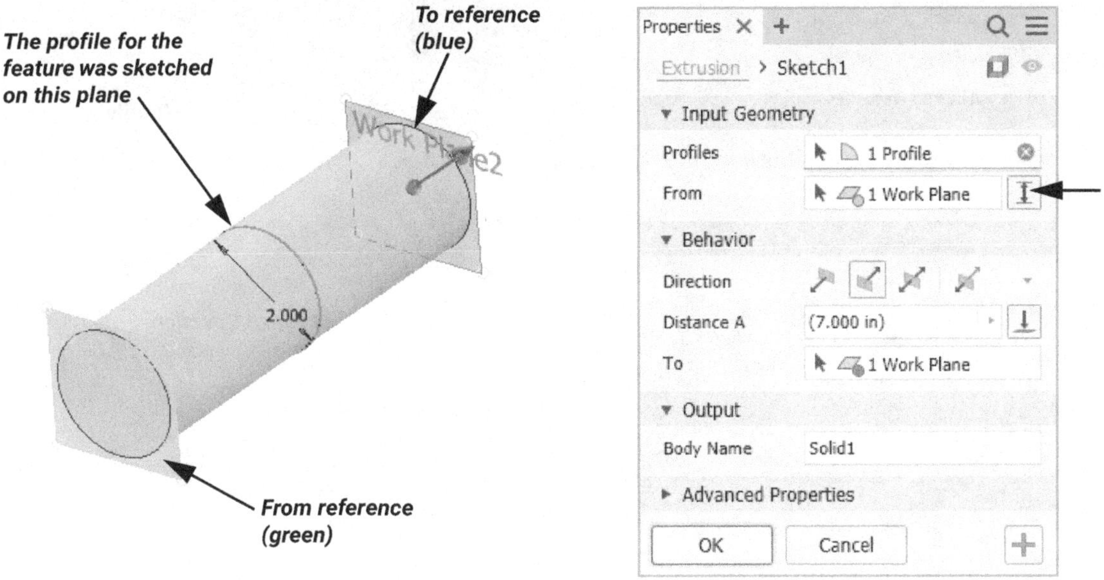

Figure 2–16

Direction

Direction icons (, , , and) set the direction to extrude/revolve from the sketch plane or how it extrudes on both sides of the plane. Extrude directions are shown in Figure 2–17 to Figure 2–20. You can select the direction using the icons in the *Properties* panel.

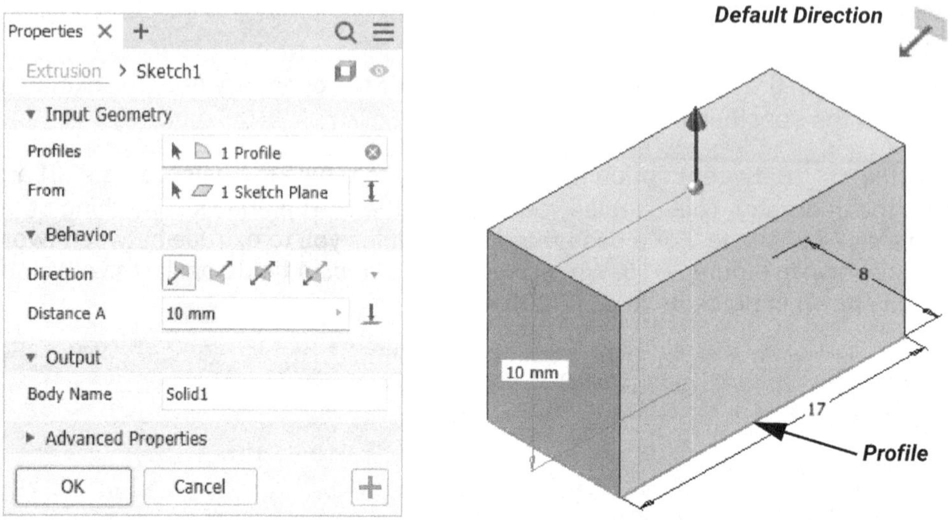

Figure 2–17

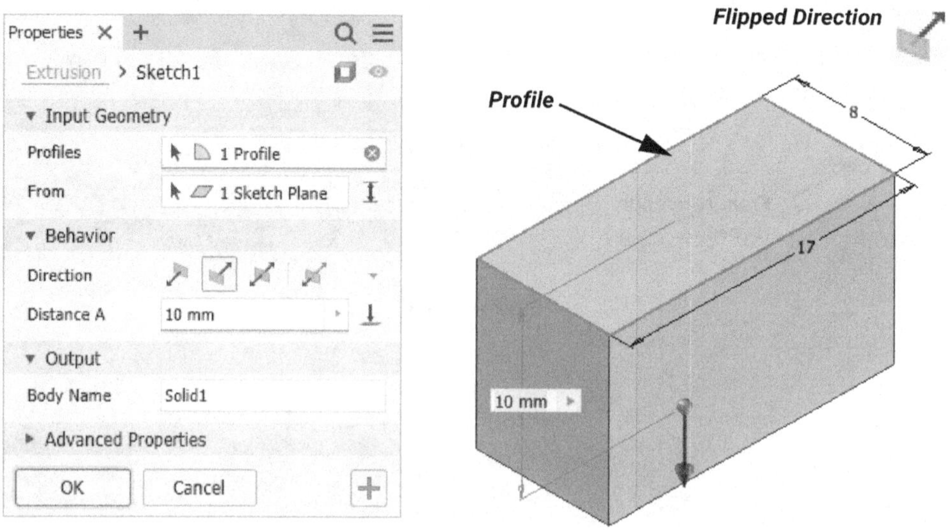

Figure 2–18

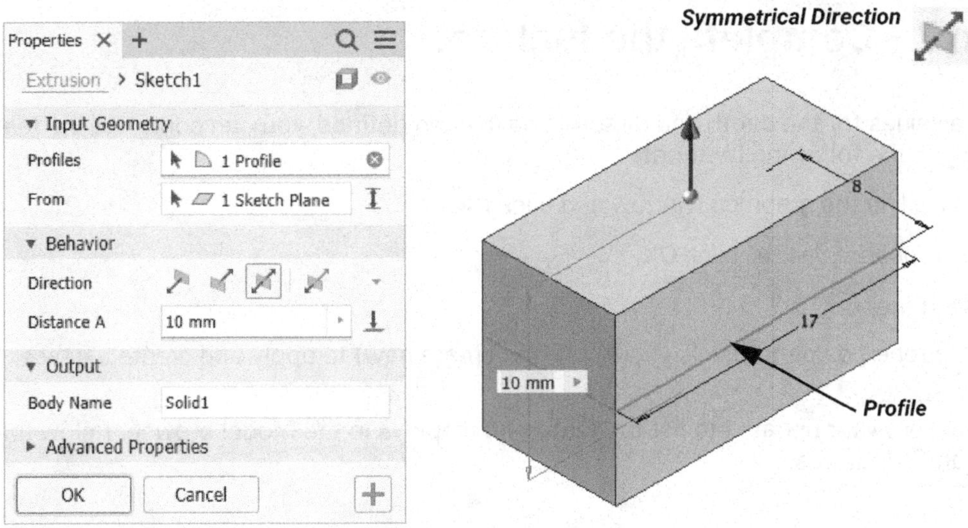

Figure 2–19

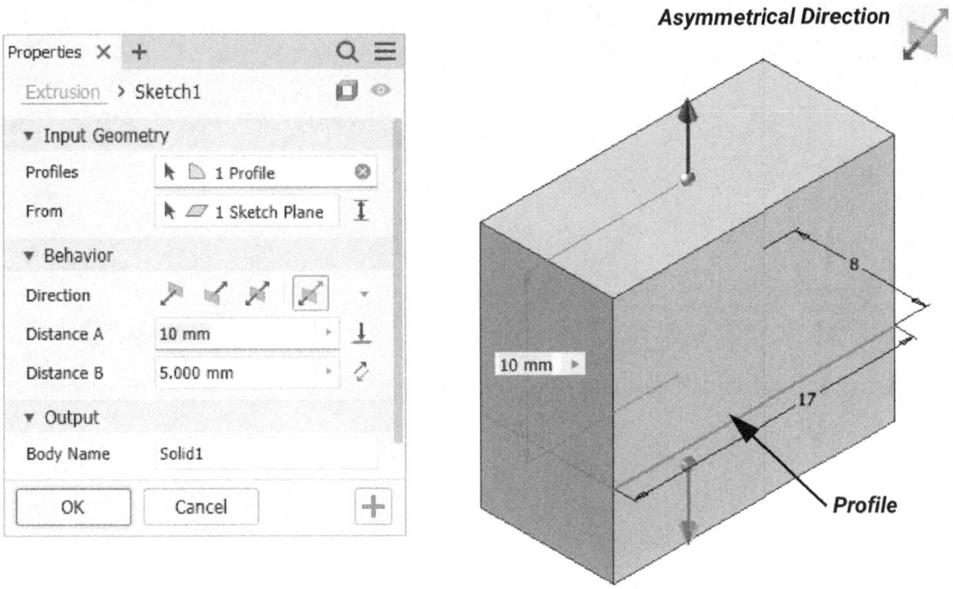

Figure 2–20

Step 7 - Complete the feature.

Once the values for the depth and direction have been defined, you can complete the feature using any of the following methods:

- Right-click in the graphics window and click **OK**.
- In the *Properties* panel, click **OK**.
- Press <Enter>.
- In the *Properties* panel, click  (Apply and create new) to apply and create a new extrude feature.

The Model browser updates to list the feature. It displays in the Model browser below the default origin features.

2.3 Editing Sketched Features

To make modifications to a feature, right-click on the feature in the Model browser and select the required option, as shown in Figure 2–21. Additional options are also available to edit a sketched feature.

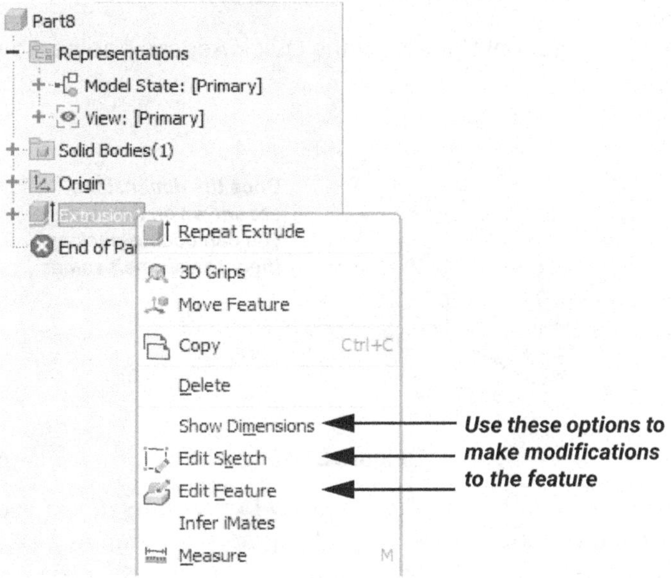

Figure 2–21

Hint: Naming a Sketch

Assigning custom names to features can help you to locate and identify features in the Model browser. To assign a custom name for the base feature you can use either of the following methods:

- At the top of the *Properties* panel, select **Extrusion** and enter a name for the sketch.
- Select the feature in the Model browser twice (do not double-click) and enter a new name.

Show Dimensions

If you are only making changes to dimension values for a feature or its sketch, right-click and select **Show Dimensions** to display the dimensions for the selected feature, as shown in Figure 2–22. This enables you to change the values by double-clicking the dimension and entering a new value in the field that displays. The dimensional changes are not automatically reflected until you click  (Local Update) in the Quick Access Toolbar to update the model.

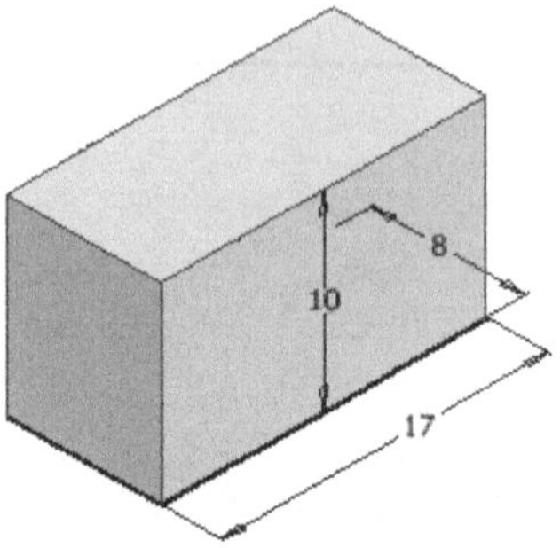

Once the dimensions are shown on the model, you can double-click on them to edit their values

Figure 2–22

__Note:__ Feature dimensions that display using __Show Dimensions__ display only until another feature is selected in the Model browser or in the graphics window.

Sketch Visibility

Once a sketch is used to create solid geometry, it is consumed within its new parent feature. By default, this sketch is not visible on the model. To make the sketch visible, expand its parent feature in the Model browser, right-click on it, and select **Visibility**. Alternatively, you can select a face to which the feature belongs and click 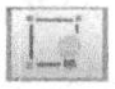. The sketch and its dimensions display on the part, as shown in Figure 2–23. Double-click on any dimension to edit its value.

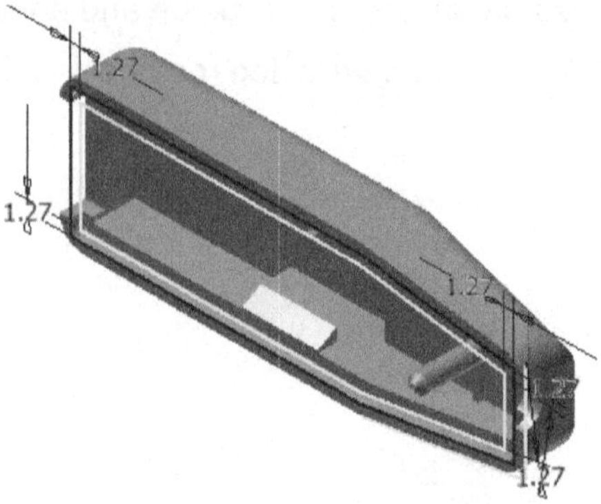

Figure 2–23

- If the screen becomes too cluttered after displaying a number of sketches, you can hide the dimensions of a selected sketch by right-clicking on the sketch in the Model browser and selecting **Dimension Visibility**. Alternatively, select the sketch in the Model browser and press <Alt>+<V>. This shortcut enables you to toggle a sketch's visibility on and off.
- You can clear the display of dimensions from all sketches in the model at once by selecting the **Sketch Dimensions** object visibility setting (*View* tab>*Visibility* panel).

Edit Sketch

To make changes to the sketch, use one of the following methods to activate the Sketch environment:

- Double-click on the sketch in the Model browser.
- In the Model browser or the graphics window, select the sketch, right-click, and select **Edit Sketch**.
- Select an entity in the sketch or in the solid feature and click  in the heads-up display on the sketch.

  Note: *To cancel any edits made to a sketch and return to the previous sketch, expand the Exit panel and click*  *(Cancel).*

Edit Feature

To make changes to the options and elements that were available when a feature (e.g., extrusion) was originally created. use one of the following methods:

- Double-click on the feature in the Model browser.
- In the Model browser or the graphics window, select the feature, right-click, and select **Edit Feature**.
- Select a face on the feature and click  in the heads-up display on the model.
- Double-click on the feature in the graphics window.

Show Input

To display the source sketch plane for a sketch, right-click on the sketch and select **Show Input**.

Change the Sketch Plane

The sketch plane for a base feature is defined when the sketch is created and the base feature becomes a child of that plane. The sketch plane can be changed after a sketch is created; however, keep in mind that references made to any existing entities or work features will be lost.

How To: Change the Sketch Plane

1. In the Model browser, right-click on the sketch and select **Redefine**. If the sketch is consumed by a solid feature, expand the solid feature name and then select the sketch plane.
2. Select another sketch plane (e.g., YZ Plane) in the Model browser.

Practice 2a
Extruded Base Features I

Practice Objectives

- Create two new part models using predefined templates.
- Create extruded and revolved base features on origin planes using a provided dimension and constraint scheme.

In this practice, you will create new models using the default template. The geometry in these models will be created using either rectangular or circular sketches to create the extrusions shown in Figure 2–24.

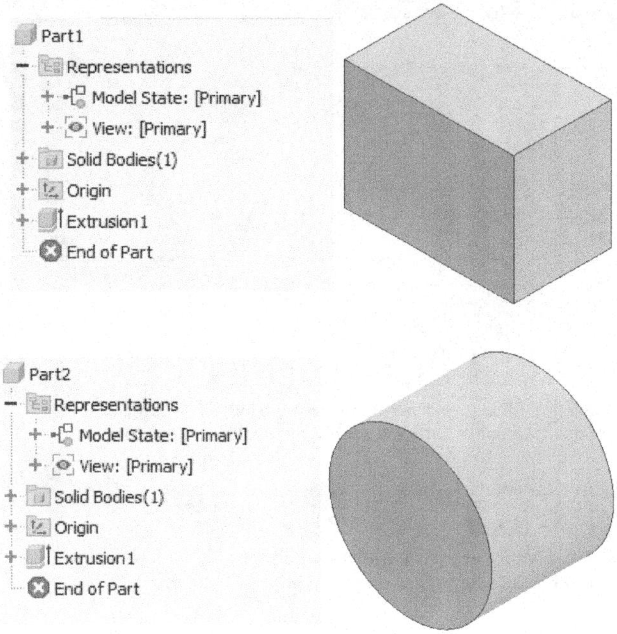

Figure 2–24

Task 1: Create a new model using a part template.

1. On the *Home* page, select **New**. The *Create New File* dialog box opens.
2. Complete the following in the *Create New File* dialog box, as shown in Figure 2–25:
   a. Expand the *Templates>en_US* folders in the left pane and select the *Metric* folder.
   b. Select **Standard (mm).ipt** in the *Part – Create 2D and 3D objects* area of the dialog box.
   c. Note that the right pane updates to show that the *Units* for the new part file is **millimeter**.
   d. Click **Create**.

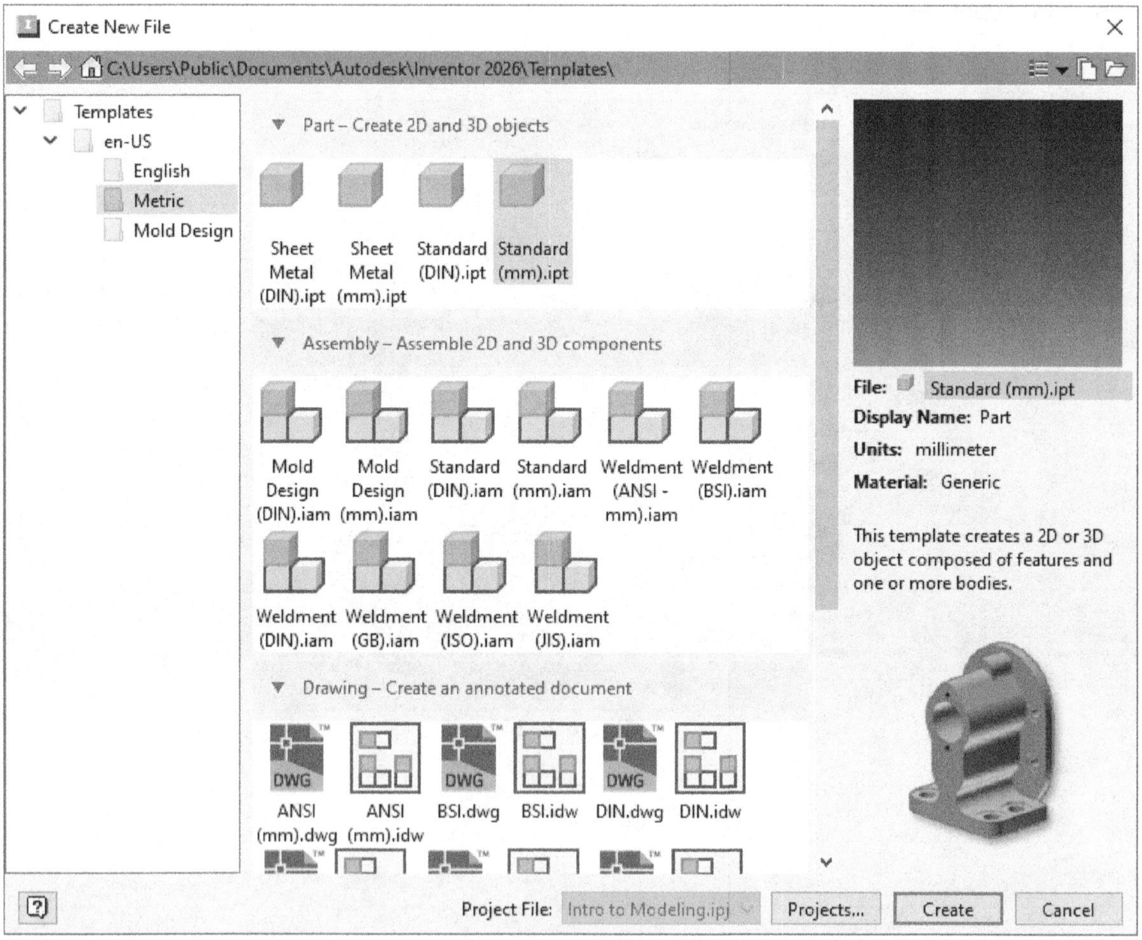

Figure 2–25

Task 2: Create a sketch.

1. In the *3D Model* tab>*Sketch* panel, click (Start 2D Sketch). Alternatively, you can right-click on the plane name in the Model browser, or in the graphics window, right-click and select **New Sketch**. The origin planes are temporarily displayed in the graphics window, as shown in Figure 2–26, so that you can select the sketch plane.

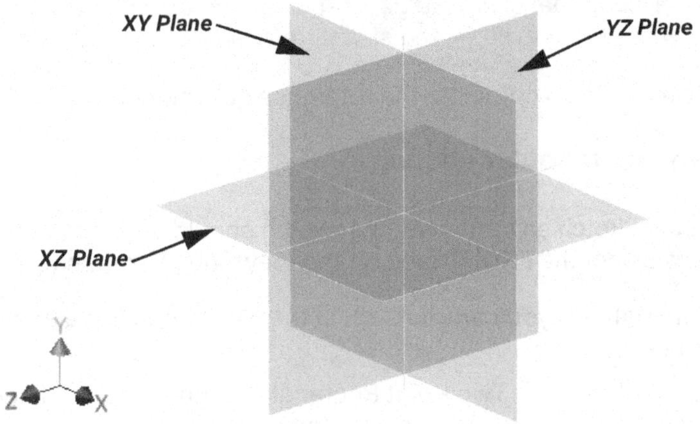

Figure 2–26

2. Hover the cursor over the origin planes in the model until you locate the XY Plane. Select the XY Plane in the graphics window to start a new sketch on this plane. You are placed in the Sketch environment, the XY Plane is the current sketch plane, and the *Sketch* tab is active.

Hint: Origin Planes in the Model Browser

The default origin planes are listed in the **Origin** node in the Model browser. To review the list, click + adjacent to the **Origin** node to expand it and hover your cursor over any of the plane names to temporarily highlight them and display their names in the graphics window.

By default, the origin center point is projected (shown in yellow) onto the XY sketch plane. It can be used as the dimensioning reference when adding geometry. By referencing the projected center point, you are directly locating the sketch relative to the origin center point of the entire model. In the next task, you will project two of the origin planes and use them as references for locating geometry in the sketch. The decision to use the projected center point or planes is based on the required design intent. By projecting planes as references, you are providing references that can be used to ensure symmetry or create revolved features. Referencing a center point is acceptable for cylindrical base features. As you gain more experience, you will learn which reference is the most appropriate to use as a reference.

Task 3: Define sketch references.

1. In the *Create* panel, click (Project Geometry), or right-click and select **Project Geometry**. Select the **YZ Plane** and **XZ Plane** in the **Origin** node of the Model browser as references to locate the sketched geometry. The references are represented as yellow lines that are projected onto the sketch plane.

   Note: *It is recommended that sketched geometry be located with respect to existing features in the part. Therefore, projected sketch reference entities are required.*

2. Right-click and select **OK** to complete the reference selection or press <Esc>.

Task 4: Sketch the rectangular section.

1. When placed in the Sketch environment, the sketch should automatically be in a 2D orientation. If not, select the **FRONT** face on the ViewCube to return to a 2D view parallel to the XY Plane. Alternatively, you can click in the Navigation Bar and select the **XY Plane** in the Model browser.
2. In the *Create* panel, click (Two Point Rectangle) or right-click and select **Two Point Rectangle** to sketch the base feature as a rectangular section.
3. Start the sketch by moving the cursor to the point at which the rectangle begins (as shown in Figure 2–27), and click.
4. Move the cursor to the point at which the rectangle ends (opposite corner), as shown in Figure 2–27, and click to complete the rectangle.

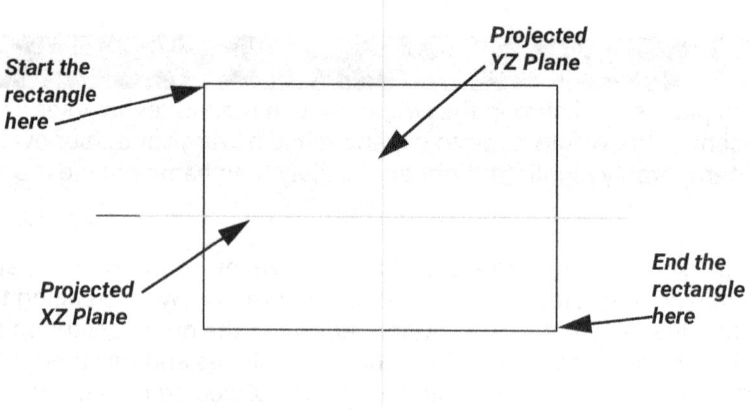

Figure 2–27

5. To complete the command you can select a new option, right-click, and select **OK**, or press <Esc>.

   Note: *To delete a sketch entity, right-click on the entity in the graphics window and select* ***Delete*** *or select the entity and press <Delete>.*

6. Note that the bottom-right corner of the main window indicates that four dimensions are required to fully locate the sketch. Two dimensions are required to fully define the size of the rectangle and two are required to locate it relative to the projected planes.
7. In the *Constrain* panel, click (Automatic Dimensions and Constraints) to locate and dimension the rectangle. The *Auto Dimension* dialog box opens, as shown in Figure 2–28. Four dimensions are required.

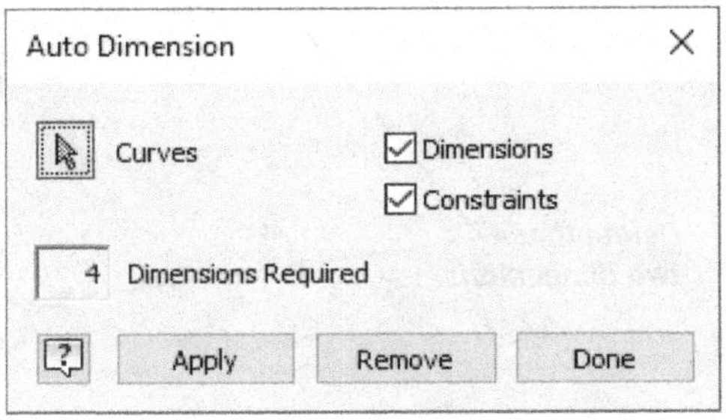

Figure 2–28

Note: Automatically dimensioning a sketch is helpful when determining a missing dimension. However, it is not recommended for use in dimensioning a full sketch, because it cannot assume your design intent for the sketch.

8. Click **Apply** to assign the dimensions, similar to Figure 2–29.

Your dimensions might be different in size and location from the dimensions shown

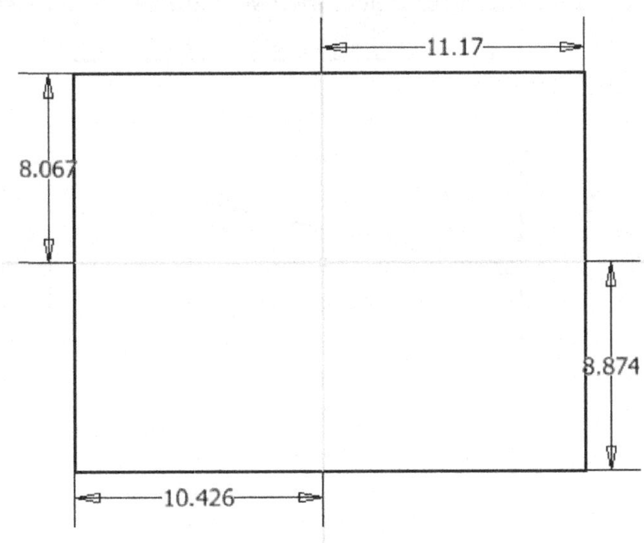

Figure 2–29

9. Click **Done** to close the dialog box.

10. Delete the two dimensions shown in Figure 2–30. To delete a dimension, right-click on it and select **Delete**. Alternatively, you can select the dimension and press <Delete>.

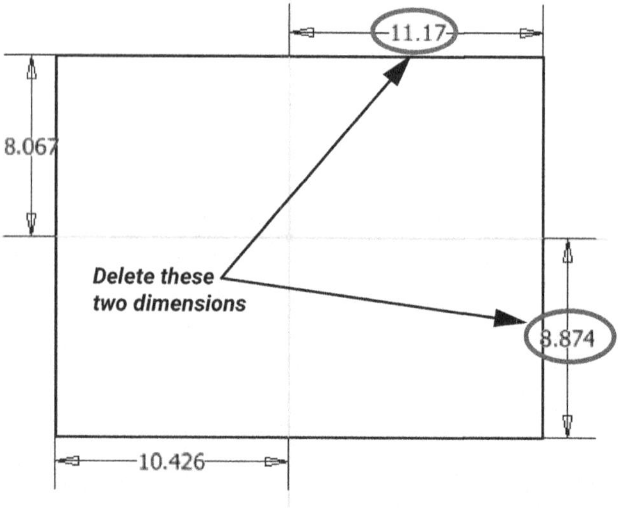

Figure 2–30

11. In the *Constrain* panel, click (Dimension) or right-click in the graphics window and select **General Dimension**. Select the two sketched entities shown in Figure 2–31.

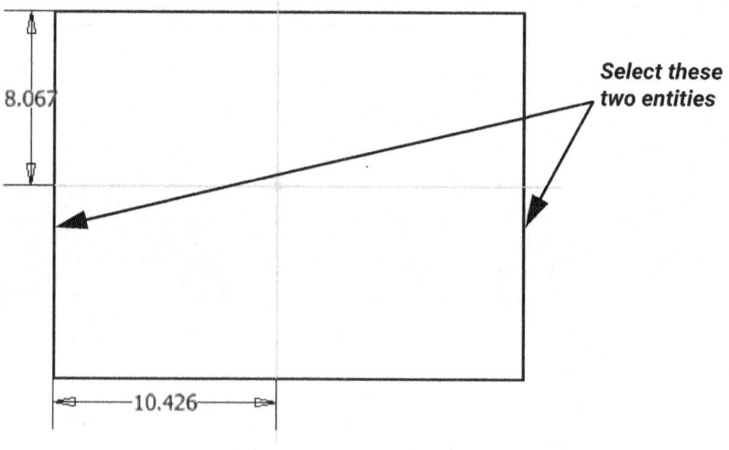

Figure 2–31

12. Move the cursor between the two selected lines and click to place the dimension in the location shown in Figure 2–32. The dimension displays as shown in Figure 2–32. Press <Enter> to accept the value, if prompted.

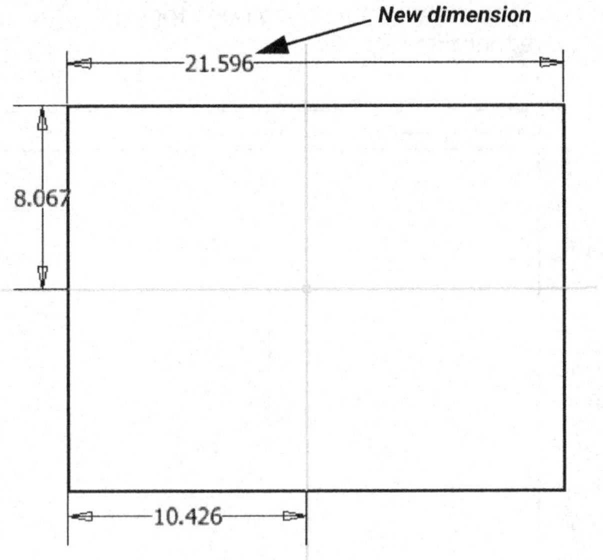

Figure 2–32

13. Note that now, in the bottom-right corner of the main window, only 1 dimension is required. Create a second dimension, as shown in Figure 2–33.

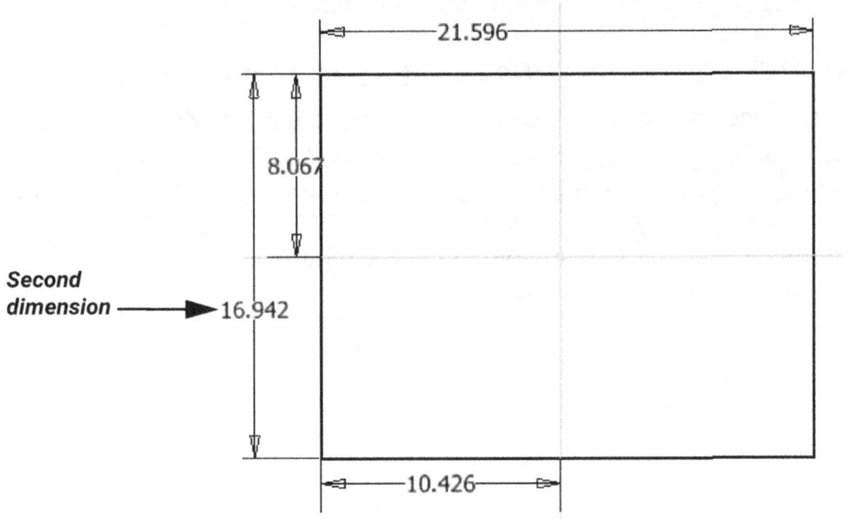

Figure 2–33

14. Modify the dimensions so that the sketch displays as shown in Figure 2–34. If (Dimension) is still toggled on, you can modify dimensions by single-clicking on them and entering the new value. If the dimensioning command is not active, double-click on a dimension to modify it. Once dimensioning has been toggled off, you can select and drag dimensions to move them as required.

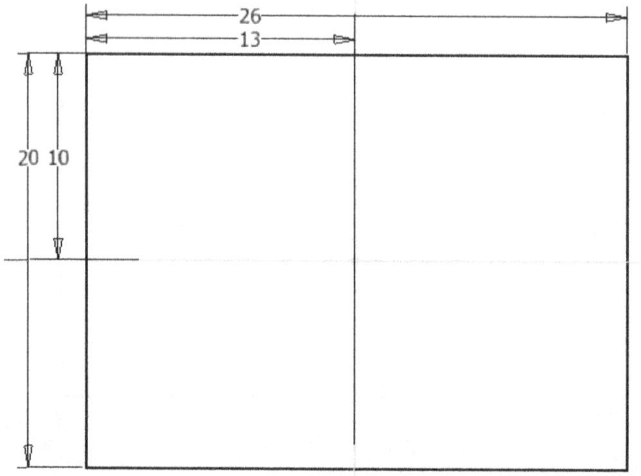

Figure 2–34

15. The base feature geometry is sketched and fully constrained. In the *Exit* panel, click (Finish Sketch), or right-click and select **Finish 2D Sketch**.

The sketch is now dimensioned relative to the origin planes and is therefore anchored, as indicated by the icon adjacent to the new Sketch feature in the Model browser. If the sketch were not fully constrained, the icon would not include a push pin ( ). Depending on the design intent, another method is to add Symmetry constraints between the sketched lines and the origin planes. Using Symmetry constraints would remove two dimension values, ensuring that the rectangle remains symmetric to the origin planes, regardless of the size of the rectangle. Constraints are discussed later in this guide.

Task 5: Select the type of feature.

1. Use any of the following methods to activate the **Extrude** option:
   - In the *3D Model* tab>*Create* panel, click  (Extrude).
   - Right-click in the graphics window and select **Extrude**.
   - In the Model browser, left-click on the Sketch name and click  in the graphics window's Heads-up display.
   - Press <E>.
2. Select anywhere on the perimeter of the sketched rectangle to select it as the profile. The *Properties* panel and a model preview display, as shown in Figure 2–35.

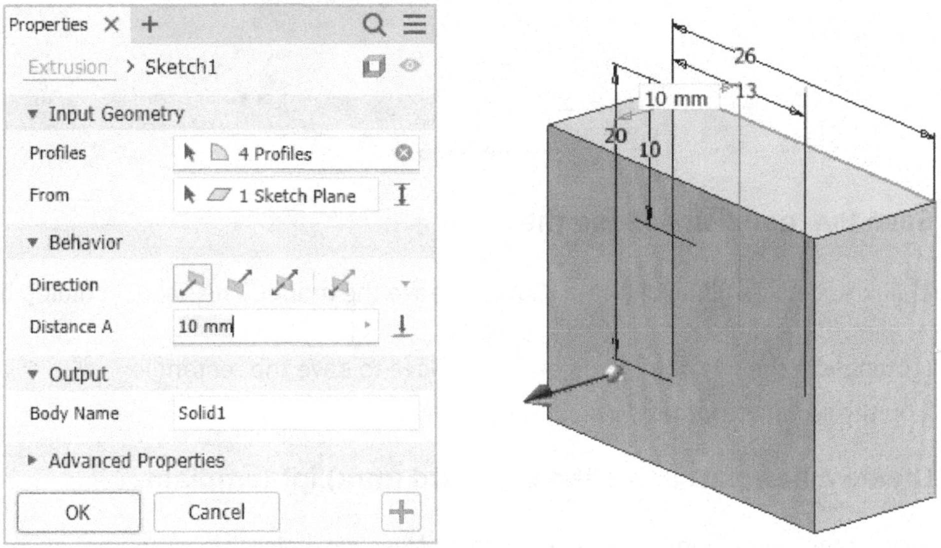

Figure 2–35

Note: *In the Properties panel, the Profile field lists four profiles. The projected work planes in the sketch divided the rectangle into four selectable profiles. You could have selected each profile individually, but by selecting the perimeter, it automatically selects all four.*

Task 6: Define the depth of the extrusion.

1. A default distance value and direction is applied. You can accept or change these defaults. Enter **15** as the *Distance A* value (depth) in the *Properties* panel or entry field on the model, or by dragging the depth handle on the model geometry. Once a value has been entered, right-click and select **OK (Enter)**, or click **OK** in the *Properties* panel. If you press <Enter> immediately after entering the *Distance A* value, the *Properties* panel also closes. This is acceptable; however, it does prevent you from reviewing any of the other options.

2. Hover the cursor over the ViewCube in the upper-right corner of the graphics window and click (home icon) to rotate the model to its default orientation. The model displays in its default view, as shown in Figure 2–36.

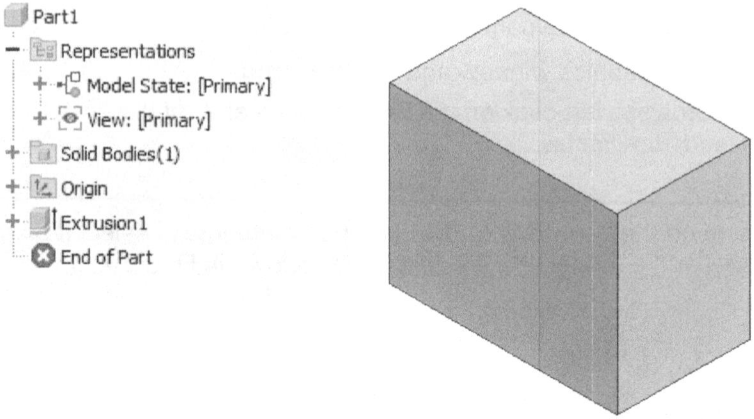

Figure 2–36

Task 7: Save the model and close the file.

1. In the Quick Access Toolbar, click (Save) to save the model. The *Save As* dialog box opens.
2. Enter **rectangle** in the *File name* field and click **Save** to save the rectangle.
3. Click **X** on the *rectangle.ipt* tab to close the file.

Task 8: Create a new part using the Standard (mm).ipt template.

1. Click **New** on the *Home* page to open the *Create New File* dialog box. Ensure that you are using the **Standard (mm).ipt** template file and click **Create**. Once created, the *3D Model* tab becomes the active tab.

Hint: Creating a Part File Using the Default Template

Using the *Create New File* dialog box enables you to review and ensure that the correct template is being used to create a new part file. This approach is recommended until you are comfortable that you understand the template assignment. Otherwise, you can use the following techniques to start a new part file using the default template directly without using the *Create New File* dialog box.

- On the *Home* page, select ˅ to expand the **New** menu and select **Part (.ipt)**.
- In the Quick Access Toolbar, expand the (New) option and select **Part**. Selecting the (New) option directly opens the *Create New File* dialog box allowing you to select the template.
- In the **File** menu, select **New>Part**. Selecting the **New>New** opens the *Create New File* dialog box allowing you to select the template.

Task 9: Create the sketch.

To create the previous sketch, you first selected the command and then selected the sketch plane. In this task, you will first select the sketch plane and then initiate the command.

1. In the Model browser, click + next to the **Origin** node to expand it.
2. Select the **XY Plane** in the Model browser. In the *3D Model* tab>*Sketch* panel, click (Start 2D Sketch). You are placed in the Sketch environment, the XY Plane is the current sketch plane, and the *Sketch* tab is active.

   Note: *Alternatively, you can also start a new sketching by clicking (Create Sketch) in the graphics window or by right-clicking on the origin plane in the Model browser or graphics window, and selecting* ***New Sketch****.*

Task 10: Sketch a circular section.

By default, the origin center point is automatically projected, so you do not need to project it. In this task, you will reference cylindrical geometry to the center point.

1. In the *Create* panel, click (Circle) or right-click and select **Center Point Circle** to sketch the base feature as a circular section.

2. Start the sketch by pressing the left mouse button at the projected center point. A green dot displays, indicating that the referenced center point has been selected. Drag the mouse away from the center point. Press the left mouse button again to define the diameter of the circle, as shown in Figure 2–37.

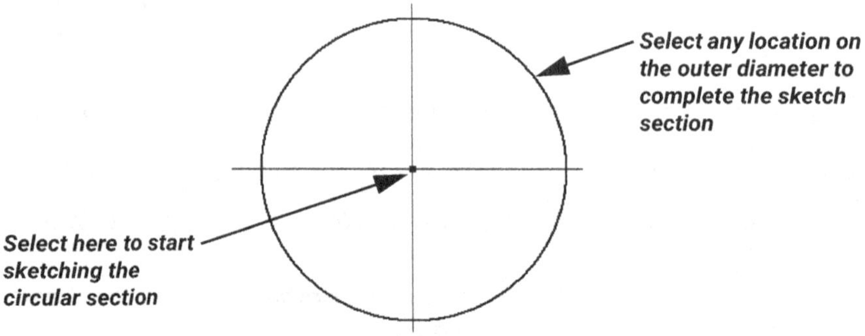

Figure 2–37

Note: To undo or redo sketching actions, click and in the Quick Access Toolbar, respectively.

3. In the *Constrain* panel, click (Dimension). Alternatively, right-click and select **General Dimension** or press <D> to dimension the circle.
4. Select the circle in the graphics window. Move the cursor away from the circle. The dimension is attached to it. Select a location outside the circle to place the dimension. The sketch displays similar to the one shown in Figure 2–38.

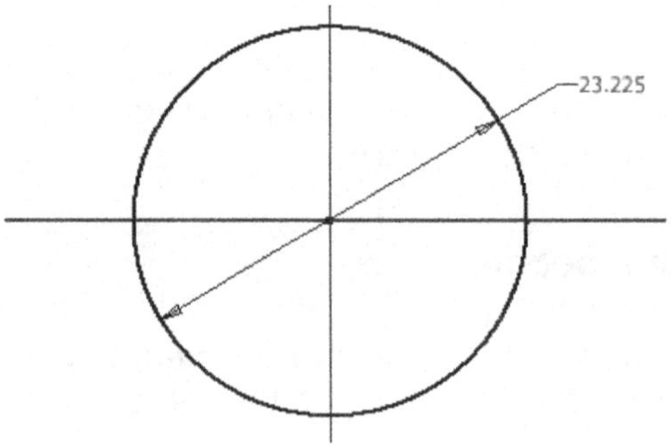

Figure 2–38

5. Select the dimension, if the *Edit Dimension* dialog box is not already active, and enter **20.00**. Press <Enter> to update the sketch.
6. In the graphics window, right-click and select **OK** to finish dimensioning.

7. The base feature geometry is sketched and fully constrained. In the *Exit* panel, click (Finish Sketch), or right-click and select **Finish 2D Sketch**.
8. Hover the cursor over the ViewCube and click (Home) to return the model to its default 3D orientation, if it does not automatically return to its default orientation.

Task 11: Select the feature type and define the depth.

1. Use any of the following methods to activate the **Extrude** option:
   - In the *3D Model* tab>*Create* panel, click (Extrude).
   - Right-click in the graphics window and select **Extrude**.
   - In the Model browser, left-click on the Sketch name and click in the graphics window's Heads-up display.
   - Press <E>.

   The *Properties* panel and a preview of the extruded model display. The circular section was automatically selected as the *Profile* because it is the only available profile in the model. It has been extruded to a default depth (*Distance A*).
2. Enter **15** as the *Distance A* value (depth). The *Distance A* value can be entered in the *Properties* panel or in the entry field on the model. Alternatively, you can drag the depth handle on the model geometry.
3. Once a value has been entered, right-click and select **OK (Enter)**, or click **OK** in the *Properties* panel. The model and Model browser display as shown in Figure 2–39.

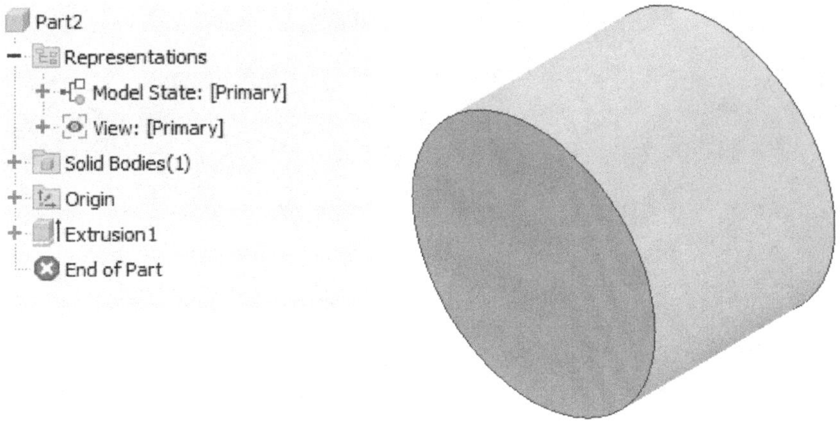

Figure 2–39

Task 12: Save the model and close the file.

1. In the Quick Access Toolbar, click (Save) to save the model. The *Save As* dialog box opens.
2. Enter **cylinder** in the *File name* field and click **Save** to save the cylinder.
3. Click **X** on the *cylinder.ipt* tab to close the file.

End of practice

Practice 2b
Extruded Base Features II

Practice Objectives

- Create a new part model using a predefined template.
- Create an extruded base feature on an origin plane, using a provided dimension and constraint scheme.
- Modify the extruded base feature to incorporate dimensional and feature direction changes.

In this practice, you will create a new model using a standard template file. The geometry is an extruded base feature, as shown in Figure 2–40. It is created by referencing the projected center point to dimension and constrain sketched line entities.

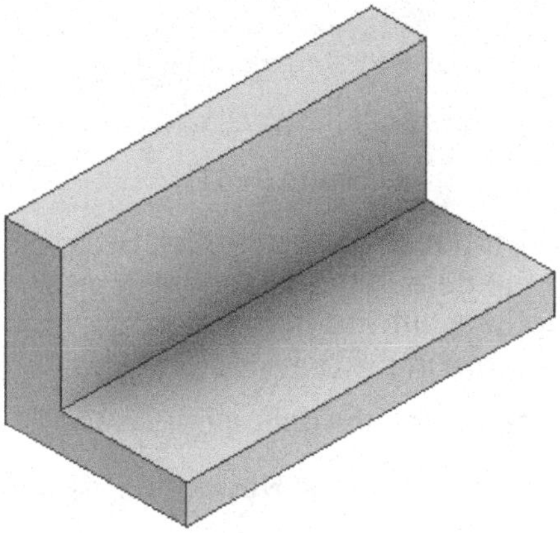

Figure 2–40

Task 1: Create a new part model and sketch its geometry.

In the previous practice, you learned to use the **New** option to open the *Create New File* dialog box and select a specific template to create new part files. In this practice, you will use the **Part** option to create a part file.

1. In the *Tools* tab, click (Application Options). Select the *File* tab in the *Application Options* dialog box and click **Configure Default Template**. The dialog box appears showing you the current units and standard for the default template. For example, Figure 2–41 shows the default templates currently assigned are in **Inches** and will use the **ANSI** drawing standard.

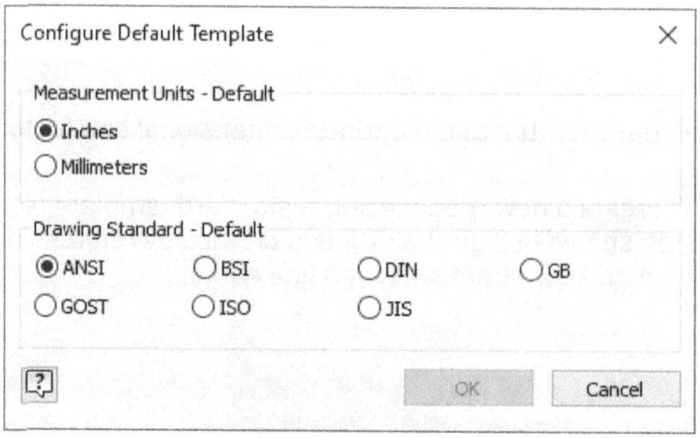

Figure 2–41

2. Select **Millimeters** and **ANSI**, if not already set. Click **OK** and confirm to **Overwrite** the default template. This sets the default template that is presented when you create a new part file; however, it does not prevent you from creating a model in inches by selecting **New** on the *Home* page as was shown in the previous practice.
3. Click **OK** to close the *Application Options* dialog box.
4. On the *Home* page, select to expand the **New** menu, as shown in Figure 2–42.

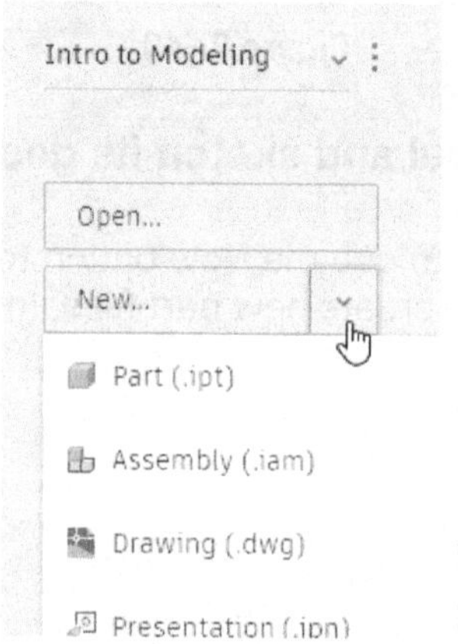

Figure 2–42

5. Select **Part (.ipt)**. This creates a new part file using the default template (which was just set to millimeter/ANSI) without having to use the *Create New File* dialog box.
6. In the Model browser, click + next to the **Origin** node to expand it.
7. In the Model browser, select the **XY Plane**. In the *3D Model* tab>*Sketch* panel, click (Start 2D Sketch) or click (Create Sketch) in the graphics window to start a new sketch. Alternatively, you can right-click on the plane name in the Model browser or in the graphics window (if displayed), right-click, and select **New Sketch**.

   Note: *You could also have initiated the command first and then selected the XY Plane as the sketching plane.*

Task 2: Sketch the base feature section.

1. In the *Create* panel, click (Line) or right-click and select **Create Line**.
2. Hover the cursor over the projected center point at the center of the sketch. The cursor should snap to this reference. Start the sketch by pressing the left mouse button at the projected center point, as shown in Figure 2–43.

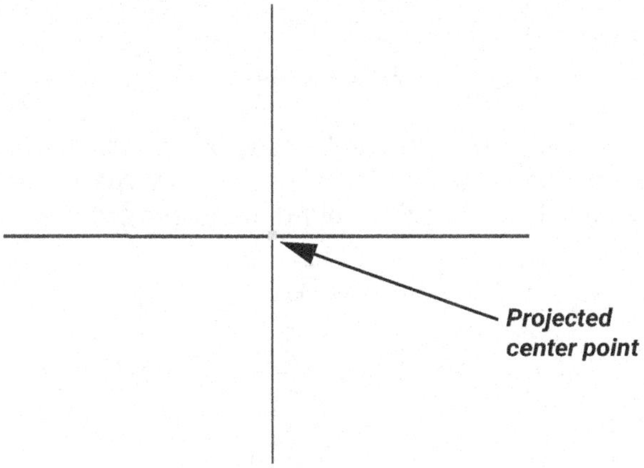

Figure 2–43

3. Sketch the six lines shown in Figure 2–44. Use the left mouse button to start and end each line segment. When drawing the lines, do not worry about their lengths, and draw the lines horizontally and vertically in a similar scale to that shown in Figure 2–44. When drawing the last line segment, which returns to the projected center point, ensure that the cursor snaps to this reference before selecting.

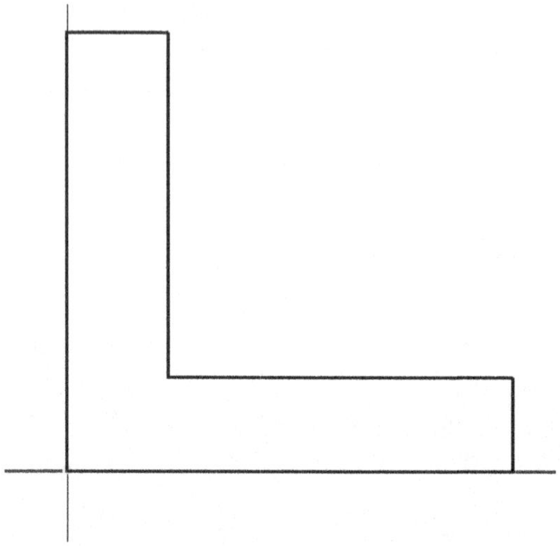

Figure 2–44

4. In the *Constrain* panel, click (Automatic Dimensions and Constraints) to reveal the number of required dimensions, as shown in Figure 2–45. Also note that the bottom-right corner of the main window indicates that four dimensions are required.

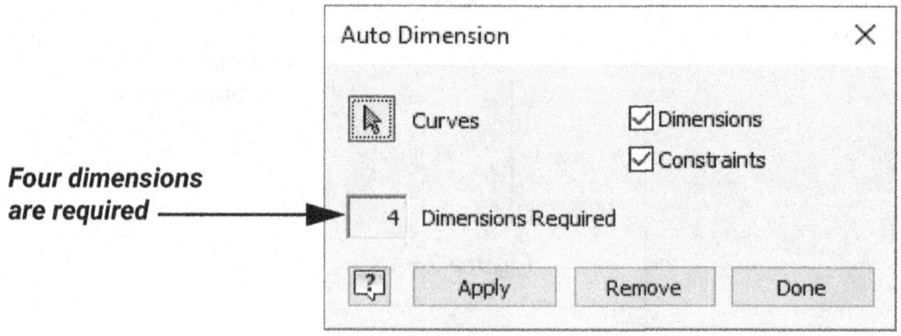

Figure 2–45

Note: *Automatically dimensioning a sketch is helpful when determining a missing dimension. However, it is not recommended for use in dimensioning a full sketch, as it does not assume your design intent for the sketch.*

5. Click **Apply** to apply the dimensions automatically.
6. Click **Done** to close the *Auto Dimension* dialog box.

7. If required, delete, recreate, and modify the dimensions to match those shown in Figure 2–46.

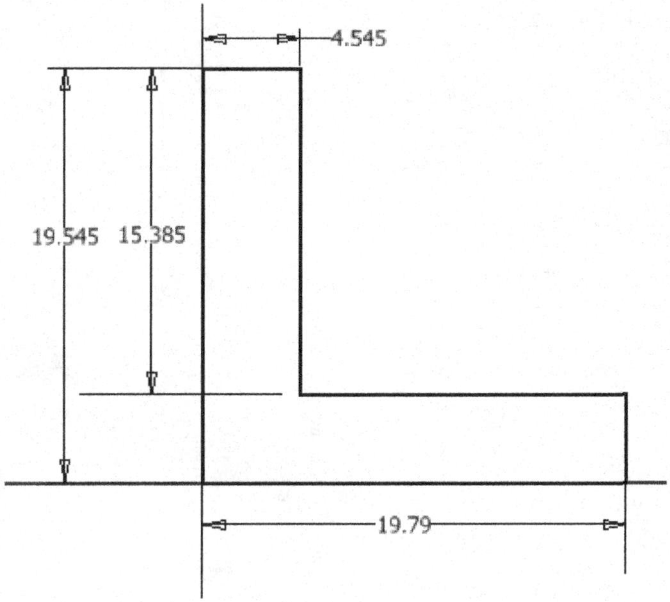

Figure 2–46

8. In the *Exit* panel, click (Finish Sketch), or right-click and select **Finish 2D Sketch**.

9. Hover the cursor over the ViewCube and click (Home) to return to the model to its default 3D orientation, if it does not automatically return to its default orientation.

Task 3: Select the feature type and define the depth.

1. Use any of the following methods to activate the **Extrude** option:

   - In the *3D Model* tab>*Create* panel, click (Extrude).
   - Right-click in the graphics window and select **Extrude**.
   - In the Model browser, left-click on the Sketch name and click in the graphics window's Heads-up display.
   - Press <E>.

   The section is automatically identified as the *Profile* because it is a single closed section and therefore has been extruded to a default depth.

2. Enter **30** as the *Distance A* value (depth) either in the *Properties* panel or in the depth field in the graphics window. Do not press <Enter> after typing the depth value. Pause for a few seconds after typing the value and the model updates with your changes. The model displays as shown in Figure 2–47.

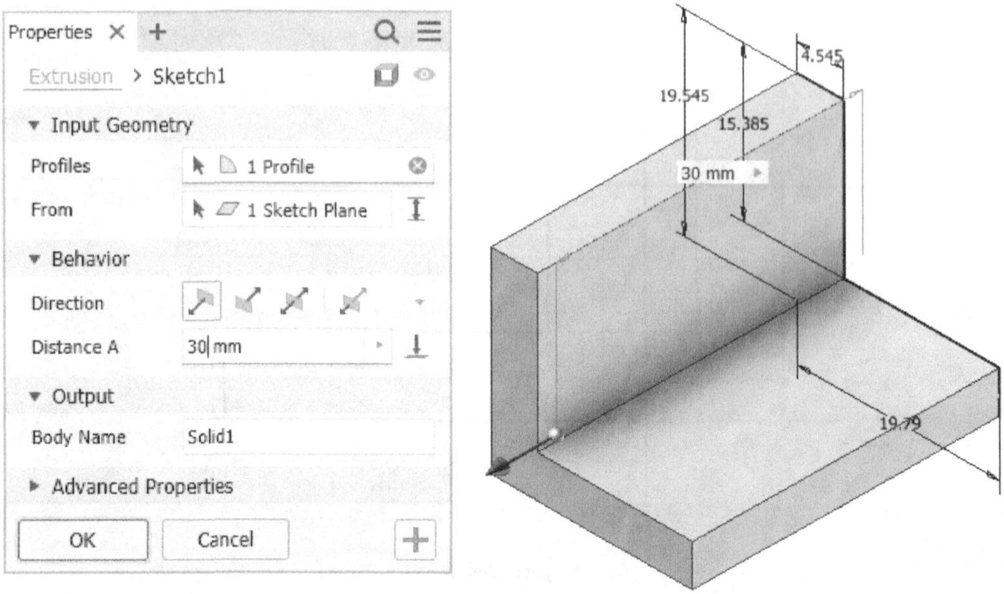

Figure 2–47

3. Once a value has been entered, right-click and select **OK (Enter)**, or click **OK** in the *Properties* panel.

Task 4: Modify dimension values associated with the extrusion.

1. Right-click on **Extrusion1** in the Model browser and select **Show Dimensions**. The extrusion dimensions display on the model.

   Note: *If you double-click on* ***Extrusion1*** *in the Model browser, the Properties panel opens, enabling you to modify the extrusion details.*

2. Double-click on the dimension that represents the thickness of the feature (in Figure 2–48, this is the dimension with the value of 4.545). Enter **6** as the new dimension value and press <Enter>.
3. Double-click on the dimension that represents the depth of the feature (in Figure 2–48, this is the dimension with the value of 30). Enter **40** as the new dimension value and press <Enter>.

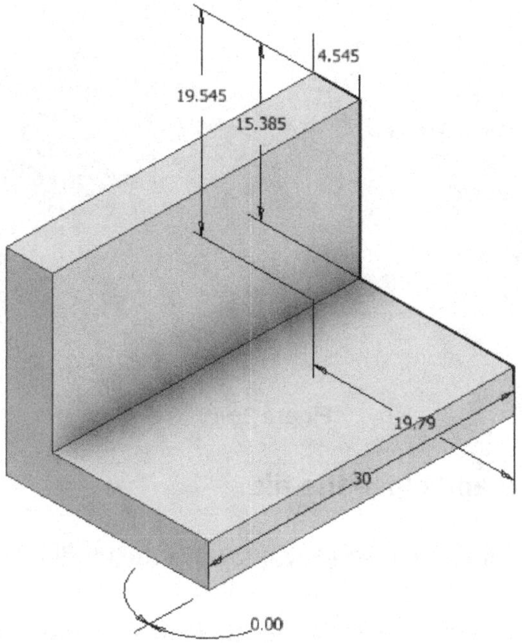

Figure 2–48

4. In the Quick Access Toolbar, click (Local Update) to update the feature.

Task 5: Redefine the extrusion direction.

1. Double-click on **Extrusion1** in the Model browser. The *Properties* panel displays. Alternatively, you can right-click on **Extrusion1** in the Model browser and select **Edit Feature** to open the *Properties* panel.
2. Click (Flipped) to flip the direction of the extrusion. Note that the preview of the extrusion flips to the opposite side of the sketch plane.
3. Click (Asymmetric) as the extent direction. The *Properties* panel updates for you to specify *Distance A* and *Distance B* values for both sides of the sketch plane. Note the preview of the extrusion.

4. Click (Symmetric) to extrude the feature equidistant from the sketch plane. Note the preview of the extrusion.
5. To assign a custom name for the base feature, select **Extrusion1** at the top of the *Properties* panel and enter **Lbracket** as the new name.
6. Click **OK**. The model and Model browser display as shown in Figure 2–49.

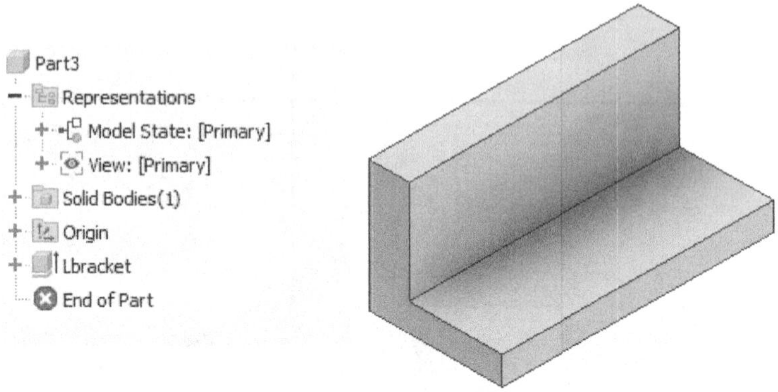

Figure 2–49

Task 6: Save the model and close the file.

1. In the Quick Access Toolbar, click (Save) to save the model. The *Save As* dialog box opens.
2. Enter **L_shape** in the *File name* field and click **Save** to save the model.
3. Click **X** on the *L_shape.ipt* tab to close the file.

End of practice

Practice 2c
Revolved Base Feature

Practice Objectives

- Create a new part model using a predefined template.
- Create a revolved base feature on an origin plane using a provided dimension and constraint scheme.

In this practice, you will create a new model using a default template. Linear geometry will be used in the model to create the revolve feature shown in Figure 2–50.

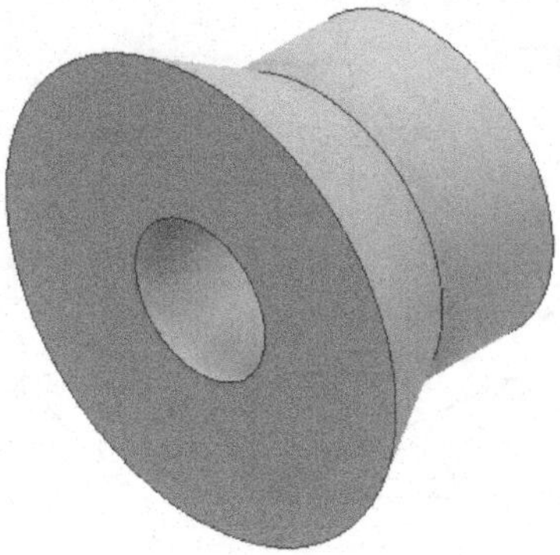

Figure 2–50

Task 1: Create a new part model and start a sketch.

1. Create a new part file using the standard metric (mm) template.
   - Remember that, in the previous practice, you had set your default template to millimeters so that you could expand the **New** option and simply select **Part (.ipt)** or you could use the **New** option and verify the template and click **Create**.
2. Using one of the techniques discussed in the previous practices, start a sketch on the XZ Plane.

Task 2: Define sketch references.

1. In the *Create* panel, click  (Project Geometry) or right-click and select **Project Geometry**. Select the **YZ Plane** and **XY Plane** as references to locate the sketched geometry. The references are represented as yellow lines that are projected onto the sketch plane.
2. Right-click and click **OK** to complete the reference selection, or press <Esc>.

Task 3: Sketch the section.

1. In the *Create* panel, click (Line), or right-click and select **Create Line** to sketch the base feature.
2. Prior to sketching, ensure that the ViewCube is oriented as shown in Figure 2–51. If not, hover your cursor over the ViewCube and select the rotation arrows to reorient. This ensures the sketch will be created in the same orientation as the images in this exercise.
3. Start the sketch by moving the cursor to the left of the projected center point, as shown in Figure 2–51, and clicking the left mouse button to start the line.
4. Move the cursor vertically upwards and click again to place another vertex. Continue to sketch the four remaining entities in the sketch, as shown in Figure 2–51.

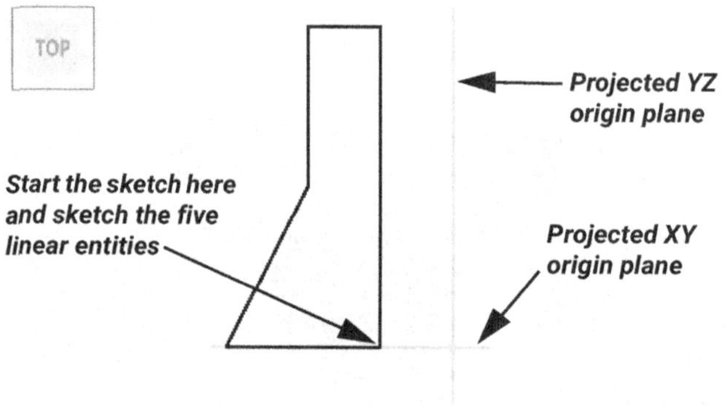

Figure 2–51

Note: To delete a sketched entity, right-click on the entity in the graphics window and select ***Delete****, or select the entity and press <Delete>.*

5. To complete the command you can select a new option, right-click and click **OK**, or press <Esc>.
6. Review the bottom-right corner of the main window. Note that it indicates that five dimensions are required to fully locate the sketch.
7. In the *Constrain* panel, click (Dimension) or right-click and select **General Dimension**. Place the vertical dimension value by selecting the upper and lower horizontal entities by clicking them. Move the cursor to the dimension's placement location and click to place the dimension. When prompted, enter **12** as the value (as shown in Figure 2–52) and press <Enter>. All of the sketch entities scale based on the modification of the first dimension in the sketch. After you add a second dimension, entity scaling will not work.

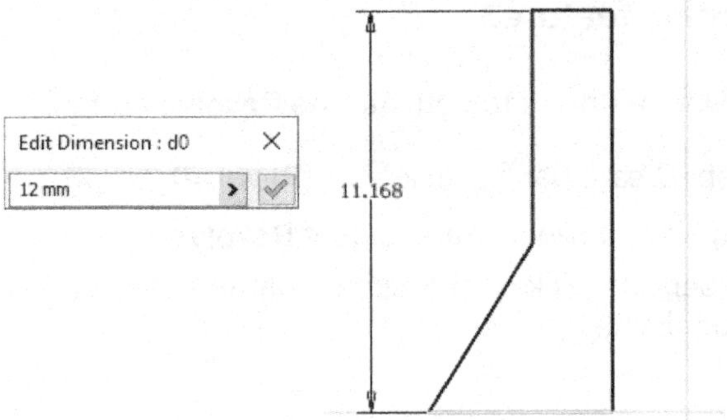

Figure 2–52

8. Place the remaining four dimensions, shown in Figure 2–53 to fully dimension the sketch. To place dimensions, select the entity or entities by clicking them. Move the cursor to the dimension's placement location and click to place the dimension.

   Note: *To select a linear entity that aligns with the projected XY Plane, you may need to use the Select Other tool. Hover the cursor over the entity until a drop-down list displays. The drop-down list displays all of the shown and hidden entities based on the current cursor location. Select the required curve from the list.*

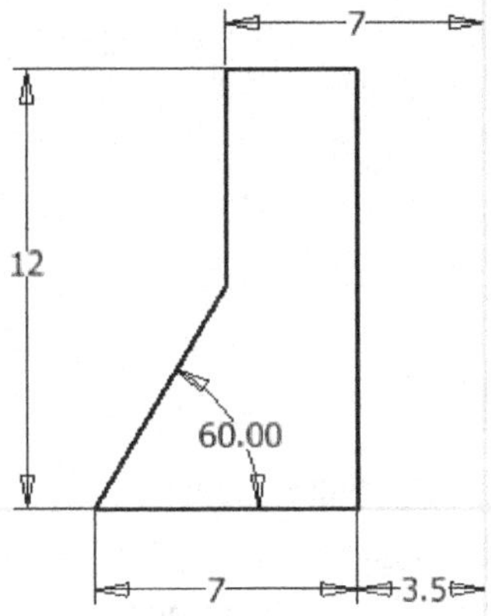

Figure 2–53

9. To complete the command you can select a new option, right-click and select **OK**, or press <Esc>. This sketch is now dimensioned relative to the origin planes, and the base feature geometry is sketched and fully constrained.

10. In the *Exit* panel, click (Finish Sketch), or right-click and select **Finish 2D Sketch**.

11. Hover the cursor over the ViewCube and click (Home) to return to the model to its default 3D orientation, if it does not automatically return to its default orientation.

Task 4: Create a Revolve feature.

1. Use any of the following methods to activate the **Revolve** option:
   - In the *3D Model* tab>*Create* panel, click  (Revolve).
   - Right-click in the graphics window and select **Revolve**.
   - In the Model browser, left-click on the Sketch name and click  in the graphics window's Heads-up display.
   - Press <R>.

   The sketched section is automatically identified as the *Profile,* as shown in Figure 2–54. However, the *Axis* has not been defined so a preview of the model cannot be provided. The axis is required to determine how the feature revolves. The profile has been preselected because it is the only section in the model. The axis must be selected manually.

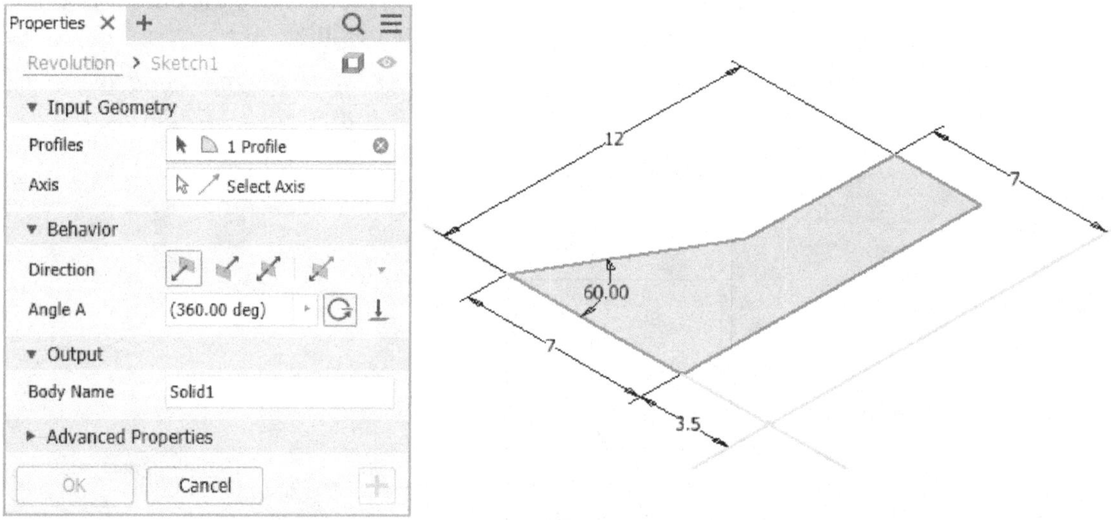

Figure 2–54

2. Select the **Z Axis** in the Model browser as the *Axis*. The section is fully revolved (360 degrees) about the selected axis. You can accept or change this. In this practice, you will maintain the full revolve.

3. Right-click and select **OK (Enter)**. Alternatively, click **OK** in the *Properties* panel. The model and the Model browser display as shown in Figure 2–55.

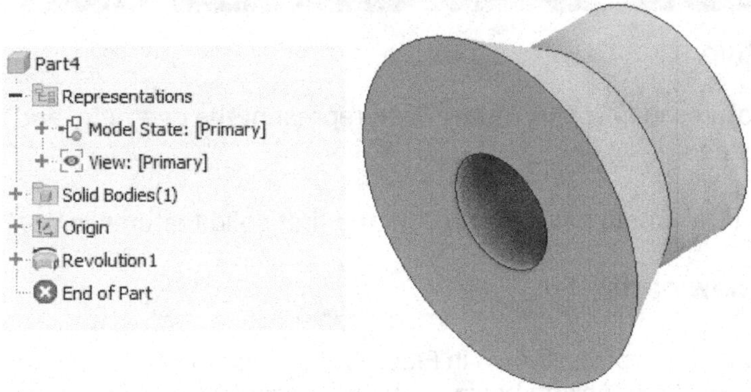

Figure 2–55

Task 5: Save the model and close the file.

1. In the Quick Access Toolbar, click (Save) to save the model. The *Save As* dialog box opens.
2. Enter **revolve** in the *File name* field and click **Save** to save the model.
3. Click **X** on the *revolve.ipt* tab to close the file.

End of practice

Practice 2d
Additional Parts

Practice Objective

- Create base features in new part models that represent the geometry and default orientation provided.

In this practice, you will create base features as the first solid features in new models.

Task 1: Create new parts.

1. Create each of the new parts shown in Figure 2–56. Use the default template and fully constrain your sketches. As you begin each part, carefully consider your sketching plane and references (origin planes or center point).

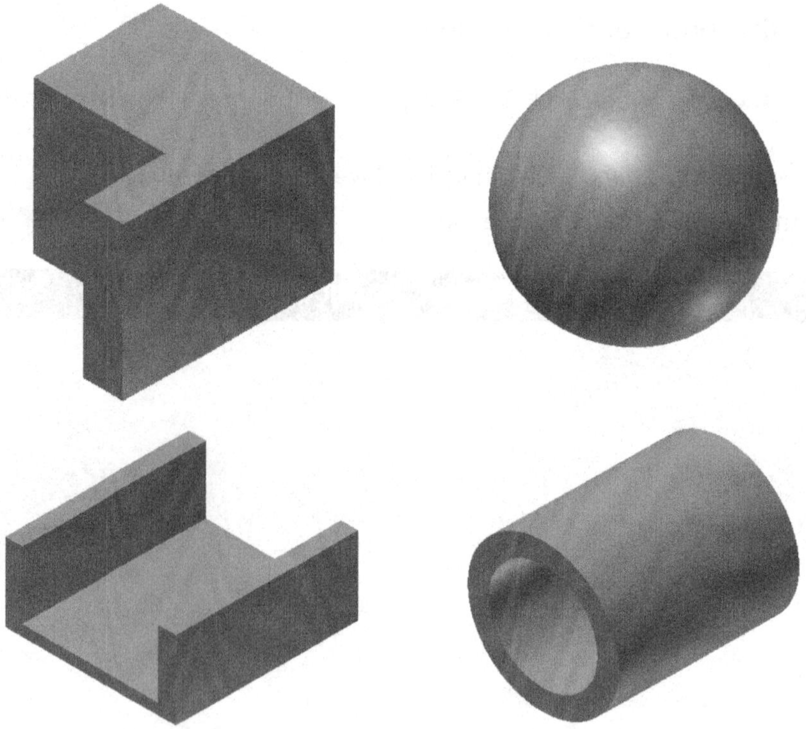

Figure 2–56

End of practice

Chapter Review Questions

1. What template would you use to create a new standard Part file?
   a. Standard.ipn
   b. Standard.idw
   c. Standard.ipt
   d. Standard.iam

2. Which of the following can be defined before sketching geometry? (Select all that apply.)
   a. Sketch Plane
   b. Sketch References
   c. Constraints
   d. Dimensions

3. An origin plane cannot be selected as a sketch plane.
   a. True
   b. False

4. Match the command in the left column to its interface icon in the right column.

a. Dimension	
b. Automatic Dimensions and Constraints	
c. Extrude	
d. Show Constraints	
e. Project Geometry	

5. The **Automatic Dimensions and Constraints** option controls whether all of the dimensions and/or constraints required to constrain a sketch are automatically added. Additionally, it controls how the dimensions are positioned in the sketch.

   a. True

   b. False

6. The sketched entities shown on the left in Figure 2–57 are fully constrained. Which of the following statements best describes the (113. 91) dimension value, as shown on the right in Figure 2–57?

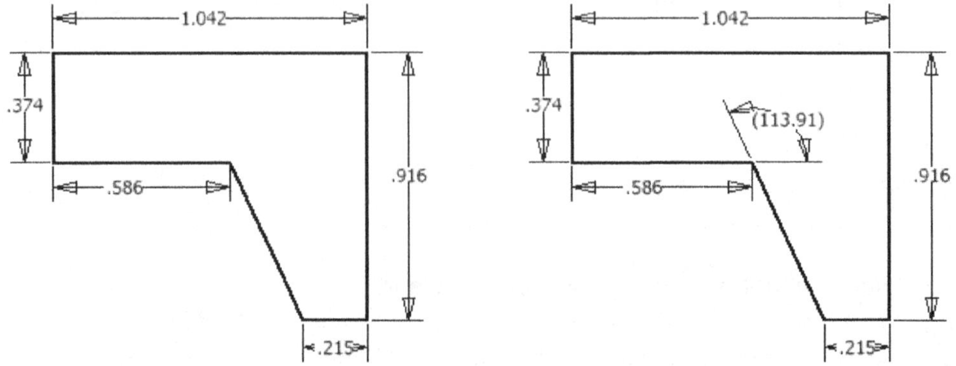

Figure 2–57

   a. The (113.91) dimension is a Driven Angular Dimension and cannot be modified to change the size of the sketch.

   b. The (113.91) dimension is a General Angular Dimension and cannot be modified to change the size of the sketch.

   c. The (113.91) dimension is a Driven Angular Dimension and can be modified to change the size of the sketch.

   d. The (113.91) dimension is a General Angular Dimension and can be modified to change the size of the sketch.

7. Match the feature form name in the left column with the geometry that would be created using this type of feature.

a. Revolve	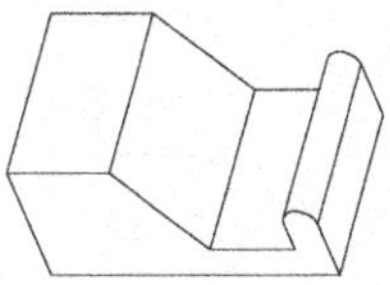
b. Sweep	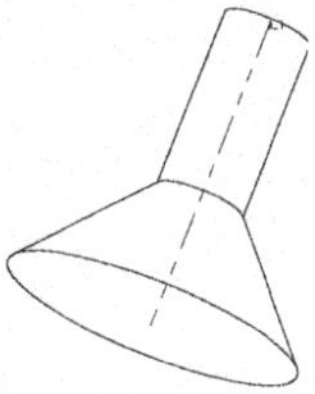
c. Loft	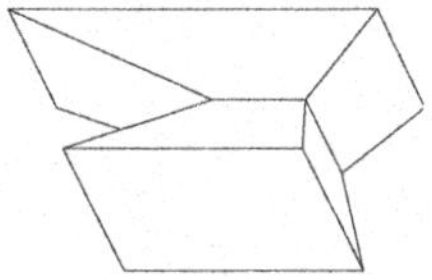
d. Extrude	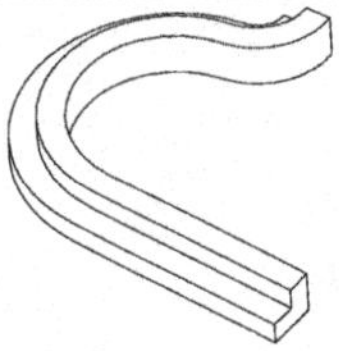

8. Which option do you use to open the feature's *Properties* panel, which would enable you to make a change to the feature (such as flipping the extrusion direction)?

a. Edit Sketch

b. Show Dimensions

c. Edit Feature

d. Properties

9. What option enables you to change the sketch plane of a feature?

a. Show Dimension

b. Edit Feature

c. Edit Sketch

d. Redefine

10. What option enables you to make changes to a sketch so that you could delete entities?

a. Show Dimension

b. Edit Feature

c. Edit Sketch

d. Redefine

Command Summary

Button	Command	Location
	**Application Options**	• **Ribbon:** *Tools* tab>*Options* panel • **File Menu:** Options
	**Automatic Dimensions**	• **Ribbon:** *Sketch* tab>*Constrain* panel
	**Circle**	• **Ribbon:** *Sketch* tab>*Create* panel • **Context Menu:** In the graphics window
 / 	**Create 2D Sketch**	• **Ribbon:** *3D Model* tab>*Sketch* panel • **Context Menu:** In the graphics window • **Heads-up Display:** In the graphics window with a face selected
	**Dimension**	• **Ribbon:** *Sketch* tab>*Constrain* panel • **Context Menu:** In the graphics window
N/A	**Dimension Visibility** (of sketch)	• **Context Menu:** In the Model browser • **Ribbon:** *View* tab>*Visibility* panel
	**Document Settings**	• **Ribbon:** *Tools* tab>Options panel
	**Edit Feature**	• **Heads-up Display:** In the graphics window with a sketch selected • **Context Menu:** In the graphics window and Model browser
	**Edit Sketch**	• **Heads-up Display:** In the graphics window with a sketch selected • **Context Menu:** In the graphics window and Model browser
	**Extrude**	• **Ribbon:** *3D Model* tab>*Create* panel • **Heads-up Display:** In the graphics window with a sketch selected • **Context Menu:** In the graphics window • **Keyboard:** <E>
	**Finish Sketch**	• **Ribbon:** *Sketch* tab>*Exit* panel • **Context Menu:** In the graphics window
	**Line**	• **Ribbon:** *Sketch* tab>*Create* panel • **Context Menu:** In the graphics window
	**Local Update**	• **Quick Access Toolbar**

Button	Command	Location
	**New**	• **Home Page** • **Quick Access Toolbar** • **File Menu**
	**Project Geometry**	• **Ribbon:** *Sketch* tab>*Create* panel • **Context Menu:** In the graphics window
	**Rectangle**	• **Ribbon:** *Sketch* tab>*Create* panel • **Context Menu:** In the graphics window
N/A	**Redefine** (sketch plane)	• **Context Menu:** In the Model browser
	**Revolve**	• **Ribbon:** *3D Model* tab>*Create* panel • **Heads-up Display:** In the graphics window with a sketch selected • **Keyboard:** <R>
	**Show All Constraints**	• **Context Menu:** In the graphics window • **Status Bar**
N/A	**Show Input**	• **Context Menu:** In the graphics window and Model browser
	**Show Selected Constraints**	• **Ribbon:** *Sketch* tab>*Constrain* panel
	**Slot**	• **Ribbon:** *Sketch* tab>*Create* panel
N/A	**Visibility** (of sketch)	• **Context Menu:** In the Model browser

Chapter 3

Additional Sketching Tools

When creating a sketch, knowledge of all of the available sketched entity types, editing tools, and dimensioning and constraining techniques enables you to create sketches that can be used to create the required solid geometry.

Learning Objectives

- Create splines and advanced rectangle, circle, and slot shaped entities in 2D sketches.
- Use the **Trim**, **Extend**, and **Mirror** editing tools that are available in a sketch to edit and modify sketched entities.
- Display the current degrees of freedom in a 2D sketch.
- Add and modify constraints in a 2D sketch to capture the required design intent.
- Customize constraint settings in a 2D sketch.
- Assign dimensions to a 2D sketch using advanced dimensioning techniques.

3.1 Advanced Sketched Entities

In the previous chapter, you learned about lines and the basic rectangle, circle, and slot commands. This section focuses on the additional sketching commands that are available. Figure 3–1 shows the drop-down lists for each entity in the *Create* panel.

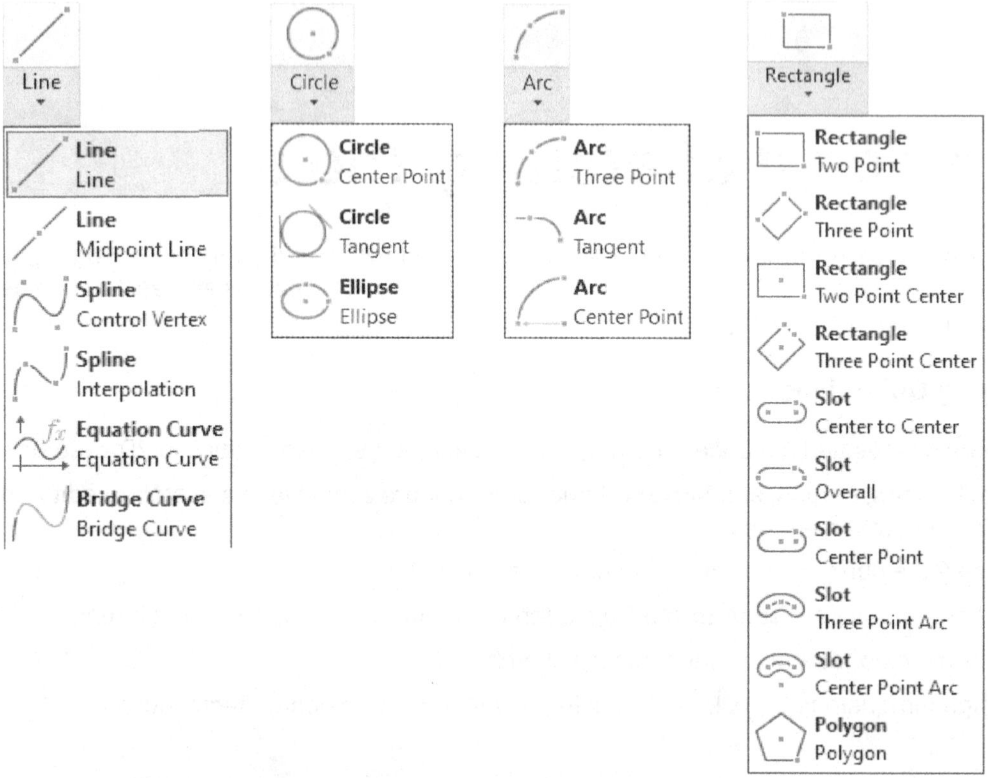

Figure 3–1

Note: *Line, Circle, Arc, and Rectangle are the default entity options that display in the Create panel. These defaults are replaced by the most recently selected entity from each drop-down list as they are used.*

Line/Spline/Curve Drop-Down List

- **(Midpoint Line):** Enables you to start a line that is symmetrical from the midpoint and then define the end point of the line.
- **(Control Vertex):** Enables you to sketch a free-form spline. Select multiple points to create it. Each point that is placed defines the vertices of the control frame.

- **(Interpolation):** Enables you to sketch a free-form spline. Select multiple points to create the spline. The spline is drawn through each point.
- **(Equation Curve):** Draws a curve based on the entry of an equation.
- **(Bridge Curve):** Draws a smooth (G2) continuous curve between two curves.

Circle/Ellipse Drop-Down List

- **(Tangent):** Draws a circle tangent to three selected lines.
- **(Ellipse):** Creates an ellipse. Select the first point to define the center. Select the second point to define its major or minor axes. Select the third point to finalize the size of the ellipse.

Arc Drop-Down List

- **(Three Point):** Draws an arc at three selected points. Select the two end points, and then select a point on the arc. The last point determines the center and radius.
- **(Tangent):** Draws an arc tangent to an existing line or arc. Select the end of the line or arc as the first point and move the cursor to define the end of the arc.
- **(Center Point):** Draws an arc at three selected points. The first point determines the center of the arc and the other two determine the ends of the arc.

Rectangle/Slot/Polygon Drop-Down List

- **(Three Point):** Draws a rectangle at any angle. Select three points to create the rectangle. The first two points define one side and the third point locates the opposite side.
- **(Two Point Center):** Draws a rectangle along the X- and Y-axes. Select two points to create the rectangle. The first point defines the center of the rectangle and the second point defines an outer corner.
- **(Three Point Center):** Draws a rectangle at any angle. Select three points to create the rectangle. The first point defines the center of the rectangle, the second defines the first side, and the third point defines the second side.
- **(Center to Center):** Draws a slot by selecting three points. Select the center points of the two arcs, then select a point to define the slot's thickness.

- **(Overall):** Draws a slot by selecting three points. The first two points define the entire length of the slot and the third selection defines the slot's thickness.
- **(Center Point):** Draws a slot by selecting three points. Select the center point of the slot, followed by the center point of one arc and finally select a point to define the slot's thickness.
- **(Three Point Arc):** Draws a slot by selecting four points. The first three points define the arc length and radius of the slot and the fourth selection defines the slot's thickness.
- **(Center Point Arc):** Draws a slot by selecting four points. The first three points define the center point of the arc, its arc length, and the radius of the slot. The fourth selection defines the slot's thickness.
- **(Polygon):** As with rectangles, polygons can be drawn with a series of lines. However, it is easier to use this command so that all of the sides and angles are equal. You can the draw polygons as:
  - **(Inscribed):** Uses the vertex between two edges to determine size and orientation.
  - **(Circumscribed):** Uses the midpoint of an edge to determine the size and orientation.

The following additional sketching tools are also useful when using the entity types to create a sketch.

Tangent Arc Using a Line

The **Line** command also enables you to sketch tangent or perpendicular arcs. These types of arcs must start at the end of an existing line or arc.

How To: Draw an Arc Tangent to or Perpendicular to a Line

1. With (Line) enabled, place the cursor at the end point of the line/arc. The yellow dot at the center of the crosshairs displays in green if you are drawing a new object or gray if you are continuing an object.
2. Press and hold the left mouse button and drag in the required direction (i.e., tangent or perpendicular).
3. Release the left mouse button to select the end point for the arc.

Tangent Line Between Two Circles/Arcs

The **Line** command can be used to sketch a line that is immediately tangent to a circle or arc. It can also be used to ensure tangency between two existing circles or arcs.

How To: Sketch a Line That Is Tangent to Two Circles/Arcs

1. Start the **Line** command.
2. Select and hold the cursor over one of the two circles.
3. While continuing to hold the left mouse button, drag it to the next circle and position the cursor so that the Tangent constraint is visible.
4. Release the mouse button to locate the tangent line, as shown in Figure 3–2.

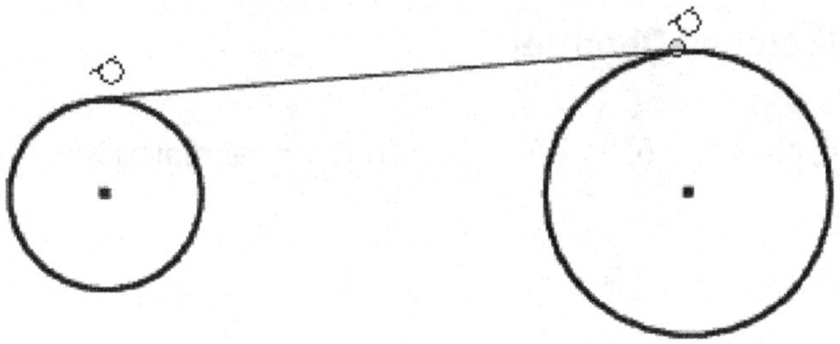

Figure 3–2

Sketched Fillets and Chamfers

The **Fillet** and **Chamfer** commands in the Sketch environment enable you to modify the intersection of two lines in a 2D sketch, as shown in Figure 3–3. Fillets and chamfers can also be created as their own independent feature types. This is discussed later in this guide.

- The fillet rounds corners in a sketch by placing an arc at the intersection of two lines. The fillet arc is always tangent to the intersecting entities.
- A chamfer is an angled corner. Its size is determined by distances along each line from their intersection, or by a distance and an angle.

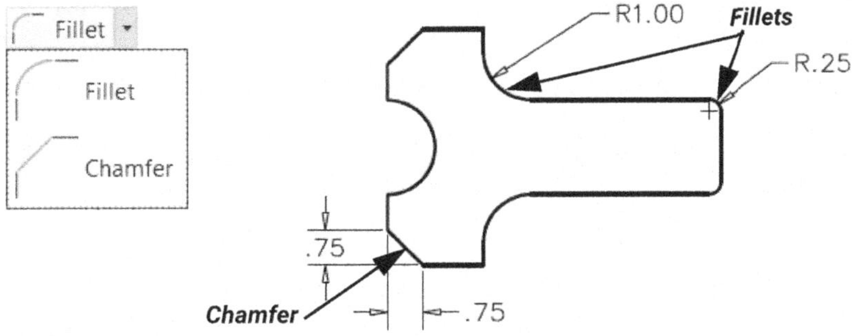

Figure 3–3

How To: Create a Sketched Fillet

1. In the *Create* panel, click (Fillet).
2. Enter a dimension value in the *2D Fillet* dialog box, but do not press <Enter>.
3. Select the intersected entities or directly at the intersection point to create the fillet. The dimension is added to the fillet arc. By default, the first fillet added includes a dimension value. Any additional fillets are driven by this value and no dimension is added. To place a fillet that has independent dimensions for each fillet, click prior to creating the fillet.
4. Continue to select entities to add additional fillets.
5. Press <Esc> or close the *2D Fillet* dialog box to end the command.

How To: Create a Sketched Chamfer

1. In the *Create* panel, click (Chamfer). The *2D Chamfer* dialog box opens, as shown in Figure 3–4.

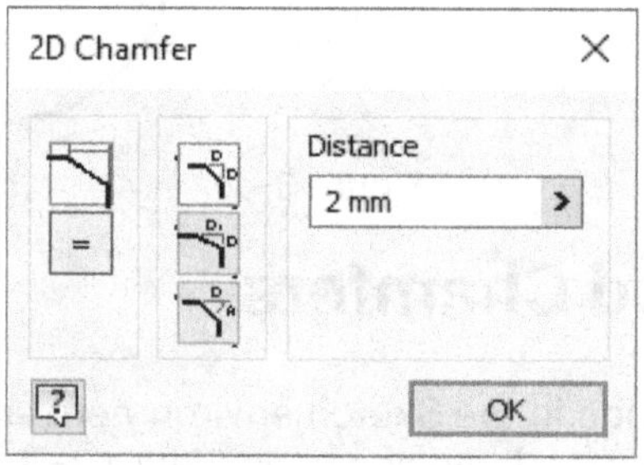

Figure 3–4

2. Select the chamfer option and dimensioning scheme.
3. Enter a dimension value(s) in the *2D Chamfer* dialog box. Do not press <Enter>.
4. Select the intersected entities to create a chamfer. The dimension is added to the chamfer.

The options in the *2D Chamfer* dialog box are as follows:

(Create dimension)	Enable this option to create a chamfer without any dimensions.
(Linked values)	Links the values for second and subsequent chamfers to the first chamfer.

(Equal distances) 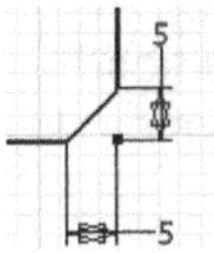	Creates a line at equal distances from the corner on each side. Enter the distance in the *Distance* field.
(Two distance) 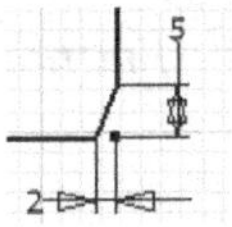	Creates a line at Distance1 along the first selected line and at Distance2 along the second selected line.
(Distance & angle) 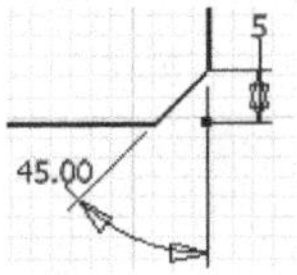	The line created is defined by a distance and an angle. The angle is between the first line you select and the new line that you create.

Hint: Part Features vs. 2D Sketched Entities

When designing a model, you can include fillets and chamfers in your 2D sketches or create them as separate fillet and chamfer part features. Consider the following:

- Chamfer and fillet features can be deleted, modified, and suppressed without needing to access the original sketch.
- If you need to change the edges selected for fillets or chamfers, you can easily edit the feature and select the edges you want to add or remove from the feature.
- The model is more robust and easier to modify if fillets and chamfers are created as features, rather than in the sketch.

Point Snaps

When sketching entities, consider right-clicking and using the **Point Snaps** options in the context menu. Snaps enable you to locate the entity points by snapping to the following points of existing entities in a sketch:

- Endpoints
- Midpoints
- Intersections
- Centers
- Quadrants
- Tangencies
- Apparent intersection points of existing entities
- The middle of two selected points

Construction Entities

Construction entities are used as references and aids in sketching. They do not create solid geometry. It is common to use construction lines when sketching to indicate that arcs or circles lie along the same line or to indicate the midpoint of a line.

In the *Format* panel, click (Construction) to sketch a construction entity (e.g., line, arc, etc.). Construction entities display as dashed lines and you can add dimensions and constraints to them. An example of circular construction entities is shown in Figure 3–5. To change a construction entity to solid geometry, select the entity and click (Construction) in the *Format* panel.

The circular construction entities were used here to create squares centered about the center point. The dimensions of each square are driven by the diameter of the construction circle.

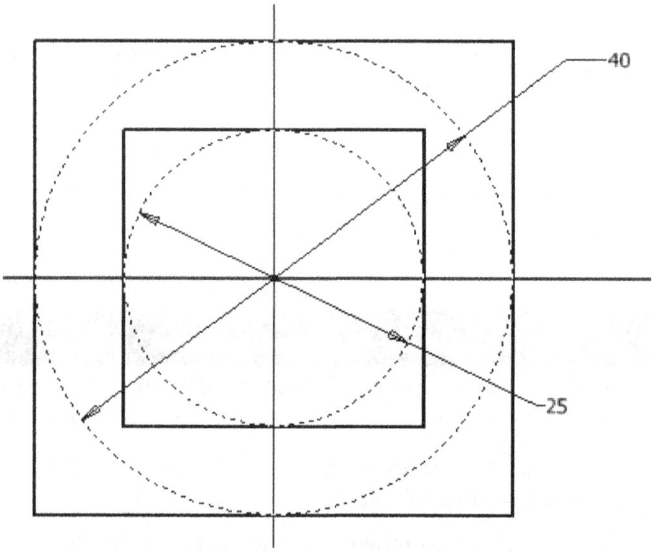

Figure 3–5

Note: *By default, when you project geometry into a sketch, it is projected as a solid sketched entity. To project selected entities as construction entities, press and hold <Shift> and then select entities to project. Projected construction entities display as yellow dashed lines.*

3.2 Basic Sketch Editing Tools

The **Trim**, **Extend**, and **Mirror** editing tools that are available on the Sketch tab provide basic editing tools that can be used to modify sketch entities.

Trim

Trim removes the segment of the entity to the nearest intersection in each direction from the selected point. The selected portion of an object (e.g., lines or arcs) is removed, as shown in Figure 3–6. Selecting an object without an intersection deletes the object. If the intersections contain multiple possibilities for trimming, move the cursor over each segment. If it can be trimmed, it displays as a red dashed entity.

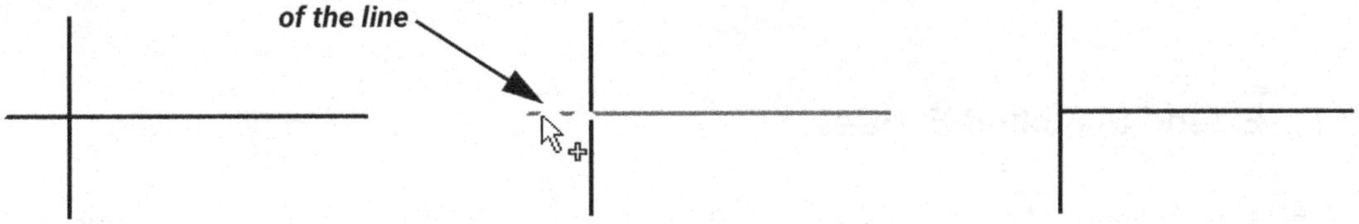

Figure 3–6

How To: Trim Sketched Entities

1. In the *Modify* panel, click  (Trim) or right-click and select **Trim.**
2. Move the cursor over the portion of the entity that you want to trim. A preview of the trim displays.
3. Click the left mouse button to remove the portion.

- Trimming can also be done dynamically once the command is initiated. Drag the freehand line over the required entities that are to be removed. Release the mouse button to remove the entities from the sketch.

Extend

Extend continues an entity to meet the next entity in its path or to close an open sketch, as shown in Figure 3–7.

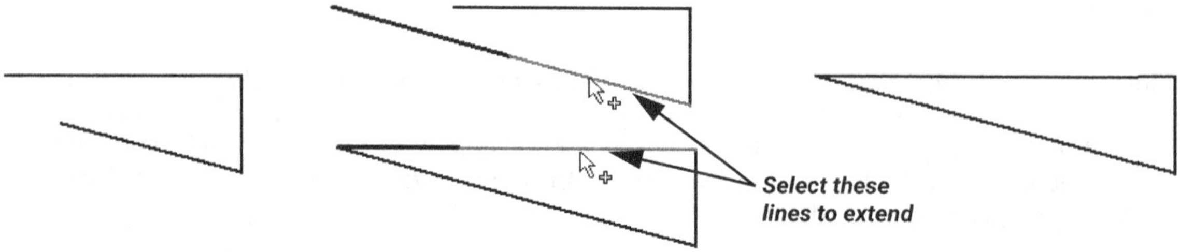

Figure 3–7

How To: Extend Sketched Entities

1. In the *Modify* panel, click (Extend) or if the **Trim** command is already active, right-click and select **Extend.**
2. Move the cursor over the portion of the entity that you want to extend. A preview of the extend displays.
3. Click the left mouse button to extend the entity.

- Extending can also be done dynamically once the command is initiated. Drag the freehand line over the required entities that are to be extended. Release the mouse button to extend the entities from the sketch.

  Note: *To toggle between* ***Trim*** *and* ***Extend*** *(or vice-versa) when a command is active, press and hold <Shift>.*

Mirror

Entities can be mirrored in a sketch. The sketch shown in Figure 3–8 is created using the **Mirror** sketch tool and a construction line as the mirror line.

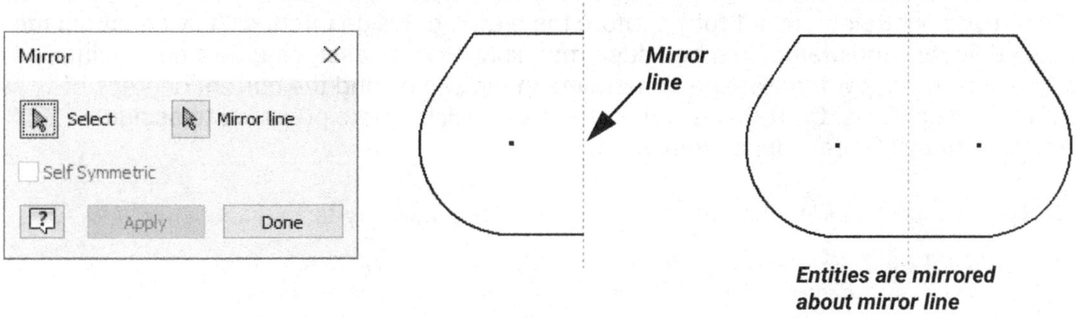

Figure 3–8

How To: Mirror a Selected Object About a Mirror Line

1. In the *Pattern* panel, click (Mirror). The *Mirror* dialog box displays.
2. Select the sketch entities that you want to mirror.
3. In the *Mirror* dialog box, click (Mirror line). The mirror line can be:
    - Entities within the geometry that are selected to mirror
    - Projected origin feature
    - Projected model edge
    - Straight sketched or construction lines
4. Select a mirror line, and click **Apply**.

3.3 Adding and Modifying Sketch Constraints

Constraints control how the sketched entities behave. As you sketch the geometry, constraints are assumed and applied when the cursor drags within a specific tolerance of other entities. Symbols display on the entity that is being sketched indicating which constraint is applied. If the assumed constraints do not fully capture the required design intent or fully constrain the sketch, additional constraints can be added manually. Prior to assigning new constraints, it is good practice to review the existing constraints in the sketch and the current degrees of freedom of the entities. Once this is understood, you will be more prepared to assign constraints that will meet your design intent.

> ***Note:*** *The icon that identifies the sketch in the Model browser displays as when the sketch is partially constrained and changes to when fully constrained.*

Reviewing Existing Constraints

To display the constraints applied to your sketch, use one of the following techniques:

- Select the entity in the sketch to temporarily display the constraint.
- To display of the all constraints in the sketch, in the Status Bar, click (Show All Constraints), or press <F8>.
- To only display the constraints applied to the selected entities, click (Show Constraints) in the *Constrain* panel. Showing the constraint using this method keeps the constraint on the screen until it is cleared.

When a constraint displays, you can select and drag it as required. Consider the following:

- Hover the cursor over a constraint symbol to highlight the entities affected.
- To hide all of the constraints from the sketch, in the Status Bar, click (Hide All Constraints) to toggle their display off or press <F9>.

Reviewing Degrees of Freedom

Reviewing the remaining degrees of freedom can help you to determine where additional constraints and dimensions are required. To display the degrees of freedom in a sketch, click (Show Degrees of Freedom) in the Status Bar.

Assigning Constraints

Once entities have been sketched, you can manually add additional constraints using the *Constrain* panel, shown in Figure 3–9. Select the required constraint icon and select the entities that you want to constrain.

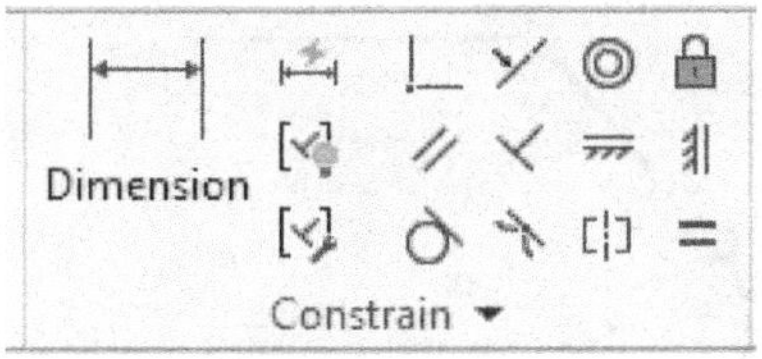

Figure 3–9

Note: *When assigning constraints, the order in which they are selected does not determine how they update. The driving entity is the first drawn in the sketch, unless there are other constraints or dimensions assigned that prevent updating.*

Parallel and Perpendicular

(Parallel) and (Perpendicular) ensure that lines are parallel or perpendicular, respectively. The lines shown in Figure 3–10 are constrained to be parallel and perpendicular.

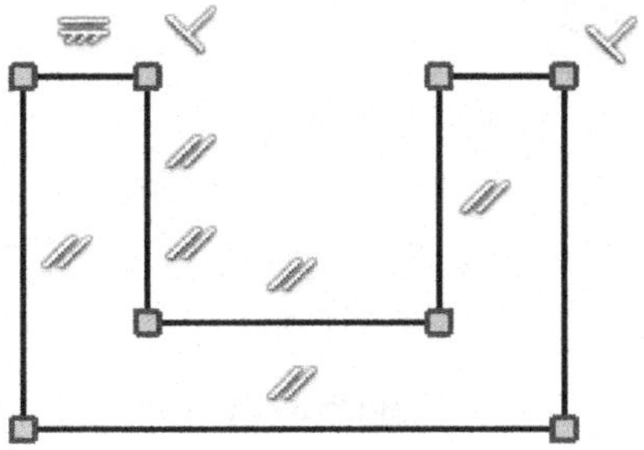

Figure 3–10

Tangent

(Tangent) ensures that the selected items are tangent. The objects do not need to touch to be tangent. The arc shown in Figure 3–11 is constrained to be tangent to the geometry lines at its end point.

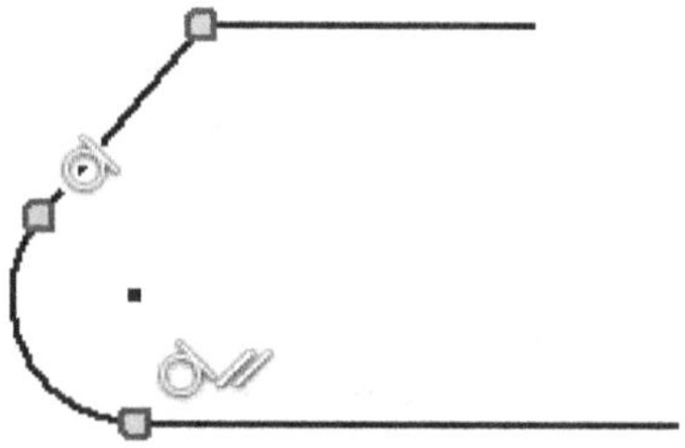

Figure 3–11

Smooth (G2)

(Smooth) ensures that the selected entities continue the same curvature values between the entities (curvature continuous). The spline shown in Figure 3–12 is constrained to be curvature continuous to the geometry line at its end point.

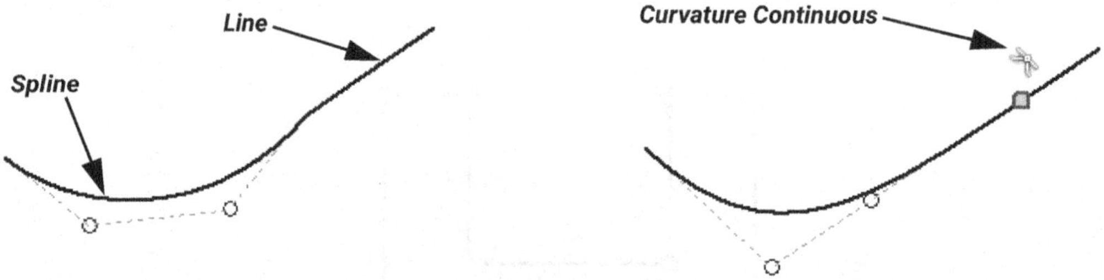

Figure 3–12

Collinear

(Collinear) ensures that selected objects lie on the same line. The constraints can be applied between lines and ellipse axes. The lines shown on the right in Figure 3–13 are constrained to be collinear.

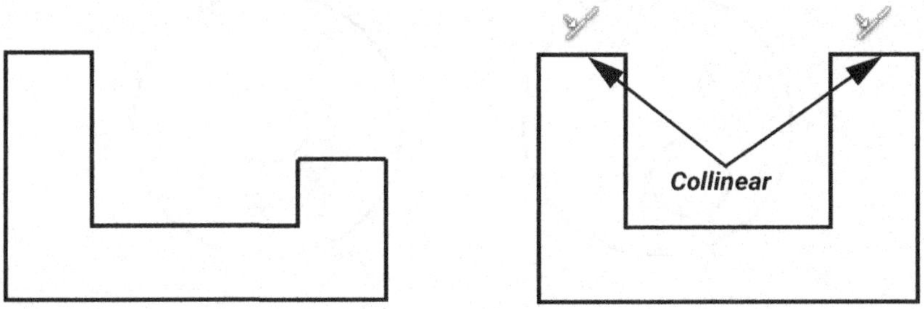

Figure 3–13

Coincident

(Coincident) ensures that two selected points are coincident. If a point and an entity are selected, the point lies on the entity or along the extension of the entity. As shown in Figure 3–14, two Coincident constraints were automatically created when the arc was sketched. They indicate that the end points of the arc lie on the horizontal line. One additional Coincident constraint was added manually (as shown on the right), so that the center of the circle lies on the center of the horizontal line. With Coincident constraints, only small yellow boxes display in a sketch when **Show Constraints** is used.

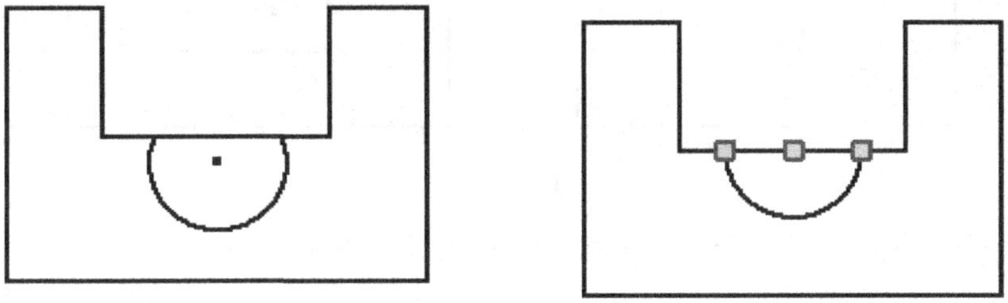

Figure 3–14

Concentric

(Concentric) ensures that the selected arcs, circles, or ellipses have the same center point. The circles shown on the right in Figure 3–15 are constrained to be concentric with one another.

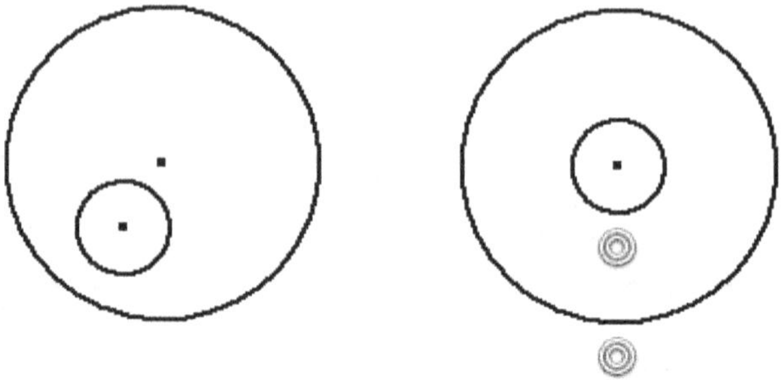

Figure 3–15

Equal

(Equal) ensures that all selected lines have the same length or that all selected circles and arcs have the same radius. The lines shown on the right in Figure 3–16 are constrained to be equal in length. The <=> keyboard key can be used as a shortcut to activate the Equal constraint.

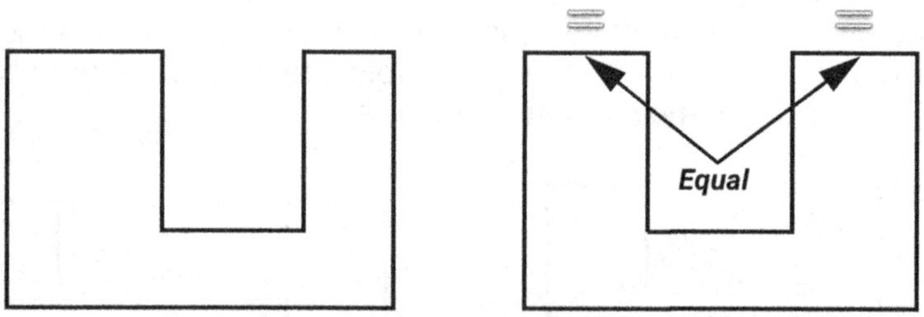

Figure 3–16

When assigning the Equal constraint, the result depends on if dimensions are present on the entities:

If...	Then...
No dimensions are present on either selected entity	The resulting entities are resized as the average size.
One dimension is present	The values of the resulting constrained entities are those of the dimension.
Dimensions are present on both entities	A prompt displays noting that the sketch is over-constrained.

Horizontal and Vertical

 (Horizontal) and  (Vertical) ensure that a line is horizontal or vertical, respectively. The lines shown on the right in Figure 3–17 are constrained to be horizontal and vertical. The <-> keyboard key can be used as a shortcut to activate the Horizontal constraint.

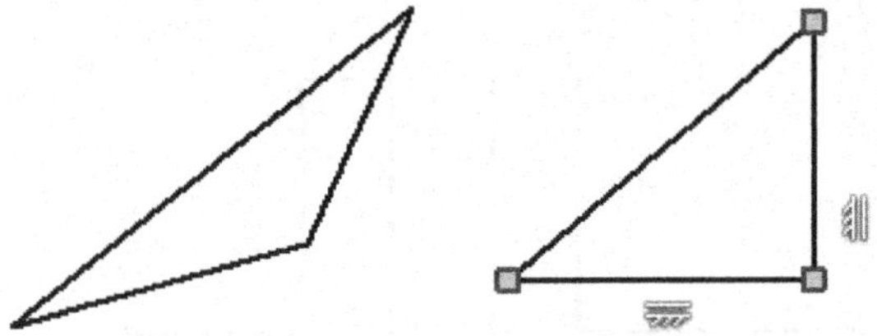

Figure 3–17

Horizontal can also be used to align two circle center points horizontally and Vertical can be used to align two circle center points vertically. The circle center points shown on the left in Figure 3–18 are constrained to line up horizontally and vertically, as shown on the right.

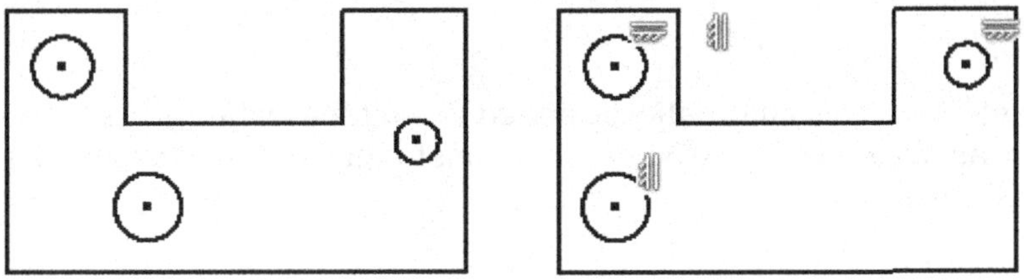

Figure 3–18

Fix

 (Fix) fixes a selected point or object relative to the default coordinate system (Sketch environment 0,0,0). The vertex shown in Figure 3–19 is fixed relative to the default coordinate system.

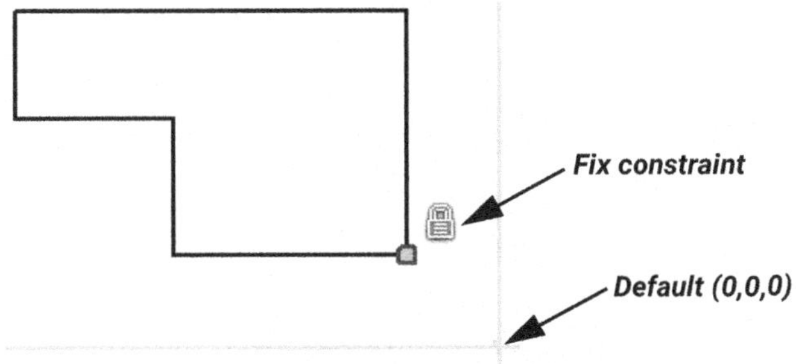

Figure 3–19

Symmetric

(Symmetric) ensures that the selected lines or points are symmetric about a selected line. To apply this constraint, select the first line or point, select the second line or point, and then select the line of symmetry. The vertical lines in Figure 3–20 are constrained to be symmetric about the centerline.

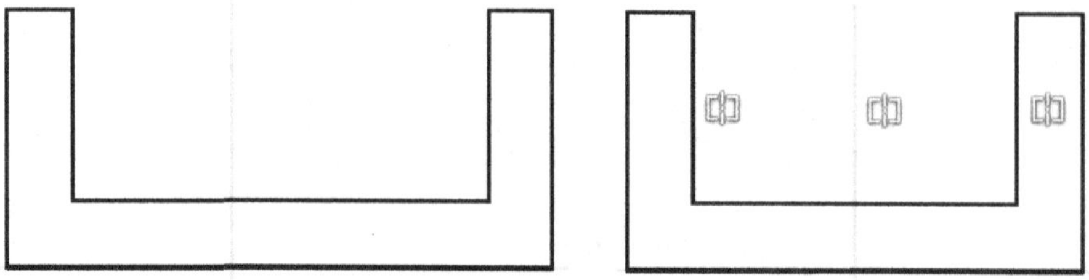

Figure 3–20

Reference

A Reference constraint is automatically added to sketches when you use the **Project Geometry** option, as shown in Figure 3–21. This constraint cannot be explicitly set using a constraint in the *Constrain* panel.

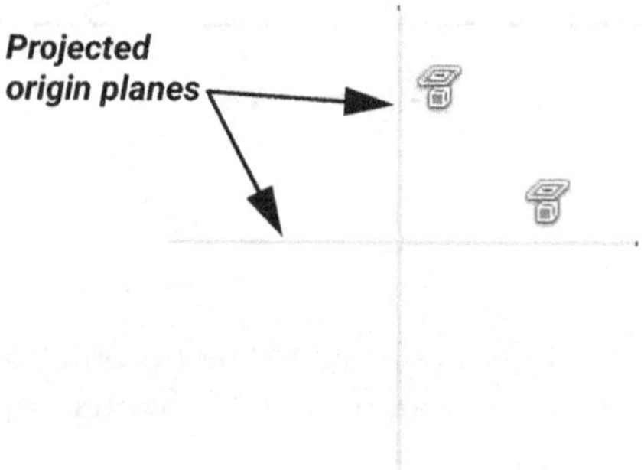

Figure 3–21

Over Constraining Entities

If you try to place a constraint that over-constrains the sketch, an error dialog box opens, as shown in Figure 3–22. You must click **Cancel** to continue. It is not possible to over-constrain a sketch. If you encounter an over-constrained sketch, keep the dimension that best suits the design intent.

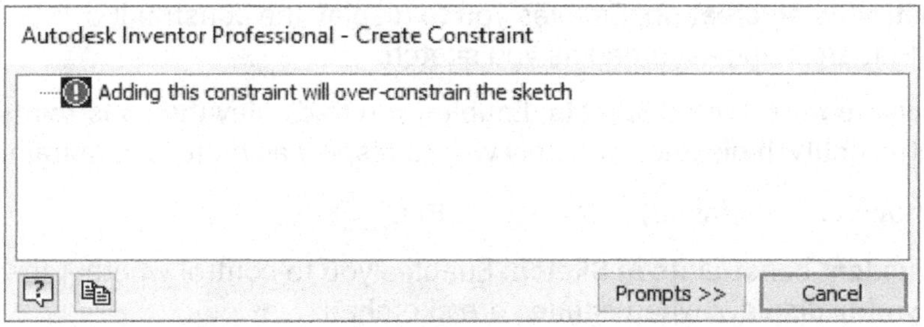

Figure 3–22

Constraint Settings

Using constraint settings enables you to customize how constraints are inferred and displayed in a sketch. To open the *Constraint Settings* dialog box, in the *Sketch* tab>*Constrain* panel, click (Constraint Settings). The *Constraint Settings* dialog box is shown in Figure 3–23.

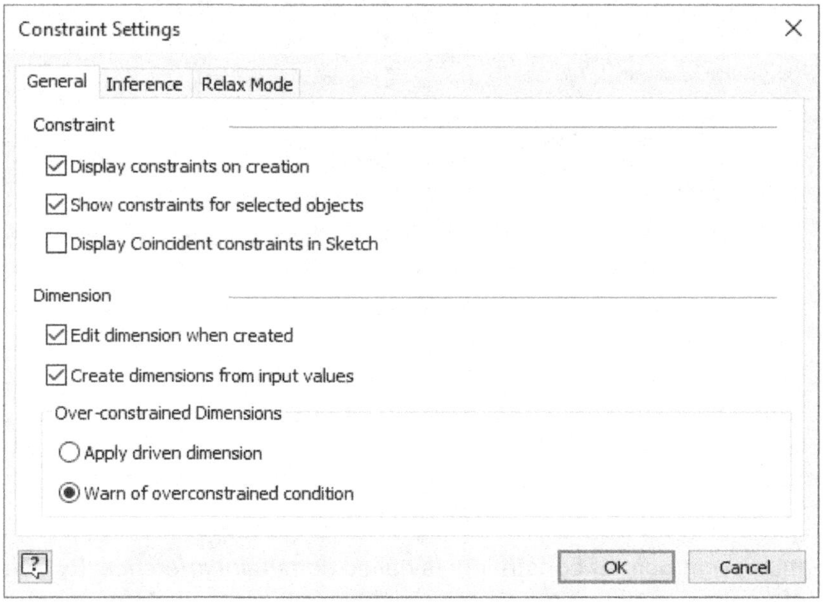

Figure 3–23

Using the *General* and *Inference* tabs in the *Constraint Settings* dialog box, you can do the following:

Control Constraint Display

In the *General* tab, you can use the following constraint options to control how constraints display when creating a sketch.

- **Display constraints on creation:** Enables you to display the constraint symbols for the constraints that are being assumed as you sketch.
- **Show constraints for selected objects:** Enables you to display the constraints associated with a selected entity. If disabled, the only way to display an entity's constraint symbols is to click  (Show All Constraints) in the Status Bar.
- **Display Coincident constraints in Sketch:** Enables you to control whether the coincident constraint symbol displays when entities are sketched.

Control Constraint Inference

The *Inference* tab (shown in Figure 3–24) in the *Constraint Settings* dialog box controls how the software assumes constraints as entities are sketched.

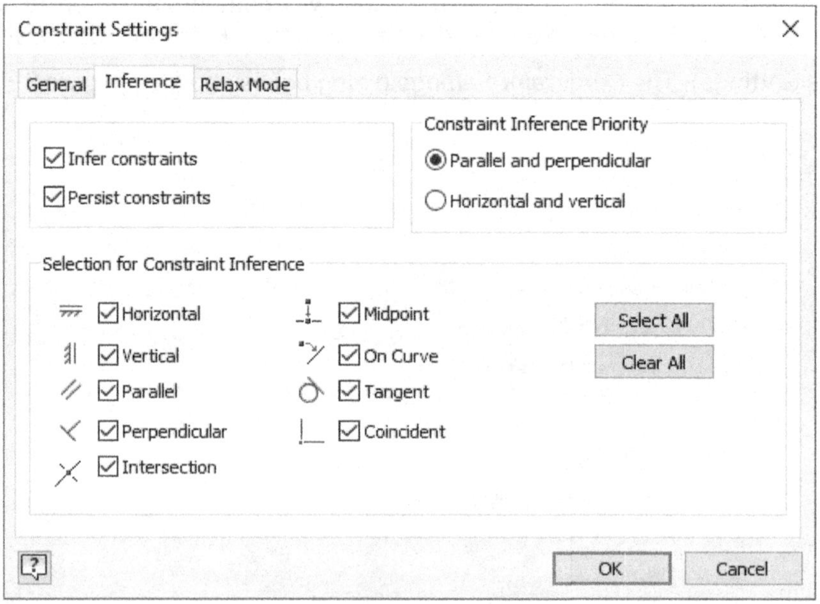

Figure 3–24

- The automatic assignment of constraints is called *constraint inference*. By default, constraint inference is enabled in a sketch. To disable it, clear the **Infer constraints** option.

- With **Infer constraints** toggled on, the additional **Persist constraints** option is also available. It controls whether the inferred constraint is permanently assigned once the entity has been placed. By default, this option is enabled in a new sketch.

  Note: *Toggling off* ***Infer constraints*** *or* ***Persist constraints*** *does not affect the creation of the Coincident constraint. This helps in preventing open profile sketches.*

- If **Infer constraints** is disabled, **Persist constraints** is automatically disabled. When enabling **Infer constraints**, ensure that **Persist constraints** is set as required.

Hint: Temporarily Controlling Constraint Inference and Persistence

When sketching geometry, you can manually enable and disable the inference and persistence options in the *Constraint Settings* dialog box. However, you can also press and hold <Ctrl> to disable them during the sketching process.

- The *Selection for Constraint Inference* area enables you to select the constraints that the software can infer during sketch creation. Select the constraint options as required. Although a constraint inference might be disabled for a specific constraint, you can still apply it manually if required.
- The *Constraint Inference Priority* area enables you to determine the priority of whether the Parallel/Perpendicular or Horizontal/Vertical constraints are inferred over one another when the sketch is created.

Constraint Inference Scope

To control the inference scope, in the expanded *Constrain* panel, click (Constraint Inference Scope). The *Constraint Inference Scope* dialog box opens and enables you to specify the geometry that can be used to infer constraints. The options include:

- **Geometry in Current Command:** Constraints are inferred to the geometry created in the current command.
- **All Geometry:** Constraints are inferred to in all of the active sketch geometry.
- **Select:** Constraints should be inferred to only selected geometry.

Deleting Constraints

To delete constraints, use one of the following:

- Display the constraint symbol that is to be deleted, select it, right-click, and select **Delete**, as shown in Figure 3–25. To display a coincident constraint symbol, hover over its yellow square icon.
- Select the required constraint symbol, and press <Delete>.
- Select entities in the sketch, right-click and select **Delete Constraints**. To delete coincident constraints, select the entities, right-click and select **Delete Coincident Constraints**. The delete options in the context menu are shown in Figure 3–25.

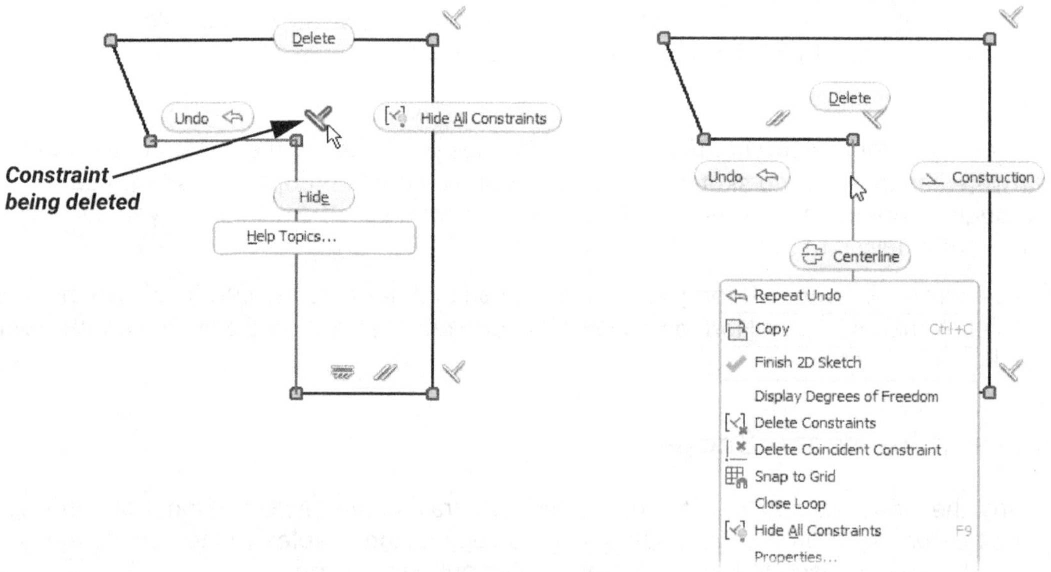

Figure 3–25

Relax Mode

Constraints can prevent entities from moving when changes are required. When enabled, Relax Mode enables you to make changes to the geometry and to apply new constraints that would otherwise not be possible without deleting constraints. Figure 3–26 shows an example of how Relax Mode can be used. Once relaxed and a sketched entity is moved, constraints are assigned based on the new placement location of the entity.

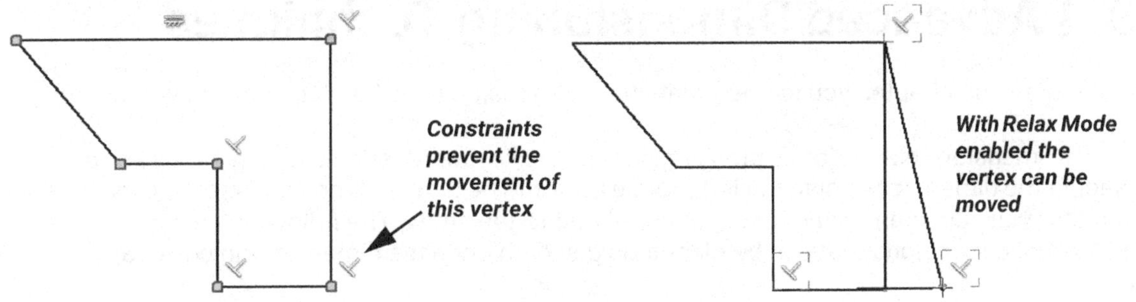

Figure 3–26

By default, Relax Mode is disabled. To enable it, use one of the following techniques:

- In the Status Bar, click (Relax Mode) to toggle it on/off.
- In the *Sketch* tab>*Constrain* panel, click (Constraint Settings), and select the *Relax Mode* tab. Select **Enable Relax Mode** to toggle it on.

The *Constraint Settings* dialog box contains added configuration options for Relax Mode. Once enabled, the *Constraints to remove in relax dragging* area becomes available, as shown in Figure 3–27. You can enable or disable specific constraints to define which constraint types are to be relaxed during dragging.

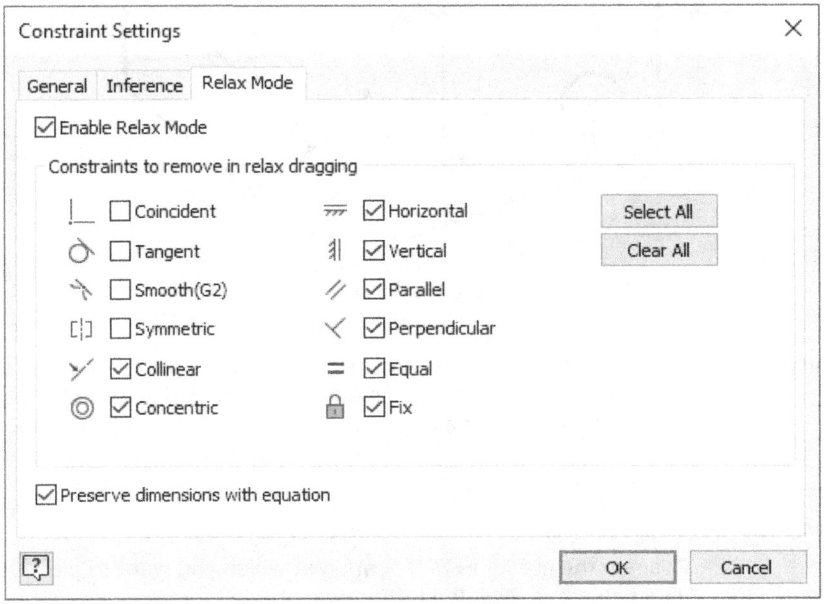

Figure 3–27

3.4 Advanced Dimensioning Techniques

In the previous chapter, you learned that linear dimensions can be placed by activating the  (Dimension) option (or by pressing <D> on the keyboard) and selecting entities and placing the dimensions using the left mouse button. The type of dimension created depends on whether you select an entity or the points related to the entity. The following are types of additional dimensions that can be placed on a sketch once the dimensioning command is active.

Center Dimensions

To create center dimensions, select the two entities to dimension the distance between circles and arcs. Move the cursor to the required location and place the dimension using the left mouse button. The different methods for dimensioning the linear entities shown in Figure 3–28 are as follows:

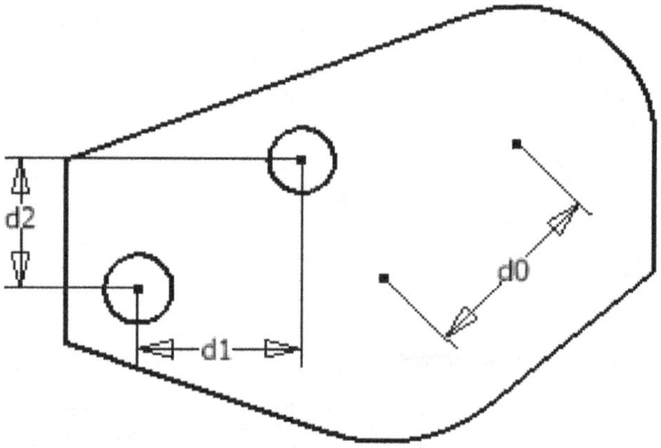

Figure 3–28

To place dimension d0	Select the centers of the arcs. Position the cursor in the location in which you want to place the dimension, right-click, and select **Aligned**. Alternatively, place the dimension at a point along a line that joins the two centers. When it displays, click the left mouse button. Move the cursor to the required location and click to locate the dimension.
To place dimensions d1 and d2	Select the centers of the circles or circular entities. Position the cursor in the location at which you want to place the dimension and click the left mouse button.

Radius/Diameter Dimensions

To create radius or diameter dimensions, select an arc or circle to create a radius dimension. Position the cursor at the location in which you want to place the dimension and press the left mouse button. By default, the dimension type for arcs is radius and the dimension type for circles is diameter, as shown in Figure 3–29.

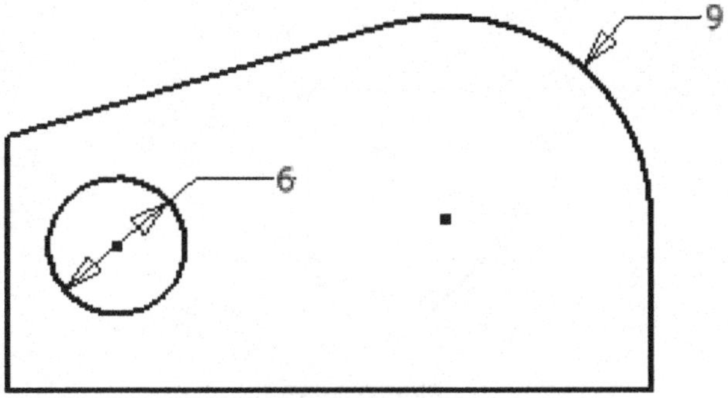

Figure 3–29

To change the type of dimensions, right-click and select **Radius** or **Diameter** from the **Dimension Type** menu before placing the dimension. Position the cursor at the location at which you want to place the dimension and click the left mouse button.

Angular Dimensions

To create angular dimensions, select lines A and B and place the angular dimension using the left mouse button. The resulting angle is dependent on the placement location of the dimension, as shown in Figure 3–30. Alternatively, you can create an angular dimension by selecting three points.

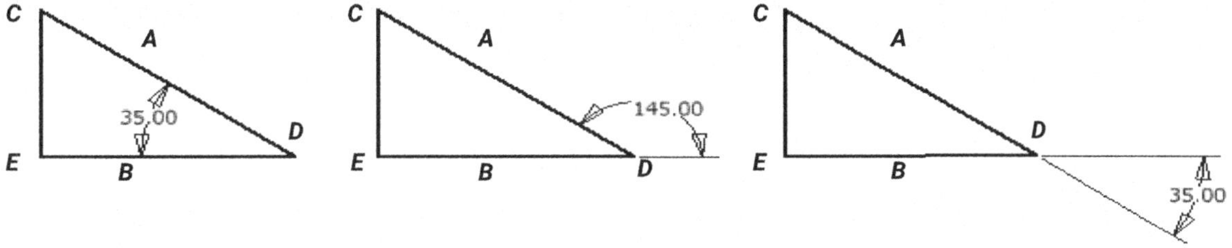

Figure 3–30

Tangent Dimensions

To create a tangent dimension, select the first arc, and move the cursor over the second arc. When displays, select the second arc and place the dimension, as shown in Figure 3–31.

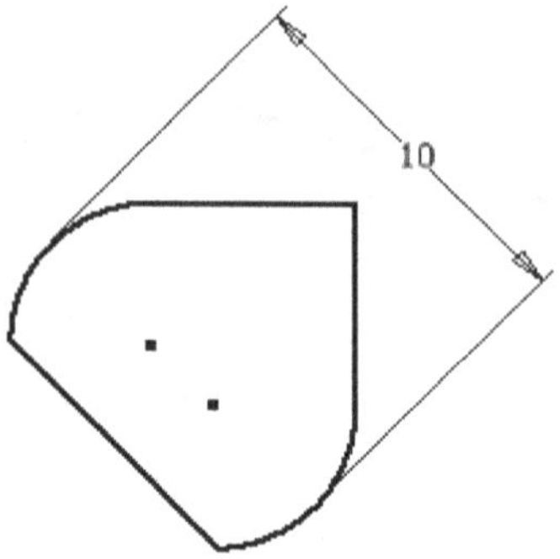

Figure 3–31

Revolved Sketch Dimensions

When sketching a cross-section of a revolved feature, only half of the section needs to be sketched. The cross-section is then revolved about the centerline at a specified angle.

To create a diameter dimension on the section of a revolved feature, select the centerline of the revolved cross-section and then the geometry, right-click, and select **Linear Diameter**. Figure 3–32 shows a revolved diameter dimension. This dimensioning scheme can also be used to dimension symmetrical entities.

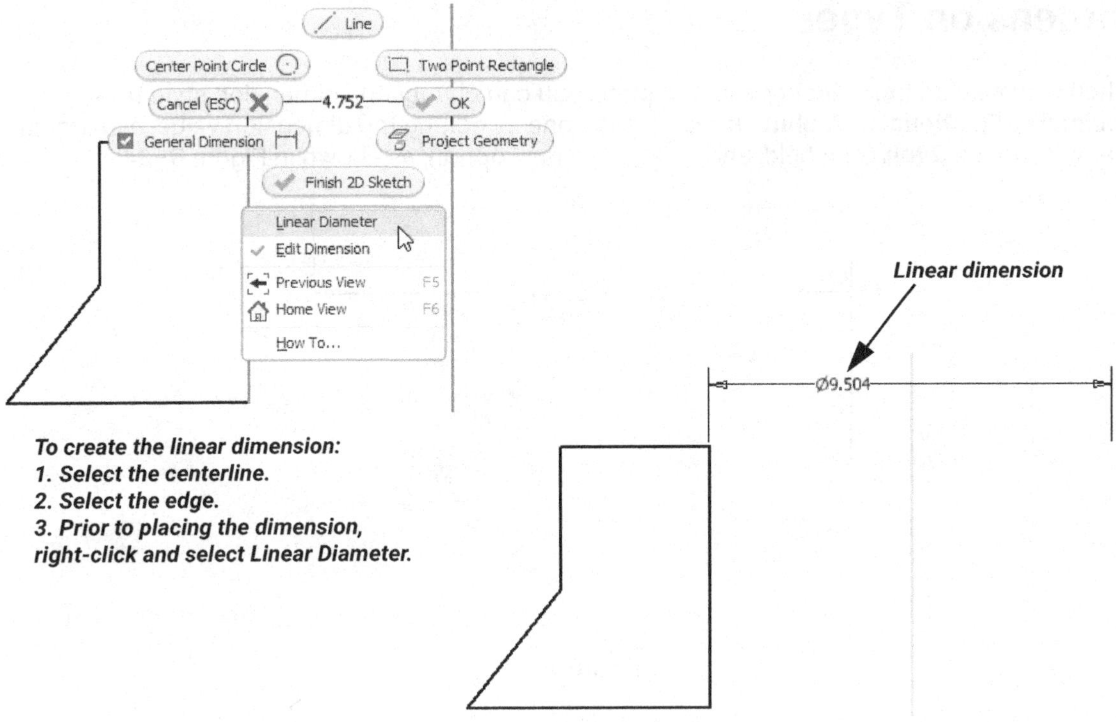

Figure 3–32

Arc Length Dimensions

To create an Arc Length dimension, select the arc, right-click, and select **Dimension Type>Arc Length**, then place the dimension, as shown in Figure 3–33.

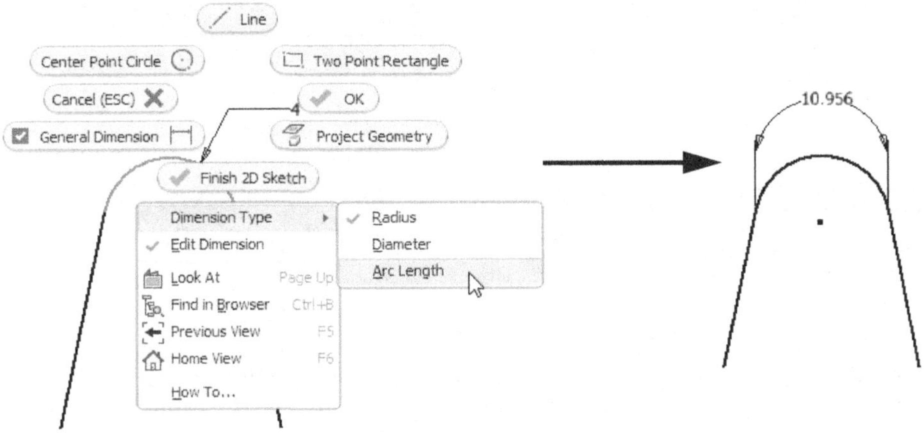

Figure 3–33

Dimension Types

When you are working in an Imperial template, you can change the dimension style from **Decimal** to **Fractional** or **Architectural**. This is done by editing the dimension value, expanding the menu in the *Dimension* field, and selecting a new option, as shown in Figure 3–34.

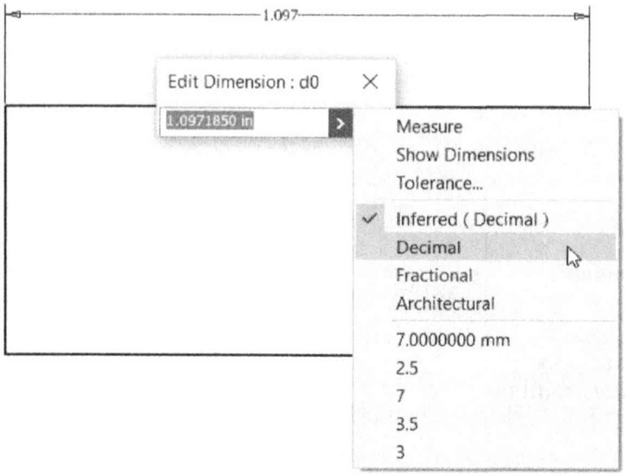

Figure 3–34

Over Dimensioned Entities

If you try to apply a dimension that is going to over-dimension the sketch, the dialog box shown in Figure 3–35 displays. You can cancel the command or place as a driven dimension. Driven dimensions display in parentheses, as shown in Figure 3–35. You cannot modify them, but they update if other dimensions are changed. If you encounter an over-dimensioned sketch, keep the dimension that best suits the design intent.

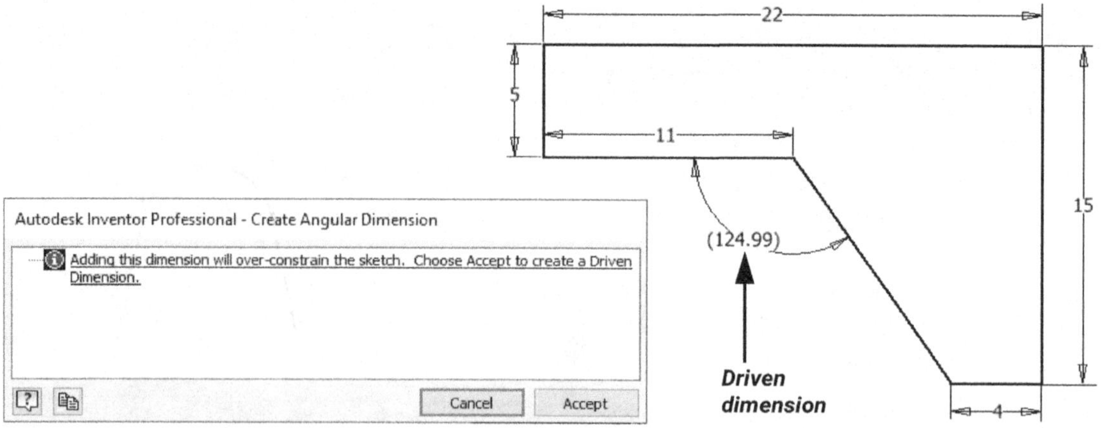

Figure 3–35

Practice 3a
Apply Constraints

Practice Objectives

- Open an existing part model and edit its sketch.
- Show existing constraints in a sketch.
- Add constraints to the sketch.
- Automatically add dimensions to ensure that the sketch is fully constrained.

In this practice, you will apply constraints to define the shape of the sketched geometry shown in Figure 3–36. You will also use automatic dimensions to fully place the geometry with respect to the sketch references.

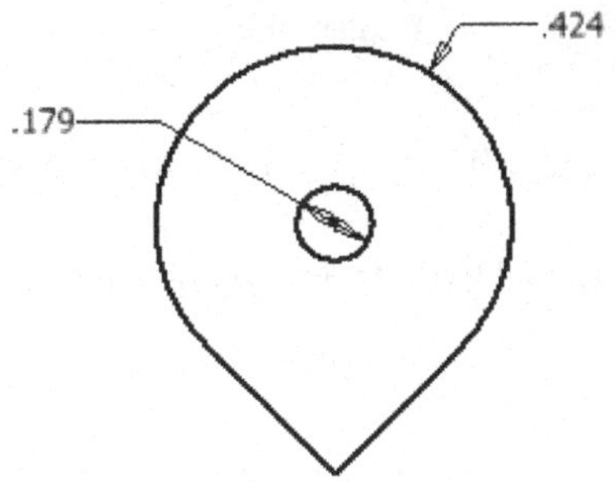

Figure 3–36

Task 1: Open a part file.

1. Open **constraints_1.ipt**.
2. In the Model browser, note that the icon adjacent to **Sketch1** does not have a push pin (). This indicates that this sketch is not fully constrained. Sketches that are fully constrained are indicated by the icon having a push pin included ().
3. Double-click on **Sketch1** in the Model browser to activate the sketch. Note the number of dimensions required to fully constrain the sketch.

4. In the Status Bar, click (Show All Constraints) to display the constraints applied in the sketch. Alternatively, you can also press <F8> to display all of the constraints. The sketch displays as shown in Figure 3–37. Review the constraints.

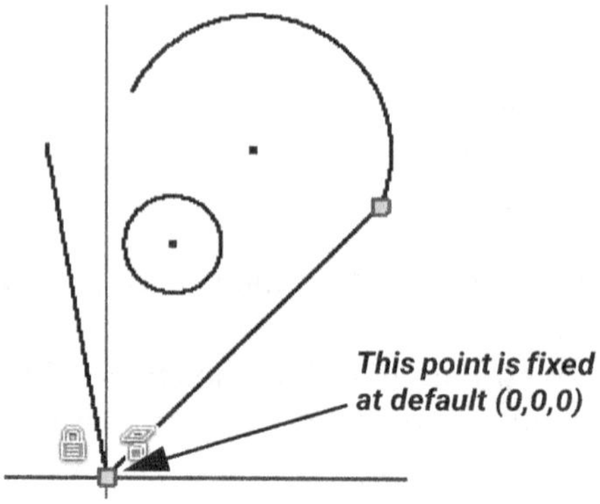

Figure 3–37

Note: If you select (Show All Constraints) in the ribbon, you must select entities in the sketch to display their constraints. Selecting it in the Status Bar shows all constraints.

5. In the Status Bar, click (Hide All Constraints) again or press <F9> to hide the constraints.

Task 2: Apply constraints.

1. In the *Constrain* panel, hover over the twelve constraint types to display their tooltip.
2. In the *Constrain* panel, click (Vertical Constraint) and select the center point of the arc followed by the projected center point, as shown on the left in Figure 3–38. The sketch displays as shown on the right.

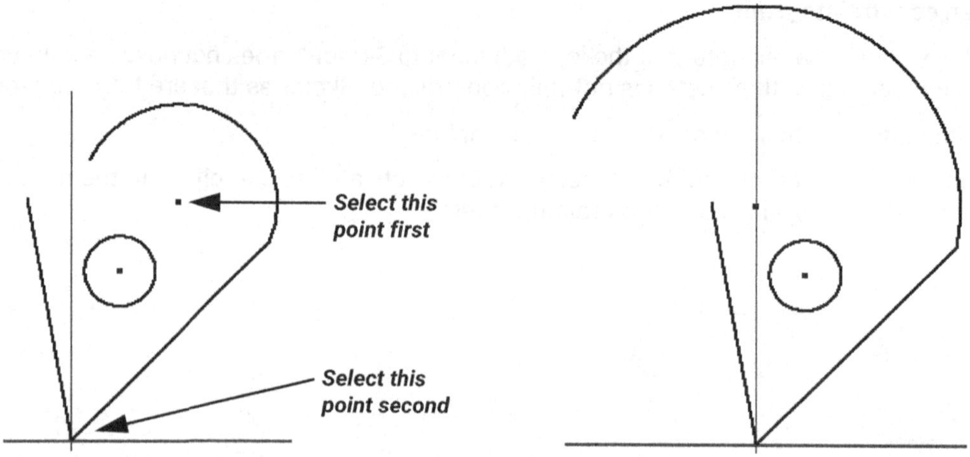

Figure 3–38

3. In the *Constrain* panel, click (Coincident Constraint) and select the end points of the arc and line, as shown on the left in Figure 3–39. The sketch displays as shown on the right.

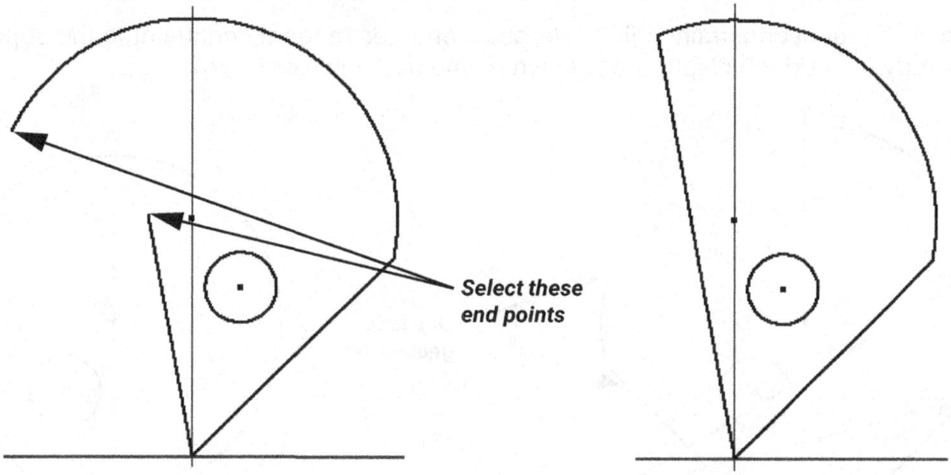

Figure 3–39

4. In the *Constrain* panel, click (Perpendicular Constraint) and select the two lines shown on the left in Figure 3–40. The sketch displays as shown on the right.

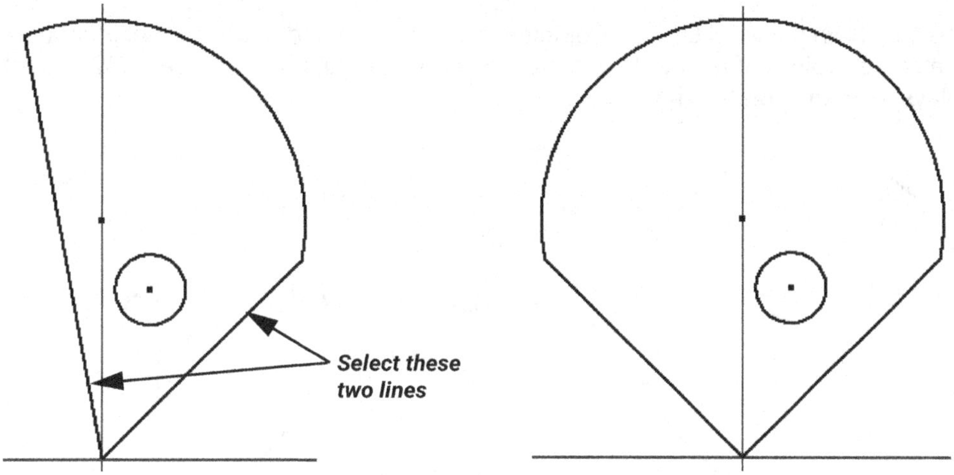

Figure 3–40

5. In the *Constrain* panel, click (Tangent Constraint) and select the arc and line shown on the left in Figure 3–41. The entities on the opposite side update automatically based on the Perpendicular constraint. However, a Tangent constraint is not added automatically.
6. With the Tangent constraint still active, apply another Tangent constraint to the opposite geometry. The sketch displays as shown on the right in Figure 3–41.

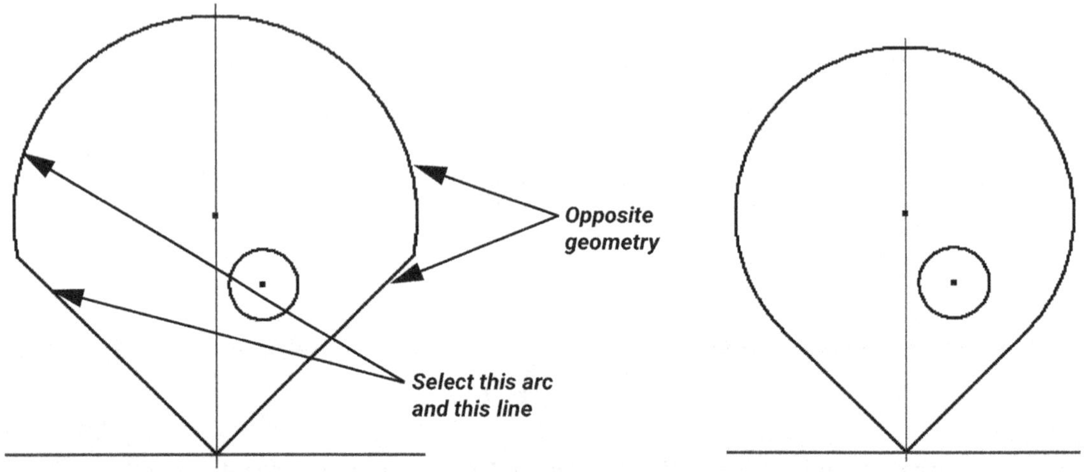

Figure 3–41

7. In the *Constrain* panel, click (Coincident Constraint) and apply a Coincident constraint to the center points of the circle and arc, as shown on the left in Figure 3–42. The sketch displays as shown on the right.

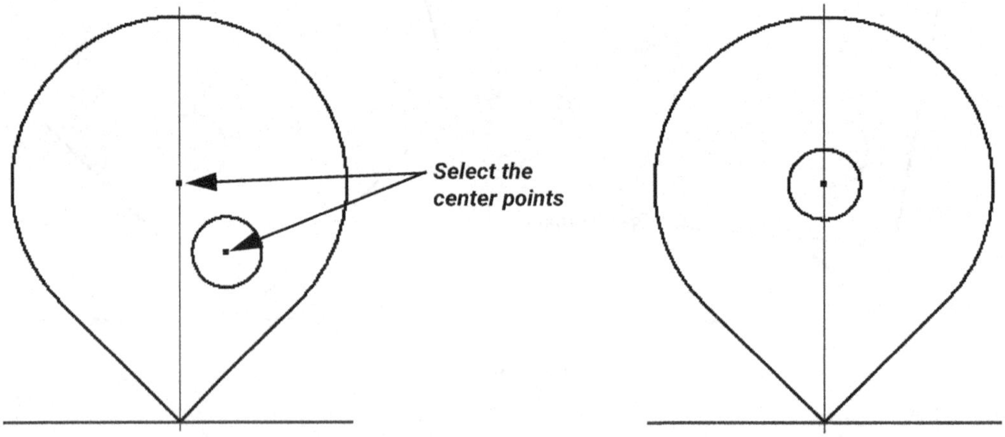

Figure 3–42

Task 3: Dimension the sketch.

The shape of the sketched geometry is defined, but some of the geometry is still not fully constrained, as indicated in the lower-right corner of the Status Bar. By assigning all of the constraints in the previous task, now only two dimensions are necessary and your design intent for the sketch is implied instead of requiring many more dimensions.

1. In the *Constrain* panel, click (Automatic Dimensions and Constraints). The *Auto Dimension* dialog box opens as shown in Figure 3–43. Two dimensions are required.

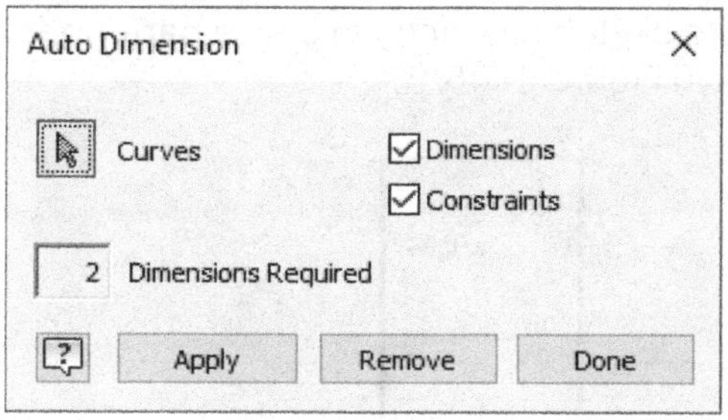

Figure 3–43

2. Click **Apply** to apply the required dimensions.
3. Click **Done** to close the dialog box.
4. Select each dimension and drag them to the locations shown in Figure 3–44.

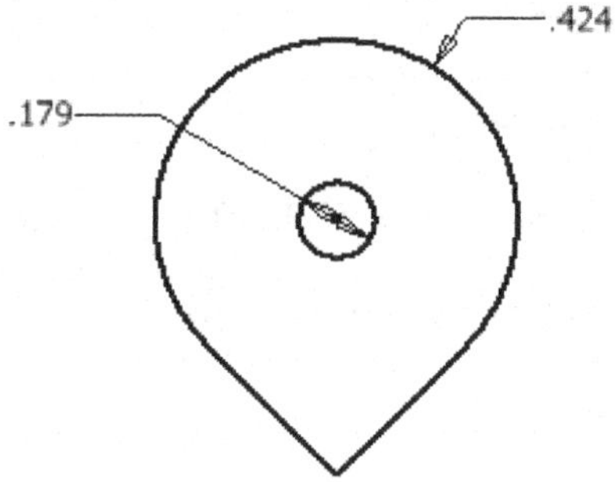

Figure 3–44

5. In the *Exit* panel, click (Finish Sketch) or right-click and select **Finish 2D Sketch**.

   Note: *To cancel any edits made to a sketch and return to the original sketch, expand the Exit panel and click (Cancel).*

6. Save the file and close the window.

End of practice

Practice 3b
Create Sketched Geometry I

Practice Objectives

- Sketch, dimension, and constrain entities to fully constrain a sketch.
- Use Relax mode to temporarily suspend constraints and dimensions to move constrained sketched entities.

In this practice, you will create sketch geometry in a new part model. The sketched geometry that you will create is shown in Figure 3–45.

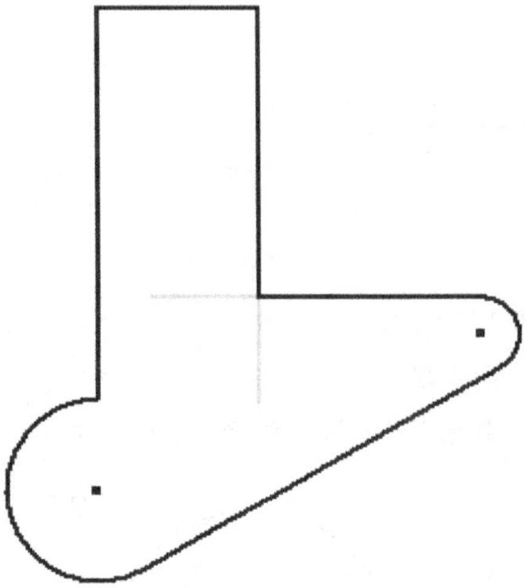

Figure 3–45

Task 1: Create a new part and create a sketch.

1. Create a new part file using the standard metric (mm) template. The *3D Model* tab is active.
2. In the *Sketch* panel, click (Start 2D Sketch) and select the XY Plane as the sketch plane.
3. In the *Create* panel, click (Project Geometry), or right-click and select **Project Geometry**. Project the YZ and XZ Planes in the sketch so that you can select them as references when locating the sketched geometry. Note that the origin center point has been projected automatically.
4. Right-click and select **OK**, or press <Esc> to complete the operation.

Task 2: Sketch the section.

1. In the *Sketch* tab>*Create* panel, click (Line) to sketch the line geometry.
2. Sketch the five linear entities as shown in Figure 3–46, beginning at the projected origin point so that the beginning of the line is coincident with the projected center point. Sketch the first vertical line (shown in Figure 3–46) so that it is approximately 40mm to determine the overall scale of the sketch.

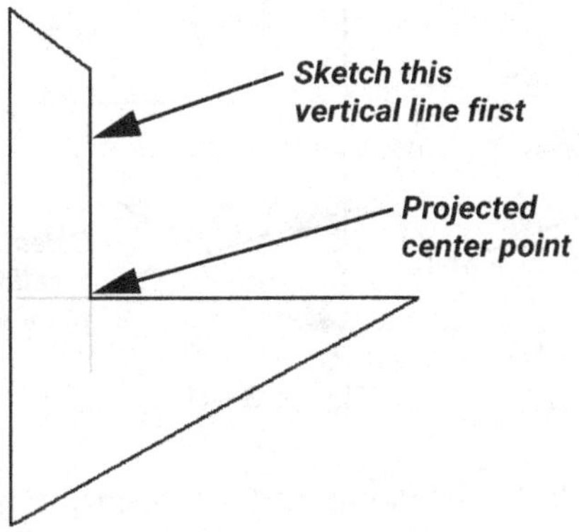

Figure 3–46

3. In the *Create* panel, click (Fillet) to sketch a fillet arc.
4. In the *2D Fillet* field, enter **5.00**. Do not press <Enter>.
5. Select the two lines shown in Figure 3–47. A fillet arc is created and the two lines are automatically trimmed.

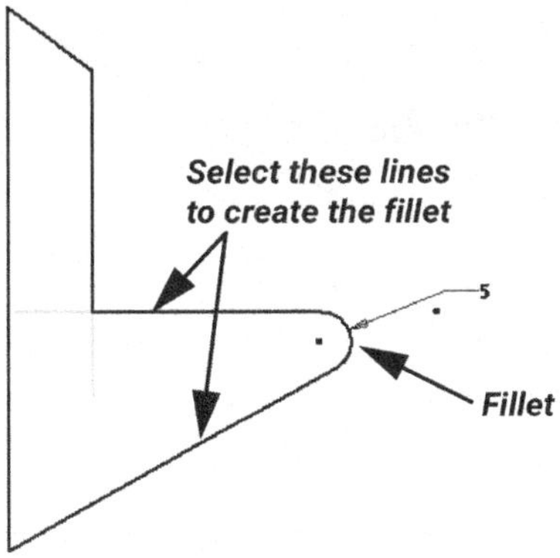

Figure 3–47

6. In the *Create* panel, click (Three Point Arc) to sketch a three-point arc.
7. Select the vertex and edge shown in Figure 3–48 to locate the arc, and drag the edge of the arc to the location shown to define the size of the arc.

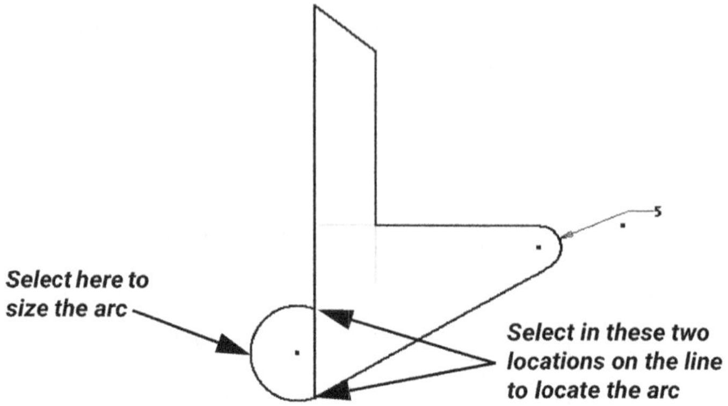

Figure 3–48

8. In the *Constrain* panel, click (Coincident Constraint) to apply a Coincident constraint to the center of the arc and the left vertical line, as shown in Figure 3–49.

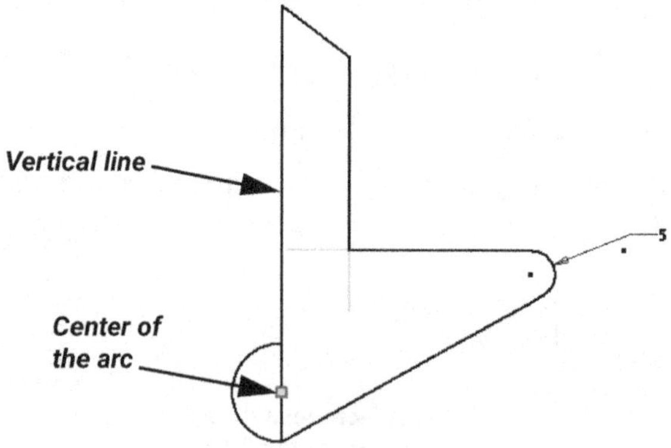

Figure 3–49

Note: *When sketching the Arc, if tangency was assumed with the vertex, assigning the Coincident constraint changes the shape of the geometry to maintain both constraint requirements. Show the constraint, delete the Tangent constraint, and assign the Coincident constraint.*

9. In the *Modify* panel, click (Trim).

10. Trim the inner intersection of the arc with the left vertical line by selecting it. The sketch displays as shown in Figure 3–50.

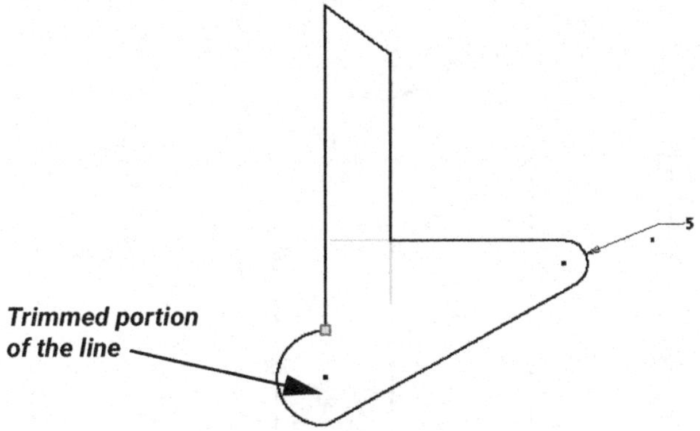

Figure 3–50

11. In the *Constrain* panel, click (Tangent Constraint) and select the arc and line shown in Figure 3–51.

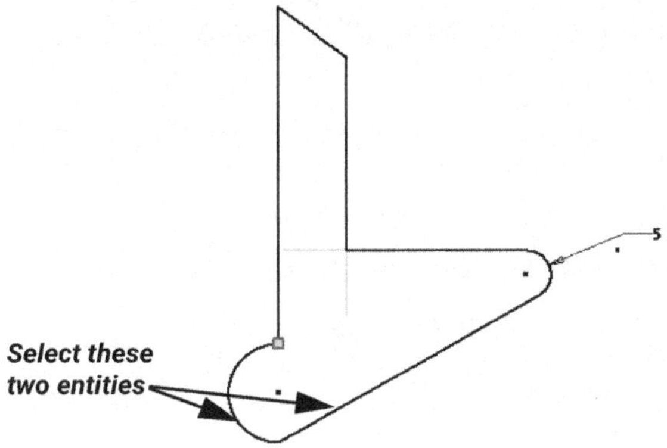

Figure 3–51

Note: *If coincidence was assumed between the arc and the vertical line, assigning the Tangent constraint changes the shape of the geometry to maintain both constraint requirements.*

12. In the *Constrain* panel, click (Dimension) or right-click and select **General Dimension**.

13. Add and modify the dimensions, as shown in Figure 3–52. To apply the 25 unit dimension, select the entity and before placement, right-click and select **Aligned**. Place the dimension by clicking at that point.

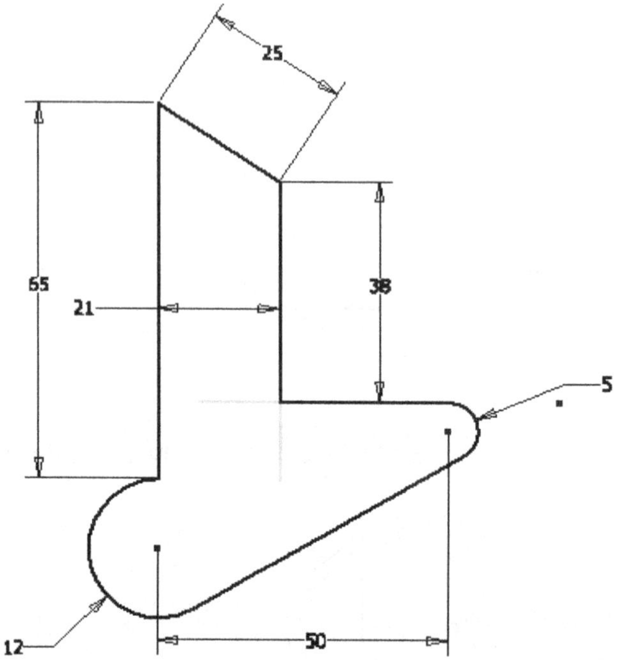

Figure 3–52

14. To finish dimensioning, right-click and select **OK**.
15. In the Status Bar, note that the sketch is Fully Constrained.

Note: *The icon that identifies the sketch in the Model browser displays as*  *while the sketch remains partially constrained and changes to*  *when it is fully constrained.*

16. Select the entity shown in Figure 3–53 and attempt to drag it downwards so that it is horizontal. This is not possible because the sketch is fully defined with dimensions and constraints.

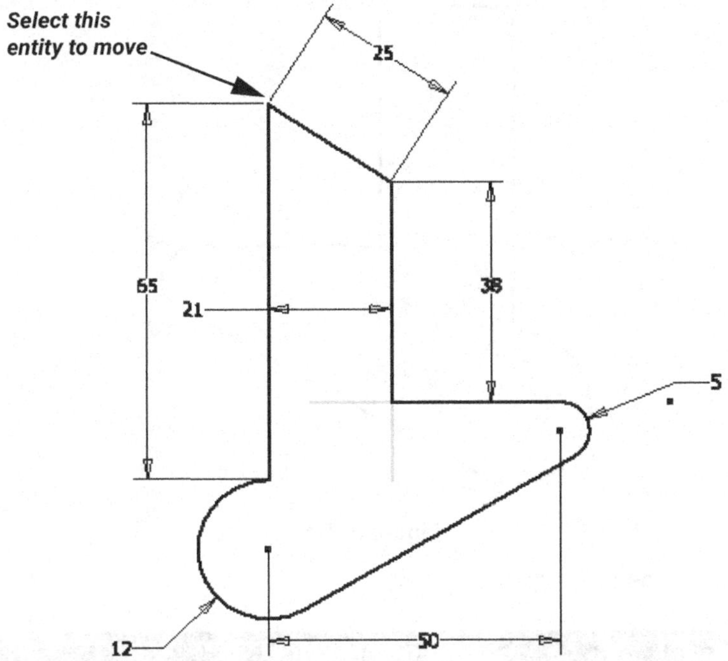

Figure 3–53

17. In the Status Bar, click (Relax Mode) to temporarily disable the constraints and dimensions so that changes can be made to the sketch. To make changes to constrained entities without using Relax Mode, you would have to delete dimensions and constraints, make the change, and then constrain the entities again.
18. Select the same entity again and drag it downwards so that it is horizontal. Note that the entity can now be moved and the sketch remains Fully Constrained.
19. In the Status Bar, click (Relax Mode) to disable Relax Mode. Note that the sketched entity remains in its moved location; however, the dimension/constraint scheme does not reflect that the top entity is horizontal.
20. Delete the dimension value that was assigned to the horizontal entity (initially it was 25). Note in the Status Bar that the sketch now requires an additional dimension.
21. In the *Constrain* panel, click (Horizontal Constraint) and select the horizontal entity that was moved. The sketch is now fully constrained.
22. In the *Exit* panel, click (Finish Sketch) or right-click and select **Finish 2D Sketch** to finish the sketch.

23. To clear the display of sketch dimensions in the graphics window, right-click on the sketch in the Model browser and disable the **Dimension Visibility** option. The Front view of the model is shown in Figure 3–54.

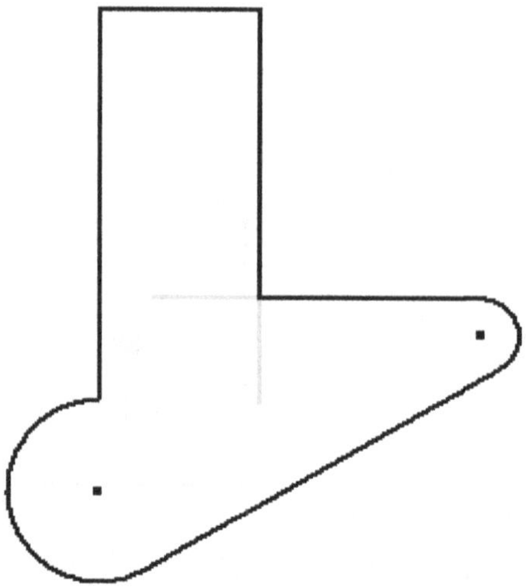

Figure 3–54

24. Save the part and close the window.

End of practice

Practice 3c
Create Sketched Geometry II

Practice Objectives

- Create a new sketch on an origin plane.
- Sketch, mirror, and trim entities to create the required shape.
- Apply dimensions and constraints so that the sketch captures the design intent and is fully constrained.

In this practice, you will create sketched geometry in a new part, as shown on the left in Figure 3–55. This geometry can be used to create the solid geometry shown on the right.

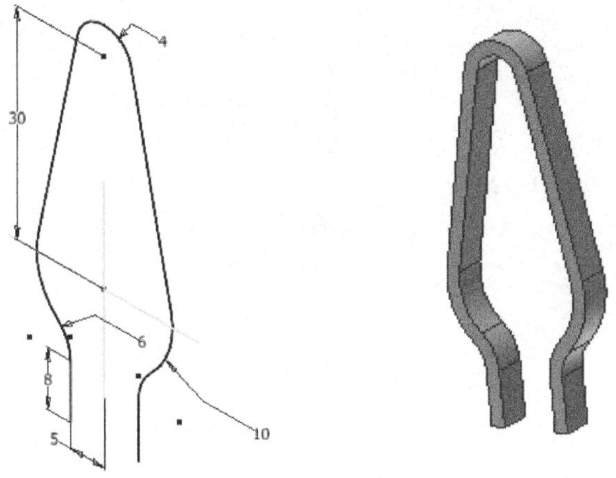

Figure 3–55

Task 1: Create a new part and create a sketch.

1. Create a new part file using the standard metric (mm) template. The *3D Model* tab is active.
2. Start the creation of a new sketch on the XY Plane.
3. In the *Create* panel, click  (Project Geometry) or right-click and select Project Geometry. Project the YZ and XZ Planes in the sketch so that you can select them as references when locating the sketched geometry. Note that the origin center point has been projected automatically.
4. Right-click and select **OK** or press <Esc> to complete the operation.

Task 2: Create the sketch geometry.

1. Start the sketch by sketching two circles, two tangent lines, and a vertical attached line, as shown in Figure 3–56. Position the circles relative to the reference entities. You might have to manually add the Tangent constraint between the lines and circles after you sketch the entities.

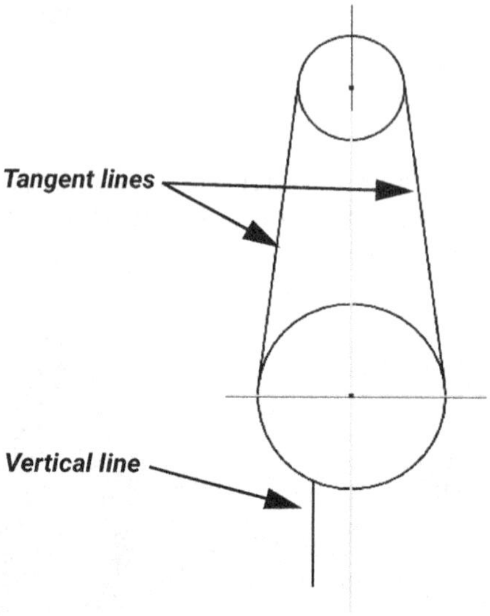

Figure 3–56

*Note: To sketch a line that is tangent to two circles, start the **Line** command, and then select and hold the cursor over one of the two circles. While continuing to hold, drag the cursor to the next circle and position it so that the Tangent constraint is visible. Release the mouse button to locate the tangent line. The same procedure can be used for tangent lines between arcs.*

2. In the *Pattern* panel, click (Mirror) to mirror the vertical line about the YZ Plane. The *Mirror* dialog box opens as shown in Figure 3–57.

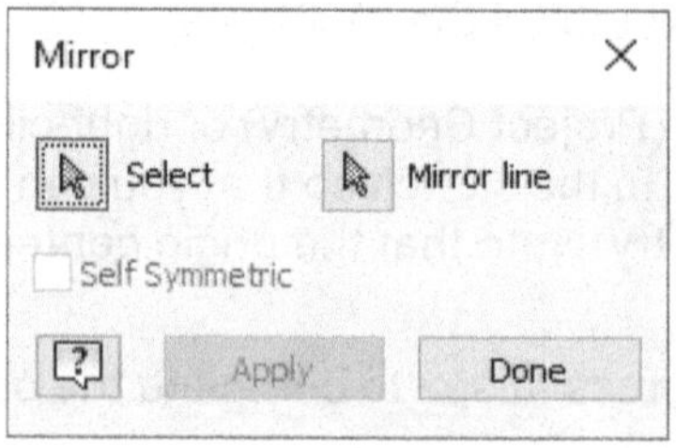

Figure 3–57

3. Select the vertical line.

4. Click (Mirror Line) in the *Mirror* dialog box and select the projected YZ Plane, as shown in Figure 3–58. Click **Apply**.

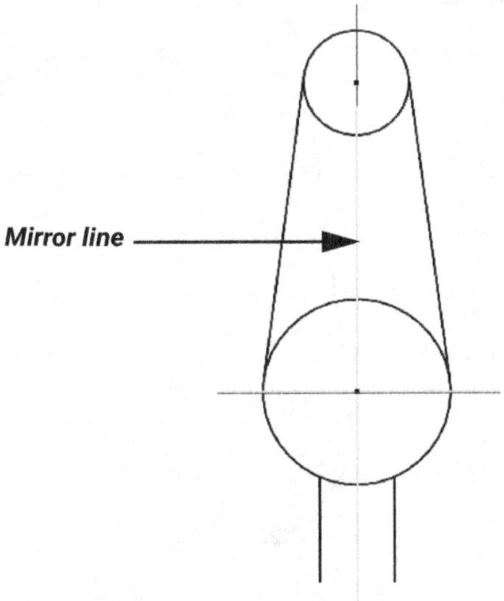

Figure 3–58

5. Click **Done**.
6. In the *Modify* panel, click (Trim) or right-click and select **Trim**. Select the unwanted segments of the circles so the sketch displays as shown in Figure 3–59. To dynamically trim, initiate the **Trim** command, press and hold the left mouse button and drag the trim line over the entities to be removed. Release the mouse button to remove the entities.

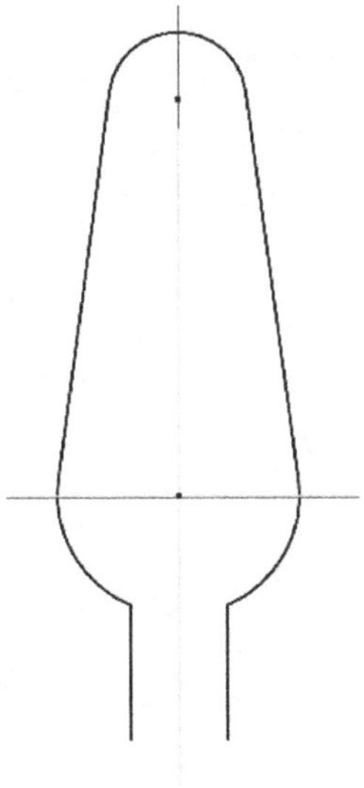

Figure 3–59

7. In the *Create* panel, click (Fillet).
8. In the *2D Fillet* field, enter **6.00**, and create fillets between the vertical lines and the arc segments, as shown in Figure 3–60.

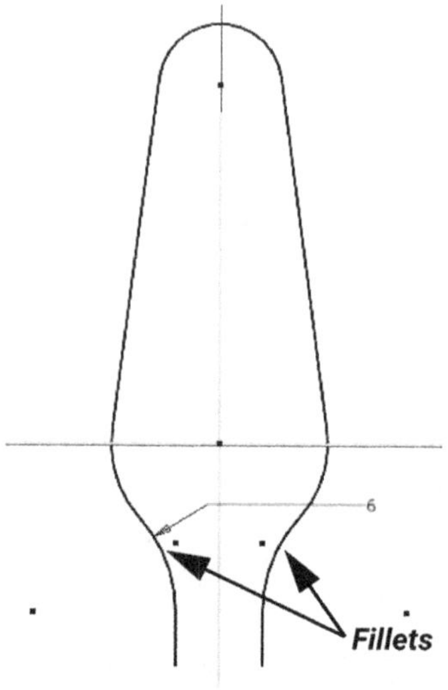

Figure 3–60

9. In the lower-right corner of the Status Bar, note that five dimensions are required.
10. Click (Show All Degrees of Freedom) in the Status Bar to display the degrees of freedom in the sketch, as shown in Figure 3–61.

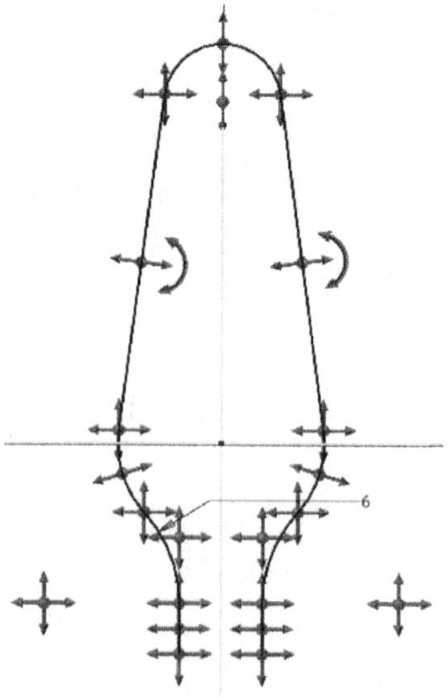

Figure 3–61

11. In the *Constrain* panel, click (Dimension) or right-click and select **General Dimension**.
12. Add and modify the dimensions as shown in Figure 3–62. Add additional constraints, if required. Note that as each degree of freedom is constrained, its symbol is removed from the sketch.

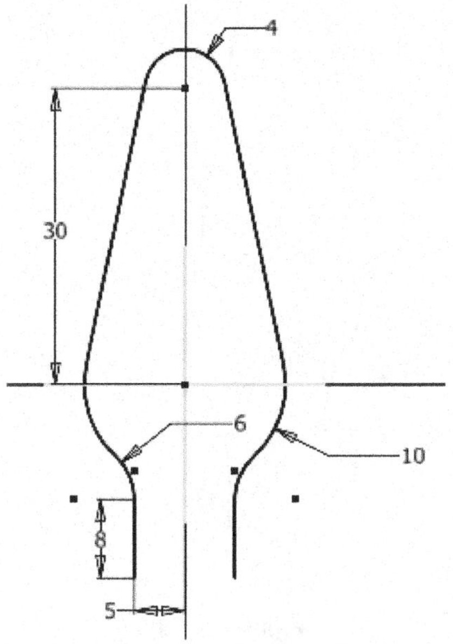

Figure 3–62

Note: *The icon that identifies the sketch in the Model browser displays as while the sketch remains partially constrained and changes to when it is fully constrained.*

13. In the *Exit* panel, click (Finish Sketch) or right-click and select **Finish 2D Sketch** to finish the sketch.

14. Hover the cursor over the ViewCube and click (Home) to return the model to its default isometric Home view, as shown in Figure 3–63.

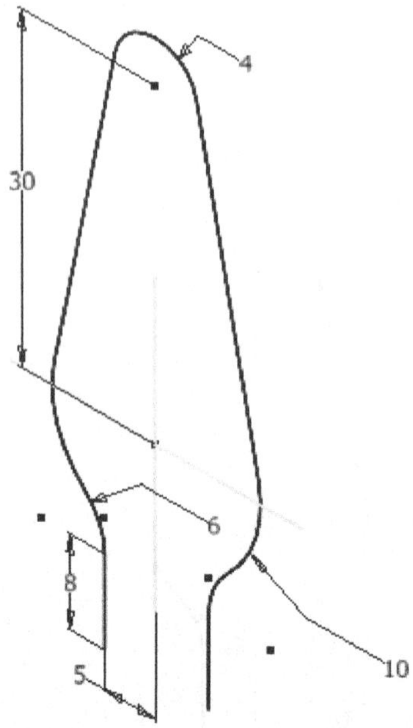

Figure 3–63

15. Save the part and close the window.

End of practice

Practice 3d
Create Sketched Geometry III

Practice Objective

- Sketch, dimension, and constrain entities to fully constrain a sketch.

In this practice, you will create the sketch shown in Figure 3–64. To successfully create this sketch you will be required to sketch linear, arc, and circular entities and ensure that they are fully dimensioned and constrained.

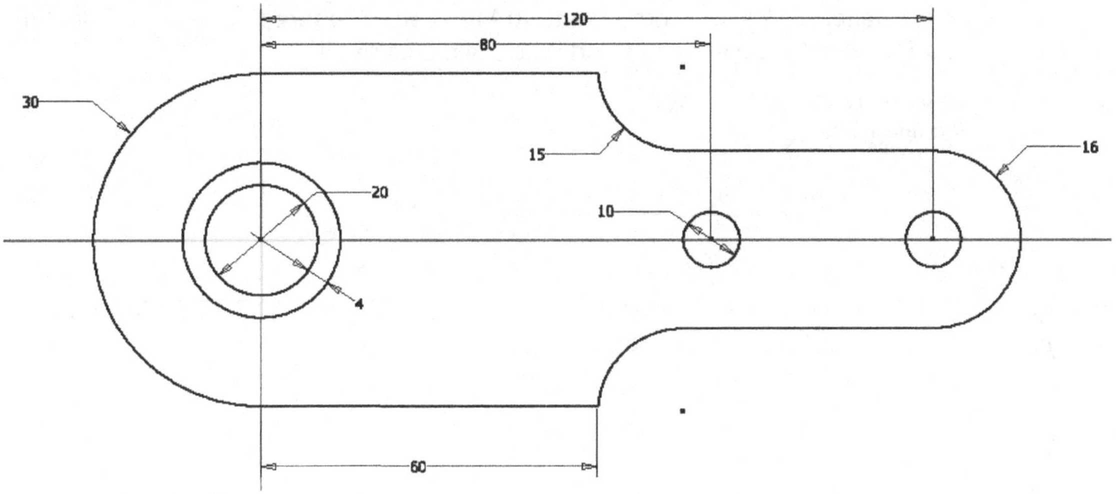

Figure 3–64

Task 1: Create a new part file and start the creation of a sketch.

1. Use the standard metric (mm) template to create a new part file. The *3D Model* tab is active.
2. Start the creation of a new sketch on the XY Plane.
3. In the *Create* panel, click (Project Geometry) or right-click and select **Project Geometry**. Project the YZ and XZ Planes in the sketch so that you can select them as references when locating the sketched geometry. Note that the origin center point has been projected automatically.
4. Right-click and select **OK** or press <Esc> to complete the operation.

Task 2: Sketch the section.

1. In the *Sketch* tab>*Create* panel, click (Line) to sketch the line geometry. Begin by sketching the top horizontal line above the projected XZ Plane, as shown in Figure 3–65.
2. Continue to sketch the additional arc and line entities to create the final sketch, similar to that shown in Figure 3–65.
   - When sketching the tangent arcs from the horizontal linear entities continue using the **Line** command by pressing and holding the left mouse button and dragging in the required direction. Release the left mouse button to select the end point for the arc.
   - In the *Create* panel, click (Three Point Arc) to sketch the three-point arcs. Select the start point followed by the endpoint and drag the arc as required.

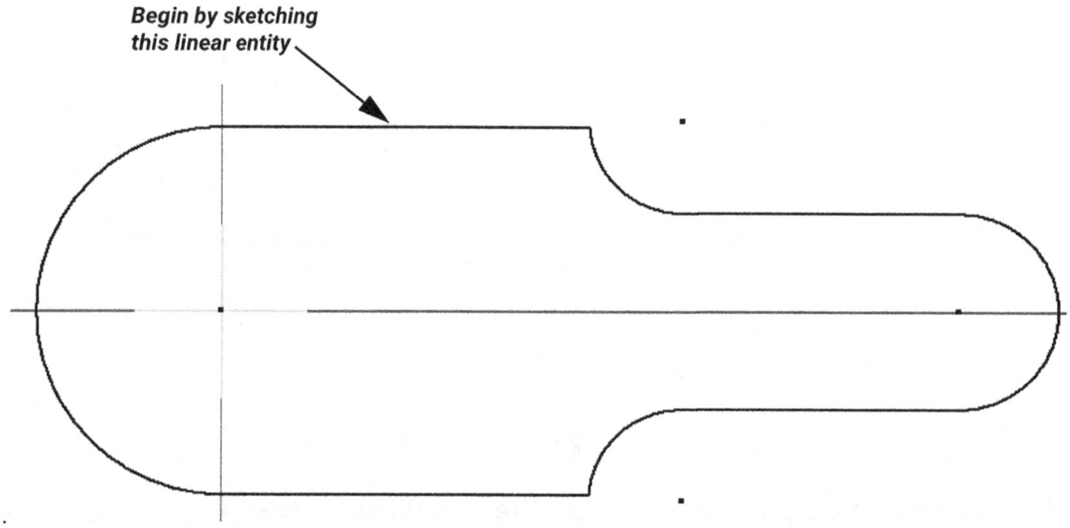

Figure 3–65

Task 3: Dimension and constrain the sketch.

1. In the *Constrain* panel, use the Horizontal, Vertical, or Coincident constraint options, as required, to ensure that the centers of the arcs on both ends of the sketch lie on the projected XZ Plane. Also ensure that the two equal arcs are aligned vertically.
2. In the *Constrain* panel, click (Dimension) or right-click and select **General Dimension**.
3. Add and modify the dimensions shown in Figure 3–66.

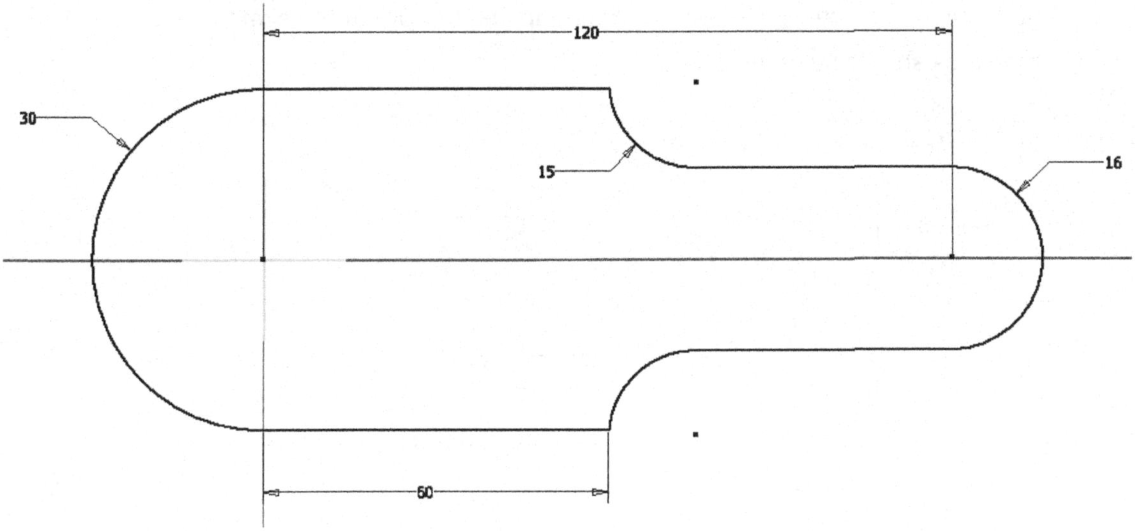

Figure 3–66

4. To finish dimensioning, right-click and select **OK**.
5. In the *Constrain* panel, click (Show Constraints) and select all of the sketched entities. All of the constraints that were implied or created when sketching are shown in the sketch. Verify the existing constraints and review the Status Bar to see how many dimensions/constraints are required to fully constrain the sketch.
6. In the Status Bar, click (Hide All Constraints) to clear the display of the constraints from the sketch.

7. Assign additional constraints (similar to those shown in Figure 3–67) to fully constrain the sketch, if not already fully constrained. The final list of constraints that you use to complete the sketch might vary, however, consider the following:
   - The four linear entities should be horizontal.
   - Tangency should be assigned between the linear entities and the arcs (4 locations).
   - The center of the large arc should be located on the project's center point origin.
   - The entities above and below the projected XZ Plane should be symmetric. This can be achieved using the Symmetric constraint or other constraints.
   - Endpoints should be aligned between the top and bottom of the sketch.
   - Small arcs should be equal in size.

   Note: *Constraints display in light gray in a model. In Figure 3–67, the constraints are selected and displayed in red for clarity.*

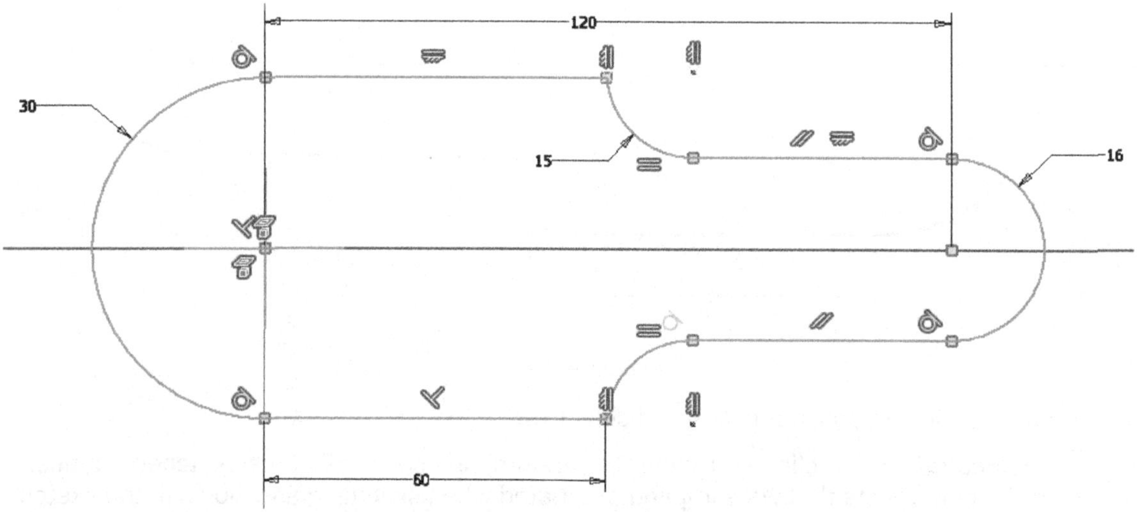

Figure 3–67

8. In the Status Bar, verify that the sketch is Fully Constrained.

9. Add the four sketch circles shown in Figure 3–68 and dimension and constrain them so that the sketch remains fully constrained. Consider the following:
   - The circles all lie on the projected horizontal XZ Plane.
   - The two smaller circles are equal in diameter. One is dimensioned from the projected center point, and the other is concentric with the right-hand arc.
   - The two circles on the left are concentric with the large arc and the dimension scheme shows one diameter and an offset distance.

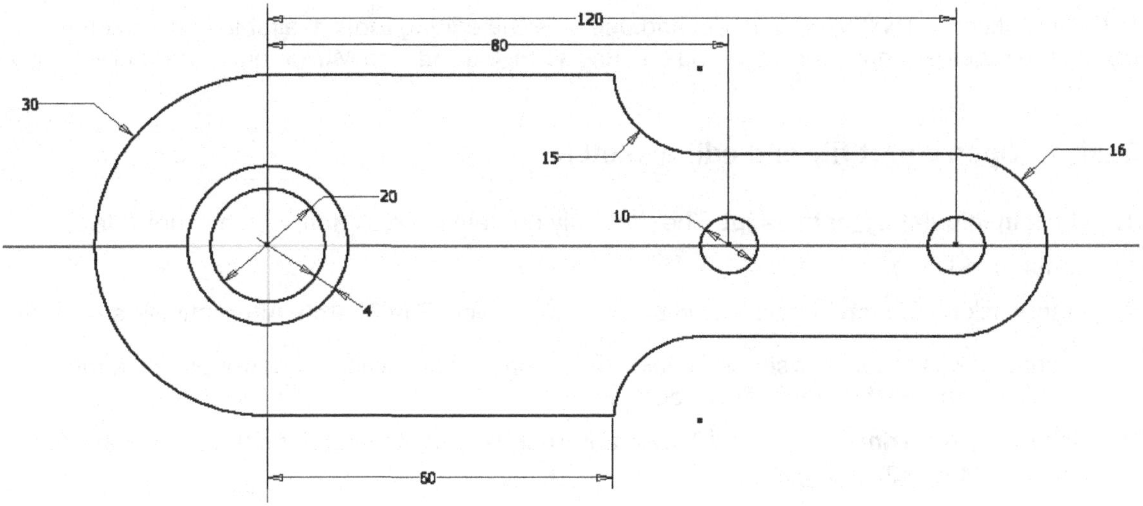

Figure 3–68

10. Finish the sketch.
11. Save the part and close the window.

End of practice

Practice 3e
(Optional) Manipulate Entities

Practice Objectives

- Open an existing part model and edit an existing sketch.
- Modify the existing entities into an alternate sketch.

In this practice, you will open a model and use only the editing tools available in the sketch to obtain the required final geometry. You can use **Trim**, **Extend**, and **Mirror**, but cannot create any new entities.

Task 1: Open a part file and edit a sketch.

1. Open **manipulating_entities.ipt**. The part only contains one sketch, which is not fully constrained ( ).
2. Right-click on **Sketch1** in the Model browser and select **Edit Sketch**. Alternatively, select the Sketch in the Model browser and click in the graphics window or double-click the sketch's name in the Model browser.
3. Using only the **Trim, Extend**, and **Mirror** commands, edit the sketch so that it displays as shown on the right in Figure 3–69.

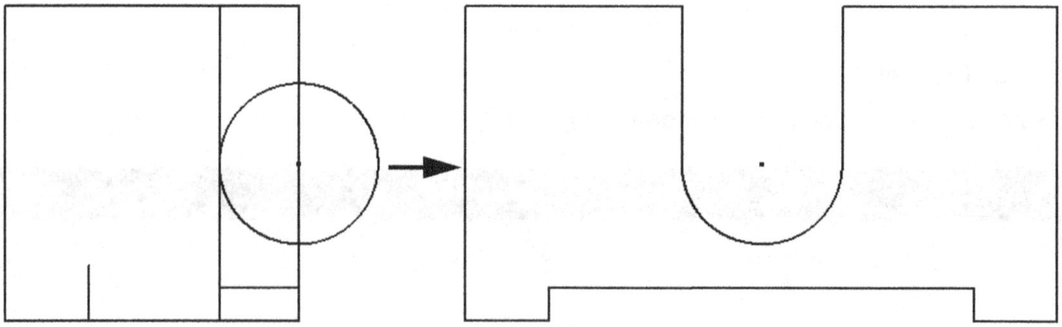

Figure 3–69

4. (Optional) Dimension the sketch.
5. Save the part and close the window.

End of practice

Chapter Review Questions

1. Construction entities can be used directly to create solid geometry.
   a. True
   b. False

2. Which of the following statements describes trimming sketch entities?
   a. Continues an entity to meet the next entity in its path or to close an open sketch.
   b. Removes the segment of the entity to the nearest intersection in each direction from the point selected.
   c. Duplicates a source entity to one or more locations in the sketch or to another sketch.
   d. Provides a specific tool for stretching sketched entities versus simply selecting and dragging them in the sketch.

3. Which of the following statements describes extending sketch entities?
   a. Continues an entity to meet the next entity in its path or to close an open sketch.
   b. Enables you to relocate original 2D sketch geometry.
   c. Duplicates a source entity to one or more locations in the sketch or to another sketch.
   d. Provides a specific tool for stretching sketched entities versus simply selecting and dragging them in the sketch.

4. How was the profile shown in Figure 3–70 created in the sketch environment?

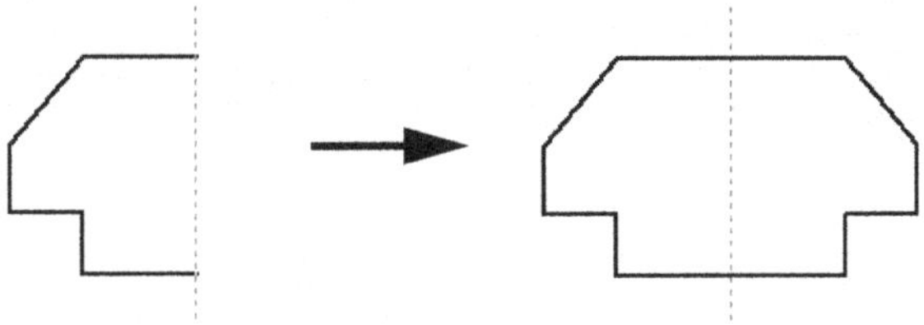

Figure 3–70

   a. Mirror
   b. Revolve
   c. Extend
   d. Trim

5. Which of the following can be made equal using (Equal Constraint)? (Select all that apply.)
   a. Angles between lines
   b. Line Lengths
   c. Arc Radii
   d. Circle Diameters

6. Which constraints enable you to create two circles with the same center? (Select all that apply.)
   a. Concentric
   b. Colinear
   c. Coincident
   d. Tangent

7. How can you control the visibility of constraint symbols in the graphics window display? (Select all that apply.)
   a. To show or hide all of the constraints on a sketch, toggle (Show All Constraints) and (Hide All Constraints) in the Status Bar.
   b. Select the entity to which it is associated.
   c. Use <F8> to show all of the constraints and <F9> to hide them.
   d. Select the symbol and press <Delete>.

8. What is the purpose of the Fix constraint, shown in Figure 3–71?

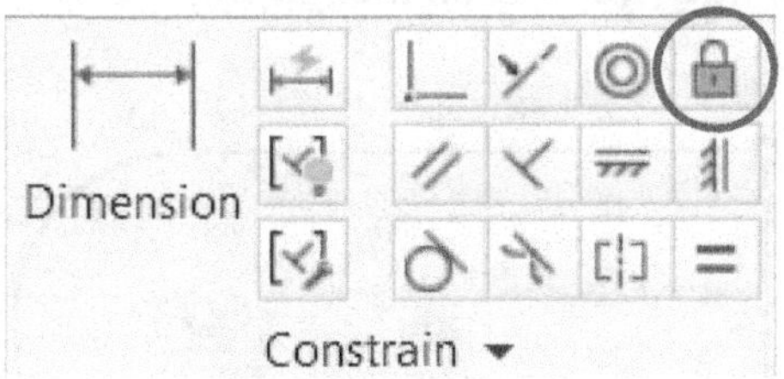

Figure 3–71

a. To position one point exactly on another.
b. To edit an existing constraint.
c. To resolve conflicts among other constraints.
d. To fix a point relative to the default coordinate system of the sketch.

9. All constraints must be manually assigned to the sketched geometry.

a. True
b. False

10. Which of the following sets of constraints was used to manipulate the geometry on the left to that on the right in Figure 3–72?

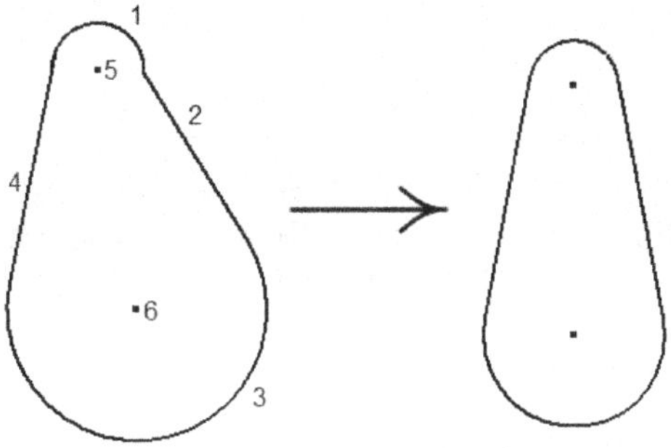

Figure 3–72

a. 1 tangent with 2, 1 tangent with 4, 5 coincident with 6.
b. 1 tangent with 2, 1 tangent with 4, 5 concentric with 6.
c. 1 tangent with 2, 1 tangent with 4, 5 collinear with 6.
d. 1 tangent with 2, 1 tangent with 4, 5 vertical with 6.

11. Based on the constraint symbols shown in Figure 3–73, which constraint types are applied to the bottom horizontal entity? (Select all that apply.)

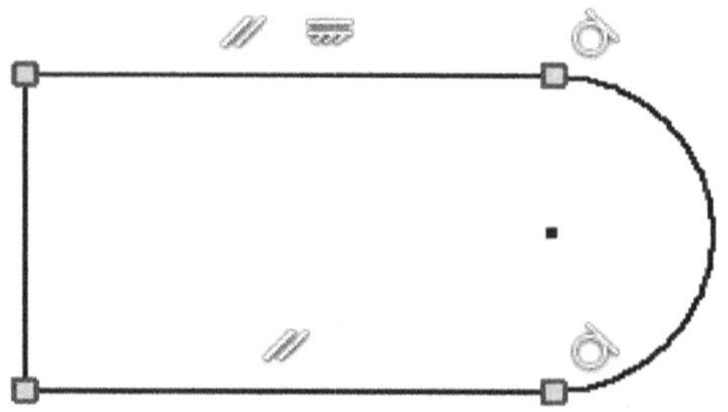

Figure 3–73

a. Symmetric

b. Parallel

c. Perpendicular

d. Tangent

e. Collinear

f. Coincident

12. Fillets and chamfers that are added in the sketch become separate Fillet and Chamfer features in the Model browser once the sketch has been completed. They can be selected and deleted independent of the sketch.

a. True

b. False

13. What types of sketch entities can you use as the mirror line when mirroring geometry? (Select all that apply.)

a. Construction line

b. Solid line

c. Projected part edge

d. Projected work plane

Command Summary

Button	Command	Location
	Bridge Curve	• **Ribbon:** *Sketch* tab>*Create* panel
	Center Point Arc	• **Ribbon:** *Sketch* tab>*Create* panel
	Center Point Arc Slot	• **Ribbon:** *Sketch* tab>*Create* panel
	Center Point Slot	• **Ribbon:** *Sketch* tab>*Create* panel
	Chamfer (sketch)	• **Ribbon:** *Sketch* tab>*Create* panel
	Coincident	• **Ribbon:** *Sketch* tab>*Constrain* panel
	Collinear	• **Ribbon:** *Sketch* tab>*Constrain* panel
	Concentric	• **Ribbon:** *Sketch* tab>*Constrain* panel
	Constraint Settings	• **Ribbon:** *Sketch* tab>*Constrain* panel
	Construction	• **Ribbon:** *Sketch* tab>*Format* panel
	Degrees of Freedom	• **Status Bar**
	Ellipse	• **Ribbon:** *Sketch* tab>*Create* panel
	Equal	• **Ribbon:** *Sketch* tab>*Constrain* panel
	Equation Curve	• **Ribbon:** *Sketch* tab>*Create* panel
	Extend	• **Ribbon:** *Sketch* tab>*Modify* panel • *(toggle between **Trim** and **Extend** using <Shift>)*
	Fillet *(sketch)*	• **Ribbon:** *Sketch* tab>*Create* panel
	Fix	• **Ribbon:** *Sketch* tab>*Constrain* panel
	Horizontal	• **Ribbon:** *Sketch* tab>*Constrain* panel

Button	Command	Location
	**Mirror**	• **Ribbon:** *Sketch* tab>*Pattern* panel
	**Overall Slot**	• **Ribbon:** *Sketch* tab>*Create* panel
	**Parallel**	• **Ribbon:** *Sketch* tab>*Constrain* panel
	**Perpendicular**	• **Ribbon:** *Sketch* tab>*Constrain* panel
	**Polygon**	• **Ribbon:** *Sketch* tab>*Create* panel
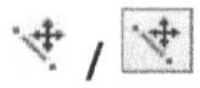	**Relax Mode**	• **Status Bar**
	**Show All Constraints/ Hide All Constraints**	• **Status Bar**
	**Show Constraints**	• **Ribbon:** *Sketch* tab>*Constrain* panel
	**Smooth (G2)**	• **Ribbon:** *Sketch* tab>*Constrain* panel
	**Spline (Control Vertex)**	• **Ribbon:** *Sketch* tab>*Create* panel
	**Spline (Interpolation)**	• **Ribbon:** *Sketch* tab>*Create* panel
	**Symmetric**	• **Ribbon:** *Sketch* tab>*Constrain* panel
	**Tangent**	• **Ribbon:** *Sketch* tab>*Constrain* panel
	**Tangent Arc**	• **Ribbon:** *Sketch* tab>*Create* panel
	**Tangent Circle**	• **Ribbon:** *Sketch* tab>*Create* panel
	**Three Point Arc**	• **Ribbon:** *Sketch* tab>*Create* panel
	**Three Point Arc Slot**	• **Ribbon:** *Sketch* tab>*Create* panel
	**Three Point Center Rectangle**	• **Ribbon:** *Sketch* tab>*Create* panel
	**Three Point Rectangle**	• **Ribbon:** *Sketch* tab>*Create* panel

Button	Command	Location
	**Trim**	• **Ribbon:** *Sketch* tab>*Modify* panel • **Context Menu:** In the graphics window • *(toggle between **Trim** and **Extend** using <Shift>)*
	**Two Point Center Rectangle**	• **Ribbon:** *Sketch* tab>*Create* panel
	**Vertical**	• **Ribbon:** *Sketch* tab>*Constrain* panel

Chapter 4

Sketch Editing Tools

The Sketch environment provides you with a variety of sketch functions and settings that enable you to efficiently create and edit sketch entities. The effective use of these tools saves time when designing and making changes to models.

Learning Objectives

- Relocate existing entities in a sketch by moving and rotating them.
- Resize existing sketched entities by scaling and stretching them.
- Split single entities into multiple entities.
- Copy sketched entities into the same or a different sketch.
- Create a circular or rectangular pattern of sketched entities.
- Customize sketching references using the *Application Options* and *Document Settings* options.

4.1 Advanced Sketch Editing Tools

Move, Copy, Rotate, Scale, and Stretch

The following describes some of the more advanced tools that can be used to edit a sketch. All of the editing tools described are located in the *Sketch* tab>*Modify* panel.

(Move)	Moves original 2D sketch geometry or copies and moves it.
(Copy)	Copies the source entities to one or more locations in the sketch or to another sketch. No relationship is established between the new and source entities. Copying entities can also be done using **Move** and **Rotate**. However, **Copy** enables you to create multiple instances at once.
(Rotate)	Rotates sketch entities about a center point.
(Scale)	Enlarges or reduces the size of sketched entities by entering a scale factor.
(Stretch)	Stretches entities versus simply selecting and dragging them. Unlike using the select-and-drag technique, which does not enable you to manipulate constrained geometry, the **Stretch** command enables you to stretch constrained geometry while maintaining its constraints.

The workflow for these sketch editing tools are similar.

How To: Edit Sketched Geometry Using These Tools

1. Select the required editing command. The associated dialog box opens, as shown in Figure 4–1.

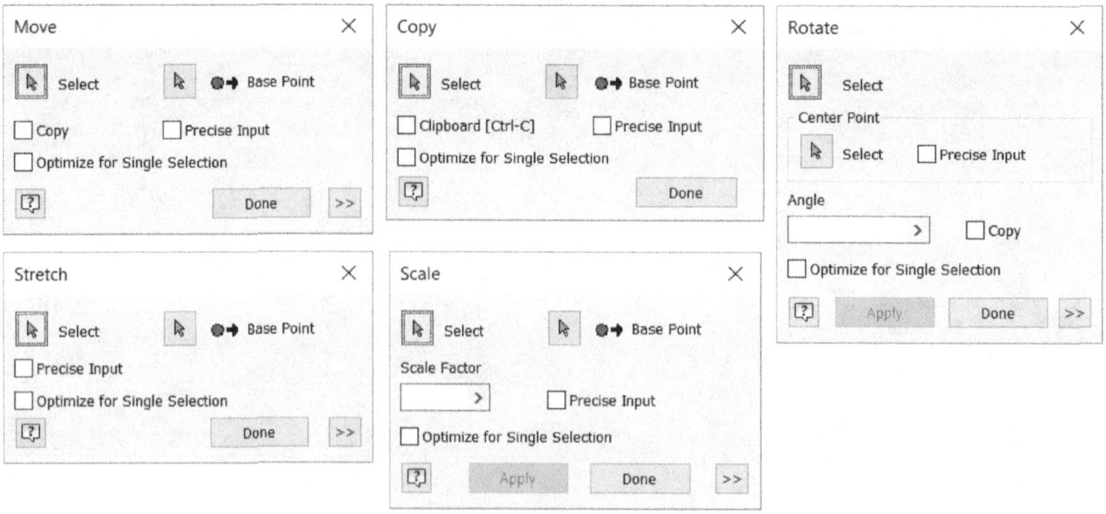

Figure 4–1

2. Select the entities to edit using  (Select). To select multiple entities, press and hold <Ctrl>, right-click and select **Select All**, or use one of the two window selection techniques shown in Figure 4–2.

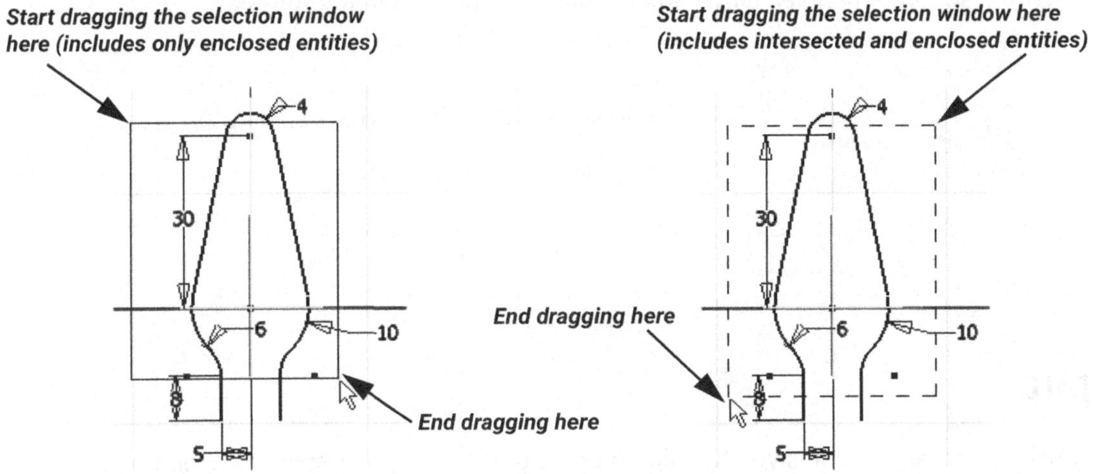

Figure 4–2

Note: *The* ***Optimize for Single Selection*** *option can be used to automatically advance to*  *(Base/Center Point) selection once a single entity has been selected for editing.*

Hint: Selection Tools

- For the **Copy** command, once entities are selected, you can use **Clipboard** to place the entities on the clipboard for pasting into the same or another sketch.
- For the **Stretch** command, entity selection (lines, points, arcs) is important, otherwise the command functions similar to the **Move** command.

3. For the **Move** and **Rotate** editing commands, you can select **Copy** in the dialog box to make a copy of the entities as you move or rotate them.
4. For the **Move**, **Copy**, **Scale**, and **Stretch**, click  (Base Point) and for **Rotate**, click  (Center Point). In both situations, select a point on the original geometry as the reference/pivot point for the operation. Alternatively, you can select **Precise Input** to enter a location for the reference.
5. Select a point to which to move, copy, scale, rotate, or stretch. As you drag the cursor, the edited sketch displays. When rotating or scaling, you can also manually enter a rotation or scale value.
6. Click **Done** to complete the operation.

Depending on the dimensional and geometric constraints, the dialog box shown in Figure 4–3 (or a similar dialog box) might open, prompting you to remove constraints or relax dimensions. Click **Yes** to remove any existing constraints; however, consider that you might want to add them again later to ensure that the design intent is maintained. You can also click Prompts to set how the software handles dimension/constraint conflicts in the future.

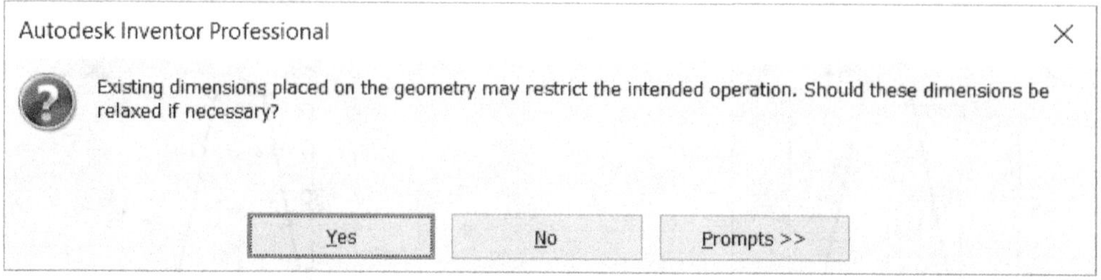

Figure 4–3

Split

The **Split** command enables you to split an entity (e.g., line, arc, or spline) based on an intersecting entity (e.g., entity, workplane, or surface). To split an entity, click (Split) in the *Modify* panel and select the entity to split. Before selecting the entity to split, hover the cursor over the entity to preview a cross mark that indicates the split location. In cases where multiple solutions are possible, the nearest one is assigned. Once split, the segments maintain all constraints, except for **Equal** and **Symmetric**, if they apply. Dimensions are also maintained when entities are split.

Copy and Paste

As an alternative to using the **Copy** command in the *Modify* panel, you can use the standard keyboard driven **Copy** (right-click and select **Copy**, or press <Ctrl>+<C>) and **Paste** (right-click and select **Paste**, or press <Ctrl>+<V>) functionality in a sketch. You can copy in the same sketch, to another sketch in the same model, or a sketch in a different model. Regardless of the target location, select the source entities and initiate the copy functionality. Once the entities are saved to the clipboard you can paste using any of the following techniques.

- Right-click and select **Paste** in the same sketch. Use the right-click **Paste** option on a Model browser Sketch node or in the graphics window if the sketch is active.
- Finish the current sketch, in the Model browser locate the target sketch in the same model, right-click and select **Paste**.
- Open a new part to copy into, locate the target sketch in the Model browser, right-click, and select **Paste**. If the sketch does not exist, create it, right-click in the graphics window, and select **Paste** while in the Sketch environment.

4.2 Rectangular Sketch Patterns

Patterning in a sketch enables you to quickly create identical entities. The sketched entities shown in Figure 4–4 are patterned horizontally and vertically using a rectangular sketch pattern.

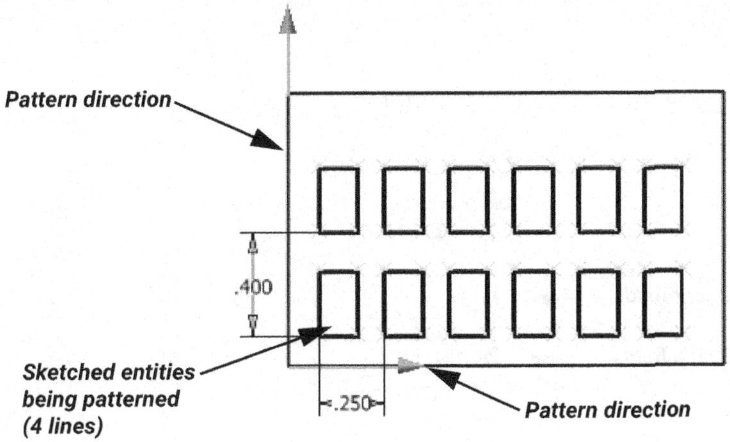

Figure 4–4

How To: Create a Rectangular Sketch Pattern

1. In the *Sketch* tab>*Pattern* panel, click (Rectangular Pattern) to open the *Rectangular Pattern* dialog box.
2. With (Geometry) selected, select the geometry to pattern.

   Note: *Drag a selection box around sketched entities to select multiple entities at once. To clear entities, press and hold <Ctrl> and reselect the entities.*

3. To define the first pattern direction, click in the *Direction 1* area and select existing linear geometry, including lines and part edges, to define the pattern direction.

4. Enter the number of occurrences (including selected) in the ∘∘∘ *(Count)* field, and the distance between each occurrence in the ◇ *(Spacing)* field, as shown in Figure 4–5.

   - To change the direction of the pattern in the first direction, click [icon] in the *Direction 1* area.
   - To pattern symmetrically from the selected entities in the first direction, click [icon] in the *Direction 1* area.

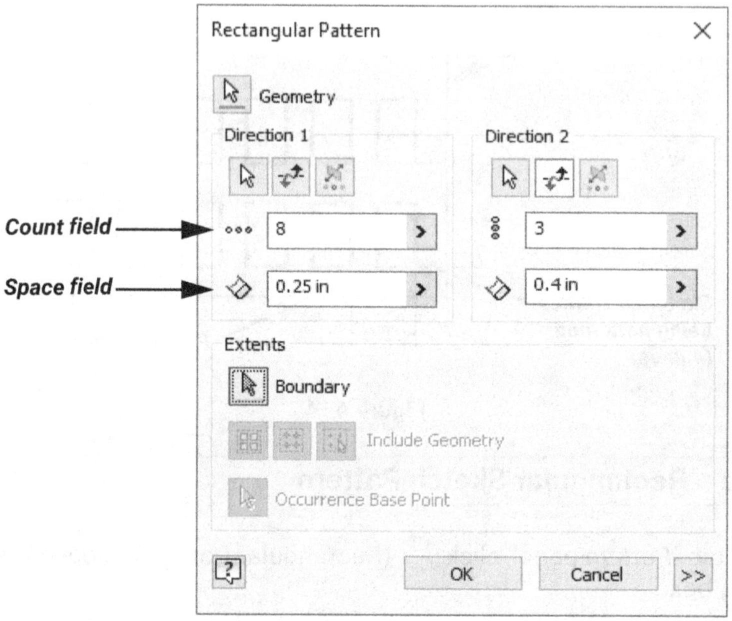

Figure 4–5

5. To define the second pattern direction, click [icon] in the *Direction 2* area and select an edge or line.

6. Enter values in the ∘∘∘ *(Count)* and ◇ *(Spacing)* fields in the *Direction 2* area to define the second direction pattern.

7. (Optional) In the *Extents* area, select (Boundary) and select a closed boundary to define the extent of the pattern. The boundary can be defined by selecting either sketched entities or projected geometry. Once selected, the area defined by the boundary displays green. Select one of the following three options to define whether the patterned instances are included/excluded at the defined boundary. The results are shown in Figure 4–6.

   - (Include Geometry) includes pattern instances that are fully enclosed by the selected boundary.
   - (Include Centroids) includes all pattern instances that have their centroid fully enclosed by the boundary.
   - (Include using occurrence base points) includes all pattern instances that have the selected base point fully enclosed by the boundary.

   Note: *Patterned entities that are displayed as solid lines are included in the pattern and hashed entities will be removed from the final pattern.*

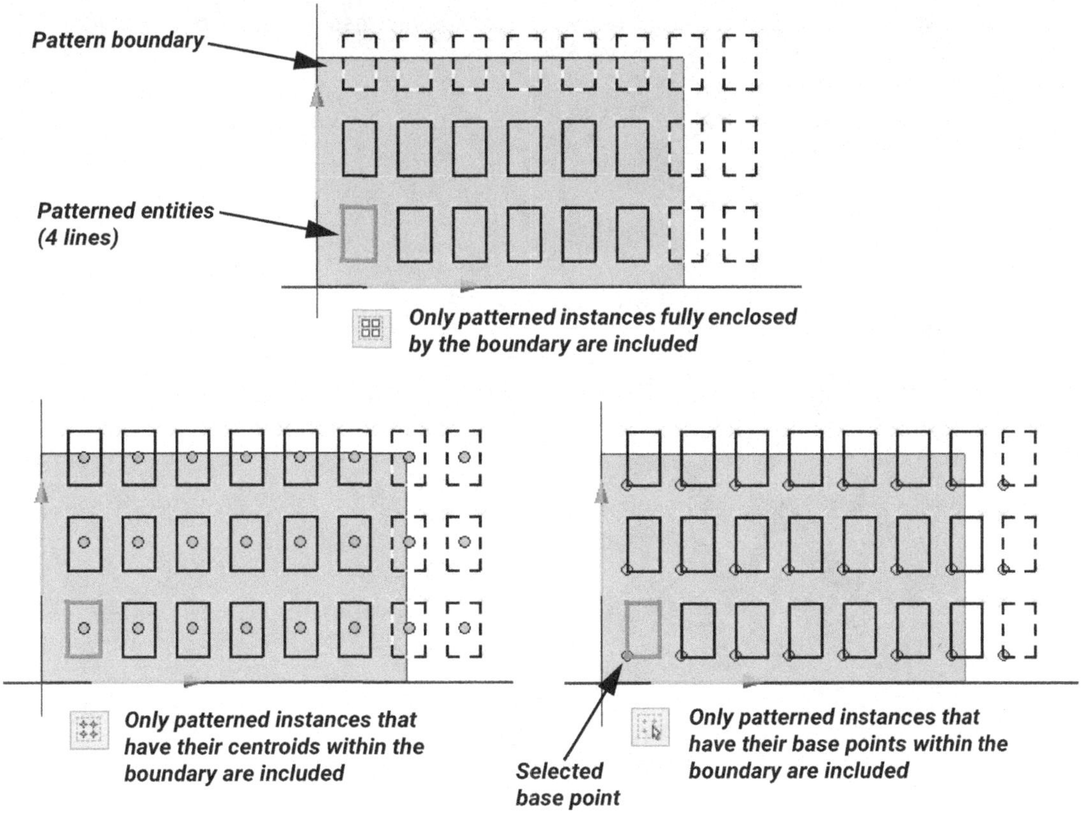

Figure 4–6

8. (Optional) Click [>>] to display the additional rectangular pattern options that can further refine the pattern.

   - Activate (Suppress) and select instances to remove from the pattern. To unsuppress, activate the option again and select again.
   - Enable the **Associative** option to maintain constant size and spacing for the pattern instances (default), even if changes are made to the original instance. If not selected, each pattern instance remains independent of the original.
   - Enable the **Fitted** option to define the pattern instances such that pattern spacing measures the overall distance for the pattern. If this option is not selected (default), the pattern spacing measures the distance between instances.

9. Click **OK** to complete the pattern.

Once a pattern is completed, you can edit the spacing values directly on the sketch by changing their dimension value. To change the number of occurrences or spacing, right-click on any of the patterned entities and select **Edit Pattern** to access the *Rectangular Pattern* dialog box.

> ***Note:*** *Sketched patterns should only be used when absolutely required. Where possible, it is better to create a feature pattern. Sketched patterns are less robust and harder to modify. They can also make sketches very large and hard to work with.*

4.3 Circular Sketch Patterns

Patterning in a sketch enables you to quickly create identical entities in your sketch. The circular sketched entity shown in Figure 4–7 is patterned using a circular pattern.

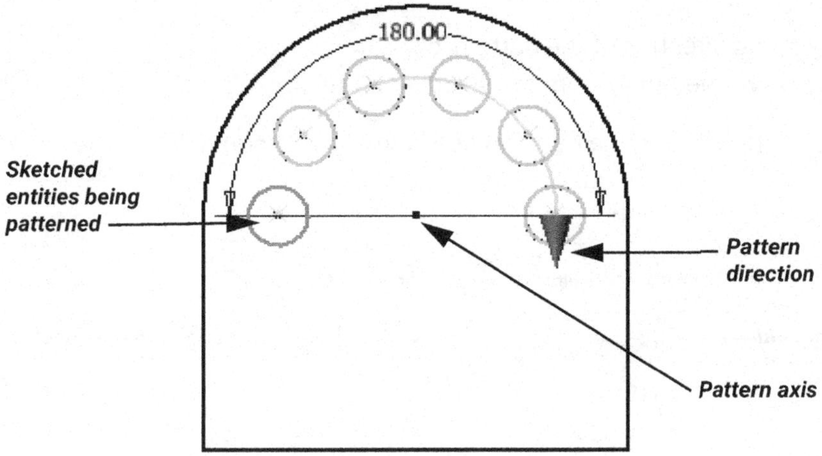

Figure 4–7

How To: Create a Circular Sketch Pattern

1. In the *Sketch* tab>*Pattern* panel, click (Circular Pattern) to open the *Circular Pattern* dialog box.

2. With (Geometry) selected, select the geometry to pattern.

   Note: *Drag a boundary box around sketched entities to select multiple entities at once. To clear entities, press and hold <Ctrl> and reselect the entities.*

3. Click (Axis) and select the axis about which to create the pattern. You can select the center of a circle or point, the end of a line, or the end point of a projected edge as the pattern axis reference.

4. Enter the number of occurrences (including selected) in the (*Count*) field, as shown in Figure 4–8.
   - To change the direction of the pattern, click .
   - To pattern symmetrically from the selected entities, click .

5. Define the angle between the occurrences in the (*Angle*) field, as shown in Figure 4–8.

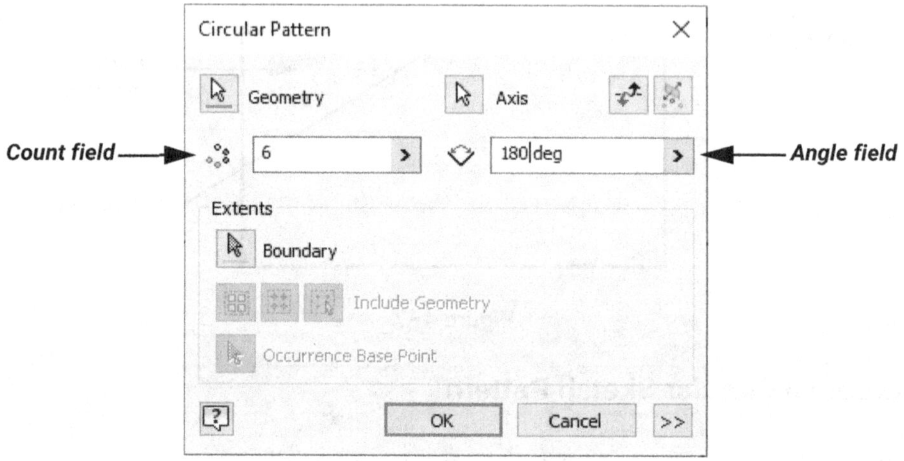

Figure 4–8

6. (Optional) In the *Extents* area, select (Boundary) and select a closed boundary to define the extent of the pattern. The boundary can be defined by selecting either sketched entities or projected geometry. Once selected, the area defined by the boundary displays green. Select one of the following three options to define whether the patterned instances are included/excluded at the defined boundary. The results are shown in Figure 4–9.

- (Include Geometry) includes pattern instances that are fully enclosed by the selected boundary.
- (Include Centroids) includes all pattern instances that have their centroid fully enclosed by the boundary.
- (Include using occurrence base points) includes all pattern instances that have the selected base point fully enclosed by the boundary.

Note: *Patterned entities that are displayed as solid lines are included in the pattern and hashed entities will be removed from the final pattern.*

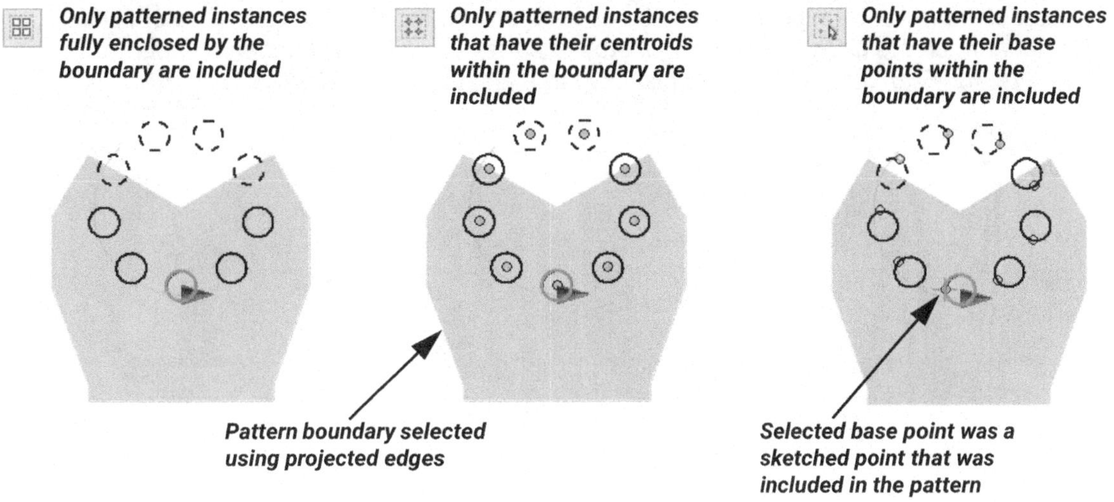

Figure 4–9

7. (Optional) Click to display the additional rectangular pattern options that can further refine the pattern.
    - Activate (Suppress) and select instances to remove from the pattern. To unsuppress, activate the option again and select again.
    - Enable the **Associative** option to maintain constant size and spacing for the pattern instances (default), even if changes are made to the original instance. If not selected, each pattern instance remains independent of the original.
    - Enable the **Fitted** option to define the pattern instances such that pattern spacing measures the overall distance for the pattern. If this option is not selected (default), the pattern spacing measures the distance between instances.
8. Click **OK** to complete the pattern.

Once a pattern is completed, you can edit the pattern by right-clicking on the pattern geometry while editing the sketch and selecting **Edit Pattern**. Change the count or angle, as required, in the *Circular Pattern* dialog box and click **OK**.

> ***Note:*** *Sketched patterns should only be used when absolutely required. Where possible, it is better to create a feature pattern. Sketched patterns are less robust and harder to modify. They can also make sketches very large and difficult to work with.*

4.4 Sketch Preferences

Sketch settings can be set to improve usage while in the Sketch environment.

Application Options

Sketch settings can be set for the software using the *Sketch* and *Part* tabs in the *Application Options* dialog box (*Tools* tab>*Options* panel, click (Application Options)).

The most commonly used options in the *Sketch* tab include:

- Click **Settings** to use the *Constraint Settings* dialog box to customize general constraint settings, such as editing and displaying constraints on creation, constraint inference, and Relax Mode settings.

  Note: *The size of dimensions on the screen can be adjusted using the Annotation scale field in the General tab in the Application Options dialog box.*

- Set the display of **Grid lines**, **Axes**, and the **Coordinate system indicator**.
- Enable/disable the **Snap to grid** option for sketch creation, as needed.
- The three autoproject options can be used to control how existing geometry is projected into a new sketch.
- Clear the **Auto-scale sketch geometries on initial dimension** option to prevent all the entities in a new sketch from rescaling to match the size of the first entity that is dimensioned.
- Enable the **Look at sketch plane on sketch creation and edit** (in the part and assembly environments) options to orient the sketch parallel to the screen by default.
- Select the **Enable Heads-Up Display** option to control how sketched entities are located in a sketch. Clearing this option enables you to place entities using the mouse only. Activating this option enables you to place entities using the mouse or by entering values dynamically as you are sketching.

The most commonly used options in the *Part* tab that affect sketches include:

- Start a new part in the Sketch environment on a specific origin plane (**Sketch on x-y plane**, **Sketch on y-z plane**, or **Sketch on x-z plane**).
- Select **Auto-consume work features and surface features** to have the work features and surface features automatically consumed when they are used in the creation of a feature.

Document Settings

The sketch grid settings for the active part can be modified in the *Sketch* tab in the *Document Settings* dialog box (*Tools* tab>*Options* panel, click (Document Settings)). The *Sketch* tab settings include the following:

- **Snap Spacing:** Sets the snap distance in the X and Y.
- **Snaps per minor:** Sets the distance between minor grid lines relative to the defined snap distance. For example, if you set the X snap distance to 1.5mm and specify two snaps per minor, the minor lines are spaced 3mm apart.
- **Minor lines:** Sets the number of minor lines to display between major lines. Major lines display heavier in the grid display.
- **Line Weight Display Options:** Controls the display of line weights. This does not affect the line weights in printed sketches.
- **Auto-Bend Radius:** Sets the radius for the corner bends that are automatically placed on 3D lines as you sketch them.

Practice 4a
Sketch Editing Tools

Practice Objectives

- Use sketch commands to copy, scale, and split sketched entities.
- Create an extruded base feature.

In this practice, you will create a sketch and use the **Copy**, **Scale**, and **Split** commands to complete the sketch. The basic sketch that you will create is shown in Figure 4–10. Using this geometry you will create solid geometry.

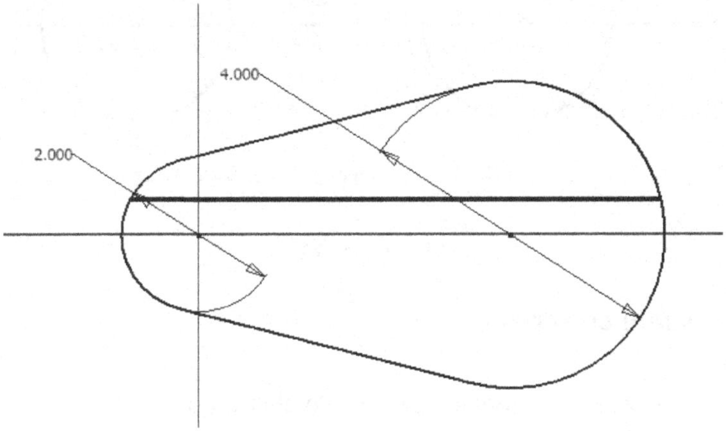

Figure 4–10

Task 1: Create a new file.

1. Create a new part file using the **Standard (in).ipt** template. If your template is set as Metric (as was done in a previous chapter), on the *Home* page, click **New** to open the *Create New File* dialog box and select the **Imperial** template.

Task 2: Start a new sketch and use the Copy command.

1. Create a sketch on the XY Plane.
2. Sketch a circle with its center on the projected origin point.
3. Add a **2.00** inch diameter dimension to the circle.
4. In the *Modify* panel, click (Copy). The *Copy* dialog box opens.
5. Select the circle.

6. Click (Base Point) and select the center of the circle as the base point.
7. Drag the copied circle to the right of the existing one and click to place.
8. Click **Done** to end the command.
9. In the *Constrain* panel, click (Dimension).
10. Add the 4 inch dimension shown in Figure 4–11. Add a horizontal constraint to ensure that the centers of both circles remain horizontal with one another.

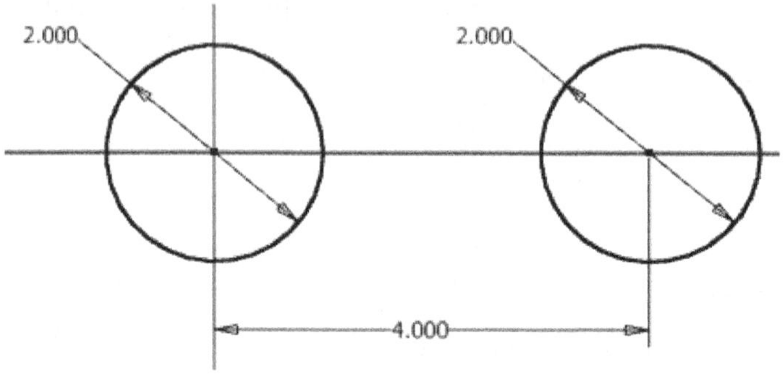

Figure 4–11

Task 3: Use the Scale command.

1. In the *Modify* panel, click (Scale). The *Scale* dialog box opens.
2. Select the circle that was created using the **Copy** command.
3. Click (Base Point) and select the center of the circle.
4. When prompted to relax existing dimensions and constraints, click **Yes** for both prompts. Note that the diameter dimension is temporarily set as a reference dimension.
5. Move the cursor to see how the scale is affected. In the *Scale* dialog box, in the *Scale Factor* field, enter **2**. Press <Enter>.
6. Click **Done** to end the command.
7. Draw two lines tangent to the circles at the top and bottom.

   Note: *To sketch the tangent lines between the circles, start the* ***Line*** *command, and select and hold the cursor over one of the two circles. While continuing to hold, drag the cursor to the next circle and position the cursor so that the Tangent constraint is visible and release the mouse button. If you do not use this technique, you must assign the Tangency constraint to the sketch.*

8. Trim the sketch as shown in Figure 4–12.

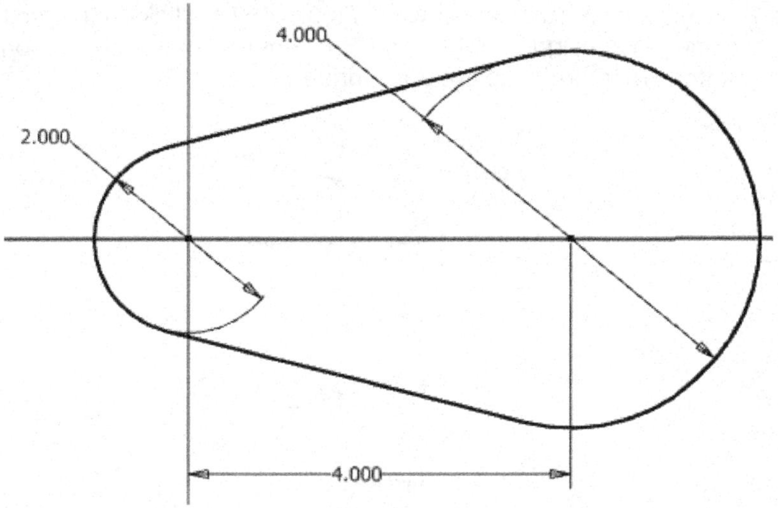

Figure 4–12

Task 4: Use the Split command.

1. Draw a horizontal line with its end point on both arcs, as shown in Figure 4–13. The exact distance above the origin point is not important.

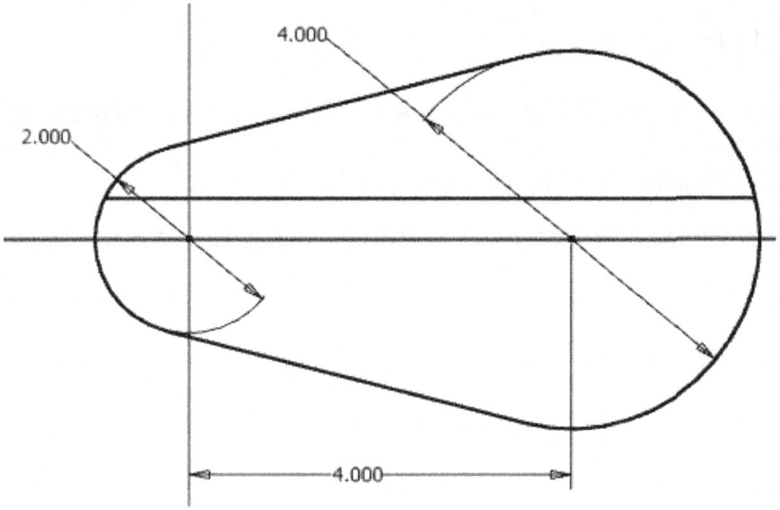

Figure 4–13

2. In the *Modify* panel, click -|- (Split). Hover the cursor over the arc on the left side. Note that the **X** marks where the arc is split, as shown in Figure 4–14. Click on the arc to split it where it intersects the line. The design intent for the part requires that both sections of the arc remain in the sketch, so trimming is not appropriate.

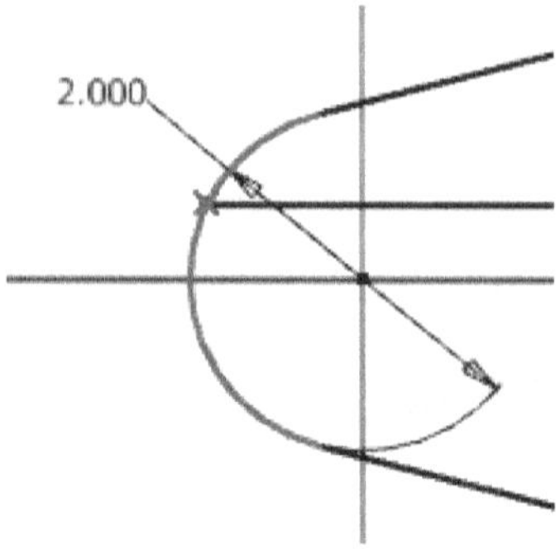

Figure 4–14

3. Repeat for the arc on the right side.
4. Right-click and select **OK** to end the command.
5. Finish the sketch.
6. Right-click on the sketch in the Model browser and clear **Dimension Visibility** to hide the dimensions in the sketch. Hiding the dimensions is not required to create an extrude, but it can help to simplify the view of the 3D geometry.

Task 5: Extrude the geometry.

1. Create an extrude feature. The profile is not automatically selected because there are two closed loops in Sketch1.
2. Select the lower half of the sketch to extrude it.
3. Extrude the feature **1** inch away from the sketch plane (behind the model when it is in the Home view).

4. Complete the feature. The model displays as shown in Figure 4–15.

Figure 4–15

5. Edit **Extrusion1**.
6. Select the *Profiles* field in the *Properties* panel and select the top half of the sketch to add it to the selection set. The **Split** tool can be used to divide a single sketch so that different closed areas can be extruded to different depths. In this case, you are adding to the existing extrusion.
7. Complete the feature. The model displays as shown in Figure 4–16.

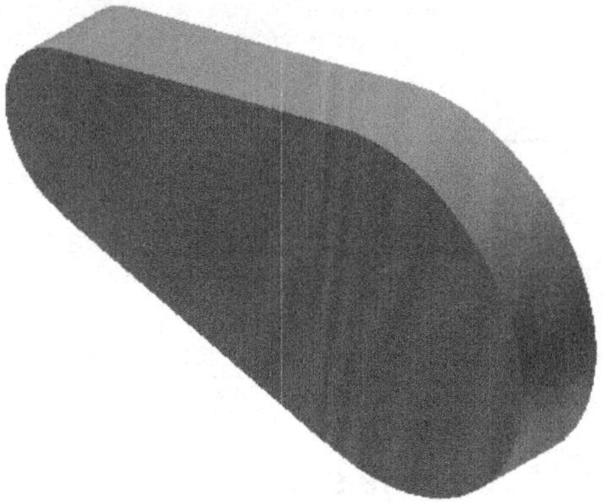

Figure 4–16

8. Save the part and close the window.

End of practice

Practice 4b
Copy and Paste a Sketch

Practice Objectives

- Use **Copy** and **Paste** to duplicate entities between different sketches.
- Move entities in a sketch.
- Apply dimensions and constraints to fully constrain a sketch.
- Create a revolved base feature.

In this practice, you will create the sketch shown on the left of Figure 4–17 by copying and pasting existing sketch geometry, and modifying it. Using this method, you can reuse a sketch in multiple models. This sketch geometry can be used to create the revolved extrusion shown on the right in Figure 4–17.

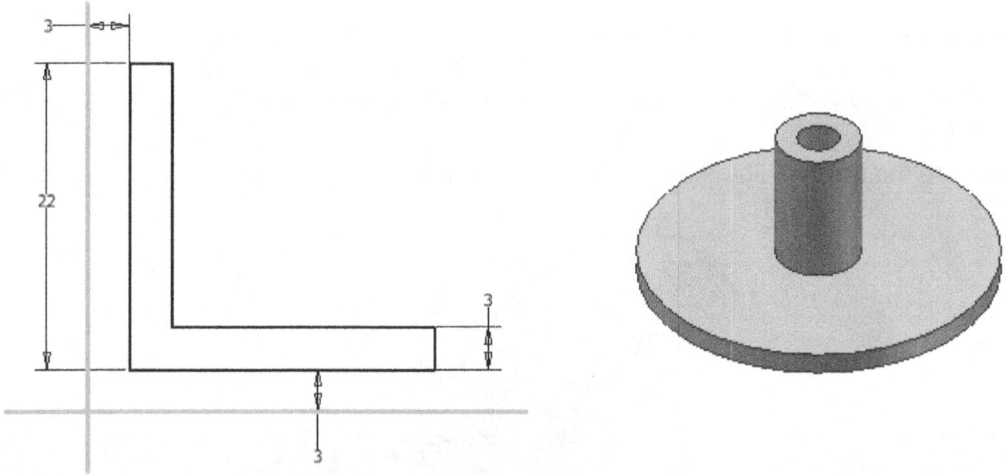

Figure 4–17

Task 1: Open a part file and copy the sketch.

1. Open **solid_base_feature.ipt**.
2. Expand **Extrusion1** in the Model browser.
3. Right-click on **Sketch1** and select **Copy**. Alternatively, you can use (Copy) (*Tools* tab> *Clipboard* panel) to copy the sketch.

Task 2: Create a new part and paste the sketch.

1. Create a new part file using the standard metric (mm) template.
2. Create a new sketch on the YZ Plane.
3. Right-click in the graphics window and select **Paste**.
4. The sketch is pasted into a new sketch. You might need to reorient the sketch to the Left view to display the orientation shown in Figure 4–18. Note that the projected reference lines from the original sketch have been copied as well. Delete the reference lines shown in Figure 4–18.

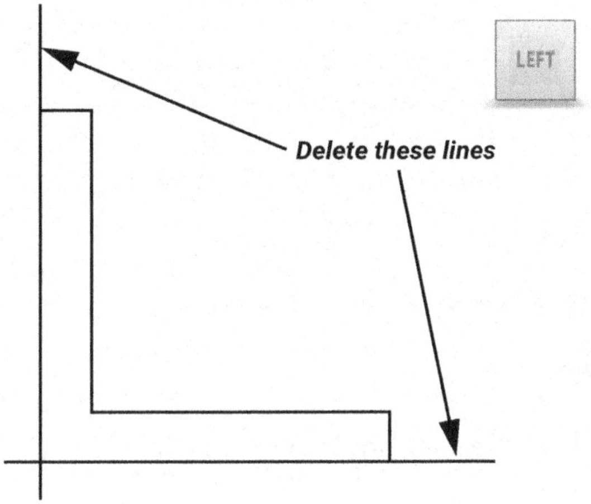

Figure 4–18

5. Project the XZ and XY Planes as a reference to locate the copied sketched geometry.

Task 3: Move the sketch.

1. Hold <Ctrl> and select all of the lines in the sketch.

2. Place the cursor on one of the lines, press and hold the left mouse button and move the sketch to the location shown in Figure 4–19. Note that the constraints appear when the entities are selected.

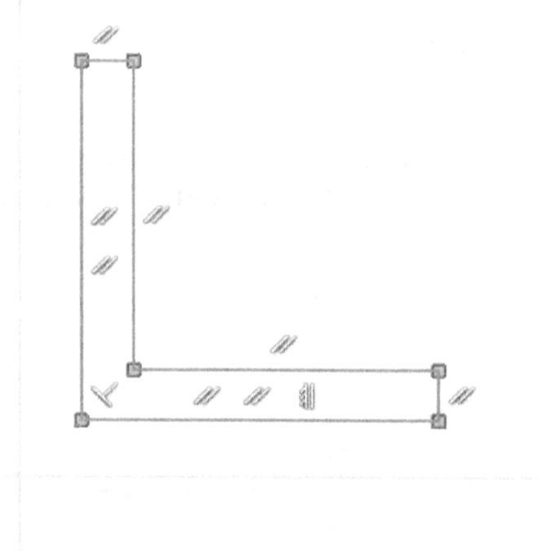

Figure 4–19

3. Click away from the entities to clear the selection.

Task 4: Apply constraints.

1. Apply Equal constraints to the lines shown in Figure 4–20.

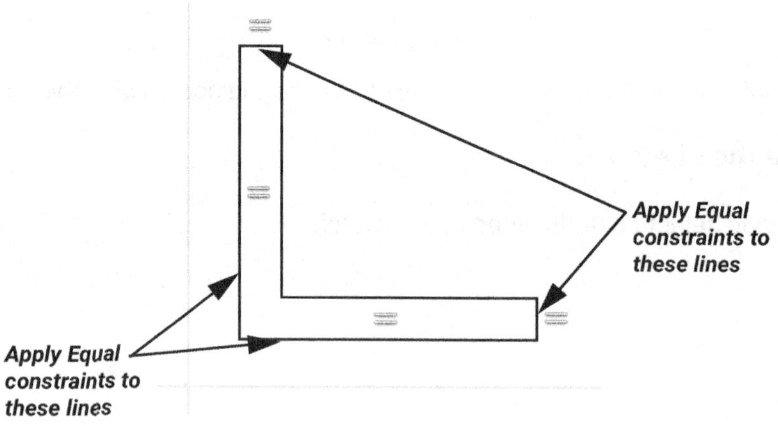

Figure 4–20

2. In the Status Bar, click [icon] to show all of the constraints. Ensure that the equal constraints were applied, if they are not already displayed. Alternatively, you can toggle the display of constraints on using <F8> and off using <F9>.
3. In the Status Bar, click [icon] to hide all of the constraints.

Task 5: Dimension the sketch.

1. Dimension the sketch and locate it with respect to the projected reference lines, as shown in Figure 4–21. Modify the dimensions as shown.

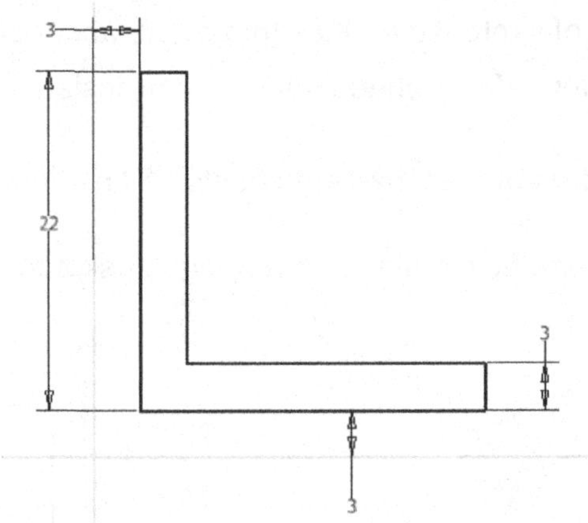

Figure 4–21

2. Finish the sketch.

Task 6: Create a solid base feature using the sketch.

1. Create a fully revolved base feature using the copied sketch. The final model should display as shown in Figure 4–22.

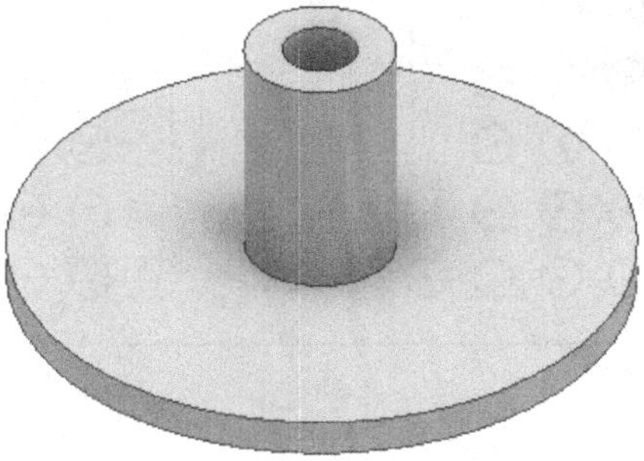

Figure 4–22

2. Save the part and close the window.
3. Close the **solid_base_feature** window without saving.

End of practice

Practice 4c
Pattern Sketched Entities

Practice Objectives

- Create a circular pattern of sketched entities that rotate about a selected point in a sketch.
- Create a rectangular pattern of sketched entities that translate along a first and second direction in a sketch.
- Create a rectangular pattern of sketched entities that fill a defined boundary.

In this practice, you will pattern the circular and rectangular sketched entities shown in Figure 4–23.

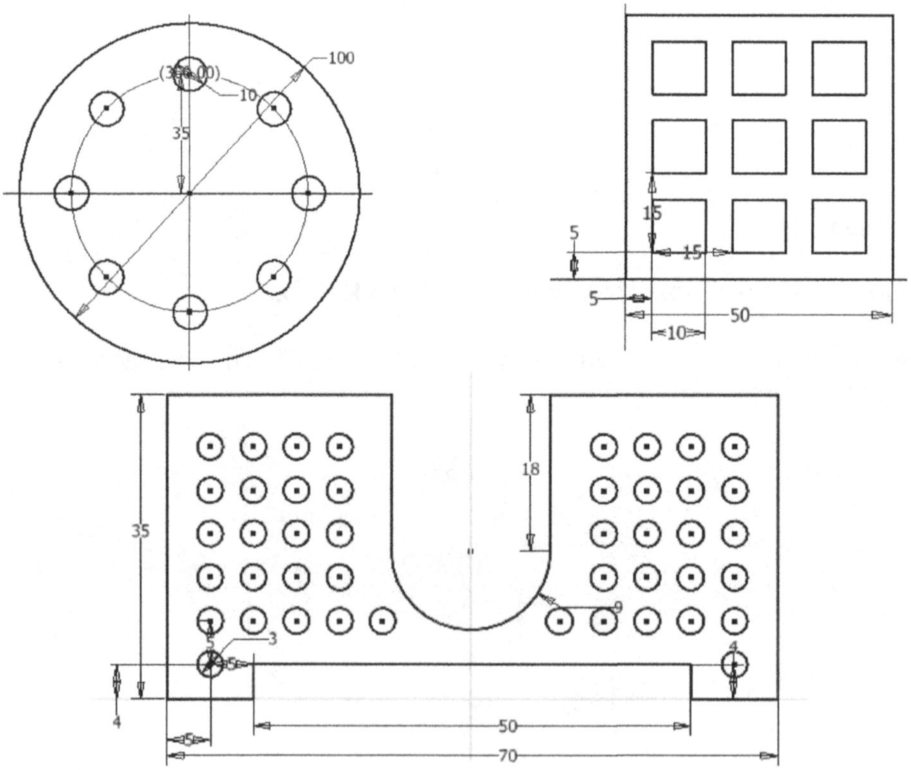

Figure 4–23

Task 1: Create a circular pattern of entities.

1. Open **pattern_circular.ipt**.
2. Edit the sketch that was provided for you in the model.
3. In the *Pattern* panel, click (Circular Pattern). The *Circular Pattern* dialog box opens, as shown in Figure 4–24.

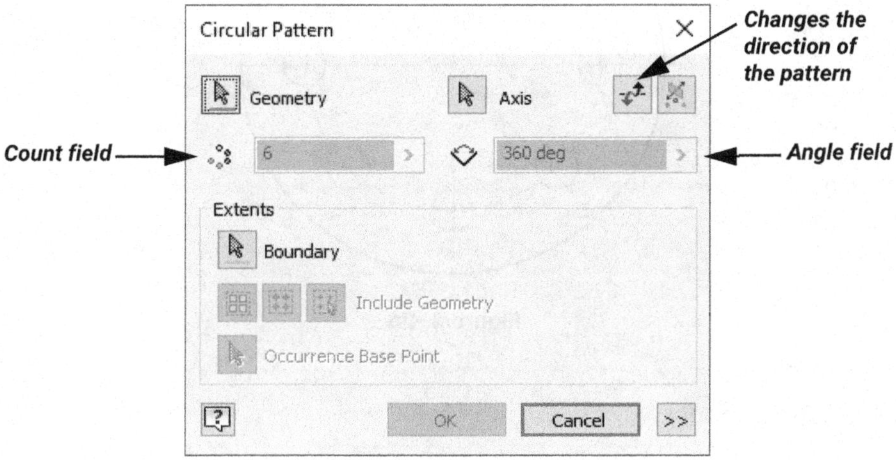

Figure 4–24

4. With (Geometry) selected, select the small circle as shown in Figure 4–25.
5. Click (Axis) and select the vertex at the center of the large circle, as shown in Figure 4–25.

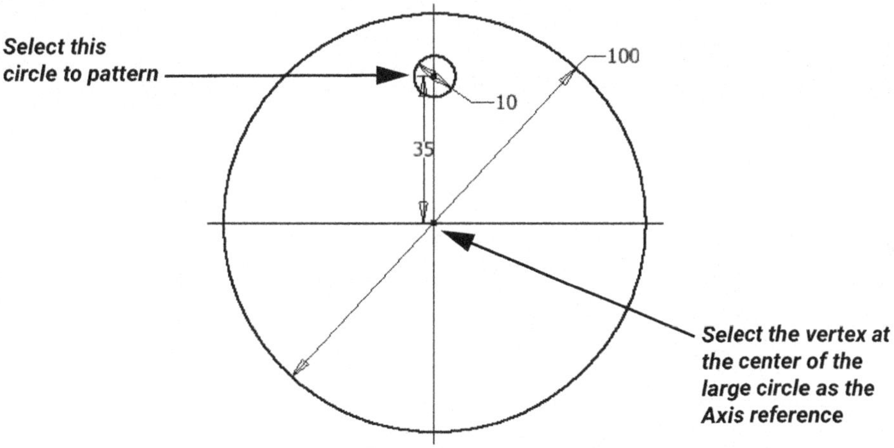

Figure 4–25

6. In the (Count) field, enter **8** and maintain the **360 deg** angular value.
7. Click **OK** to complete the pattern. The sketch displays as shown in Figure 4–26.

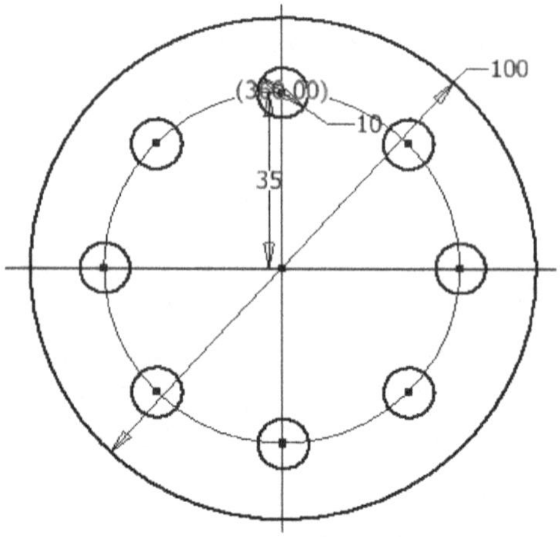

Figure 4–26

8. Finish the sketch.
9. Save and close the model.

Task 2: Create a rectangular pattern of entities.

1. Open **pattern_rectangular.ipt**.
2. Edit the Sketch that was provided for you in the model.

3. In the *Pattern* panel, click (Rectangular Pattern). The *Rectangular Pattern* dialog box opens, as shown in Figure 4–27.

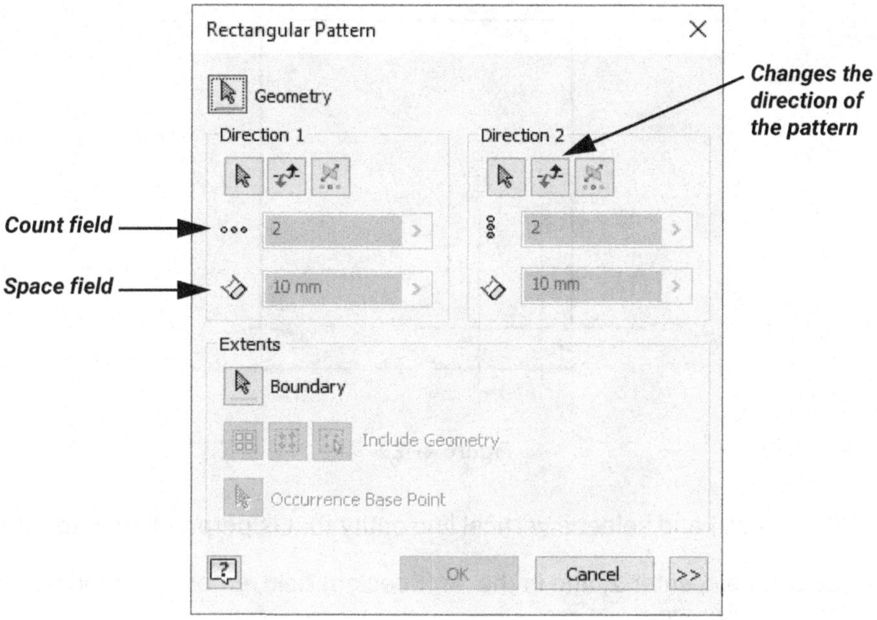

Figure 4–27

4. With (Geometry) selected, select the four entities of the rectangle, as shown in Figure 4–28.

5. Click (Direction1) and select the horizontal line entity, as shown in Figure 4–28.

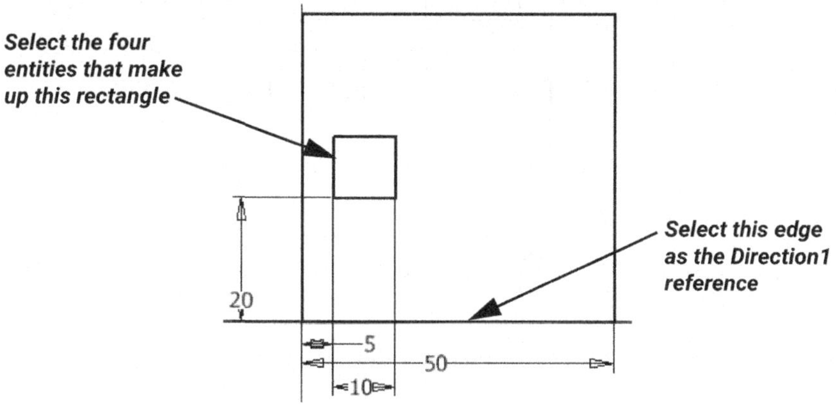

Figure 4–28

6. In the (Count) field, enter **3**, and in the (*Spacing*) field, enter **15** as the distance between each occurrence. The pattern previews as shown in Figure 4–29.

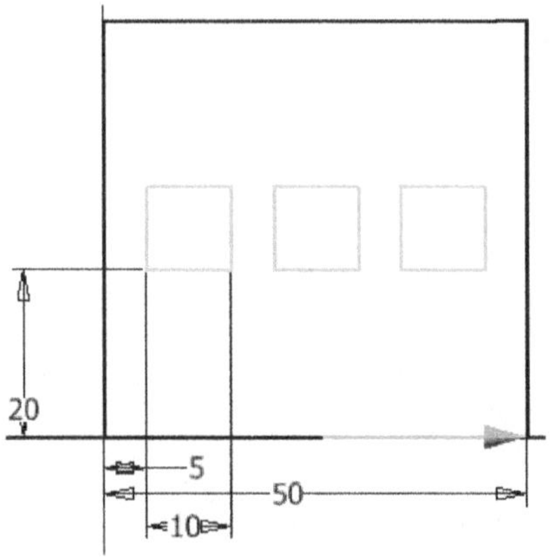

Figure 4–29

7. Click (Direction2) and select a vertical line entity that is perpendicular to **Direction1**.

8. In the (Count) field, enter **2**, and in the (*Spacing*) field, enter **15** as the distance between each occurrence.

9. In the *Direction2* area, click to change the direction of the pattern.

10. Click **OK** to complete the pattern. The sketch displays as shown in Figure 4–30.

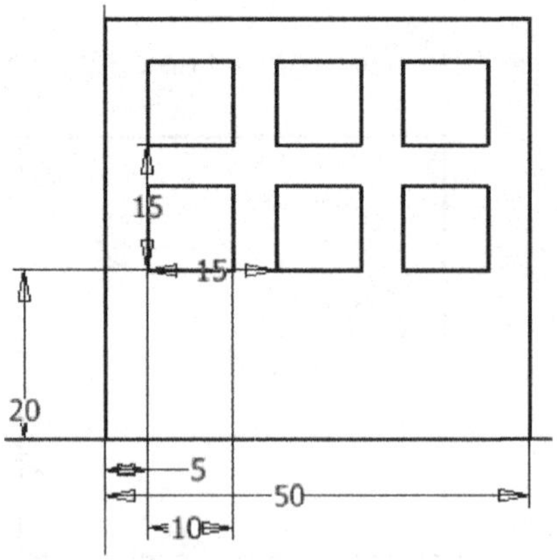

Figure 4–30

11. Double-click on the **20** dimension and enter **5**. Note how the entire pattern updates to reflect the change, as shown in Figure 4–31. This is because all of the occurrences are located with respect to the initial entities that were selected for patterning.

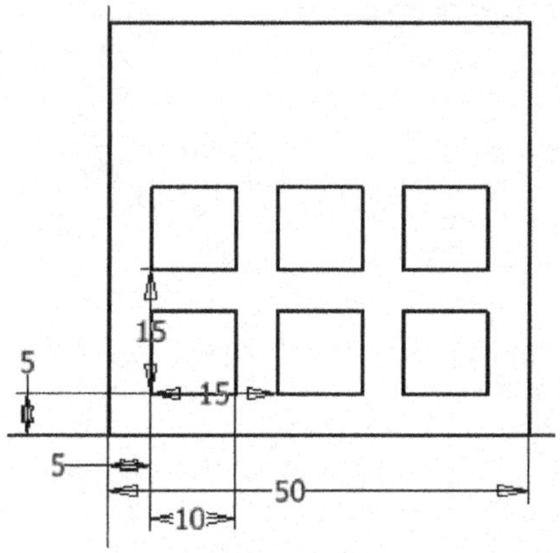

Figure 4–31

12. Right-click on any one of the patterned entities and select **Edit Pattern** in the marking menu. The *Rectangular Pattern* dialog box opens.
13. Change the value in the *Count* field for *Direction 2* to **3**. Click **OK** to complete the pattern.
14. Finish the sketch. The completed sketch displays as shown in Figure 4–32.

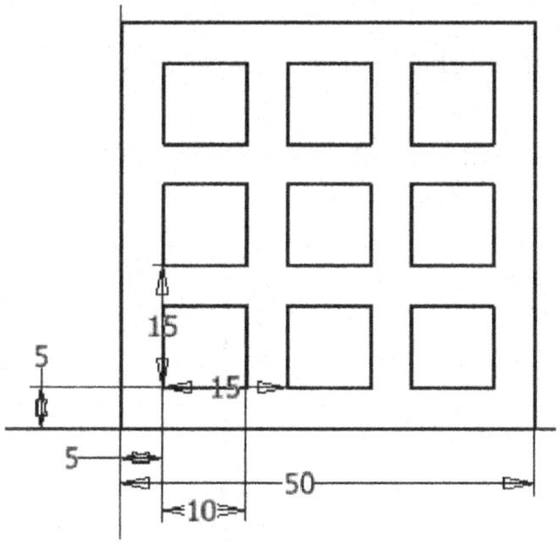

Figure 4–32

15. Save the model and close the window.

Task 3: Create a rectangular pattern of entities defined by a boundary.

1. Open **pattern_boundary.ipt**.
2. Edit the sketch that was provided for you in the model.

3. In the *Pattern* panel, click (Rectangular Pattern). The *Rectangular Pattern* dialog box opens, as shown in Figure 4–33.

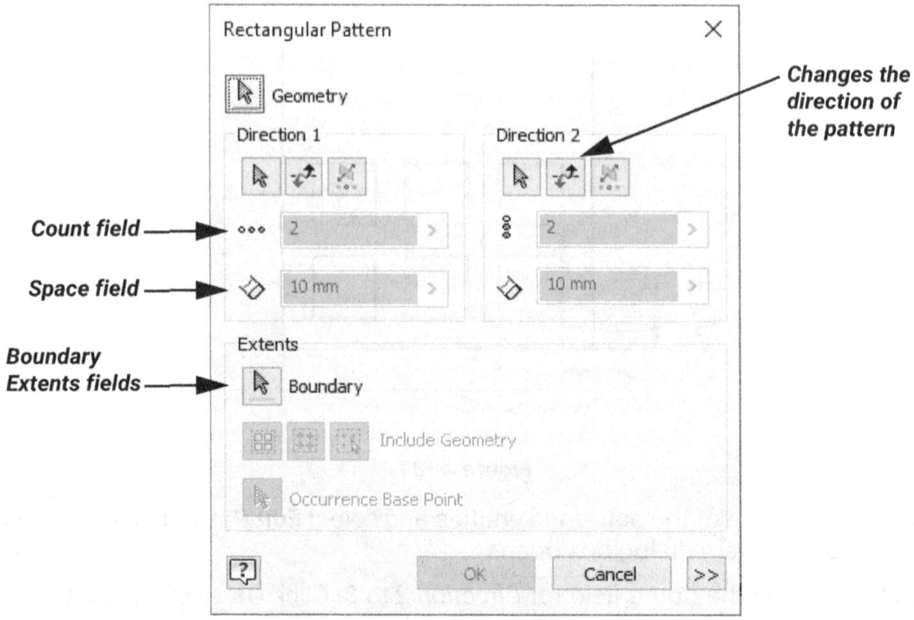

Figure 4–33

4. With (Geometry) selected, select the circular entity, as shown in Figure 4–34.

5. Click (Direction1) and select the horizontal line entity, as shown in Figure 4–34.

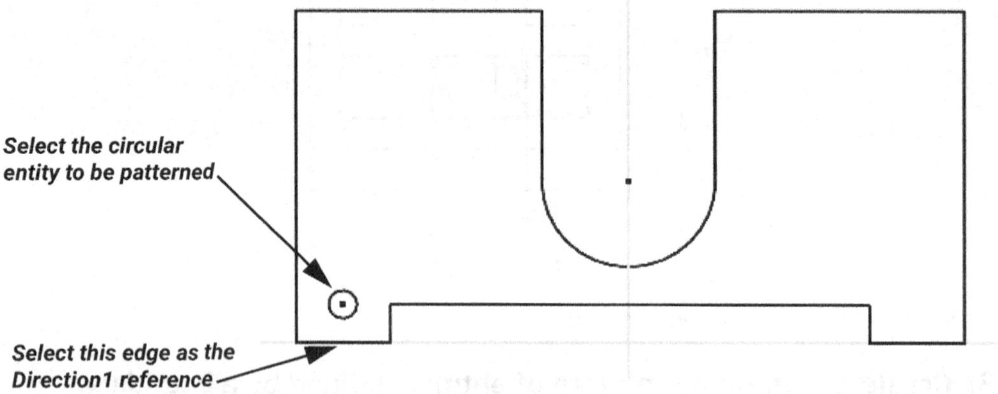

Figure 4–34

6. In the (Count) field, enter **15**, and in the (*Spacing*) field, enter **5** as the distance between each occurrence. Click to change the direction of the pattern, if needed. The pattern previews as shown in Figure 4–35.

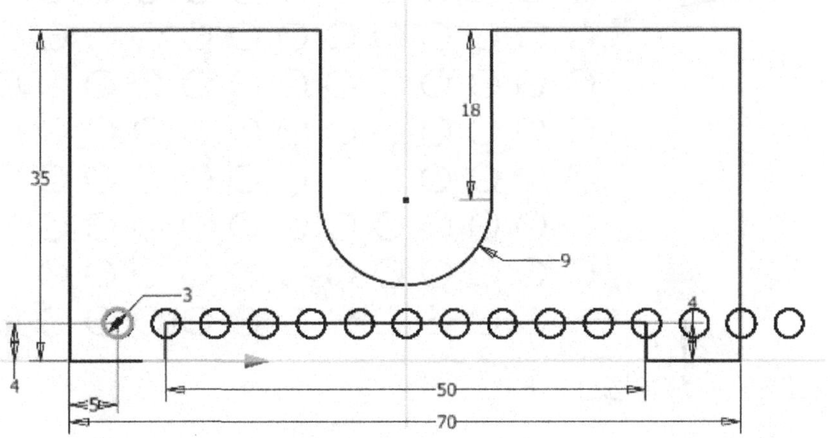

Figure 4–35

7. Click (Direction2) and select a vertical line entity that is perpendicular to **Direction1**.
8. In the (*Count*) field, enter **8**, and in the (*Spacing*) field, enter **5** as the distance between each occurrence.
9. In the *Direction2* area, flip the direction of the pattern, if needed, to pattern upwards, as shown in Figure 4–36.

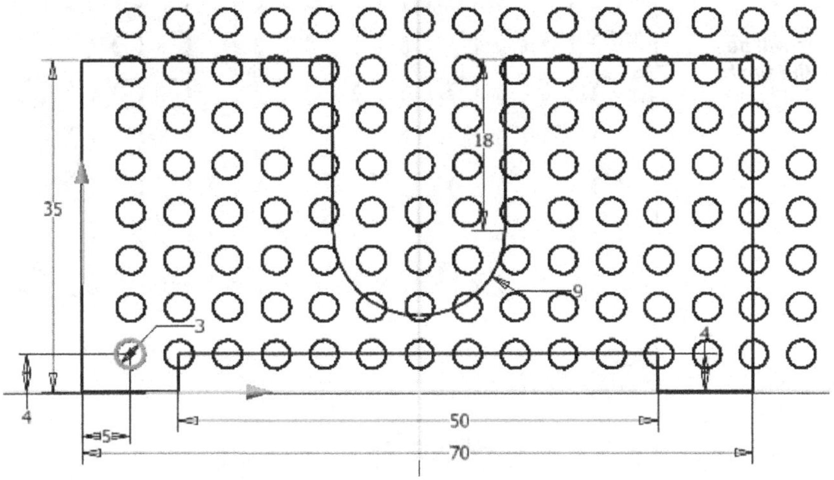

Figure 4–36

10. In the *Extents* area, click (Boundary) and select the boundary of the sketch, as shown in Figure 4–37. Once selected, the area defined by the boundary displays green.

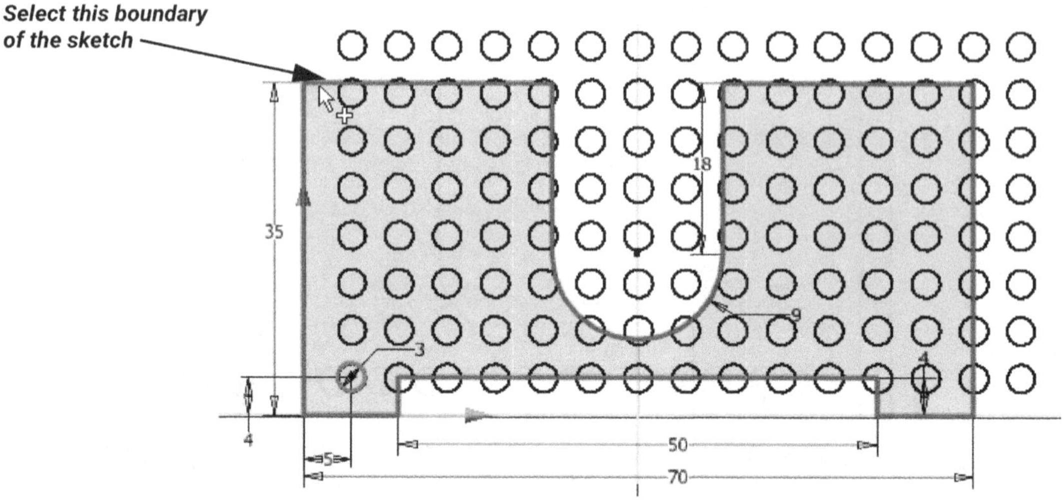

Figure 4–37

11. Ensure that (Include Geometry) is selected in the *Extents* area. Note that any patterned circular entity that is fully enclosed by the boundary displays as a solid circle and any that are fully outside or intersect with the boundary are displayed with a hashed line, as shown in Figure 4–38. Hashed entities will be removed from the final pattern.

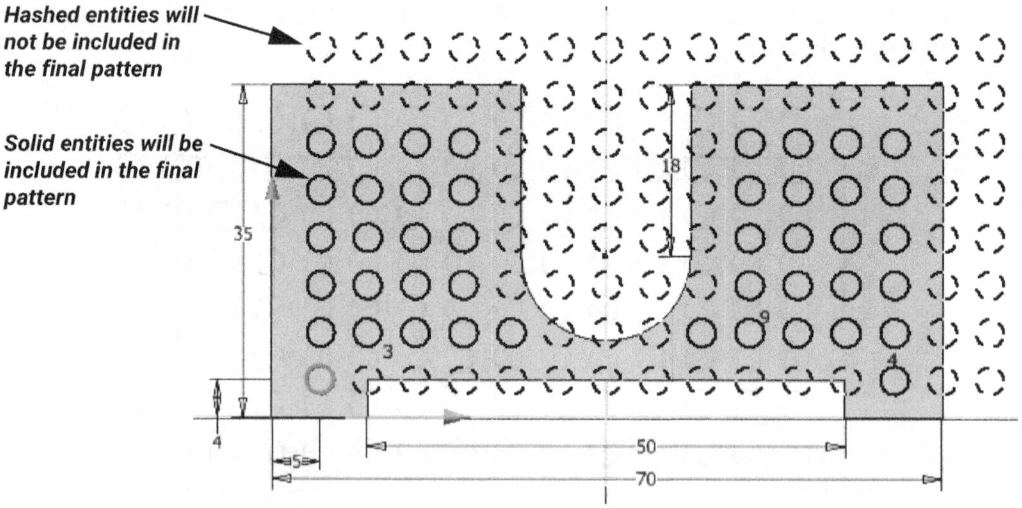

Figure 4–38

12. Select (Include Centroids) in the *Extents* area. Note that a centroid is included at the center of the circular entities. Any patterned circular entity that has its centroid fully enclosed by the boundary displays as a solid circle and any that are fully outside are displayed with a hashed line, as shown in Figure 4–39. Hashed entities will be removed from the final pattern.

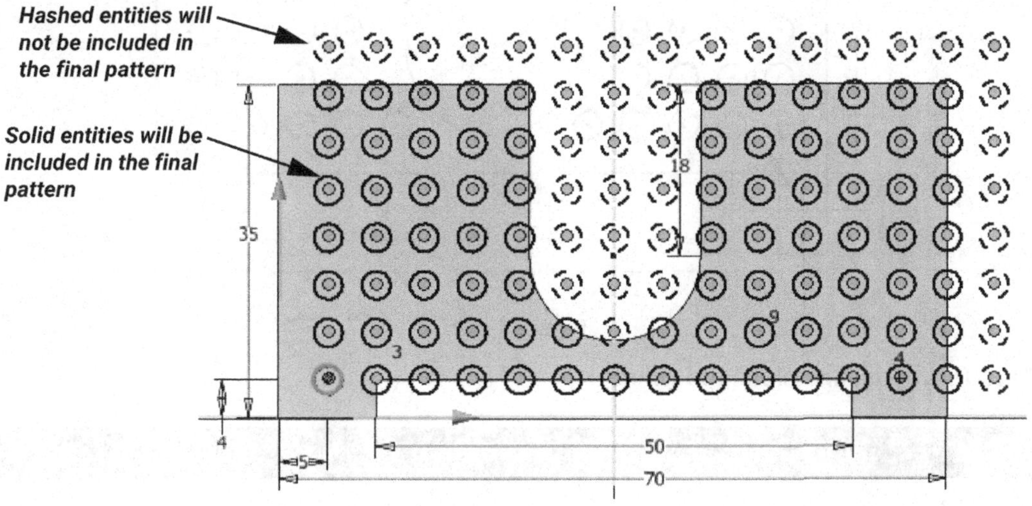

Figure 4–39

13. Note that with the (Include Centroids) option set, circular entities will be created that will cut the boundary. This is not what is required, so select (Include Geometry) again.

Note: The (Include using occurrence base points) option can be used to define a specific vertex in the first occurence that must lie inside the boundary to be included in the pattern. In this case for a circular entity, there is no vertex other than the center to select unless you add a point to the sketch, pattern it, and use it as the base point.

14. Click **OK** to complete the pattern. All patterned occurrences are shown; however, those that intersect or are outside the boundary are hashed, indicating they are not going to be generated.

15. Finish the sketch. The completed sketch displays as shown in Figure 4–40.

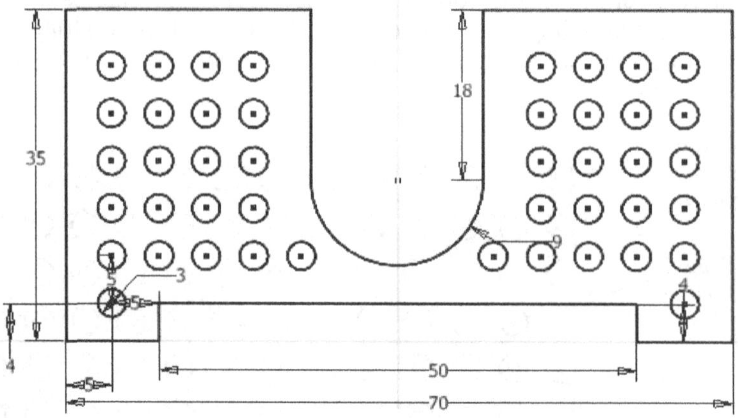

Figure 4–40

16. Save the model and close the window.

End of practice

Chapter Review Questions

1. Which commands can be used to copy sketched entities? (Select all that apply.)
   a. Copy
   b. Trim
   c. Move
   d. Extend

2. Which of the following statements describes the **Move** command for sketch entities?
   a. Continues an entity to meet the next entity in its path or to close an open sketch.
   b. Enables you to relocate original 2D sketch geometry.
   c. Removes the segment of the entity to the nearest intersection in each direction from the point selected.
   d. Provides a specific tool for stretching sketched entities versus simply selecting and dragging them in the sketch.

3. You can rotate and make a copy of the entities at the same time.
   a. True
   b. False

4. Which of the following statements best describes the difference between the **Stretch** command and the select and drag technique for manipulating constrained geometry?
   a. The Stretch command enables you to stretch constrained geometry, maintaining established constraints, whereas the select and drag technique cannot be used to manipulate constrained geometry.
   b. The select and drag technique enables you to stretch constrained geometry, maintaining established constraints, whereas the Stretch command cannot be used to manipulate constrained geometry.

5. What is the purpose of defining the base point for the **Move, Copy, Scale**, and **Stretch** sketching tools?
   a. The base point defines a point on the original geometry as the reference point for the operation.
   b. The base point defines the location to which you are copying the selected entities.

6. You can copy a sketch from one part into another part.
   a. True
   b. False

7. Which of the following are required when creating a rectangular pattern in two directions, as shown in Figure 4–41? (Select all that apply.)

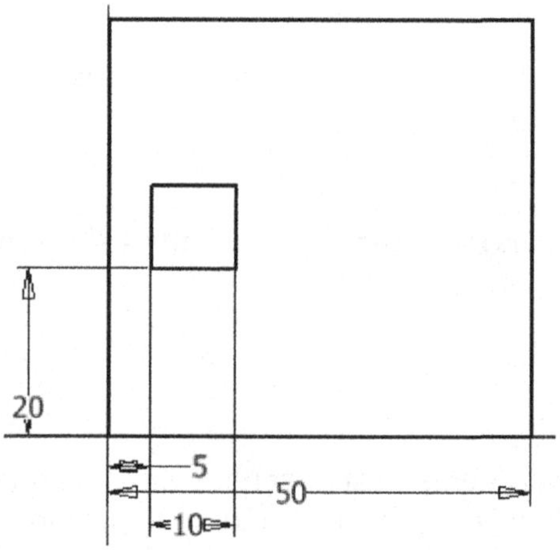

Figure 4–41

   a. Geometry to pattern (e.g., circular sketch)
   b. First pattern direction
   c. Second pattern direction
   d. Angle between occurrences
   e. Pattern axis
   f. Count and Space in the first direction
   g. Count and Space in the second direction

8. Which of the following boundary extent options should be used to ensure that a generated pattern of sketched entities all lie within a defined boundary?

a.  (Include Geometry)

b.  (Include Centroids)

c.  (Include using occurrence base points)

9. Which of the following tools enables you to customize the sizing of the grid display for a sketch?

a. Application Options

b. Document Settings

Command Summary

Button	Command	Location
	**Application Options**	• **Ribbon:** *Tools* tab>*Options* panel • **File Menu**: Options
	**Circular Pattern (sketch)**	• **Ribbon:** *Sketch* tab>*Pattern* panel
	**Copy**	• **Ribbon:** *Sketch* tab>*Modify* panel • **Context Menu**: In the graphics window with an entity selected • **Keyboard**: <Ctrl>+<C>
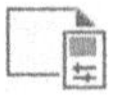	**Document Settings**	• **Ribbon:** *Tools* tab>*Options* panel
	**Move**	• **Ribbon:** *Sketch* tab>*Modify* panel
N/A	**Paste**	• **Context Menu**: In the graphics window • **Keyboard**: <Ctrl>+<V>
	**Rectangular Pattern (sketch)**	• **Ribbon:** *Sketch* tab>*Pattern* panel
	**Rotate**	• **Ribbon:** *Sketch* tab>*Modify* panel
	**Scale**	• **Ribbon:** *Sketch* tab>*Modify* panel
	**Split**	• **Ribbon:** *Sketch* tab>*Modify* panel
	**Stretch**	• **Ribbon:** *Sketch* tab>*Modify* panel

Chapter

5

Sketched Secondary Features

Sketched secondary features, such as extrusions, add or remove material from a model. As features and design intent become more complex, additional options are available to help you create more advanced secondary features.

Learning Objectives

- Create extruded and revolved secondary features.
- Create offset entities that reference existing features.
- Project geometry to create references between sketched entities and existing features.
- Share existing sketches so they can be used again to create model geometry.
- Create sketched entities by entering starting locations and size values in the Dynamic Input fields.
- Create sketched entities by entering coordinate values in the Precise Input toolbar.
- Insert 2D AutoCAD data into an Inventor sketch to use for creating 3D geometry.

5.1 Creating Sketched Secondary Features

A secondary feature is any geometry that is added after base feature creation. It can be created as a sketch or added as a pick and place feature. Sketched features require the selection of an existing sketch to create additional geometry. A pick and place feature is a feature in which the shape is implied. You are not required to sketch the section (e.g., chamfer, fillets, holes). This chapter covers sketched secondary features. Pick and place features are covered later in this guide.

The workflow for creating a sketched secondary feature is the same as that for sketched base feature creation. The following differences and available tools should be noted:

- As an alternative to selecting an origin plane as the sketching plane, you can also select planar faces.
- Reference projection is done the same way as for base feature creation. However, because they now exist, you can project part edges to be used as constraint and dimension references. Additionally, as you reference model edges while sketching (i.e., dimensioning or offsetting), these edges or vertices are automatically projected.

Hint: Projecting Geometry

It is strongly recommended to use origin features as references for sketched geometry when intended references are not required between features. Origin features are more stable than feature edges and the result is a robust model that is easy to modify.

- When the sketch plane is located in or behind other geometry, you can temporarily remove the portion of the model that is in front of the sketch plane using the **Slice Graphics** option. To use this option, orient the model so that the portion you want to remove is in front of the sketching plane and then right-click on the graphics window and select **Slice Graphics**, as shown in Figure 5–1. Alternatively, you can click (Slice Graphics) in the Status Bar.

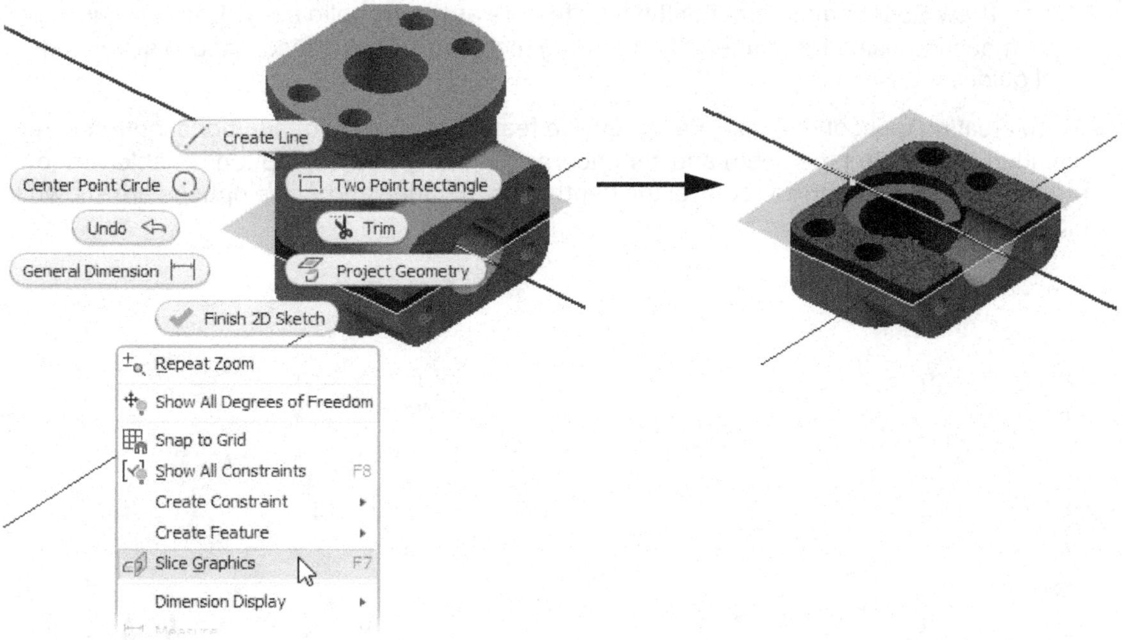

Figure 5–1

- When creating a base feature only the (Join) option is available; however, when creating a secondary extrude or revolve feature, the (Join), (Cut), and (Intersect) options are all available. These options enable you to specify whether the feature will add material (Join), remove material (Cut), or create the feature as an intersection (Intersect), as shown in Figure 5–2. The **Intersect** option creates geometry from the shared volume of the new and existing features and removes material outside the shared volume.

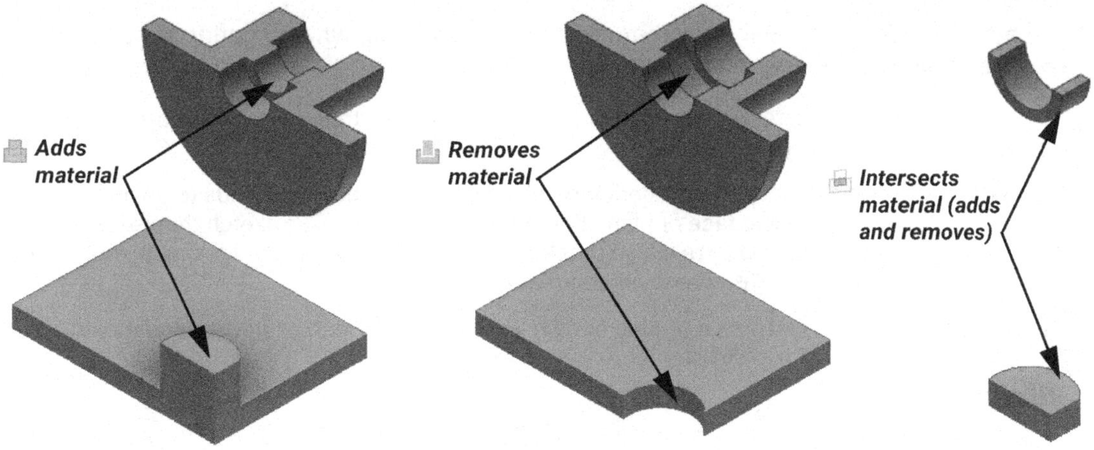

Figure 5–2

- The (New Solid) option creates the new feature as a new solid body. This is required when modeling using the multi-body modeling technique. This is discussed in advanced level guides.
- When creating a secondary extrude or revolve feature, a number of additional options are provided for defining the depth and distance/angle. Many of these options enable you to reference other geometry to control the depth. The *Distance* and *Angle* options are shown in Figure 5–3.

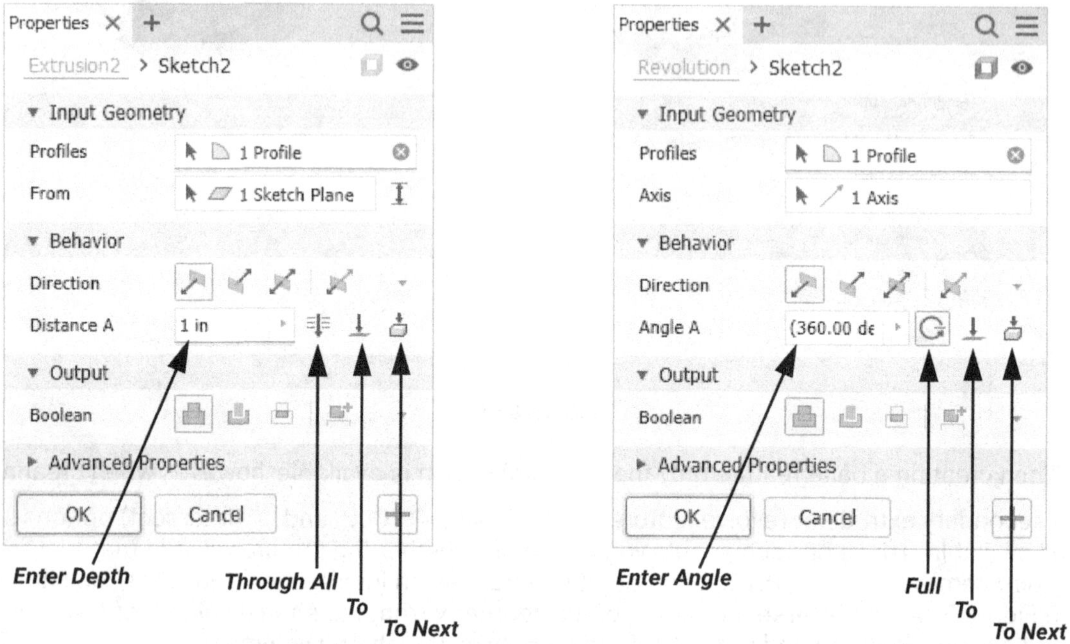

Figure 5–3

The additional *Distance* and *Angle* options that are available when creating secondary sketched features are defined as follows:

To	Creates an extruded or revolved feature so that it extends to a selected reference face.
To Next	Creates an extruded or revolved feature so that it extends to the next possible face or plane that it fully encounters. The sketch that is being extruded or revolved must fully intersect the face or body that it encounters for the feature to be created.
Through All/Full	Creates an extruded or revolved feature through all of the geometry in a defined direction.

- The (Between) option adjacent to the *From* field can be used to customize a start and end plane for the geometry. This option enables you to define these planes as something other than the profile's sketch plane, as shown in Figure 5–4. When used, the *Distance A* field populates with a reference dimension shown in brackets (e.g., **(7.085mm)**).

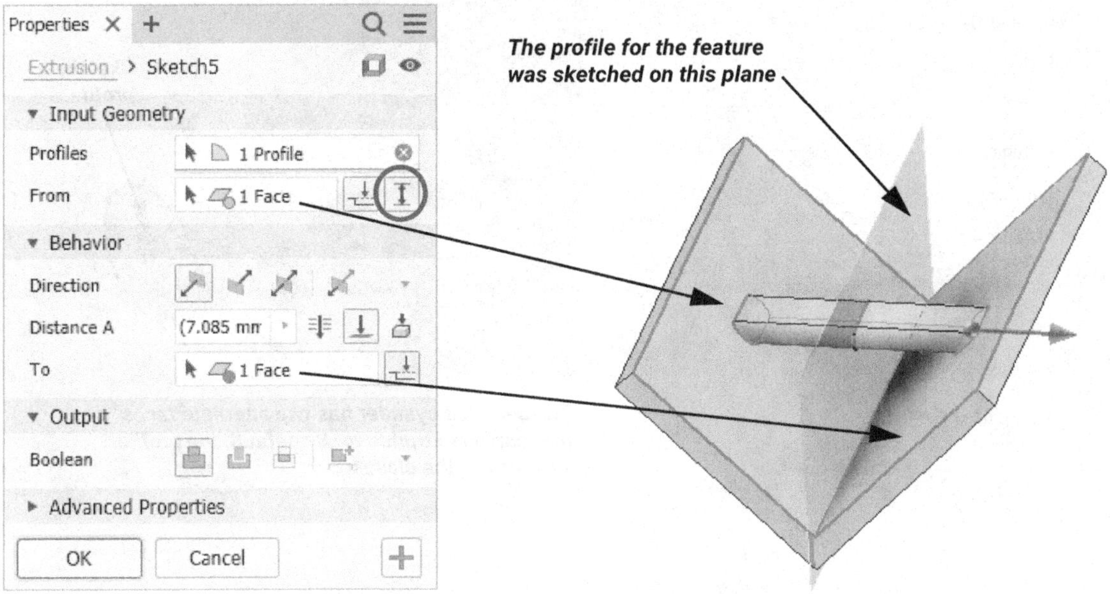

Figure 5–4

Note: *The (Between) option is available for base features where the references can be work planes instead of existing solid geometry.*

Alternate Solution

There may be situations when an irregular surface or a cylinder is selected as a termination surface. In these situations, the extend location on the face might not be clear (e.g., it could be on either side of the cylinder), or there might be multiple intersection locations. The

(Alternate Solution) option in the *Properties* panel can be selected to toggle through the available options.

Figure 5–5 shows how this option can be used when the extrude reference has two possible solutions.

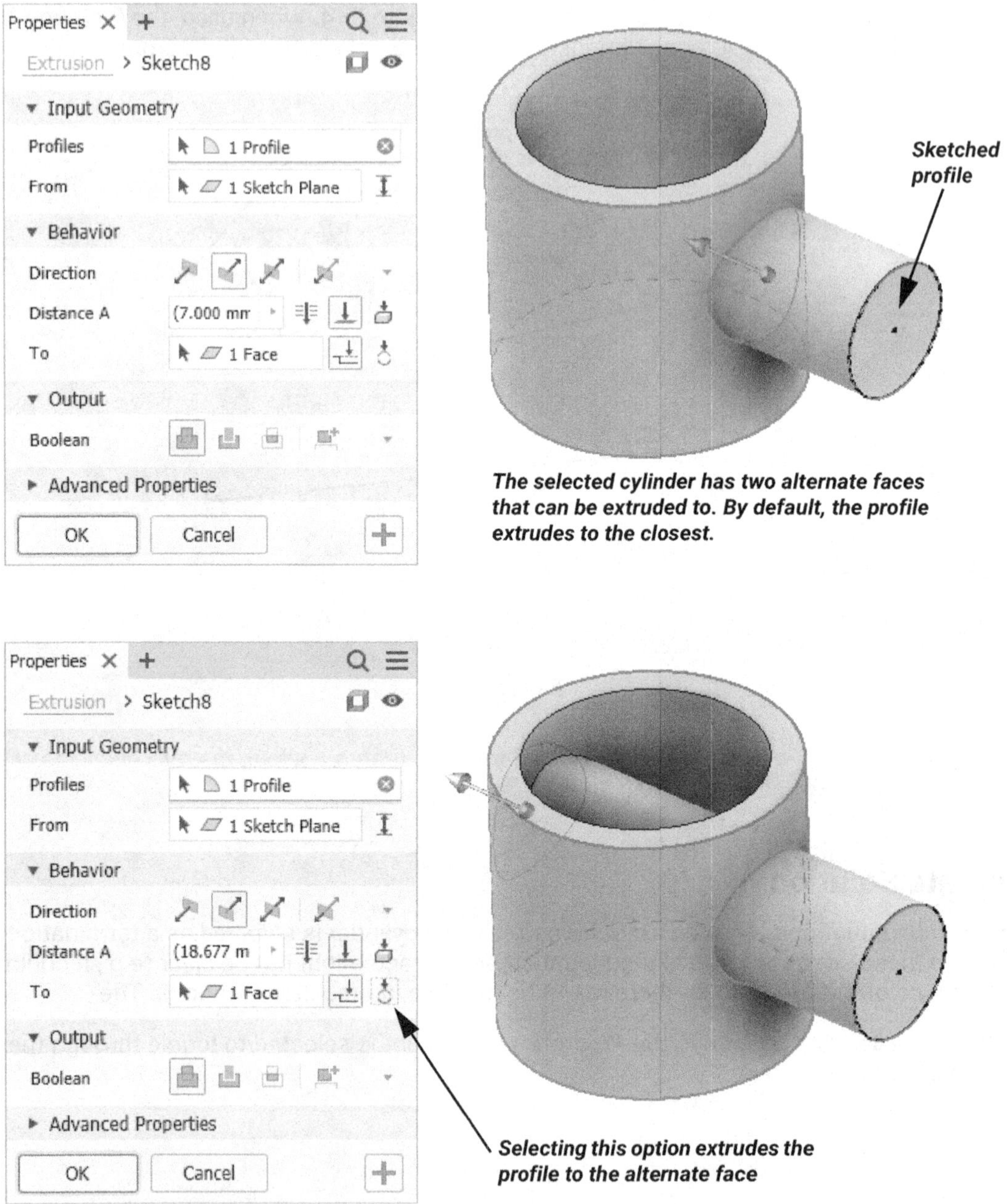

Figure 5–5

Taper

Tapering enables you to specify an angle for an extruded feature. A positive taper angle increases the cross-section, while a negative taper angle decreases the cross-section. To taper, expand the *Advanced Properties* area in the *Properties* panel and enter a taper angle, as shown in Figure 5–6.

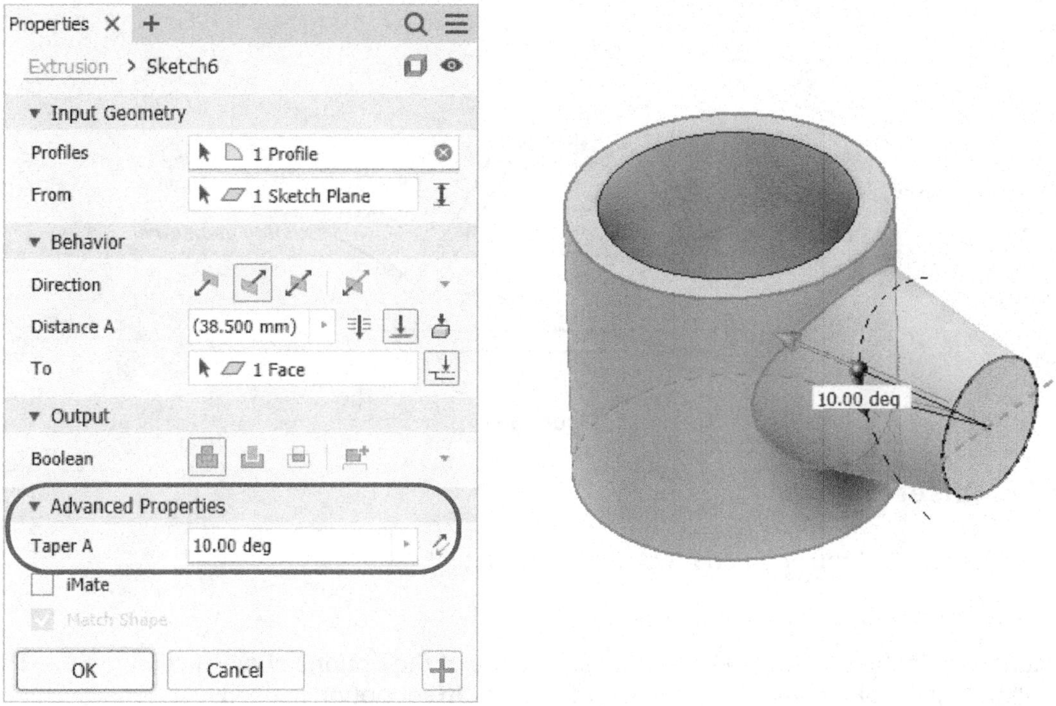

Figure 5–6

5.2 Offsetting Sketch Geometry

The **Offset** option enables you to create new entities by offsetting existing feature edges. Rather than sketching each set of entities separately, offsetting enables you to create a copy of the new or projected geometry and positions it at an offset distance from the original. An example of a sketch created by offsetting feature edges is shown in Figure 5–7.

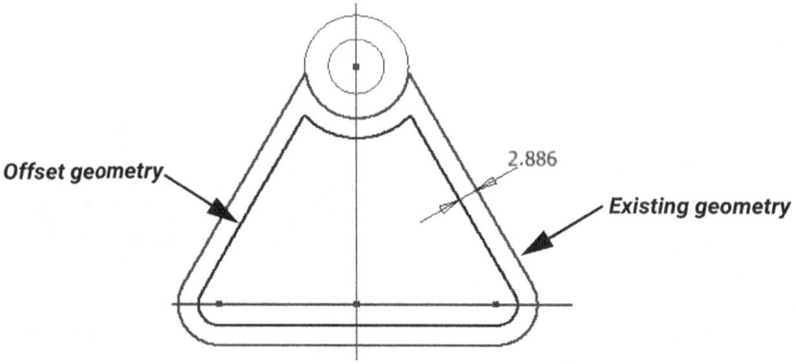

Figure 5–7

How To: Offset Entities

1. Sketch or project the geometry that is to be offset.
2. In the *Modify* panel, click (Offset).
3. Right-click in the graphics window and select one of the options shown in Figure 5–8. The option that is set is maintained the next time the **Offset** option is used.

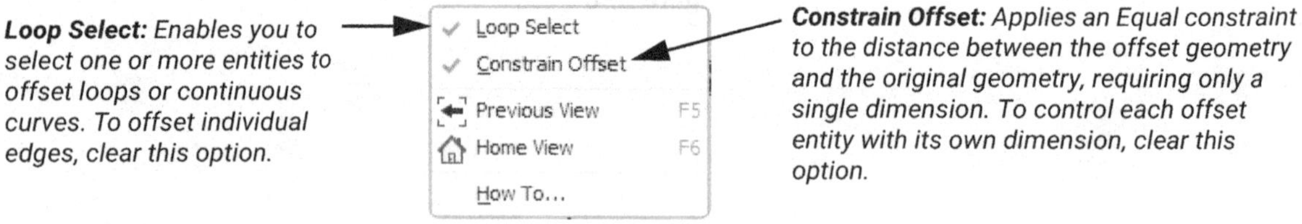

Figure 5–8

4. Select the entities or projected geometry to offset.
5. Drag the entities to the offset location and click to place them. As the entities are dragged and reach zero length, they are removed from the offset geometry set.
6. To complete the offset, right-click and select **OK,** press <Esc>, or select a new command.
7. Dimension and constrain the offset geometry as required to fully locate it in the sketch. Offset geometry only needs one dimension to fully locate it relative to its parent entities.

5.3 Projecting Geometry

Incorporating the use of projected geometry into a sketch enables you to build relationships between features. For example, in Figure 5–9, the extrusion was built from the projected silhouette edges of the hole shown. If the hole diameter changes, the extrude's size will automatically update.

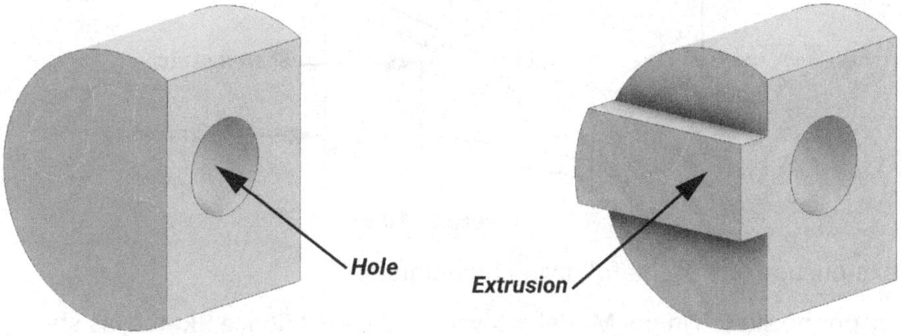

Figure 5–9

Consider the following when projecting geometry into a sketch:

- To project an edge into a sketch, in the *Create* panel, click  (Project Geometry) and select the entity.
- Existing geometry or origin/work features can be projected.
- Constraining and dimensioning sketch geometry to an edge automatically projects the part edge onto the sketch plane.
- To project all edges that are intersected by the sketch plane, click  (Project Cut Edges). If all edges are not required, select an edge and change it to construction or delete it.
- By default, all entities are projected as solid entities. To project as a construction entity, enable **Project objects as construction geometry** on the *Sketch* tab in the *Application Options* dialog box.
- If the projected source geometry changes, the projected geometry updates. To break the link, right-click on the projected geometry in the sketch and select **Break Link**.

Hint: Automatically Projecting Edges on a Sketch Plane

To automatically project all of the edges that exist on a sketch plane when you select the sketch plane, enable **Autoproject edges for sketch creation and edit** on the *Sketch* tab in the *Application Options* dialog box.

5.4 Sharing a Sketch

As soon as a sketch is used as a profile in a feature, it is consumed in that feature. Once shared, that single sketch can be used to create multiple features, as shown in Figure 5–10.

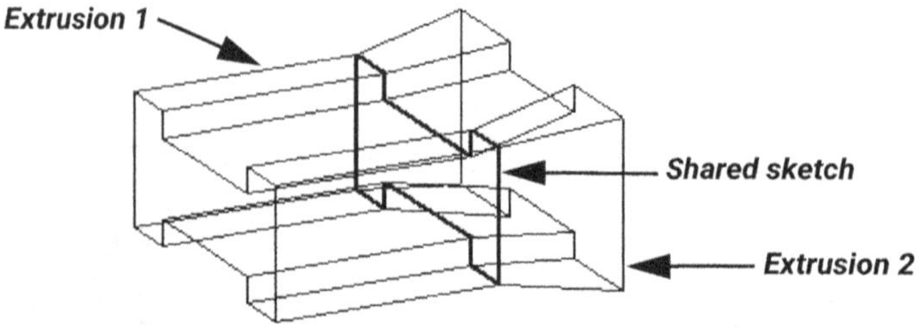

Figure 5–10

To reuse a sketch, use one of the following techniques:

- Right-click on the sketch in the Model browser and select **Share Sketch**, as shown on the left in Figure 5–11.
- Select a face in the model that was generated by the sketch and select (Share Sketch) in the toolbar.
- Select the consumed sketch and drag it to the top level of the Model browser to share it.
- Select a visible sketch as a profile in creating a new solid feature.

When you share a sketch, it is listed with the same name in the Model browser before the original feature or wherever it was placed when dragging, as shown on the right in Figure 5–11. By default, when shared, both the sketched geometry and its dimensions are displayed. To control the visibility of the sketch and/or its dimensions, right-click on the shared sketch and select or clear the **Visibility** or **Dimension Visibility** options, respectively. In order to use a shared sketch, its visibility must be toggled on, but its dimension visibility can be either on or off.

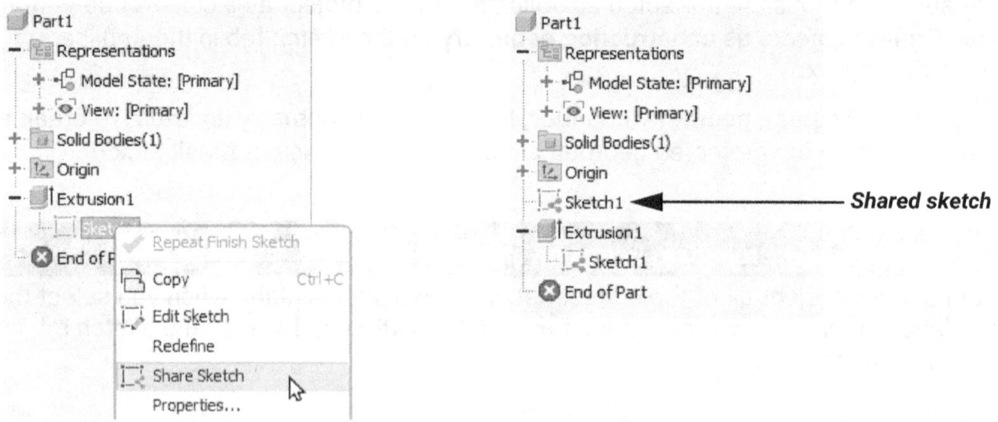

Figure 5–11

5.5 Sketching Using Dynamic Input

When creating a Line, Rectangle, Circle, Arc, Slot, or Point entity, a dynamic input line displays as soon as you drag the cursor onto the graphics window. This line provides input fields to define the start location of an entity (relative to 0,0,0), values to extend the entity, and angular values to position the entity, as shown in Figure 5–12. The field highlighted in blue is the active value. To toggle to alternate fields, press <Tab>.

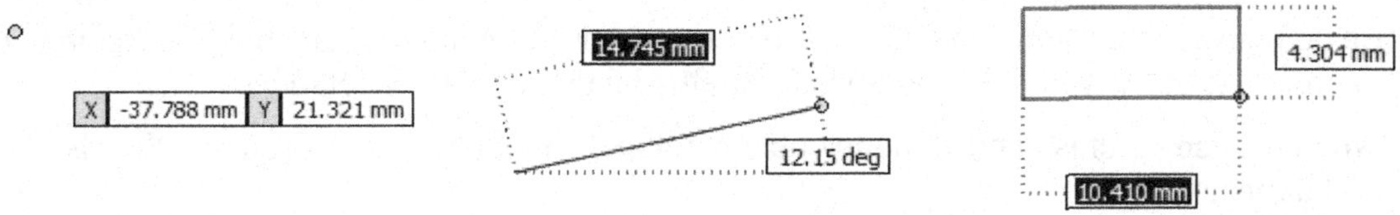

Figure 5–12

Note: *When sketching entities using dynamic input, the dimensions default to using polar coordinates while measuring relative. To change the coordinate type, right-click and expand the Coordinate Type options.*

As soon as you enter a value into a dynamic input field and press <Enter>, the entity is placed and a dimension is automatically created. If multiple values must be entered in various fields, enter a value, press <Tab> to toggle to the next field, and enter its value. Only press <Enter> once all values are defined. Note that any entities located with the cursor must be explicitly dimensioned.

- When creating a primitive as the base feature, you must use the Dynamic Input method to create dimensions that are associated with the feature.
- To disable dynamic input, in the *Application Options* dialog box (*Tools* tab>*Options* panel>  (Application Options)), in the *Sketch* tab, clear the **Enable Heads-Up Display (HUD)** option. Additionally, you can select **Settings** and specify whether Cartesian or Polar Coordinates are used for pointer and dimension input.
- To disable the automatic creation of dimensions when entities are created using dynamic input, in the *Constraint Settings* dialog box, in the *General* tab, clear the **Create dimensions from input values** option.

5.6 Sketching Using Precise Input

Similar to dynamically entering coordinate and entity values upon entity placement, precise input also enables more precise sketching using coordinates rather than simply selecting points on the screen.

- Unlike dynamic input, precise input is available for Spline, Ellipse, and Polygon entities, and is the only option for precise location in a 3D sketch.
- Using precise input, you can enter coordinates either by typing their absolute Cartesian coordinates or by typing the distances from the last point you selected.
- When precise input is used, dimensions are not automatically placed. You must explicitly add dimensions.

Note: Precise Input is also available for many of the sketch editing tools (e.g., ***Move****,* ***Copy****,* ***Rotate****, etc.).*

How To: Enter Precise Values When Creating Geometry

1. Select the type of entity to sketch in the *Create* panel.
2. Expand the *Create* panel by clicking ▾ and then click (Precise Input), as shown in Figure 5–13. The Precise Input mini-toolbar opens.

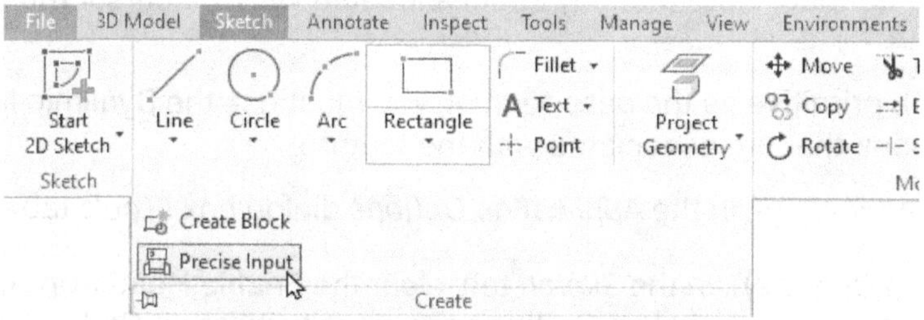

Figure 5–13

3. Select a precise input type from the drop-down list, as shown in Figure 5–14 for a 2D sketch. These options enable you to define how you enter the precise values to locate your geometry. The options vary depending on if you are working with a 2D or 3D sketch. For example, if you use precise input for a 3D sketch you only have one option which is to enter an X, Y, and Z value.

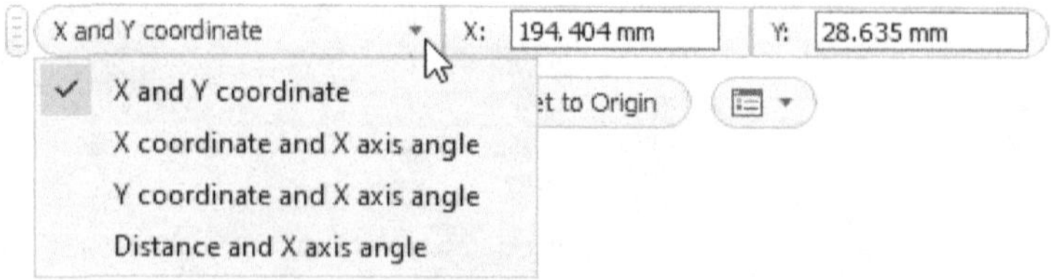

Figure 5–14

4. Relocate the origin, if required. By default, all values are measured from the model origin.

   - To change the location of the origin (triad), click **Reposition Triad**. The origin displays on the model as a triad symbol. Select the blue sphere at the center of the origin and select a new location. A red dot displays under the cursor when you hover over a possible location for the origin. This location must be fully located in the model (e.g., a vertex, point, etc.). Select to relocate the triad (origin) in the new location.
   - The newly defined origin for precise input remains until it is explicitly changed. To reset the origin back to the model origin, in the Inventor Precise Input toolbar, click **Reset to Origin**.

5. Define whether to enter values as absolute (relative to the origin) or relative to the previous point, by selecting **Relative** or **Absolute** from the drop-down list.The **Relative** option enables you to enter relative to the last point rather than from the origin (0,0,0). This is not available for the placement of the first point as it is defined from the origin.
6. Enter dimensional values in the mini-toolbar, measured as relative or absolute values, to locate the sketch entities.

   - Once you have entered a value, it constrains movement of the cursor based on what was entered. For example, if you select the **X coordinate and X axis angle** input type, and set the X value to 10 and the angle field to 15, the line shown in Figure 5–15 is created.

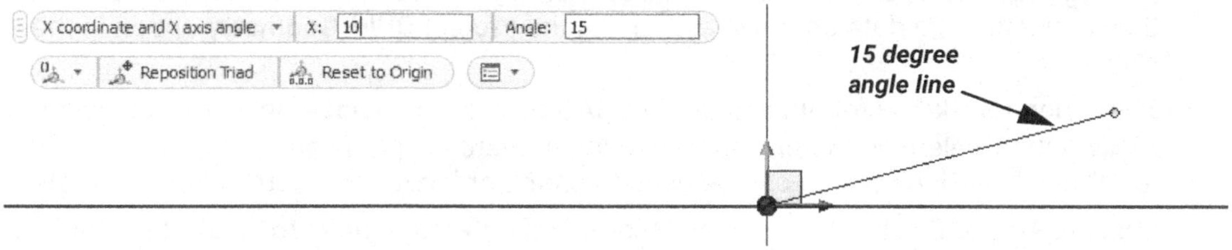

Figure 5–15

   - Once you enter the required values to define a point, press <Enter> to locate it. Continue to enter points as required to fully define the entity that has been selected. For example, if you are creating a two point rectangle you must enter two points to define the extent of the rectangle. Alternatively, you can select a point without entering values.

5.7 Using AutoCAD Data in Inventor

There are two workflows that can be used to incorporate AutoCAD® .DWG data into the Autodesk® Inventor® software for use in creating 3D geometry. The choice of whether to use either workflow is dependent on whether you require an associative link to be maintained with the AutoCAD .DWG data.

- When creating a sketch, the (Insert ACAD File) option on the *Insert* panel enables you to select and import an AutoCAD .DWG file into a sketch to create 3D geometry.
    - During import you can select which layers and selectively choose entities that are to be imported onto the active sketch. The data is imported as native Autodesk Inventor data and no associative link is maintained to the .DWG file.
    - You can add dimensions and/or constraints as required to capture your design intent and use the sketch to create solid geometry.
- An AutoCAD .DWG file can also be inserted directly into a part file and used to create 3D geometry or placed in an assembly file and used to constrain geometry. This option enables you to maintain an associative link between the AutoCAD .DWG and the part file, so that any changes to the .DWG data updates in the part file.
    - The general workflow for inserting an AutoCAD part file includes inserting the file (*Manage* tab>*Insert* panel, click (Import)) on a selected planar face or work plane and then projecting the data onto a sketch using the **Project DWG Geometry** option in the sketch.
    - The general workflow for placing an AutoCAD part file in an assembly involves using the **Place** option, selecting the file, and selecting a reference plane and point to locate the .DWG file. The **Place** option can be used to create or locate geometry in an assembly.
    - Multiple AutoCAD .DWG files can be inserted on different planes to create the required 3D geometry.

Note: *More information on this workflow is covered in the Advanced guide, or you can search for Associative DWG or DWG Underlay in the Help documentation.*

Practice 5a
Create a Sketched Revolve

Practice Objectives

- Create a revolved base feature using a provided sketch.
- Create a secondary extrude feature that references a face and entities in the base feature to fully constrain it.

In this practice, you will create a revolved base feature from an existing sketch and create an extruded cut on a face of the base feature, as shown in Figure 5–16.

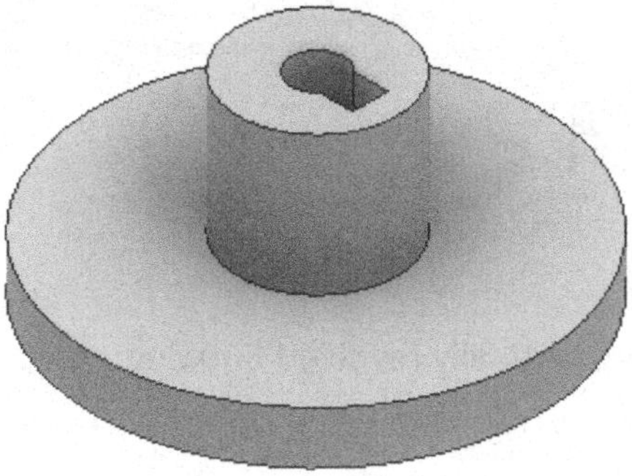

Figure 5–16

Task 1: Open a part file and create a revolved base feature.

1. Open **rev_flange_1.ipt**.
2. In the *Create* panel, click (Revolve).

3. The sketch is automatically selected as the Profile. Select the line (projected XZ Plane) shown in Figure 5–17 as the axis of rotation.

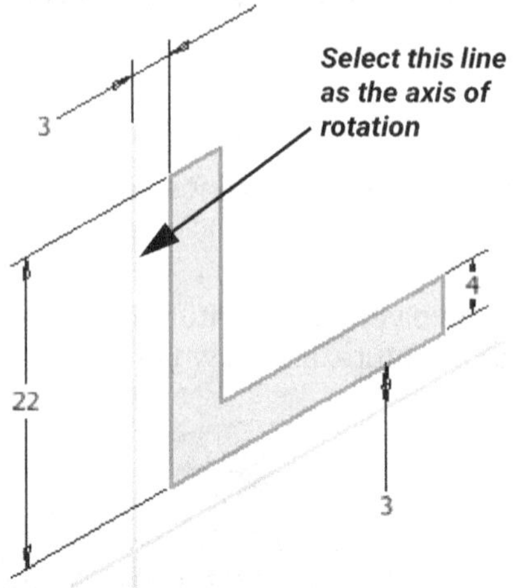

Figure 5–17

4. The revolved feature is automatically revolved 360 degrees ((Full)), as shown in Figure 5–18.

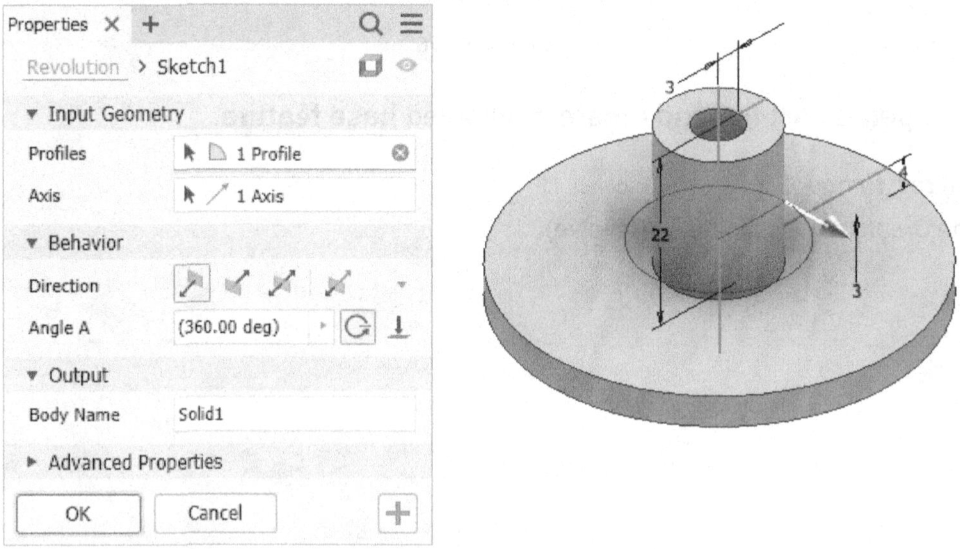

Figure 5–18

5. To change the value of the revolved angle, click in the *Angle* field and enter **220**.

6. Click to change the direction of the feature creation. The *Properties* panel and the revolved feature geometry display as shown in Figure 5–19.

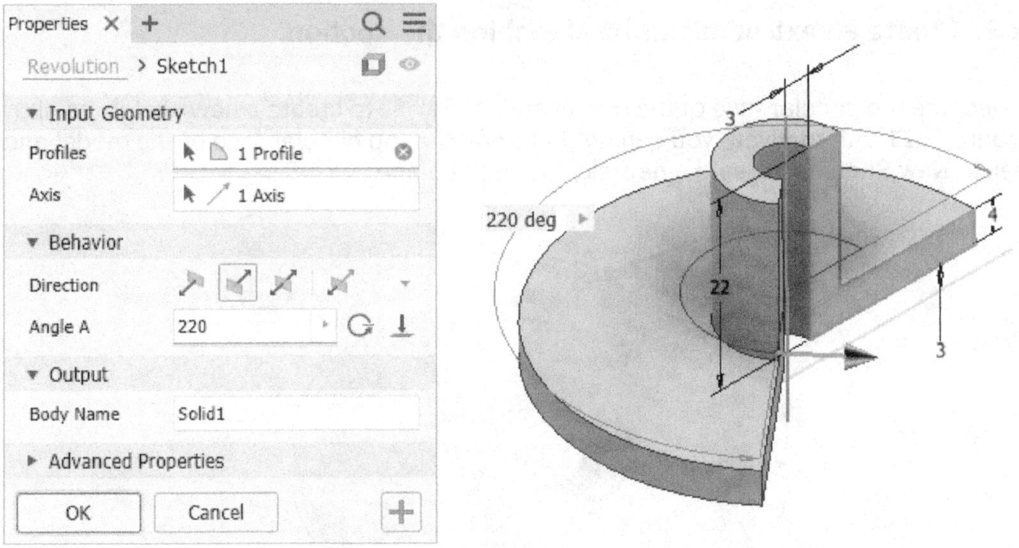

Figure 5–19

7. Click **OK** to complete the feature.

Task 2: Modify the feature.

1. Right-click on **Revolution1** in the Model browser and select **Show Dimensions**.
2. Double-click on the *220* degrees dimension, as shown in Figure 5–20, and change the angle value to **360** degrees.
3. Double-click on the *4* dimension, as shown in Figure 5–20, and change the value to **6**.

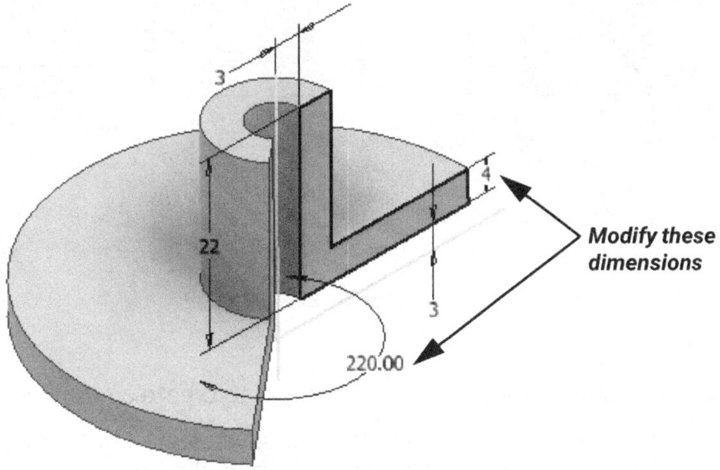

Figure 5–20

4. In the Quick Access Toolbar, click  (Local Update) to update the model.

Task 3: Create an extruded cut by sketching the section.

1. Select the top circular face of the model and click to create a new sketch, as shown in Figure 5–21. Alternatively, you can right-click on the top circular face of the model and select **New Sketch** to create a new sketch on the plane.

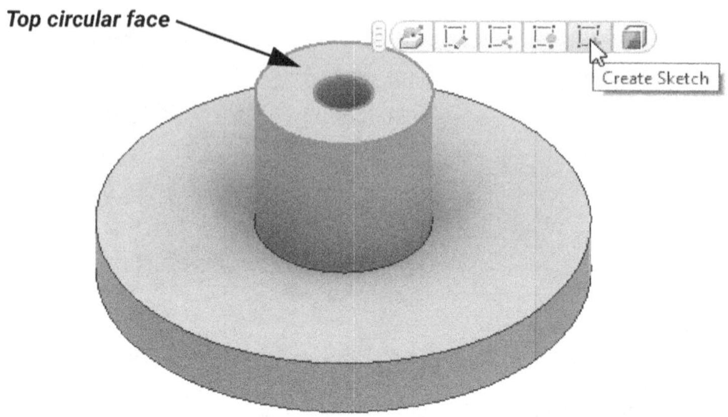

Figure 5–21

2. Sketch and dimension three lines with respect to the center point of the circular edge, as shown in Figure 5–22. Project the XZ Plane and apply the Symmetric constraint to the two parallel horizontal lines to fully constrain the sketch.

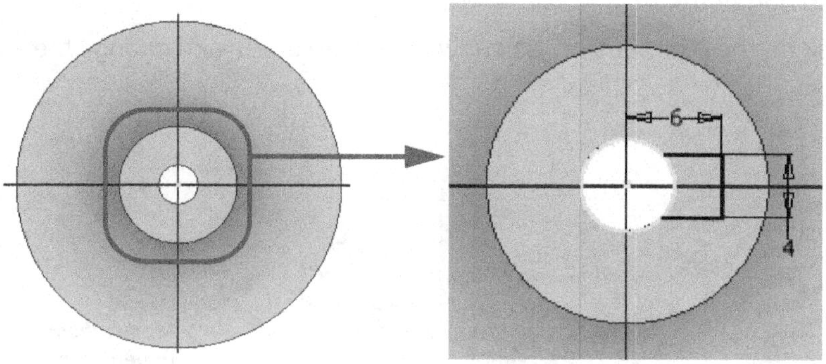

Figure 5–22

3. Finish the sketch.
4. In the *3D Model* tab>*Create* panel, click (Extrude) to create a cut using this sketch.
5. Select the new sketched profile. It is not automatically selected because there are now two closed sections in the part. Both of the sections exist in the newly created sketch.
6. Click (Cut) to remove material, if not already set.

7. Enter **16** in the *Distance A* field.
8. Ensure that the cut is extruded inside the part. If required, change its direction.
9. Click **OK** to complete the feature. The model displays as shown in Figure 5–23.

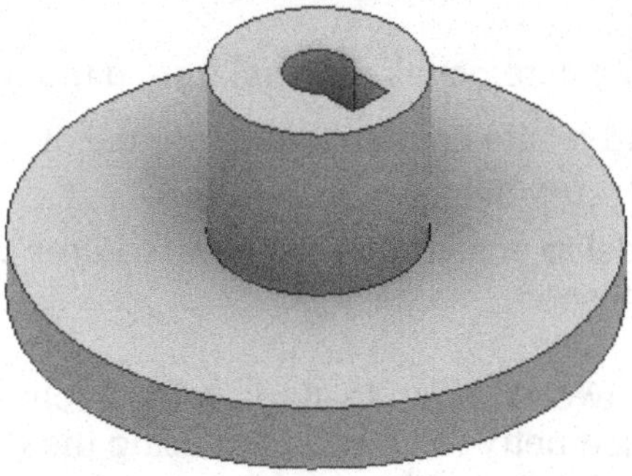

Figure 5–23

10. Save the part and close the window.

End of practice

Practice 5b
Create Sketched Extrusions

Practice Objectives

- Create geometry that adds and removes material from a model.
- Use the **Offset** command to create entities that reference other features so that the design intent is built into the model.
- Modify features in the model to ensure that the new features update based on the references that were established.

In this practice, you will create two extruded features using geometry that exists in a model that is provided for you. The new geometry will be created using the **Offset** command. The initial and final models are shown in Figure 5–24.

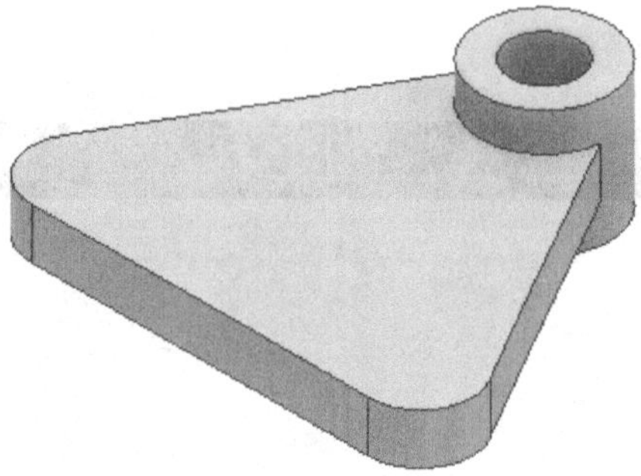

Initial model

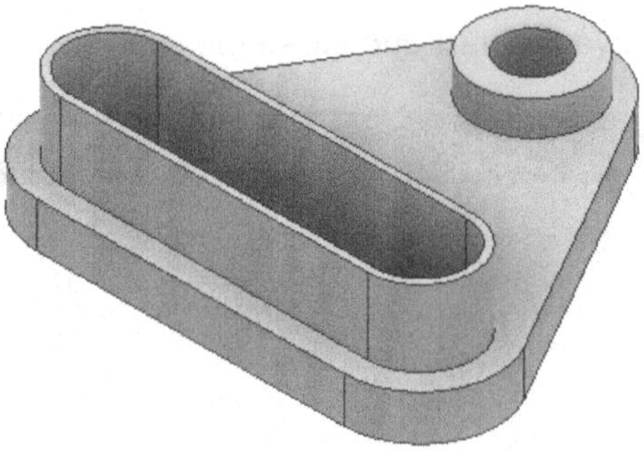

Final model

Figure 5–24

Task 1: Open a part file and create offset geometry.

1. Open **Offset.ipt**.

2. In the *Sketch* panel, click (Start 2D Sketch) and select the top face of the bracket, as shown in Figure 5–25, as the sketching plane.

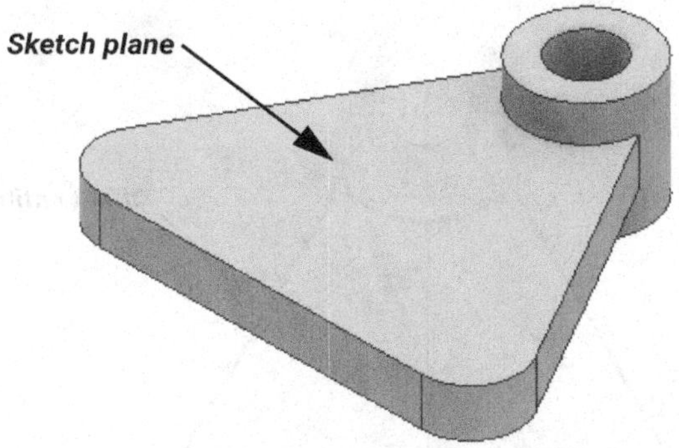

Figure 5–25

Note: *If a model is not automatically oriented into 2D on sketch creation, you can select a face and click (Look at) in the Navigation Bar to look at the plane, or you can select a face on the ViewCube. If the orientation is not as expected, spin the model into the approximate location using the arrows around the outer extent of the ViewCube.*

3. In the *Create* panel, click (Project Geometry) or right-click and select **Project Geometry**. Select the face shown in Figure 5–26 to project the six edges that define the face onto the sketch plane.

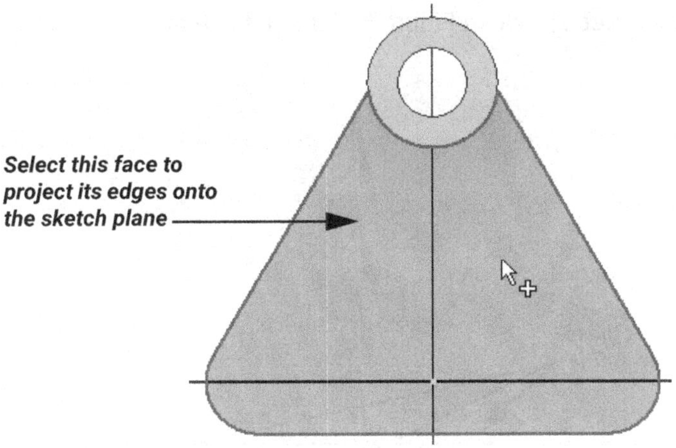

Figure 5–26

4. In the *Sketch* tab>*Modify* panel, click (Offset).

5. Select a location on any of the projected entities. Drag the cursor towards the center of the model. Note that the loop of projected entities are automatically being offset, as shown in Figure 5–27.

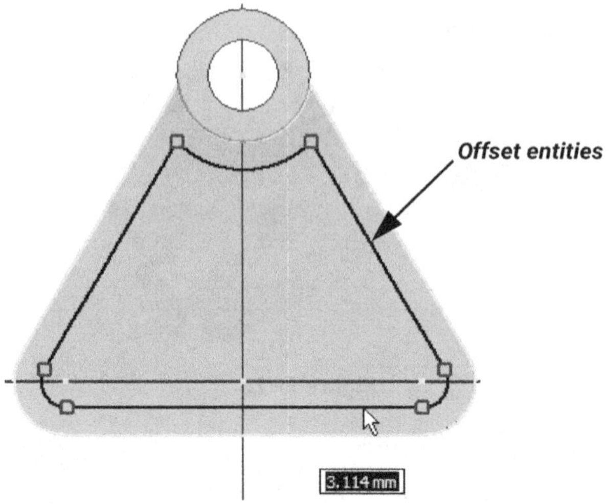

Figure 5–27

6. Right-click and select **Cancel** to cancel the command or press <Esc>.
7. In the *Modify* panel, click (Offset) again.
8. Right-click in the graphics window and toggle off **Loop Select**. This enables you to individually select entities to offset.
9. Select the three entities shown in Figure 5–28 to be offset.

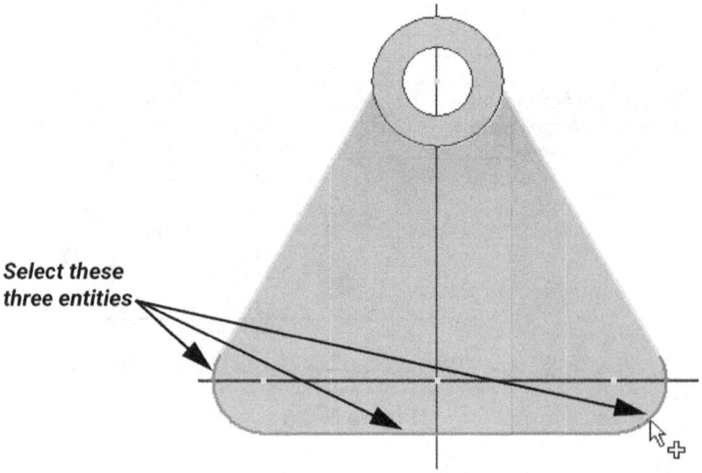

Figure 5–28

10. Right-click and select **Continue**. Drag the entities to the location shown in Figure 5–29 and select to place them.

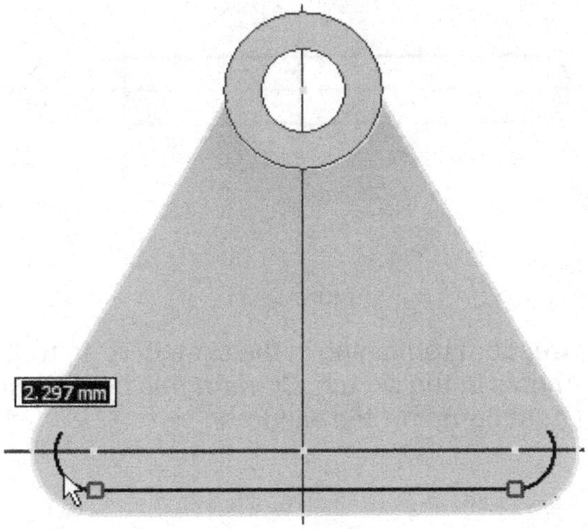

Figure 5–29

Task 2: Sketch a line and apply a Tangent constraint.

1. Sketch a horizontal line shown in Figure 5–30.

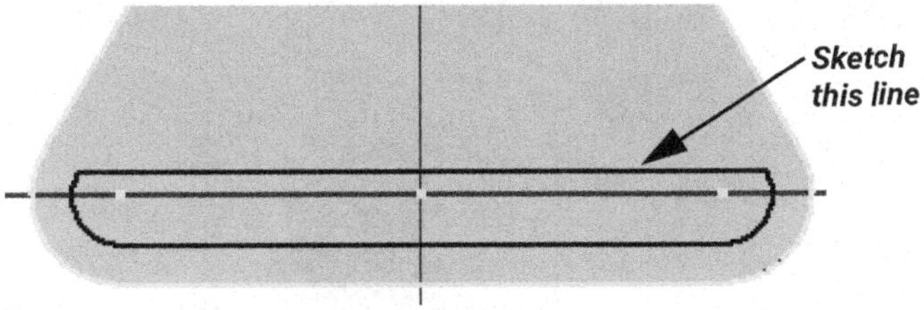

Figure 5–30

2. At the bottom of the screen, the Status Bar indicates that dimensions are required to fully constrain the sketch. Click  (Show all degrees of Freedom) in the Status Bar. The arrows that display on the screen indicate the degrees of freedom remaining in the sketch. Select the option again to clear their display.
3. Apply tangent constraints to the line and arcs, as required. Depending on how the horizontal line was sketched, you might require an additional Coincident constraint at the right end.

4. Apply and modify a vertical linear dimension to the lines shown in Figure 5–31 to fully locate the geometry.

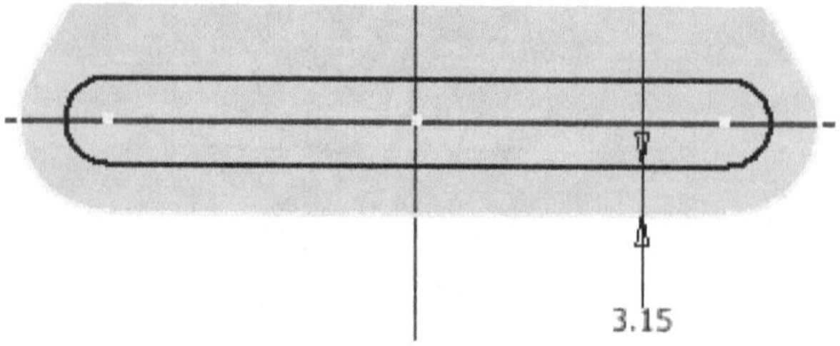

Figure 5–31

5. Review the degrees of freedom remaining in the sketch. Note that there are no remaining degrees of freedom symbols in the sketch. Confirm this by reviewing if any dimensions are required in the bottom-right corner of the window.
6. Finish the sketch.

Task 3: Extrude the sketch.

1. In the *Create* panel, click  (Extrude) to create an extrusion. Select the profile such that the extrusion displays similar to that shown in Figure 5–32.

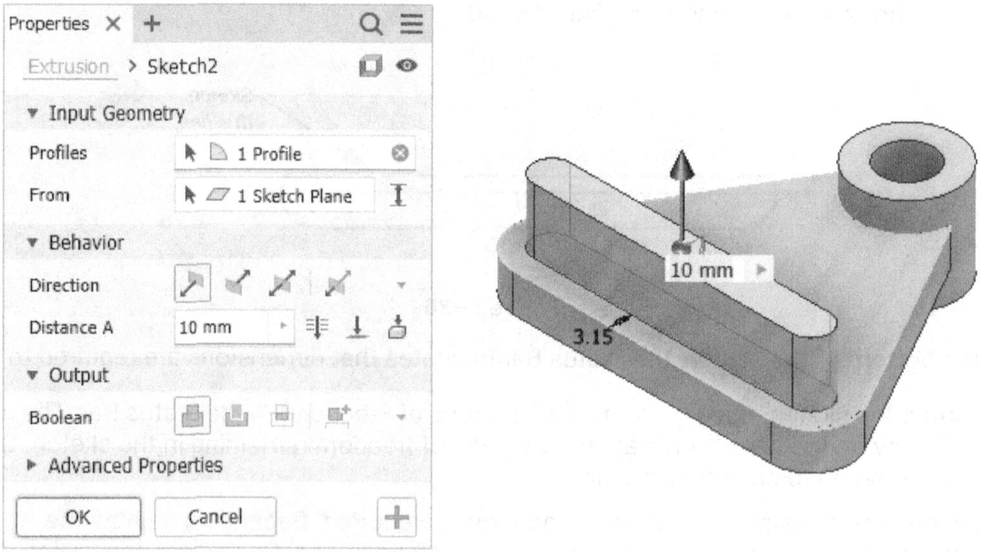

Figure 5–32

Note: *Because the face was selected as the Project Geometry reference, there are two closed sections in the sketch. This means that the required closed section is not automatically selected to be extruded. Consider changing the projected entities to construction lines if the edges are not required.*

2. Set *Distance A* to **10mm**, if not already set.
3. Complete the extrusion.

Task 4: Offset projected edges.

1. Select the top face you have just created and click [icon] to create a new sketch on this face, as shown in Figure 5–33.

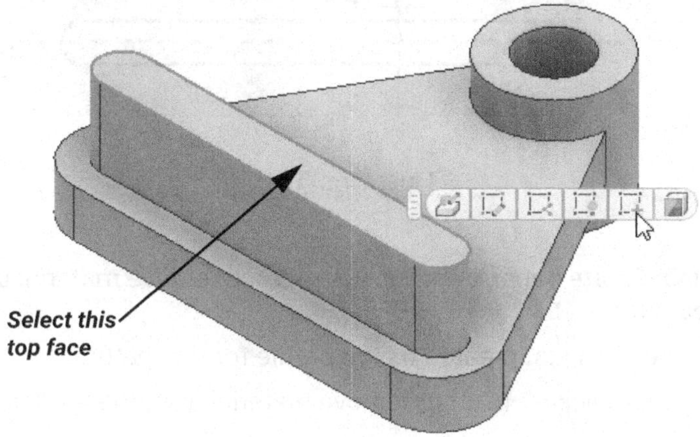

Figure 5–33

2. In the *Create* panel, click [icon] (Project Geometry). Select the face used as the sketch plane to project its edges.
3. In the *Sketch* tab>*Modify* panel, click [icon] (Offset).
4. Right-click and select **Loop Select**. Because the option was cleared in the previous task it must be enabled again.
5. Select one of the edges of the extrusion, as shown in Figure 5–34.

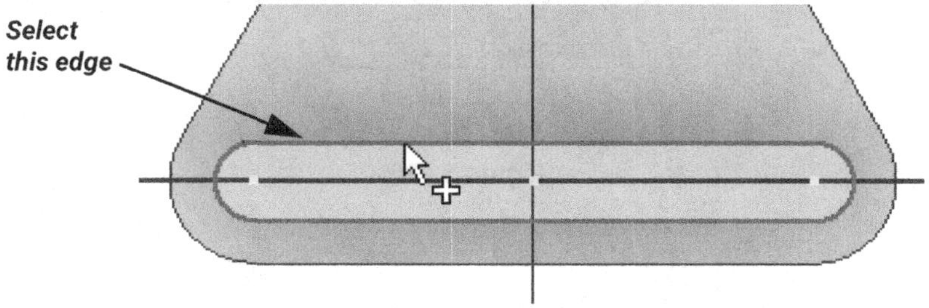

Figure 5–34

6. Offset (to the inside), enter **1** in the entry field, and press <Enter>. The entities are offset and the dimension is automatically added to the sketch, as shown in Figure 5–35. Note that in the previous task, the dimension did not immediately appear because you did not enter a value in the offset field. In that case, you had to manually add the dimension.

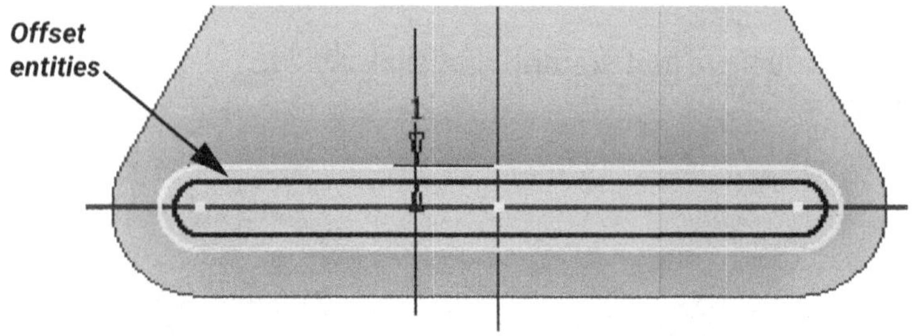

Figure 5–35

7. Finish the sketch.
8. In the *3D Model* tab>*Create* panel, click (Extrude) to remove material using the sketch you have just created.
9. Select the sketch that was just created as the profile for the feature.
10. In the *Properties* panel, click (Cut) to remove material from the model, if not already set.
11. Accept the defaults and complete the cut. The model displays as shown in Figure 5–36.

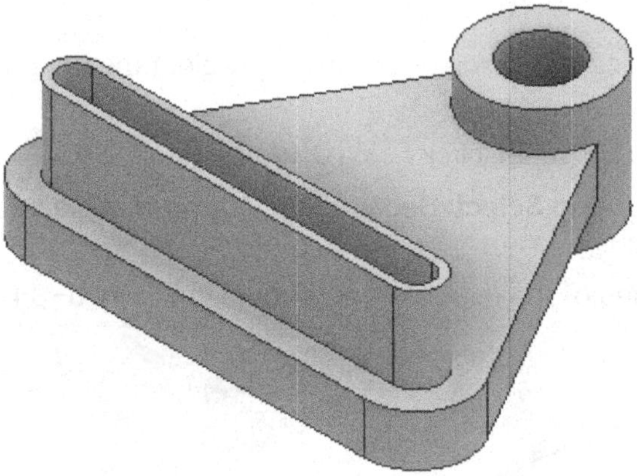

Figure 5–36

Task 5: Edit the model.

1. Right-click on the last extrusion that you have created (cut) in the Model browser and select **Edit Feature**. You can also double-click the feature in the Model browser, or select a surface that makes up the feature and click . The *Properties* panel for the feature displays.
2. Click (Through All) to extrude the cut through the entire part.
3. Complete the feature.
4. Double-click on **Sketch1** (below the **Origin** node in the Model browser). This sketch is a shared sketch that was used to create multiple features in the model. Change the fillet from 6 units to **10**. Finish the sketch. The model displays as shown in Figure 5–37. Both of the extrusions that you created update based on the change to Sketch1 because of the established relationships.

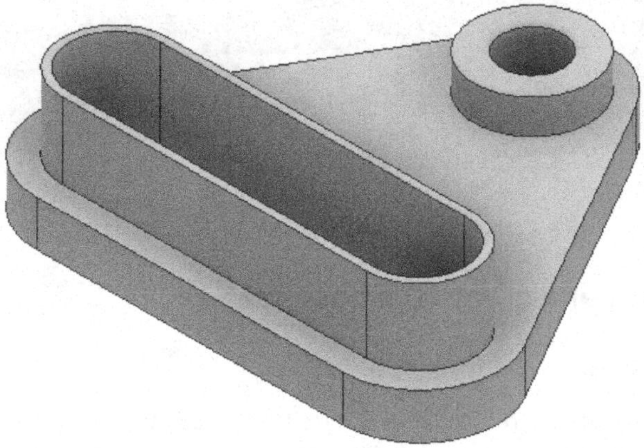

Figure 5–37

5. Save the model and close the window.

End of practice

Practice 5c
Share Sketch

Practice Objectives

- Appropriately reuse a shared sketch to create required geometry in the model.
- Control the visibility of sketched entities and dimensions.

In this practice, you will use a single sketch to create four extrusions to create the geometry shown in Figure 5–38. To use the same sketch for multiple features you will use the **Share Sketch** command to add it as an independent node in the model so that it can be reused.

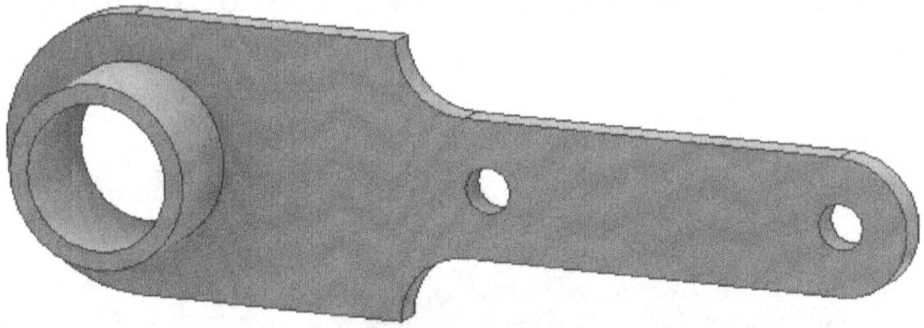

Figure 5–38

Task 1: Open the part and create the base feature.

1. Open **Shared Sketch.ipt**.
2. Create the extrusion shown in Figure 5–39 using the sketch provided. The depth of the extrusion should be **6** and it should be extruding in the **+Y** direction. You must select multiple closed sections to obtain geometry. To select multiple closed sections at one time, you can manually select them or drag a crossing window around all the closed sections. Alternatively, if you select the outer edge that encompasses all the sections, you can select the entire section at once.

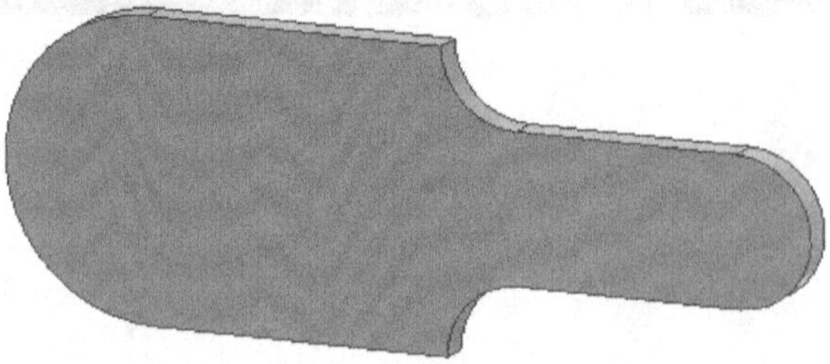

Figure 5–39

Task 2: Share the sketch.

1. Note that the sketch is now consumed in **Extrusion1**. To use this sketch again, it must be shared. Expand **Extrusion1** in the Model browser.
2. In the Model browser, right-click on the **Sketch1** and select **Share Sketch**. Alternatively, select a face in the model and select  (Share Sketch) in the toolbar. The sketch is shared and is now listed as an independent node, as shown in Figure 5–40. The shared sketch can now be used for additional features without having to create a new sketch.

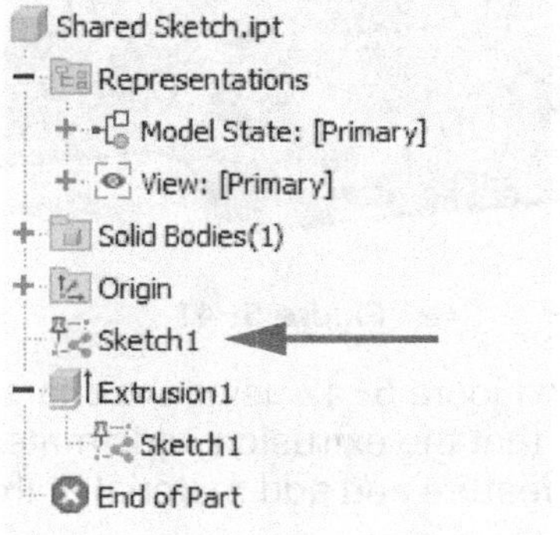

Figure 5–40

Note: A shared sketch is not consumed by the extruded features which are created from it. It can be found in the Model browser under any features that use it, and in the tree on its own. Keep in mind that it is a shared sketch and any change will reflect in changes to all features that use it.

3. When a sketch is shared, its sketched entities and dimensions are set as visible. To clear the dimensions (not entities) from the display, right-click **Sketch1** in the Model browser and select **Dimension Visibility** to clear it. A sketch must remain visible if it is to be used to create geometry; however, dimension visibility is not required.

Task 3: Create additional features.

1. Create the extrusion shown in Figure 5–41 using the shared sketch. Both cuts are created as a single extruded feature and they are to remove all material through the entire model.

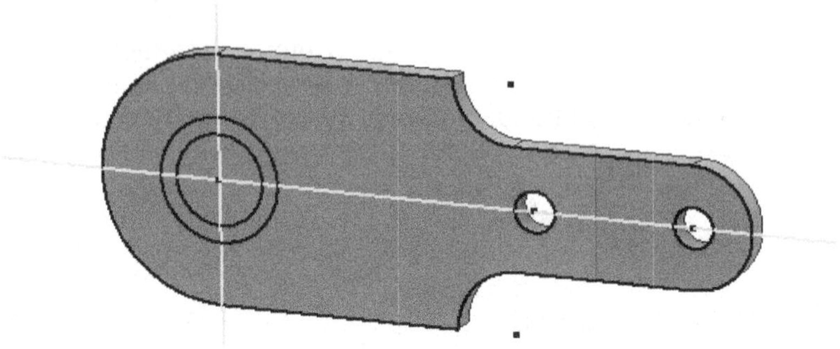

Figure 5–41

2. Create the extrusion shown in Figure 5–42 using the shared sketch. The depth of the extrusion should be **20**. Note that the extrusion adds material to the model. The extrusion cannot cut through the base feature and add material at the same time.

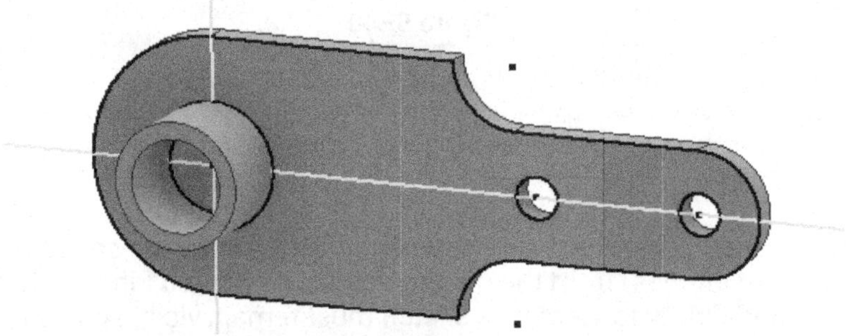

Figure 5–42

3. Create another extrusion that removes the material shown in Figure 5–43.

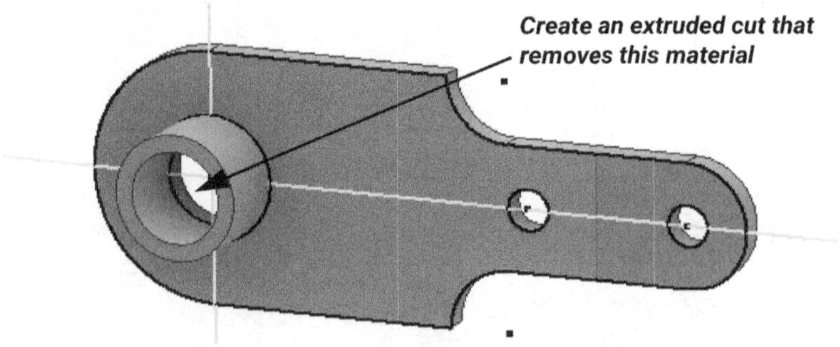

Figure 5–43

Task 4: Modify the sketch.

1. Right-click on **Sketch1** and select **Dimension Visibility** to toggle on the display of dimensions.

   ***Note:** Dimension Visibility can be controlled using either the **Sketch1** node at the top of the Model browser's feature list or the **Sketch1** node in **Extrusion1**.*

2. Double-click on the *120* dimension and enter **160**.
3. Double-click on the *30* diameter dimension and enter **40**.
4. In the Quick Access Toolbar, click  (Local Update) to update the model. Note how all of the features that referenced the sketch update.
5. In the Model browser, right-click on **Sketch1** (in either location) and select **Visibility** to remove the sketch from the display.
6. Save the model and close the window.

End of practice

Practice 5d
(Optional) Create a Sketch Using Precise Coordinates

Practice Objectives

- Create sketched entities by entering their starting locations and dimension sizes.
- Reposition the origin triad in a sketch so that dimensions can be entered relative to a defined location rather than the origin of the model.
- Create sketched entities by entering their extents using the *Precise Input* dialog box versus sketching and dimensioning them independently.

In this practice, you will create a part. For some sketch features, you will use either dynamic input or precise input to create the entities in the model. The completed part is shown in Figure 5–44.

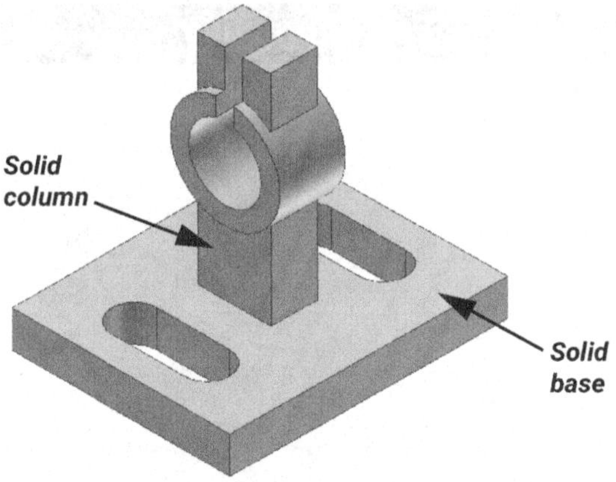

Figure 5–44

Task 1: Create a new part file and its base geometry.

The sketch for the solid base is a 300 X 240mm rectangle.

1. Use the standard metric (mm) template to create a new part file.
2. Start the creation of a new sketch on the XZ Plane. Ensure the ViewCube appears as shown in Figure 5–45; if it does not, rotate it. This ensures that your sketch will have the same orientation as the images in this exercise.
3. In the *Create* panel, click (Project Geometry) or right-click and select **Project Geometry**. Project the YZ and XY Planes onto the sketch plane to locate and dimension the sketch.

4. In the *Create* panel, click (Rectangle).
5. Press <Tab> to activate the *X* field in the dynamic input display. Enter **120** in the *X* field, press <Tab> to toggle to the *Y* field, and enter **150** in the *Y* field. The point is measured from the absolute origin (0,0). Press <Enter> after you have entered the values.
6. Enter **240** in the *X* field, press <Tab>, and enter **300** in the *Y* field. Press <Enter> after you have entered the values. The point is measured from the previous point (120,150). The rectangle displays as shown in Figure 5–45 with the defined dimensions.

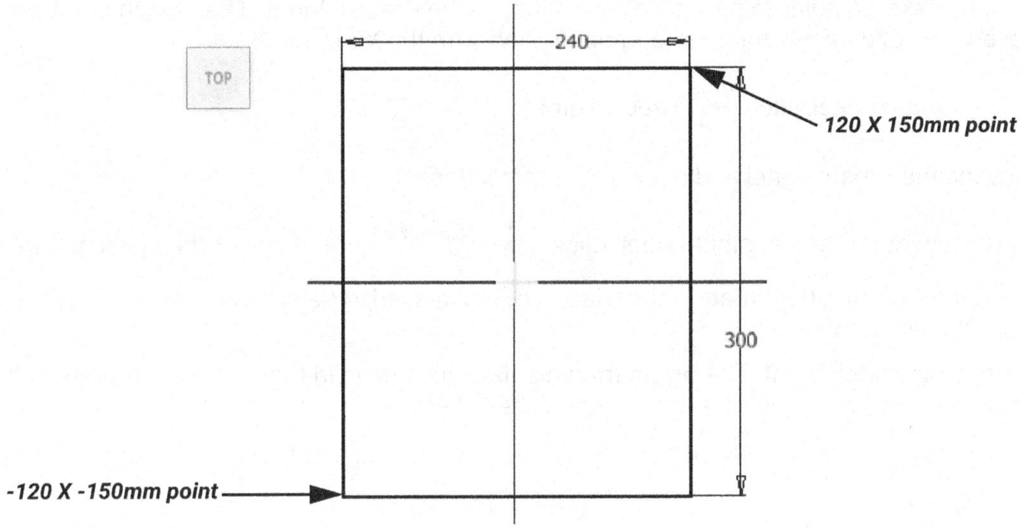

Figure 5–45

7. Press <Esc> to cancel the command.
8. Constrain the sketch to ensure symmetry with respect to the projected work planes.
9. Finish the sketch. Extrude the sketch by **40mm** in the positive Y-direction. The extrusion displays as shown in Figure 5–46. The model is displayed in the isometric Home view.

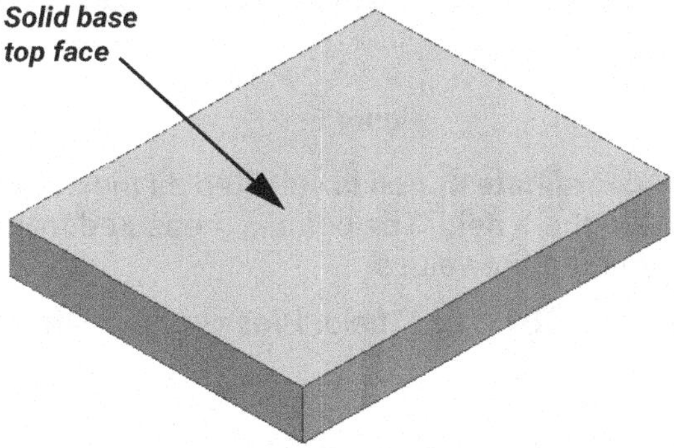

Figure 5–46

Task 2: Create the solid column.

The sketch for the solid column is a 240 X 80mm rectangle. The coordinates for a solid column sketch are given from the center of the solid base top face.

1. In the Model browser, right-click on the **XY Plane** and select **New Sketch**, or use any of the other options to create a new sketch.
2. Project the YZ Plane onto the sketch plane to locate and dimension the sketch.
3. Create a sketch point to provide a reference for the Precise Input. The sketch point should lie on the solid base's top face and be aligned with the YZ Plane.
4. In the *Create* panel, click  (Rectangle).
5. Expand the *Create* panel and click  (Precise Input).
6. In the Inventor Precise mini-toolbar, click 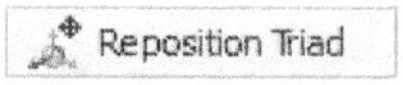

and select the black sphere at the center of the origin triad. If the triad is not displayed, reselect the  (Rectangle) option again to activate it.
7. Select the sketch point. The origin triad displays as shown in Figure 5–47. Your sketch might be displayed from the other side of the XY Plane.

   Note: *The new location you define remains the active origin until you select a new point or you reset it back to the model origin using* 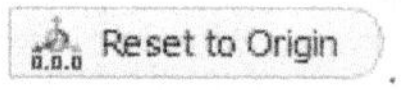

.

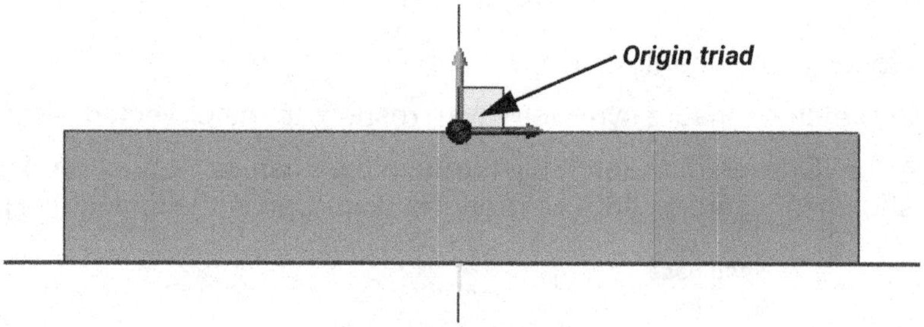

Figure 5–47

8. Ensure that the **X and Y coordinate** option is selected as the measuring type and then enter **40** in the *X* field and **240** in the *Y* field. The point is measured from the relative origin. Press <Enter> after you have entered the values.
9. Enter **-40** in the *X* field and **0.00** in the *Y* field. Press <Enter> after you have entered the values.

10. Dimension and constrain the sketch, as shown in Figure 5–48. You will need to assign the symmetric and coincident constraints.

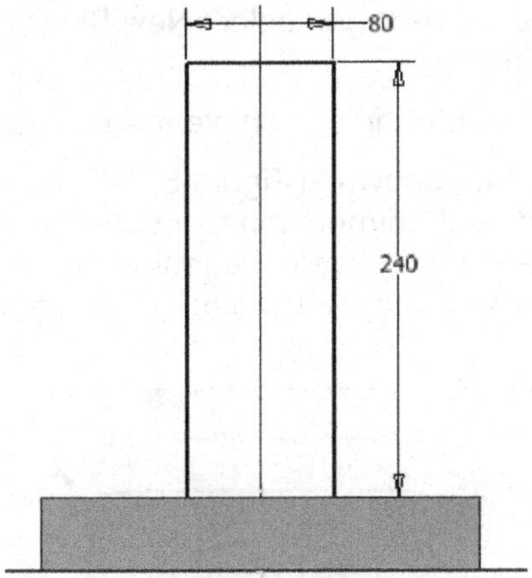

Figure 5–48

Note: *In this case, Precise Input enabled you to change the origin point from which the dimensions were entered. Although it would have been easier to adjust the coordinate entries for values that were relative to the origin, Precise Input can be valuable if the provided values are more complex. In addition, consider that you had to manually assign the dimensions, while with dynamic input, they were assigned for you.*

11. The Precise Input mini-toolbar remains open and enabled while you are sketching entities, unless explicitly closed. Expand the *Options* drop-down list () and select **Close**.
12. Finish the sketch.
13. Extrude the sketch by 25mm on either side of the XY Plane by entering **50mm** as the *Distance A* value.
14. Click **OK**. The extrusion displays in its isometric Home view as shown in Figure 5–49.

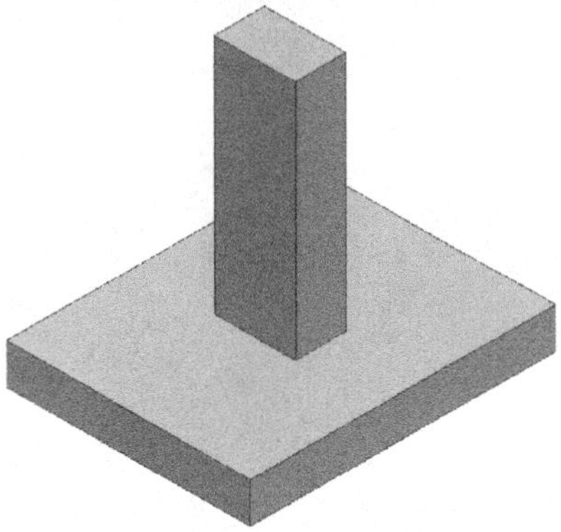

Figure 5–49

Task 3: Create the slots in the solid base.

1. Right-click on the solid base top face and select **New Sketch**, or use any of the other options to create a new sketch.
2. Project the YZ and XY Planes onto the sketch plane to locate and dimension the sketch.
3. Sketch the Center to Center Slot shown in Figure 5–50. Use dynamic input to enter the dimensions. Add the additional **70** dimension to locate the slot and assign a symmetry constraint to fully locate the slot. To create the radius measurement, you may need to right-click and select **Radius** to change it from the Diameter measurement option.

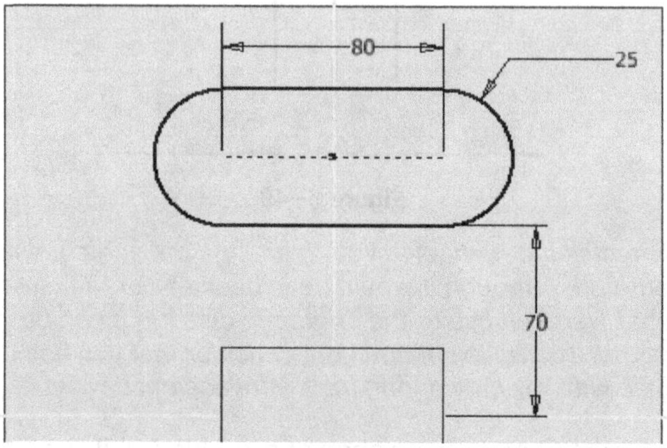

Figure 5–50

4. Finish the sketch and extrude the sketch as a cut through the entire model.
5. Mirror the slot using the XY Plane as the mirroring plane. The model displays as shown in Figure 5–51.

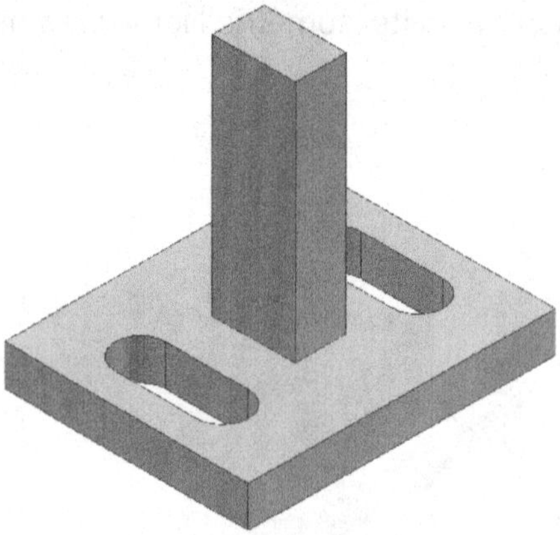

Figure 5–51

Task 4: Create the extrusion.

1. Create the extrusion shown in Figure 5–52. Select the XY Plane as the sketching plane. Locate the center of the circular sketch using either dynamic input or precise input. Locate the center of the circular sketch at **0, 180** with a diameter of **120mm**. Extrude the sketch by **35mm** on either side of the XY Plane. Ensure that the sketch is fully constrained.

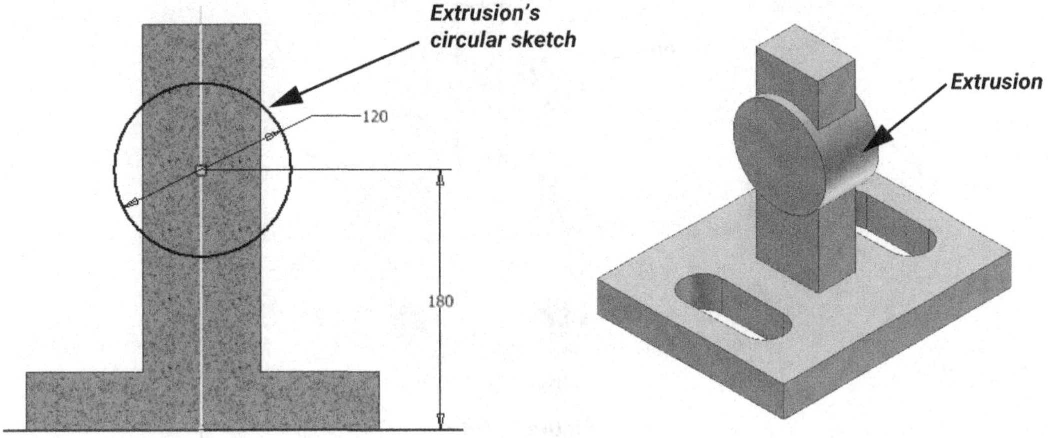

Figure 5–52

Note: *Consider enabling (Slice Graphics) in the Status Bar to see the entire sketch.*

Task 5: Create a Through All hole.

1. Create the concentric, through circular cut shown in Figure 5–53. The hole diameter is **80mm**.

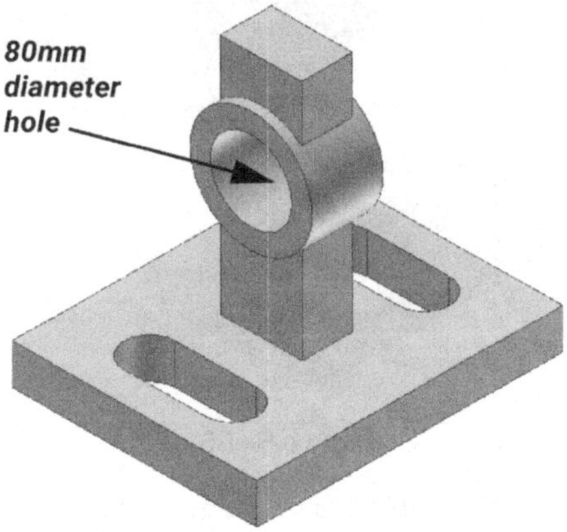

Figure 5–53

Task 6: Create an extruded cut.

1. Select the XY Plane as the sketching plane and sketch the section shown in Figure 5–54. The cut should always cut through to the concentric hole. By referencing existing geometry and using constraints you can create the section using only one dimension.

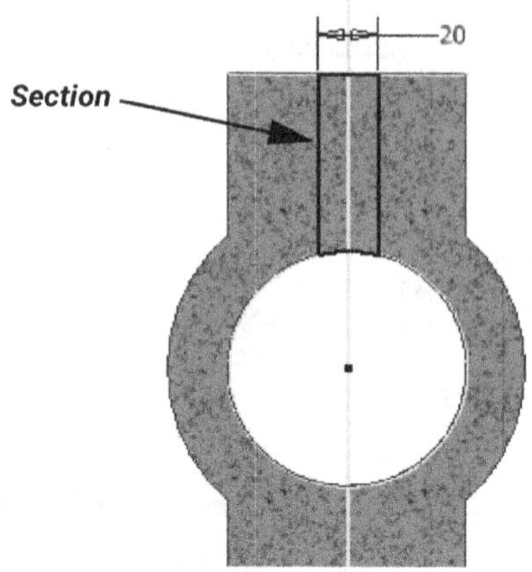

Figure 5–54

Note: *Consider enabling (Slice Graphics) in the Status Bar to see the entire sketch.*

2. Finish the sketch.
3. Create an extruded cut through both sides of the XY Plane. The model displays as shown in Figure 5–55.

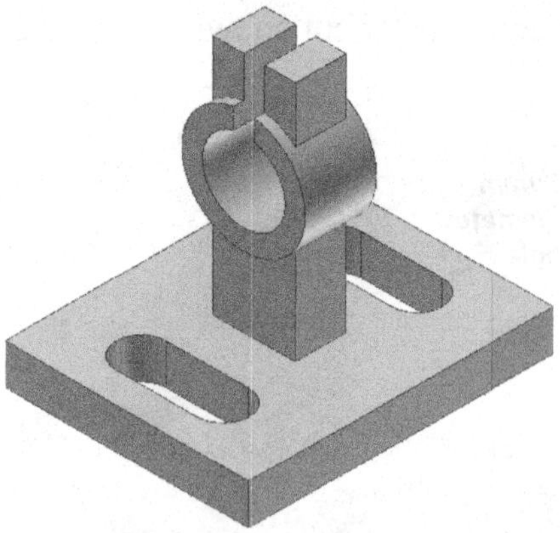

Figure 5–55

4. Save the part as **Precise_Input.ipt** and close the model.

End of practice

Chapter Review Questions

1. The **Offset** option is commonly used to create sketched entities offset from projected geometry. In the sketch shown in Figure 5–56, how many dimensions are required to fully constrain the sketch? Assume **Constrain Offset** and **Loop Select** are toggled on.

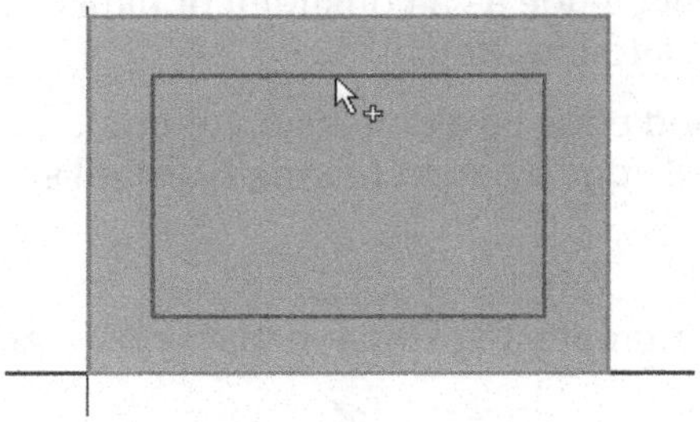

Figure 5–56

   a. 1
   b. 2
   c. 3
   d. 4
   e. More than 4

2. To create a new feature, you are required to reuse a sketch that was created for **Extrusion2**, as shown in Figure 5–57. Is this possible? If so, which option would you use?

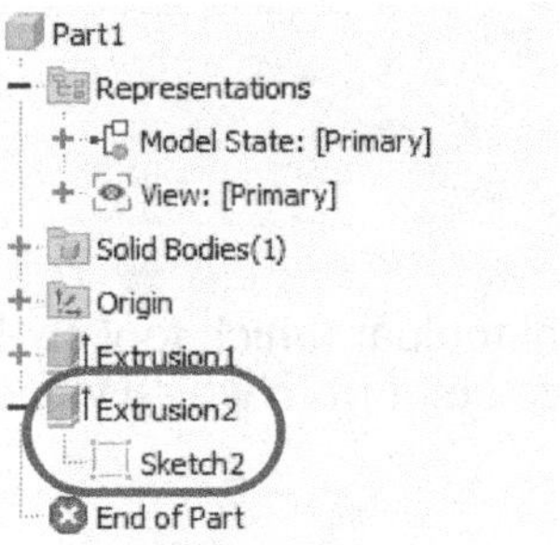

Figure 5–57

   a. You cannot reuse an existing sketch; you must recreate it using projected geometry.
   b. It is possible using the **Visibility** option.
   c. It is possible using the **Edit Sketch** option.
   d. It is possible using the **Share Sketch** option.

3. Which of the following is true regarding projected geometry in a sketch?

a. You can only project edges into a sketch that lie in the same plane as the sketching plane.

b. When selecting a work plane as a sketching plane, the edges that lie in the plane are automatically projected into the sketch.

c. When selecting an existing edge as a constraint or dimension reference, it is automatically projected into the sketch.

d. When you use a projected edge as a dimension reference, no relationship between the sketch and the projected edge's parent feature is established.

4. Which command is used to create an extrusion that adds material to existing solid geometry?

a.  (Join)

b. (Intersect)

c.  (Cut)

d.  (Solid)

5. Which tool temporarily hides the portion of a part that is above the sketch plane to display the plane more clearly for sketching?

a. Slice Graphics

b. Relax Mode

c. Look At

d. Hidden Edge Display

6. In the Inventor Precise Input mini-toolbar, which tool enables you to change the origin point so that it is used as the reference point from which values are measured?

a. 

b. 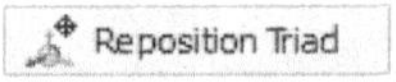

c. 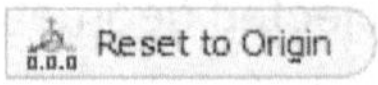

7. The custom placement of the origin used with the Precise Input tool is only set as long as the entity that was being sketched at the time is active.
   a. True
   b. False

8. Which of the following statements are true regarding dynamic input and dimensioning when creating sketched entities? (Select all that apply.)
   a. Dynamic input is available for all sketched entity types.
   b. When dynamically entering the first dimension value (the locating dimension value) for an entity, the coordinate entry is always measured from (0,0,0).
   c. By default, values entered in a dynamic input field automatically display as dimensions in the sketch.
   d. Dynamic input cannot be disabled for sketched entities.

Command Summary

Button	Command	Location
	**Import** (into model)	• **Ribbon:** *Manage* tab>*Insert* panel
	**Insert ACAD File** (into sketch)	• **Ribbon:** *Sketch* tab>*Insert* panel
	**Offset**	• **Ribbon:** *Sketch* tab>*Modify* panel
	**Precise Input**	• **Ribbon:** *Sketch* tab>expand *Create* panel
	**Project Cut Edges**	• **Ribbon:** *Sketch* tab>*Create* panel, expanded *Project Geometry* drop-down list
	**Project Geometry**	• **Ribbon:** *Sketch* tab>*Create* panel • **Context Menu:** In the graphics window
N/A	**Share Sketch**	• **Context Menu**: In Model browser with sketch selected
	**Slice Graphics**	• **Status Bar** • **Context Menu:** In the graphics window

Chapter

6

Creating Pick and Place Features

Chamfers, fillets, and holes are known as pick and place features. This means that the shape of the feature is implied; therefore, you are not required to sketch the section. Pick and place features can be added once the model's base feature has been created.

Learning Objectives

- Create a chamfer by defining its dimension scheme and placement references.
- Create constant and variable fillets by defining placement references, dimensions, and shape settings.
- Create a face fillet between faces that do not share an edge.
- Create a full round fillet between three adjacent faces.
- Create a hole by defining its type, placement reference, dimensions, and depth options.
- Create a thread on a cylindrical face.
- Use the editing options available for Pick and Place features to show dimensions, edit a sketch, and edit a feature.

6.1 Edge Chamfers

A chamfer adds a beveled edge between two adjacent surfaces, as shown in Figure 6–1. An edge chamfer can add or remove material.

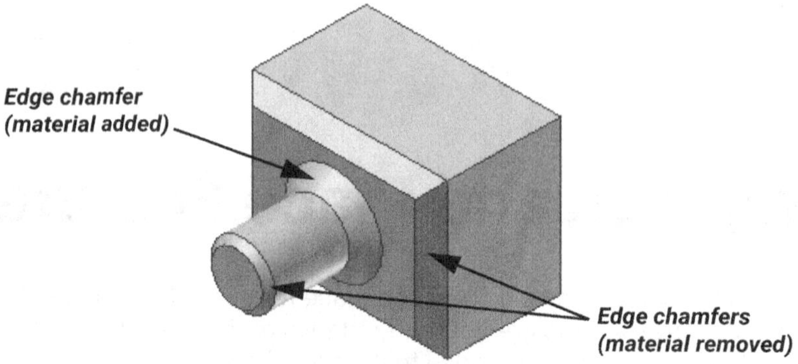

Figure 6–1

Use the following general steps to create an edge chamfer along the entire length of an edge:

1. Start the creation of the feature.
2. Define the dimensioning scheme.
3. Select the placement references and enter distances.
4. Select additional options, as required.
5. Select references to create a partial chamfer, as required.
6. Complete the feature.

Step 1 - Start the creation of the feature.

Use one of the following methods to create an edge chamfer:

- Select the edge(s) to be chamfered and click in the heads-up display on the model.
- In the *3D Model* tab>*Modify* panel, click (Chamfer) to start the creation of an edge chamfer.

Once the command is selected, the *Chamfer* dialog box opens. By default, the display of the mini-toolbar is toggled off. On the *View* tab, expand **User Interface** and enable the **Mini-Toolbar** option to display it. To collapse the dialog box, click the up arrow at the bottom of the dialog box.

Step 2 - Define the dimensioning scheme.

Edge chamfers have three alternative dimension types that can be used. Select the type from the lists shown in Figure 6–2. Changing dimension types clears the reference edge selection. It is recommended that you define the dimension type before selecting a placement reference.

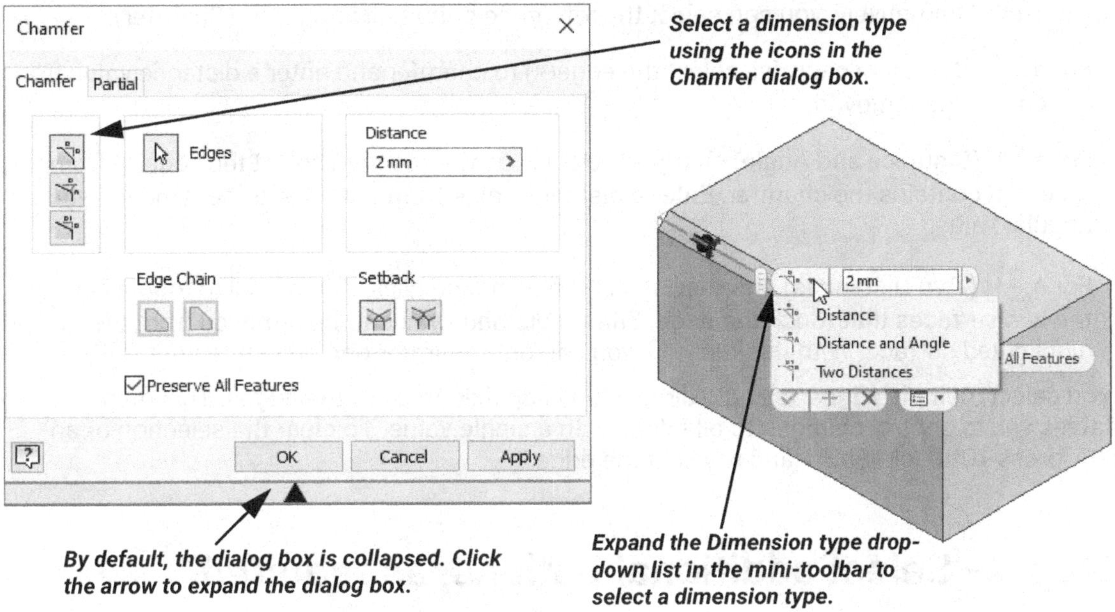

Figure 6–2

The dimension types are as follows:

(Distance)	The chamfer is created at the same distance from the edge on each face.	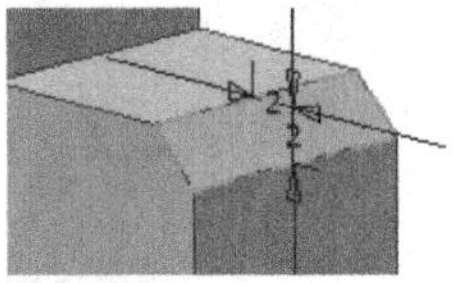
(Distance and Angle)	The chamfer is created at a distance from the edge on one face and at an angle to that face.	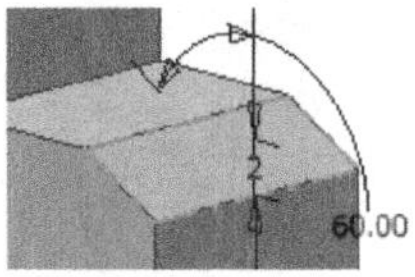
(Two Distances)	The chamfer is created at one distance from the edge of one face and a different distance from the edge of another.	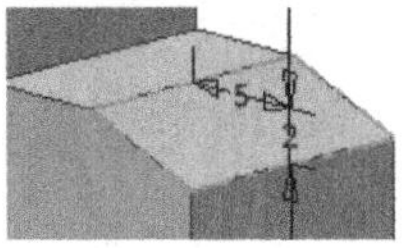

Step 3 - Select the placement references and enter distances.

The references and dimensions required to locate a chamfer depend on the dimension type that is used. Alternatively, you can select the reference before clicking (Chamfer).

- For a (Distance) chamfer, select the edge(s) to chamfer and enter a distance value from the edge to be removed.
- For a (Distance and Angle) chamfer, select the face and then select the edge(s) from the face that contains the chamfer. Enter a distance value from the edge to be removed and an angular value.
- For a (Two Distances) chamfer, select the edge and click or to toggle between the two surfaces that touch the edge. Enter a distance value to be removed from the highlighted surface. With this method, you can only chamfer one edge at a time.

If you select multiple edges, a single dimension is applied to all of the edges. This method enables you to control changes to all edges with a single value. To clear the selection of an edge, press <Ctrl> or <Shift> and reselect the edge.

Step 4 - Select additional options, as required.

Additional options (shown in Figure 6–3) enable you to further define the edges of the chamfer.

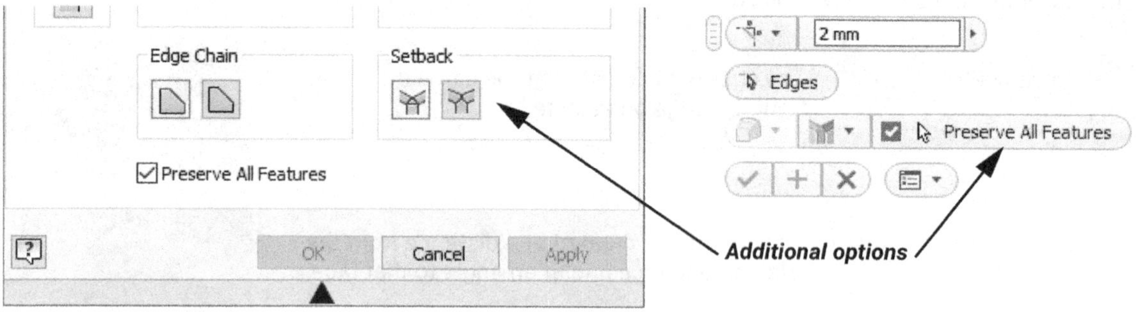

Figure 6–3

Note: *To toggle between the fields in the mini-toolbar, press <Tab> or select the field to activate it.*

The additional options are as follows:

- The **Edge Chain** options determine how edges with curves are selected.
  - Click (All tangentially connected edges) to select all of the tangent edges.
  - Click (Single edge) to select each edge individually.
  - In the mini-toolbar, the options are available as shown in Figure 6–4.

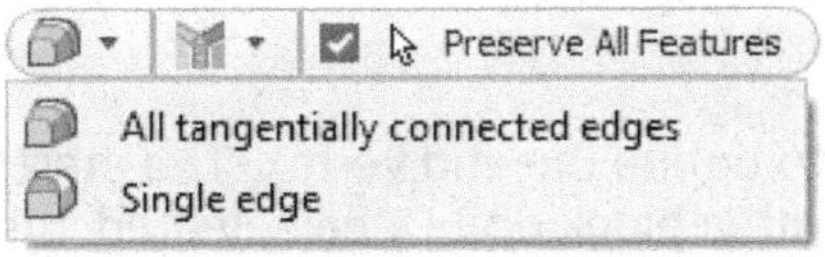

Figure 6–4

- Setback options control how chamfers meet at corners and are only available when using (Distance) chamfer type. The setback options are shown in Figure 6–5.

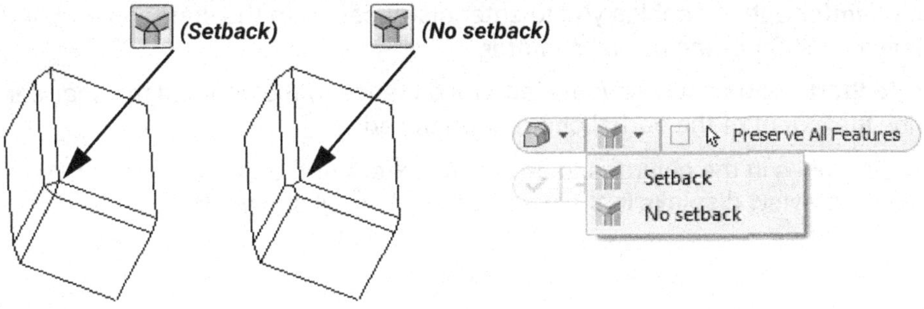

Figure 6–5

- The **Preserve All Features** option retains the existing features affected by the chamfer (e.g., a hole near the chamfered edge).

Step 5 - Select references to create a partial chamfer, as required.

To create a chamfer that does not fully extend the length of a selected reference edge, you can use the options on the *Partial* tab of the *Chamfer* dialog box. A partial chamfer cannot be defined using the mini-toolbar options. To define a partial chamfer on a selected reference, complete the following:

1. Select the *Partial* tab.
2. Select a point on the edge to define the end vertex. The start point is automatically set on the edge and is identified with a black dot. Once selected, the partial chamfer previews in the model and values populate in the dialog box.
3. The *Set Driven Dimension* option is set to **To End** by default. This sets the *To End* field as driven and prevents you from editing it. All changes to the size of the chamfer are made using the *To Start* and *Chamfer* fields. To adjust which fields are modifiable, you can change the option in the *Set Driven Dimension* option to **To Start** or **Chamfer**.
    - The **Chamfer** option enables you to enter distances from the start and end of the line to define the extent of the partial chamfer.
    - The **To Start** option enables you to enter a distance to the end and the chamfer length to define the extent of the partial chamfer on the edge.
4. Modify the values in the columns to define the extent of the partial chamfer. As changes are made, a preview displays in the graphics window, as shown in Figure 6–6.

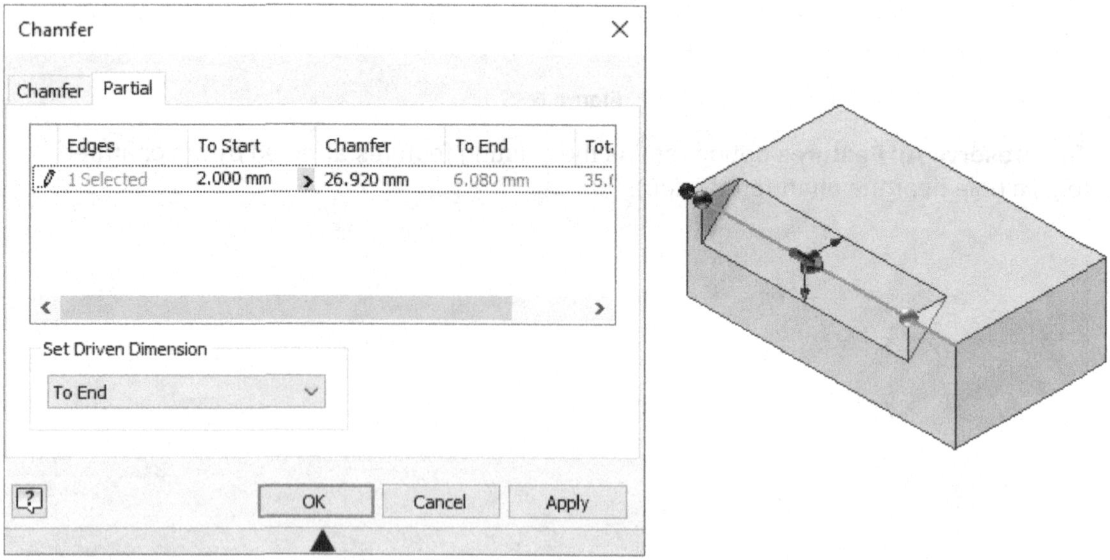

Figure 6–6

Step 6 - Complete the feature.

Once the edge chamfer is defined, you can complete the feature using any of the following options:

- Click  in the mini-toolbar.
- Right-click in the graphics window and select **OK (Enter)**.
- Click **OK** in the *Chamfer* dialog box.
- Press <Enter>.
- Click **Apply** to add the chamfer and remain in the dialog box to continue adding additional chamfers.

The Chamfer feature is identified with the  icon in the Model browser once created. If the  icon displays in the mini-toolbar, it indicates that the chamfer cannot be created.

6.2 Constant Fillets

Fillets can add or remove material, as shown in Figure 6–7. A constant edge fillet has a constant radius along its entire reference edge.

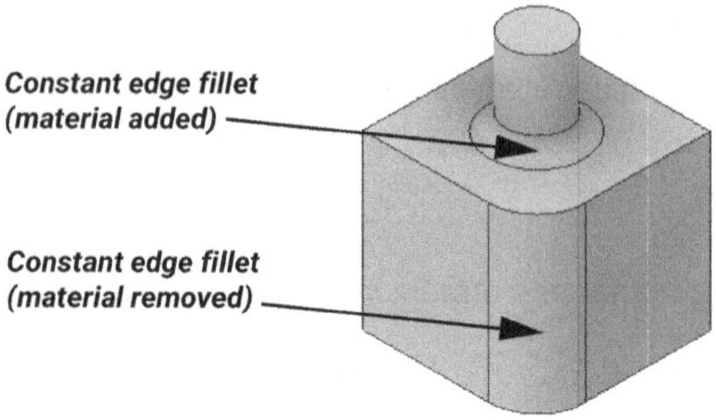

Figure 6–7

Use the following general steps to create a constant fillet:

1. Start the creation of the feature.
2. Select placement references.
3. Define the fillet size and shape.
4. Define the setbacks, as required.
5. Complete the feature.

Step 1 - Start the creation of the feature.

Use one of the following methods to create a fillet:

- Select the edge(s) to be filleted and click  in the heads-up display on the model.
- In the *3D Model* tab>*Modify* panel, click  (Fillet).
- Right-click anywhere in the graphics window and select **Fillet**.

Once the **Fillet** command is selected, the *Properties* panel and the tool palette open, as shown in Figure 6–8. The *Properties* panel enables you to define the properties and values for the fillet and the tool palette enables you to define the type of fillet and the reference selection priority.

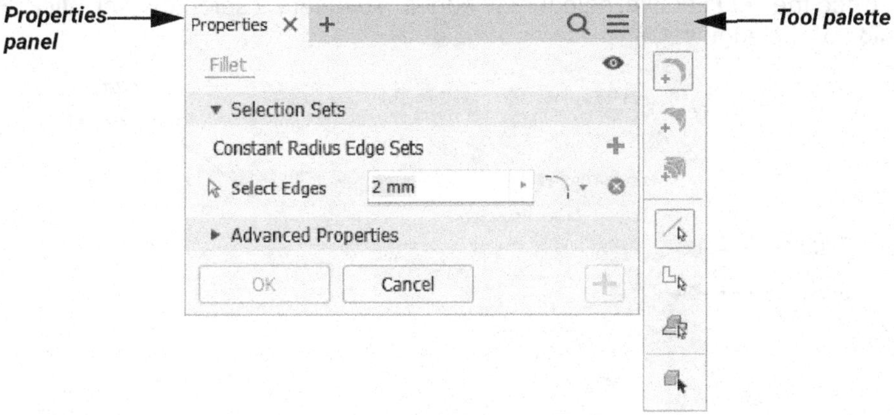

Figure 6–8

Step 2 - Select placement references.

On the tool palette, enable the required reference selection priority. This determines the type of entity that is to be selected as the placement reference for the fillet. The options are as follows:

	Selects one edge at a time. To select multiple edges to fillet, select each one independently.
	Selects all of the edges on a selected face.
	Selects all of the edges on a selected feature.
	Selects all of the edges on a selected solid body.

Based on the selection priority that is set, select edges, faces, or features to fillet them. If the  option is selected and there is only one solid body in the model, all edges are automatically selected.

Note: *To clear the selection of an edge, hold <Ctrl> or <Shift> and reselect the edge.*

By default, all selected edges are included in one set and are controlled by a single radius value. To add edges with unique radius values in the same feature, you must add additional sets. To add a set, select + (Add constant radius edge set) in the *Properties* panel, as shown in Figure 6–9. Once the set is active, select new edges. To delete a selection set, click ⊗ on the right-hand side of the edge set.

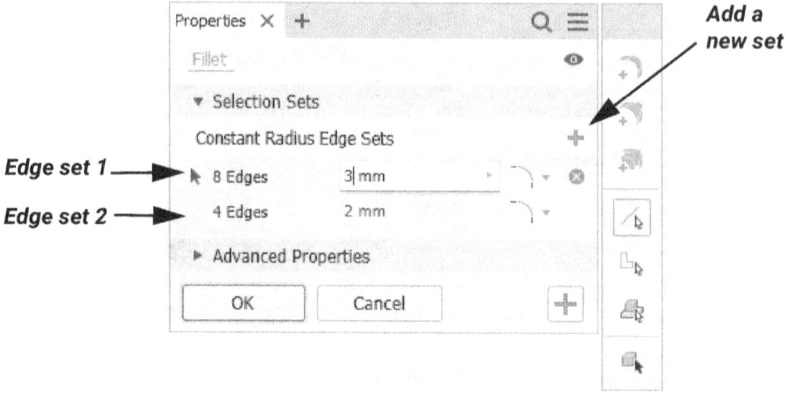

Figure 6–9

Step 3 - Define the fillet size and shape.

By default, the radius value that was last set during fillet creation is used as the default value. To modify the radius of the fillet, enter the new value in the on-screen entry field or in the *Properties* panel, as shown in Figure 6–10. As an alternative, you can also select and drag the radius handle that displays on the model to resize the fillet.

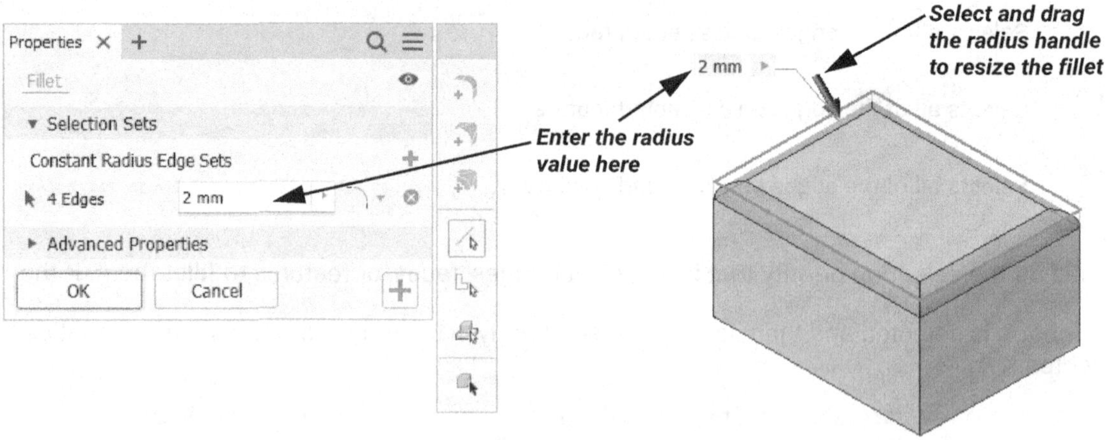

Figure 6–10

Continuity

Edge fillets can use one of three continuity options to further define the shape of the fillet geometry. The available options are shown in Figure 6–11.

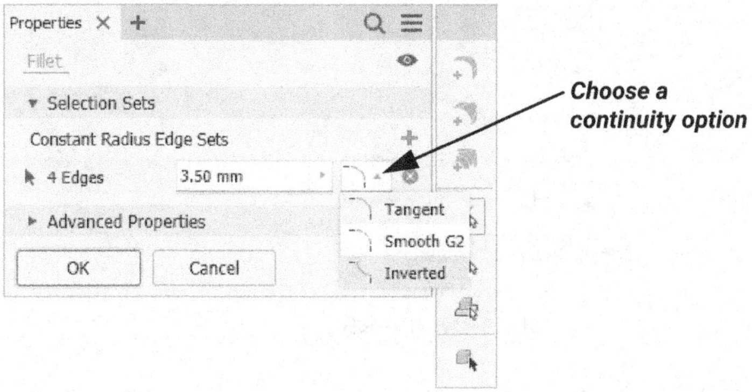

Figure 6–11

The continuity options are described as follows and are shown in Figure 6–12. Once the reference geometry is selected, you can assign a continuity option for each selection set.

- The **Tangent** setting ensures that the transition between the fillet and adjacent surfaces is tangent.
- The **Smooth G2** setting ensures the transition between the fillet and the adjacent surfaces is tangent and has a common curvature.
- The **Inverted** setting ensures that the transition between the fillet and the adjacent surfaces is perpendicular. This produces both concave and convex edges.

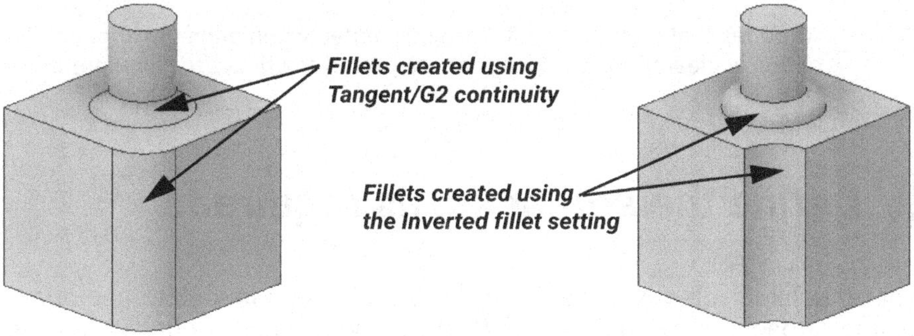

Figure 6–12

Additional Fillet Options

To display additional fillet options, expand the *Advanced Properties* area in the *Properties* panel, as shown in Figure 6–13.

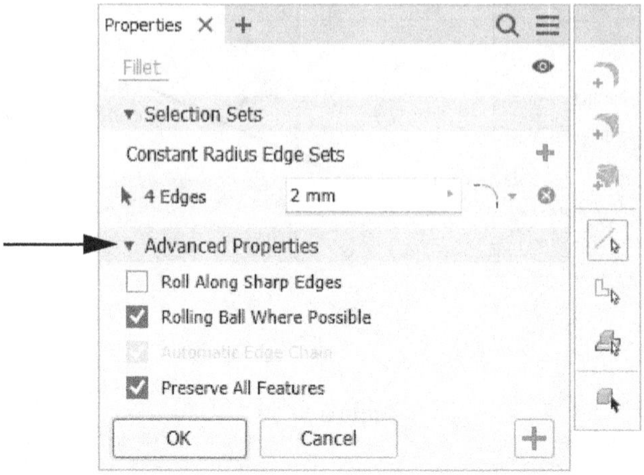

Figure 6–13

The options in the expanded area are as follows:

Roll Along Sharp Edges	Varies the radius of the fillet, if required, to preserve the edges of the adjacent faces.
Rolling Ball Where Possible	Sets the corner style for fillets. If selected, the shape of surfaces that contain adjacent edges to which fillets are applied is maintained. The corner is not rounded.
Automatic Edge Chain	Determines how edges that contain curves are selected. When selecting an edge, any edge that is tangent to it is also selected.
Preserve All Features	All edges that intersect a fillet are calculated when a fillet is applied. When this option is cleared, only edges that are part of the fillet are calculated.

Step 4 - Define the setbacks, as required.

When three or more fillets intersect, you can define tangent continuous transitions between them by enabling setbacks in the tool palette. Examples with and without setback distances are shown in Figure 6–14.

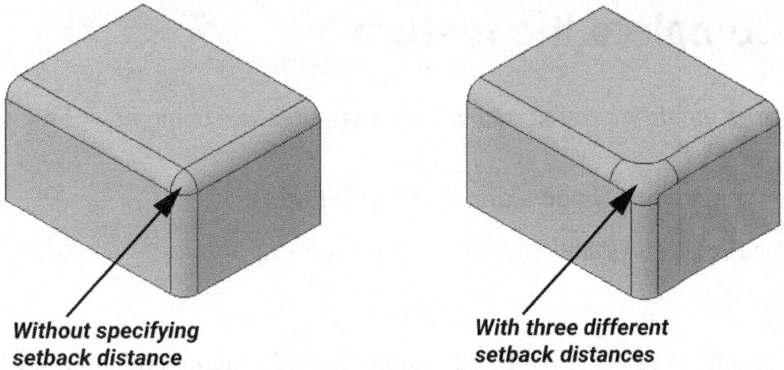

Figure 6–14

How To: Add a Setback

1. In the tool palette, click  (Add corner setback).
2. Select a vertex where the fillets intersect. Once selected, the intersecting edges are listed in the *Properties* panel, as shown in Figure 6–15.
3. In the *Properties* panel, enter setback values for each edge. The **Minimal** option enables you to define the setback values as the minimum allowable for that vertex.

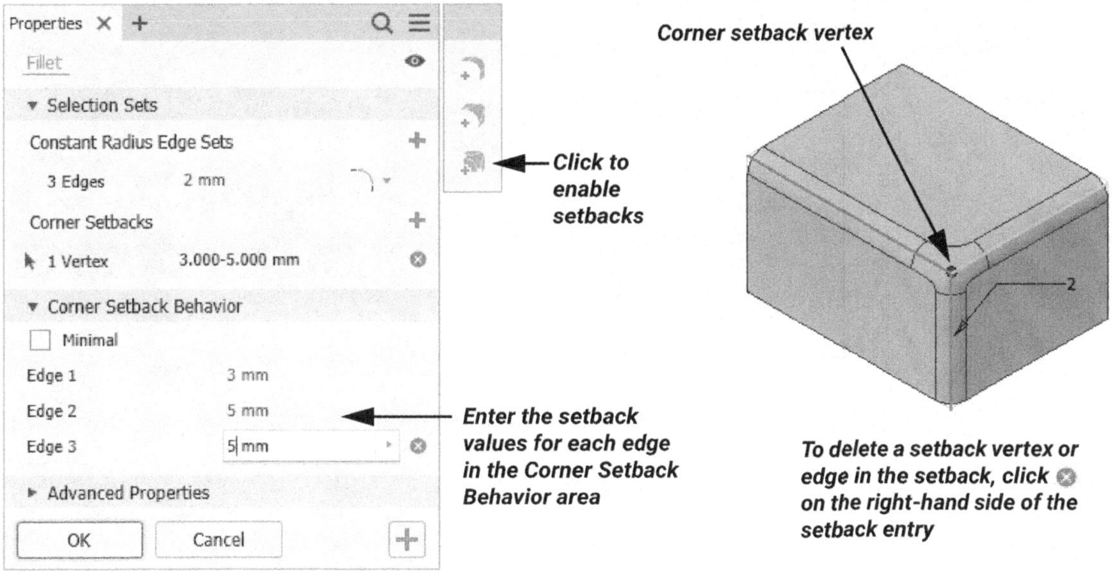

Figure 6–15

Step 5 - Complete the feature.

Once the references are defined, you can complete the feature using any of the following options:

- Right-click in the graphics window and select **OK (Enter)**.
- Click **OK** in the *Properties* panel.
- Press <Enter>.
- Click (Apply) to create the fillet and remain in the *Properties* panel to create another.

Once the fillet is created, the Model browser's fillet icon reveals whether the fillet was created as tangent ( ), smooth G2 ( ), or inverted ( ).

Hint: Constant Fillet Failures

The icon displays at the top of the *Properties* panel when the feature cannot be created. Click to open a window that attempts to describe why the fillet has failed. Click **Close** to return to the *Properties* panel to edit the fillet and resolve the failure.

6.3 Variable Fillets

A variable fillet's radius changes along the length of the edge. Radii values are applied to the ends of the edge and at intermediate points, if required. Each value can be independent. Two examples of variable fillets are shown in Figure 6–16.

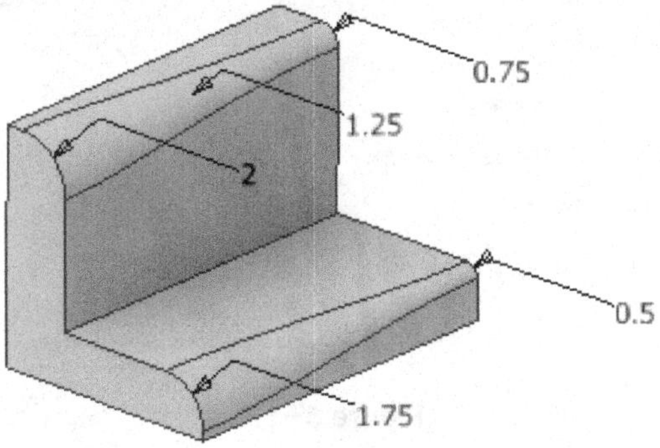

Figure 6–16

Use the following general steps to create a variable fillet:

1. Start the creation of the feature.
2. Select placement references.
3. Define the fillet size.
4. Define additional options, as required.
5. Complete the feature.

Step 1 - Start the creation of the feature.

Use one of the following methods to create a fillet:

- Select the edge(s) to be filleted and click  in the heads-up display on the model.
- In the *3D Model* tab>*Modify* panel, click  (Fillet).
- Right-click anywhere in the graphics window and select **Fillet**.

Once the **Fillet** command is selected, the *Properties* panel and the tool palette open. By default, constant fillet is the default option. In the tool palette, click (Add variable radius fillet) to define a variable fillet. The *Properties* panel and tool palette update as shown in Figure 6–17. The *Properties* panel enables you to define the properties and values for the variable fillet.

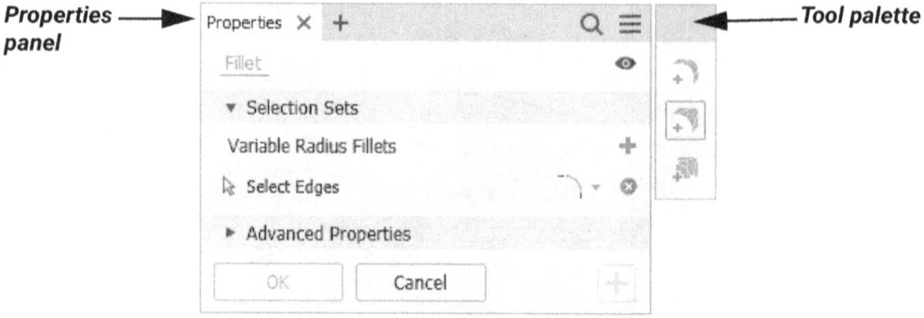

Figure 6–17

Step 2 - Select placement references.

Select an edge on the model to assign the variable fillet to. Only a linear or tangent edge can be selected for an individual fillet set. To clear the selection of an edge, hold <Ctrl> or <Shift> and reselect the edge.

To add other reference edges with unique radius values in the same feature, you must add additional sets. To add a set, select (Add variable radius fillet) adjacent to the *Variable Radius Fillets* area in the *Properties* panel, as shown in Figure 6–18. Once the set is active, select new edges. To delete a selection set, click on the right-hand side of the edge set.

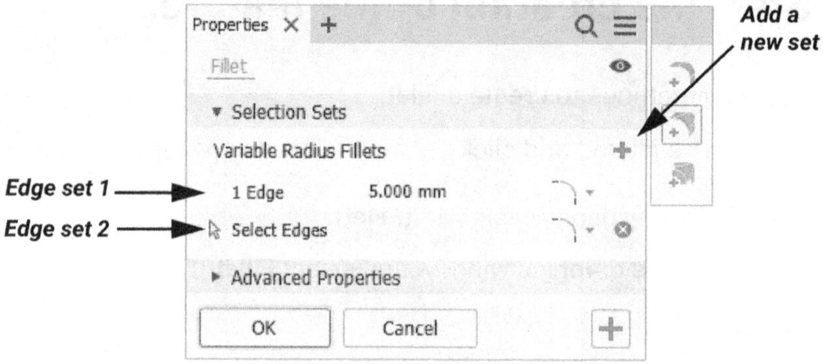

Figure 6–18

Step 3 - Define the fillet size.

By default, the radius value that was last set during fillet creation is used as the default value at both ends of the reference entity. To modify the radius values of the variable fillet, activate the required field (i.e., either end) and enter the new value in the on-screen entry field or in the *Properties* panel, as shown in Figure 6–19. As an alternative, you can also select and drag the radius handle that displays on the model to resize the fillet.

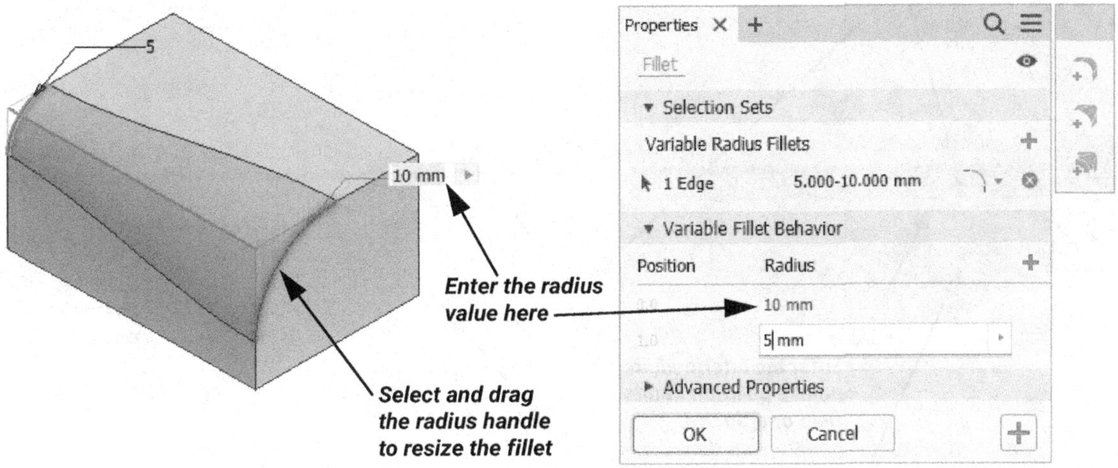

Figure 6–19

To vary the radius between the endpoints, you can add an intermediate point(s) using either of the following methods:

- In the *Properties* panel>*Variable Fillet Behavior* area, click +.
- In the graphics window, use your mouse and select a location on the edge that is being filleted.

If the intermediate point is added using the *Properties* panel, the point is automatically added at the midpoint of the edge (0.5 position). If you selected on the filleted edge, the point location is based on the selection location. Once the point is added, you can select the *Position* cell in the *Properties* panel or drag the point on the edge to modify its placement location. To modify the intermediate point's radius value, activate the radius handle or the *Radius* field in the *Properties* panel and modify it as needed. Figure 6–20 shows how an intermediate point was added, and where its position and radius can be modified.

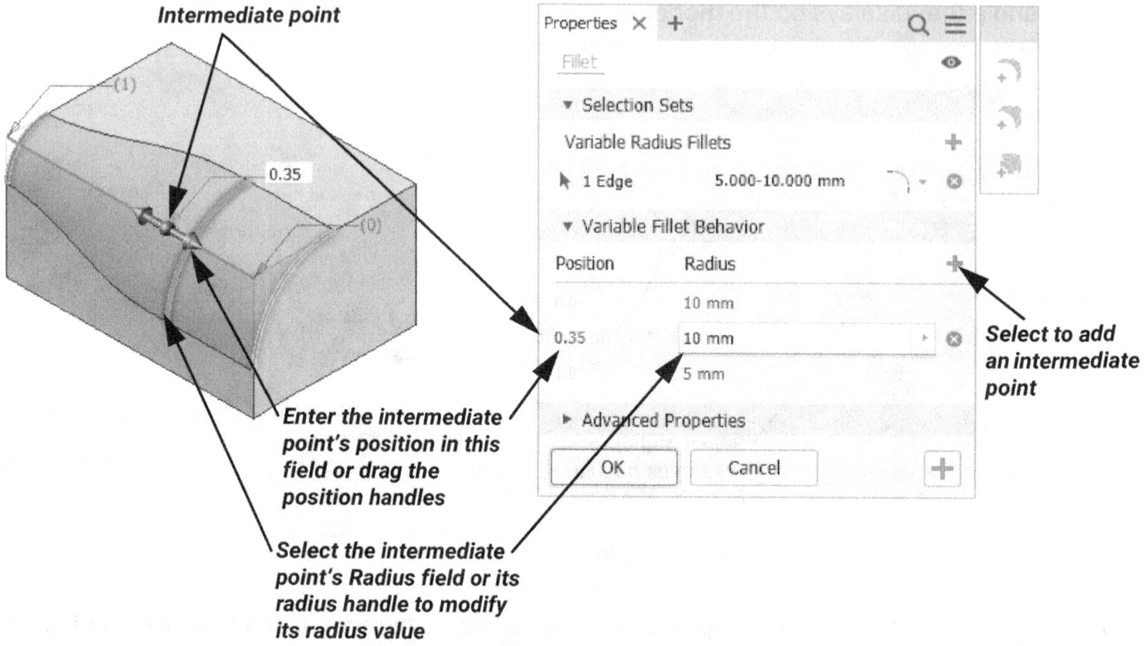

Figure 6–20

Step 4 - Define additional options, as required.

Consider using the following options to further control the variable fillet:

- Variable edge fillets are created with Tangent continuity by default. The continuity of a variable edge fillet can be changed to **Smooth G2**; however, unlike with constant edge fillets, you cannot invert a variable edge fillet. Defining continuity for a variable edge fillet is the same process as for a constant fillet, as shown in Figure 6–21.

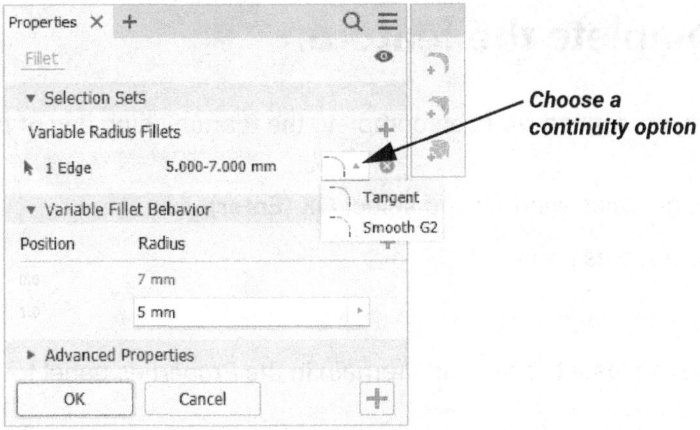

Figure 6–21

- Depending on how variable fillets and/or other fillets intersect, you may be able to define the setback for the intersecting vertex to customize the shape of the geometry. To add a corner setback, click  (Add corner setback) in the tool palette. Once active, you will be prompted to select the intersecting vertex. If a vertex is unavailable, it will be identified in the *Properties* panel.
- Similarly to creating a constant fillet, you can access the same additional options to control the fillet's shape by expanding the *Advanced Properties* area, as shown in Figure 6–22. For variable fillets, the **Smooth Radius Transition** option can also be set to define how the fillet transitions between points. When enabled, the transition between adjacent points is a complex curve. This produces a fillet surface that is tangent to its adjacent surfaces. When disabled, the transition between the points is a straight line and is not necessarily tangent to its adjacent surfaces.

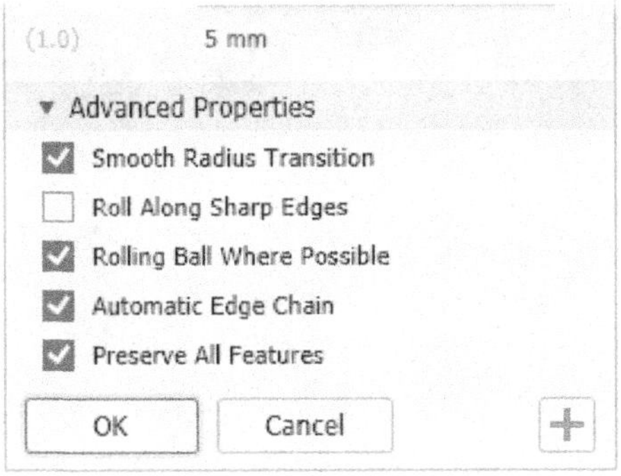

Figure 6–22

Step 5 - Complete the feature.

Once the references are defined, you can complete the feature using any of the following options:

- Right-click in the graphics window and select **OK (Enter)**.
- Click **OK** in the *Properties* panel.
- Press <Enter>.
- Click (Apply) to create the fillet and remain in the *Properties* panel to create another.

Once the fillet is created, the Model browser's fillet icon reveals whether the fillet was created as a tangent ( ) or smooth G2 ( ) variable fillet.

Hint: Variable Fillet Failures

The icon displays at the top of the *Properties* panel when the feature cannot be created. Click to open a window that attempts to describe why the fillet has failed. Click **Close** to return to the *Properties* panel to edit the fillet and resolve the failure.

6.4 Face Fillets

Use a face fillet when traditional edge-based filleting is not suitable for your geometry. It creates fillets between two sets of faces that do not share an edge. An example of a face fillet is shown in Figure 6–23.

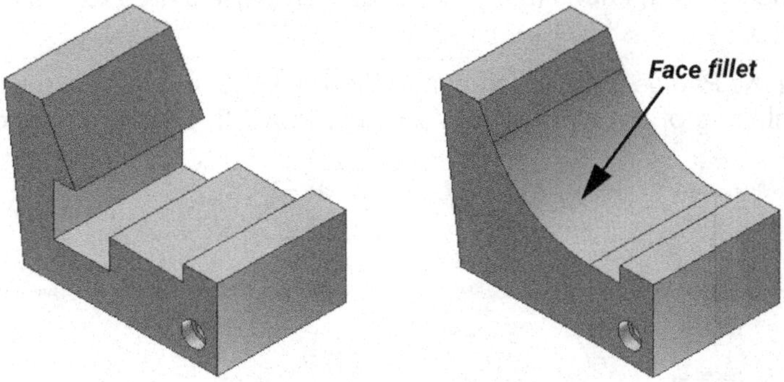

Figure 6–23

How To: Create a Face Fillet

1. In the *3D Model* tab>*Modify* panel, expand the **Fillet** command and click  (Face Fillet). The *Properties* panel opens, as shown in Figure 6–24. The *Properties* panel enables you to define the references and size for the face fillet. You cannot initiate the creation of a face fillet by preselecting the faces and then selecting the **Face Fillet** option.

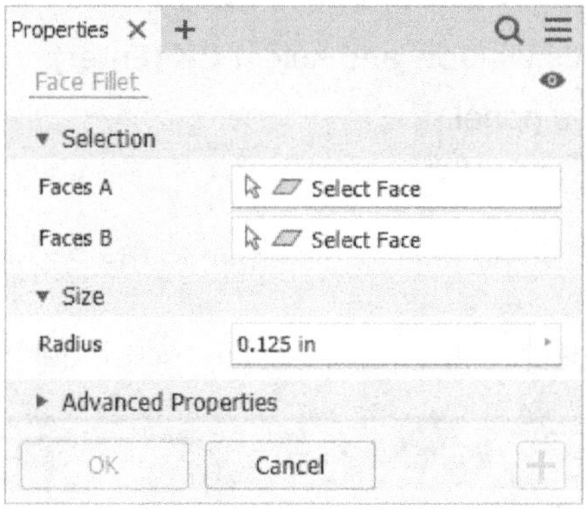

Figure 6–24

***Note:** The **Optimize for Single Selection** option in the Advanced Properties area enables a single selection before automatically prompting for the next reference. Clear this option to select more than one reference at a time.*

2. The *Faces A* field is active by default as soon as the Face Fillet is activated; if not, select it to activate it. Select a face in the model to include as the first face set.
3. Once the first reference face is selected, the *Faces B* field should be automatically activated; if not, then select it. Select a second face in the model to include as the second face set.
   - Select **Include Tangent Faces** in the *Advanced Properties* area to automatically fillet adjacent faces.
4. Enter a value in the *Radius* field, as shown in Figure 6–25. By default, a value appears that allows for the filleting of the two faces. You can modify this value as needed.

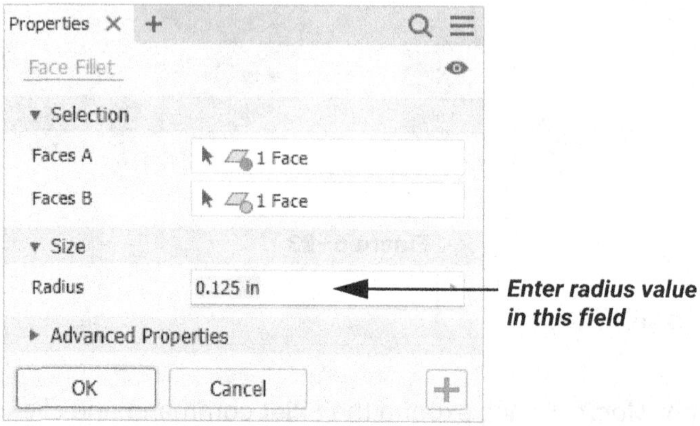

Figure 6–25

5. Once the references are defined, you can complete the feature using any of the following options:
   - Right-click in the graphics window and select **OK (Enter)**.
   - Click **OK** in the *Properties* panel.
   - Press <Enter>.
   - Click (Apply) to create the fillet and remain in the *Properties* panel to create another.

The **Face Fillet** feature is identified with the icon in the Model browser once created.

Hint: Face Fillet Failures

Face fillets fail if the radius value is not large enough to span between the faces, or if the specified radius is so large that it extends beyond the two faces. The icon displays at the top of the *Properties* panel when the feature cannot be created. Click to open a window that attempts to describe why the fillet has failed. Click **Close** to return to the *Properties* panel to edit the fillet and resolve the failure.

6.5 Full Round Fillets

Full round fillets can be used for rounding ribs and other geometry that might be difficult or impossible to fillet using edge-based fillets. A full round fillet enables you to create a constant or variable radius fillet between three adjacent faces. The radius value for the fillet is not modifiable. An example of a full round fillet is shown in Figure 6–26.

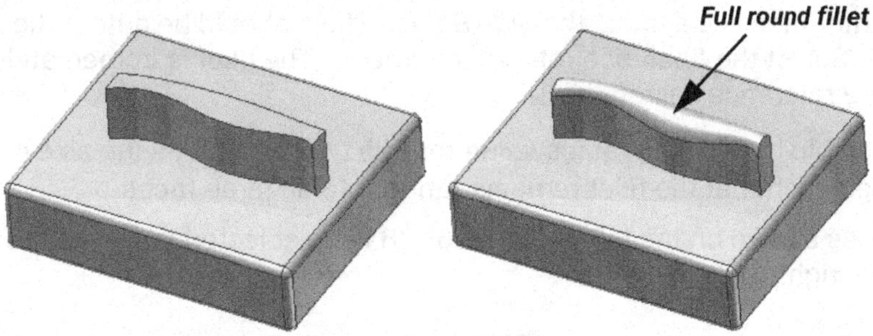

Figure 6–26

How To: Create a Full Round Fillet

1. In the *3D Model* tab>*Modify* panel, expand the **Fillet** command and click (Full Round Fillet). The *Properties* panel opens, as shown in Figure 6–27. The *Properties* panel enables you to define the references for the full round fillet. You cannot initiate the creation of a full round fillet by preselecting the faces and then selecting the **Full Round Fillet** option.

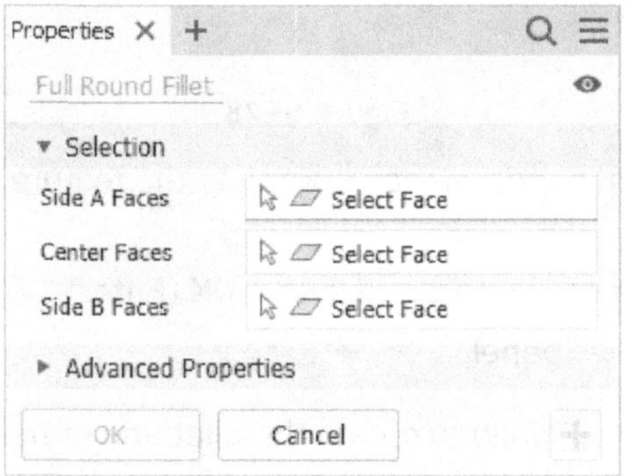

Figure 6–27

Note: The ***Optimize for Single Selection*** *option in the Advanced Properties area enables a single selection before automatically prompting for the next reference. Clear this option to select more than one reference at a time.*

2. The *Side A Faces* field is active by default as soon as the Full Round Fillet is activated; if not, select it to activate it. Select a face in the model to include as the first face set.
3. Once the first reference face is selected, the *Center Faces* field should be automatically activated; if not, select it. Select the face that lies between the selected side A face and the face that will be selected as the side B reference.
   - The faces are not required to be adjacent.
4. Once the center face is selected, the *Side B Faces* field should be automatically activated; if not, select it. Select the final face reference (side B). The fillet is immediately created to fillet the three reference selections.
   - You are unable to assign a radius value for this type of fillet as the size of the fillet is determined such that the fillet remains tangent to all three faces.

   The references shown on the left in Figure 6–28 were selected to create the full round fillet shown on the right.

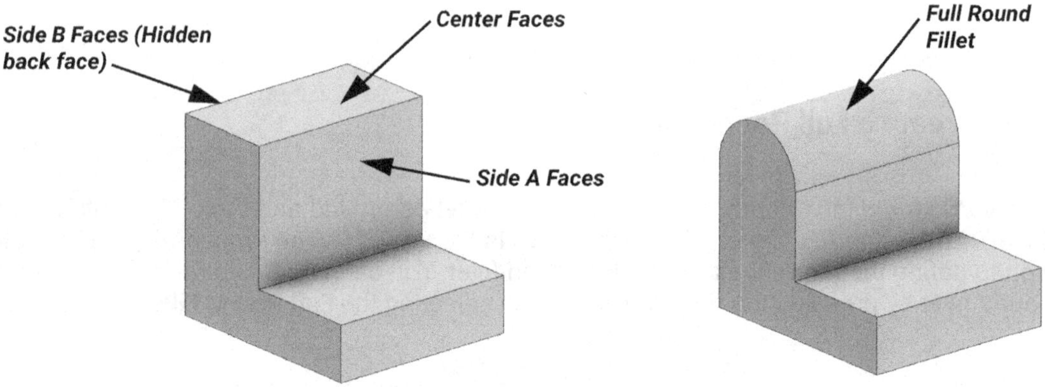

Figure 6–28

5. Once the references are defined, you can complete the feature using any of the following options:
   - Right-click in the graphics window and select **OK (Enter)**.
   - Click **OK** in the *Properties* panel.
   - Press <Enter>.Click (Apply) to create the fillet and remain in the *Properties* panel to create another.

The **Full Round Fillet** feature is identified with the icon in the Model browser once created.

6.6 Holes

Holes remove material from the model. Using the hole creation options that are available in the *Properties* panel, you can define multiple types of holes (as shown in Figure 6–29) that start and terminate in different configurations.

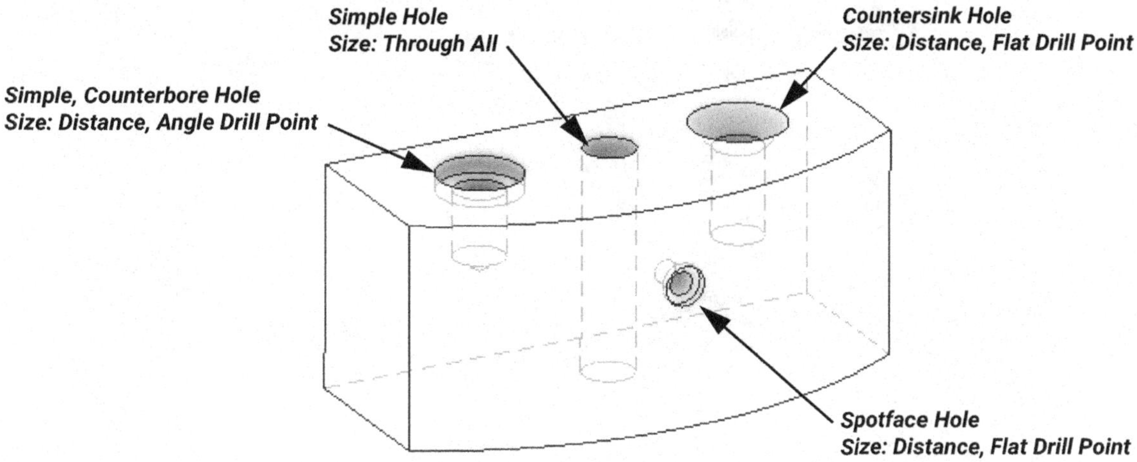

Figure 6–29

Use the following general steps to create a simple hole:

1. Start the creation of the feature.
2. Define the placement location for the hole.
3. Fully locate the hole on the placement plane.
4. Define the type of hole.
5. Define the size of the hole.
6. Complete the feature.

Step 1 - Start the creation of the feature.

The following methods can be used to create a new hole in a model:

- In the *3D Model* tab>*Modify* panel, click  (Hole).
- Right-click anywhere in the graphics window and select **Hole**.
- Preselect a sketched point and click  in the heads-up display on the model.

The *Properties* panel opens, similar to that shown in Figure 6–30.

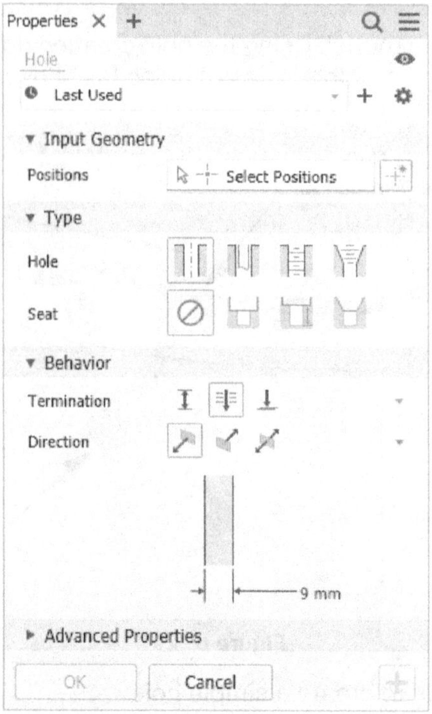

Figure 6–30

Note: *By default,* ***Last used*** *is set as the hole preset at the top of the Properties panel. This presets all of the hole options to those that were used in the last hole operation. Creating unique hole presets are discussed later in the section.*

Step 2 - Define the placement location for the hole.

To locate the hole you must select a placement reference on which to locate the hole. Placement references can include the following:

- Sketch Points
- Faces
- Work Points

When selecting a placement location, you can use the **Allow Center Point Creation** option that is adjacent to the *Positions* field to control the type of reference that can be selected to locate a hole. Consider the following:

- When the **Allow Center Point Creation** option is OFF, its icon appears as in the *Properties* panel and only sketch geometry (i.e., points) or workpoints can be selected.
- When the **Allow Center Point Creation** option is ON, its icon appears as in the *Properties* panel and sketch geometry (i.e., points) or workpoints and faces can be selected.

Hole Placement on Sketched Points

If a single sketch is visible (and not consumed) and contains any sketched points, all of its points are automatically preselected as hole placement references. If two sketches are visible, no preselections are made by Inventor. Holes located based on the selection of a sketch point are extended perpendicularly from the face/sketch plane. References are listed in the *Input Geometry* area of the *Properties* panel, as shown on the left in Figure 6–31.

Hole Placement on a Face

To place a hole on a planar face, the (Allow Center Point Creation option ON) must be enabled in the *Properties* panel. Once on, select a hole placement location on a face using the left mouse button. A center point is added to the face and a preview of the hole displays. Holes located based on the selection of a face are extended perpendicular to the face. References are listed in the *Input Geometry* area of the *Properties* panel, as shown on the left in Figure 6–31.

Hole Placement on a Work Point

To place a hole on a work point, select it directly in the graphics window. Holes located using a work point require that an orientation reference also be selected. References are listed in the *Input Geometry* area of the *Properties* panel, as shown on the right in Figure 6–31.

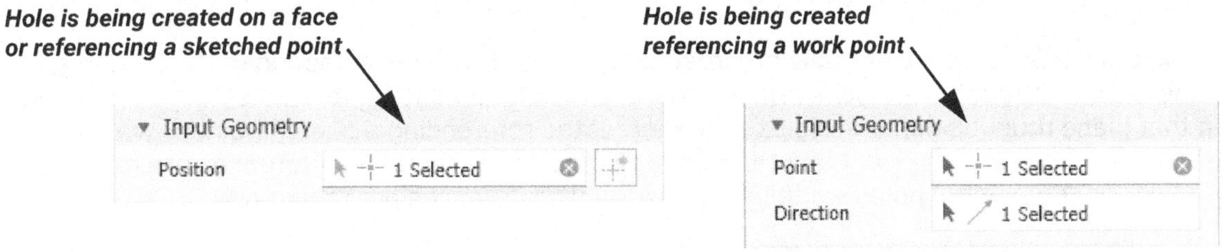

Figure 6–31

Note: *To clear a hole placement selection, you can either click adjacent to the field or press and hold <Ctrl> and select the point on the model to clear its selection.*

Hint: Sketch Creation

Consider the following:

- When you select a planar face for hole placement, a sketch is immediately created and listed at the top of the *Properties* panel, as shown in Figure 6–32. In Step 3, you will learn how to access the sketch to fully locate the hole.

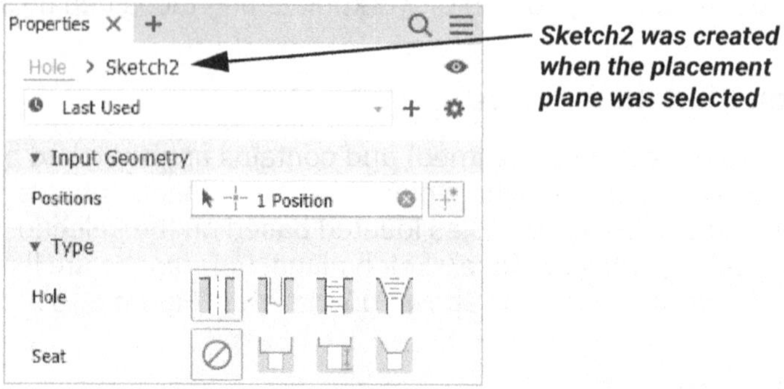

Figure 6–32

- If a sketch point is selected for hole placement, its sketch is listed at the top of the *Properties* panel. If a hole is added and subsequently removed, the center point remains in the sketch unless deleted in the Sketch environment.
- If a work point is selected for hole placement, no sketch is created because the work point alone fully defines its location in the model.

Step 3 - Fully locate the hole on the placement plane.

A hole placed on a face is not fully parametrically located with the selection of the placement plane alone. Although the hole is previewed once the placement plane is selected, its location on that plane must be defined. Holes that are created referencing a sketch point or work point are located based on the location of the points so no further location references are required. For linear or concentric holes, additional placements references are required.

Linear Placement

To fully locate a hole, you must constrain the center of the hole in two directions on its placement face. This can be done using different methods:

- In the graphics window, select the first linear edge and then select the second. Dimensions are created between each selected reference and the hole's center point, as shown in Figure 6–33. You can select on each entry field to activate it and modify the dimension value.

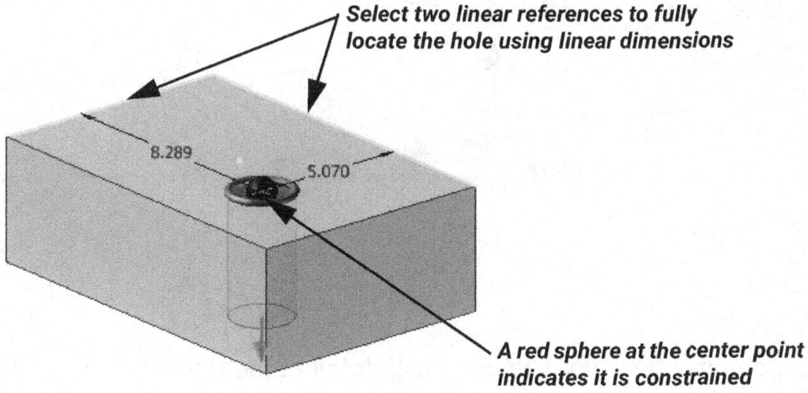

Figure 6–33

- In the graphics window, select and drag the center point of the hole so that it is coincident with the projected (fully constrained) origin point. A green circle displays when it snaps to the origin. Once you release the mouse button, a red sphere displays indicating the point is fully constrained. Figure 6–34 shows examples of how the center point can be constrained to the projected origin.

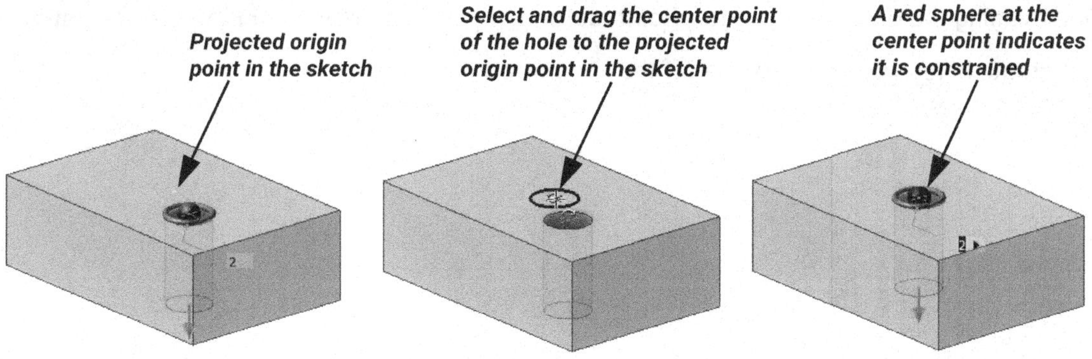

Figure 6–34

- In the header of the *Properties* panel, click **Sketch#** to open the hole's sketch, which provides access to the familiar Sketch ribbon, as shown in Figure 6–35. You can use all of the standard sketch tools to fully dimension and constrain the center point of the hole.

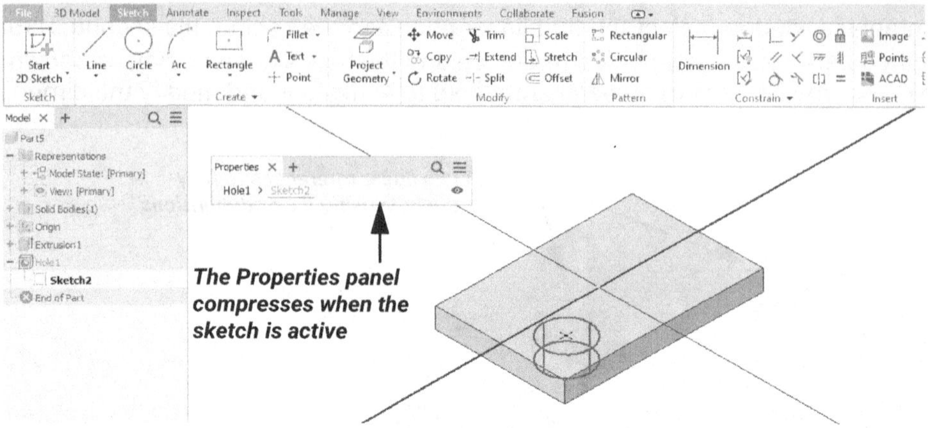

Figure 6–35

Once the center point has been constrained, click **Hole#** at the top of the *Properties* panel or click (Return to Hole) in the Sketch ribbon to reactivate the hole. If you select **Finish Sketch**, the hole is completed and placed based on the settings that were previously set in the *Properties* panel.

Hint: Point Creation in a Hole's Sketch

During hole creation (with the sketch active), additional holes are added if you place new points using the default (Center Point) setting. If you require points in the sketch that do not create holes, you must toggle off the button in the *Format* panel.

Concentric Placement

To locate a hole concentrically once it is placed on a plane, hover the cursor over the outside cylindrical face. Once the symbol displays adjacent to the cursor (as shown in Figure 6–36), select the face. This assigns the hole as a concentric hole to the selected face. Once the hole is constrained concentrically, a red sphere displays on the center point of the hole indicating it is fully constrained.

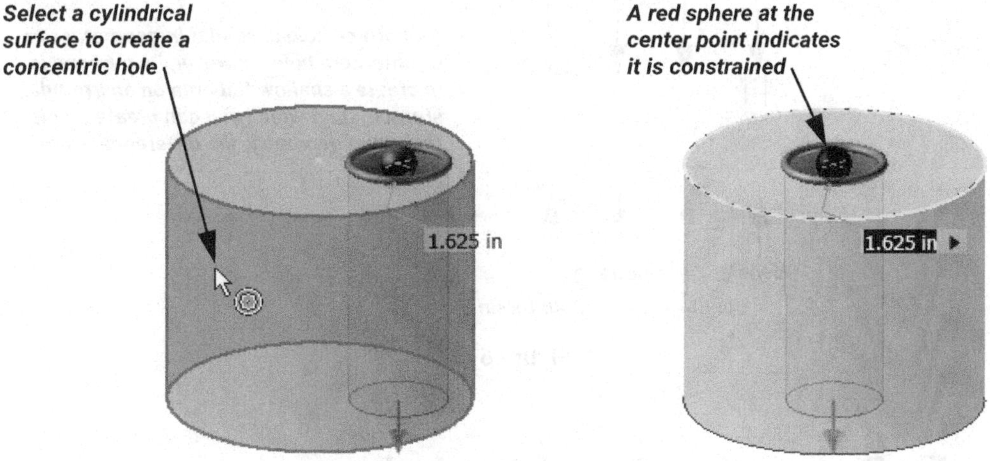

Figure 6–36

A sketch is created whenever a hole is placed on a plane. For a concentric hole, this sketch is still created; however, you are not required to access it unless you wanted to break the concentric alignment.

Hint: Fully Locating a Hole

A hole can be completed without its center point being parametrically constrained. This is not recommended! You should ensure that the center point is parametrically placed in such a way that it defines the hole's intent. To ensure it is fully located on its placement plane, confirm that a red sphere displays on the center point prior to completing the hole. Alternatively, hover the cursor over the center point and review the cursor symbol that displays. If the symbol displays adjacent to the cursor, it indicates the center point can be dragged and is therefore not constrained.

Step 4 - Define the type of hole.

The options available in the *Type* area enable you to define the hole. Its options are divided into how the hole is created and the type of seating that is to be assigned, as shown in Figure 6–37.

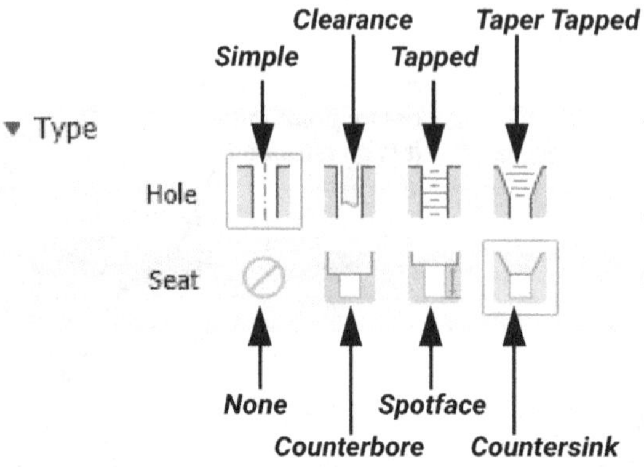

A Spotface hole is similar in geometry to a Counterbore hole, However, its purpose is to create a shallow flat area on an irregular surface, from which you can create a hole. On planar geometry, the difference is not obvious.

Figure 6–37

Step 5 - Define the size of the hole.

The options available in the *Behavior* area define how the hole is terminated, its direction, and the drill point type at the bottom of the hole, as shown in Figure 6–38.

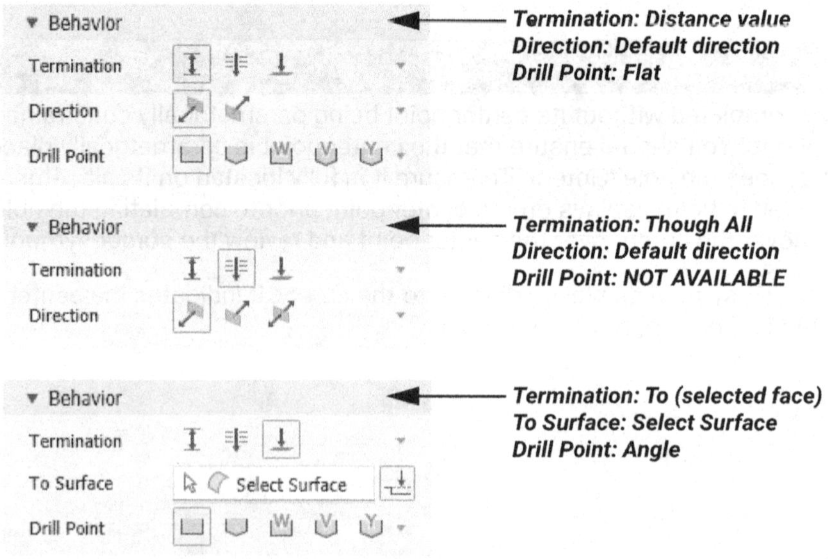

Figure 6–38

The termination options are as follows:

Distance ( )	Creates a blind hole of a specified depth. Using the direction buttons you can define the direction of the hole.
Through All ( )	Creates a hole through the entire model. Using the direction buttons you can define the direction of the hole. For drilled simple holes, the direction can also be defined as symmetric.
To ( )	Creates a blind hole that terminates at a selected plane or at the extension of the selected plane. Toggle the (Terminate feature by extending the face ON) option when the selected termination plane does not completely intersect the hole.

Hint: Extend Start

You can enable the **Extend Start** option in the *Advanced Properties* area to extend the start plane to remove fragments, similar to the example shown in Figure 6–39. In this example, a hole and a fillet are intersecting and you can remove the material on the fillet using the **Extend Start** option. This option is only available to extend the start face in a single body.

Extend Start disabled ***Extend Start enabled***

Figure 6–39

Hole size values can edited in the *Behavior* area by selecting and activating each dimension field and entering a value. The values can also be modified in the graphics window. To switch between fields, select the fields in the *Properties* panel or the graphics window, or select the gold rings and arrows that display on the model. Figure 6–40 shows two examples of holes.

Simple None-Seated Hole

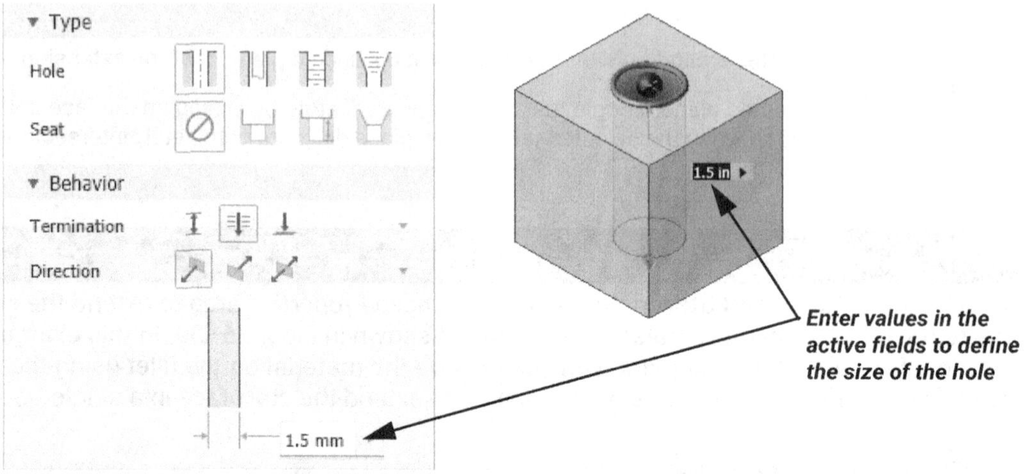

Simple Counterbore Hole

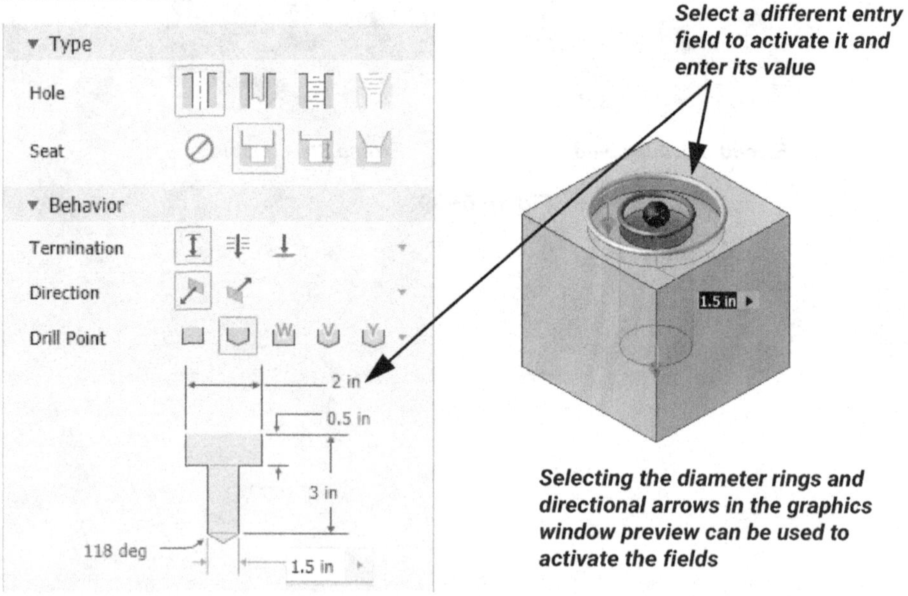

Figure 6–40

Step 6 - Complete the feature.

Once the hole is defined, you can complete the feature using any of the following options:

- Right-click in the graphics window and select **OK (Enter)**.
- Click **OK** in the *Properties* panel.
- Press <Enter>.
- Click (Apply) to create the hole and remain in the *Properties* panel to create another.

The **Hole** feature is identified with the icon in the Model browser once created.

Placing Multiple Holes

When the *Properties* panel is active, you can continue to place new center points to define multiple holes in the one Hole feature. All holes created in this way have the same settings and sizes. For unique settings, you must create a new hole feature.

Hole Presets

The **Hole** feature enables you to create and save unique and commonly used hole presets. By default, the preset list at the top of the *Properties* panel indicates that the **Last used** preset is active. This means that all of the settings that were used to create the last hole will be used for the creation of the new hole.

To create a custom preset, set the hole options in the *Type* and *Behavior* areas and click (Create new preset) adjacent to the preset list, as shown in Figure 6–41. The preset is created with a system-defined name and you can immediately enter a new descriptive name.

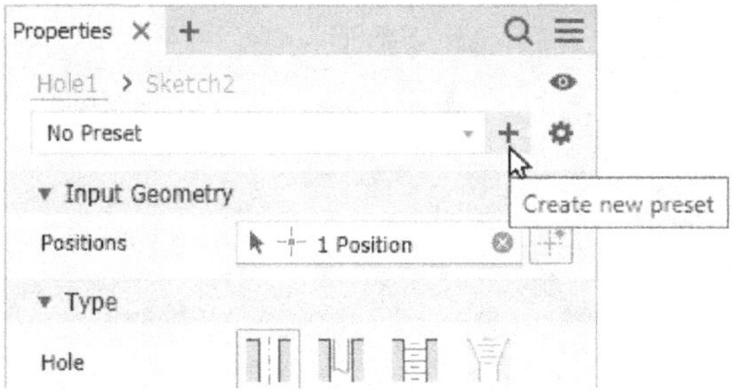

Figure 6–41

To use a saved preset, simply select it once the Hole feature has been activated, as shown in Figure 6–42. The hole is created using all the options that were saved when the preset was created.

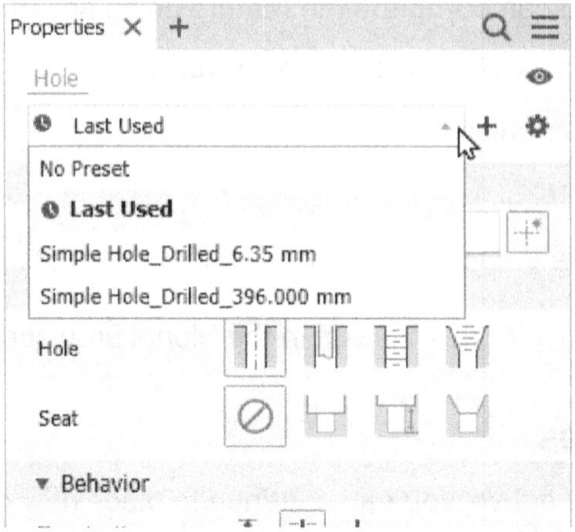

Figure 6–42

The preset settings are available by selecting (Preset Settings) adjacent to the preset list, as shown in Figure 6–43. These options enable you to save changes to a preset, rename a preset, and delete a preset. Additionally, you can customize the sort order for the preset list and define whether a new hole uses the **Last Used** or the current preset to create new holes.

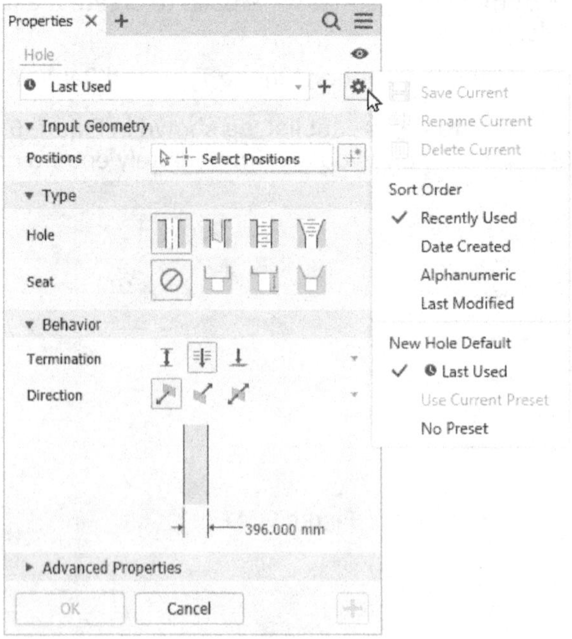

Figure 6–43

6.7 Threads

You can use the **Thread** tool to add a cosmetic image of a thread to holes, shafts, bolts, and pins, as shown in Figure 6–44. Thread information can also be assigned or read from a spreadsheet so that it can be used when detailing the model. Alternatively, you can use the **Hole** option to create threaded holes (as previously discussed).

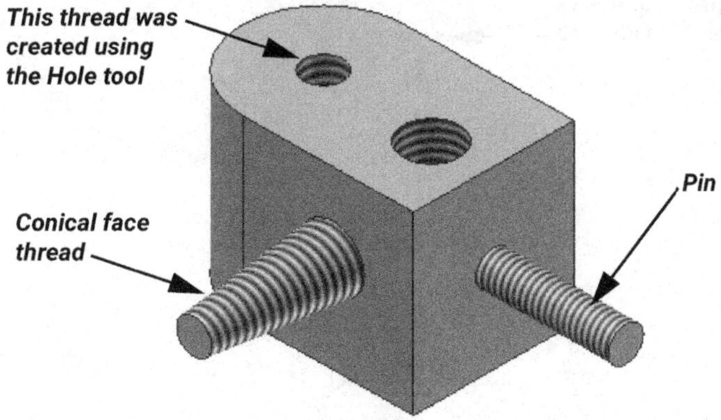

Figure 6–44

How To: Create a Thread Feature

1. In the *3D Model* tab>*Modify* panel, click (Thread) to create a thread. The *Properties* panel opens, as shown in Figure 6–45.

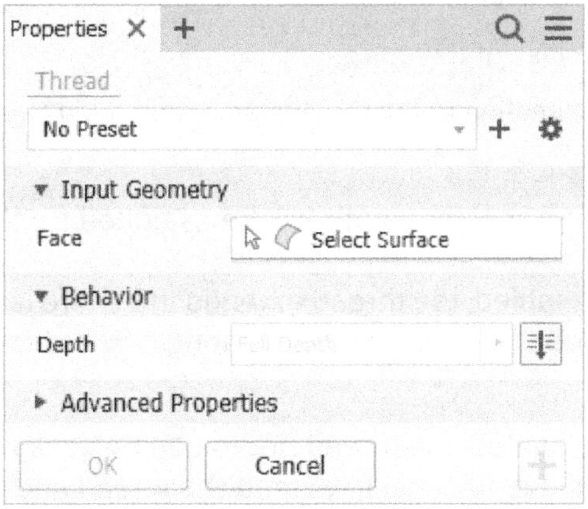

Figure 6–45

2. Select a cylindrical or conical face on which to create the thread. A thread can only be created on one face at a time.

3. Define the thread specifications in the *Threads* area (shown in Figure 6–46).

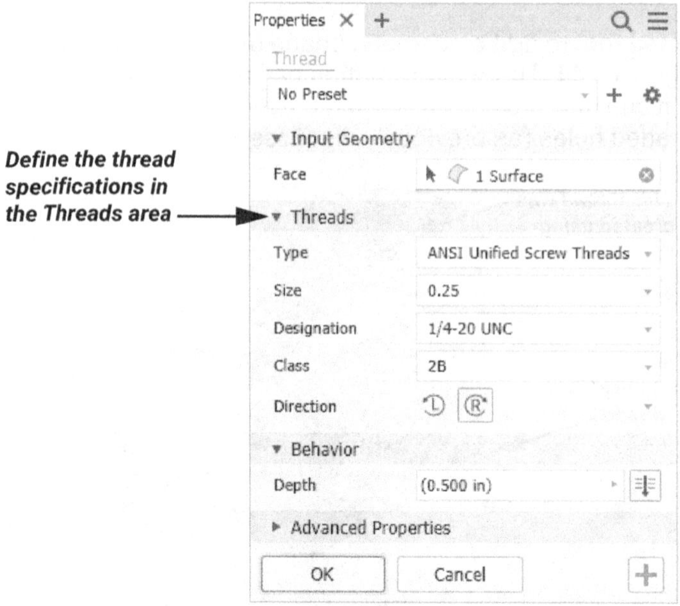

Figure 6–46

The options are as follows:

Type	Sets the series of threads to apply.
Size	Sets the diameter size of the selected thread type.
Designation	Sets the number of threads based on the unit of length and bolt size.
Class	Sets the class of threads.
Direction	Sets the direction of the threads as a right-hand twist or a left hand twist.

4. In the *Behavior* area, define how the depth will be assigned for the thread.

   - With (Full Depth) enabled, the thread extends the entire length of the selected face. A value appears in brackets (e.g., (0.5 in)), indicating it is a reference value being read from the model geometry.
   - With (Full Depth) disabled, the thread depth can be assigned with a *Depth* and *Offset* value. The offset value enables you to extend the thread such that it is offset from the bottom edge by the specified value.

5. (Optional) To control whether the thread is displayed on the model geometry or not, expand the *Advanced Properties* area and set the **Display thread in model** option, as needed.

6. Once the thread is defined, you can complete the feature using any of the following options:
   - Right-click in the graphics window and select **OK (Enter)**.
   - Click **OK** in the *Properties* panel.
   - Press <Enter>.
   - Click (Apply) to create the thread and remain in the *Properties* panel to create another.

The Thread feature is identified with the icon in the Model browser once created.

6.8 Editing Pick and Place Features

Once you have created a pick and place feature, you might need to modify it by changing dimension values, editing the properties of the feature, or in the case of a hole modify its location by editing the sketch that was generated when it was created. The following options enable you to make these changes.

- **Show Dimensions:** Displays the dimensions associated with the feature. You can double-click on the values once displayed to make dimensional changes.
- **Edit Sketch:** Accesses the feature's sketch to redefine any of the elements used to define the sketch. For pick and place features, this only applies to Hole features that generate a sketch during creation.
- **Edit Feature:** Opens the *Properties* panel or feature dialog box to redefine the settings used to define the feature.You can also double-click on the feature in the Model browser as an equivalent method to using the **Edit Feature** command.

The options can be accessed in the Model browser by right-clicking on the feature, as shown on the left in Figure 6–47, in the graphics window by selecting any face that is generated by the feature to bring up the toolbar options (shown in the center image), or by right-clicking on a feature geometry, as shown on the right.

To access the options in the right-click menu in the graphics window, you must have the Select Features Priority filter set in the Quick Access Toolbar

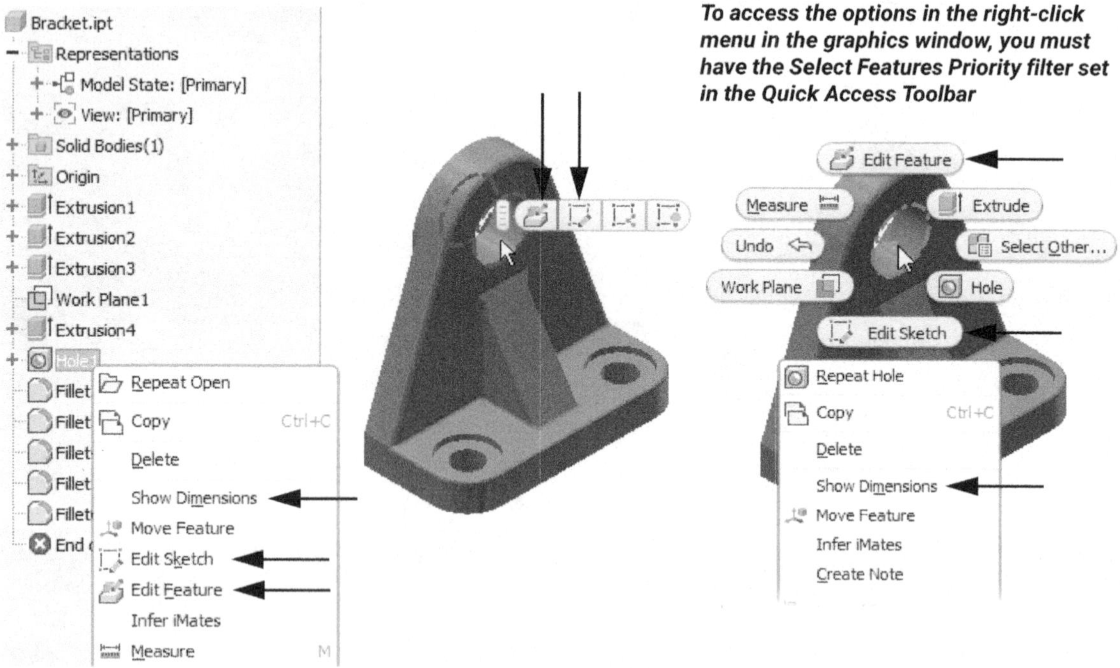

Figure 6–47

6.9 Creation Sequence

Feature-based modeling involves creating features, one by one, on a base feature until the model is complete. By this point in this guide you have learned to create sketched and pick and place based features. These are the main components in the modeling process. The flowchart in Figure 6–48 shows the paths available when creating these features.

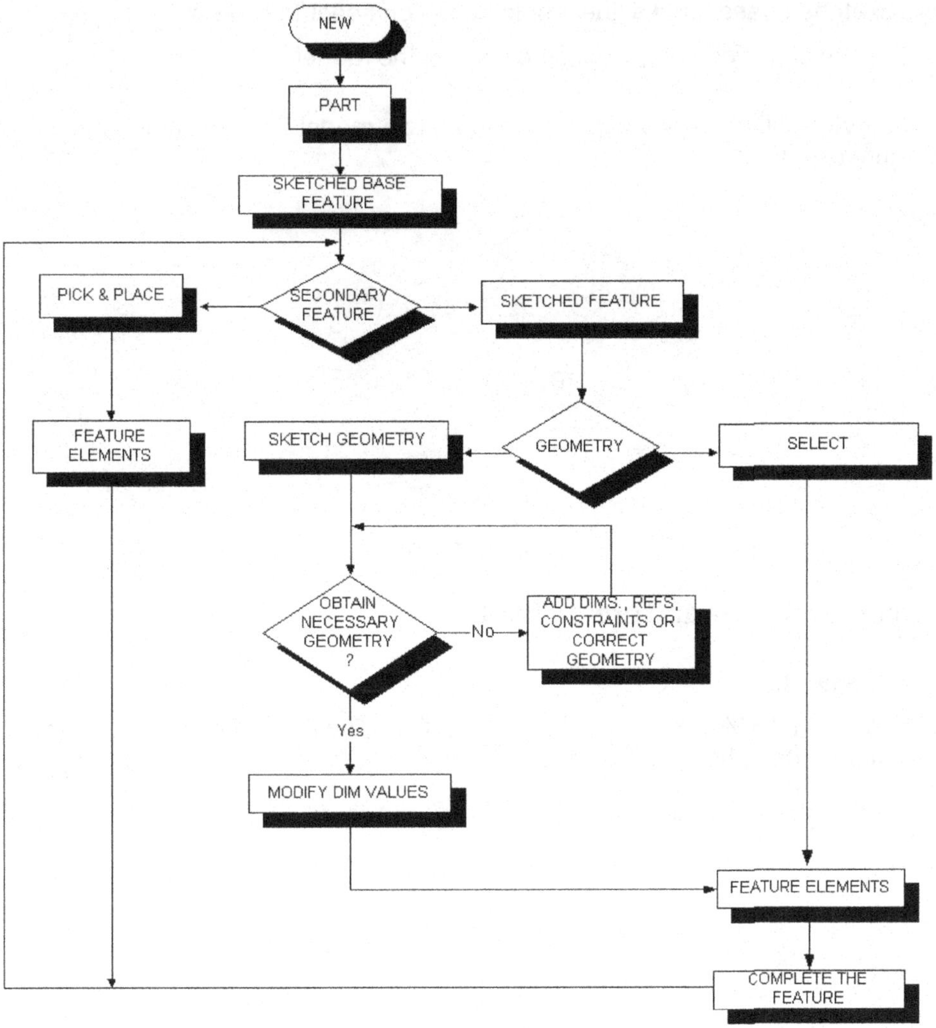

Figure 6–48

When creating features, it is important to consider your design intent. Every aspect of feature creation, such as specifying the references, dimensioning, and constraining the model, affect design intent and the design sequence.

Practice 6a
Add Fillets, Holes, and a Chamfer

Practice Objectives

- Create constant and variable edge fillets along specific edges in the model.
- Create a sketched-based and a linear hole based on specific criteria.
- Create an edge chamfer along a specific edge in the model.

In this practice, you will add pick and place features to a model. The resulting model displays as shown in Figure 6–49.

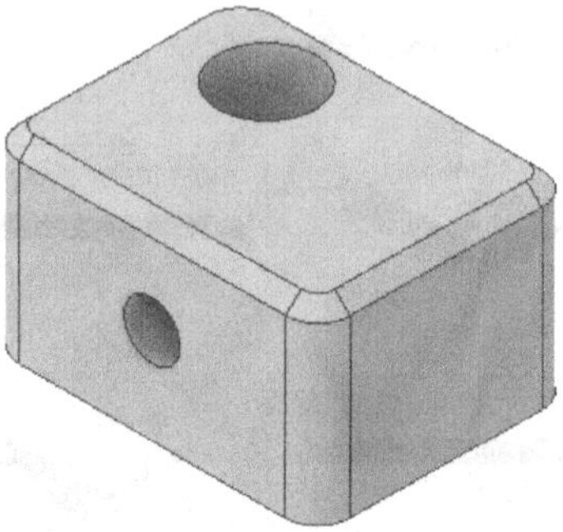

Figure 6–49

Task 1: Open a part file and create fillets.

1. Open **rectangle_1.ipt**.
2. In the *3D Model* tab>*Modify* panel, click  (Fillet). The *Properties* panel and tool palette open, similar to that shown in Figure 6–50.

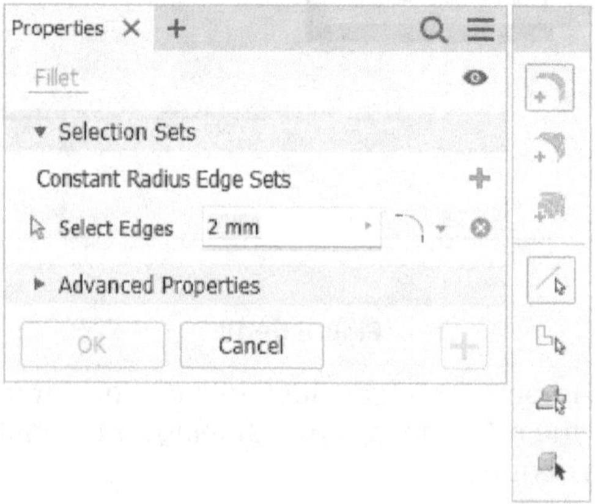

Figure 6–50

3. In the tool palette, click  (Add constant radius edge set) to create a constant fillet, if not already active.
4. In the tool palette, click  (Sets selection priority to edges), if not already active. Select the edges of the model shown in Figure 6–51. Selecting multiple edges ensures that the fillets are all the same radius and are driven by one dimension value. A default fillet automatically displays on the model.

   Note: *To clear the edges selected for fillets, press and hold <Ctrl> or <Shift> and select the referenced edge a second time.*

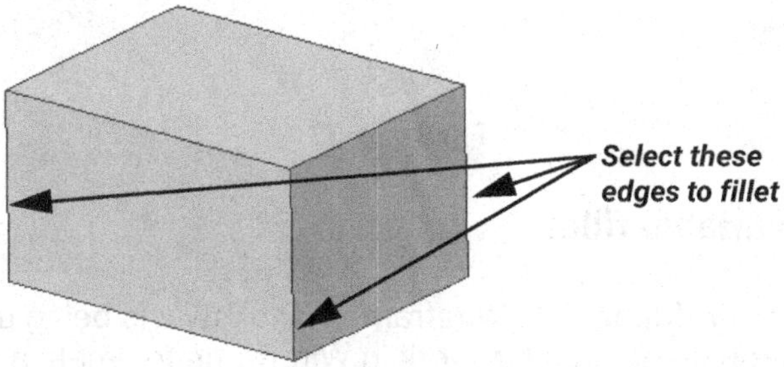

Figure 6–51

5. In the radius on-screen entry field or in the *Properties* panel, enter **2.54** as the radial dimension for the fillets, as shown in Figure 6–52. All three fillets act as one and update dynamically.

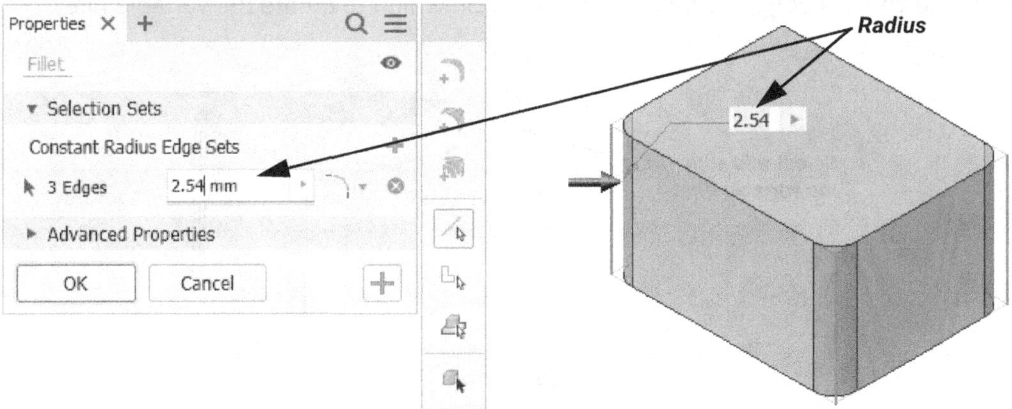

Figure 6–52

6. Click **OK** to complete the simple fillet. The model is shown in Figure 6–53. Note how the Model browser updates to display the single fillet feature.

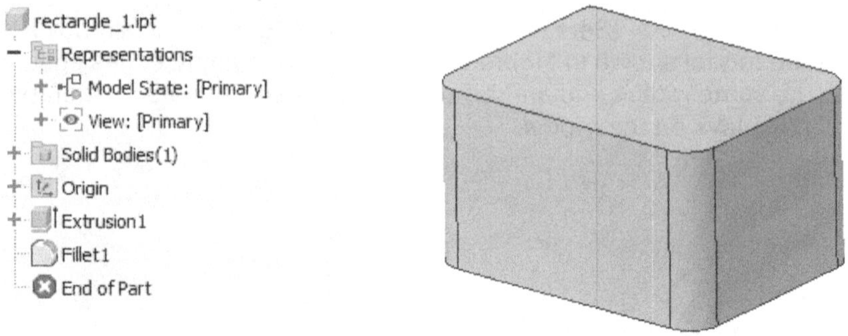

Figure 6–53

Task 2: Create the variable fillet.

1. Switch the model to **Wireframe**. The Wireframe visual style is being used for clarity in the upcoming images. You do not need to work in Wireframe to create a variable fillet.
2. In the graphics window, right-click and select **Fillet**.
3. In the tool palette, select (Add variable radius fillet). Note that the selection filters are cleared from the tool palette for a variable fillet because only linear edges can be selected as references for variable fillets.
4. Select the vertical edge shown in Figure 6–54 on which to create the variable fillet.

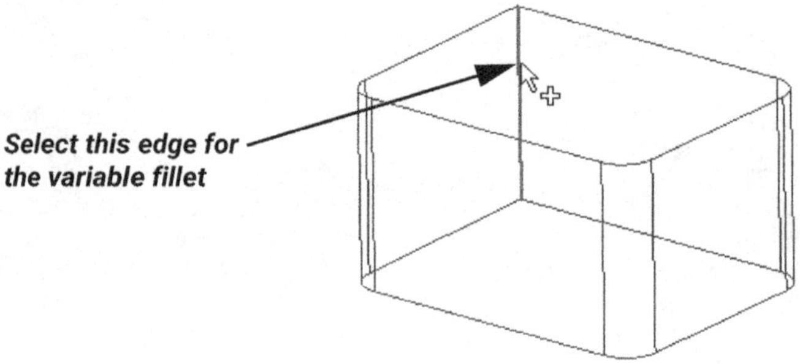

Figure 6–54

5. A variable fillet with the same radius at both ends is created by default. Modify the radius of both the start point (position 0,0) and end point (position 1,0) to **3.81** in the radius on-screen entry field or in the *Properties* panel, as shown in Figure 6–55.

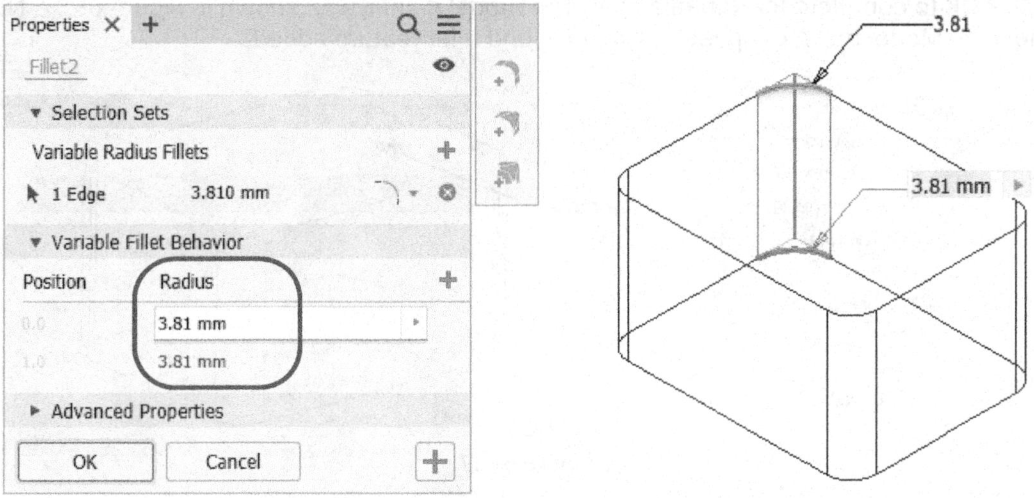

Figure 6–55

6. In the *Variable Fillet Behavior* area, click + (Add variable fillet point) to add an intermediate point on the same edge. The point is added at the midpoint of the line by default.
7. In the *Properties* panel, hover your cursor over the **0.5** *Position* field and note that you can edit this value if necessary. For this fillet, maintain the 0.5 position value to keep it at the midpoint of the selected edge.
8. Modify the radius of the intermediate point (position 0.5) to **7.62** in the radius on-screen entry field or in the *Properties* panel, as shown in Figure 6–56.

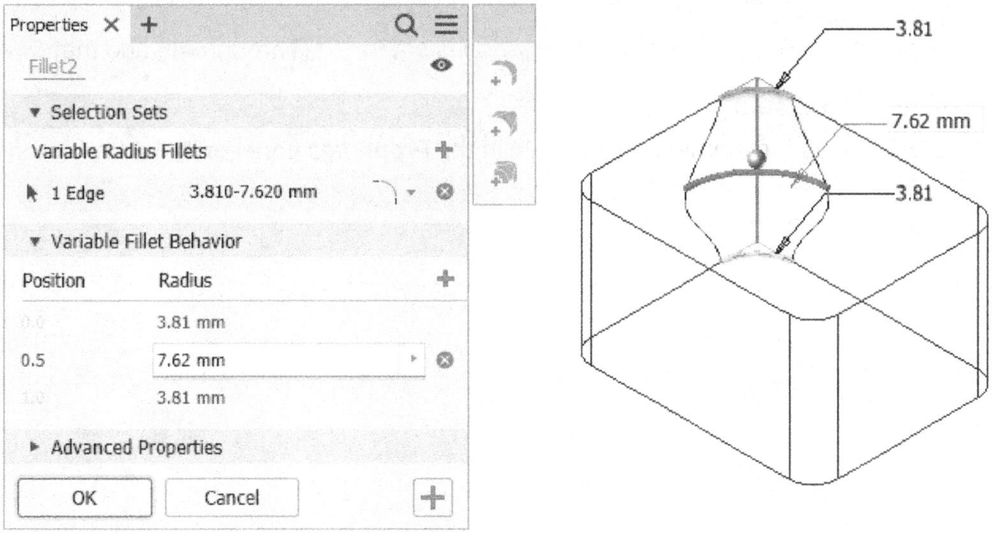

Figure 6–56

9. Click **OK** to complete the variable fillet. The model displays as shown in Figure 6–57. Note how the Model browser updates with a second fillet feature added.

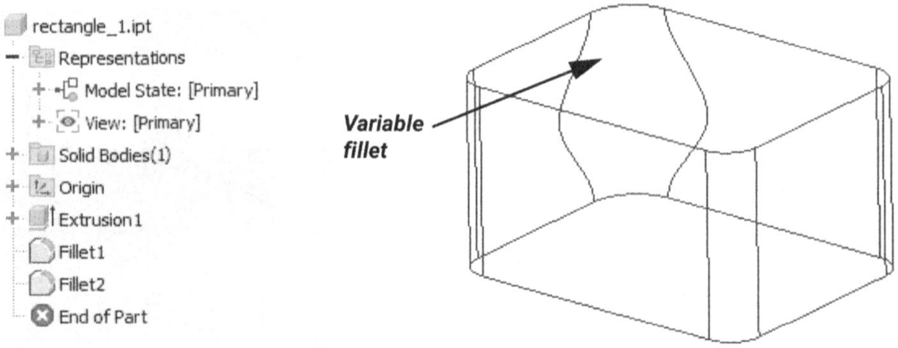

Figure 6–57

Task 3: Create a hole.

1. In the *Modify* panel, click (Hole).
2. Complete the following in the *Properties* panel or graphics window (as shown in Figure 6–58). A preview of the hole displays in the graphics window as you make selections.
   - Select the location shown in Figure 6–58 to place the hole.
   - In the *Type* area, ensure that *Hole* is set to (Simple) and that *Seat* is set to (None).
   - In the *Behavior* area, ensure that *Termination* is set to (Through All) and that *Direction* is set to (Default).
   - Enter **7.5mm** as the diameter of the hole in the *Properties* panel or in the on-screen entry field.

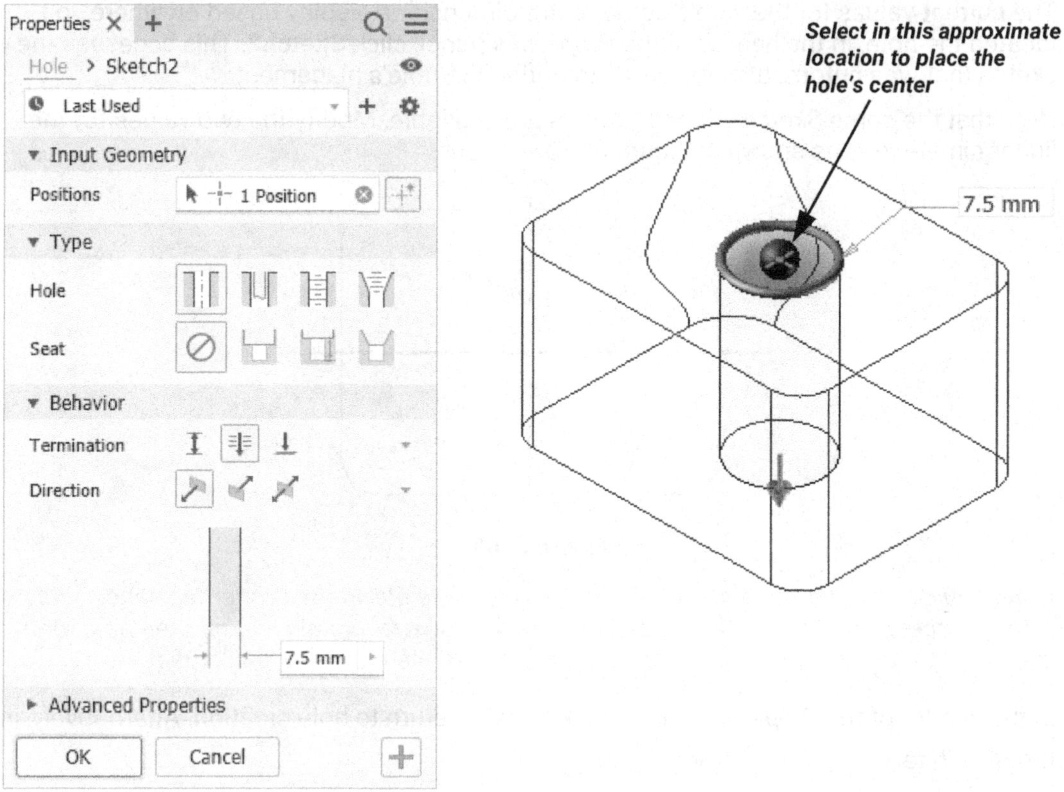

Figure 6–58

3. To fully locate the hole, additional positional references are required. Select the two edges shown in Figure 6–59 to create two linear dimensions that fully locate the hole.

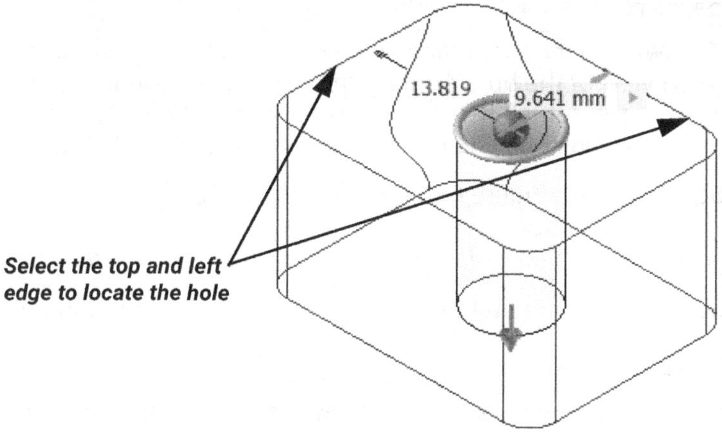

Figure 6–59

4. Reorient the model to the **TOP** view using the ViewCube.

5. The current values for the hole's center point dimensions display based on where you located the hole. In the header of the *Properties* panel, click **Sketch2**. This accesses the sketch that was automatically created to define the hole's placement.
6. Note that the same *Sketch* tab and options are available. Modify the two values for the linear dimensions as shown in Figure 6–60.

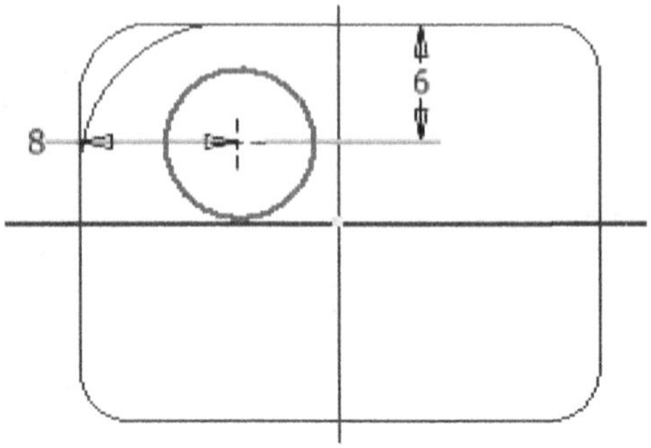

Figure 6–60

Note: *You could have also edited the dimensions while still in the Properties panel, without accessing the sketch. This step is simply shown to explain that all sketching tools and constraints are still available to you to further define the hole's placement.*

7. In the header of the *Properties* panel, click **Hole** to return to hole creation. Alternatively, in the *Sketch* tab, click (Return to Hole).
8. Click **OK** to complete the hole.

Task 4: Create a second hole.

1. In the *Modify* panel, click (Hole).
2. Complete the following in the *Properties* panel or graphics window (as shown in Figure 6–61). A preview of the hole displays in the graphics window as you make selections. Note that the default settings in the *Properties* panel are consistent with those used in creating the previous hole because **Last used** is selected at the top of the panel.
   - Select the point shown in Figure 6–61 to place the hole.
   - In the *Type* area, ensure that *Hole* is set to (Simple) and *Seat* is set to (None).
   - In the *Behavior* area, ensure that *Termination* is set to (Through All) and *Direction* is set to (Default).
   - Enter **4.5** as the diameter of the hole in the *Properties* panel on in entry field.

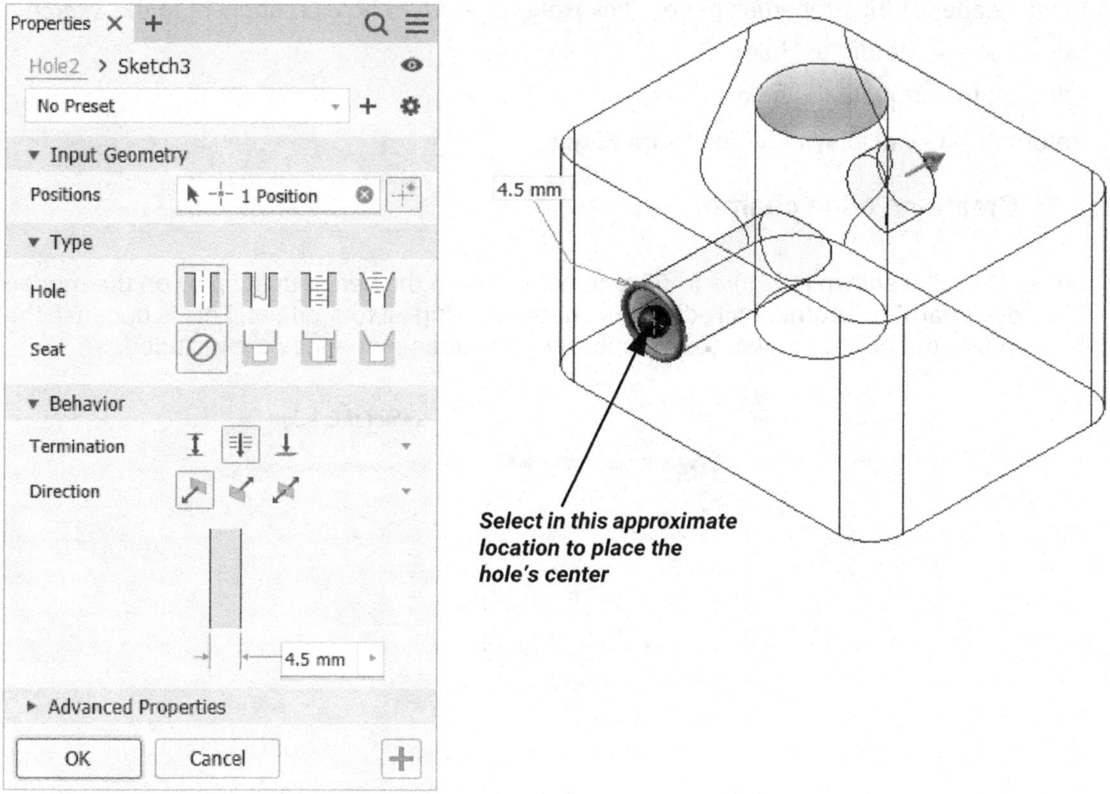

Figure 6–61

3. To fully locate the hole, additional positional references are required. The design intent requires that the hole is centered on the face. To accomplish this with constraints, you must go directly to the sketch. In the header of the *Properties* panel, click **Sketch3**.
4. The projected origin point exists in the middle of the face. Use the **Coincident** constraint to constrain the hole center and the projected origin point, as shown in Figure 6–62. Alternatively, drag the center point to the projected origin point without accessing the sketch.

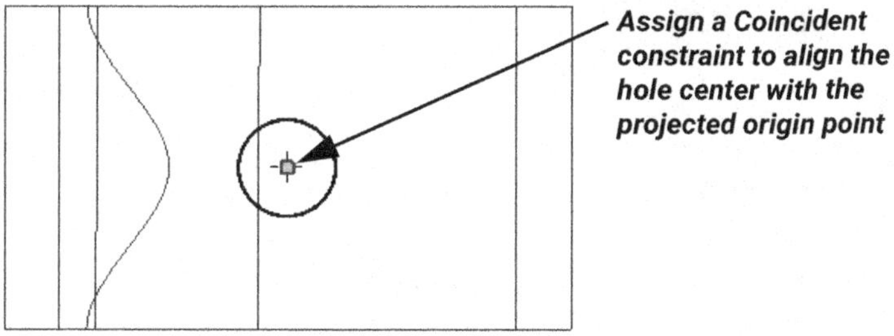

Figure 6–62

5. In the header of the *Properties* panel, click **Hole** to return to hole creation, or in the *Sketch* tab, click (Return to Hole).
6. Click **OK** to complete the hole.
7. Return the view display to **Shaded with Edges**.

Task 5: Create an edge chamfer.

1. Select the edge shown in Figure 6–63, and click in the heads-up display on the model. The edge chamfer automatically displays encompassing all four edges. This is because the fillets made the edges tangent to one another and all tangent edges are included.

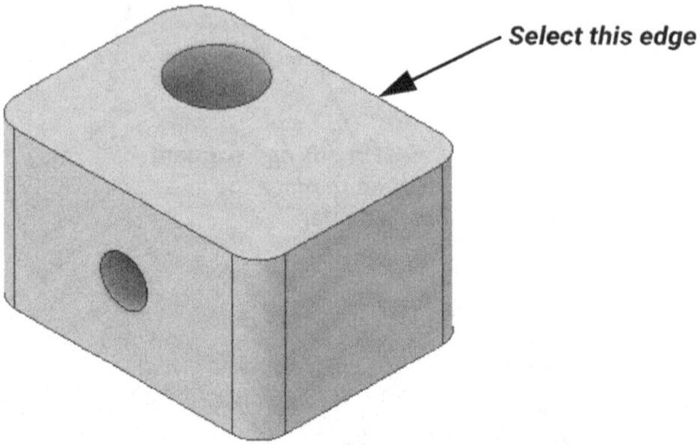

Figure 6–63

2. In the mini-toolbar, enter **1.20** in the *Distance* field, as shown in Figure 6–64.

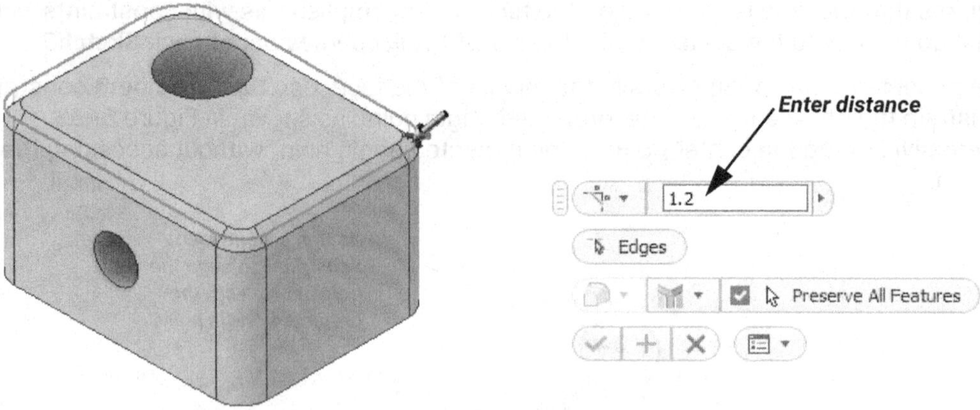

Figure 6–64

3. Click  to complete the chamfer. The model displays as shown in Figure 6–65.

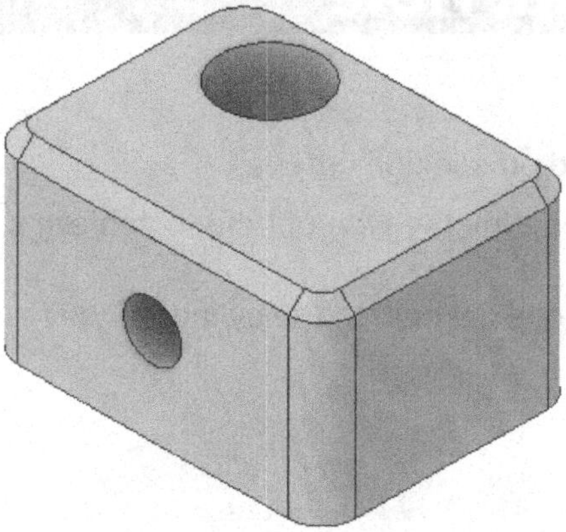

Figure 6–65

4. Save the model and close the window.

End of practice

Practice 6b
Create a Coaxial Hole

Practice Objectives

- Create a coaxial hole based on specific criteria.
- Make modifications and redefine the type of hole to achieve a required result.

In this practice, you will add a coaxial hole to the cylinder. The resulting model displays as shown in Figure 6–66.

Figure 6–66

Task 1: Open a part file and create a concentric hole.

1. Open **cylinder_1.ipt**.
2. Right-click in the graphics window, and select **Hole**.
3. Complete the following in the *Properties* panel or graphics window (as shown in Figure 6–67). A preview of the hole displays in the graphics window as you make selections.
   - Select a location on the top face of the cylinder to place the hole.
   - Hover the cursor over the outside cylindrical face. Once the symbol displays adjacent to the cursor, select the face. This assigns the hole as a concentric hole and centers it on the top face.

- In the *Type* area, set *Hole* to (Simple) and *Seat* to (None), if not already set.
- Enter **7.5** as the diameter of the hole in the *Properties* panel or in the on-screen entry field.
- In the *Behavior* area, ensure that *Termination* is set to (Distance), *Direction* is set to (Default), and *Drill Point* is set to (Flat).
- Enter **13.5** as the depth of the hole in the *Properties* panel or in the on-screen entry field.

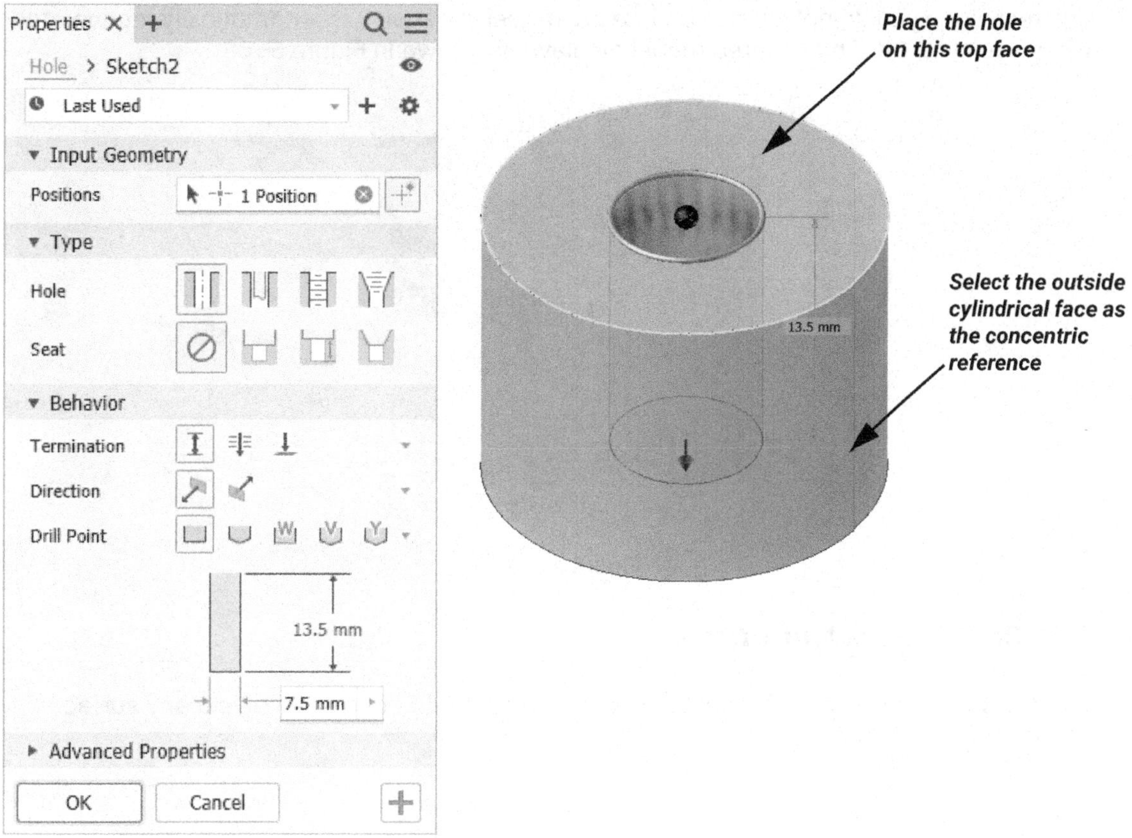

Figure 6–67

4. For Concentric holes, as described above, no additional references are required to define the hole's placement. Although a sketch is created, it does not need to be accessed unless its placement location is to be changed (i.e., linear dimensions are required). Click **OK** to complete the hole.

Task 2: Change the diameter of the coaxial hole.

1. Right-click on **Hole1** in the Model browser and select **Show Dimensions**.
2. Double-click on the diameter dimension in the graphics window.
3. Enter **9.00** in the *Hole Diameter* field in the *Hole Dimensions* dialog box.
4. Click **OK** to close the dialog box.
5. In the Quick Access Toolbar, click (Local Update). Alternatively, you can double-click on the hole in the Model browser and simply edit the value in the *Properties* panel. Using this technique you do not have to update the model because it is automatically regenerated when you click **OK**. The updated model displays as shown in Figure 6–68.

Figure 6–68

Task 3: Redefine the type of hole.

1. Right-click on **Hole1** in the Model browser and select **Edit Feature**, or select any surface on the hole and click . The *Properties* panel opens.
2. In the *Type* area, set (Countersink) as the *Seat* type.
3. Activate the countersink diameter field (as shown in Figure 6–69) and enter **15.25**.

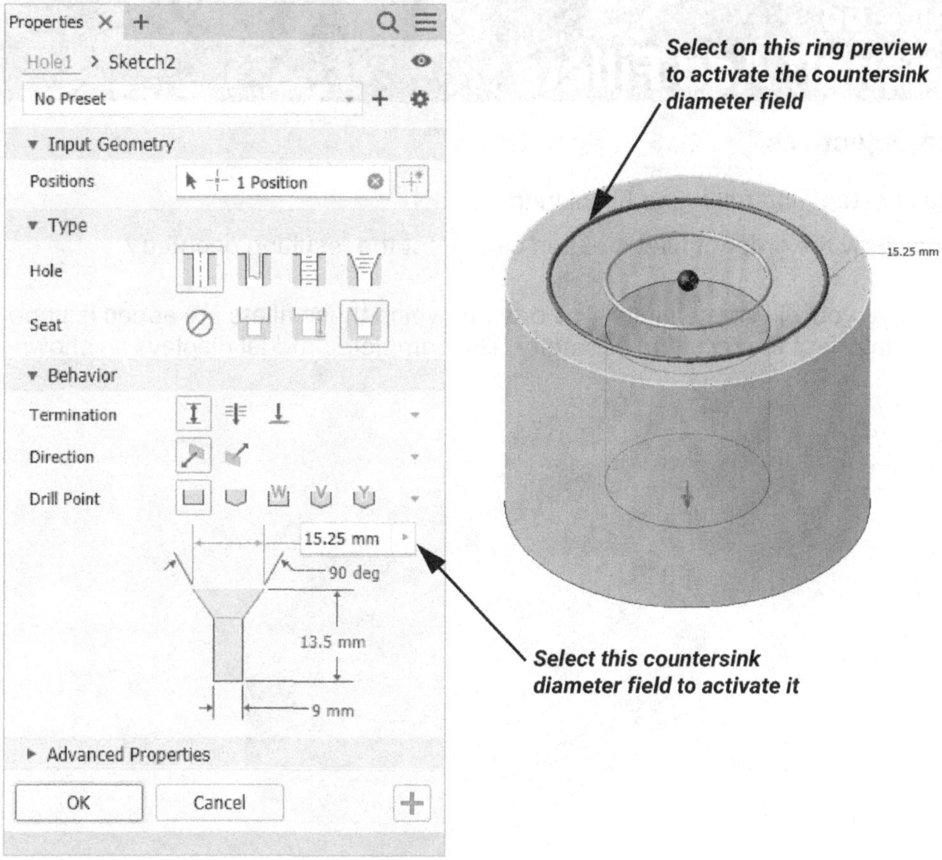

Figure 6–69

4. Click **OK** to complete the feature. The model displays as shown in Figure 6–70.

Figure 6–70

5. Save the model and close the window.

End of practice

Practice 6c
(Optional) Add Fillets

Practice Objectives

- Create constant and full round fillets in the model.
- Describe how the order of fillet creation can affect the resulting geometry.

In this practice, you will create fillets. The order in which these fillets are added is important because it can affect the resulting geometry. The completed model displays as shown in Figure 6–71.

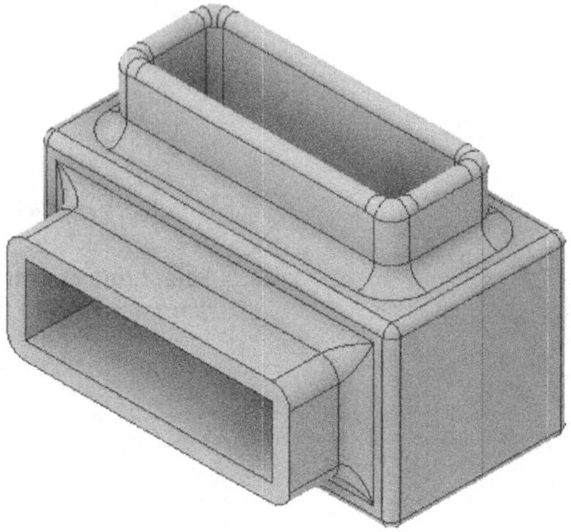

Figure 6–71

Task 1: Open a part file and create a fillet.

1. Open **fillet.ipt**.

2. In the *Modify* panel, click (Fillet). The *Properties* panel and tool palette display, similar to that shown in Figure 6–72.

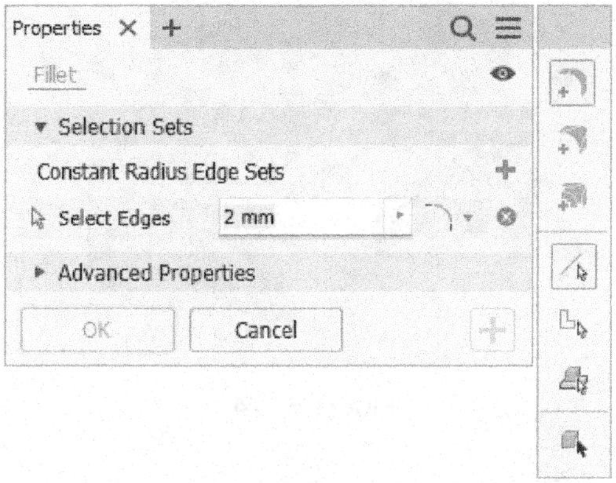

Figure 6–72

Note: *Alternatively, you can preselect the edges to be filleted and click in the heads-up display on the model. If you select an edge in error, press and hold <Ctrl> and select the edge again to clear it.*

3. Ensure that and are selected in the tool palette. Select all four outside edges of **Extrusion4**, as shown in Figure 6–73. The fillet automatically previews on the model.

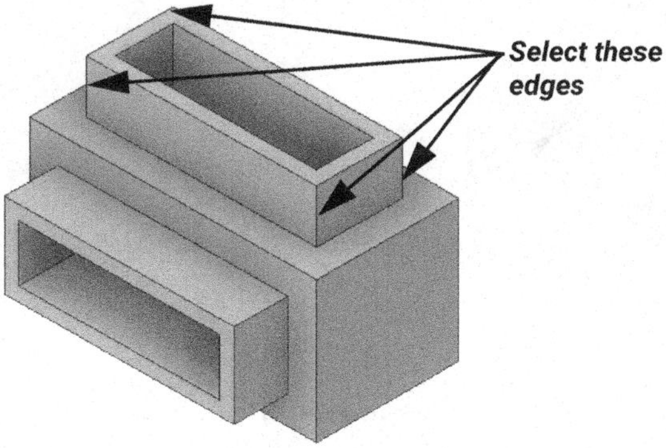

Figure 6–73

4. In the on-screen entry field or in the *Properties* panel, modify the fillet radius to **20.00**.

5. Click **OK** to complete the feature. The model displays as shown in Figure 6–74.

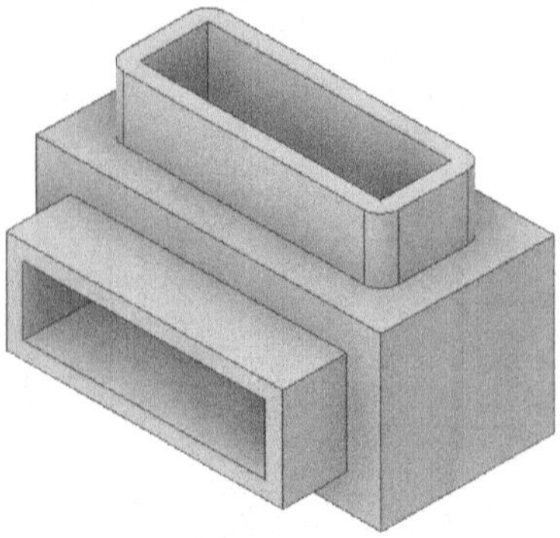

Figure 6–74

Task 2: Create a second fillet.

1. Select the edge shown on the left in Figure 6–75.
2. Activate the **Fillet** command in the ribbon or shortcut menu. All of the tangent edges are automatically selected.
3. Modify the radius to **20.00**. Click **OK** to complete the feature. The model displays as shown on the right in Figure 6–75.

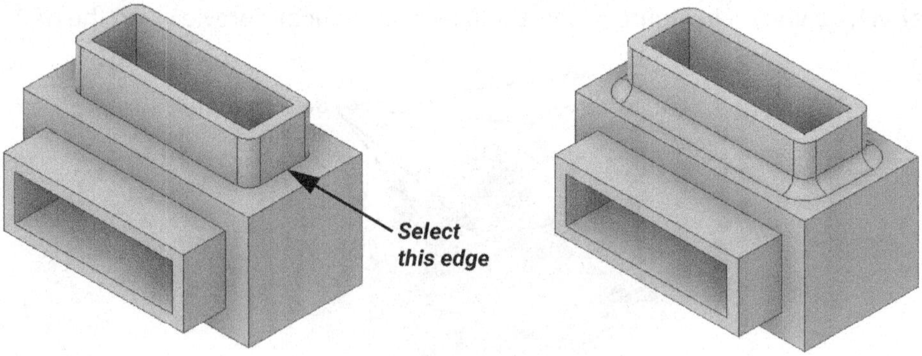

Figure 6–75

Task 3: Create a third fillet.

1. Activate the **Fillet** command in the ribbon or shortcut menu and select the edges shown on the left of Figure 6–76.
2. Modify the radius to **20.00**, if not already set, and complete the feature. The model displays as shown on the right side of Figure 6–76.

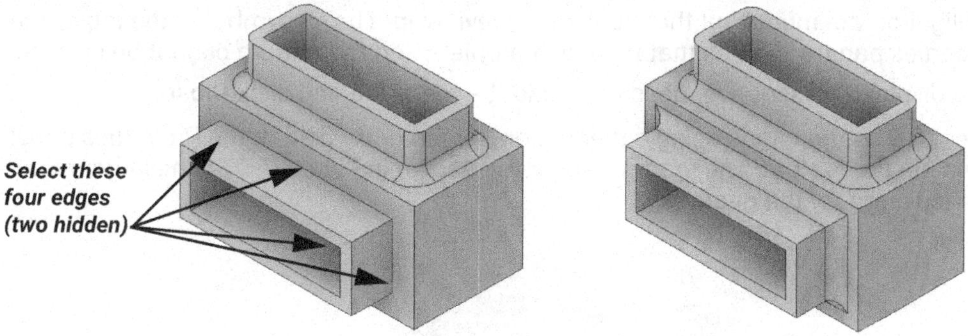

Figure 6–76

Task 4: Create a fourth fillet.

1. Activate the **Fillet** command and select the four edges shown on the left in Figure 6–77. When you select the edges, all of the tangent edges highlight automatically.
2. Ensure the radius is **20.00** and complete the feature. The model displays as shown on the right in Figure 6–77.

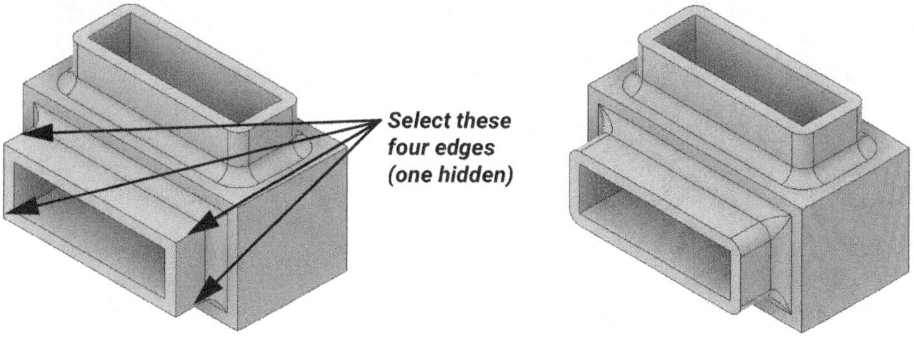

Figure 6–77

3. Note the difference in the fillets that were created on this feature and previously on **Extrusion4**. This is because the order in which the edges were selected were different.

Task 5: Create a fifth fillet.

1. Activate the **Fillet** command.
2. In the tool palette, maintain the selection and select to enable feature selection.
3. Select **Extrusion1** in the Model browser to add a constant fillet to all of its edges.
4. The default radius is 20 because this was the one previously used. Note that the edges highlight on the model but that no fillet is previewed. The symbol at the top of the *Properties* panel indicates that there is a problem and the feature cannot be created. Click to display a descriptive message. Read the message and click **Close**.
5. Enter **10.0** as the radius using either the on-screen entry field or the *Properties* panel and complete the feature. The model displays as shown in Figure 6–78. The larger radius value was too large for the geometry.

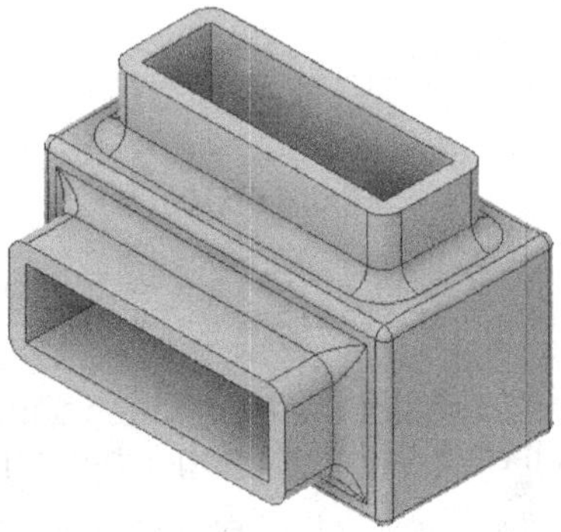

Figure 6–78

Task 6: Create a sixth fillet.

1. Activate the **Fillet** command and attempt to select the four inside edges of **Extrusion5**, as shown on the left in Figure 6–79. The  feature selection option remains active from the previous feature. Select  to enable edge selection and select the edges again.
2. Ensure that the fillet radius is **10.00** (same as the previously assigned value) and complete the feature. The model displays as shown on the right in Figure 6–79.

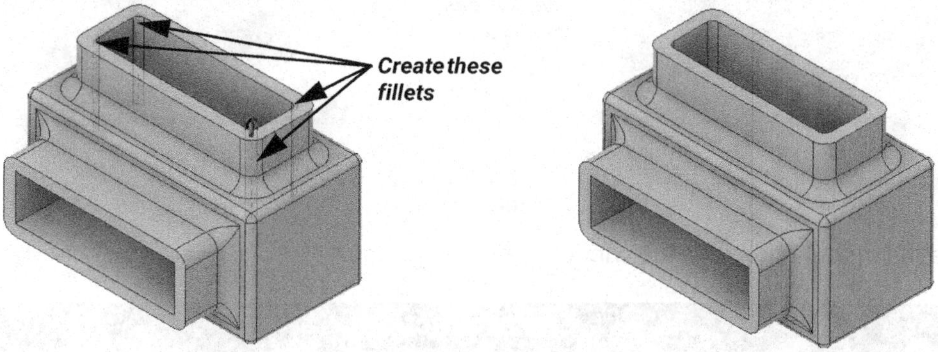

Figure 6–79

Task 7: Create a full round fillet.

1. Expand the **Fillet** command on the ribbon and click  (Full Round Fillet). The *Properties* panel appears, as shown in Figure 6–80.

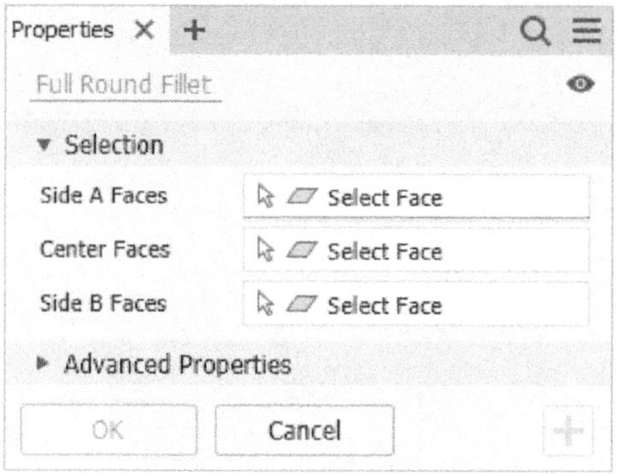

Figure 6–80

2. Select the references, as shown on the left in Figure 6–81.
3. Complete the feature. The model displays as shown on the right in Figure 6–81.

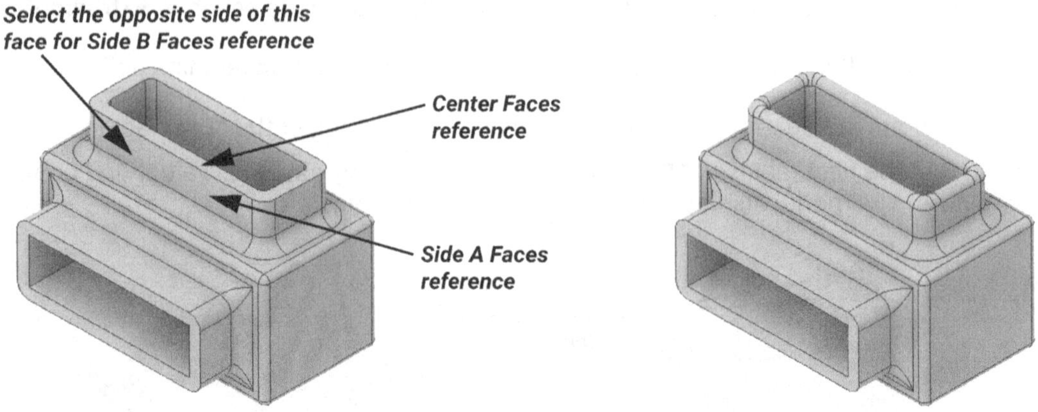

Figure 6–81

4. Save the model and close the window.

End of practice

Practice 6d
(Optional) Add Pick and Place Features

Practice Objective

- Create appropriate hole, chamfer, and fillet features to create the required geometry.

In this practice, you will continue to practice placing pick and place features on a model. The completed model displays as shown in Figure 6–82. Minimal instruction is provided for this practice.

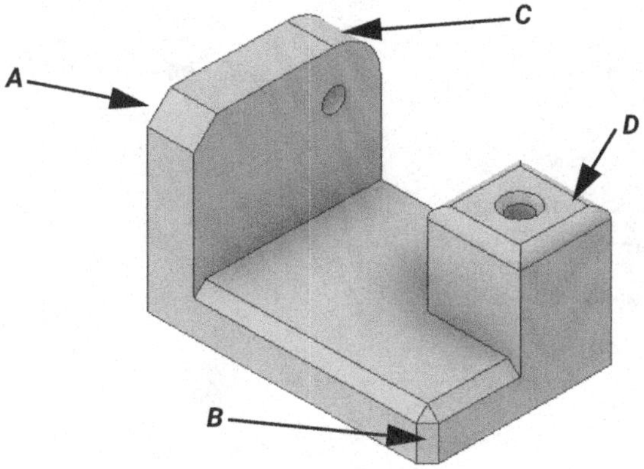

Figure 6–82

Task 1: Open a part and add features.

1. Open **placed_features.ipt**.
2. Add a **.5** chamfer to edge **A** and a **.25** chamfer to the three edges meeting at corner **B**.
3. Add a **1.0** constant radius fillet at edge **C**.
4. Create a **.5 dia.** hole through the part, concentric to fillet **C**.
5. Add a through all hole with a **.5** diameter and a **.75** countersink in the center of the surface **D** that is 2in by 2in.
6. Fillet the loop on surface **D**. Use a radius of **0.25**.
7. Save the model and close the window.

End of practice

Chapter Review Questions

1. Which chamfer type requires you to select a reference surface?
    a. Distance
    b. Distance and Angle
    c. Two Distances

2. In the fillet tool palette, shown in Figure 6–83, which option enables you to fillet all of the edges of a feature?

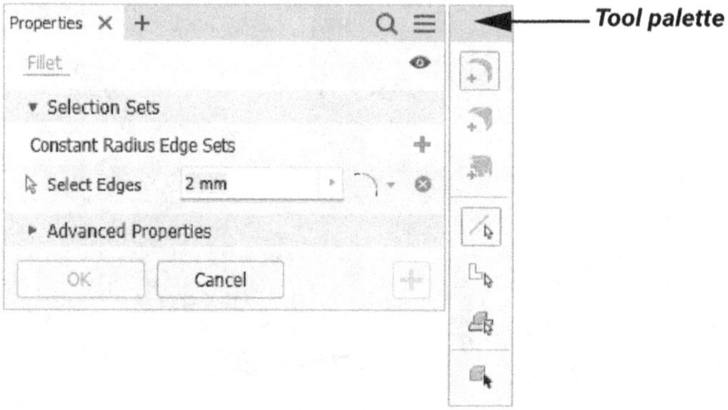

Figure 6–83

a. 

b. 

c. 

3. Chamfer features always remove material.
    a. True
    b. False

4. Fillet features can add or remove material.

a. True

b. False

5. Which keys on the keyboard can be used to clear the edges selected for a fillet or chamfer feature? (Select all that apply.)

a. <Tab>

b. <Ctrl>

c. <Shift>

d. <Alt>

6. Fillets on multiple edges can be controlled by one dimension.

a. True

b. False

7. How many separate Fillet features are listed in the Model browser if you click **OK** to create Fillet2, shown in the *Properties* panel in Figure 6–84?

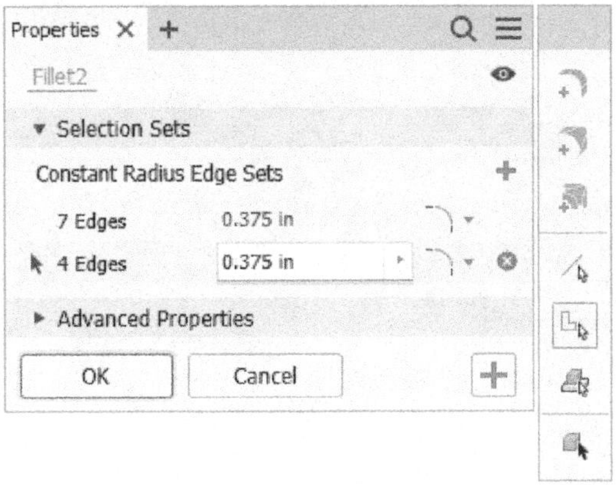

Figure 6–84

a. 1

b. 2

c. 4

d. 11

8. You can add threads to both cylindrical faces and conical faces.

a. True

b. False

9. When defining the location reference for a concentric hole, which of the following can be selected?

a. Planar Face

b. Cylindrical Face

10. How can you modify an existing placed feature, such as a fillet or chamfer?

a. Return to the sketch mode and change the sketch profile.

b. Double-click on the feature in the model or in the Model browser.

c. Select the same tool used to create the feature to edit it.

11. Which option do you select to change the reference edges for a chamfer?

a. Show Dimensions

b. Edit Feature

c. Edit Sketch

d. Suppress Features

Command Summary

Button	Command	Location
	**Chamfer (feature)**	• **Ribbon:** *3D Model* tab>*Modify* panel • **Heads-up Display:** In the graphics window with an entity selected
	**Face Fillet**	• **Ribbon:** *3D Model* tab>*Modify* panel>expanded Fillet command
	**Fillet**	• **Ribbon:** *3D Model* tab>*Modify* panel • **Context Menu:** In the graphics window • **Heads-up Display:** In the graphics window with an entity selected
	**Full Round Fillet**	• **Ribbon:** *3D Model* tab>*Modify* panel>expanded Fillet command
	**Hole**	• **Ribbon:** *3D Model* tab>*Modify* panel • **Context Menu:** In the graphics window
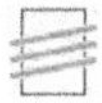	**Thread**	• **Ribbon:** *3D Model* tab>*Modify* panel

Chapter 7

Work Features

During the design process, the features that currently exist in the model might not provide the references required to place a new feature. In these situations, you can use work features to create the required references.

Learning Objectives

- Use the work plane creation types to create new work planes in a model.
- Use the work axes creation types to create new work axes in a model.
- Use the work point creation types to create new work points in a model.
- Describe how using work planes, work axes, and work points in a model can assist you in creating geometry that cannot otherwise be created using existing planes or geometry.

7.1 Work Planes

Work planes are non-solid features. They do not have thickness or mass and are used as references when creating other features in a model. When creating a part, three origin work planes are automatically created in the default templates.

Additional work planes can be created if a feature's sketching plane is not satisfied by any of the three origin work planes or existing geometry. Multiple work planes might be required to create a required work plane.To create the extrusions shown in Figure 7–1, additional work planes were required.

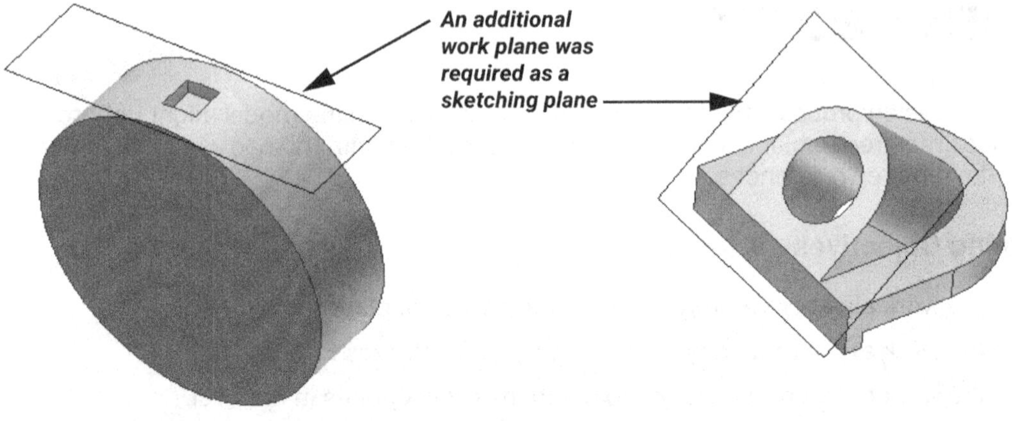

Figure 7–1

How To: Create a Work Plane

1. Start the creation of a work plane using one of the following techniques. The end result of any of these methods is the same. However, by selecting a plane placement type you are guided as to which references to select.
   - In the *3D Model* tab>*Work Features* panel, click (Plane).
   - In the *3D Model* tab>*Work Features* panel, expand (Plane) and select a plane placement type. Note that some of the methods are not available in Assembly mode.
   - In the graphics window, right-click and select **Work Plane**.
2. Once you have started the creation of a work plane, you must select references to locate it. References can include origin features, work features (plane, axis, point), edges, construction lines, vertices, or faces (planar or cylindrical). The reference type required depends on the work plane being created. Once the selected references fully define the work plane's placement, it displays. Alternatively, you can select the reference before clicking (Plane).

The different work plane placement types are as follows:

Type	Example
Offset from Plane: Creates a work plane parallel to an existing plane. Place the cursor over a reference plane or face, hold the left mouse button, and drag away from the face. Enter the required offset distance.	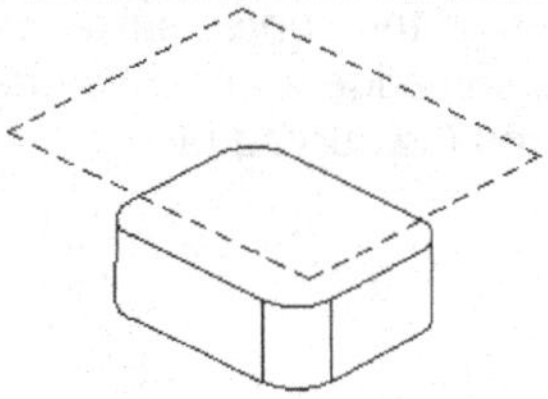
Parallel to Plane through Point: Creates a work plane that is parallel to another plane or face and passes through an edge, axis, or point. Select the reference plane and then select a point.	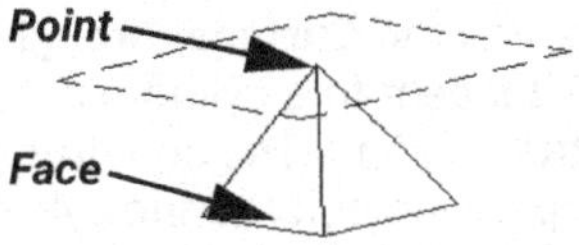
Midplane between Two Planes: Creates a work plane in the middle of two planes (parallel or non-parallel). Select two planes to create a work plane evenly spaced between them.	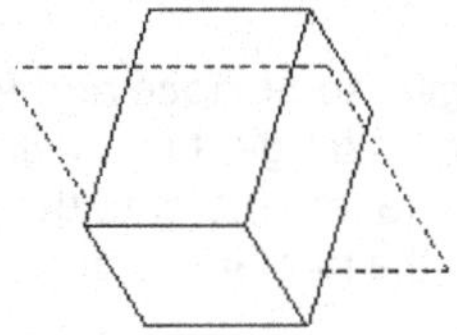
Midplane of Torus: Creates a work plane through the center or mid-plane of a torus. Select the torus to place the plane at its mid-plane.	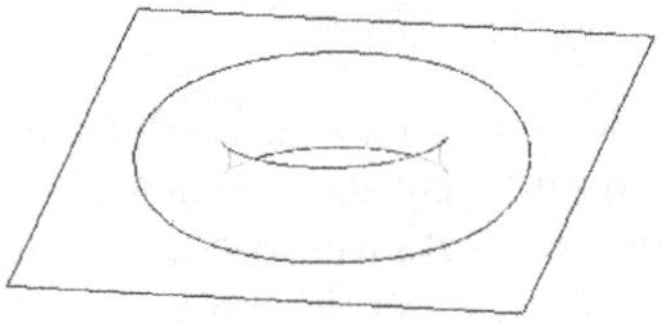
Angle to Plane around Edge: Creates a work plane at an angle to an existing plane or face. Select the plane to which the work plane is referenced. Select the edge or axis through which the work plane passes. Enter the required angle in the mini-toolbar to create a plane perpendicular to another plane.	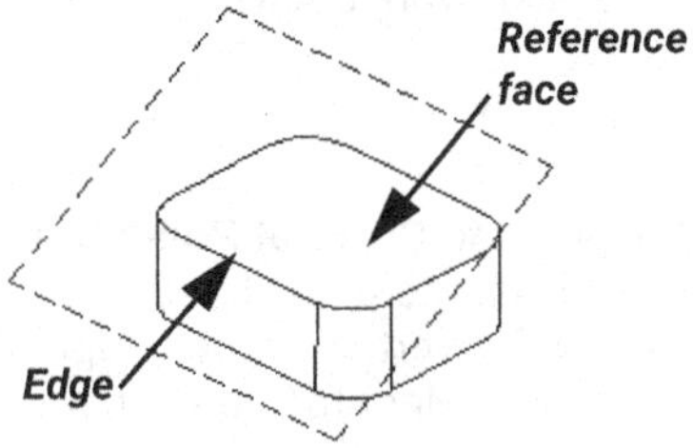
Three Points: Creates a work plane through three selected points (midpoints, end points, and/or work points). Select three point references to place the plane.	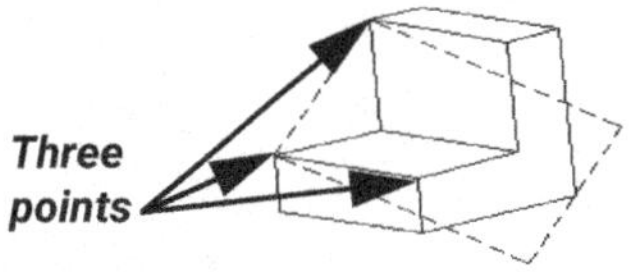
Two Coplanar Edges: Creates a work plane by selecting two coplanar straight edges or work axes. Select the two linear references to place the plane.	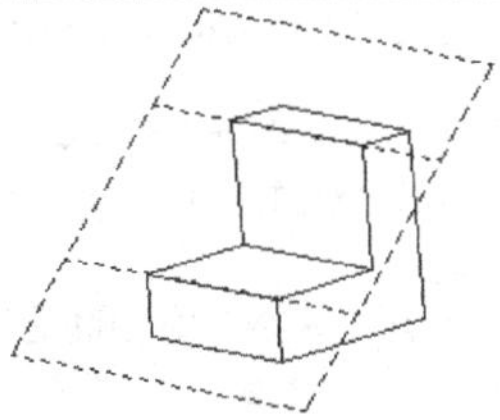

Type	Example
Tangent to Surface through Edge: Creates a work plane that lies on the curved surface or its projection and passes through an edge or axis. To create the work plane, select the edge and the curved face.	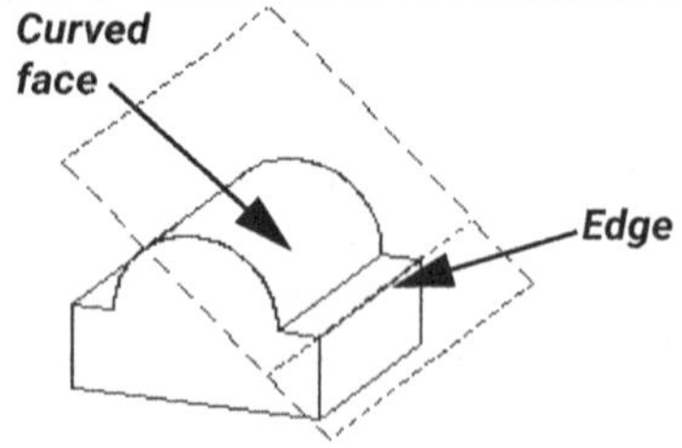
Tangent to Surface through Point: Creates a work plane that is tangent to a cylindrical face at a point defined by a construction line. The construction line should be drawn on a plane perpendicular to the cylindrical surface and from the centerline of the cylinder to a point on the cylinder	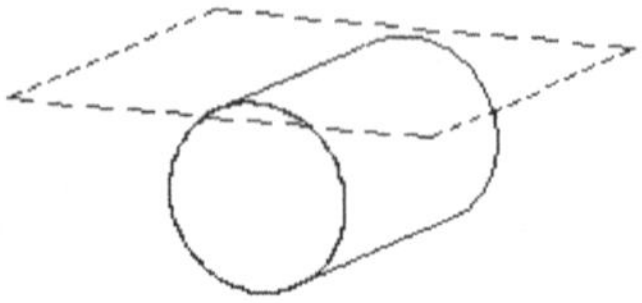
Tangent to Surface and Parallel to Plane: Creates a work plane that is tangent to a cylindrical face and parallel to a planar surface. To create the work plane, select the cylindrical face and the planar surface.	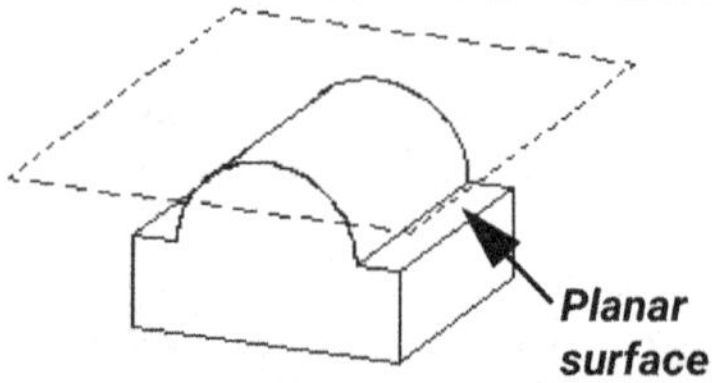
Normal to Axis through Point: Creates a work plane that is perpendicular to an axis and passes through a selected point. To create the work plane, select the axis or edge to which it is perpendicular and select the point (i.e., end point, midpoint, or work point).	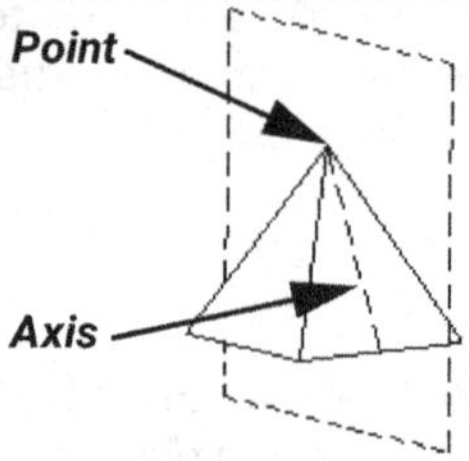
Normal to Curve at Point: Creates a work plane that is perpendicular to a non-linear sketch curve at a work point, sketch point, vertex, or the midpoint of an edge. To create the work plane, select the edge or sketch curve and select the point.	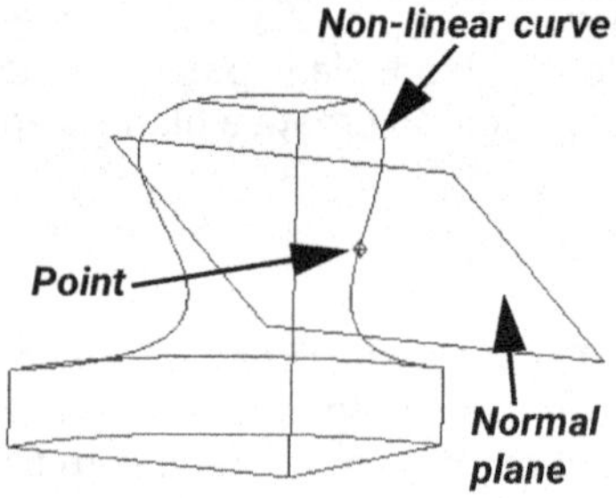

Consider the following when working with work planes:

- In situations where you have started to define a sketch and realize that a required plane does not exist, you can create an offset work plane on-the-fly. To create an offset work plane while (Start 2D Sketch) is active, select and drag the plane from a reference plane, and enter an offset value.

- Work axes and work points can be created during work plane creation and used as references. To do so, start the creation of the work plane (using either the **Plane** option or a specific work plane placement type), right-click, and select **Create Point** or **Create Axis**, as shown in Figure 7–2. Once the references have been selected, the work plane is created.

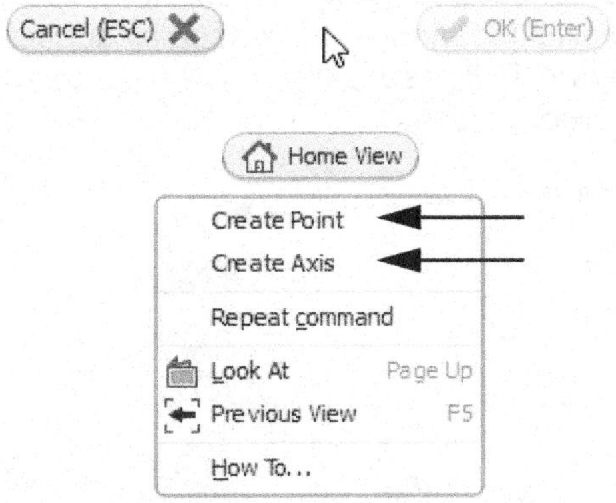

Figure 7–2

- To change the name of the work plane, select it in the Model browser and select it again (do not double-click) and enter a new name.
- To redefine the references of a work plane, right-click on the work plane, select **Redefine Feature**, and select new references.
- To modify the dimension values associated with work planes, double-click on the work plane in the graphics window or Model browser or right-click and select **Edit Dimension**. Once the dimension value displays, enter a new value.
- Work planes are infinite in size, but are sized to fit the geometry. To change its size, select its corner, wait until  displays, and drag. To automatically resize to fit the model, right-click on the work plane and select **Auto-Resize**. To manually change size, **Auto-Resize** must be toggled off.
- The two sides of a work plane are different colors. The normal side is a lighter color than the non-normal side. The normal side of the work plane can be reversed by right-clicking on the work plane and selecting **Flip Normal**. When entering offset values, the positive direction is always taken from the normal side of the plane.
- To toggle a work plane's visibility, right-click on the work plane and select **Visibility**. Alternatively, you can select the work plane in the Model browser and press <Alt>+<V>.
- To globally control work plane display, use the  (Object Visibility) options (*View* tab> *Visibility* panel).

7.2 Work Axes

A work axis is a type of feature that can be used to help create work planes, revolved features, or any other feature in the model. For example, a construction line can be sketched to serve as the axis of rotation for rotational features. However, creating a permanent work axis in the model is more efficient if the axial location is referenced by subsequent features (e.g., work plane). The plane shown in Figure 7–3 passes through the center of the rotational feature (work axis) and at an angle to the vertical face.

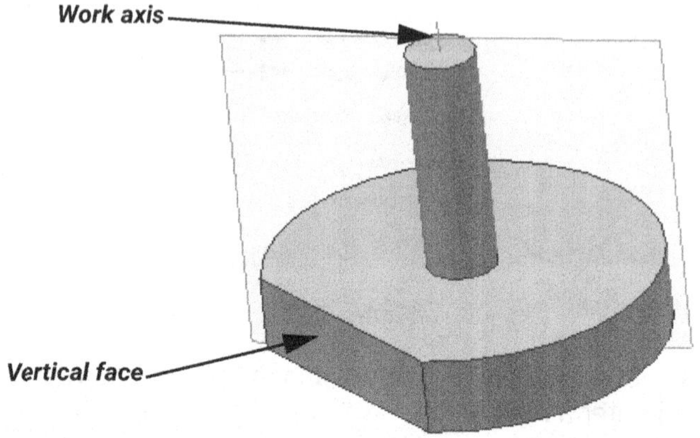

Figure 7–3

How To: Create a Work Axis

1. Start the creation of a work axis using one of the following methods. The end result of either method is the same. However, by selecting an axis placement type option, you are guided as to which references to select.
   - In the *3D Model* tab>*Work Features* panel, click (Axis).
   - In the *3D Model* tab>*Work Features* panel, expand (Axis) and select an axis placement type.
2. Once you have started the creation of a work axis, you must select references to locate it. References can include edges/curves, planar faces, work planes, cylindrical surfaces, work points, vertices, or sketched lines. The reference type required depends on the work axis being created. Once the selected references fully define the work axis' placement, the work axis displays. Alternatively, you can select the reference before clicking (Axis).

The different work axis placement types are as follows:

Type	Example
On Line or Edge: Select a line or linear edge. The resulting axis is along that line or edge.	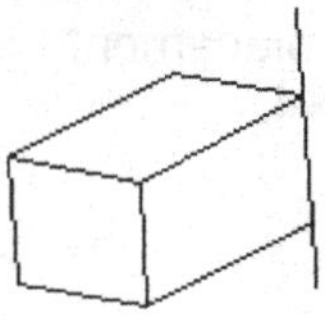
Parallel to Line through Point: Select a point and then an edge, work axis, or sketched line. The resulting axis is parallel to the edge, work axis, or sketched line and goes through the point.	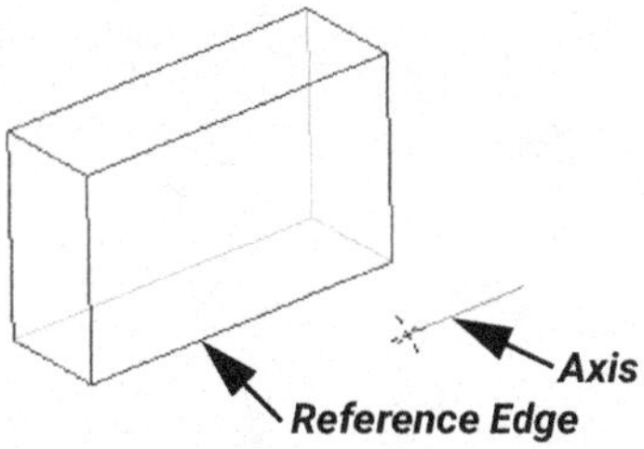
Through Two Points: Select two end points, center points, or work points. The resulting axis passes through those points.	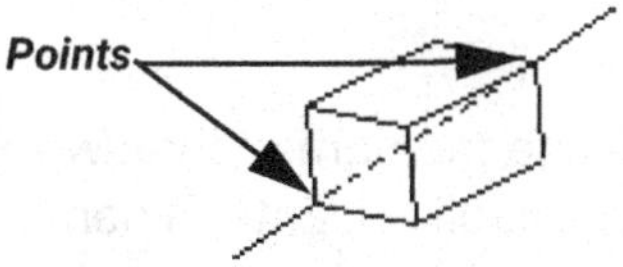
Intersection of Two Planes: Select two work planes or planar faces. The resulting axis is located along the intersection of the two planes.	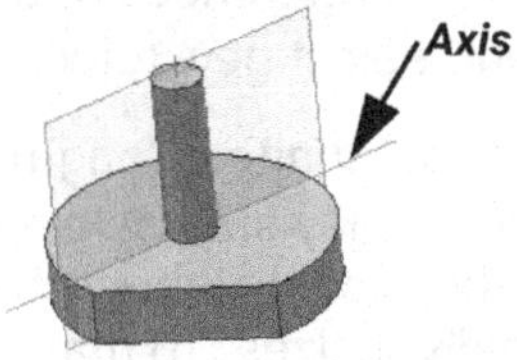
Normal to Plane through Point: Select a point and a surface. The resulting axis is normal to the surface and goes through the point.	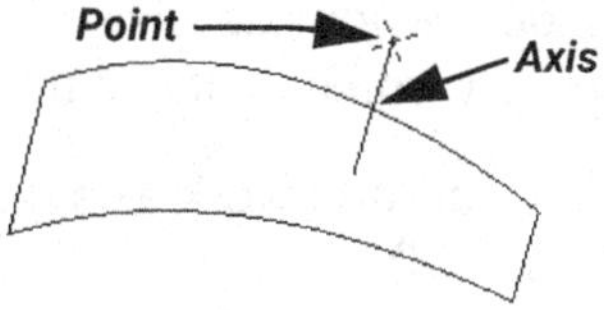
Through Center of Circular or Elliptical Edge: Select an edge of a circular or elliptical feature. The resulting axis passes through the centerline of the edge.	
Through Revolved Face or Feature: Select a face or feature of a revolved feature to create an axis that passes through the feature's centerline.	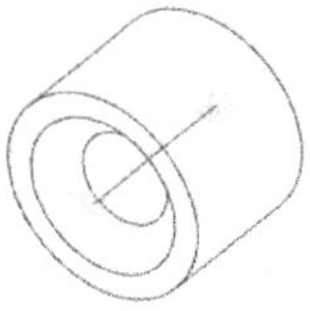

Consider the following when working with work axis:

- Work planes and work points can be created during work axis creation and used as references. To do so, start the creation of the work axis (using either the **Axis** option or a specific work axis placement type), right-click, and select **Create Plane** or **Create Point**, as shown in Figure 7–4.

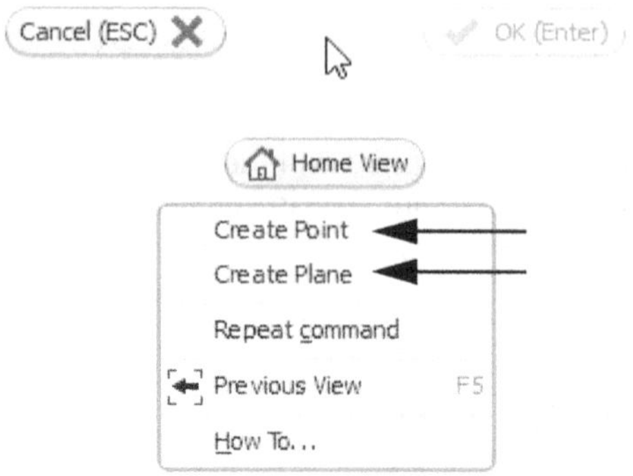

Figure 7–4

- To change the name of the work axis, select it in the Model browser and select it again (do not double-click). Enter a name.
- To redefine the references of a work axis, right-click on the work axis, select **Redefine Feature**, and select new references.
- Work axes are infinite in length, but on screen they are sized to fit the overall geometry. To change the display size, select one of its ends and drag it. To automatically resize the work axis to fit the model, right-click on it and select **Auto-Resize**. Once toggled on, the work axis automatically resizes. To manually change the size, **Auto-Resize** needs to be toggled off.
- To change a work axis' visibility, right-click on the work axis and select **Visibility**. Alternatively, you can select the work axis in the Model browser and press <Alt>+<V>.
- To globally control work axis display, use the (Object Visibility) options (*View* tab> *Visibility* panel).

7.3 Work Points

Work points can be used as references when creating work planes, work axes, or other features in the model. In the example shown in Figure 7–5, various methods are used to create work points.

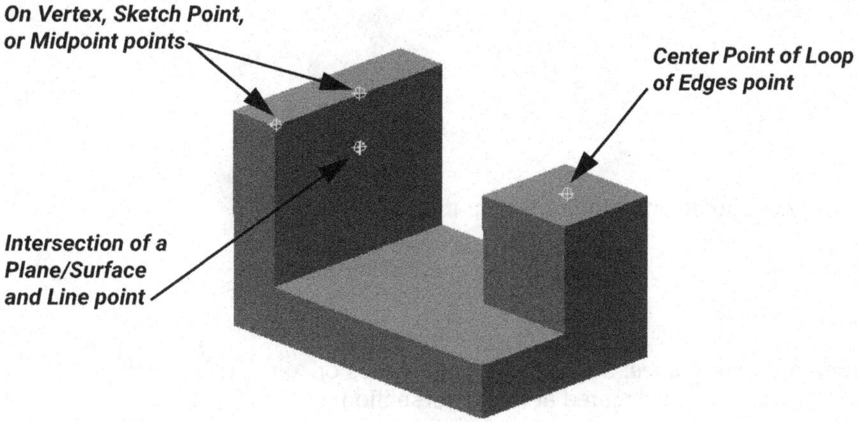

Figure 7–5

How To: Create a Work Point

1. Start the creation of a work point using one of the following methods. The end result of either method is the same. However, by selecting a point placement type, you are guided as to which references to select.
   - In the *3D Model* tab>*Work Features* panel, click (Point).
   - In the *3D Model* tab>*Work Features* panel, expand (Point) and select a point placement type.
2. Once you have started the creation of a work point, you must select references to locate it. References can include work points, vertices, sketched points, midpoints, work planes, edges, work axes, or solid geometry. The reference type required depends on the work point being created. Once the selected references fully define the work point's placement, it displays. Alternatively, you can select the reference before clicking (Point).

The different work point placement types are as follows:

Type	Example
Grounded Point: Select an existing point and convert it to a grounded point. Grounded work points have all degrees of freedom removed and are fixed in space.	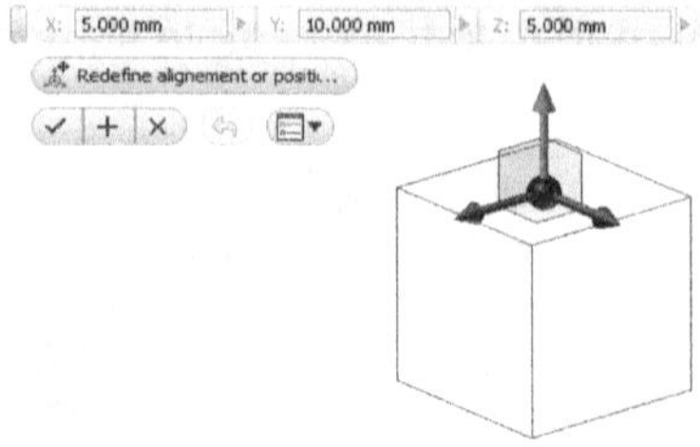
On Vertex, Sketch point, or Midpoint: Select the end point or midpoint.	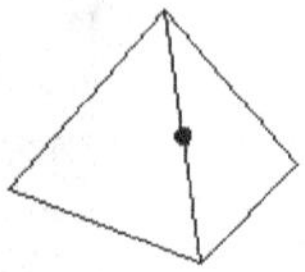
Intersection of Three Planes: Select three work planes or planar faces. The work point is located at their intersection.	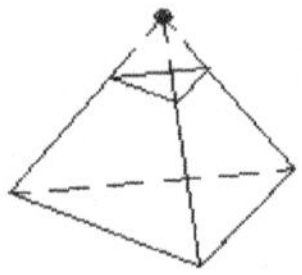
Intersection of Two Lines: Select the two edges, work axes, or lines. The work point is located at their intersection.	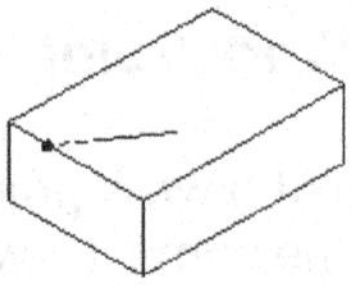
Intersection of a Plane/Surface and Line: Select a plane and sketch line, curve, edge, or axis. The work point is located at their intersection.	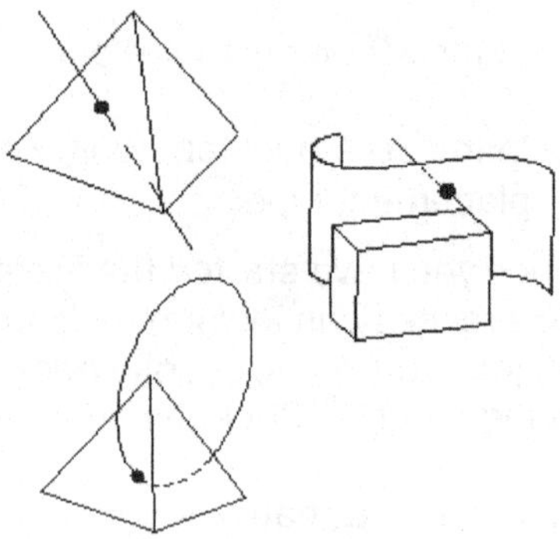
Center Point of Loop of Edges: Toggle on Loop Select Mode in the shortcut menu and select a circle, arc, or edge. A point is created at the center of the loop whether it is circular or not.	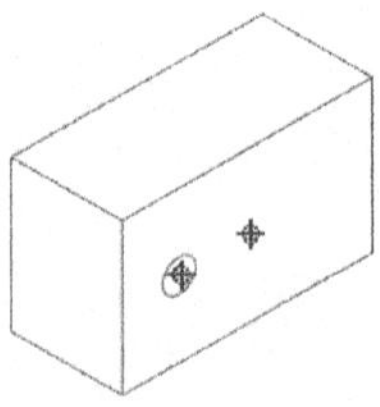

Type	Example
Center of Torus: Select the torus surface. A point is created at the center of the selected surface.	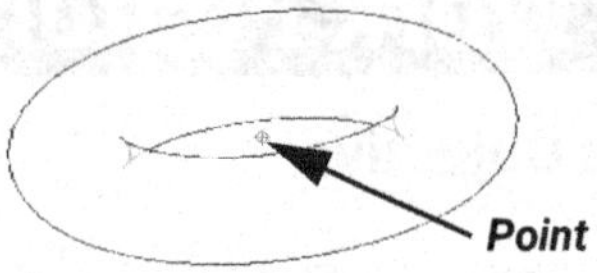
Center of Sphere: Select the sphere surface. A point is created at the center of the selected surface.	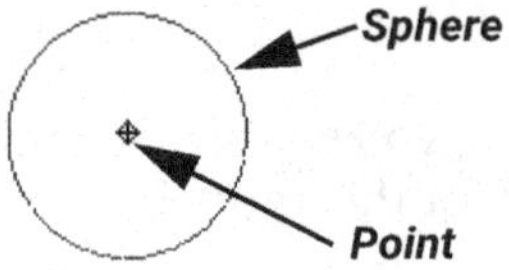

Consider the following when working with work points:

- Work planes and work axes can be created during work point creation and used as references. To do so, start the creation of the work point (using either the **Point** option or a specific work point placement type), right-click, and select **Create Axis** or **Create Plane**, as shown in Figure 7–6.

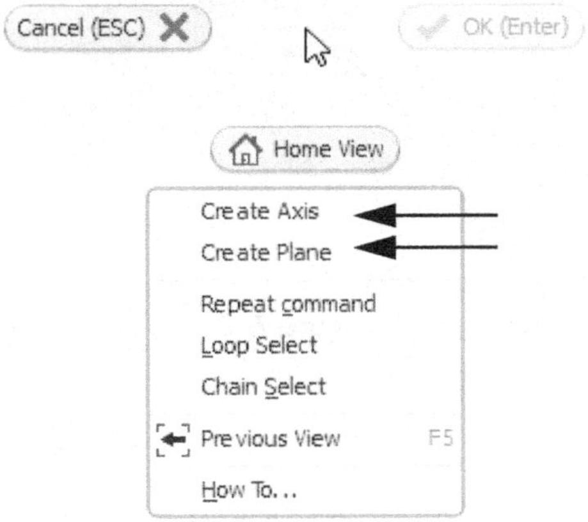

Figure 7–6

- To change the name of the work point (feature) select it in the Model browser and select it again (do not double-click). Enter a new name.
- To redefine the references of a work point, right-click on the work axis, select **Redefine Feature**, and select new references.
- To change a work point's visibility, right-click on the work point and select **Visibility**. Alternatively, you can select the work point in the Model browser and press <Alt>+<V>.
- To globally control work point display, use the (Object Visibility) options (*View* tab> *Visibility* panel).

Practice 7a
Use Work Features to Create Geometry I

Practice Objective

- Create work planes that can be used as references in the creation of a solid geometry feature.

In this practice, you will create the post/handle for the model shown in Figure 7–7. To create the geometry for this model, you need to create two additional work planes.

Figure 7–7

Task 1: Open a part file.

1. Open **fork.ipt**.
2. Display the XZ Plane in the model.

Task 2: Create the post for the fork.

1. In the *Work Features* panel, expand (Plane) and select **Tangent to Surface and Parallel to Plane** to create a work plane.

2. Select the bottom circular surface of **Extrusion1** as the reference for the work plane to be tangent to, as shown in Figure 7–8.
3. Select the XZ Plane as the plane to be parallel to. A new work plane displays, as shown in Figure 7–8.

   Note: *Alternatively, you can click*  *(Plane) and select the tangent and parallel references without enabling* ***Tangent to Surface and Parallel to Plane****. Based on the selected references, the software knows the type of plane that should be placed.*

4. In the Model browser, select the new work plane once and then again. Enter **Post Tangent Ref** as the new name of the work plane and press <Enter>.

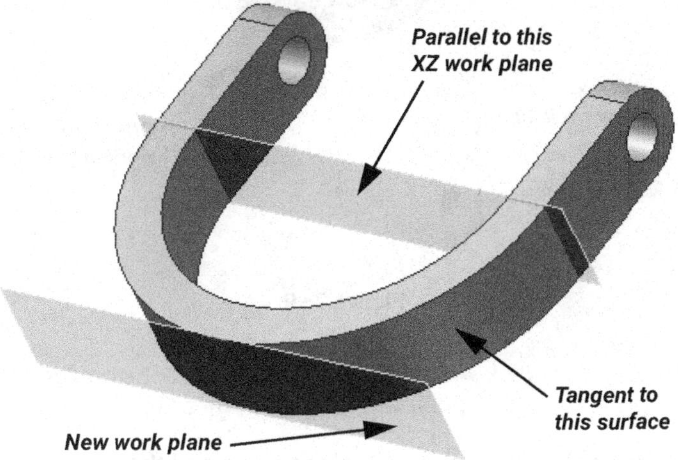

Figure 7–8

The next steps create the post portion of the fork. There are many different ways that this can be accomplished. These steps take into account that the post must be exactly 7.5 in length. To meet this design requirement and create a robust model if changes are required, you will create an additional work plane offset 7.5 from the Post Tangent Ref work plane. A circular section will be placed on this work plane and extruded back to the fork portion of the model. Completing the model like this ensures that if dimensional changes are required, there is an easy and efficient way to make changes to the model.

5. In the *Work Features* panel, expand  (Plane) and select **Offset from Plane** to create a work plane.
6. Select the **Post Tangent Ref** work plane.

7. Enter **-7.5 in** when prompted and click ✓ in the mini-toolbar. The work plane is created as shown in Figure 7–9.

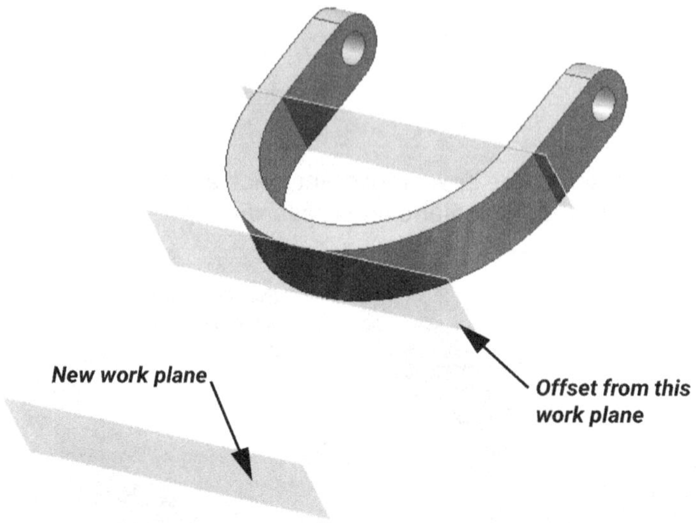

Figure 7–9

Note: *Alternatively, you can click (Plane), hover the cursor over the reference work plane, hold the left mouse button, and drag to position the new offset plane.*

8. In the Model browser, select the new work plane once and then again. Enter **Post Depth** as the new name of the work plane and press <Enter>.
9. Review the Model browser and notice that the **Post Tangent Ref** work plane is now embedded within the node for **Post Depth**. This is because it is a child of the new work plane. It can be referenced/selected in this node as needed, or it can be shared to have a copy brought out to the top level.
10. Select the new **Post Depth** work plane, right-click and select **New Sketch**, or click in the heads-up display on the model.

11. Sketch a circular entity centered on the projected origin point and dimension, as shown in Figure 7–10.

    Note: *You might need to change to the Wireframe visual style and enable (Slice Graphics) in the Status Bar to see the projected origin point and the sketch once it has been created.*

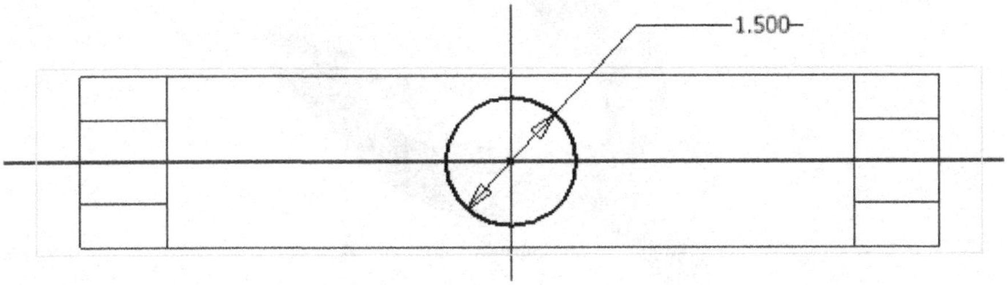

Figure 7–10

12. Finish the sketch.
13. In the *3D Model* tab>*Create* panel, click (Extrude) to create an extruded feature.
14. The circular section is automatically selected as the profile. Extrude the section using the (To Next) distance option. Complete the feature. The model displays as shown in Figure 7–11.

    Note: *By using the (To Next) distance option you ensure that the post extends as required to lie against the entire circular section of the fork.*

Figure 7–11

15. Change the length of the post to 9 inches by editing the offset dimension on the Post Depth work plane to **-9 in**. Update the model, if required.

16. Right-click on **Extrusion1** and select **Show Dimensions**. Edit the value of the current radius dimension from 4 (as shown in Figure 7–12) to **.5 in**.

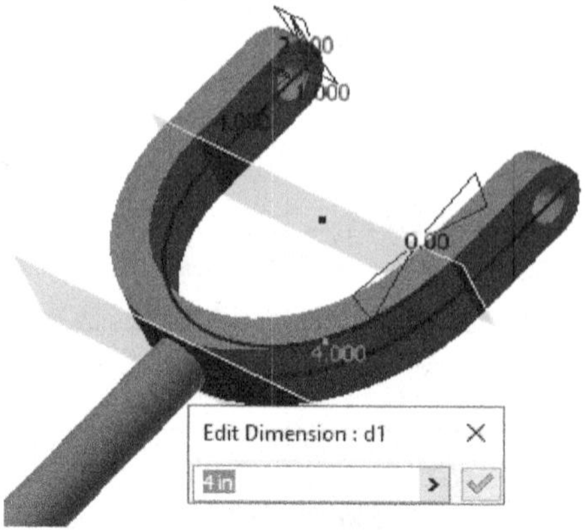

Figure 7–12

17. Update the model. Your updated model should appear as shown in Figure 7–13.

Figure 7–13

18. Save the model and close the window.

End of practice

Practice 7b
Use Work Features to Create Geometry II

Practice Objective

- Create a work plane that can be used as a reference in the creation of a solid geometry feature.

In this practice, you will create the Spotface hole shown in Figure 7–14. To create the geometry for this model, you need to create additional work planes.

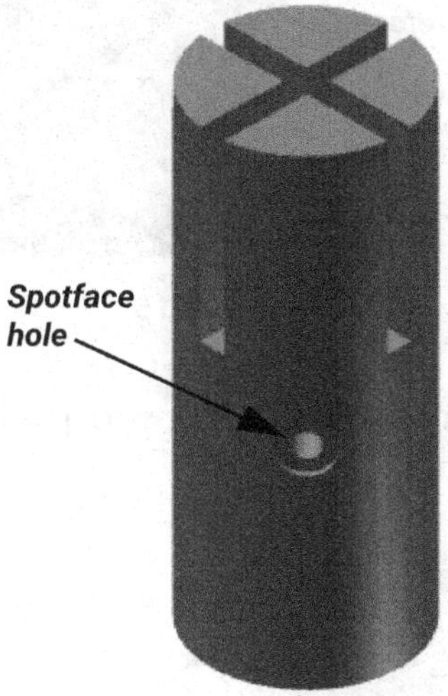

Figure 7–14

Task 1: Open a part file and create work features required to create a hole.

1. Open **cylindrical_surf.ipt**.
2. In the *Work Features* panel, expand (Plane) and select **Angle to Plane around Edge** to create a work plane.

3. Select the XY Plane as the angular reference for the work plane. The model is shown in Figure 7–15.
4. Select the **Y-axis** in the **Origin** node of the Model browser as the linear reference to measure the angle about, as shown in Figure 7–15.

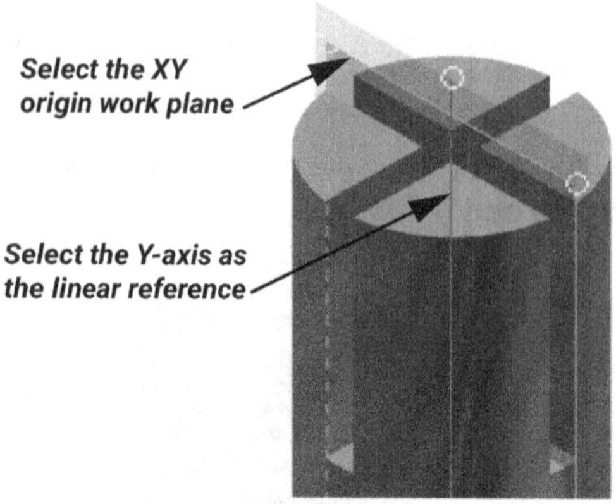

Figure 7–15

5. Enter **45** and click  in the mini-toolbar. The work plane displays, as shown in Figure 7–16.

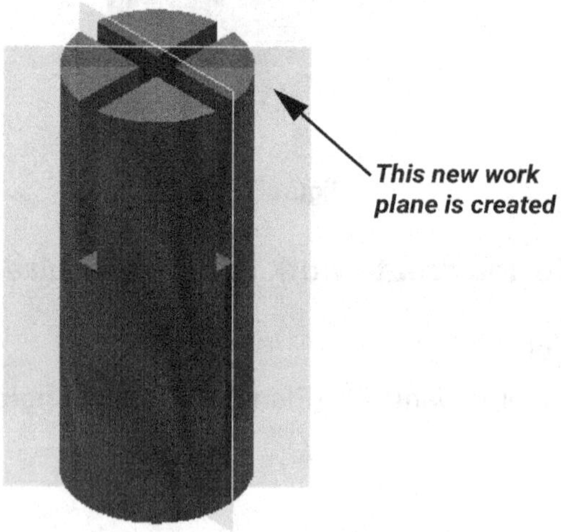

Figure 7–16

Note: *Alternatively, you can click*  *(Plane) and select the references without enabling* ***Angle to Plane around Edge****. Based on the selected references, the software knows the type of plane that should be placed.*

6. In the Model browser, select the new work plane once and then again. Enter **Angular Ref** as the new name of the work plane and press <Enter>.
7. In the *Work Features* panel, expand (Plane) and select **Tangent to Surface and Parallel to Plane** to create a work plane.
8. Select the **Angular Ref** work plane and select the cylindrical surface, as shown on the left in Figure 7–17. The work plane is created as shown on the right.

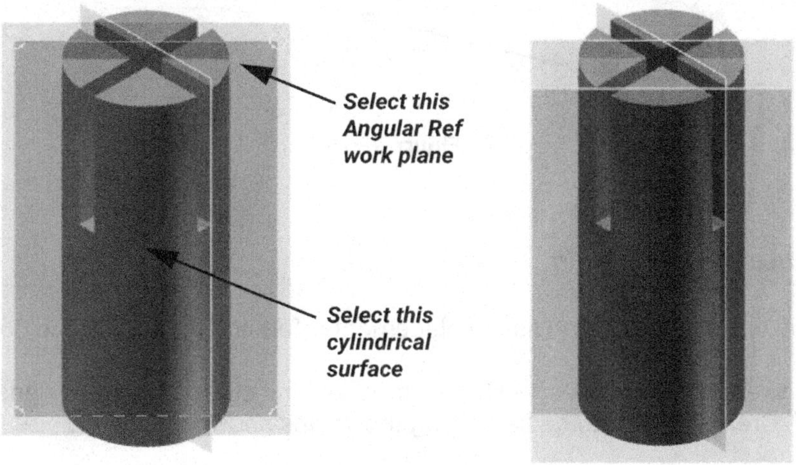

Figure 7–17

Note: *Alternatively, you can click (Plane) and select the tangent and parallel references without enabling* ***Tangent to Surface and Parallel to Plane****. Based on the selected references, the software knows the type of plane that should be placed.*

9. In the Model browser, select the new work plane once and then again. Enter **Hole Sketch Plane** as the new name of the work plane and press <Enter>.

Task 2: Create the sketch required to create the hole.

In this task, you will use **Hole Sketch Plane** (work plane) as the sketch plane for a point. In the next task, you will then use this point to create a hole.

1. Select the new **Hole Sketch Plane** work plane, right-click, and select **New Sketch**, or click in the heads-up display on the model.
2. Project the Y-axis.
3. Project the top edge of the cylinder to use as a dimension reference for the Sketch Point. This dimension reference will control the position of the hole from the top of the cylinder.

4. In the *Create* panel, click (Point). Place and dimension the point, as shown in Figure 7–18.

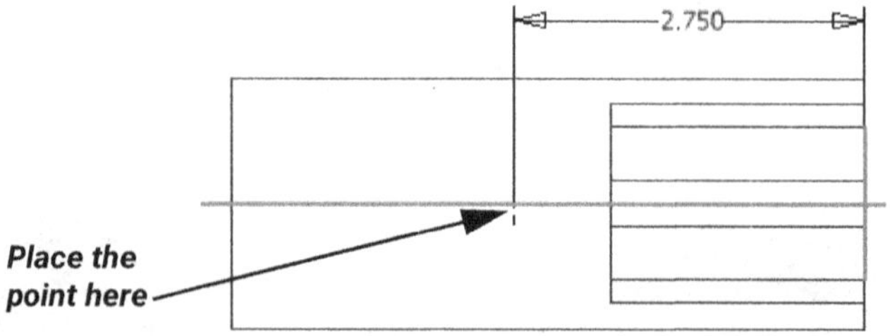

Figure 7–18

5. Finish the sketch.

Task 3: Create the hole.

In this task, you will use the sketch as the placement reference for a Spotface hole.

1. Select the sketch of the point in the Model browser and click in the heads-up display on the model. Create the **Spotface** hole using the values shown in Figure 7–19.

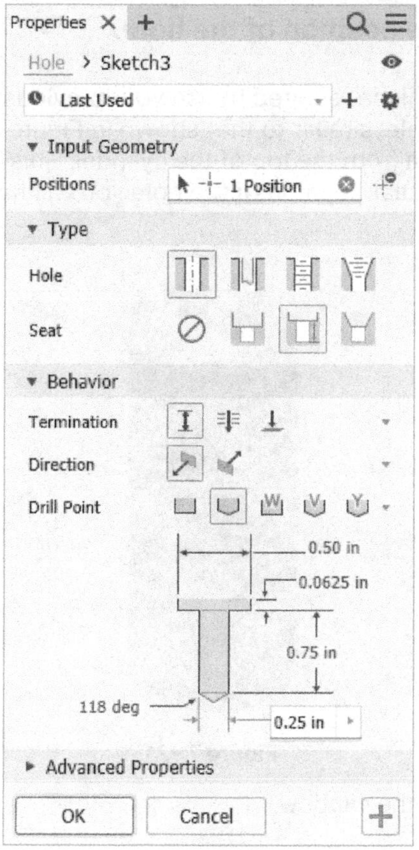

Figure 7–19

2. Complete the feature. The model displays as shown in Figure 7–20.

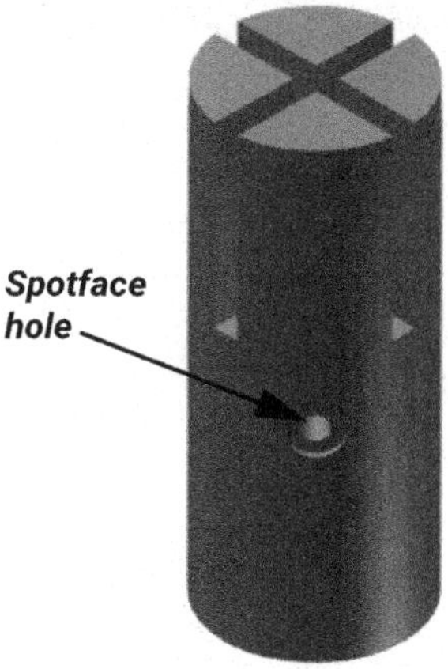

Figure 7–20

Task 4: (Optional) Edit the position of the hole.

1. In this optional task, you will be required to use your previous knowledge to change the position of the Spotface hole, similar to that shown in Figure 7–21. To do so you will have to edit the linear dimension from the top of the cylinder. This dimension was established in the sketch. To edit the angular position of the hole you will have to edit the angle on the Angular Ref work plane.

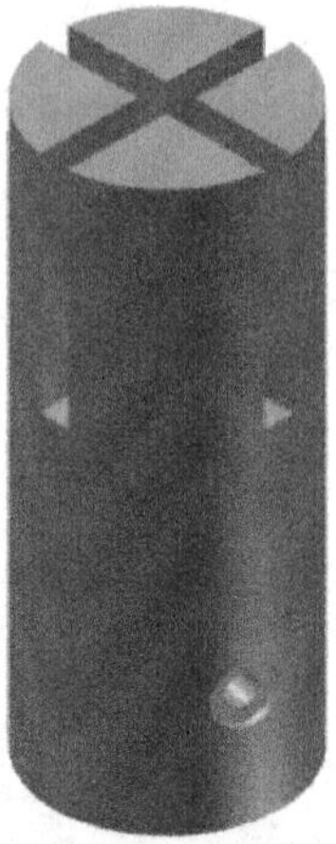

Figure 7–21

2. Save the model and close the window.

End of practice

Practice 7c
(Optional) Use Work Features to Create Geometry III

Practice Objective

- Create a work plane and work axis that can be used as references in the creation of a solid geometry feature.

In this practice, you will create the model shown in Figure 7–22. To create the geometry for this model, you need to create an additional work plane and axis.

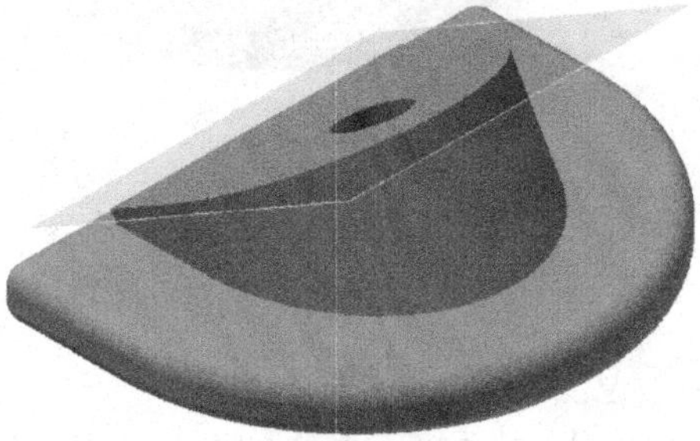

Figure 7–22

Task 1: Create a new part and create a sketch.

1. Create a new part using the standard metric (mm) template.
2. Create a sketch on the XZ Plane.
3. Project the YZ and XY work planes as references to locate the sketched geometry.
4. Sketch and dimension the section as shown in Figure 7–23.

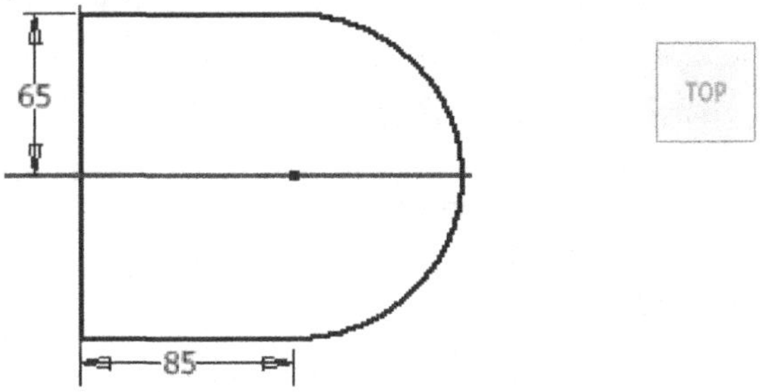

Figure 7–23

5. Finish the sketch.

6. In the *3D Model* tab>*Create* panel, click (Extrude).
7. Select the required profiles, enter **20.00** in the *Distance A* field, and complete the feature. The model displays as shown in Figure 7–24. Depending on the orientation of the sketch plane, the default view of the model might vary. Spin as required, to reorient the model.

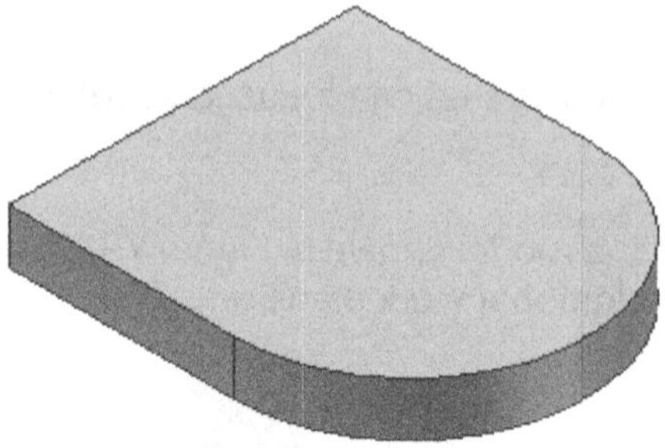

Figure 7–24

Task 2: Create a fillet.

1. In the *Modify* panel, click (Fillet) to create a fillet.
2. Adjacent to the *Properties* panel, select in the tool palette to enable feature selection. Select **Extrusion1** to add fillets to all of its edges.
3. Enter **7.00** as the radius.
4. Complete the feature. The model displays as shown in Figure 7–25.

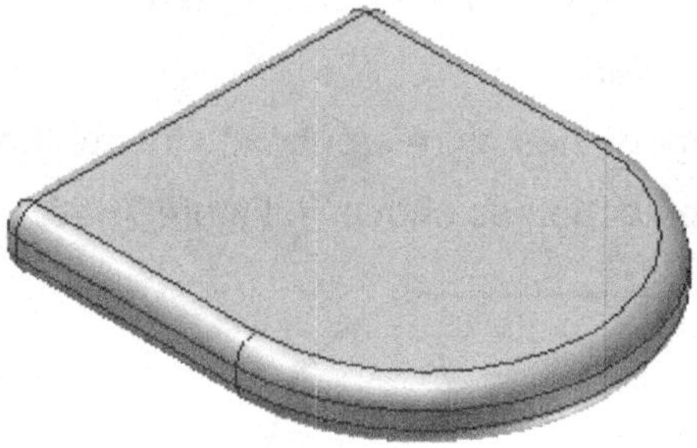

Figure 7–25

Task 3: Create work features.

In the remaining tasks, you will create the extrusion shown in Figure 7–26. In this task, you will create a work axis at the intersection of two faces on the base feature and a work plane referencing the axis.

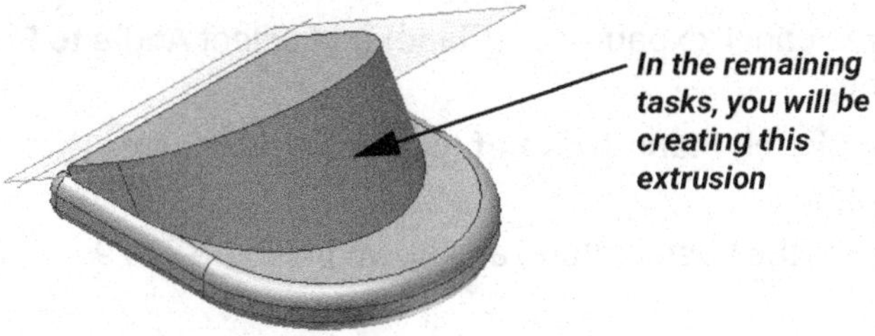

Figure 7–26

1. In the *Work Features* panel, expand (Axis) and select **Intersection of Two Planes** to create a work axis.
2. Select the two faces shown in Figure 7–27 to create a work axis at their intersection.

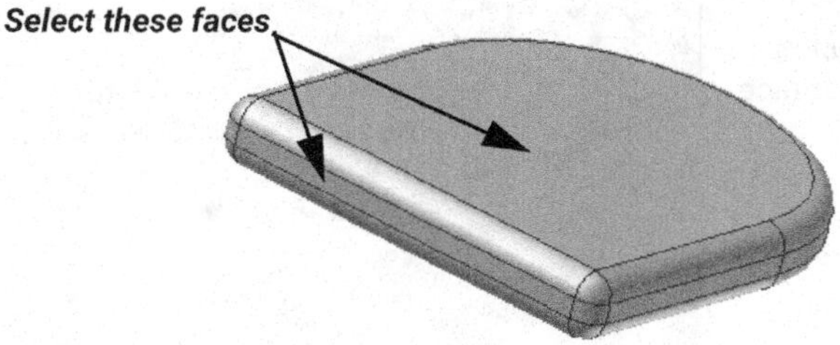

Figure 7–27

The work axis is created at the intersection of the faces, as shown in Figure 7–28.

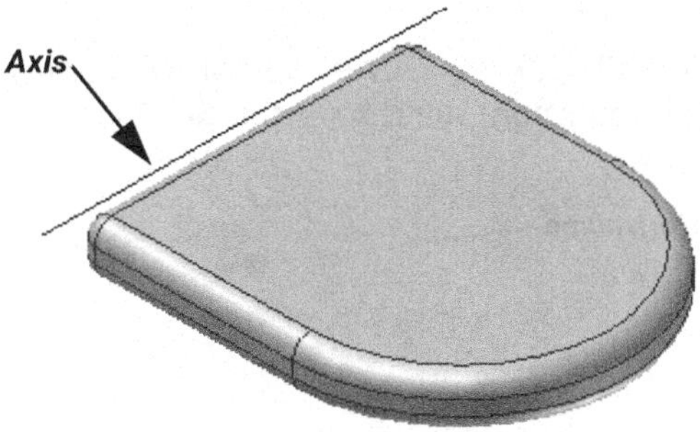

Figure 7–28

Note: *Alternatively, you can click (Axis) and select the two planes without enabling* ***Intersection of Two Planes****. Based on the selected references, the software knows the type of plane that should be placed.*

3. In the Model browser, select the work axis once and then again. Enter **Angular Sketch Plane Axis Ref** as the new name of the work axis and press <Enter>.

4. In the *Work Features* panel, expand (Plane) and select **Angle to Plane around Edge** to create a work plane.
5. Select the **Angular Sketch Plane Axis Ref** (previously Work Axis1) in the Model browser or the graphics window.
6. Select the top face of the base feature, as shown in Figure 7–29.

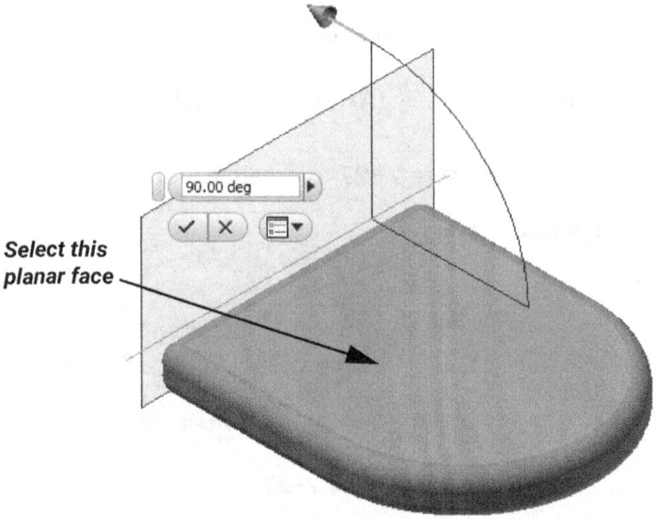

Figure 7–29

7. Enter **30** in the *Angle* field and click . The work plane displays as shown in Figure 7–30. Depending on your model, you might need to enter **-30** to obtain the result.

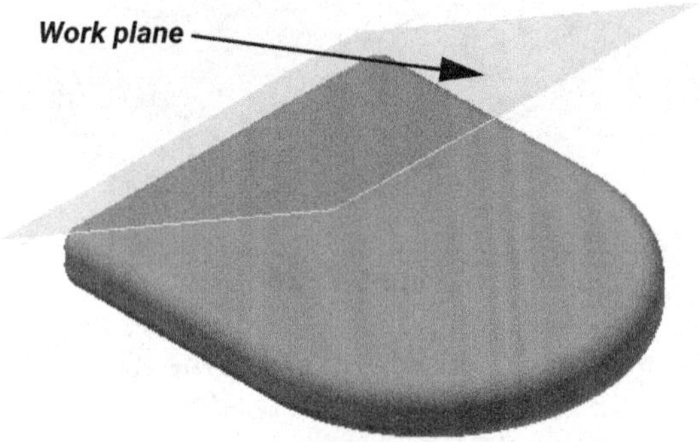

Figure 7–30

Note: *Alternatively, you can click (Plane) and select the references without enabling* ***Angle to Plane around Edge****. Based on the selected references, the software knows the type of plane that should be placed.*

8. In the Model browser, select the work plane once and then again. Enter **Angular Sketch Plane** as the new name of the work plane and press <Enter>.

Task 4: Create the angled extrusion.

1. Create a sketch on the new work plane (**Angular Sketch Plane**).
2. Project the XY Plane and the newly created axis (**Angular Sketch Plane Axis Ref**).

   ***Note:** The **Angular Sketch Plane Axis Ref** was consumed by **Angular Sketch Plane**. Expand the workplane's node in the Model browser to select the axis.*

3. Press <Esc> to complete the operation.
4. Sketch the section with the dimensions and constraints shown in Figure 7–31. The sketch is displayed in wireframe for clarity.

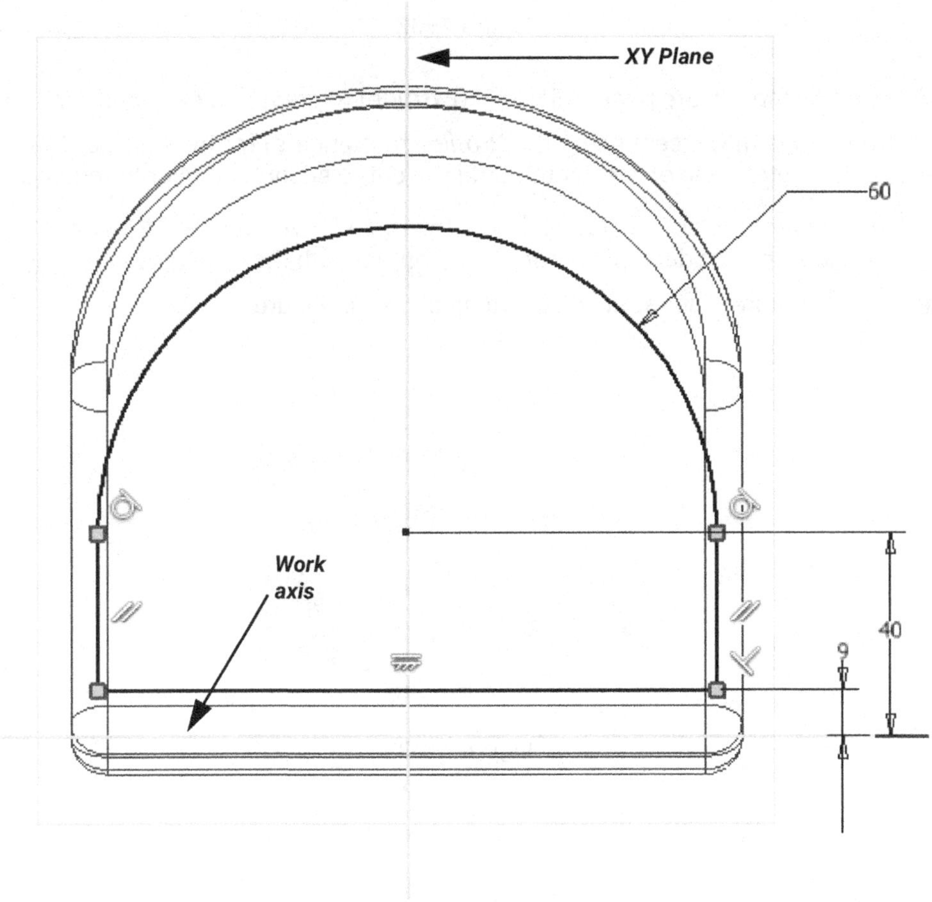

Figure 7–31

5. Finish the sketch. The sketch displays as shown in Figure 7–32.

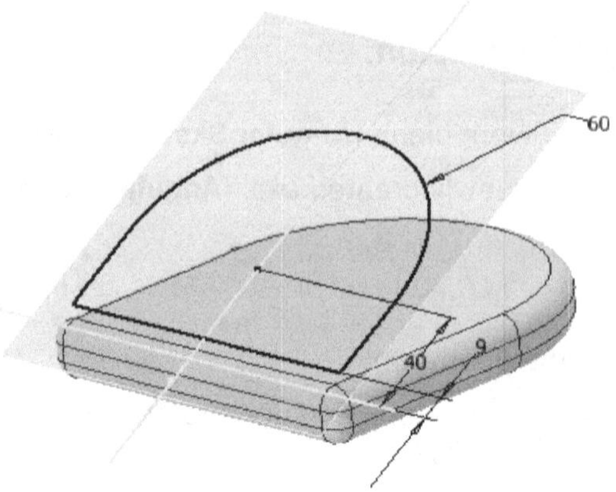

Figure 7–32

6. In the *3D Model* tab>*Create* panel, click (Extrude) to create an extruded feature.
7. Select both halves of the section as the *Profiles* reference(s) for the feature. Alternatively, hover over the outer edge of the sketch until the entire section highlights red and select it.
8. In the *Behavior* area, select (To Next) as the *Distance A* reference for extruding the sketch. The sketch extrudes until it comes in contact with the next face.
9. Complete the feature. The model displays as shown in Figure 7–33.

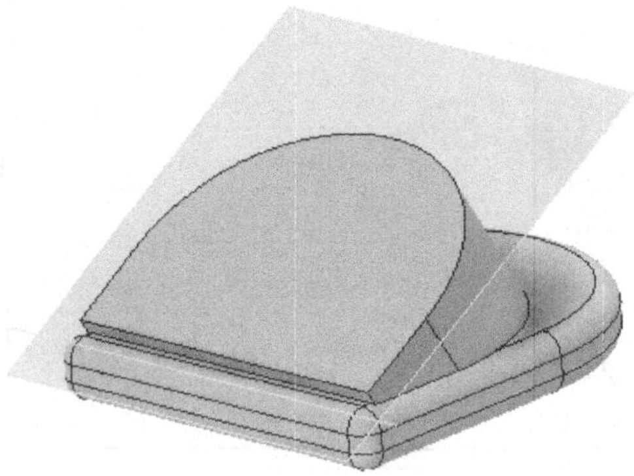

Figure 7–33

Task 5: Create a hole that remains centered on a face.

In this task, you will create a hole that will remain centered on a selected face, regardless of changes to the model that would change the size of the face. To accomplish this, you will create a work point and create the hole based on the point. You will make changes to the model to ensure that the hole placement updates correctly.

1. In the *Work Features* panel, expand (Point) and select **Center Point of Loop of Edges** to create a work point.
2. Rotate the model and select the loop of edges, as shown in Figure 7–34.

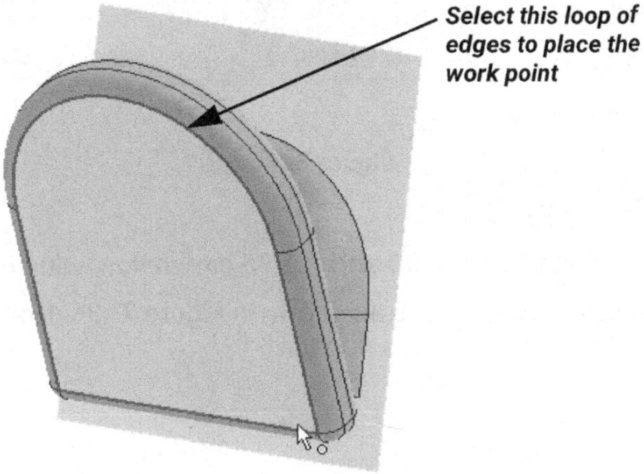

Figure 7–34

3. A point displays, centered on the face that is bounded by the selected loop.
4. Right-click in the graphics window and select **Hole**.
5. Place the hole on the work point that was just created and define the hole's direction in the Y-axis cutting into the model. Further define the hole as a simple hole that cuts through the entire model.
6. Set the diameter for the hole to **25mm**.

7. Complete the feature. The model displays as shown in Figure 7–35.

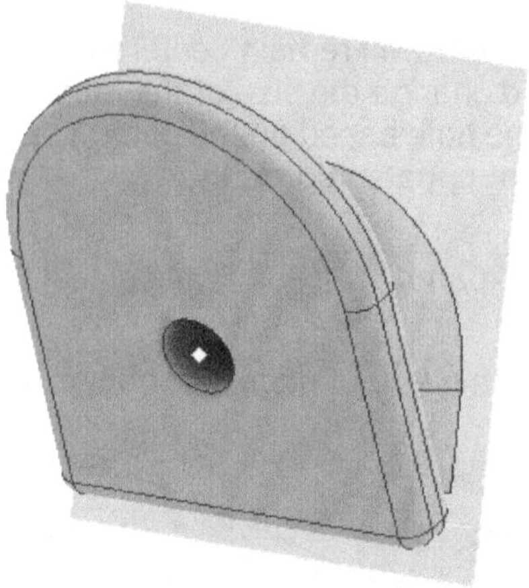

Figure 7–35

8. Show the dimensions for **Extrusion1**.
9. Change the *65* dimension value to **100** and the 85 dimension value to **50**.
10. Update the model. The model displays as shown in Figure 7–36. Note that the hole remains centered on the face after the model is updated.

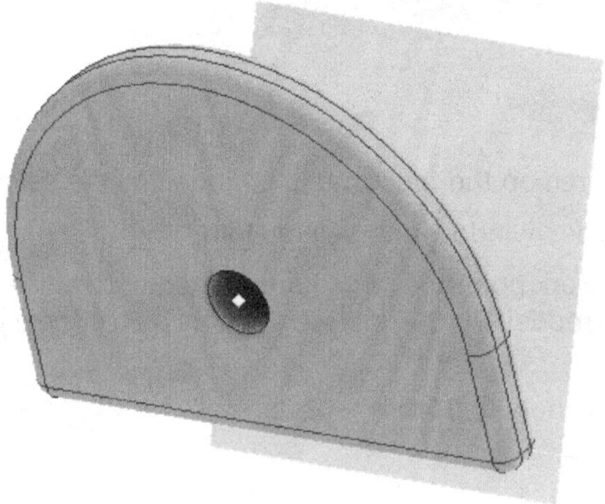

Figure 7–36

11. Save the model and enter **work_features** as the name.
12. Close the window.

End of practice

Chapter Review Questions

1. Origin planes are the only work planes that can exist in a model.
   a. True
   b. False

2. Which of the following are possible uses for work planes similar to those shown in Figure 7–37? (Select all that apply.)

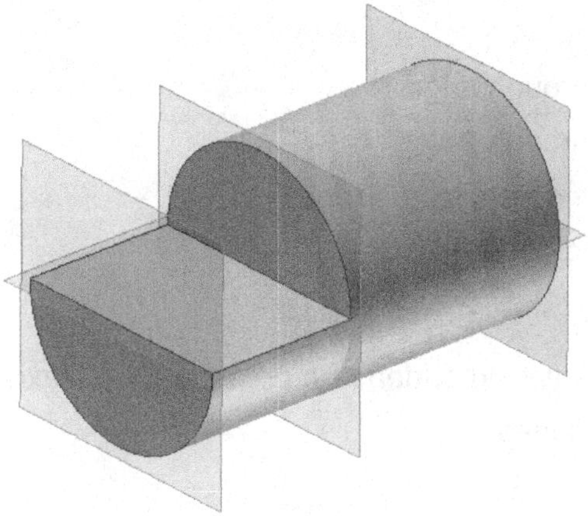

Figure 7–37

   a. To create another work plane.
   b. To define a sketch plane.
   c. To serve as the boundary for the depth of an extrusion.
   d. To set up a drawing sheet.

3. Which of the following are valid options to create a work plane? (Select all that apply.)
   a. Through a Plane and Parallel to an Axis
   b. Offset from Plane
   c. Tangent to Surface and Parallel to Plane
   d. Three Points

4. Which option enables you to create the work plane shown in Figure 7–38?

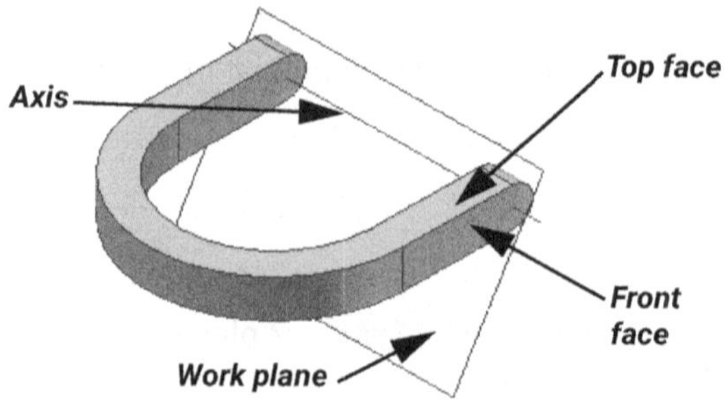

Figure 7–38

a. Tangent to Surface through Edge
b. Tangent to Surface through Point
c. Tangent to Surface and Parallel to Plane
d. Angle to Plane around Edge

5. Which of the following are valid options for creating a work axis? (Select all that apply.)

a. Intersection of Two Planes
b. Through Two Points
c. Parallel to a Line
d. On Line or Edge

6. A work axis can be used as a reference when creating a work plane.

a. True
b. False

7. Which option creates a work point centered on a face and remains centered even after the size of the face changes?

a. On Vertex, Sketch Point, or Midpoint
b. Center Point of Loop of Edges
c. Center of Torus
d. Through Center of Circular or Elliptical Edge

8. You can create work planes during work point creation to reference and constrain the work point.

a. True

b. False

Command Summary

Button	Command	Location
	**Angle to Plane around Edge**	• **Ribbon:** *3D Model* tab>*Work Features* panel>expand **Plane**
	**Axis**	• **Ribbon:** *3D Model* tab>*Work Features* panel
	**Center Point of Loop of Edges**	• **Ribbon:** *3D Model* tab>*Work Features* panel>expand **Plane**
	**Center Point of Sphere**	• **Ribbon:** *3D Model* tab>*Work Features* panel>expand **Plane**
	**Center Point of Torus**	• **Ribbon:** *3D Model* tab>*Work Features* panel>expand **Plane**
	**Grounded Point**	• **Ribbon:** *3D Model* tab>*Work Features* panel>expand **Plane**
	**Intersection of a Plane/ Surface and Line**	• **Ribbon:** *3D Model* tab>*Work Features* panel>expand **Plane**
	**Intersection of Three Planes**	• **Ribbon:** *3D Model* tab>*Work Features* panel>expand **Plane**
	**Intersection of Two Lines**	• **Ribbon:** *3D Model* tab>*Work Features* panel>expand **Plane**
	**Intersection of Two Planes**	• **Ribbon:** *3D Model* tab>*Work Features* panel>expand **Axis**
	**Midplane between Two Planes**	• **Ribbon:** *3D Model* tab>*Work Features* panel>expand **Plane**
	**Midplane of a Torus**	• **Ribbon:** *3D Model* tab>*Work Features* panel>expand **Plane**
	**Normal to a Curve at Point**	• **Ribbon:** *3D Model* tab>*Work Features* panel>expand **Plane**
	**Normal to Axis through Point**	• **Ribbon:** *3D Model* tab>*Work Features* panel>expand **Plane**
	**Normal to Plane through Point**	• **Ribbon:** *3D Model* tab>*Work Features* panel>expand **Axis**
	**Offset from Plane**	• **Ribbon:** *3D Model* tab>*Work Features* panel>expand **Plane**
	**On Line or Edge**	• **Ribbon:** *3D Model* tab>*Work Features* panel>expand **Axis**

Button	Command	Location
	**On Vertex, Sketch point, or Midpoint**	• **Ribbon:** *3D Model* tab>*Work Features* panel>expand **Plane**
	**Parallel to Line through Point**	• **Ribbon:** *3D Model* tab>*Work Features* panel>expand **Axis**
	**Parallel to Plane through Point**	• **Ribbon:** *3D Model* tab>*Work Features* panel>expand **Plane**
	**Plane**	• **Ribbon:** *3D Model* tab>*Work Features* panel • **Context Menu:** In the graphics window
	**Point**	• **Ribbon:** *3D Model* tab>*Work Features* panel
	**Tangent to Surface and Parallel to Plane**	• **Ribbon:** *3D Model* tab>*Work Features* panel>expand **Plane**
	**Tangent to Surface through Edge**	• **Ribbon:** *3D Model* tab>*Work Features* panel>expand **Plane**
	**Tangent to Surface through Point**	• **Ribbon:** *3D Model* tab>*Work Features* panel>expand **Plane**
	**Three Points**	• **Ribbon:** *3D Model* tab>*Work Features* panel>expand **Plane**
	**Through Center of Circular or Elliptical Edge**	• **Ribbon:** *3D Model* tab>*Work Features* panel>expand **Axis**
	**Through Revolved Face or Feature**	• **Ribbon:** *3D Model* tab>*Work Features* panel>expand **Axis**
	**Through Two Points**	• **Ribbon:** *3D Model* tab>*Work Features* panel>expand **Axis**
	**Two Coplanar Edges**	• **Ribbon:** *3D Model* tab>*Work Features* panel>expand **Plane**

Chapter 8

Equations and Parameters

Equations help incorporate design intent into a model, which ensures that the model behaves as intended when changes occur. They are established by creating mathematical relationships between dimensions and/or parameters.

Learning Objectives

- Change the dimension display type to identify dimension values, names, or equations.
- Create equations between dimensions to incorporate design intent into the model.
- Describe the difference between model parameters and user-defined parameters.
- Create user-defined parameters in a model.

8.1 Creating Equations

Features and sketches generate dimensions in a model. Each dimension has a unique dimension name. The dimension name starts with the letter "d" followed by a unique number (e.g., d0 or d1). Relationships can be defined between these dimensions, enabling you to control a dimension value based on a function of another dimension's value. These relationships are called *equations*. Equations can also include user parameters. When one dimension is referencing another, the referenced dimension in the equation is considered the driving dimension. The model in Figure 8–1 shows a hole being located based on an equation. When fx displays as part of a dimension name, it indicates that the dimension contains an equation.

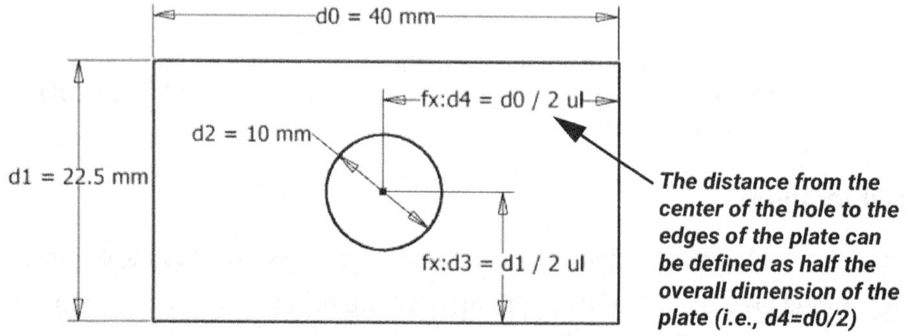

Figure 8–1

Use the following general steps to add an equation:

1. Display the dimension symbols.
2. Create equations.
3. Flex the model.
4. Edit the equations, as required.

Step 1 - Display the dimension symbols.

To create equations, you must use dimension names. To display dimension names, right-click in the graphics window, select **Dimension Display**, and click **Name**, as shown in Figure 8–2. Additional styles are listed in the following table. To control the display of dimensions in a sketch, expand (Dimension Display) in the Status Bar and select an option. The options are the same as those in the Part environment.

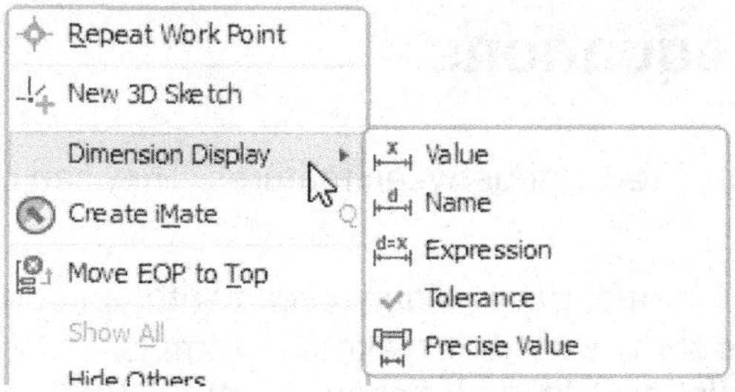

Figure 8–2

<table>
<tr><td>Value</td><td>Displays the numeric values of the dimensions.
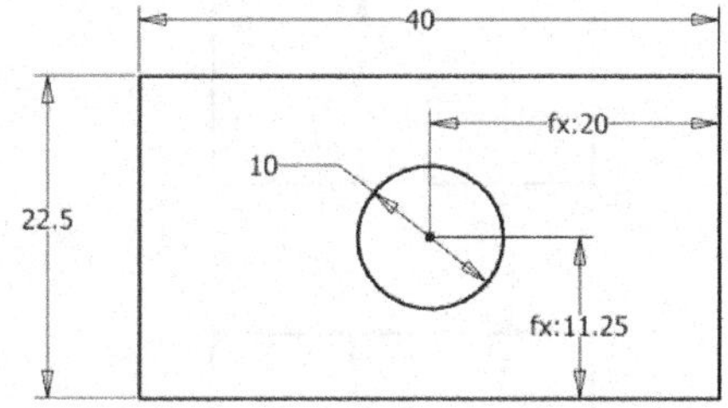
</td></tr>
<tr><td>Name</td><td>Displays the dimension names (e.g., d4 or d5).
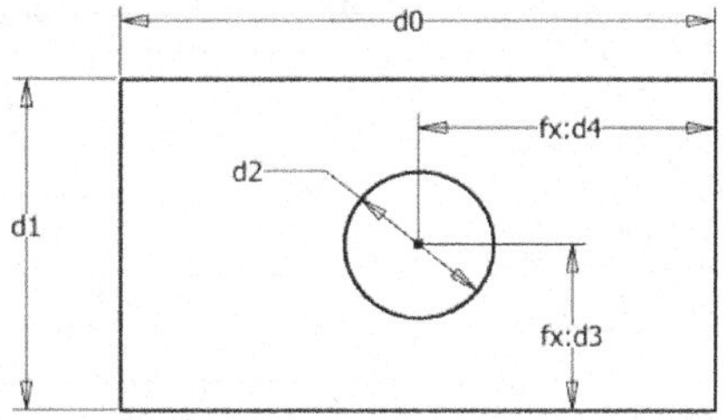
</td></tr>
<tr><td>Expression</td><td>Displays the dimension names with their numeric values or the equations that result in the numeric values (e.g., d2=d0/3 or d4=d5).
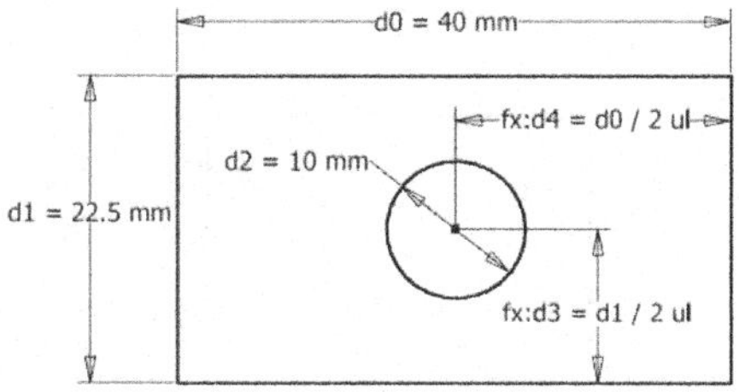
</td></tr>
<tr><td>Tolerance</td><td>Displays the tolerances defined on any dimensions.</td></tr>
<tr><td>Precise value</td><td>Displays the precise numeric values of dimensions (not rounded). The Precise value option also displays the actual value of a dimension if a tolerance is applied. For example, if the dimension is 2.00 +/- 0.05 and is evaluated at the maximum tolerance, the value is 2.0500000000.</td></tr>
</table>

Step 2 - Create equations.

Equations can be created in a sketch or between features. They can be created using any one of the following techniques:

- When editing a sketch or feature dimension you can enter an equation directly in the *Edit Dimension* dialog box, as shown in the two sketch examples in Figure 8–3. Alternatively, you can also select a dimension to add its dimension name to the Edit Dimension field for use in an equation.

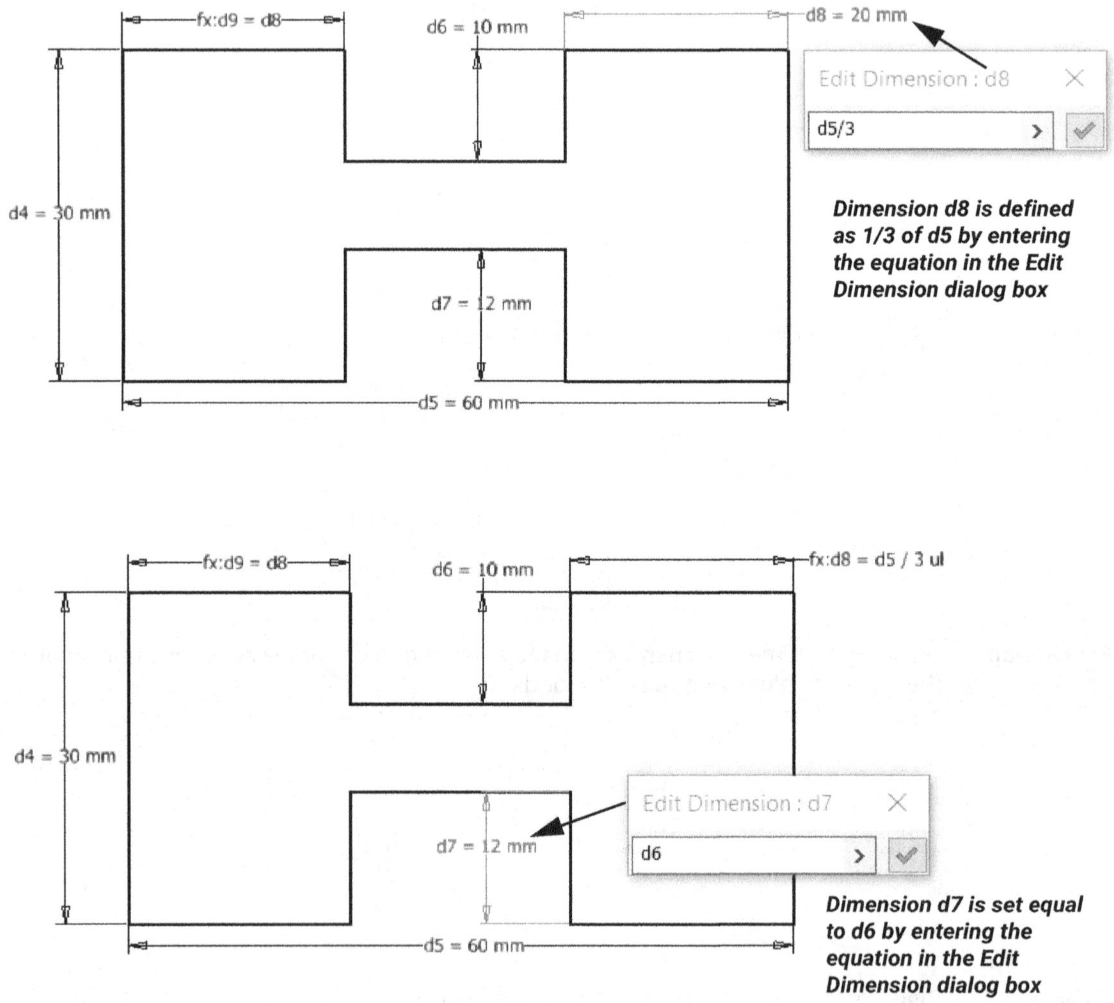

Figure 8–3

- During feature creation, you can enter an equation in the entry fields, as shown in Figure 8–4.

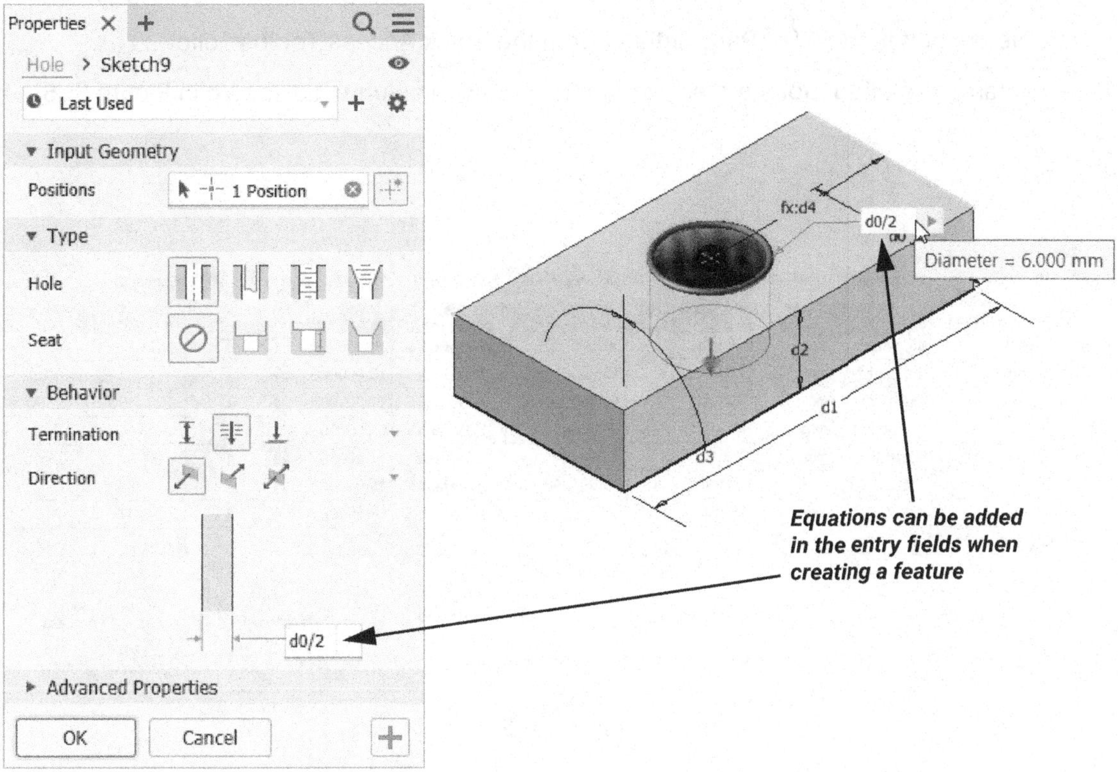

Figure 8–4

Hint: Selecting Dimension Symbols for Equations

When in a sketch, you can select other dimension symbols in the sketch to include them in an equation. If an equation requires a reference to another feature, right-click on it in the Model browser and select **Show Dimensions** so that the required dimension symbol can be selected for inclusion. When creating equations between features show all dimensions, edit the required dimension and select other dimension symbols to include them in the equation.

During Hole creation, in the expanded dimension field, click **Reference Dimension** to show the dimension symbols for other features. Select them, as required, to incorporate their dimension symbol into an entry field to establish a relationship. To establish a relationship between the placement references in a hole, press and hold <Ctrl> while selecting.

- Equations can be entered after sketch or feature creation using the *Parameters* dialog box. This dialog box enables you to review the complete list of all of the parameters (dimension names) and existing equations. To open the *Parameters* dialog box, in the *Manage* tab> *Parameters* panel, click f_x (Parameters), or in the Quick Access Toolbar, click f_x (Parameters). Equations are entered in the *Equation* column, as shown in Figure 8–5.

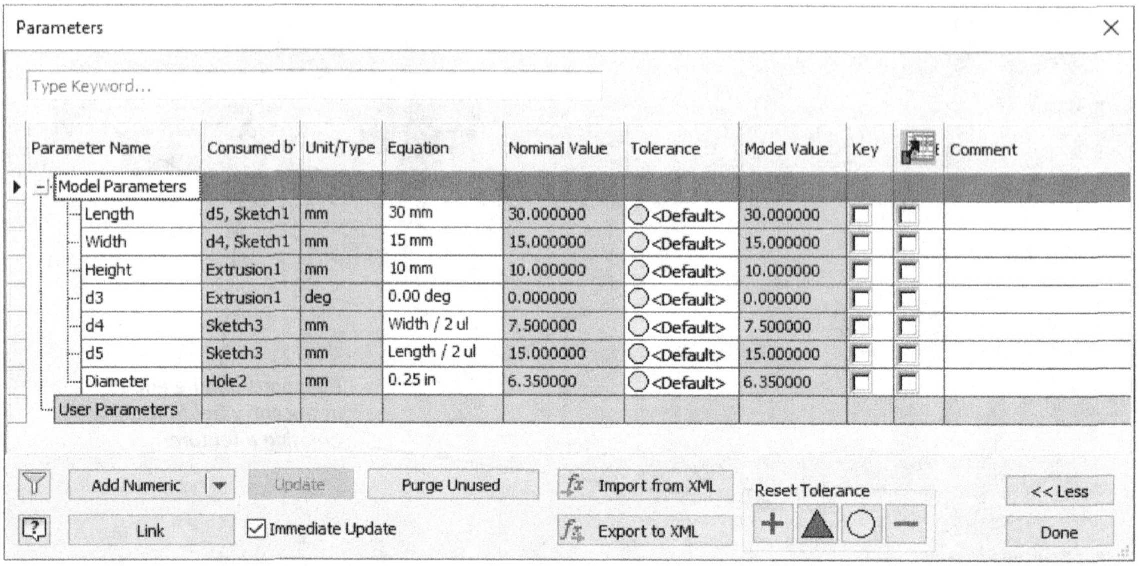

Figure 8–5

Note: *Model parameters can also be renamed in the Parameters dialog box to help recognize what the parameter is controlling. If* ***ul*** *displays next to a value, it indicates that the value is unitless.*

Equations can be written using any of the following operators or functions.

Mathematical Operators

The following operators can be used in equations:

+	Addition
-	Subtraction
/	Division
*	Multiplication
^	Exponentiation
()	Expression delimiter

> **Note:** *The software can resolve equations that use some operators (+, -, *, /). However, for operators such as exponents, units should be assigned (e.g., 3in^2ul).*

Functions

The following functions can be used in equations:

sin( )	tanh( )	sinh( )
cos( )	sqrt( )	cosh( )
tan( )	log( )	ceil( ) converts arbitrary real numbers to close integers. The ceil function of a real number x, ceil(x) returns the next highest integer (e.g., ceil(3.2) =4).
asin( )	ln( )	
acos( )	exp( )	floor( ) converts arbitrary real numbers to close integers. The floor function of a real number x, floor(x) returns the next smallest integer (e.g., floor(3.8) =3).
atan( )	abs( )	

Units

Units are assigned to each value, if you do not assign them first. Some of the symbols used for units of distance are as follows:

Unitless	ul
Inches	in, inch, or "
Feet	ft, foot
Meter	m, meter
Centimeter	cm
Millimeter	mm

Step 3 - Flex the model.

Once you finish adding an equation, test the model to verify that the equation captures the required design intent. This is called flexing the model and should involve editing the driving dimension values to verify that the model changes as expected.

> ***Note:*** *To help identify which features the model parameters were created by, you can review the Consumed by column in the Parameters dialog box. The column lists the feature that the parameter was created in to help identify it.*

Step 4 - Edit the equations, as required.

If flexing the model did not result in the required behavior, you can make required changes. This can be done by editing a dimension or feature, or using the *Parameters* dialog box.

8.2 Model and User Parameters

As features are created in a model, dimensions are used to define the model's shape. The name and value of the dimension are considered model parameters. Model parameters are listed in the *Parameters* dialog box. The *Parameters* dialog box also enables you to create user-defined parameters, which can be used in equations to help you control the model. Once created, user-defined parameters are listed under the *User Parameters* area in the *Parameters* dialog box. To open the *Parameters* dialog box, in the *Manage* tab>*Parameters* panel or the Quick Access Toolbar, click f_x (Parameters).

Model Parameters

Model parameters are the dimensions that are automatically assigned as you add sketch dimensions and features to the model. They use default dimension names (e.g., d0, d1, d2, etc.), and are listed at the top of the *Parameters* dialog box, as shown in Figure 8–6.

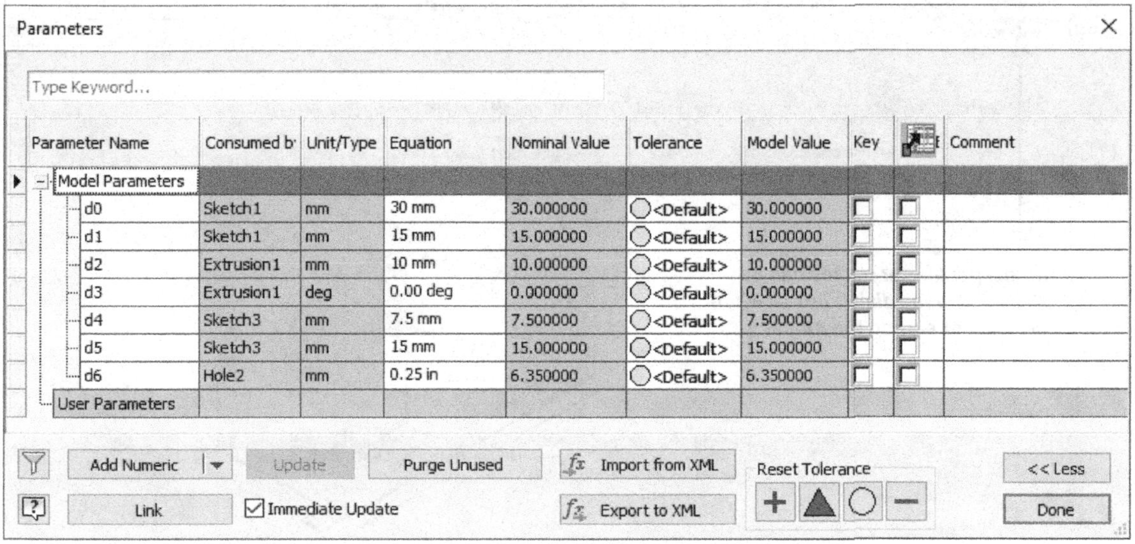

Parameter Name	Consumed b	Unit/Type	Equation	Nominal Value	Tolerance	Model Value	Key		Comment
Model Parameters									
d0	Sketch1	mm	30 mm	30.000000	<Default>	30.000000			
d1	Sketch1	mm	15 mm	15.000000	<Default>	15.000000			
d2	Extrusion1	mm	10 mm	10.000000	<Default>	10.000000			
d3	Extrusion1	deg	0.00 deg	0.000000	<Default>	0.000000			
d4	Sketch3	mm	7.5 mm	7.500000	<Default>	7.500000			
d5	Sketch3	mm	15 mm	15.000000	<Default>	15.000000			
d6	Hole2	mm	0.25 in	6.350000	<Default>	6.350000			
User Parameters									

The sketch and feature dimensions are listed in the Model Parameters area

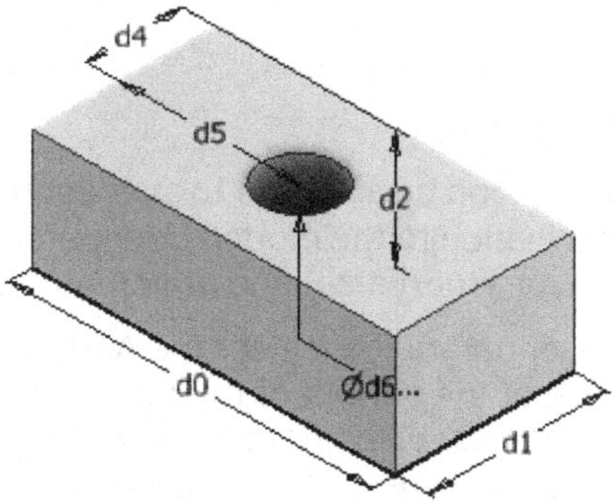

Figure 8–6

Renaming model parameters enables you to identify the parameter in the context of the entire model. To rename a model parameter, enter a new name in the *Parameter Name* column of the *Parameters* dialog box, as shown in Figure 8–7. Alternatively, enter a new name in the entry fields when creating or modifying dimensions associated with the feature you want to rename.

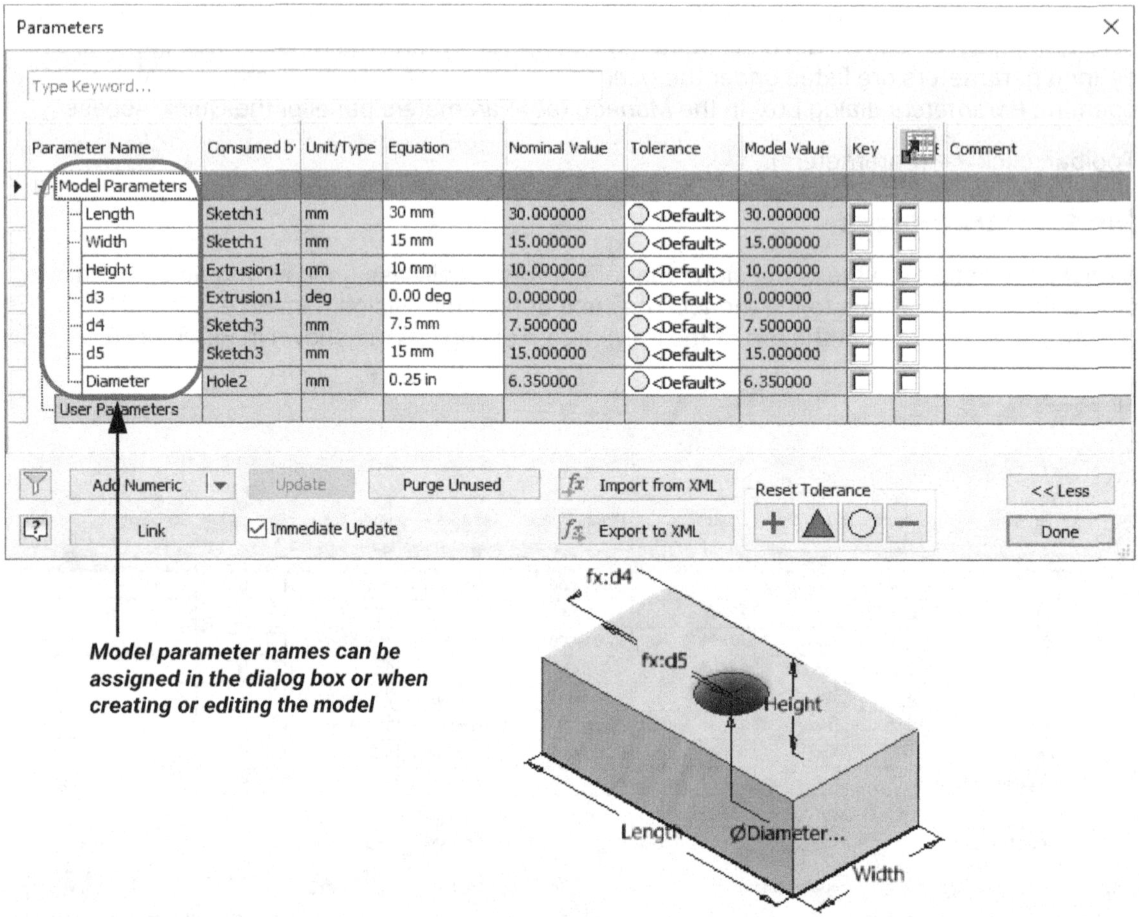

Figure 8–7

User Parameters

User parameters can be added to further capture the model's design intent for use in equations or to add information to the model. User parameters can be any one of three types (i.e., Numeric, Text, or True/False) and are created in the *Parameters* dialog box.

To create a user parameter, select the Add option that is associated with the required parameter type at the bottom of the *Parameters* dialog box, as shown in Figure 8–8. Once added, the parameter displays in the *User Parameters* area at the bottom of the *Parameters* dialog box. Enter a name, unit (if applicable), and value for the new parameter.

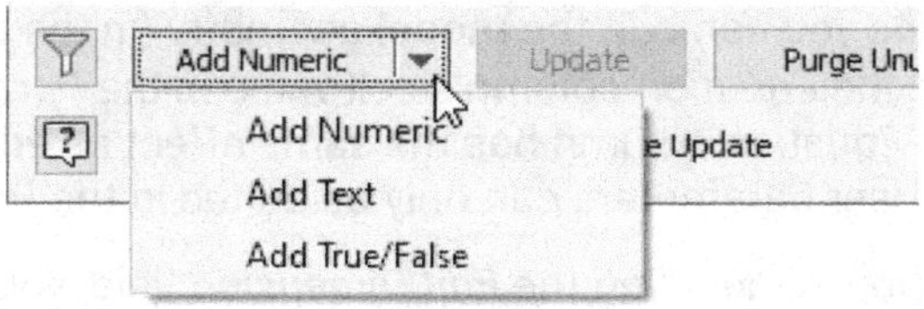

Figure 8–8

- Parameter names must be unique. They are case-sensitive and cannot begin with a numeric digit, nor can they contain spaces or mathematical operators.
- Some names are reserved by the software for specific operations and for mathematical use. If the name is unavailable for use you will be prompted that the parameter cannot be created.
- Numeric and text parameters can be either a single-value or a multi-value parameter. To set a parameter as multi-value, right-click on any cell in its row and select **Make Multi-Value**. Using the *Value List Editor* dialog box (shown in Figure 8–9), multiple values can be added. Enter the possible values in the *Add New Items* area in the dialog box and click **Add** to include them in the multi-value list and reorder the list, if needed, using the up and down arrows. Multi-value parameters display all of the available values in a drop-down list in the *Equation* column, as shown on the right of in Figure 8–9.

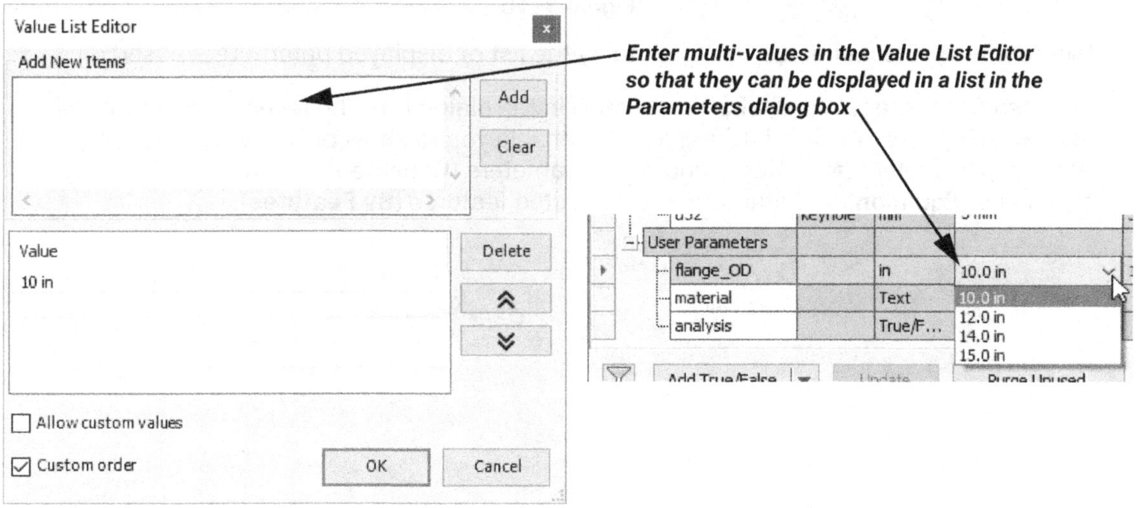

Figure 8–9

Note: *Multi-value parameters can also be assigned for use with model parameters.*

- Text parameters provide static text as their value.
- Similar to multi-value parameters, True/False parameters also display a drop-down list in the *Equation* column, enabling you to select the **True** or **False** value.

- To edit parameter values you can edit the model geometry (in the case of model parameters) or change the *Equation* column's cell value in the *Parameters* dialog box. Editing the value in the *Equation* column has the same effect as editing the dimension value directly on the model. User parameters can only be edited in the *Parameters* dialog box.
- When editing a dimension value using the *Edit Dimension* field, you can select from the list to efficiently create equations. Click  when editing and select **List Parameters** to open and directly select from the list of renamed parameters, as shown in Figure 8–10. Only renamed parameters are shown in this list.

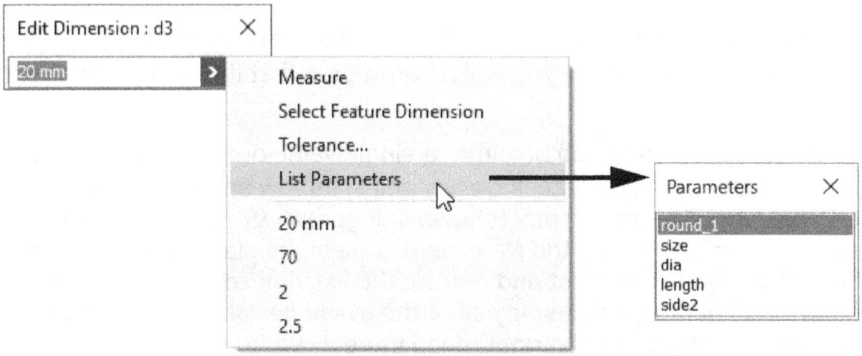

Figure 8–10

- Incorporating filters enables you to simplify the list of displayed parameters based on a selected filter type. To filter, click  (Filter) in the dialog box and select a filter type, as shown in Figure 8–11. The filtering options enable you to show only key parameters (**Key**), non-key parameters (**Non-Key**), renamed parameters (**Renamed**), parameters driven by equations (**Equation**), or parameters for selected features (**By Features**).

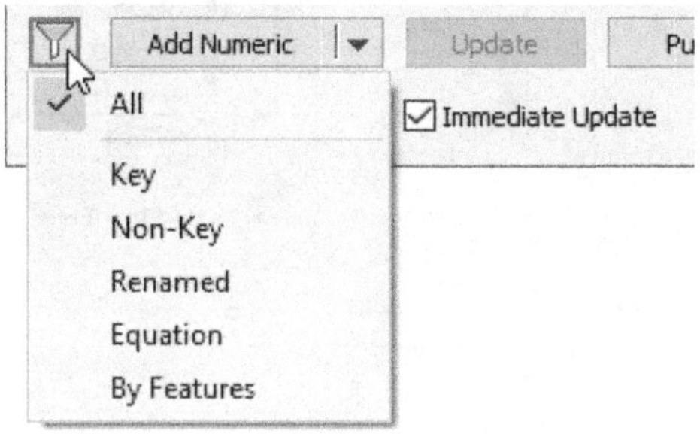

Figure 8–11

- To delete individual user-parameters, right-click on the parameter name and select **Delete Parameter**. Alternatively, you can delete multiple unused parameters at once by, clicking **Purge Unused** and selecting the parameters in the *Purge Parameters* dialog box.
- User parameters can be grouped together for better organization. To group, right-click on the parameter name and select **Add to Group**. You can either select an existing group to add to or create a new group.

Hint: Searching the Parameters Dialog Box

The *Type Keyword* field at the top of *Parameters* dialog box enables you to search all parameters for keywords that exist in any of the columns in the dialog box. Once you type a keword in the field, the results are immediately filtered to only show the rows that contain it. Additionally, the located keyword is highlighted in yellow. Note that if a filter is active in the dialog box, only the rows displayed are searched. If you want to search all data, ensure that the **All** option is enabled in the *Filter* drop-down list. Commonly used formats include:

- Entering a single keyword to search all fields (for example, **Extrusion**).
- Entering multiple keywords separated by spaces searches the first keyword and then further refines the list based on the second keyword (for example, **Extrusion d12**).
- Entering a keyword(s) in quotes searches all fields for a phrase (for example, **"length"**).
- Entering the column name followed by a colon prior to the keyword searches all fields in the column (for example, **Equation:Width**). If the column name has multiple words, use quotation marks for the column name (for example, **"Parameter Name":Length**).

For more information on additional search criteria that you can use in the *Type Keyword* area, search on "Search Options Reference" in Help.

- Some of the other options in the *Parameters* dialog box are as follows:

Tolerance column	Sets the tolerance setting: (Upper), (Median), (Nominal), or (Lower).
Consumed by column	Displays the feature or sketch name that contains the parameter. This enables you to identify where the parameter was created.
Model Value column	Displays the calculated value for the parameter based on the tolerance.
Key column	Identifies existing model/user parameters and flags them as critical (key).
Export Parameter column	Adds the parameter to the custom properties for the model. Custom properties can be used in bill of materials and part lists.
Comment column	Enables you to add a comment about the parameter.
Link	Links a parameter to a spreadsheet or to another file (part, assembly).
Immediate Update	Enables you to specify whether or not the model updates immediately when a change is made. If disabled, you must manually update the model.
Import from XML	Imports parameters from an XML file as user parameters. Parameters with duplicate names will not be imported.
Export to XML	Exports all model and user parameters to an XML file.
Reset Tolerance	Changes the Tolerance setting for all of the parameters.
Less and **More**	Customizes the display by displaying less or more of the dialog box.

Practice 8a
Add Equations

Practice Objectives

- Show dimensions in a model and obtain their expression value for use in an equation.
- Add equations to a model using the *Edit Dimension* dialog box and feature creation dialog box.

In this practice, you will modify dimensions in a part using dimension equations. The completed part is shown in Figure 8–12.

Figure 8–12

Task 1: Open a part file.

1. Open **equation.ipt**.
2. Right-click anywhere in the graphics window and select **Dimension Display>Name**.

3. Right-click on **Extrusion1** and select **Show Dimensions**. The dimensions display as shown in Figure 8–13.

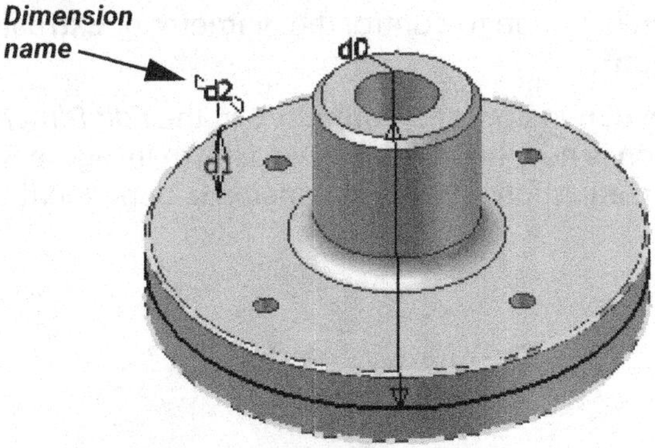

Figure 8–13

4. In the Model browser, note how **Extrusion1** remains selected. Click the left mouse button anywhere in the graphics window to clear the feature selection in the Model browser.
5. Right-click anywhere in the graphics window and select **Dimension Display>Expression**. The dimensions display as equations, as shown in Figure 8–14.

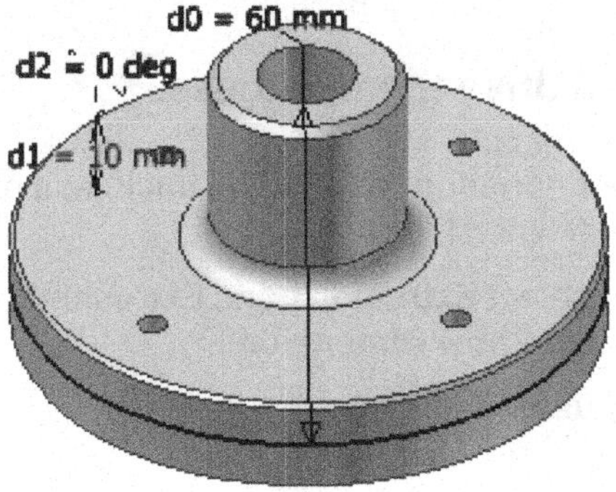

Figure 8–14

*Note: To display dimensions for multiple features at the same time, select the features using <Shift>, right-click on any of the features in the Model browser, and select **Show Dimensions**.*

6. Note the diameter and thickness of the extrusion:
   - *Diameter:* **d0 = 60mm**
   - *Thickness:* **d1 = 10mm**
7. Display the dimensions for **Extrusion3**.
   - *Diameter:* **d6 = 10mm**

Task 2: Add an equation to control the diameter.

In this task, you will add an equation to control the diameter of **Extrusion3** so that it will be 1/6 of the diameter of **Extrusion1**.

1. Double-click on the d6 dimension, and enter **d0/6** in the *Edit Dimension* dialog box. Press <Enter>. The expression is now **fx:d6=d0/6ul**, as shown in Figure 8–15. The fx indicates the dimension contains an equation. The d6 dimension is dependent on the d0 dimension.

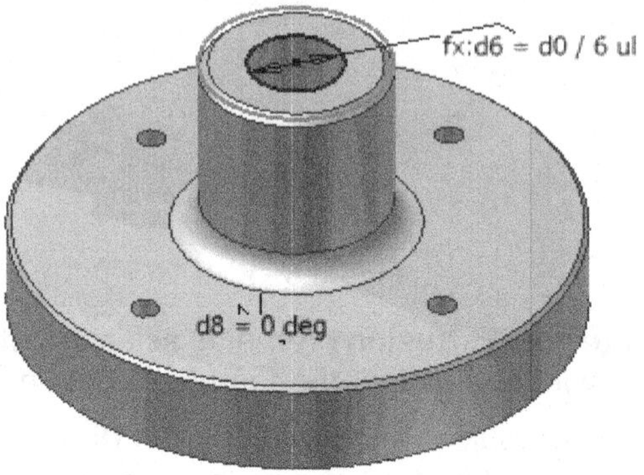

Figure 8–15

Task 3: Add an equation to drive the thickness.

In this task, you will add another equation to drive the thickness of **Extrusion2** so that it is twice as much as the thickness of **Extrusion1**.

1. Press and hold <Shift> and select **Extrusion1** and **Extrusion2**. Right-click on either feature in the Model browser and select **Show Dimensions**.
2. Note the thickness for **Extrusion2**:
   - d4 = 20mm
3. Double-click on the d4 dimension and enter **2*d1** in the *Edit Dimension* dialog box. Press <Enter>. The expression is now **fx:d4=2ul*d1**. The d4 dimension is controlled by the d1 dimension (the thickness of **Extrusion1**).
4. Modify the thickness of **Extrusion1** from 10mm to **12mm**.
5. In the Quick Access Toolbar, click (Local Update) to update the part.
6. Modify the diameter of **Extrusion1** to **72mm** and then update the part to see the changes.

Task 4: Add an equation to control the diameter.

1. Right-click on **Hole1** and select **Edit Feature**.

2. The diameter of the hole is 3mm. Change the diameter to **d6/2**. The hole's diameter is now controlled by the d6 dimension (**Extrusion3** diameter). Close the *Properties* panel. The model displays as shown in Figure 8–16.

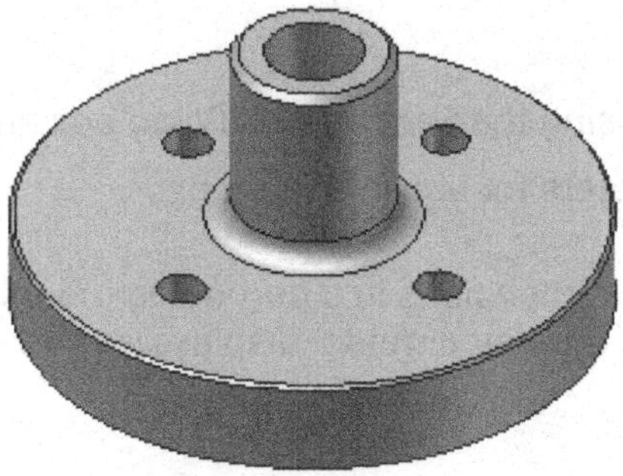

Figure 8–16

3. Select the *Manage* tab. In the *Parameters* panel, click f_x (Parameters). The *Parameters* dialog box opens, as shown in Figure 8–17. Alternatively, click the same icon in the Quick Access Toolbar to open the *Parameters* dialog box.

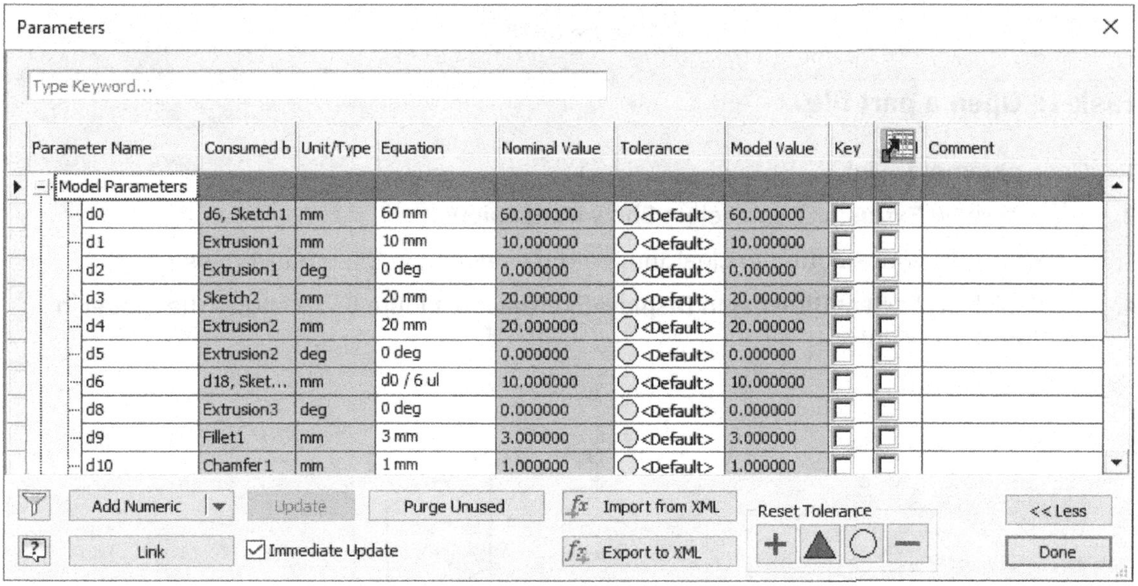

Parameter Name	Consumed b	Unit/Type	Equation	Nominal Value	Tolerance	Model Value	Key		Comment
Model Parameters									
d0	d6, Sketch1	mm	60 mm	60.000000	<Default>	60.000000			
d1	Extrusion1	mm	10 mm	10.000000	<Default>	10.000000			
d2	Extrusion1	deg	0 deg	0.000000	<Default>	0.000000			
d3	Sketch2	mm	20 mm	20.000000	<Default>	20.000000			
d4	Extrusion2	mm	20 mm	20.000000	<Default>	20.000000			
d5	Extrusion2	deg	0 deg	0.000000	<Default>	0.000000			
d6	d18, Sket...	mm	d0 / 6 ul	10.000000	<Default>	10.000000			
d8	Extrusion3	deg	0 deg	0.000000	<Default>	0.000000			
d9	Fillet1	mm	3 mm	3.000000	<Default>	3.000000			
d10	Chamfer1	mm	1 mm	1.000000	<Default>	1.000000			

Figure 8–17

4. Scroll through the list, reviewing and note the equations that were created in the *Equation* column. Close the *Parameters* dialog box.
5. Save the model and close the window.

End of practice

Practice 8b
Add Parameters

Practice Objectives

- Add equations to a model using the *Parameters* dialog box and feature dialog boxes.
- Create user-defined parameters for use in equations.

In this practice, you will modify dimensions in a part using model parameters and then add user-defined parameters. The completed model displays as shown in Figure 8–18.

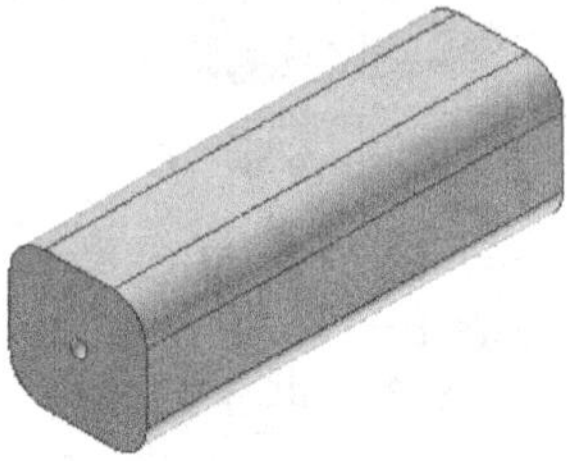

Figure 8–18

Task 1: Open a part file.

1. Open **parameters.ipt**.
2. Right-click on **Extrusion1** and select **Show Dimensions**.
3. Click the left mouse button to clear the feature selection in the Model browser.
4. Right-click and select **Dimension Display>Expression**. Figure 8–19 shows the model in wireframe, for clarity.

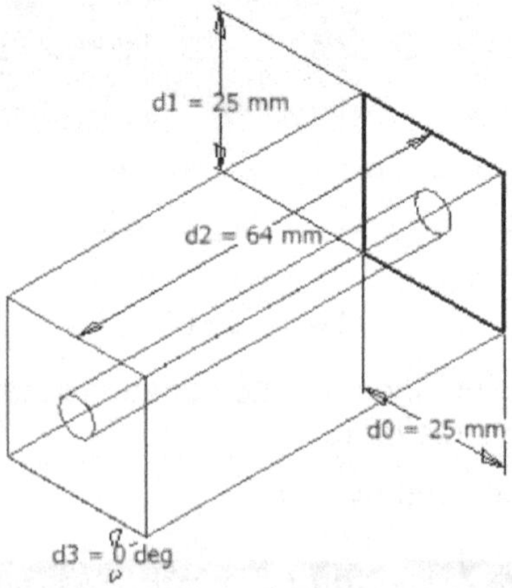

Figure 8–19

Task 2: Change the model parameter names.

1. In the Quick Access Toolbar, select fx (Parameters) to open the *Parameters* dialog box.

   Alternatively, in the *Manage* tab>*Parameters* panel, click fx (Parameters).

2. In the *Parameter Name* column in the *Parameters* dialog box, do the following:
   - Change the name to d0 to **side1**.
   - Change the name of d1 to **side2**.
   - Change the name of d2 to **length**.
   - Change the name of d4 to **dia**.

3. Select the **side2** *Equation* column and enter **side1**. The side2 dimension is now driven by the side1 value. The *Parameters* dialog box should be as shown in Figure 8–20.

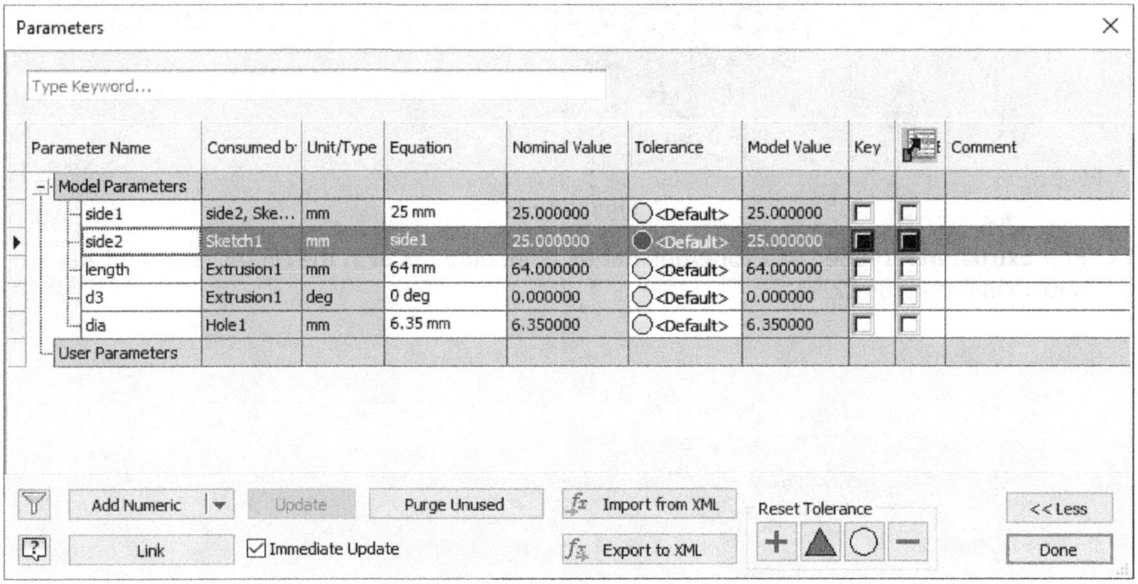

Figure 8–20

4. Click **Done** to close the *Parameters* dialog box.

5. Display the **Extrusion1** and **Hole1** dimensions. To display dimensions for multiple features at the same time, select the features using <Shift>, right-click on any of the features in the Model browser, and select **Show Dimensions**. Note the parameter names that you assigned.

6. In the Quick Access Toolbar, select fx (Parameters) to open the *Parameters* dialog box.

7. Select the length *Equation* column, enter **side1*3**, and press <Enter>. The entry in the *Model Value* column changes.

8. Click **Done** to close the *Parameters* dialog box.

9. Update the model, if it does not automatically update on its own.

   Note: *To update the part, click*  *(Local Update) in the Quick Access Toolbar.*

10. Display the **Extrusion1** dimensions. The model displays as shown in Figure 8–21.

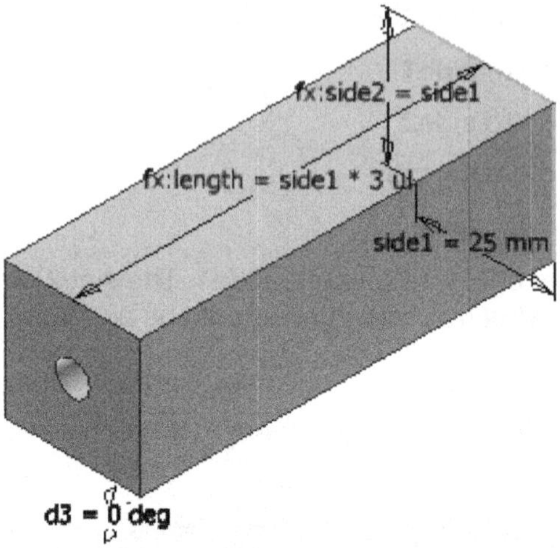

Figure 8–21

11. Edit **Extrusion1** to open its *Properties* panel. Note **side1*3 ul** in the *Distance A* field, as shown in Figure 8–22.

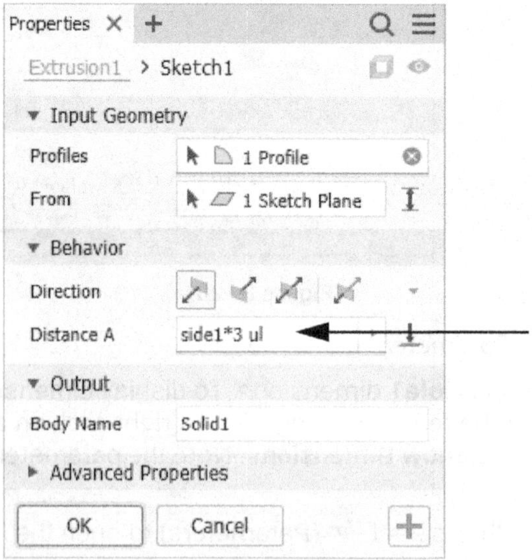

Figure 8–22

12. Close the *Properties* panel.

Task 3: Add a user-defined parameter.

1. In the Quick Access Toolbar, select f_x (Parameters) to open the *Parameters* dialog box.
2. Click **Add Numeric** in the *Parameters* dialog box to add a user-defined parameter to the model.
3. In the *User Parameters* area, enter **size** in the *Parameter Name* column.
4. Select the *Unit/Type* column. The *Unit Type* dialog box opens.
5. Delete **mm** in the *Unit Specification* field. Expand the **Unitless** branch and select **Unitless (ul)**.
6. Click **OK** to close the *Unit Type* dialog box.
7. In the *User Parameters* area, enter **1 ul** in the *Equation* column and enter **determine overall size** in the *Comment* column. Press <Enter>. The size parameter should display in the *Parameters* dialog box as shown in Figure 8–23.

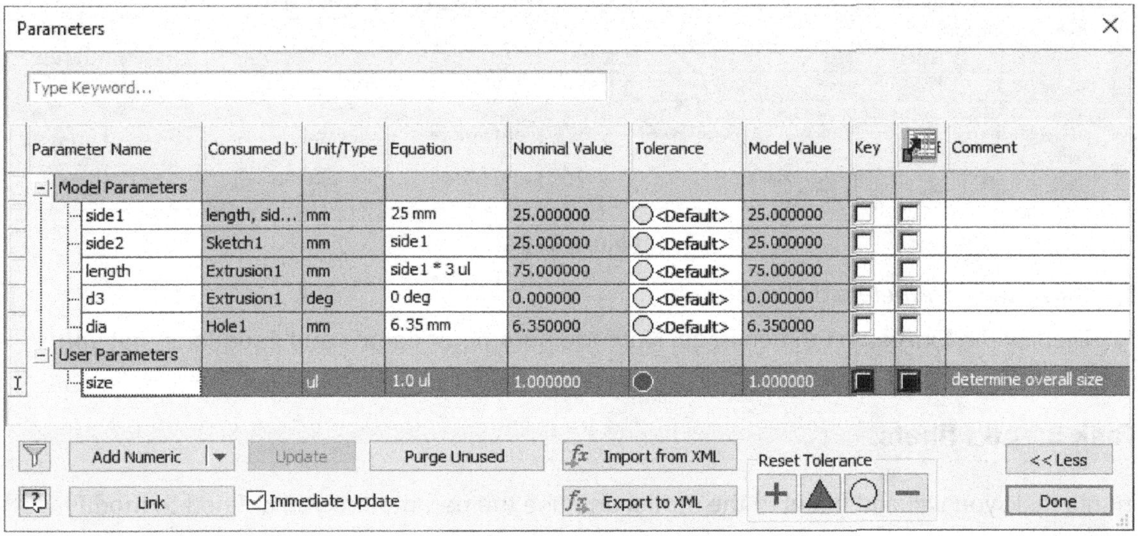

Figure 8–23

Task 4: Add a second user-defined parameter.

1. Click **Add Numeric** to add a second user parameter.
2. Enter **round_1** in the *Parameter Name* column in the second row of the *User Parameters* area.
3. If units are not set to mm, select the *Unit* column, expand the *Length* branch, and select **millimeter (mm)**.

4. In the *User Parameters* area, enter **3.175** in the *Equation* column and **fillet radius** in the *Comment* column.

5. Select the *Equation* column's cell for **side1**and enter **25mm*size**. The *Parameters* dialog box should be as shown in Figure 8–24. The user-defined size parameter is going to drive the side1 dimension. Since the size parameter is unitless, you must multiply it by a distance to obtain a distance value.

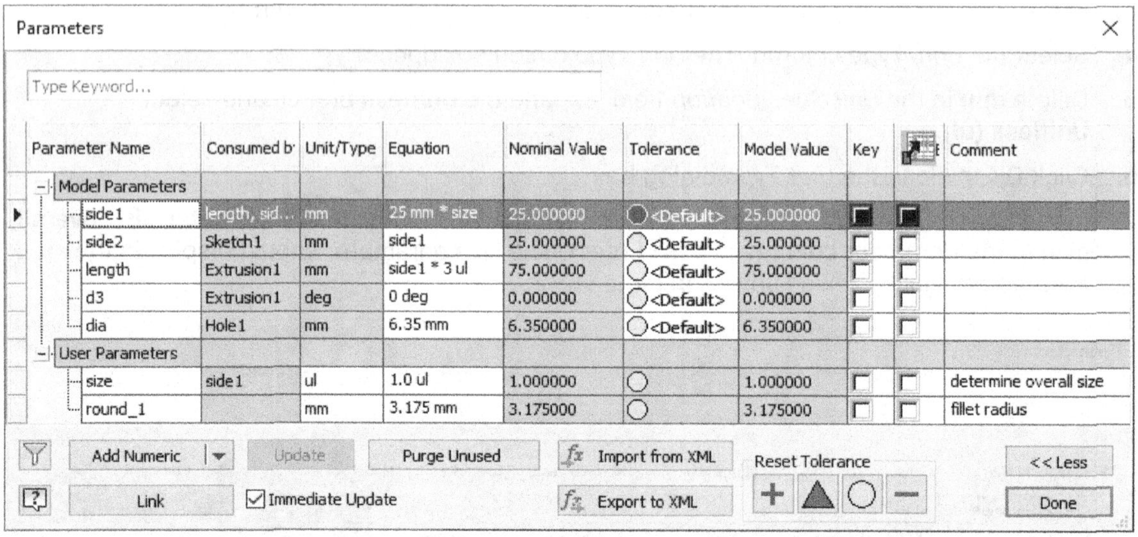

Figure 8–24

6. Close the *Parameters* dialog box.

7. Display the **Extrusion1** dimensions. Note the parameter names and equations that you assigned.

Task 5: Add fillets.

In this task, you will add fillets to the model and use the parameters you defined to modify the fillets.

1. Start the creation of the fillet.

2. Select the four long edges of the part to add fillets to.

3. In the *Selection Sets* area, expand the flyout menu associated with the fillet radius, as shown in Figure 8–25.

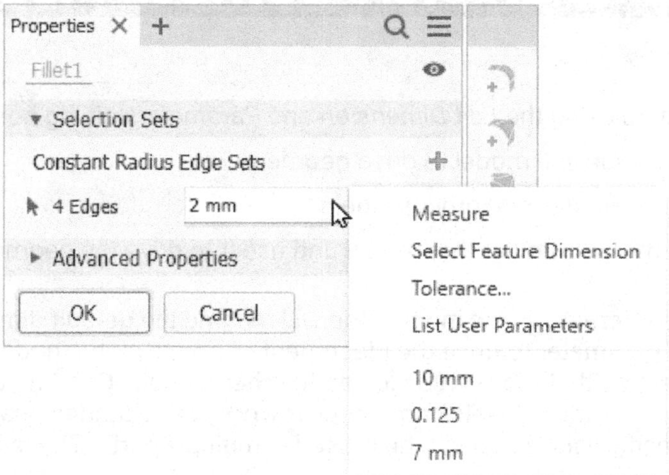

Figure 8–25

4. Select **List Parameters** and select **round_1** in the list that displays. The fillets radii are now controlled by the **round_1** parameter.
5. Complete the fillet.
6. Open the *Parameters* dialog box and ensure that **Immediate Update** is selected.
7. Change the equation of the **round_1** parameter to **12.5** in the *Parameters* dialog box and press <Enter>. The model displays as shown on the left in Figure 8–26.
8. Change the equation of the size parameter to **4**. The updated model displays as shown on the right in Figure 8–26. Close the *Parameters* dialog box.

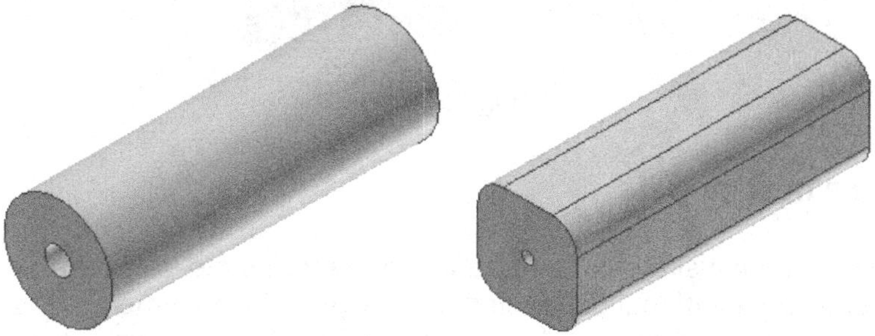

Figure 8–26

9. Save the model and close the window.

End of practice

Practice 8c
Reference Parameters Between Models

Practice Objectives

- Rename parameters using the *Edit Dimension* and *Parameters* dialog boxes.
- Use a driven dimension in a model to drive geometry.
- Export a parameter for use in another model.
- Reference a parameter from another model and use it to drive the geometry.

In this practice, you will create a new model. You will rename the default dimension parameters and use a reference parameter to drive the placement of points in the model. In addition, you will export parameters so that they can be linked to other models. Creating and linking reference parameters to other models can reduce rework and redundancy by enabling designs to carry non-part-specific values that can be reused in multiple parts. The model that you create is shown in Figure 8–27.

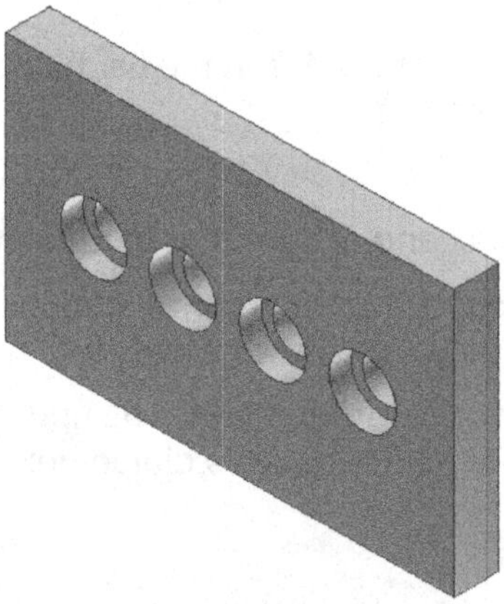

Figure 8–27

Task 1: Create a new model.

In this task, you will create a sketch of a rectangle and four points, and fully dimension the sketch. You will add one additional dimension to provide a driven dimension. This will be used as a parameter to drive the placement of all points so that they are always equally spaced in the rectangle. To complete the task, you will rename the reference parameter and set it so that it can be referenced by other models.

1. Create a new model using the standard imperial (in) template.

2. Sketch a rectangle centered about the origin of the sketch, as shown in Figure 8–28.

3. Click (Line) and draw a line connecting the two midpoints of the vertical edges. Select the line, click (Construction) to convert it to a construction line, as shown in Figure 8–28.

   Note: *Alternatively, enable (Construction) before creating the line.*

4. Click (Dimension) and place dimensions along the top and the side of the rectangular sketch, as shown in Figure 8–28. Press <Esc> to finish the command. Assign a Symmetric constraint, as required, to ensure that the sketch is fully constrained.

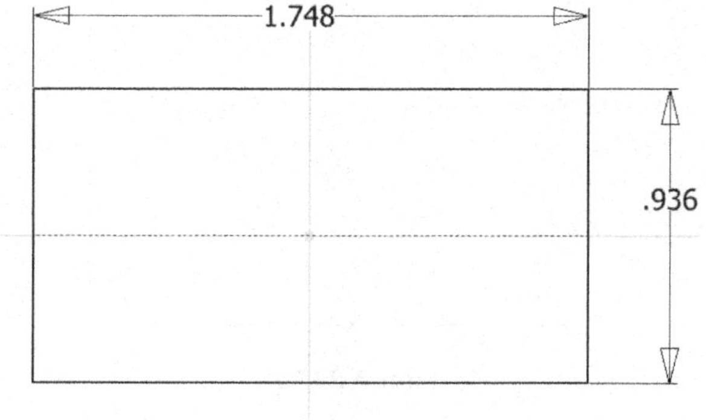

Figure 8–28

5. Double-click on the longer dimension value to edit it. Enter **Length = 2.5** in the *Edit Dimension* dialog box. Edit the width value in the same way. The *Edit Dimension* dialog boxes are shown in Figure 8–29. By entering the parameter name in the dialog box, you are renaming the default d0 and d1 dimension names to *Length* and *Width* without having to rename them in the *Parameters* dialog box.

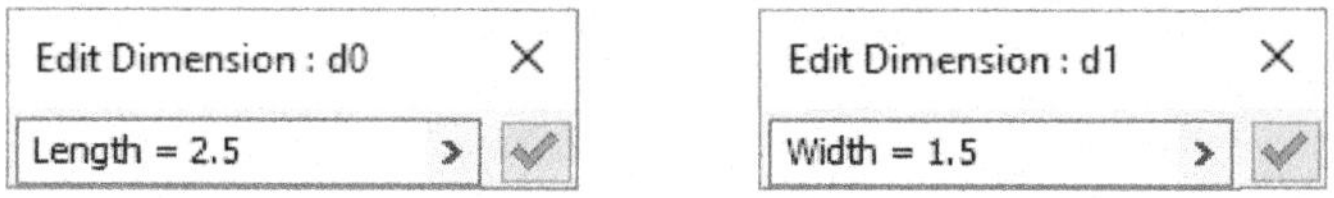

Figure 8–29

6. Click (Point) and sketch four points on the construction line, as shown in Figure 8–30.

7. Click (Dimension) and place dimensions, as shown in Figure 8–30, so that the left-most point is dimensioned from the left vertical edge, and the remaining points are dimensioned from each other. Dimension the last point to the right-most vertical edge. Once this dimension is placed, it will indicate that the sketch is over-dimensioned. Accept this dimension so that it is created as a driven dimension.

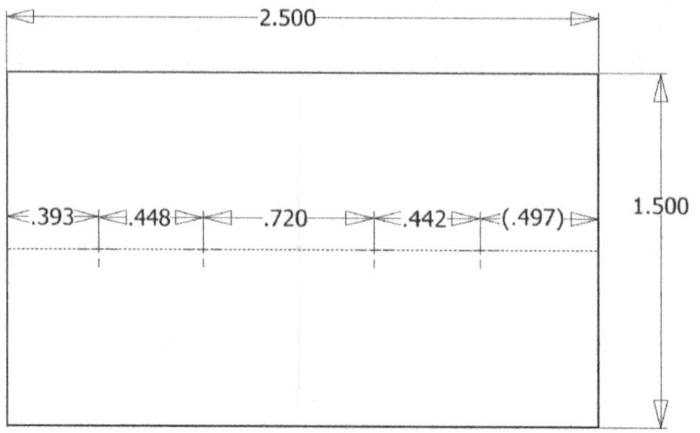

Figure 8–30

8. Expand (Dimension Display) on the Status Bar and select **Name** to display the parameter name for the dimensions. Note that *Length* and *Width* are now the names for the first two dimensions that you created.

9. Double-click on the **d2** dimension value and enter **d3** in the *Edit Dimension* dialog box, as shown in Figure 8–31.

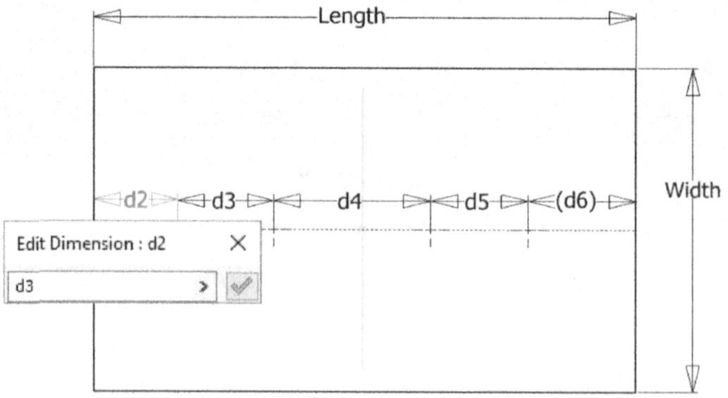

Figure 8–31

10. Continue to edit the remaining dimension values so that **d3 = d4**, **d4 = d5**, and **d5 = d6**. The sketch updates once you have entered all of these values, as shown in Figure 8–32. By establishing relationships to the driven dimension in the model, you force the points to stay equally spaced based on the overall length of the rectangle.

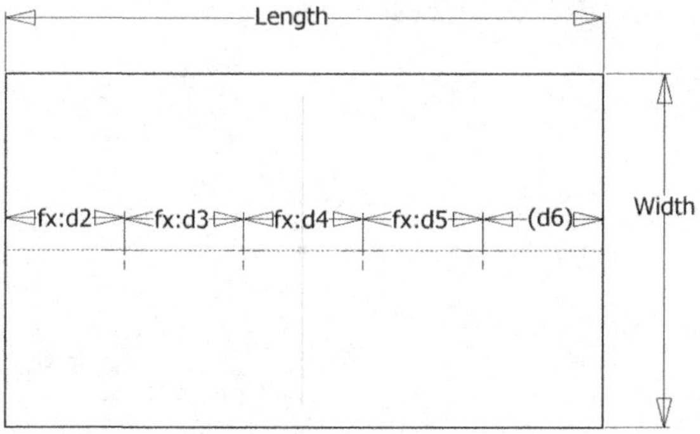

Figure 8–32

11. In the Quick Access Toolbar, select *fx* (Parameters) to open the *Parameters* dialog box. Review all of the parameters and equations that you established in the sketch.

12. In the *Reference Parameters* area, rename the **d6** parameter to **Hole_Spacing** and select the checkbox in the *Export* column, as shown in Figure 8–33. The reference parameter has to be renamed in the *Parameters* dialog box because it is not an editable value; it is a driven value.

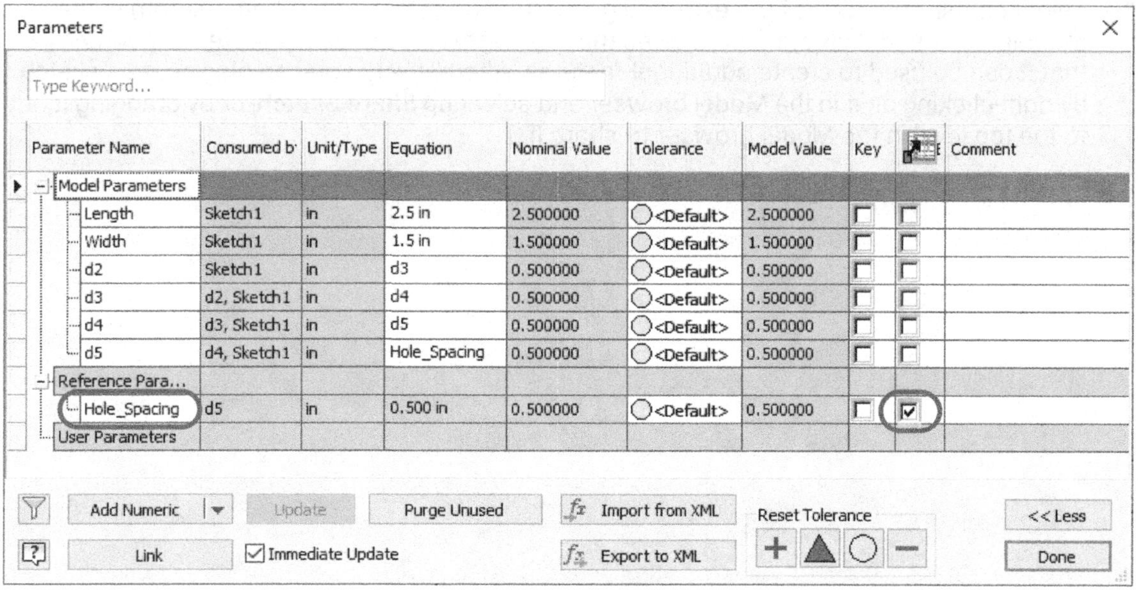

Parameter Name	Consumed b	Unit/Type	Equation	Nominal Value	Tolerance	Model Value	Key	Export	Comment
Model Parameters									
Length	Sketch1	in	2.5 in	2.500000	<Default>	2.500000	☐	☐	
Width	Sketch1	in	1.5 in	1.500000	<Default>	1.500000	☐	☐	
d2	Sketch1	in	d3	0.500000	<Default>	0.500000	☐	☐	
d3	d2, Sketch1	in	d4	0.500000	<Default>	0.500000	☐	☐	
d4	d3, Sketch1	in	d5	0.500000	<Default>	0.500000	☐	☐	
d5	d4, Sketch1	in	Hole_Spacing	0.500000	<Default>	0.500000	☐	☐	
Reference Para...									
Hole_Spacing	d5	in	0.500 in	0.500000	<Default>	0.500000	☐	☑	
User Parameters									

Figure 8–33

13. Click **Done** to close the *Parameters* dialog box.
14. Finish the sketch.
15. Extrude the sketch as shown in Figure 8–34.

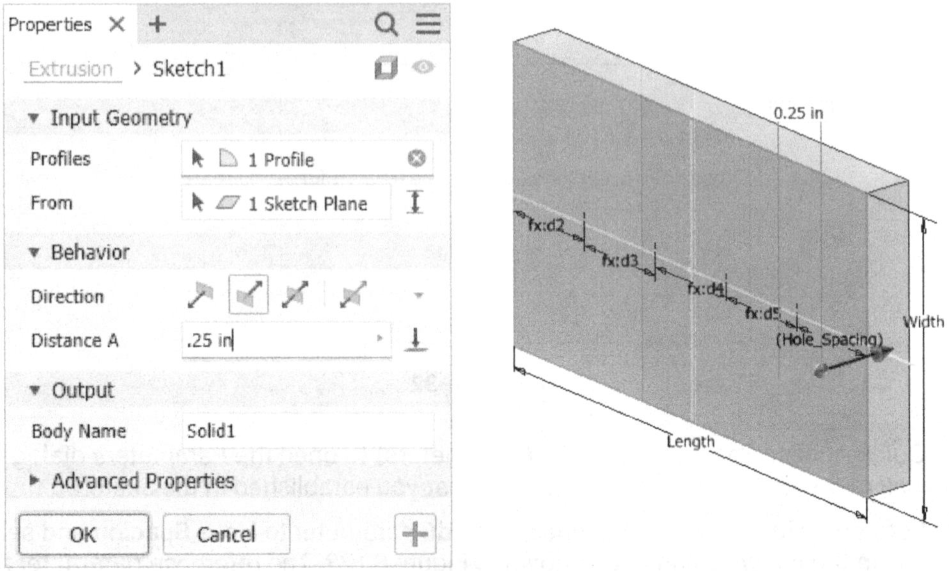

Figure 8–34

16. Select on the front face of the extruded geometry and select (Share Sketch) in the toolbar menu that displays. This shares the sketch that was used to create the geometry so that it can be used to create additional features. Alternatively, you can also share a sketch by right-clicking on it in the Model browser and selecting **Share Sketch**, or by dragging it out to the top level in the Model browser to share it.

17. In the *Modify* panel, click  (Hole). Create holes that are located on the four sketched points and are sized as shown in Figure 8–35.

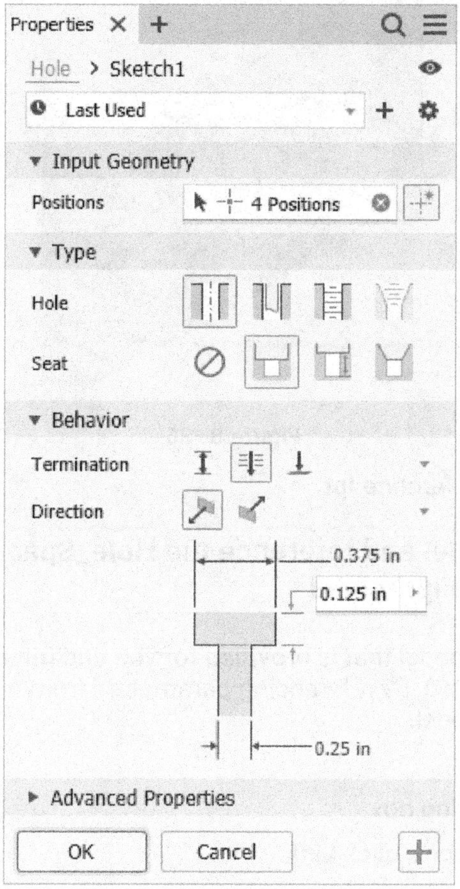

Figure 8–35

18. Complete the feature.

19. Toggle off the visibility of **Sketch1**. The model displays as shown in Figure 8–36.

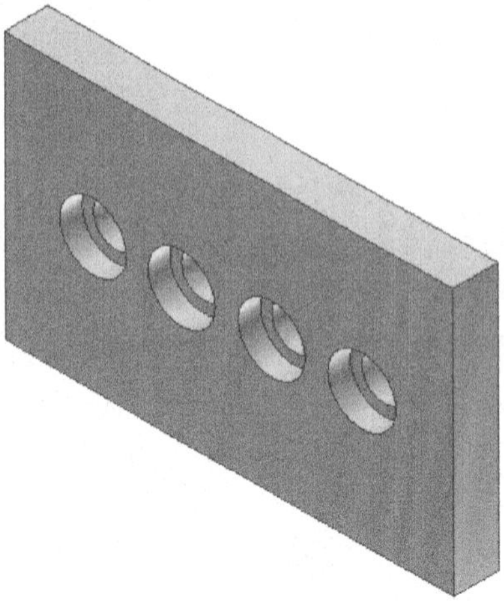

Figure 8–36

20. Save the file as **DrivenReference.ipt**.

Task 2: Open a new model and reference the Hole_Spacing parameter in the DrivenReference.ipt model.

In this task, you will open a model that is provided for you and reference parameters from the part model that you just created. By referencing parameters from another part, you will drive the geometry in this provided model.

1. Open **Placement.ipt**.
2. Open the *Parameters* dialog box.
3. In the *Parameters* dialog box, click **Link**.
4. Change the *Files of type* drop-down list option to **Inventor Files (*.ipt, *.iam)**. Browse to the location of the **DrivenReference.ipt** file, select it, and click **Open**.

5. The *Link Parameters* dialog box opens, listing all of the parameters from the **DrivenReference.ipt**. Click next to the **Hole_Spacing** reference parameter. Once selected, it displays as , indicating it can be referenced. Click **OK**. The *Parameters* dialog box updates as shown in Figure 8–37.

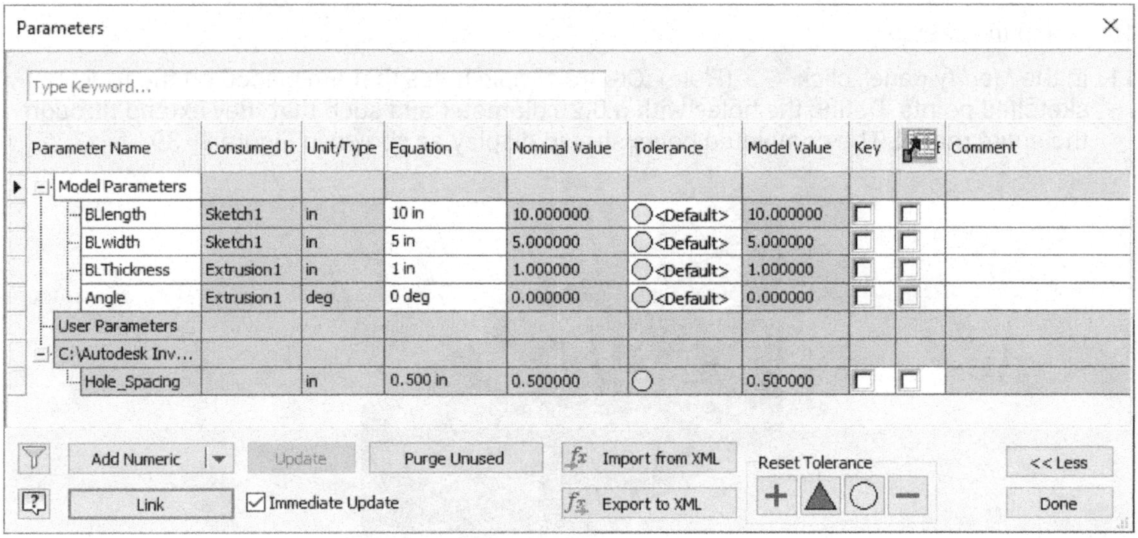

Figure 8–37

A link has been created as a User Parameter to the **DrivenReference.ipt** file. This can be edited or deleted by right-clicking on the row in the *Parameters* dialog box and selecting the required option on the shortcut menu. Ensure that the file is always maintained in this location and is not deleted. This ensures that the reference is not lost. This is also true if a spreadsheet is used as the reference location for parameters.

6. Close the *Parameters* dialog box.
7. Edit **Sketch2**.
8. Click (Dimension) and place dimensions between the points, as shown in Figure 8–38.

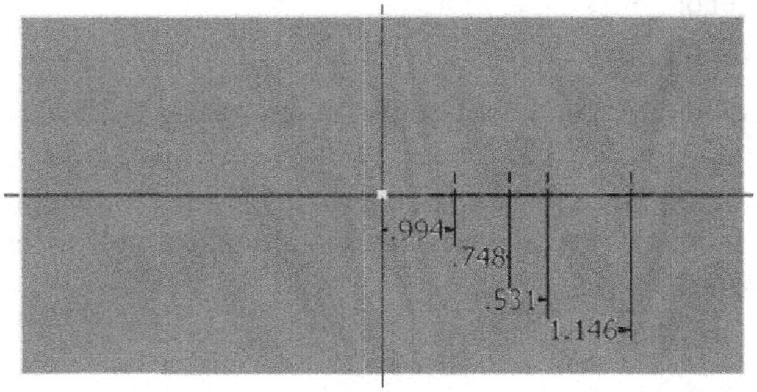

Figure 8–38

9. Edit the values of the dimensions so that they are equal to the **Hole_Spacing** parameter.

   *Note: As an alternative to typing the **Hole_Spacing** parameter value, when editing, click and select **List Parameters** to display the list of available parameters. Select **Hole_Spacing** in the Parameters dialog box.*

10. Finish the sketch.
11. In the *Modify* panel, click (Hole). Create simple holes that are placed on the four sketched points. Define the holes with a 0.25 diameter and such that they extend through the entire model. The completed holes should display as shown in Figure 8–39.

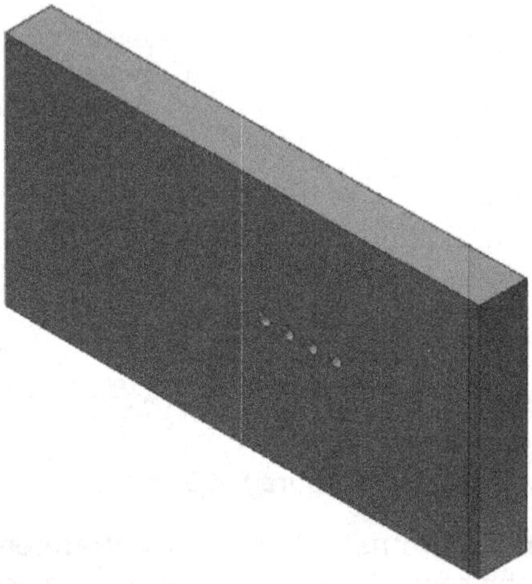

Figure 8–39

12. Save the model.

Task 3: Make modifications in the DrivenReference model to test the referenced parameters.

In this task, you will open the **DrivenReference.ipt** model and make changes to it to ensure that the **Placement.ipt** model updates as expected.

1. Activate **DrivenReference.ipt**.
2. In the *Parameters* dialog box, edit the **Length** parameter from *2.5 in* to **5 in**. Close the dialog box.
3. Return to the **Placement.ipt** model and perform an update. The model updates to reflect the change. This functionality would be useful in an Assembly environment if these two models were assembled.
4. Save and close the models.

End of practice

Chapter Review Questions

1. You can only add an equation to a model in the *Parameters* dialog box.

a. True

b. False

2. Which of the following statements regarding equations are true? (Select all that apply.)

a. Dimensions and parameters can be used in an equation to drive a value.

b. Equations can be manually entered in the *Edit Dimension* dialog box.

c. Equations can be created by selecting dimensions directly from the model.

3. Which combination of equations centers the hole if the length and width are equivalent, as shown in Figure 8–40? (Select all that apply.)

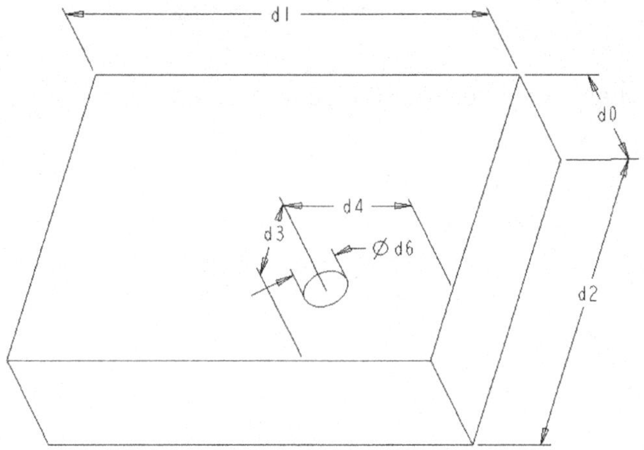

Figure 8–40

a. d4 = d1 / 2
d3 = d2 / 2

b. d1 = d4 / 2
d2 = d3 / 2

c. d1 = d2
d4 = d1 / 2
d3 = d2 / 2

4. Which dimension display type is set to display the dimensions in the model shown in Figure 8–41?

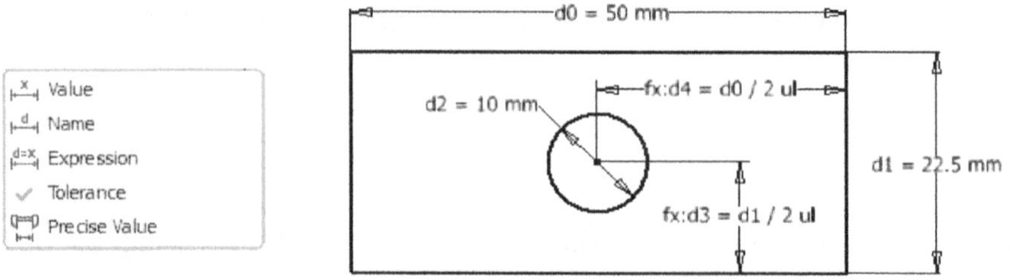

Figure 8–41

a. Value

b. Name

c. Expression

d. Tolerance

e. Precise Value

5. Which description best describes how the equation shown in Figure 8–42 affects the model?

d0 = 3 * d6
d3 = d4

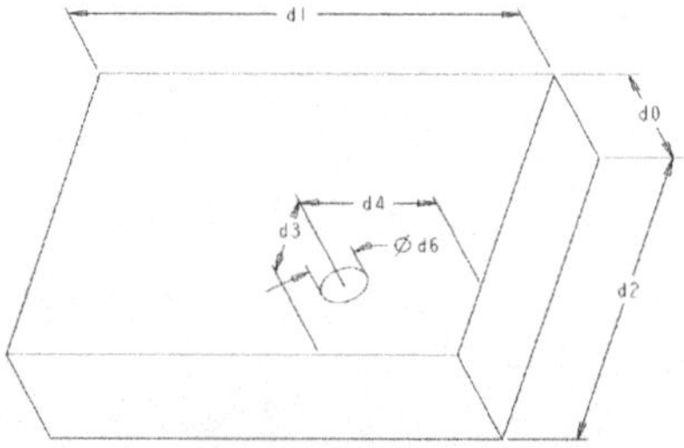

Figure 8–42

a. The depth of the base extrusion is equal to the diameter of the hole and the hole is centered on the base extrusion.

b. The depth of the base extrusion is equal to three times the diameter of the hole and the hole is centered on the base extrusion.

c. The depth of the base extrusion is equal to three times the diameter of the hole, and the values of the horizontal and vertical hole dimensions are equivalent.

d. The depth of the base extrusion is equal to three times the diameter of the hole, the values of the horizontal and vertical hole dimensions are equivalent, and d1 and d2 are equivalent.

6. Fill in the parameter type, **Model** or **User-Defined**, for the method in which it is created in a model.

   a. _____ parameters are created using the *Parameters* dialog box where you select the type, name, and enter values.

   b. _____ parameters are automatically assigned each time you add a dimension or feature to a part.

7. Which of the following best describes what **fx** is identifying in the sketch shown in Figure 8–43?

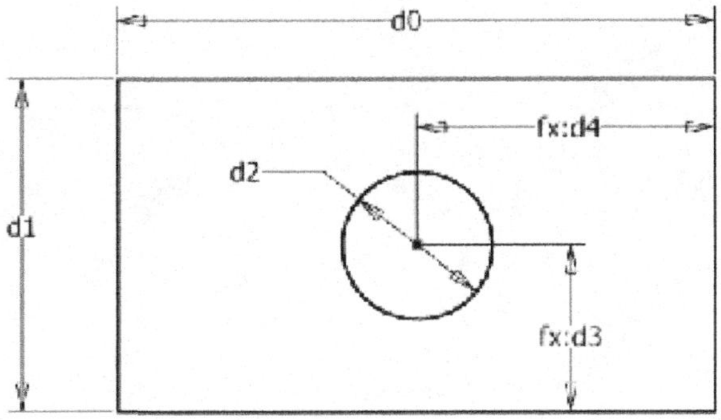

Figure 8–43

   a. d3 and d4 are reference dimensions.

   b. d3 and d4 are equal.

   c. d3 and d4 are generated based on a user-defined equation.

   d. d3 and d4 have a tolerance assigned.

Command Summary

Button	Command	Location
f_x	**Parameters**	• **Ribbon:** *Manage* tab>*Parameters* panel • **Quick Access Toolbar**

Chapter

9

Additional Features

Numerous combinations of features can be used to build a model. These can include standard sketched features and pick and place features. Drafts, shells, and ribs are advanced features that can be incorporated into the model to create geometry.

Learning Objectives

- Create a face edge draft where the draft pull direction is defined along a selected edge.
- Create a face edge draft where the draft pull direction is normal to the selected plane or face.
- Create a face edge draft where the draft is applied above and below a parting line reference.
- Use the **Split** command to split a face or solid based on a split reference tool.
- Create a shell feature that removes faces and assigns uniform or unique wall thickness to the remaining faces in the model.
- Create a rib feature from a sketched section.
- Create boss and draft geometry in a rib feature.

9.1 Creating Drafts

A draft creates sloped surfaces and is often used to remove a part from a mold. You can apply draft over the entire profile, to one face, or apply drafts to different faces, as shown in Figure 9–1. If you apply draft to a face, draft is also applied to all faces that are tangent to it.

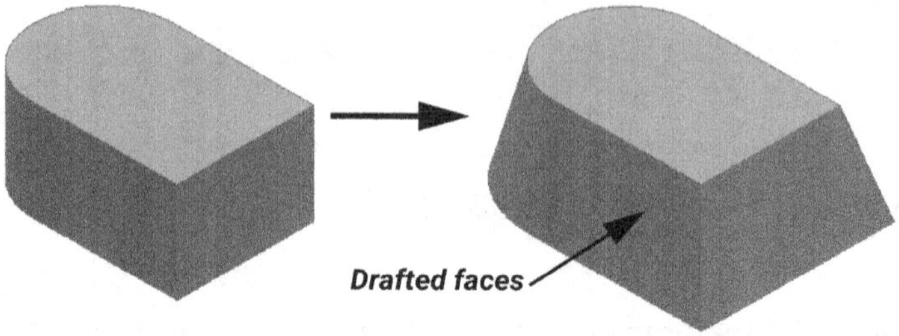

Figure 9–1

Use the following general steps to create a draft:

1. Start the creation of the face draft.
2. Select the draft type.
3. Select the draft references.
4. Select faces to draft.
5. Enter the draft angle.
6. Complete the feature.

Step 1 - Start the creation of the face draft.

In the *3D Model* tab>*Modify* panel, click (Draft) to create a face draft. The *Face Draft* dialog box and mini-toolbar display.

Step 2 - Select the draft type.

You can create three types of drafts: **Fixed Edge**, **Fixed Plane**, and **Parting Line**. Select the type of draft in the dialog box or in the drop-down list in the mini-toolbar, as shown in Figure 9–2.

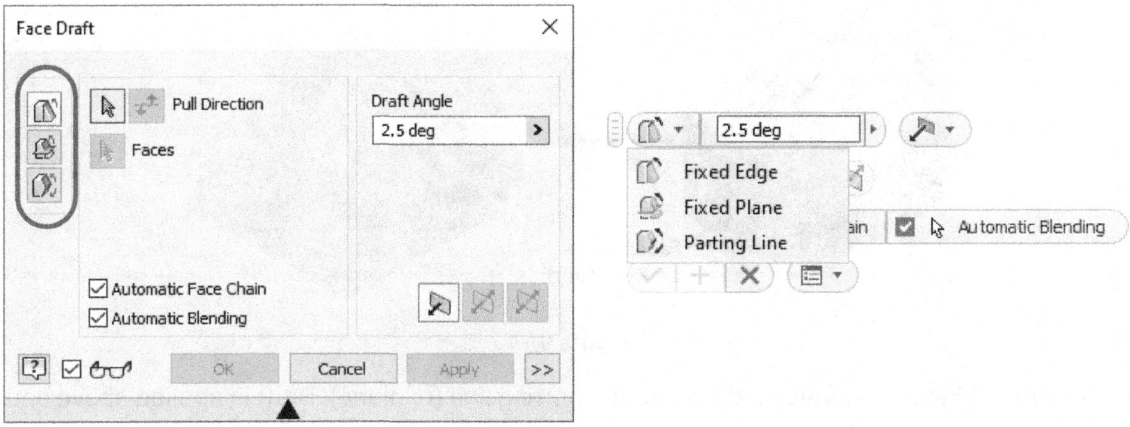

Figure 9–2

The three draft types are described as follows:

- A **Fixed Edge** draft creates a draft about one or multiple tangent fixed edges for a selected face(s), as shown in Figure 9–3. To create a fixed edge draft, click (Fixed Edge) in the *Face Draft* dialog box or select **Fixed Edge** in the drop-down list in the mini-toolbar.

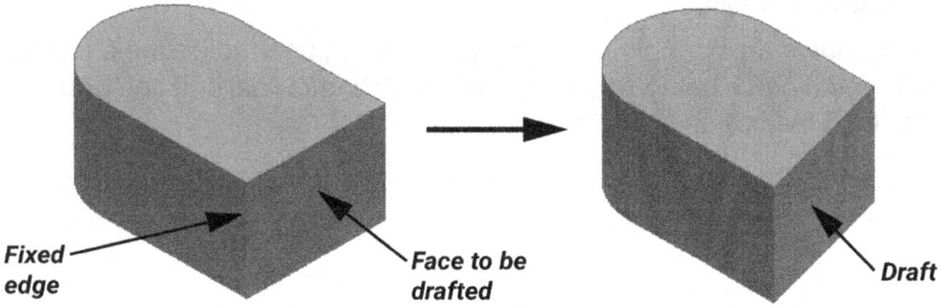

Figure 9–3

- A **Fixed Plane** draft creates a draft about a fixed plane for a selected face(s), as shown in Figure 9–4. To create a fixed plane draft, click (Fixed Plane) in the *Face Draft* dialog box or select **Fixed Plane** in the drop-down list in the mini-toolbar.

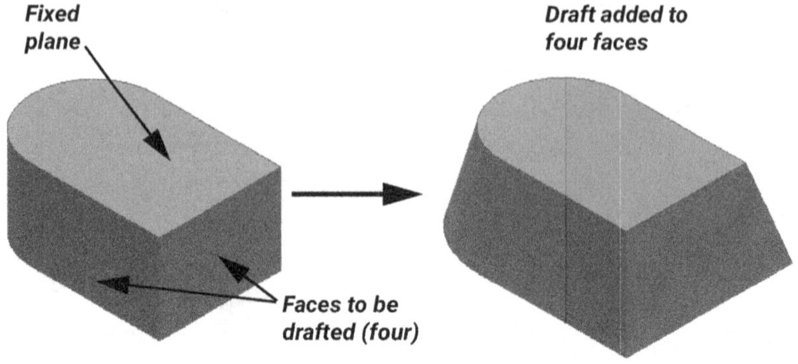

Figure 9–4

- A **Parting Line** draft creates a draft about a parting line (or plane). Draft is applied above and below the parting line for a selected face(s). To create a parting line draft, click (Parting Line) in the *Face Draft* dialog box or select **Parting Line** in the drop-down list in the mini-toolbar.
  - By default, a parting line draft is created using the (Fixed Parting Line) option, which ensures that the geometry remains the same size at the parting line and draft is added above or below. Alternatively, the (Move Parting Line) option can be selected to add material at the parting line.
  - Figure 9–5 shows an example of a work plane being used to define a fixed parting line draft (top) and a curve being used as the parting line for parting line draft that uses the **Move Parting Line** option (bottom).

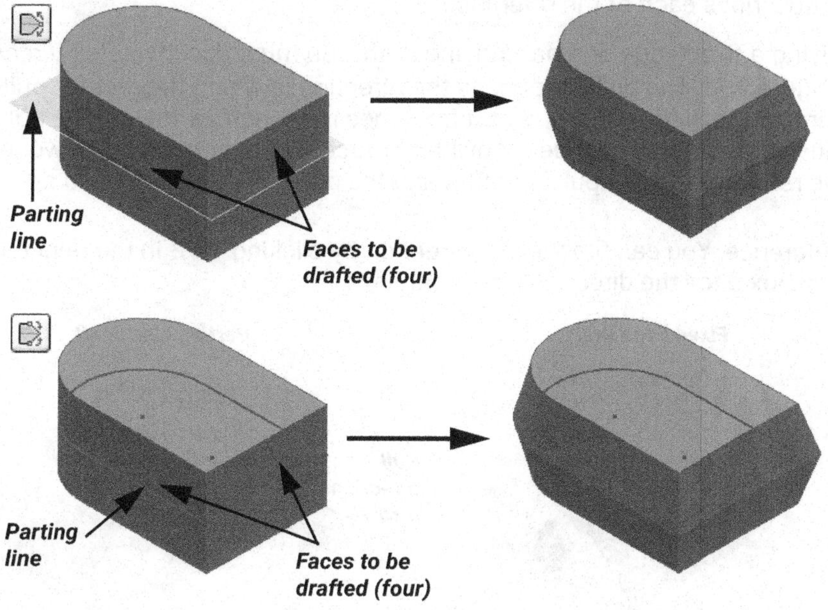

Figure 9–5

Step 3 - Select the draft references.

The references that are required to place a face draft depends on the type of draft that is being created. The following summarizes the reference selections that are required and which draft types require them.

Required Reference	Draft Type
Pull Direction	Fixed Edge and Parting Line
Fixed Plane	Fixed Plane
Parting Tool	Parting Line

To select a reference, ensure that its associated reference button ( ) is active in the *Face Draft* dialog box or that its option is selected in the mini-toolbar drop-down list.

The following describes each of the references:

- When applying a fixed edge or a parting line draft, you must specify a *Pull Direction*, as shown in Figure 9–6. The pull direction is the direction in which the mold is pulled from the part. The draft is applied so that the part becomes more narrow toward the pull direction, when positive draft angles are used. Any planar face, edge, work plane, or work axis can be used as the reference for the pull direction and the pull direction is defined as normal to this selected reference. You can flip the pull direction by clicking in the mini-toolbar or in the dialog box once the direction arrow displays.

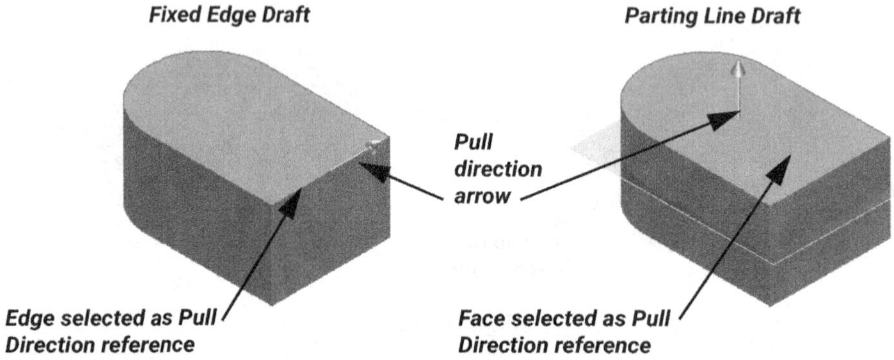

Figure 9–6

- When creating a fixed plane draft, a fixed plane reference must be defined. The fixed plane defines the plane that remains unchanged (fixed) and defines the pull direction. A work plane or planar face can be used as the reference for a fixed plane. Figure 9–7 shows the fixed plane reference and the resulting pull direction for the fixed plane draft shown previously.

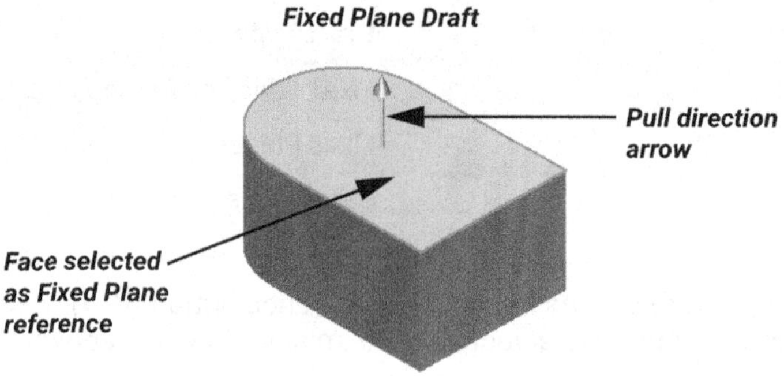

Figure 9–7

- When creating a parting line draft, a *Parting Tool* reference must be defined. The parting tool reference can be a 2D or 3D sketch, a plane, or a surface and defines where two halves of a mold meet. Figure 9–8 shows the parting tool reference for the parting line draft shown previously. The reference used as the draft pull direction should be normal to the parting tool.

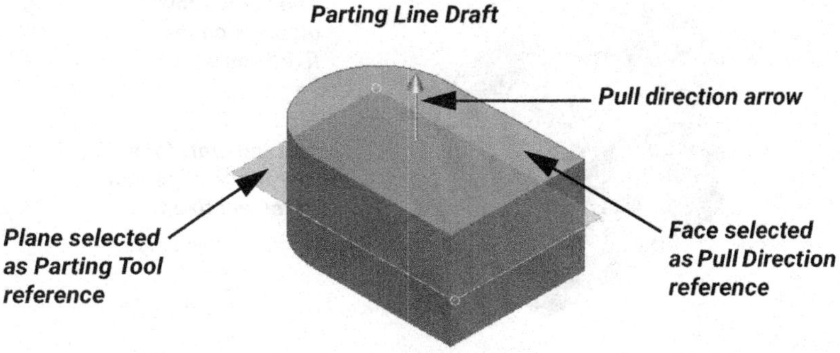

Figure 9–8

Step 4 - Select faces to draft.

All three draft types require the selection of face(s) that are to be drafted. To select the face(s) to be drafted, ensure that (Faces) is active in the *Face Draft* dialog box or that **Faces** is selected in the mini-toolbar (shown in Figure 9–9), and then select the required faces.

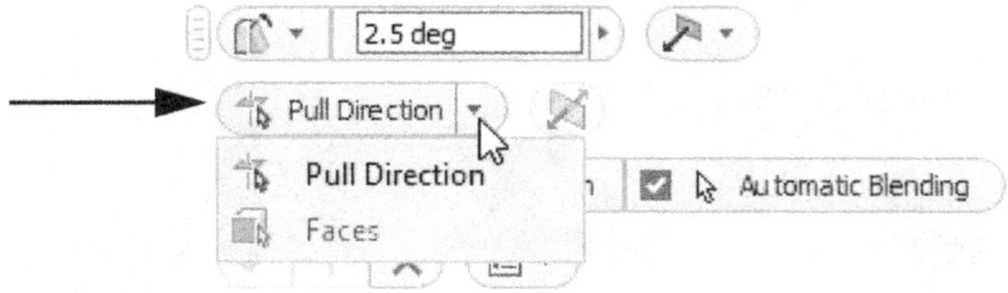

Figure 9–9

- Both face and edge references can be selected to define the geometry that is to be drafted.

- For fixed edge drafts, select the draft face closer to the edge that is to be fixed, as shown in Figure 9–10. The angle preview displays on the fixed edge. If the draft does not display as required, clear the face selection by holding <Ctrl> while selecting the reference again.

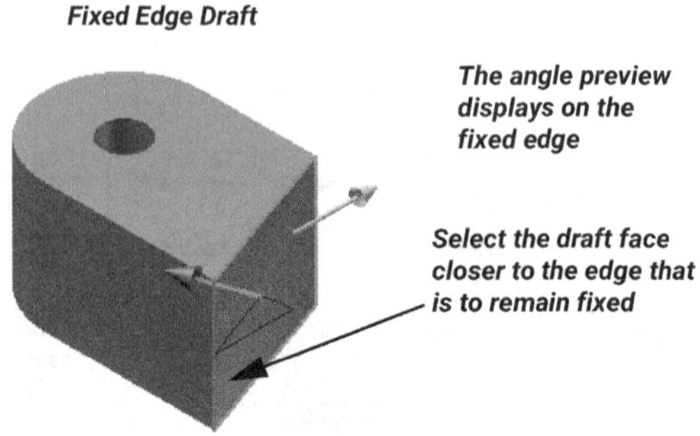

Figure 9–10

- Multiple faces or edges can be selected for drafting; however, their draft angles are controlled by one value. Create separate face drafts to individually control the draft angles of individual faces.
- Select **Automatic Face Chain** to automatically include any faces that are tangent to the selected face. This option is available for all three types of drafts.
- Select **Automatic Blending** to blend the resulting draft with adjacent filleted faces. This option is available for all three types of drafts. Figure 9–11 shows that a single face has been selected for drafting (**Automatic Face Chain** was cleared) and the **Automatic Blending** option is on or off.

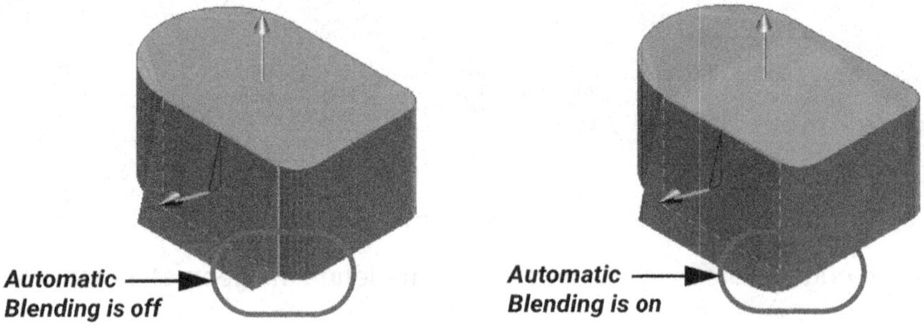

Figure 9–11

- When creating a parting line draft that uses the (Move Parting Line) option, you can further customize the draft by setting static edges on the draft geometry. To do so, enable (Fixed Edges) once draft faces have been selected and select the individual edges that will not change.
  - Alternatively, click (Select Boundary) to select multiple edges automatically.
  - To clear all selected fixed edges, click (Clear All). The selection of fixed edges can only be customized in the *Face Draft* dialog box and not the mini-toolbar.

Step 5 - Enter the draft angle.

A default *Draft Angle* value is automatically assigned once all references have been selected. The draft displays in preview mode with this value. To change the value, enter a new value in the *Draft Angle* field in the mini-toolbar or *Face Draft* dialog box, as shown in Figure 9–12. Draft values can be between 0 and 89 degrees. A negative angle value reverses the pull direction.

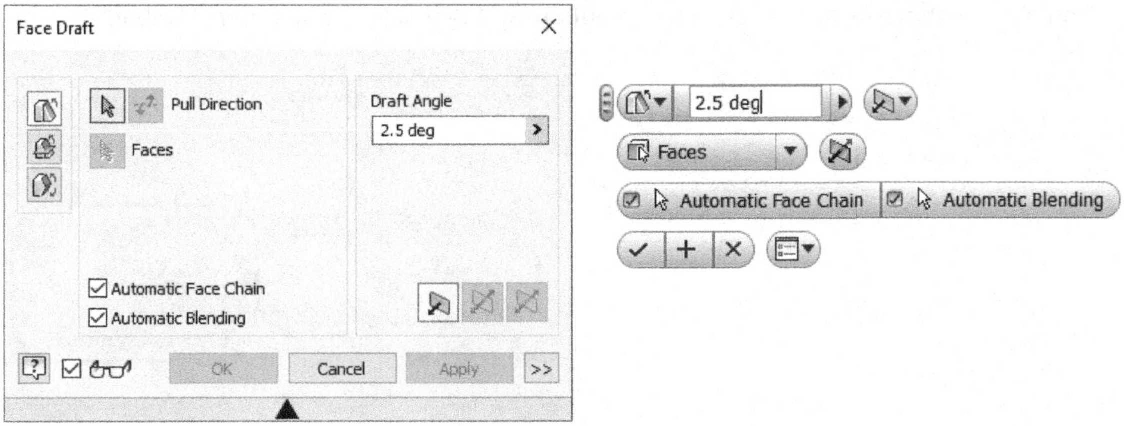

Figure 9–12

- For fixed edge drafts, the draft value is measured from the fixed edge.
- For fixed plane and parting line drafts that use the (Fixed Parting Line) option, the draft value is measured from the fixed plane or parting line reference.

- The (Symmetric) and (Asymmetric) side options can be used to further define the draft angles on either side of the reference plane. For an asymmetric draft, the draft angle can be different above and below. To toggle between the draft angles on the model, press <Tab>. Alternatively, enter the draft angle values using the dialog box. Figure 9–13 shows how these options can be accessed in the mini-toolbar.

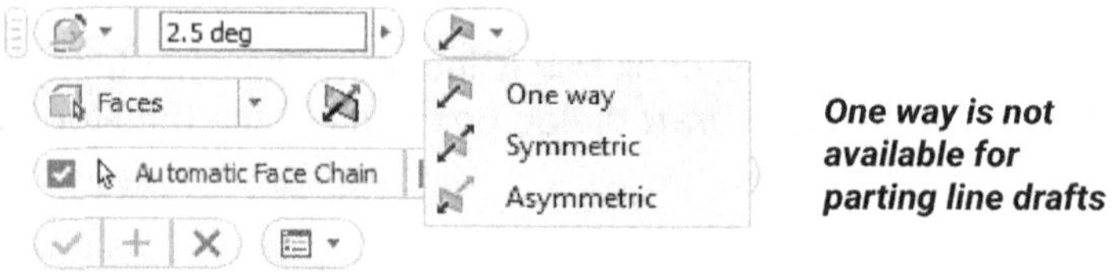

Figure 9–13

- For parting line drafts that use the (Move Parting Line) option, the draft value can be specified so that it is on both sides using the (Angle for Both), (Angle for Top), or (Angle for Bottom) options. Once activated, enter a value in the *Min. Draft Angle* field. Figure 9–14 shows how to access these options in the dialog box and mini-toolbar.

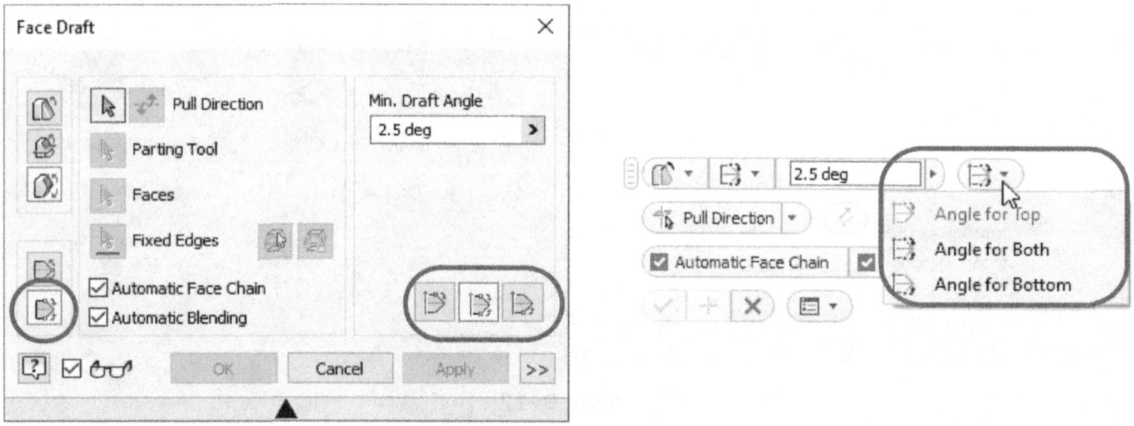

Figure 9–14

Step 6 - Complete the feature.

Click **OK** or to complete the face draft and close the *Face Draft* dialog box and mini-toolbar. Alternatively, right-click and select **OK (Enter)** or press <Enter>.

9.2 Splitting a Face or Solid

You can split a face or a solid to manipulate each portion of the geometry separately. For example, if a portion of a face is required to be drafted, it can be split so that the resulting drafted faces can have different draft angles. This can be helpful for mold creation. In Figure 9–15, an example is shown where the same split tool is being used; however, faces and solids are selected to vary the result.

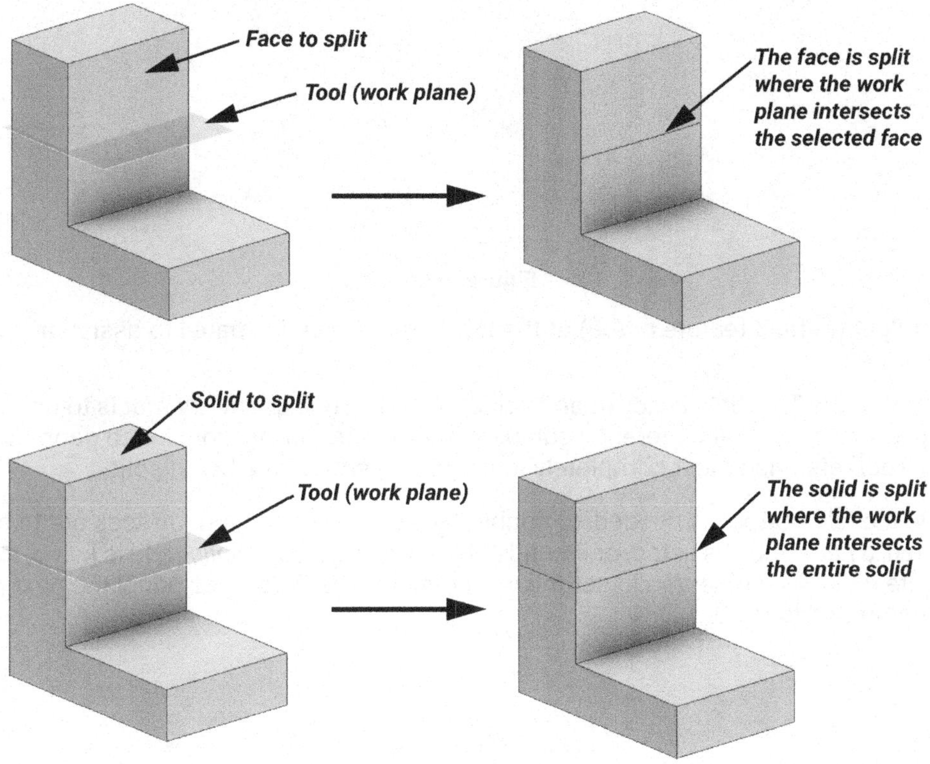

Figure 9–15

How To: Split a Face or Solid

1. In the *3D Model* tab>*Modify* panel, click (Split). The *Properties* panel opens, as shown in Figure 9–16.

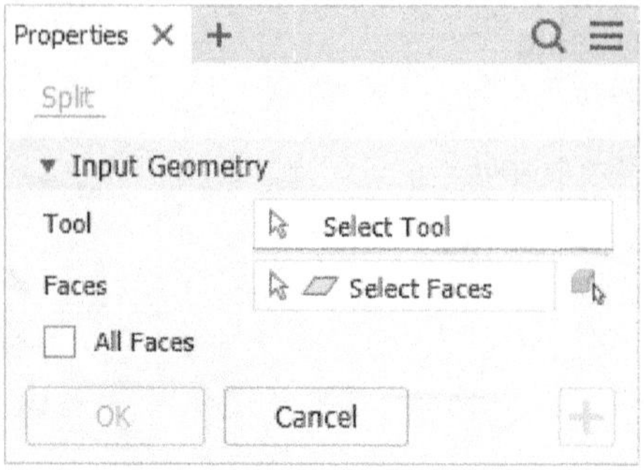

Figure 9–16

2. Select **Split** (default feature name) at the top of the *Properties* panel to assign a name for the feature.
3. Ensure that the *Tool* field is active and select the reference geometry that is to define where the split is to occur. This reference can be a work plane, surface, or sketch geometry. The split's *Tool* reference must completely intersect the entire face being split.
4. Toggle the button, as needed, to enable face or solid selection. If faces are to be selected, a *Faces* field is listed, or if solids are to be selected, a *Solid* field is listed, as shown in Figure 9–17. The faces/solid setting will persist in the *Properties* panel the next time the Split command is started.

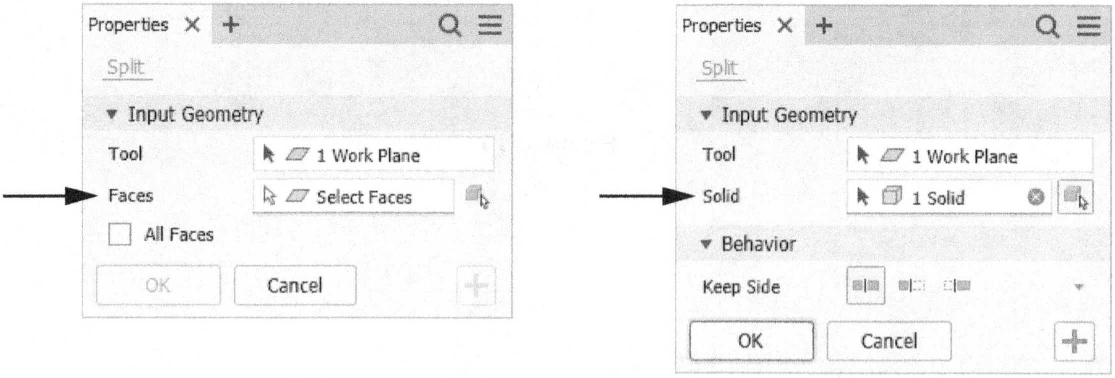

Figure 9–17

5. Ensure that the *Faces* or *Solid* field is active and, depending on whether the split is being conducted on faces or a solid, complete one of the following:
    - If faces are being split, select a single face or multiple faces, as needed. To quickly select all faces in the model, click **All Faces**.
    - If a solid is being split, Inventor will automatically pre-select it if there is only one solid in the model. If there are multiple solids, you must explicitly select the solid(s) to be split.
6. When splitting a solid, the *Properties* panel provides additional settings in the *Behavior* area. This enables you to use the split to remove geometry from the model. By default, both sides of the split are kept ( ); however, you can select or to remove one side of the split or the other. When one of these side options are selected, a red arrow appears on the model indicating the side that will be removed. Toggle these options, as needed, to remove the required side.
7. Click **OK** or to complete the split. Alternatively, right-click and select **OK (Enter)** or press <Enter>.
    - To continue creating additional split features without closing the panel, click (Apply) and define the references as needed. Once all splits have been completed, click **OK**.

Hint: Splitting Using Multiple Entities in the Same Sketch

If multiple entities exist in a single sketch and each entity is to be used to create a separate split operation, consider enabling the **Keep sketch visible on (+)** option in the (Advanced Settings Menu). You can then use (Apply) to continue selecting entities without the sketch visibility being turned off, as is done when the feature is completed.

Figure 9–18 shows examples of a split that is done for both a face (top two images) and solid (bottom four images) using a work plane as the splitting tool.

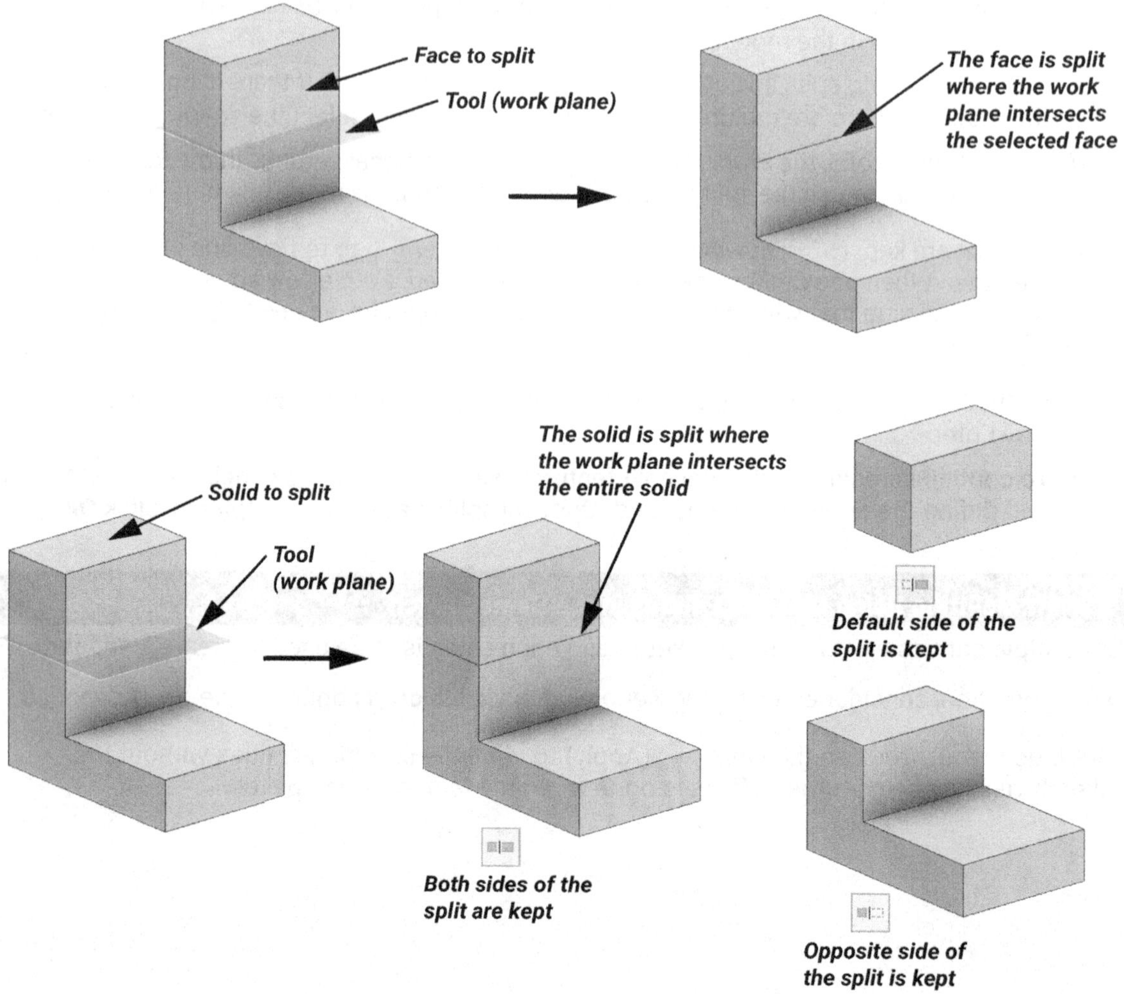

Figure 9–18

9.3 Shells

A shell feature is a feature that hollows a solid leaving a specified wall thickness. You can only vary the thickness of the walls between faces if the faces are not tangent. For this reason, you should normally shell the part before you add fillets. The model shown in Figure 9–19 has been shelled to remove the top and side face. Shell features cannot create tapered geometry; they are most often used for models with a constant thickness. Shell features can also be used for castings and molded parts.

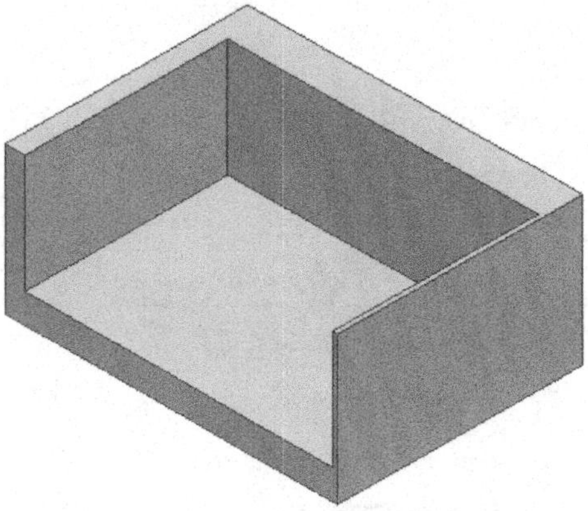

Figure 9–19

Use the following general steps to create a shell:

1. Start the creation of the shell.
2. Select the faces to remove.
3. Select the direction of shell removal.
4. Define the shell type.
5. Define the thickness of the wall.
6. Complete the feature.

Step 1 - Start the creation of the shell.

In the *3D Model* tab>*Modify* panel, click (Shell) to create a shell. The *Properties* panel opens, as shown in Figure 9–20.

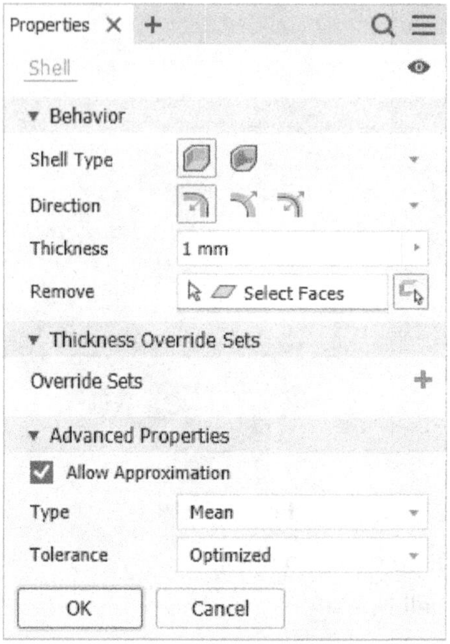

Figure 9–20

Step 2 - Select the faces to remove.

Ensure the *Remove* field is active and select the model faces to remove. The remaining faces are left as the shell walls. Removing a face creates an opening on that side of the part, as shown in Figure 9–21. If no model faces are selected to be removed, the shell cavity is entirely enclosed in the part, as shown on the right in Figure 9–21.

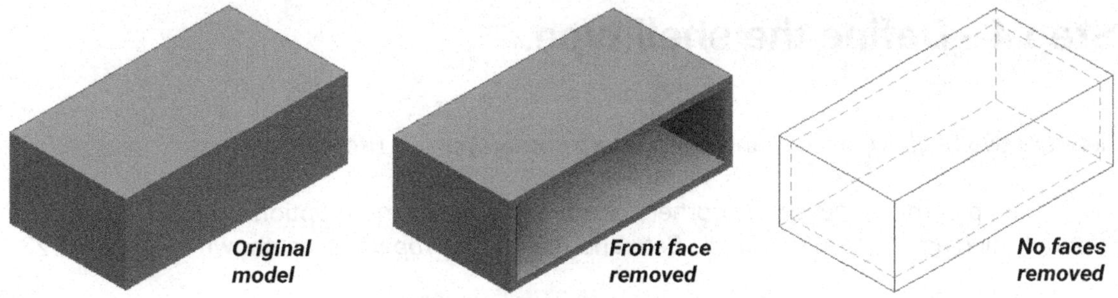

Figure 9–21

- To restore a face that has been selected for removal, hold <Ctrl> and select the face again.
- To automatically select all of the surfaces that are tangent to the surface that is selected for removal, click (Automatic Face Chain) in the *Properties* panel. Clear this option to select only the selected surface. Figure 9–22 shows the resulting shelled geometry when this option is both enabled and disabled.

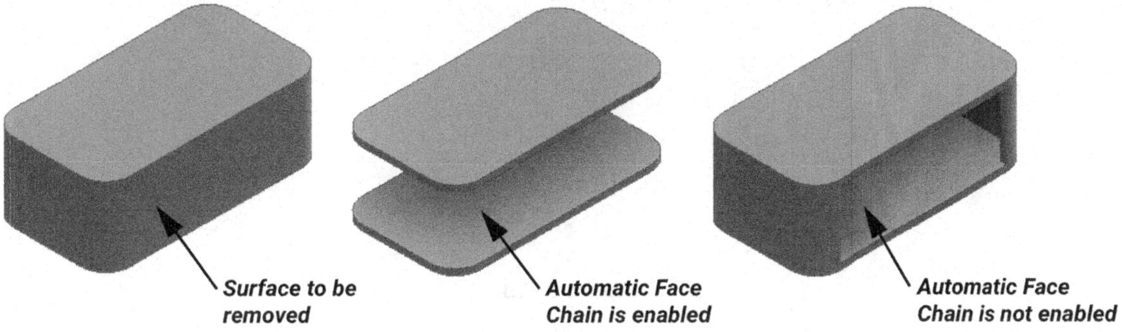

Figure 9–22

Step 3 - Select the direction of shell removal.

The shell direction options enable you to define the side to which the shell is added. The options are as follows:

(Inside)	Creates the shell inside the existing part boundaries with a specified thickness.
(Outside)	Creates the shell outside the existing part boundaries with a specified thickness.
(Both)	Existing part boundaries define the midpoint of the walls of the new part.

Step 4 - Define the shell type.

There are two *Shell Types* available: (Sharp corners) or (Round corners).

- (Sharp corners) leaves the corners sharp and enables more options in the *Properties* panel, such as *Thickness Override Sets* and *Advanced Properties*, as shown in Figure 9–23.

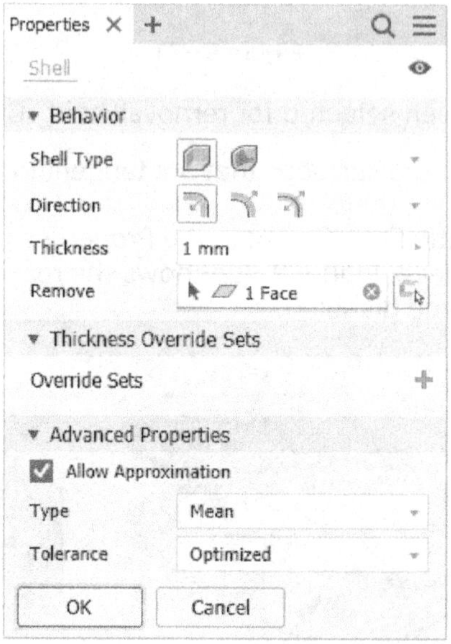

Figure 9–23

- (Round corners) rounds the corners of the geometry during shell creation. If you select round corners, the *Properties* panel reduces the available options, as shown in Figure 9–24.

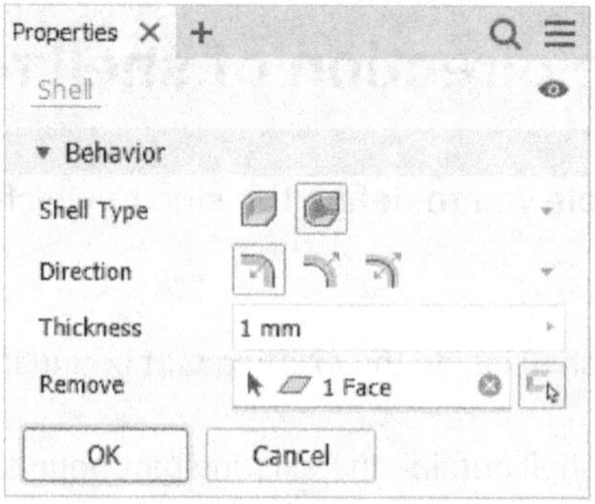

Figure 9–24

Step 5 - Define the thickness of the wall.

The wall thickness for a shell can be uniform, or you can assign unique wall thickness values to individual faces.

- To assign a uniform thickness for either a sharp corners or round corners shell, enter a value in the *Thickness* field in the *Properties* panel. Expand the *Thickness* field to select from a list of recent values.
- A unique face thickness can be added using the *Thickness Override Sets* area in the *Properties* panel. Unique thicknesses can only be assigned for sharp corners shells.To add a unique thickness value to individual faces, click + to add a new override set. Click **select faces** to select a face for which you are defining a unique thickness. Enter a dimension next to the selected face(s), as shown in Figure 9–25. Multiple faces can be selected and assigned the same value, or you can add a new override set and assign it a different thickness, as shown in Figure 9–25. To delete an entry, select it and click the ⊗ icon that appears for the entry.

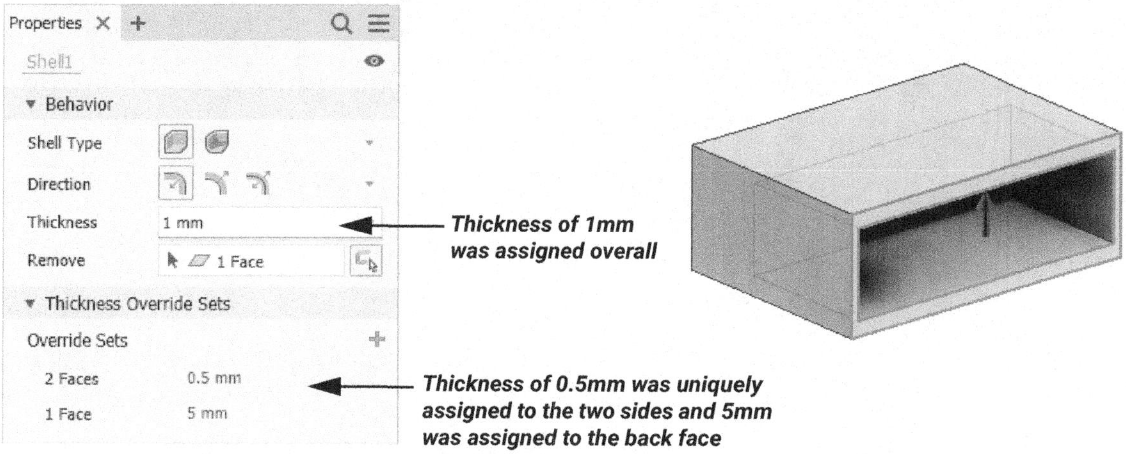

Figure 9–25

Step 6 - Complete the feature.

Click **OK** to complete the shell feature. Alternatively, right-click and select **OK (Enter)** or press <Enter>.

Hint: Shell Restrictions

The model geometry controls whether a shell can be added to a model or not. Note the following restrictions:

- Two tangent faces cannot have different thickness values. This restriction is generally due to the use of fillets. To apply different thickness values, add fillets after the shell.
- The face being removed for a shell must be surrounded by edges (i.e., not a fully revolved feature). Alternatively, use a closed shell, followed by an extruded cut feature.

9.4 Ribs

The **Rib** command enables you to create solid extrusions with open geometry. Typically, a rib is a feature that supports adjoining geometry. The rib can be constructed so that it is parallel to (rib) or perpendicular to (web) the plane of the sketched geometry, as shown in Figure 9–26.

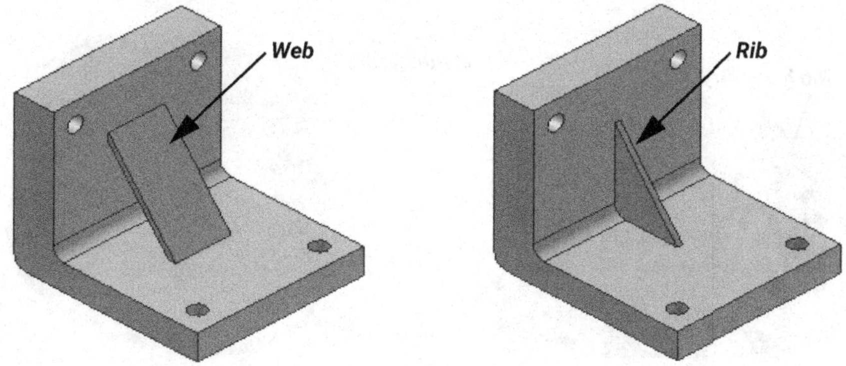

Figure 9–26

> ***Note:*** *Consider using the* ***Extrude*** *command to create rib and web features with closed geometry.*

Use the following general steps to create a rib:

1. Create the rib sketch.
2. Start the creation of the rib.
3. Define the shape of the rib.
4. Define the thickness of the rib.
5. Extend the rib.
6. Define additional features.
7. Complete the feature.

Step 1 - Create the rib sketch.

Rib geometry can be defined by sketching on work planes, or existing planar faces. The profile can be drawn so that it does not meet the part. When the rib is created, it is extended to the part, as shown in Figure 9–27. Once the sketch geometry has been defined, you can create the rib.

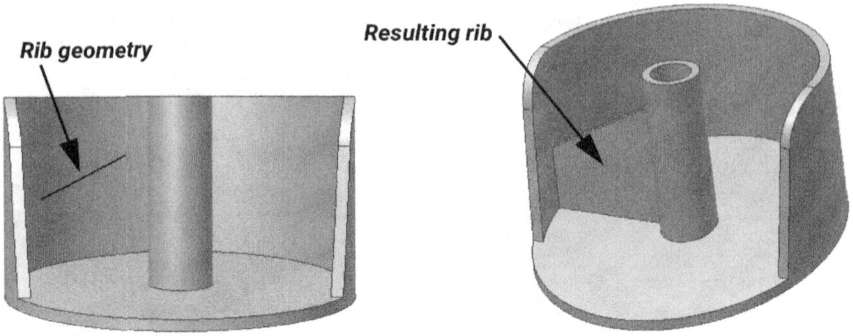

Figure 9–27

__Note:__ You can use several entities at the same time to create a series or network of ribs. The profile lines can intersect, but a single profile cannot be self-intersecting.

Step 2 - Start the creation of the rib.

In the *3D Model* tab>*Create* panel, click  (Rib) to create a rib. The *Rib* dialog box opens, as shown in Figure 9–28. The mini-toolbar is not available for creating ribs.

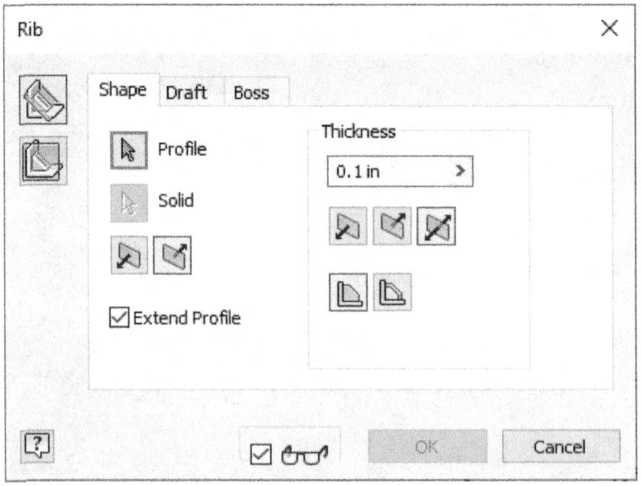

Figure 9–28

Step 3 - Define the shape of the rib.

Select the rib sketch if it is not automatically selected. Click (Normal to Sketch Plane) to create a rib perpendicular to the sketch plane (web) or click (Parallel to Sketch Plane) to create a rib parallel (rib) to the sketch plane. Figure 9–29 shows a rib being created both perpendicular (web) and parallel (rib) to the sketch plane of a sketched line.

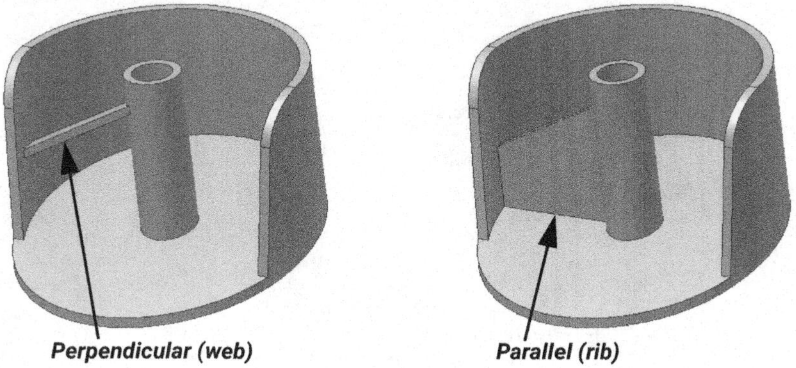

Figure 9–29

To further refine the direction of the feature, use the appropriate direction icon (or).

Step 4 - Define the thickness of the rib.

Enter a value for the thickness of the rib or select a value in the drop-down list. By default, the rib is extruded symmetrically on both sides of the sketching plane (). To switch the feature creation from both sides to one side of the sketching plane, select the appropriate direction icon (or).

Step 5 - Extend the rib.

The two options at the bottom of the *Thickness* area specify how the rib terminates. The difference between these extent options is shown in Figure 9–30.

- To extend the rib feature to the part face(s), click (To Next).
- To extend the rib feature to a specified distance, click (Finite) and enter a value for the rib extent.

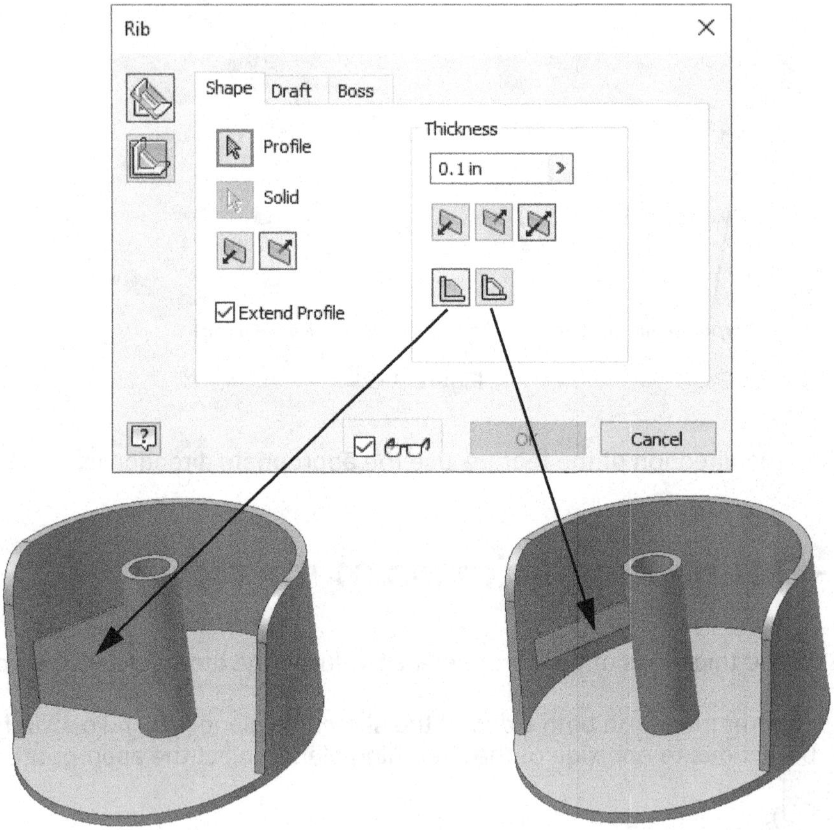

Figure 9–30

- The **Extend Profile** option extends the profile to intersect the model faces. It is only available when you are creating a finite extension.

Hint: Preview Not Displaying

If the preview does not display, it usually means that the geometry cannot be created with the options currently selection, consider changing the direction and extent options.

Step 6 - Define additional features.

For rib features that are created normal to a sketch plane, draft and boss features can be added to the rib during creation. This avoids having to create the features in separate steps.

To add draft to the rib, select the *Draft* tab, as shown in Figure 9–31. Enter the *Draft Angle* and specify where the thickness is controlled. Thickness can be controlled at the sketch plane (**At Top**) or at the intersection of the rib and the next feature face (**At Root**).

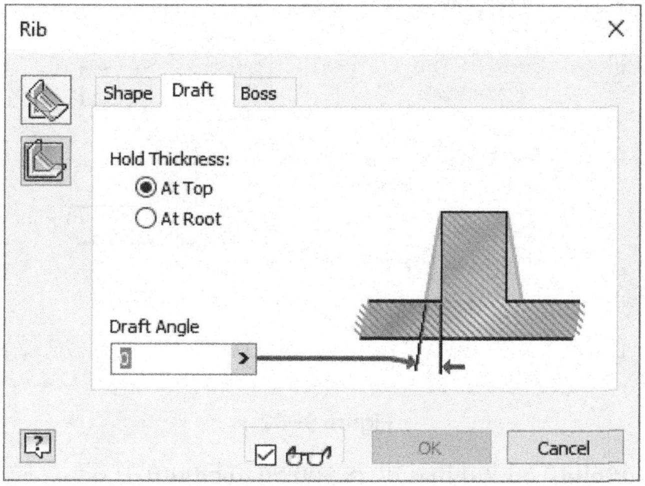

Figure 9–31

A boss feature can be added to the rib from the *Boss* tab, as shown in Figure 9–32. To create a boss feature, point(s) must first be created in the rib sketch. The point(s) represent the center point of the boss. If points are present in the sketch, they are selected automatically. To specify specific points around which to create the bosses, clear the **Select All** option, click

 (Centers), and select the points.

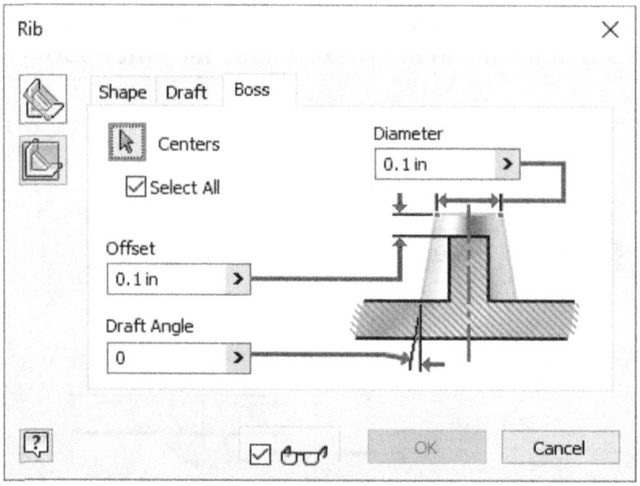

Figure 9–32

An example of a boss feature added to a rib is shown in Figure 9–33.

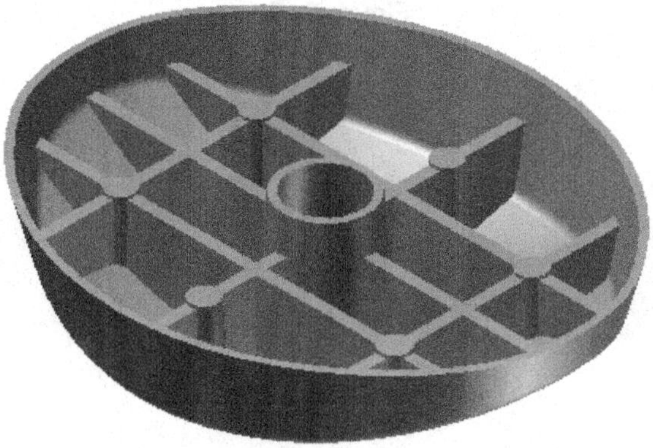

Figure 9–33

Step 7 - Complete the feature.

Click **OK** to complete the feature. Alternatively, right-click and select **OK (Enter)** or press <Enter>.

Practice 9a
Create a Shell and Ribs

Practice Objectives

- Create a shell feature that removes required geometry from the model.
- Add unique wall thickness for selected faces that remain after a shell operation.
- Create a rib feature from a sketched section.

In this practice, you will add a shell and rib feature to create the geometry shown in Figure 9–34.

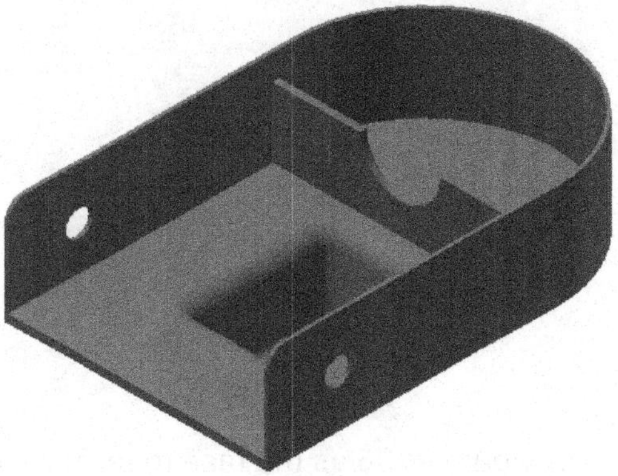

Figure 9–34

Task 1: Shell the model.

1. Open **shell.ipt**.

2. In the *Modify* panel, click  (Shell). The *Properties* panel opens, as shown in Figure 9–35.

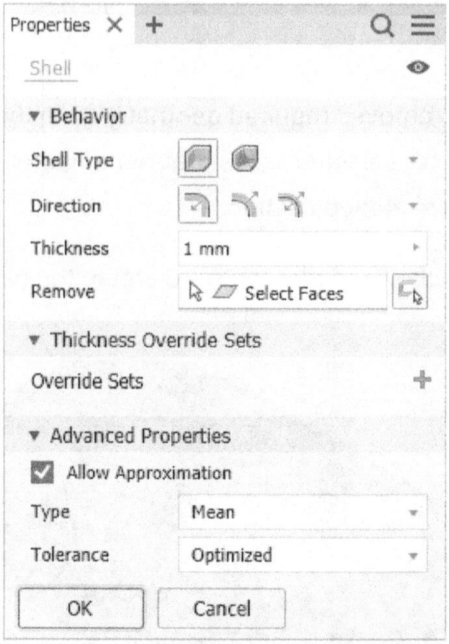

Figure 9–35

3. Select the surface shown in Figure 9–36 as the face to remove. Maintain the default 1mm thickness.

Figure 9–36

4. Complete the shell. The model displays as shown in Figure 9–37. The hole in the model did not shell as expected because its surface was not selected for removal.

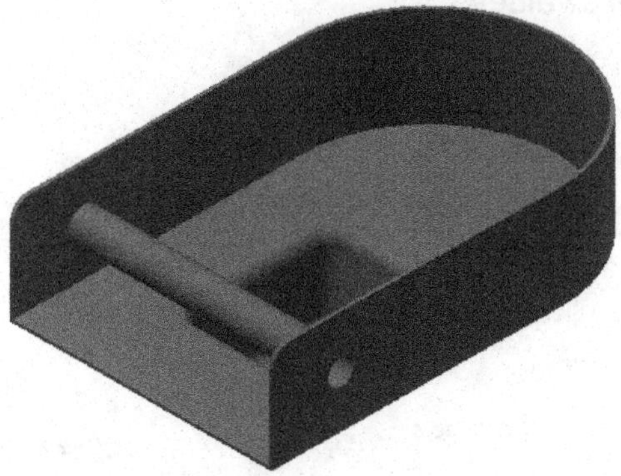

Figure 9–37

5. Edit the **Shell**. Select in the *Remove* field to activate it, then select the surface of the hole to be removed. The *Remove* field should now indicate that **4 Faces** will be removed.
6. Complete the shell. The model displays as shown in Figure 9–38.

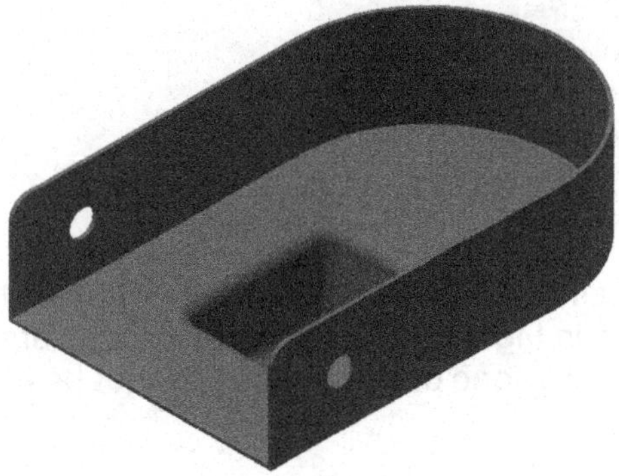

Figure 9–38

Note: *As an alternative to selecting the surface of the hole as an additional surface to be removed, you can also reorder features. To reorder the hole after the shell, select the hole and drag it after the shell in the Model browser.*

7. Edit the **Shell**. In the *Properties* panel, click + in the *Thickness Override Sets* area, as shown in Figure 9–39, to add an override set. This area enables you to create sets of faces that can have unique thickness values.

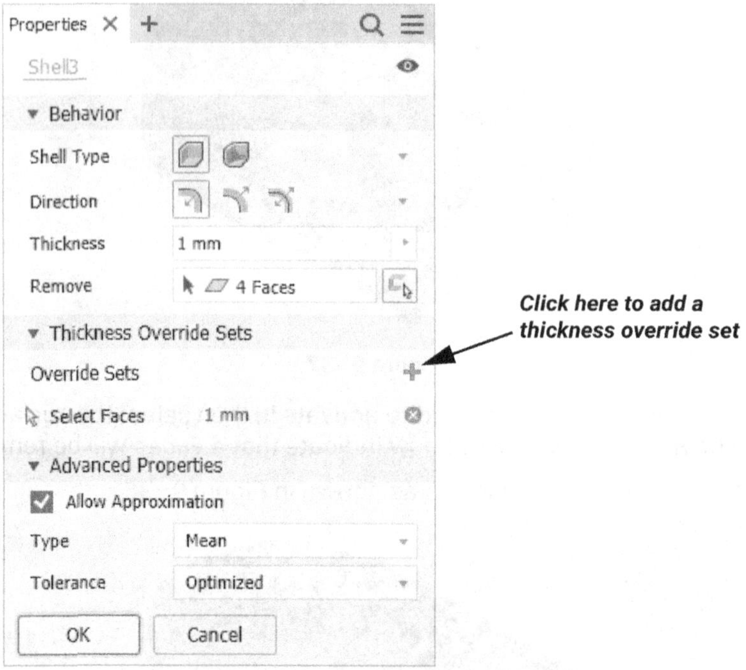

Figure 9–39

8. In the *Override Sets* area, click **Select Faces** in the override set that was just created and select the face shown in Figure 9–40. Twenty-six faces are selected because they are all tangent to one another. Any one of these faces cannot be assigned a unique wall thickness on its own.

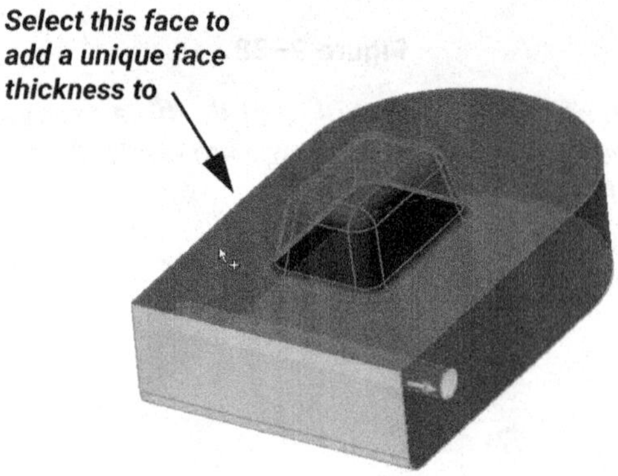

Figure 9–40

9. Enter **2.5** next to the selected face.
10. Complete the shell. The model displays as shown in Figure 9–41. Note the two wall thickness values that are assigned.

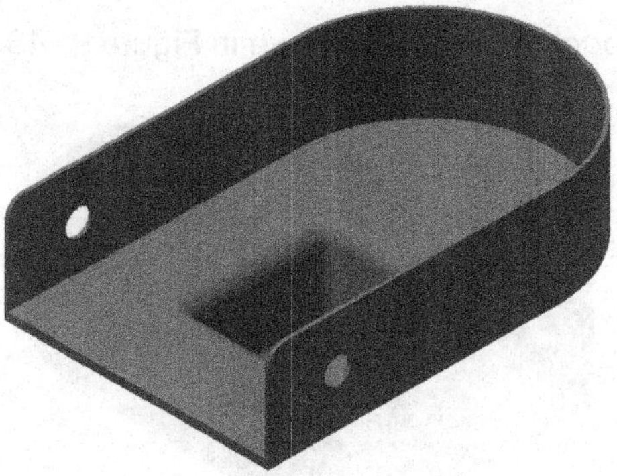

Figure 9–41

Task 2: Create a rib using a provided sketch.

1. In the Model browser, right-click on **Rib Sketch** and select **Visibility**. This sketch will be used to create a rib.
2. In the *Create* panel, click  (Rib).
3. Select the sketch as the profile for the rib feature.
4. Click  (Parallel to Sketch Plane) to create a rib.
5. Ensure  (Direction1) is specified.
6. Select  (To Next) as the extent. The dialog box and model display as shown in Figure 9–42.

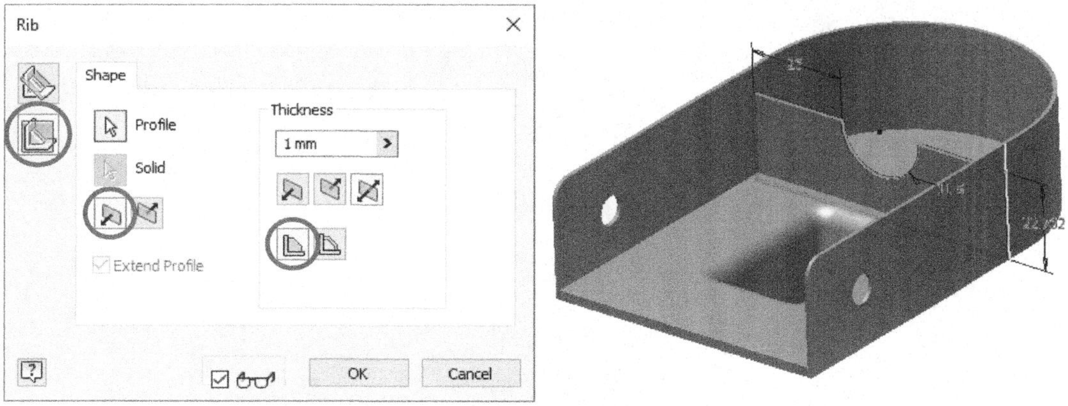

Figure 9–42

7. In the *Rib* dialog box, change the *Thickness* to **2.00**.

8. In the *Thickness* area in the dialog box, click  to add material to the far side of the sketch (based on the orientation shown previously in Figure 9–42).

9. Complete the rib. The model displays as shown in Figure 9–43.

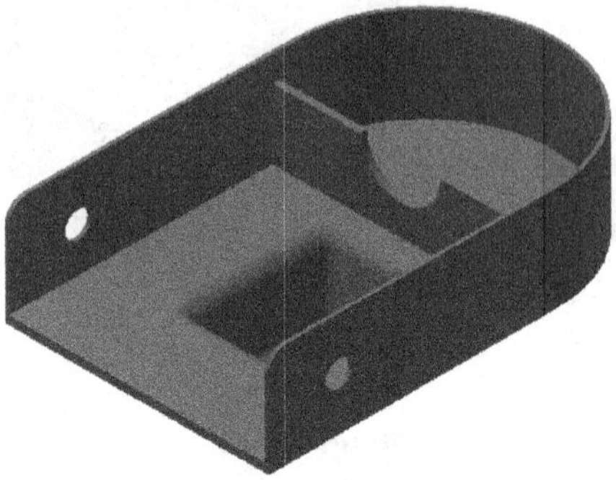

Figure 9–43

10. Modify the offset value of **Work Plane 1** to **-50mm**. Note how the rib updates with the change.

11. Save the model and close the window.

End of practice

Practice 9b
Create Ribs with Bosses

Practice Objectives

- Create a sketch that can be used to create a rib feature.
- Create a rib feature with boss geometry.

In this practice, you will create the model shown in Figure 9–44. To create the geometry, you will sketch the profile of the rib and then using the sketch create a rib with boss geometry.

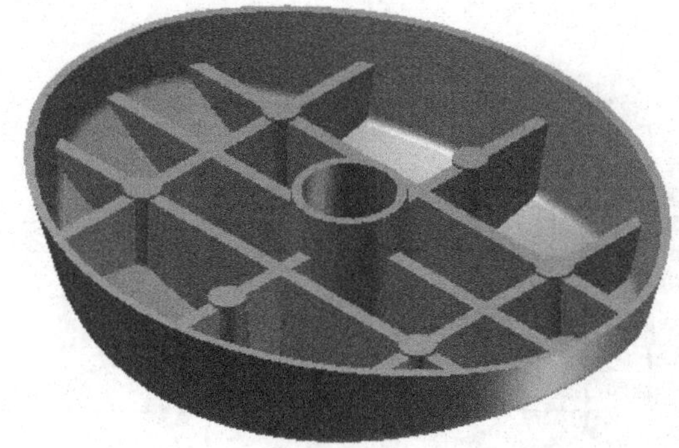

Figure 9–44

Task 1: Create the profile sketch for the rib feature.

1. Open **Complex_Rib.ipt**.
2. In the *Work Features* panel, expand (Plane) and select **Offset from Plane** to create a work plane.
3. Select the thin top face of the model as the plane to offset from, as shown in Figure 9–45. Enter **-12.7mm** as the *Offset* value. Complete the plane.

Figure 9–45

4. Rename the new work plane as **Rib Plane**.
5. Create a new sketch on **Rib Plane**.
6. Project the YZ and XZ origin planes.
7. Sketch the six entities as shown in Figure 9–46. Note the orientation of the ViewCube in the image to confirm orientation. Ensure that the horizontal and vertical lines are symmetric about the projected YZ and XZ origin planes and that the central lines are also constrained to the YZ and XZ origin planes. Add the two dimensions shown.

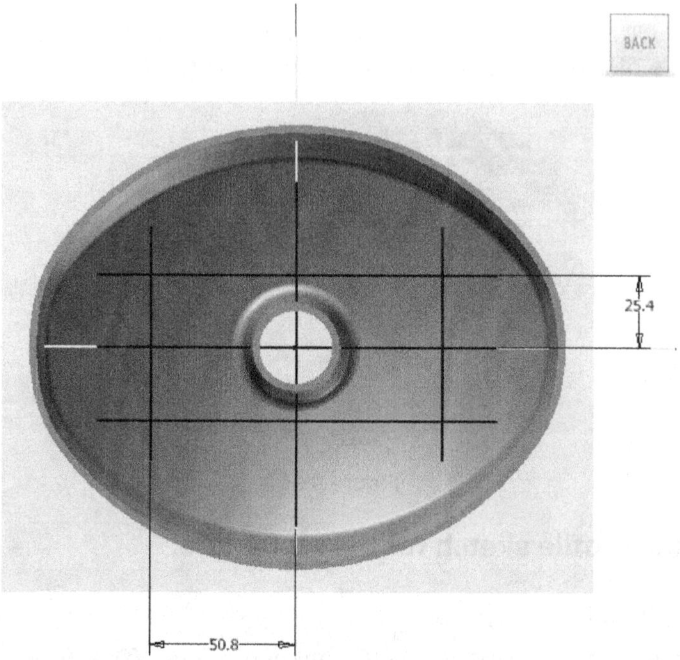

Figure 9–46

Note: *Additional dimensions are required to fully constrain the sketch, however they are not required to successfully create a rib. Rib features automatically project the sketch to the nearest geometry. In creating the sketch for a rib, ensure that you create the correct network; the lengths of the entities are not required.*

8. Bosses can be added as part of a rib feature. To do this, sketched points must be included in the sketch. Add the six sketch points, as shown in Figure 9–47. The two points that are on the vertical centerline should be symmetric with one another and dimensioned as shown. The remaining four points are aligned at the intersection of the sketched entities.

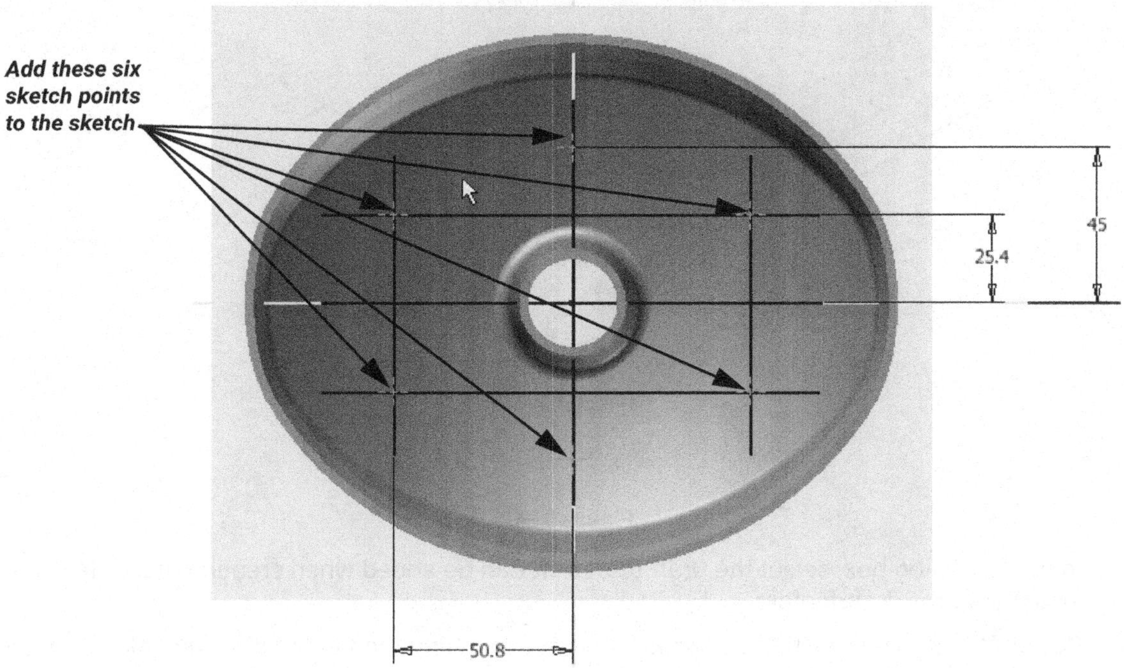

Figure 9–47

9. Finish the sketch.

Task 2: Create the rib feature.

1. In the *Create* panel, click (Rib).
2. Click (Normal to Sketch Plane) to create the rib so that it is normal to the sketch plane.
3. Select any one of the sketched entities. A rib should be previewed on the model. If not, toggle the feature direction using or as required until the geometry displays.
4. Ensure that is selected in the *Thickness* area so that the rib is created evenly on both sides of the sketched entity.
5. Enter **4mm** as the *Thickness* value.

6. Click (Profile) and select the remaining 5 sketched entities. The model previews as shown in Figure 9–48. Ensure that you select the sketched entity that lies on the projected YZ Plane and not the projected entity.

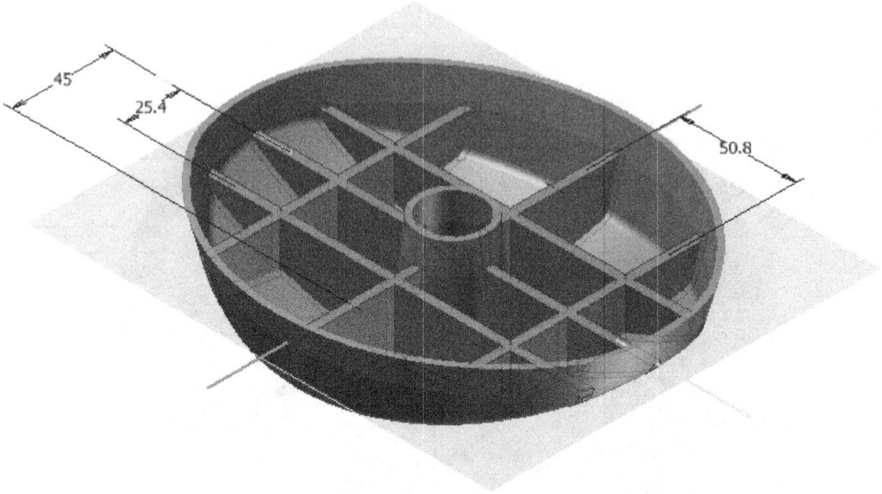

Figure 9–48

7. In the *Rib* dialog box, select the *Draft* tab. Draft can be added when creating the rib feature, instead of as a draft feature.
8. Select **At Top** to ensure that the **4mm** thickness is maintained at the sketched plane once draft is added.
9. Enter **4** as the *Draft Angle* value. Note the small change to the preview as the draft is added.
10. In the *Rib* dialog box, select the *Boss* tab.
11. Boss features can also be incorporated directly as part of the rib feature. Bosses are placed based on sketched points in the sketch. Select **Select All** in the *Rib* dialog box to ensure that all sketched points are automatically selected.
12. Enter **10mm** as the diameter of the boss geometry. Prior to changing the diameter, you will not see the boss geometry as the default diameter is smaller than the rib wall.
13. Maintain the default offset value of the boss above the rib.
14. Enter **4** as the *Draft Angle* value.
15. Click **OK** to complete the rib feature.

16. Toggle off the display of the **Rib Plane** work plane. The model displays as shown in Figure 9–49. If bosses do not display on the rib along the YZ Plane, it is possible that you selected the projected entity and not the sketched line so the sketched points are not being recognized.

Figure 9–49

17. Save the model.

End of practice

Practice 9c
Split a Face

Practice Objectives

- Create a split feature that splits a selected face based on a sketched profile.
- Create a face draft feature to add draft to a selected face in a model.
- Create a split feature that trims a solid based on a selected reference.

In this practice, you will use the **Split** and **Face Draft** commands to refine a block-shaped part. The completed part displays as shown in Figure 9–50.

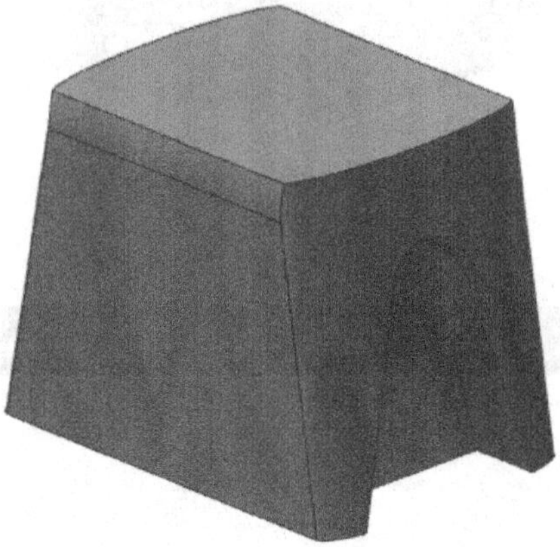

Figure 9–50

Task 1: Create geometry to define a split.

1. Open **split.ipt**.

2. Sketch, constrain, and dimension the profile for the split on one of the flat faces that contains an arced edge, as shown in Figure 9–51.

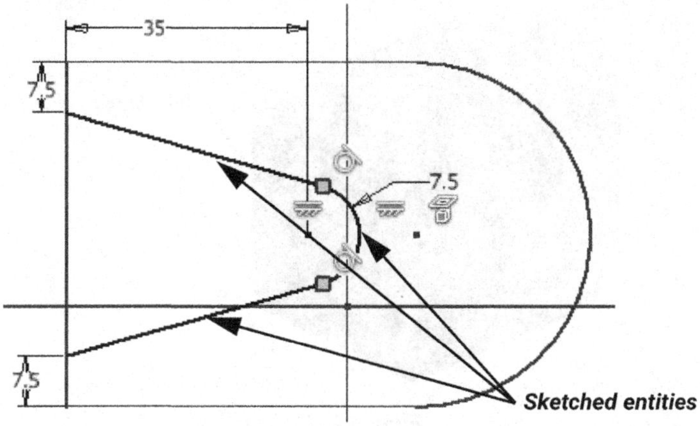

Figure 9–51

3. Finish the sketch.

Task 2: Create the split.

1. In the *Modify* panel, click (Split). The *Properties* panel opens, as shown in Figure 9–52.

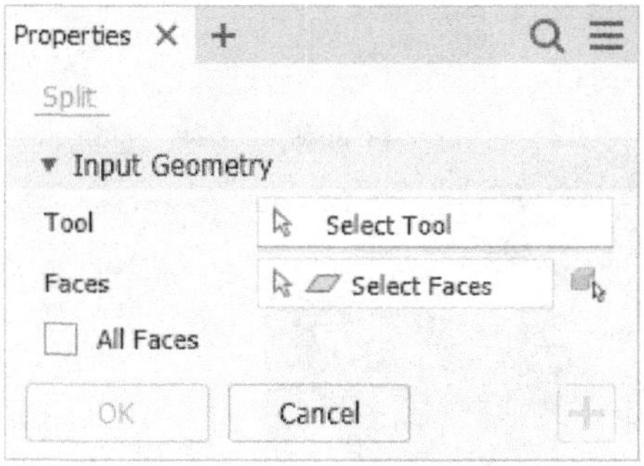

Figure 9–52

2. Select the sketch that you just created as the *Tool* reference. Three curves are assigned.
3. The *Faces* field should activate automatically; if not, select it. Select the face that you used as the sketch plane for the sketch as well as the opposite face as the faces to be split. Two faces are assigned.
4. Click **OK** to split the faces.

5. Select the split surfaces. They highlight individually (below the curve and above the curve), as shown in Figure 9–53.

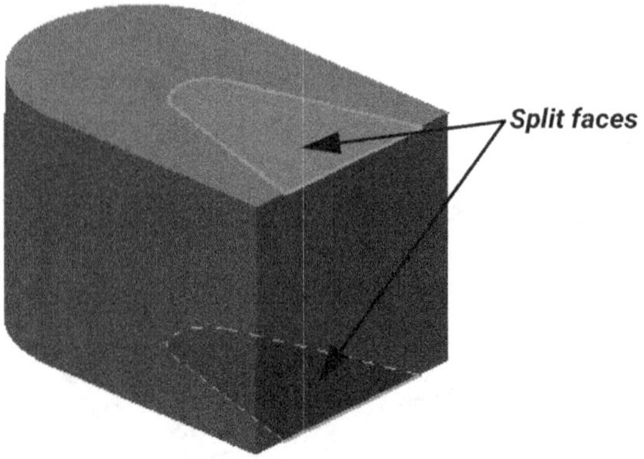

Figure 9–53

Task 3: Create draft faces.

1. In the *Modify* panel, click (Draft) to create a face draft. The *Face Draft* dialog box and the mini-toolbar open.
2. Select the pull direction reference shown in Figure 9–54. Click , as required, to set the pull direction towards the cylindrical end of the part.

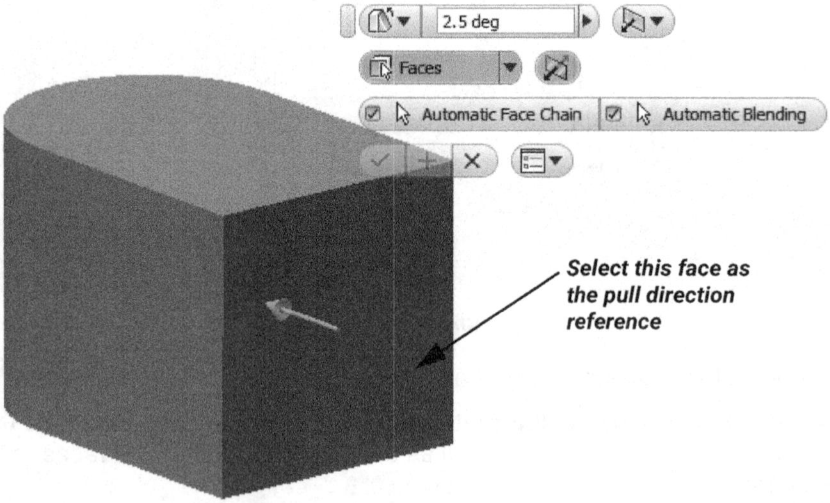

Figure 9–54

3. Select the face near the edge, as shown in Figure 9–55. Ensure that the draft angle directions display as shown.

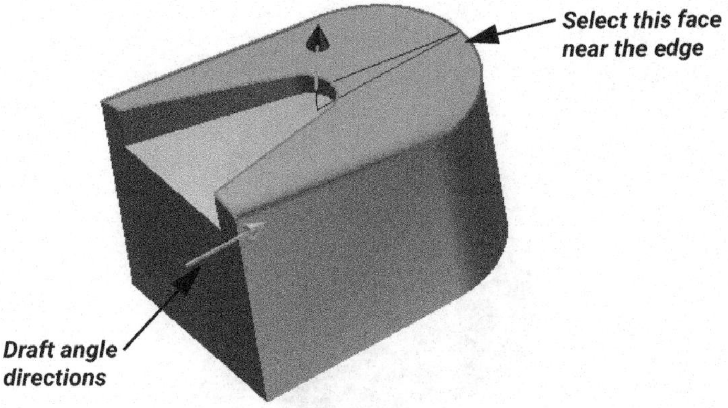

Figure 9–55

4. Set the angle to **10** degrees.
5. Click **OK** to draft the face. The model displays as shown in Figure 9–56.

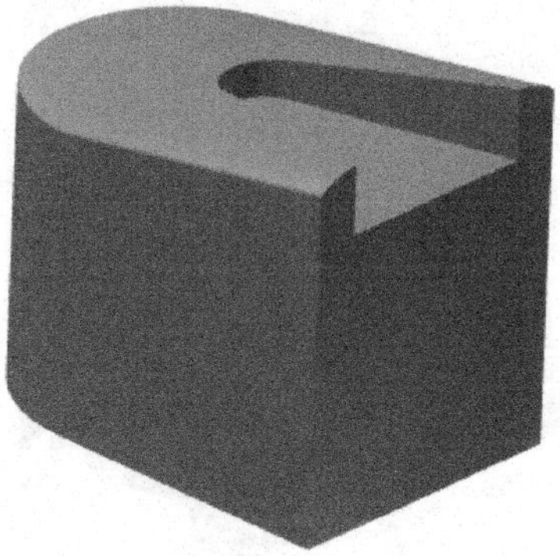

Figure 9–56

6. Repeat Steps 1 to 5 to draft the opposite face that was also split.

Task 4: Create another split.

1. Create a work plane parallel to the bottom face (now H-shaped), inside the part at an *Offset* value of **-57mm**.
2. In the *Modify* panel, click (Split). The *Properties* panel opens.
3. Select the work plane as the split's *Tool* reference.
4. By default, the split is set to allow the selection of faces. In this task, you must trim a solid.

   Click (Solid) to enable solid selection. The entire solid is assigned automatically because there is only one solid in the model.

5. In the *Behavior* area, select  (Split the solid and keep the default side). The arrow points towards the smaller section, as shown in Figure 9–57. This is the area that will be removed after the split.

Figure 9–57

6. Click **OK**. The model displays as shown in Figure 9–58.

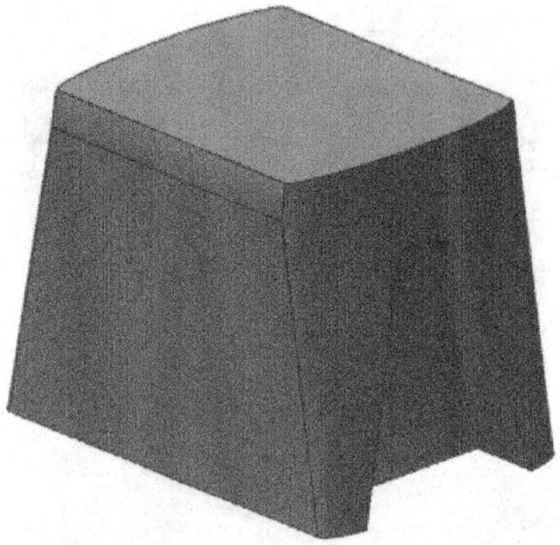

Figure 9–58

7. Save and close the part.

End of practice

Chapter Review Questions

1. Which of the following statements is true for creating a draft?
   a. Multiple surfaces can be selected for drafting.
   b. Multiple faces can be selected when defining the pull direction.
   c. Only existing edges on the model can be selected to define the pull direction.

2. If the *Behavior* area of the split's *Properties* panel is displayed, is a face or a solid being split?
   a. Face
   b. Solid

3. You can shell the part without removing model faces.
   a. True
   b. False

4. Which of the following is true for shell features?
   a. To create a shell, you must select the face(s) to remove.
   b. A single face that is tangent to another face cannot be removed unless the tangent face is also removed.
   c. A closed shell cannot have walls of varying thickness.
   d. Wall thickness can be added to the inside or outside of a model.

5. When creating a shell, how can you leave one side of the part open, as shown in Figure 9–59?

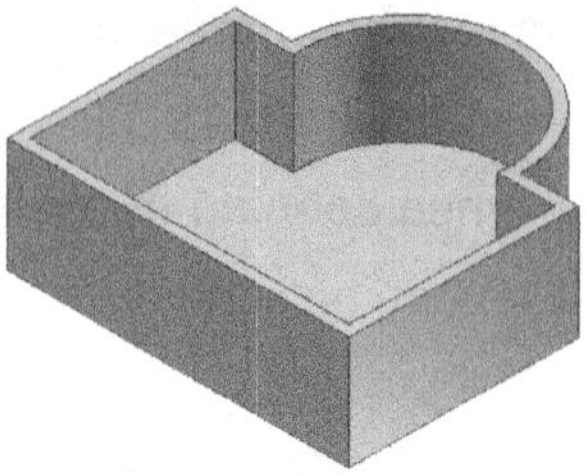

Figure 9–59

a. Use the *Remove* field in the *Properties* panel.

b. Set the *Thickness* for that face to 0.

c. Delete the face after the shell has been created.

d. Set the *Thickness* for that face to the negative of the general thickness.

6. What can you do with the **Rib** command that you cannot do with the **Extrude** command?

a. Create a surface object.

b. Cut through an existing solid.

c. Select multiple profiles for the feature.

d. Create a solid from an open profile.

Command Summary

Button	Command	Location
	**Draft**	• **Ribbon:** *3D Model* tab>*Modify* panel
	**Rib**	• **Ribbon:** *3D Model* tab>*Create* panel
	**Shell**	• **Ribbon:** *3D Model* tab>*Modify* panel
	**Split**	• **Ribbon:** *3D Model* tab>*Modify* panel

Chapter 10

Model and Display Manipulation

Learning how to manipulate and control existing and new features in your model provides flexibility in designing and making changes to your models. Tools such as section and design views provide additional viewing tools to review the model.

Learning Objectives

- Change the order of features in the Model browser.
- Use the End of Part marker to change the location in which new features are added to a model.
- Remove a feature temporarily from being included in the model geometry.
- Create quarter, half, and three-quarter section views in a model to help visualize the interior of a 3D model.
- Create and activate custom design views that store display settings for a model.

10.1 Reordering Features

A model is generated in the order in which the features display in the Model browser. In certain situations, the resulting geometry varies, depending on the feature creation order. To achieve the required geometry, you can reorder the features to change the way the part is constructed. To reorder a feature, select it in the Model browser and drag it below or above its current position. You cannot drag a feature above a feature that it references or below a feature that references it.

Consider the following example shown in Figure 10–1. Shell and fillet features are to be added to the model. Due to the order in which the existing features were initially added, the resulting geometry after the addition of the shell is not wanted. Reordering the hole after the shell and adding the fillet before the shell results in the completed part shown in Figure 10–1.

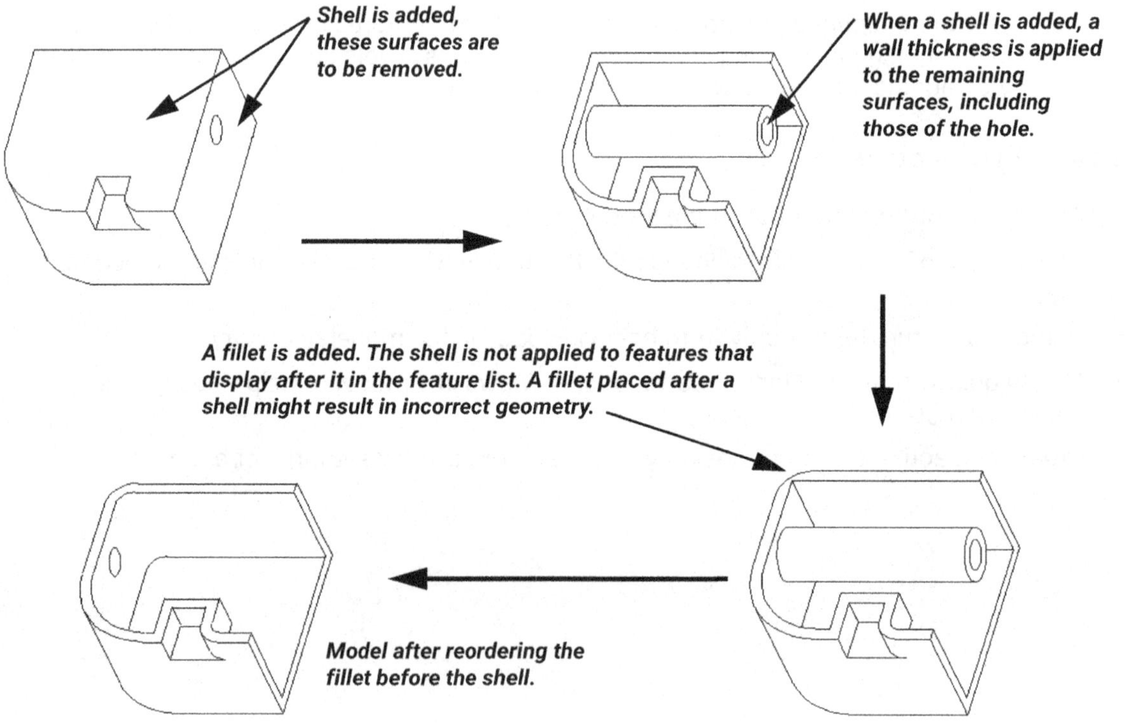

Figure 10–1

10.2 Inserting Features

By default, when features are added to the model, they are added to the end of the feature list. To insert features at any earlier point, you must move the End of Part marker from the bottom of the Model browser to the location at which you want to insert a feature. You can use this technique when you need to create a feature earlier in the design process. Use any of the following techniques to move the End of Part marker:

- Right-click a feature in the Model browser and select **Move EOP Marker**. The End of Part is placed after the feature.
- Select and drag the End of Part marker in the Model browser to the location at which you want to insert a feature.

Figure 10–2 shows an example of a model and its Model browser before (left-hand side) and after (right-hand side) moving the End of Part marker. Once moved, all of the features below it are temporarily removed from the model and a new feature can be added.

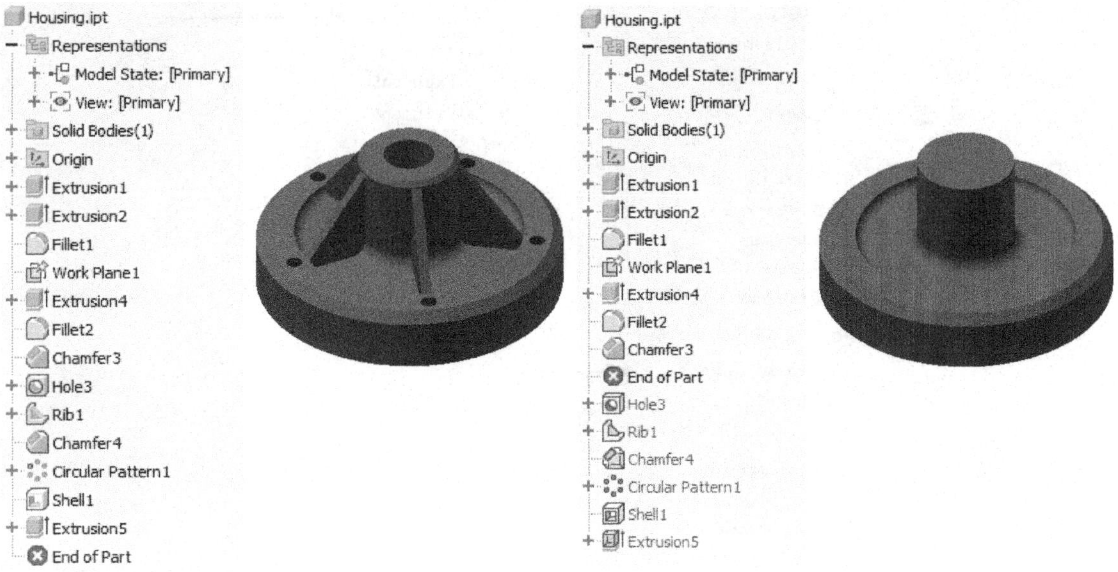

Figure 10–2

To return the End of Part marker to the bottom of the Model browser use one of the following techniques:

- Right-click End of Part and select **Move EOP to End**.
- Drag the End of Part to the bottom of the Model browser.

10.3 Suppressing Features

As you work on a complex part, you might find it difficult to identify or select features in the graphics window. You can simplify the model appearance by suppressing a feature to make it temporarily invisible. To suppress a feature, right-click on it in the Model browser and select **Suppress Features**, as shown on the left in Figure 10–3. If you suppress a feature, all of its dependent features are also suppressed. Suppressed features and their dependent features are displayed in gray and are crossed out in the Model browser, as shown on the right in Figure 10–3.

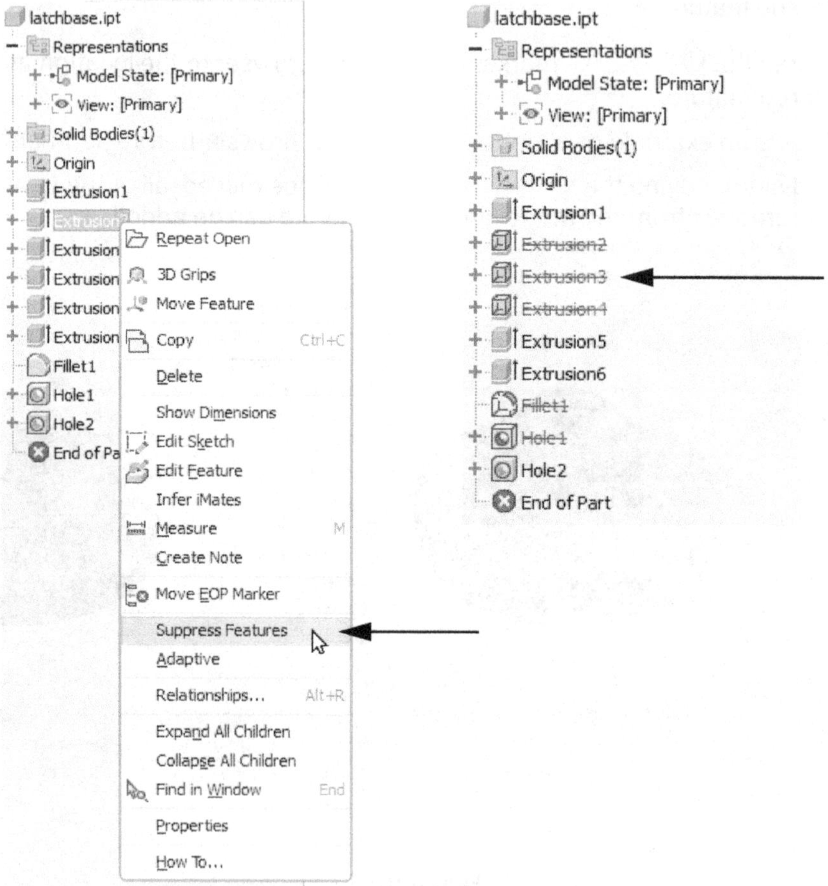

Figure 10–3

Note: *You can select features for suppression directly in the graphics window if the* ***Select Features*** *feature priority setting is set.*

To unsuppress a feature, right-click on the feature in the Model browser and select **Unsuppress Features**. The dependent features that were suppressed are also unsuppressed.

Hint: Rule-Based Suppression

Using the *Feature Properties* dialog box, you can establish rule-based suppression. To access the dialog box, right-click the feature and select **Properties**. In the *Suppress* area of the dialog box, you can set the appropriate situation for suppressing the feature. The suppression options are shown in Figure 10–4. When using the **If** suppression condition, you can:

- define a dimension-related situation (e.g., d14=12mm, d14>5mm, or d14<10mm).
- assign a True/False user parameter in the *Parameters* dialog box and base the suppression's If condition on whether the parameter value is set to True or False.

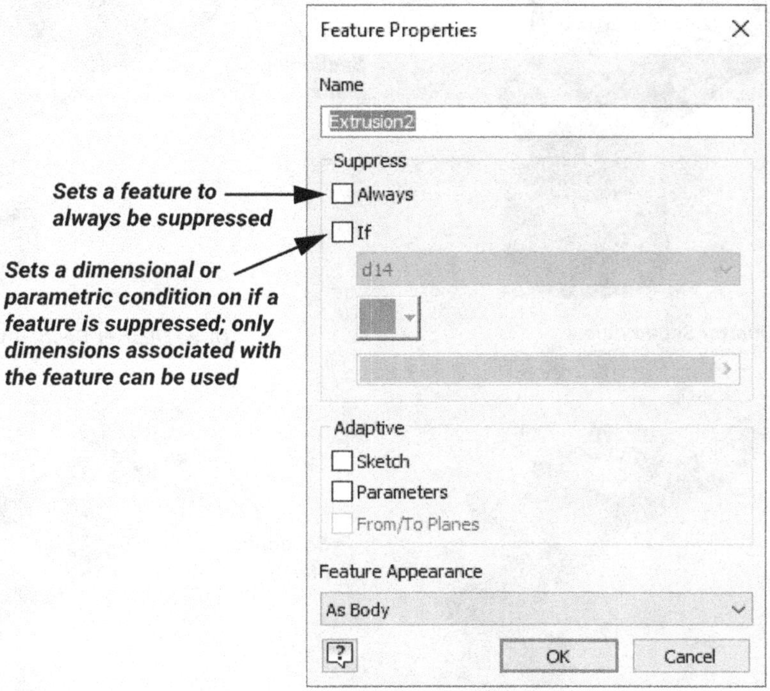

Figure 10–4

If a suppression condition is set, you must unsuppress it to return it to the model. Just unsuppressing the parent geometry does not resume it.

10.4 Sectioning Part Models

Section views help visualize a 3D model by providing a section view of it. There are three types of section views that can be created. Figure 10–5 shows these views and the selected planes required to create them.

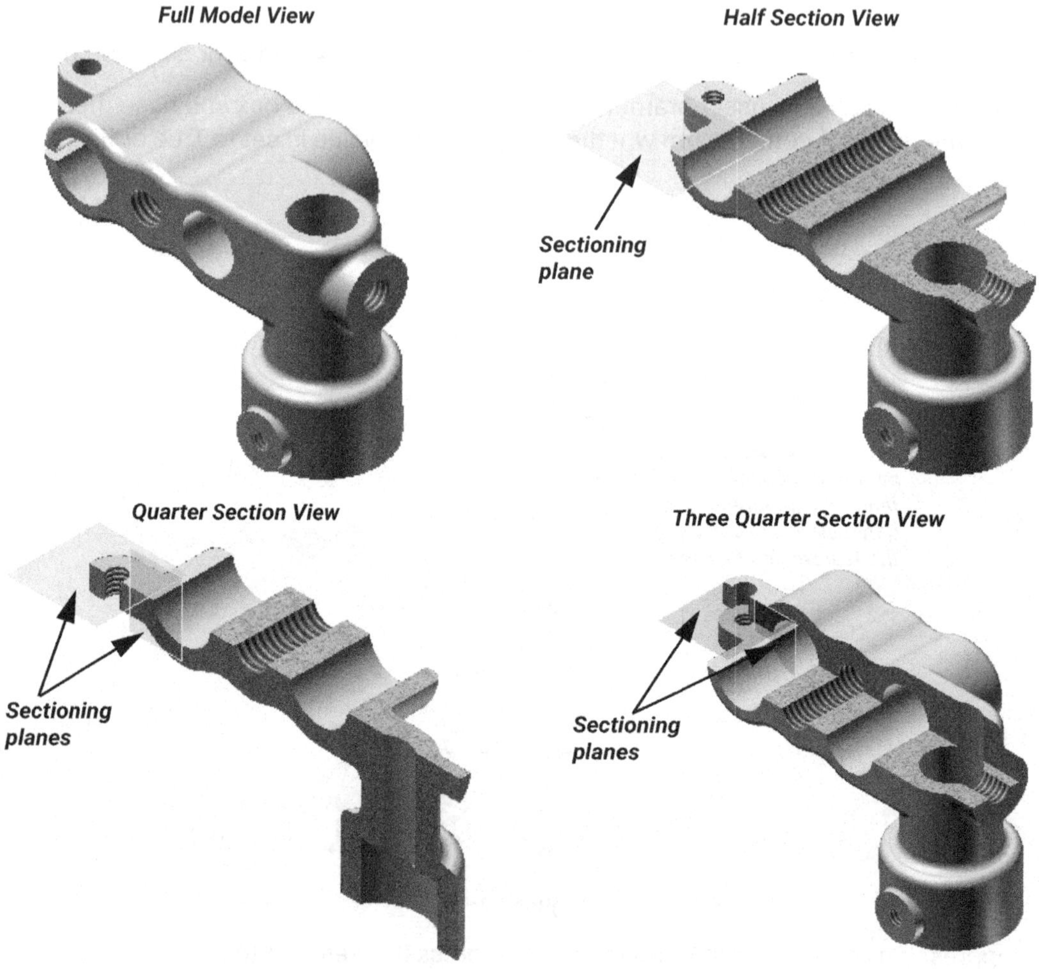

Figure 10–5

How To: Section a Part

1. In the *View* tab>*Visibility* panel, select the type of section view in the *Section View* drop-down list, as shown in Figure 10–6.

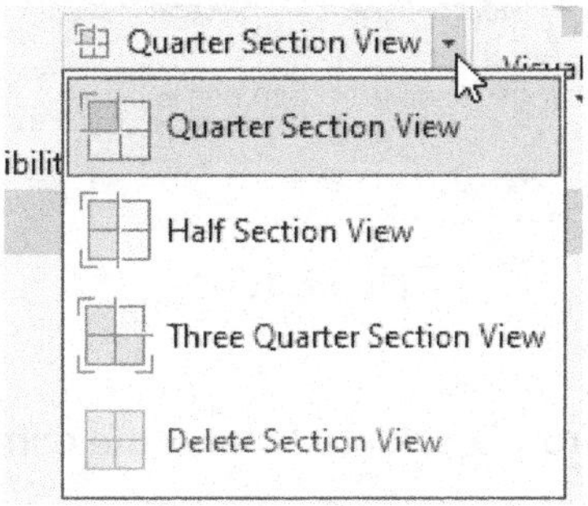

Figure 10–6

2. Select the plane to section about. The mini-toolbar appears in the graphics window as shown in Figure 10–7.

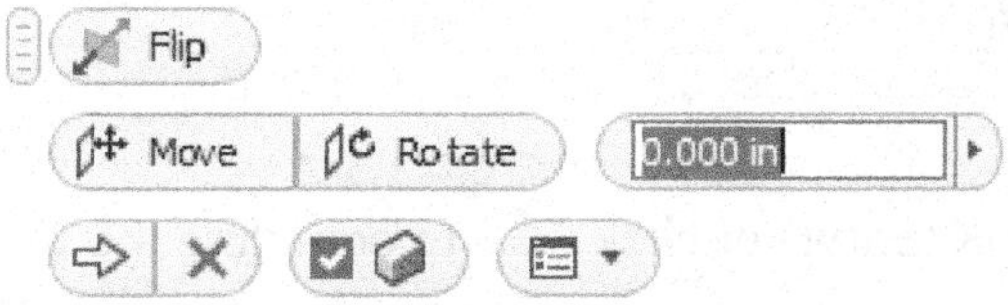

Figure 10–7

3. If required, move the selected plane using one of the following techniques with the  option selected.
   - In the mini-toolbar, enter a value in the offset field.
   - In the graphics window, drag the arrow that appears on the section plane.
   - In the mini-toolbar, use the scroll wheel in the Offset field to offset incrementally. To change the scroll increments when modifying section plane placement, right-click in the graphics window and select **Scroll Step Size**, enter an increment value, and click .

Note: *To rotate the plane, select*  *and enter or drag the rotation handle as needed.*

4. If required, flip the section about the plane by selecting .

5. If creating a quarter or three quarter section view, click  to continue or click  to combine the section.

6. Select an additional plane to section about. If required, enter an offset value or flip the direction of the new plane using the same techniques as mentioned above. The mini-toolbar appears as shown in Figure 10–8 when a quarter or three quarter section view is being created.

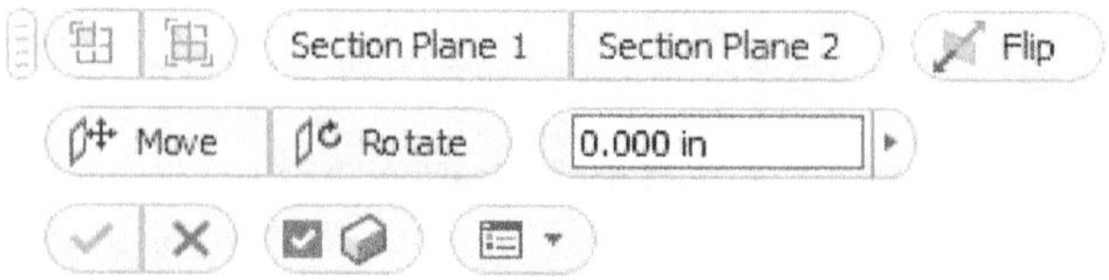

Figure 10–8

7. To further modify the offset from a selected plane, the correct plane must be active. In the mini-toolbar select Section Plane 1 or Section Plane 2, as needed, to switch the active plane and then modify as required.

   Note: *If creating a Quarter Section or a Three Quarter Section View you can toggle between the two. This can be done in the mini-toolbar by selecting (Three Quarter Section View) or (Quarter Section View), as needed.*

8. Right-click and select **OK (Enter)** or click to complete the view.
9. To return to a view of the entire part, select **Delete Section View** in the *Section View* drop-down list.

Section views are temporary unless used in conjunction with design views. Once you select **Delete Section View**, the created section view is lost and must be recreated if required again. If created in a design view, do not select **Delete Section View** to maintain the section view in the design view. Unless a section view is saved as a design view, it cannot be redefined and you would need to recreate it to make changes. If stored in a design view, you can modify the section, by right-clicking its name and selecting **Section View>Edit** to make changes to the section or **Section View>Suppress** to suppress the section view in the design view.

10.5 Part Design Views

A representation of the part's display can be saved using a design view. Model configuration settings that you might want to save include: part color, work feature (not origin features) and sketch visibility, camera position, section views, orientation, and zoom level. Any of these settings can be saved using a design view. Additionally, design views can be used when creating drawing views.

How To: Save a Design View

1. Expand the *Representations* folder in the Model browser, right-click on the **View** node, and select **New**, as shown in Figure 10–9.

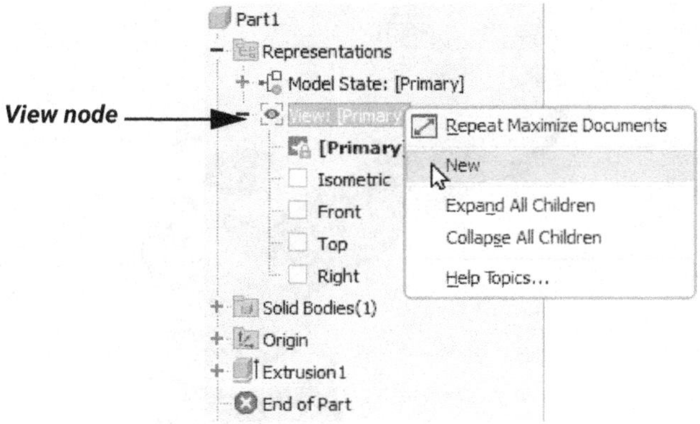

Figure 10–9

__Note:__ As of Autodesk Inventor 2017, models created with a default template contain four additional default design views. For models created prior to 2017, only a single Primary design view is provided in the default template.

2. Enter a name for the new view or press <Enter> to accept the default name.

   __Note:__ Once a view is created, it can be renamed by slowly selecting the view name twice (do not double-click), entering a new name, and pressing <Enter>.

3. Configure the view display (e.g., change the part orientation, set a section view, set the part color, toggle off the visibility of work features or sketches, or change the camera position).
4. (Optional) To lock the design view, right-click on the view name in the Model browser and select **Lock**. Locking restricts you or others from making changes to the design view representation.

When a new view is created, it is automatically set to be active. To display an alternate design view, right-click on its name in the Model browser and select **Activate**. Alternatively, you can double-click on its name.

Practice 10a
Section and Design Views

Practice Objectives

- Create section views using a work plane as the cutting reference.
- Create a design view to capture a model's view display.

In this practice, you will work with a part model and create both section and design views in the model. The model that will be used is shown in Figure 10–10.

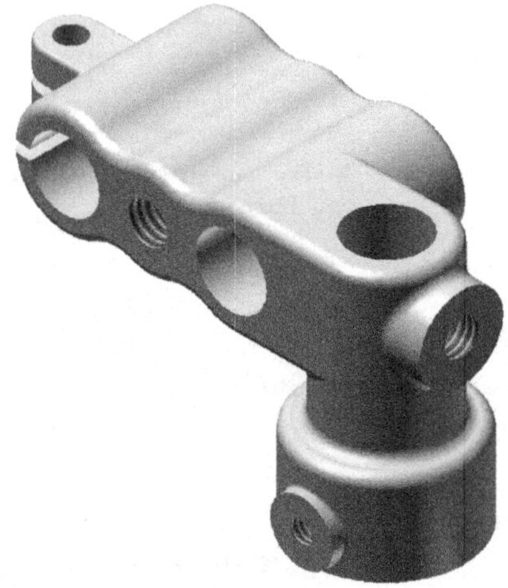

Figure 10–10

Task 1: Create design views in a model.

1. Open **Bracket_Display.ipt**.
2. In the Model browser, right-click on the **View** node and select **New**.
3. Expand the **View** node of the Model browser, if it does not automatically expand. A new **View1** design view is created.

4. Enter **Quarter Section View** as its name and press <Enter>. It is set to be active (indicated by the bolded text and checkmark). The new view appears as shown in Figure 10–11. If you are not immediately able to enter the new name, select the **View1** node and then select it again to activate it for renaming.

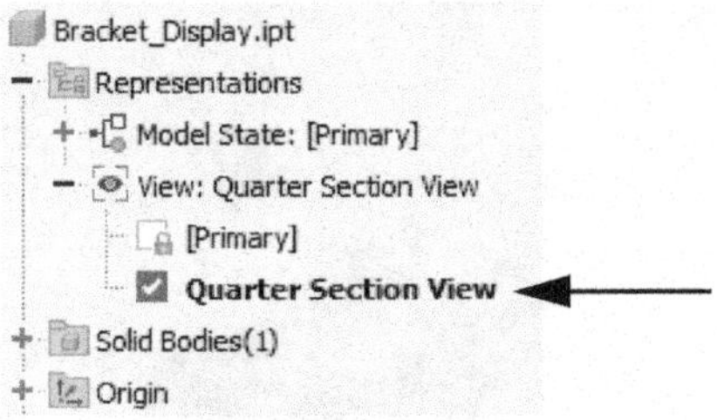

Figure 10–11

5. Select the *View* tab>*Visibility* panel and expand the *Section View* drop-down list. The command displayed will vary depending on which command was last selected.

6. Click (Half Section View), as shown in Figure 10–12, if not already active.

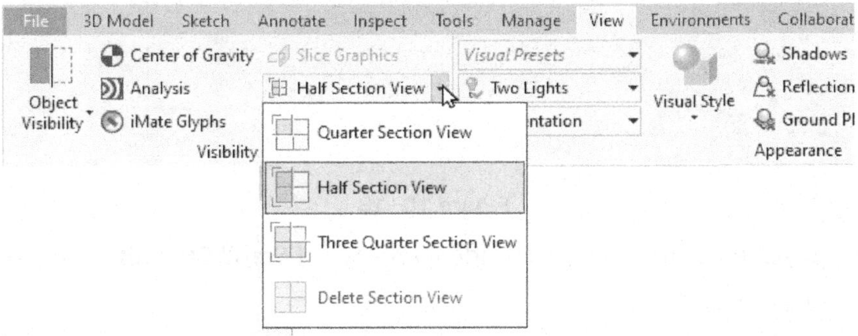

Figure 10–12

7. Select **XY Plane** in the Model browser. In the offset prompt that displays you can enter an offset value to reposition the section plane. For this section, leave the value at 0.00 in. The model displays as shown in Figure 10–13.

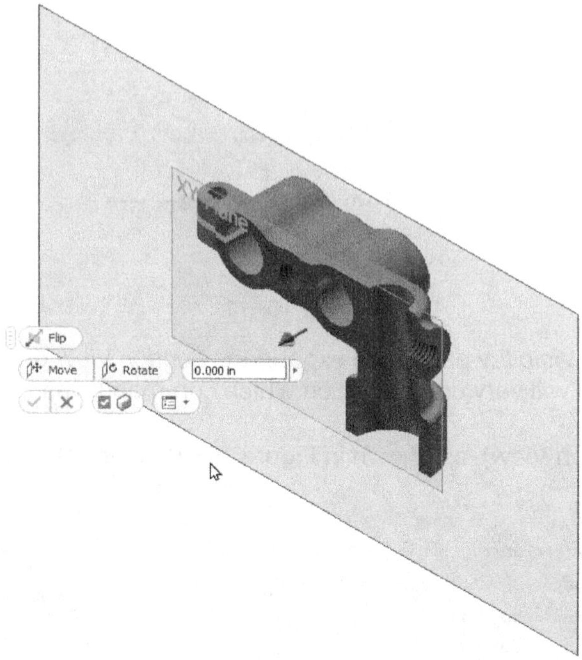

Figure 10–13

8. Right-click anywhere in the graphics window and select **Scroll Step Size**. Accept the default value of .25 in and click .
9. Place the cursor in the *Offset* entry field and scroll the middle mouse button. The sectioning plane moves in .25 in increments to progress you through multiple section views.
10. Alternatively, you can hover the cursor over the offset direction arrow and drag it. The drag uses a smaller increment to produce a more gradual sectioning movement.
11. Click to complete the section view at its current offset value.
12. In the *Visibility* panel, expand the *Section View* drop-down list and click (Delete Section View) to delete the section view.
13. Expand the *Section View* drop-down list again and click (Quarter Section View).
14. Select **XY Plane** in the Model browser. In the offset prompt that displays, accept the 0.00 in offset and click to continue to the selection of the second plane.

15. Select **XZ Plane** in the Model browser. In the offset prompt that displays, accept the 0.00 in offset. The model displays as shown in Figure 10–14.

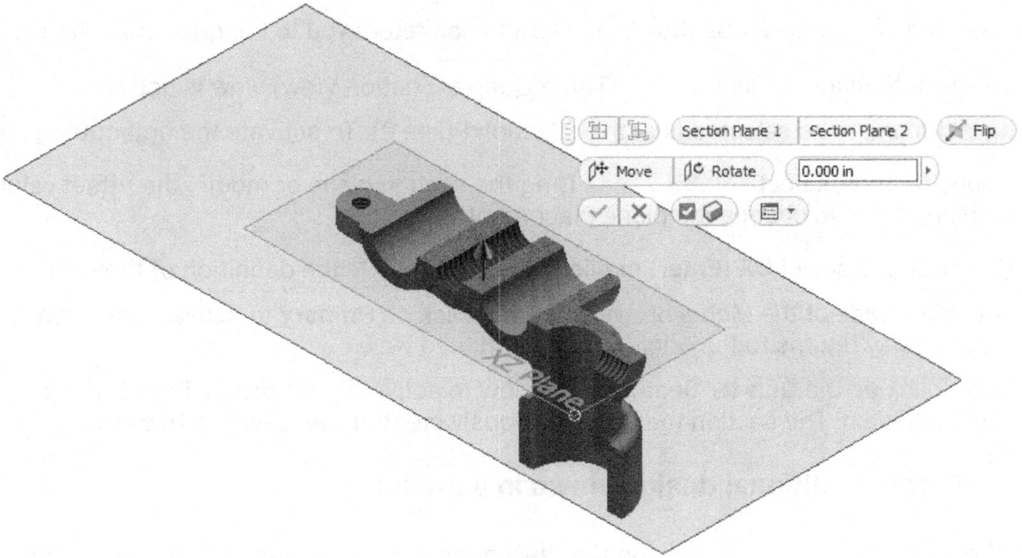

Figure 10–14

16. Select Flip. This flips the direction of section based on the currently active **Section Plane 2**, as shown in Figure 10–15.

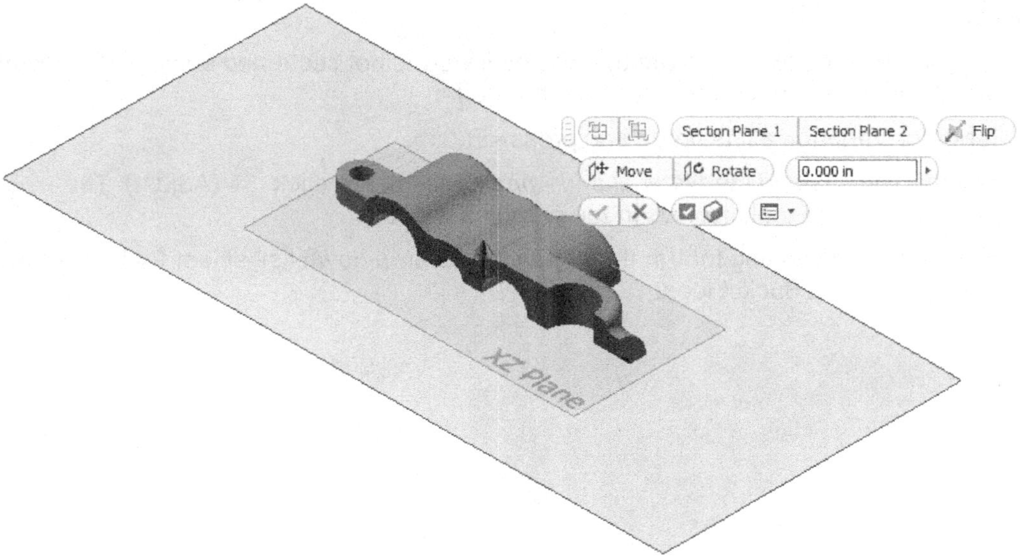

Figure 10–15

17. In the mini-toolbar, select (Three Quarter Section View). Because two planes would also be required to create a three quarter view, you can quickly switch between these two views. The (Quarter Section View) option can return you to the quarter section view.
18. Before continuing, ensure the (Three Quarter Section View) view is active.
19. The last plane to be selected is active (Section Plane 2). To activate the first cutting plane for modification, select Section Plane 1. Drag the section plane or modify the offset value in the mini-toolbar to change the plane placement.
20. Right-click and select **OK (Enter)** or click to complete the definition of the section view.
21. In the *View* node of the Model browser, double-click on **Primary** to activate this view. The model display returns to the original, non-sectioned view.
22. Double-click on the **Quarter Section View** view to activate it. The model displays as sectioned again. The section that was previously created was saved in this view.

Task 2: Create additional design views in a model.

1. In the Model browser, right-click on the **View** node and select **New**. A new design view is created and is set as active (indicated by the checkmark).
2. Note that the new design view displays the sectioned view. This is because it was the active view when the new one was created.
3. Right-click on **View1** and select **Delete**. Once deleted, the **Primary** view becomes the active view.
4. Create another design view. Note that the new view is not sectioned because the **Primary** view was active when the new view was created.
5. Enter **Color Variation** as its name and press <Enter>.
6. Select the *Tools* tab. In the *Material and Appearance* panel, click (Adjust). The appearance editing tool displays in the graphics window.
7. In the appearance editing tool, in the *Appearances* drop-down list, select **Red**. The cursor displays as a Paint Bucket icon.

8. Hover the cursor over the model so that it highlights, as shown in Figure 10–16.

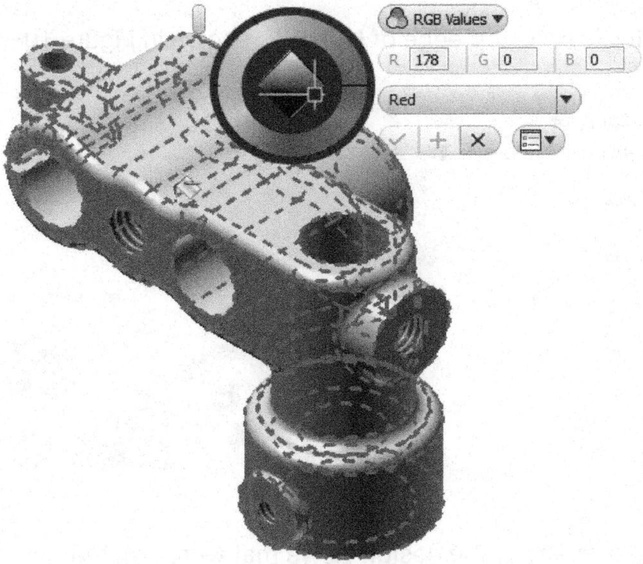

Figure 10–16

9. Select the model. Click . This assigns red as the color of the model for this design view. In this case, the color was used to help identify that the view is an informational view.
10. Activate the **Primary** view and create a third design view called **Additional Info**.
11. Right-click on **Sketch2** and select **Visibility** to display the feature's sketch.
12. Zoom in on the sketch to change the zoom level and change the view orientation, as required.
13. Return to the **Primary** view. It initially holds the view orientation and zoom level. Return to the model Home view using the ViewCube.
14. Return to the **Additional Info** design view. The sketch visibility, view orientation, and zoom are stored with this view.
15. Return to the Home view in the **Primary** view.

Task 3: Add additional solid features to the model.

1. Create a fillet feature on the top edge of **Hole6** as shown in Figure 10–17. Use a radius value of **0.05 in**.

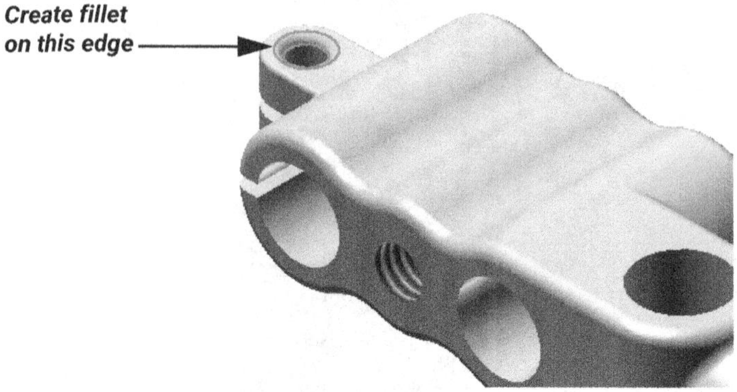

Figure 10–17

2. Once created, return to any of the design views that were created and note that the fillet exists in all of the views. Feature creation does not affect design views. Design views only store visual changes in the model, such as color, visual display of work features, sketches, view orientation, and zoom, as well as sectioning changes to the model.
3. Save the part and close the window.

End of practice

Practice 10b
Feature Order

Practice Objectives

- Change the order of features in the Model browser to obtain required geometry.
- Use the End of Part marker to insert a new feature at a point other than the end of the feature list.

In this practice, you will explore the impact of feature order on a part. You will create a switch plate as shown in Figure 10–18. Once complete, you will reorder and insert features in the part and observe the results.

Figure 10–18

Task 1: Create a new part file.

1. Create a new part using the standard imperial (in) template.

2. Create the sketch on the XY Plane, as shown in Figure 10–19. Create the sketch symmetrically about the YZ and XZ origin planes.

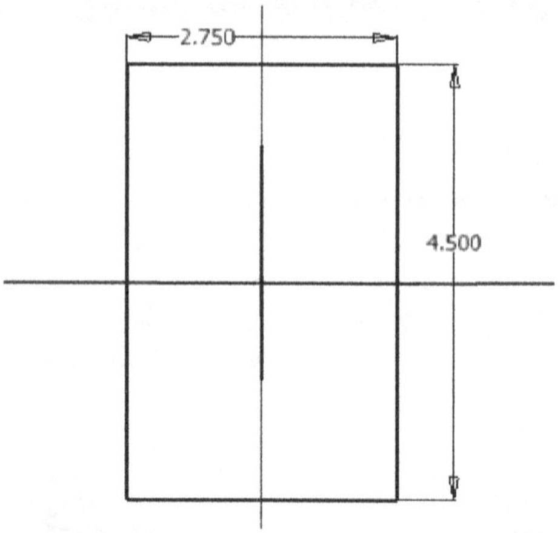

Figure 10–19

3. Extrude all four quadrants of **Sketch1, 0.25 in** away from the sketch plane (behind the model when it is in the Home view).

Task 2: Create holes in the geometry.

1. Begin the creation of a hole on the front face of the extruded geometry. Two holes will be created at the same time. To locate the holes, select two points on the face, similar to that shown in Figure 10–20.

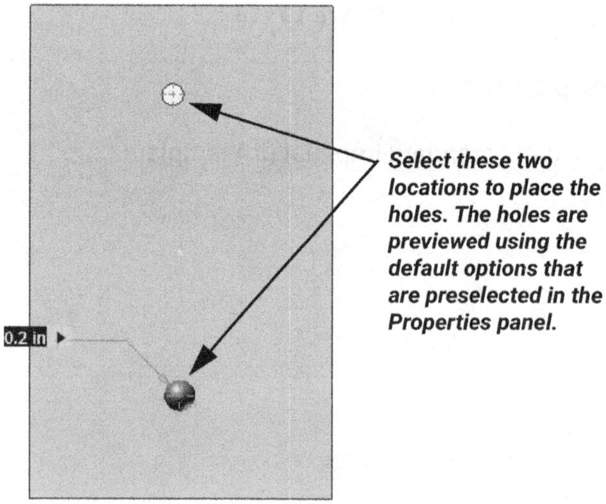

Figure 10–20

2. To fully define the location of the holes, you must access the associated sketch for the hole. This sketch was automatically created when you located the holes. In the header of the *Properties* panel, select **Sketch 2** to activate it.
3. Using the standard sketching tools, complete the following (as shown in Figure 10–21):
   - Project the YZ Plane and align the sketch points (center points of the holes) to it.
   - Add linear dimensions to locate the holes equally at **1.1 in** from the top and bottom of the geometry.
   - Edit the value of one of the dimensions and set it equal to the dimension symbol of the other. This establishes a relationship between the holes that sets the top and the bottom dimensions to be equal.

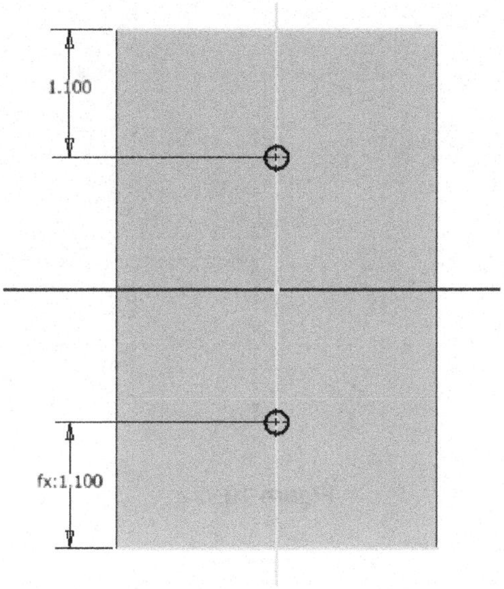

Figure 10–21

4. <u>Do not</u> select **Finish Sketch**. In the header of the *Properties* panel, select **Hole** to return to creating the hole. Alternatively, in the *Sketch* tab>*Exit* panel, click  (Return to Hole).

5. Modify the hole diameter to **0.188 in** and set the hole to cut though the entire part, as shown in Figure 10–22.

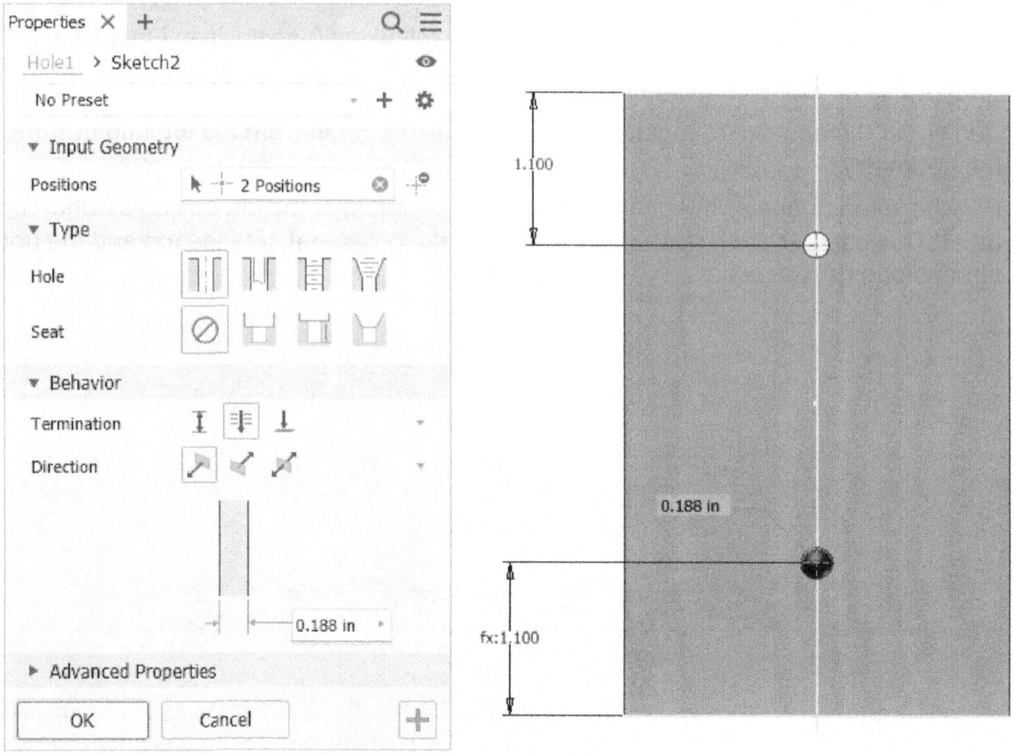

Figure 10–22

6. Click **OK** to complete the holes.

Task 3: Create an extrude feature.

1. Create and dimension the sketch shown in Figure 10–23, using the front surface of **Extrusion1** as the sketching plane. Create the sketch symmetrically about the YZ and XZ origin planes.

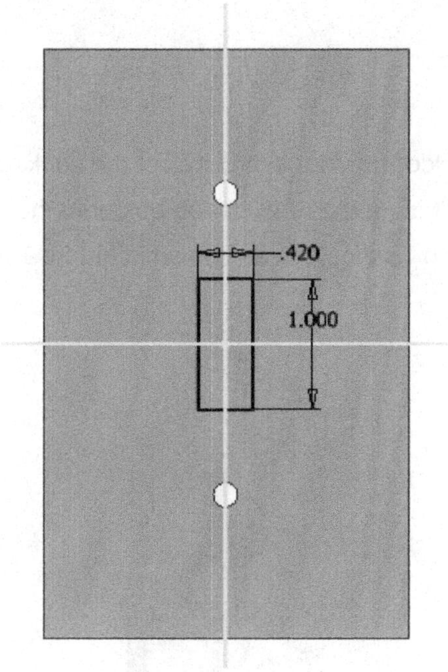

Figure 10–23

2. Create an extruded cut feature that cuts through the entire model, as shown in Figure 10–24.

Figure 10–24

Task 4: Shell the model.

1. In the *Modify* panel, click (Shell).
2. Reorient to look at the back of the model and select the back surface as the face to remove.
3. Enter a *Thickness* of **0.063 in,** in the *Shell* dialog box or in the mini-toolbar.
4. Complete the shell. The model displays as shown in Figure 10–25.

Figure 10–25

Task 5: Insert and reorder model features.

Extrusion2 does not display as required. It should not have a wall thickness applied to it. In this task, you will reorder **Extrusion2** after the shell feature to correct this.

1. Delete **Shell1**.
2. Select and drag the End of Part marker above **Extrusion2**. All features below the marker are suppressed, as shown in Figure 10–26.

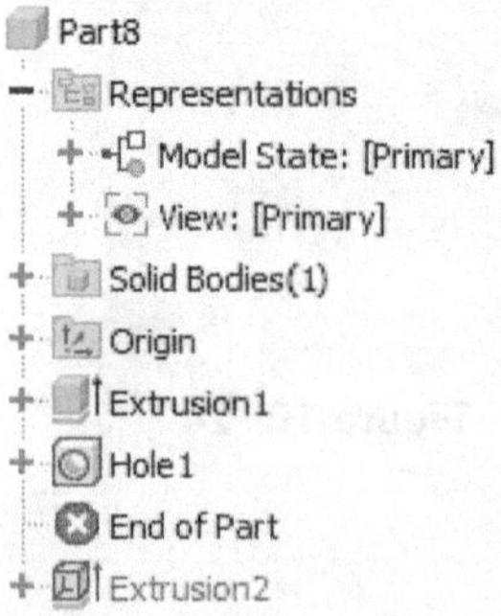

Figure 10–26

3. Recreate the Shell feature.
4. Right-click in the graphics window and select **Move EOP to End**. **Extrusion2** is resumed without a wall thickness, as shown in Figure 10–27. Alternatively, you can also click and drag the End of Part marker to the bottom of the Model browser.

Figure 10–27

5. Return to the Home view.
6. Create a **0.175 in** fillet on the four outside edges of the model, as shown in Figure 10–28.

Figure 10–28

7. Orient the model to view its back. Note that the fillet is not applied to the back.

8. Select **Fillet1** in the Model browser. Click and hold the left mouse button and drag **Fillet1**.

   Try to drag **Fillet1** above **Extrusion1**. Note that the cursor changes to ⦸ as shown in Figure 10–29. This indicates that you cannot move **Fillet1** above **Extrusion1**.

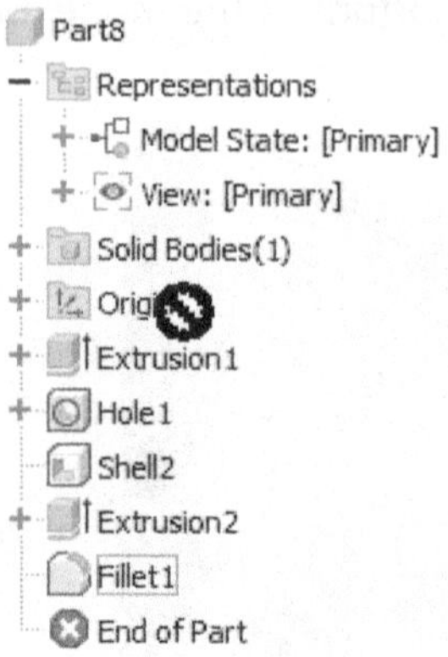

Figure 10–29

Fillet1 cannot be moved above **Extrusion1** because it is its child. **Fillet1** uses the edges of **Extrusion1** as reference. Therefore, **Fillet1** cannot exist unless **Extrusion1** has been created.

9. In the Model browser, drag **Fillet1** above **Shell2**. Note that the fillet is now created on the back as well, as shown in Figure 10–30.

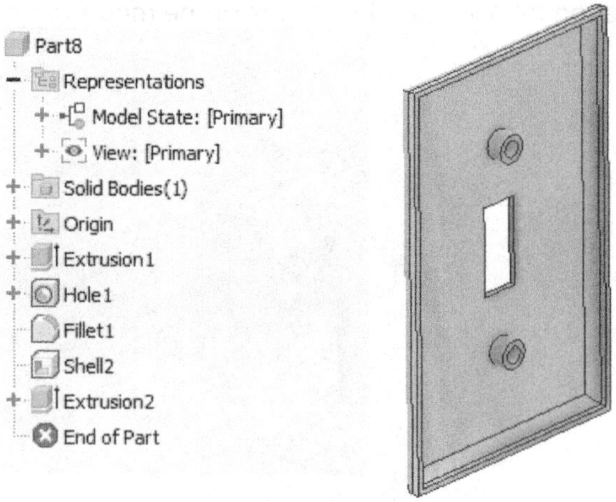

Figure 10–30

10. Save the model. Enter **Switch** as the name of the file.
11. Close the window.

End of practice

Chapter Review Questions

1. In the example shown in Figure 10–31, **Hole1** is a **Through All** hole and **Extrusion2** is the solid cylindrical feature. What can you do to include **Extrusion2** in the **Hole1** feature (i.e., have the hole pass through the cylinder)?

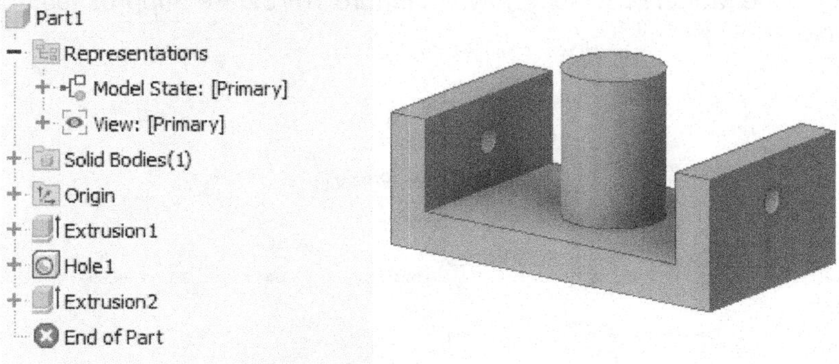

Figure 10–31

   a. Suppress Hole1 and then recreate Extrusion2.
   b. In the Model browser, drag the End of Part marker above Hole1.
   c. Make Extrusion2 Adaptive.
   d. In the Model browser, drag Extrusion2 above Hole1.

2. Which of the following statements are true for reordering features in a model? (Select all that apply.)
   a. Reordering enables you to drag and drop features so that you can rearrange the feature creation order.
   b. When reordering, features can be moved anywhere.
   c. Base features can be moved anywhere in the model.
   d. You can insert new features between existing features.

3. Any features below the End of Part marker in the Model browser are still displayed, but you cannot select them as references when creating new features.
   a. True
   b. False

4. If you suppress a feature, all dependent features are also suppressed.

a. True

b. False

5. Which items in the Model browser shown in Figure 10–32 are *Suppressed* in the model? (Select all that apply.)

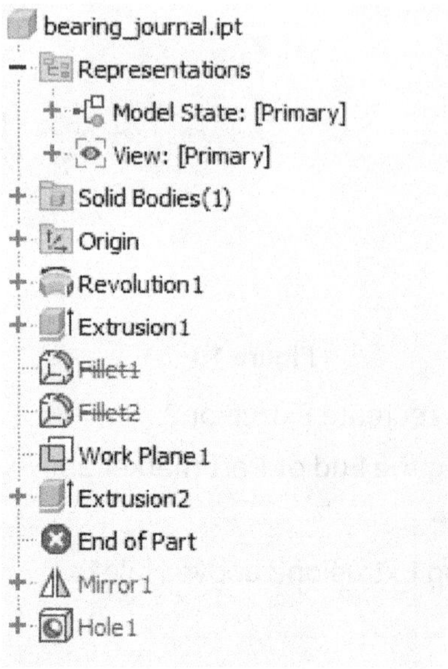

Figure 10–32

a. Solid1

b. Sketch3

c. Fillet1

d. Fillet2

e. Work Plane1

f. Mirror1

g. Hole1

6. How can a section view be saved with the model?

a. A section view is saved with the model and can be retrieved in the Navigation Bar.

b. A section view is saved with the model and can be retrieved in the *Appearance* panel in the *View* tab.

c. A section view is saved with the model in a design view and can be retrieved in the Model browser.

d. A section view cannot be saved with the model.

7. Once completed, a section view can be modified.

a. True

b. False

8. Which of the following can be manipulated and stored in a design view? (Select all that apply.)

a. Part color

b. Sketch and feature visibility

c. Display of origin planes

d. Section views

e. Model orientation

f. Model zoom level

Command Summary

Button	Command	Location
	**End Section View**	• **Ribbon:** *View* tab>*Visibility* panel
	**Half Section View**	• **Ribbon:** *View* tab>*Visibility* panel
N/A	**Move EOP Marker**	• **Context Menu:** In Model browser with a feature selected
N/A	**Move EOP to End**	• **Context Menu:** In Model browser with the *End of Part* node selected
N/A	**New (Design View)**	• **Context Menu:** In Model browser with the *View* node selected
	**Quarter Section View**	• **Ribbon:** *View* tab>*Visibility* panel
N/A	**Suppress Features**	• **Context Menu:** In Model browser with a feature selected • **Context Menu:** In graphics window with a feature selected
	**Three Quarter Section View**	• **Ribbon:** *View* tab>*Visibility* panel
N/A	**UnSuppress Features**	• **Context Menu:** In Model browser with a suppressed feature selected

Chapter 11

Fixing Problems

When a parent feature is deleted or modified, its dependent features are affected. This might result in a variety of design problems (e.g., geometry that does not form a closed loop for a solid feature, dimensional changes that result in geometry that cannot be updated, changes to the model that interfere with other features, etc.). When errors occur, you can use error tracking and recovery tools to correct the design error or accept the errors and correct them later. You might also have to edit other features to correct the error.

Learning Objectives

- Identify the dialog boxes that display when you over-dimension or over-constrain a sketch.
- Use the Sketch Doctor to diagnose and correct failures that occur due to problems in a sketched section.
- Use the Design Doctor to diagnose and correct feature failures that occur for reasons other than problems in the sketch.

11.1 Sketch Failure

In the Sketch environment, an error can occur if you try to over-dimension or over-constrain a sketch. A dialog box opens, similar to the one shown in Figure 11–1, outlining the reasons for the failed operation. The symbol that displays next to the message indicates the seriousness of the problem, as follows:

	This symbol (internal white highlight) indicates a partially failed operation.
	This symbol (internal yellow highlight) indicates a failed operation.

You can click **Cancel** to cancel the change or click **Apply** to apply the change, investigate, and/or recover the feature.

- In Figure 11–1, the dialog box indicates that adding a dimension over-constrains the sketch ( ). You can cancel the command or accept the warning and place a driven dimension (displayed in parentheses).

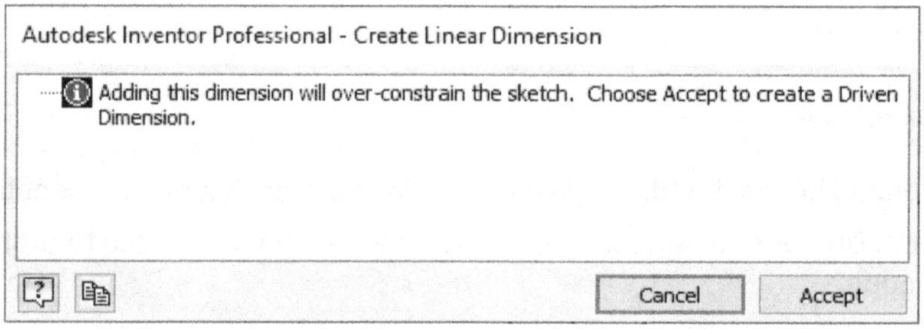

Figure 11–1

- In Figure 11–2, the dialog box indicates that a constraint already exists in the sketch and that the operation has failed ( ). To resolve the problem, cancel the operation.

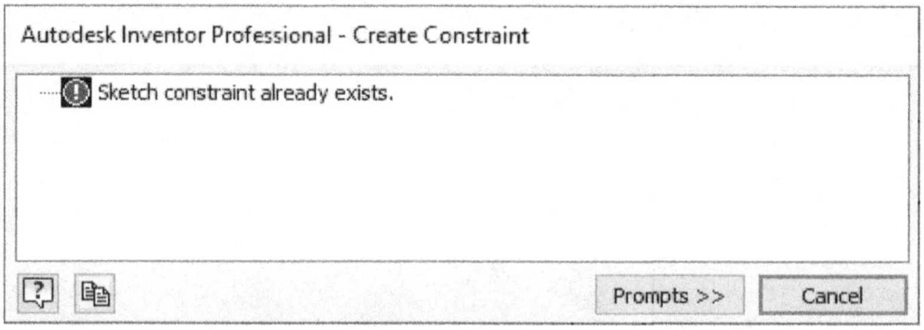

Figure 11–2

Hint: Error Prompts

To control the timing of when error prompts are presented, click **Prompts** at the bottom of the dialog box. Select the required option from the list, as shown in Figure 11–3. These options are not available in all error dialog boxes.

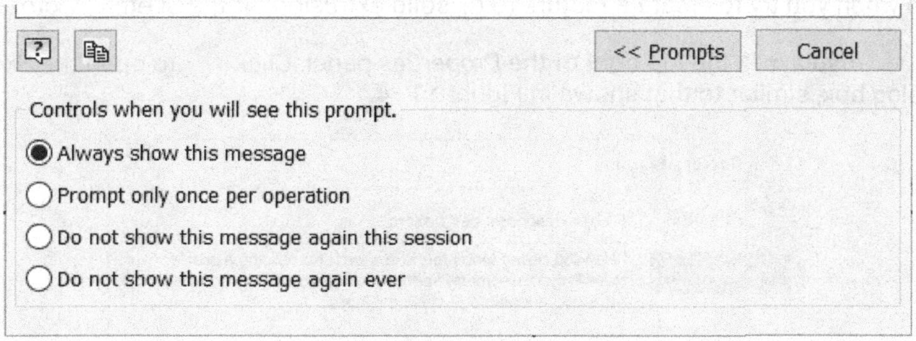

Figure 11–3

11.2 Sketch Doctor

The Sketch Doctor is an error tracking and recovery tool that examines errors in the sketch that affect feature creation, and also suggests solutions for the problem. For example, your sketch might include errors, such as open loops. As a result, the software might be unable to interpret the sketch when you try to create a feature (e.g., solid extrusion). If the Sketch Doctor is available, displays in the top right of the *Properties* panel. Click to open the *Sketch Doctor* dialog box, similar to that shown in Figure 11–4.

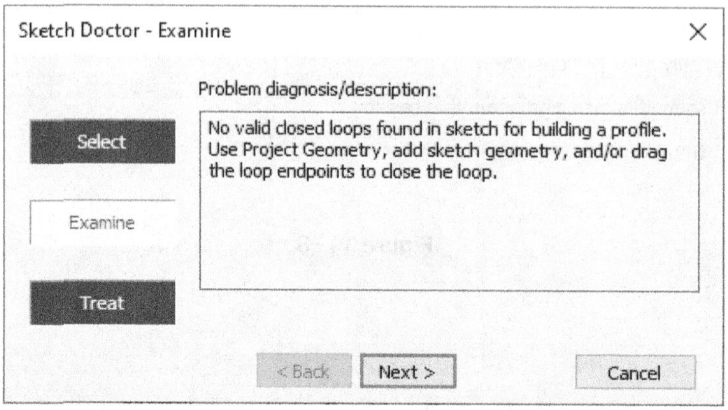

Figure 11–4

Using **Next** and **Back**, you can toggle between three solution steps in the *Sketch Doctor* dialog box: **Select**, **Examine**, and **Treat**.

- **Select:** Lists all of the errors in the sketch in the *Problem diagnosis/description* area.
- **Examine:** Provides information on the error and suggests solutions. The problem is described in the *Problem diagnosis/description* area, as shown above in Figure 11–4. Click **Next** to highlight the problem geometry on the sketch.
- **Treat:** Lists the method(s) you can use to correct the problem(s) with the sketch, as shown in Figure 11–5.

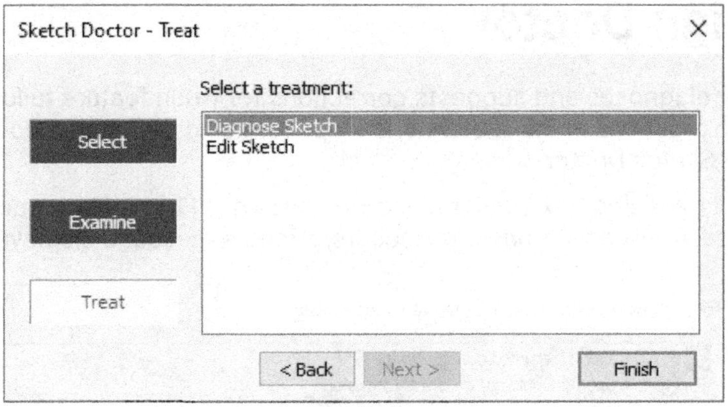

Figure 11–5

To correct the error in the sketch, select one of the recommended methods in the *Select a treatment* area and click **Finish**. The various methods you can use to correct the problem(s) are as follows:

Diagnose Sketch	Enables you to specify which tests to perform on the sketch. 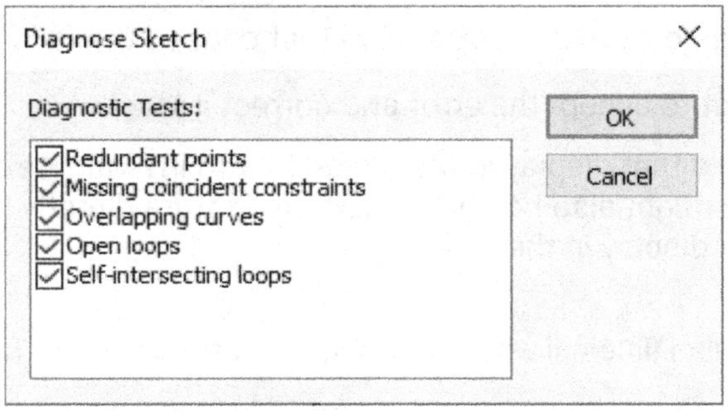
Close Loop	Enables you to select sketch entities to close an open loop.
Edit Sketch	Returns to the Sketch environment to enable you to fix the problem in the sketch.

11.3 Design Doctor

The Design Doctor diagnoses and suggests corrections for when feature failures occurs for reasons other than problems in the sketch. The steps for using the Design Doctor are similar to those used for the Sketch Doctor.

When a feature fails, a dialog box similar to the one shown in Figure 11–6 opens, listing the errors that occurred. If more than one error occurs, a failure message displays for each error.

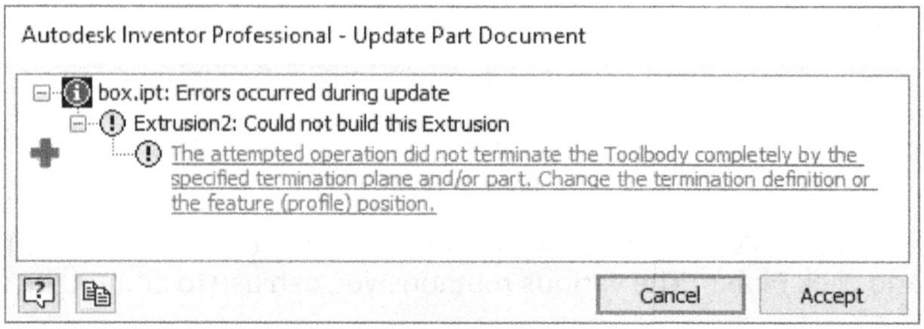

Figure 11–6

When a feature fails, you can perform one of the following operations:

- Click **Cancel** to cancel the operation that caused the failure.
- Click **Accept** to accept the error and correct it later.

Use the symbols that display in the dialog box to investigate and resolve the failure. In some situations, you might also be able to edit the feature directly in the dialog box. The following symbols might display in the dialog box:

	This symbol (internal white highlight) indicates a partially failed operation.
	This symbol (internal yellow highlight) indicates a failed operation.
	This symbol enables indicates tips for resolving the failure.
	This symbol enables you to open the *Design Doctor* dialog box to recover the failure.

To fix a failure, select the symbol and click **Yes** to accept the changes and start the recovery process. The *Design Doctor* dialog box opens, as shown in Figure 11–7.

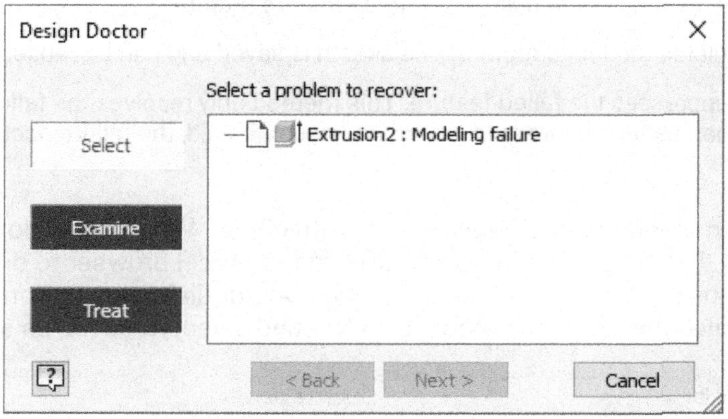

Figure 11–7

Using **Next** and **Back**, you can toggle between the three solution steps in the Design Doctor: **Select**, **Examine**, and **Treat**.

- **Select:** Lists all of the errors.
- **Examine:** Provides information on the error and suggests solutions.
- **Treat:** Lists the method(s) to correct the problem(s).

To fix a feature failure, select one of the recommended methods, as shown in Figure 11–8, and click **Finish**.

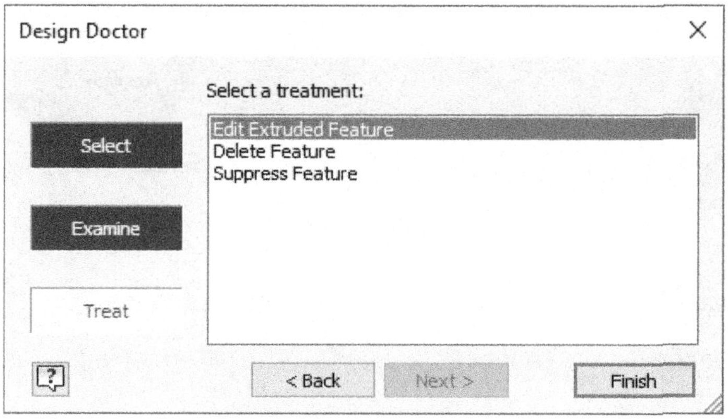

Figure 11–8

The various methods of resolving a feature failure are as follows:

Edit	Opens the feature dialog box or *Properties* panel. Enables you to modify any element and dimension used to create the feature.
Delete	Deletes the failed feature. The sketch is saved and can be reused.
Suppress	Suppresses the failed feature. This method only resolves the failure temporarily. As soon as the suppressed feature is unsuppressed, the failure occurs again.

Failed features are marked in the Model browser with either ⓘ or ⚠, as shown on the left in Figure 11–9. Hover the cursor over failed features in the Model browser to display their pre-failure state in the model. If you close the *Design Doctor* dialog box before fixing a problem, right-click on the failed feature in the Model browser and select **Recover**, as shown on the right.

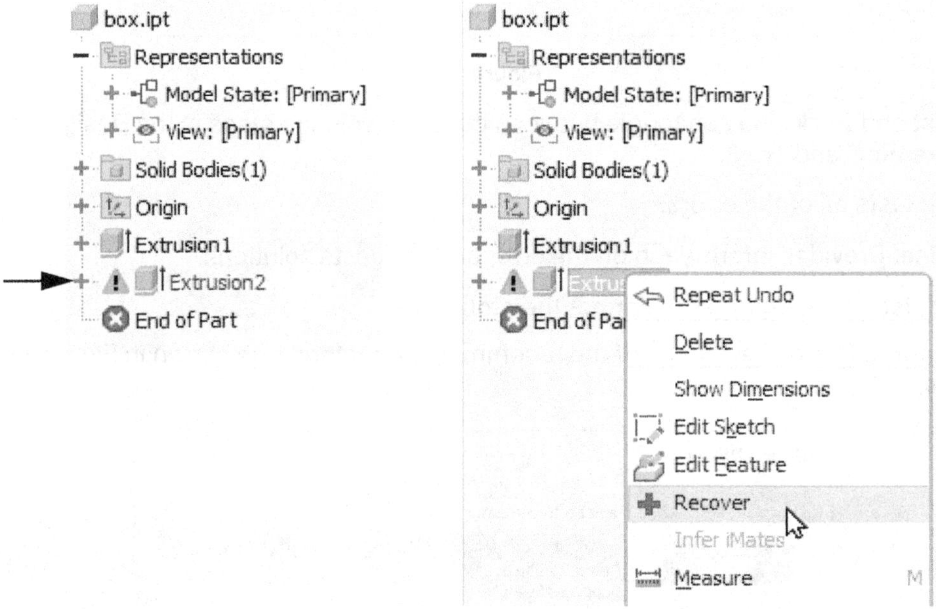

Figure 11–9

Note: ⚠ *displays in the mini-toolbar for **Fillets**, **Chamfers**, **Shells**, and **Thicken/Offset** commands when the feature cannot be created. Click* ⚠ *to open the Design Doctor.*

Practice 11a
Resolve Sketch Problems

Practice Objectives

- Use the *Sketch Doctor* dialog box to examine problems in a sketch that are causing an Extrusion to fail.
- Use the *Sketch Doctor* dialog box to select a treatment option to resolve problems in a sketch that are causing an Extrusion to fail.
- Edit a sketched section to resolve problems that are causing an Extrusion to fail.

In this practice, you will use the Sketch Doctor to diagnose a problem in the sketch.

Task 1: Open a part file and create an extrude.

1. Open **sketch_doctor.ipt**. The part file consists of a single sketch. By simply reviewing the sketched section (as shown in Figure 11–10), it appears to be a closed, fully constrained sketch. For the purposes of the exercise, ignore the fact that the sketch icon in the Model browser indicates that the sketch is not fully constrained (this would normally be a good clue to you that the sketch is not constrained).

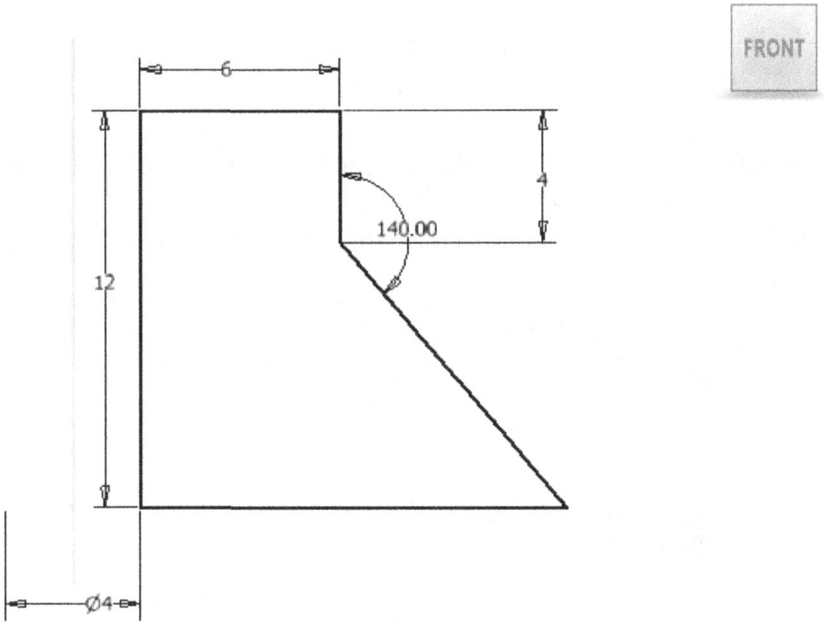

Figure 11–10

2. In the *Create* panel, click (Extrude).
3. Note that surface mode is active by default. Click in the header of the *Properties* panel to toggle to solid mode. The button displays, as shown in Figure 11–11, indicating that there are problems with the profile. This is why surface mode was active by default—a surface extrusion could be created, but a solid could not.

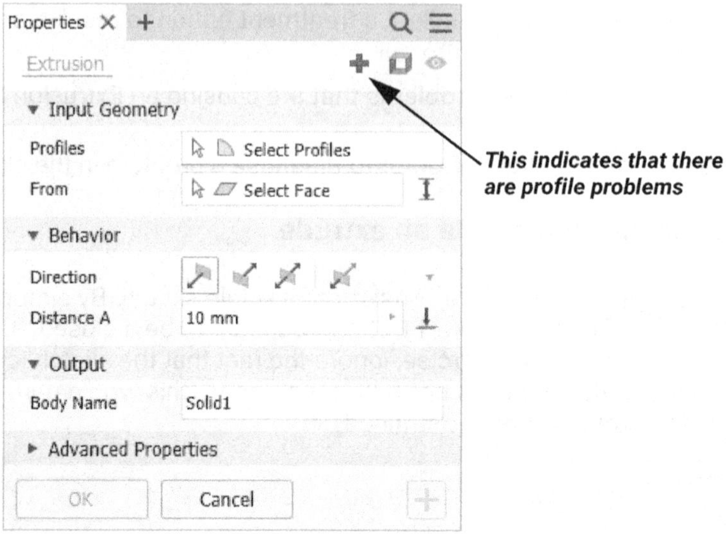

Figure 11–11

4. Click to open the *Sketch Doctor* dialog box, as shown in Figure 11–12. An open loop is highlighted in the graphics window.

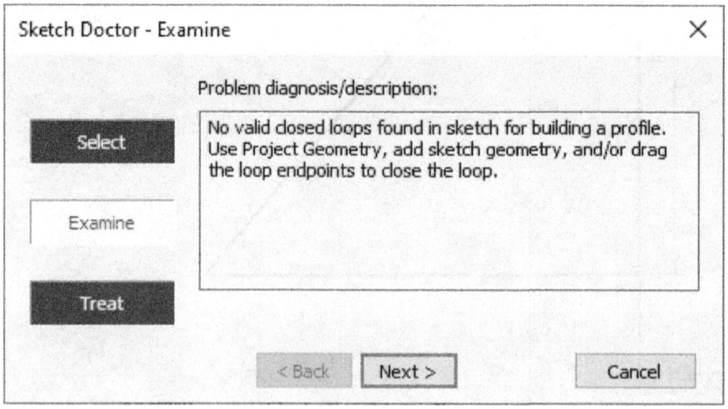

Figure 11–12

5. Click **Next**. The treatment options display as shown in Figure 11–13.

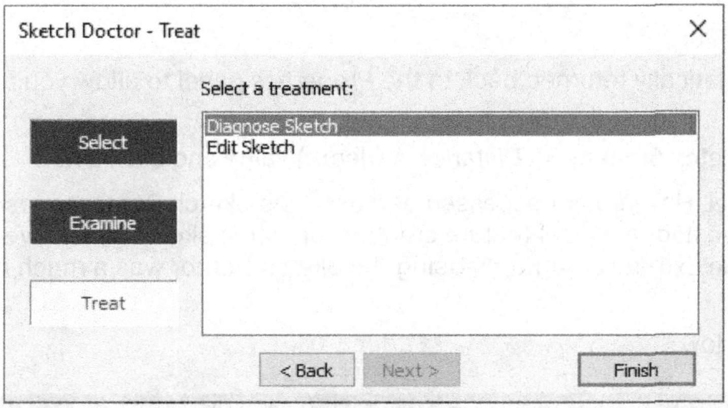

Figure 11–13

6. Select **Edit Sketch** and click **Finish**. You are placed in the Sketch environment.
7. Review the sketch to locate the open section. You can do this by zooming in on the sketch and reviewing all the vertices, or you can show all sketch contraints. In the *Constrain* panel, click  (Show Constraints) and drag a bounding box around all the entities in the sketch. Notice how there is no Coincident constraint on the entities in the lower-left corner of the sketch, as shown in Figure 11–14. This indicates the section is not closed.

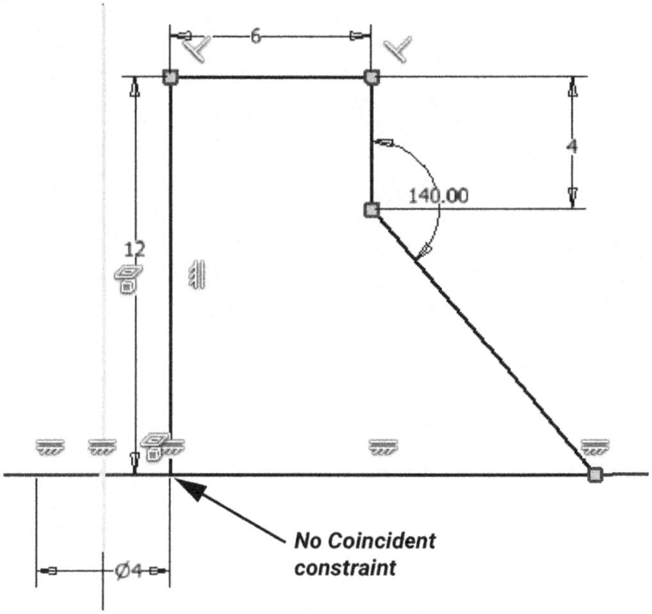

Figure 11–14

8. Use the **Extend** tool to close the loop. The Coincident constraint should appear automatically.
9. Finish the sketch.
10. You are automatically returned back to the *Properties* panel to allow you to finish creating the feature.
11. Extrude the sketch **5mm** as its *Distance A* (depth) value and click **OK**.
12. Save the model. Had you not accessed and used the Sketch Doctor to resolve the sketch, you would have had to cancel feature creation, open the sketch to resolve the issue, and then restart the Extrude command. Using the Sketch Doctor was a much more efficient method.
13. Close the window.

End of practice

Practice 11b
Resolve Feature Failure

Practice Objectives

- Use the *Design Doctor* dialog box to examine problems causing a model to fail after a dimensional modification.
- Use the *Design Doctor* dialog box to select a treatment option to resolve modeling problems.
- Edit a feature to resolve problems caused by a dimensional modification.

In this practice, you will find and fix errors using *Design Doctor*.

Task 1: Investigate and modify the part.

1. Open **box.ipt**. Review the Model browser to understand the hierarchy of the model.
2. Edit **Extrusion2**. Note that *Distance A* is set as (To) and the termination face is set as the back face of the model. Using this setting, the entire sketch must land on the termination face when extruded in order to be successfully created.
3. Close the *Properties* panel.
4. Modify the diameter dimension of **Extrusion2** from *25mm* to **50mm** and update the model.
5. An error message displays. Expand the nested messages in the dialog box to view the details, as shown in Figure 11–15. This indicates that the extrusion has failed because the cut is not completely terminated by the termination plane.

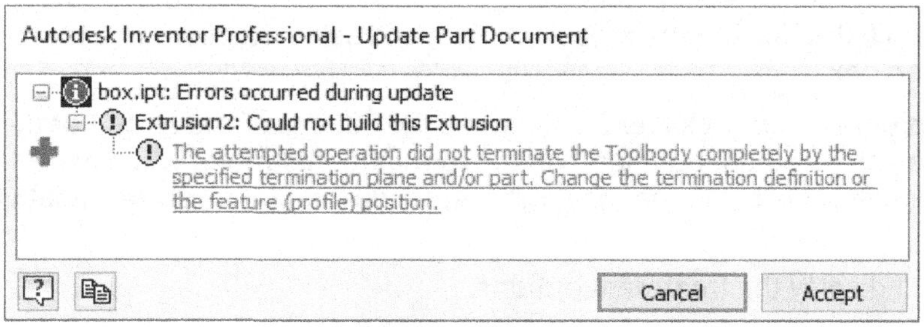

Figure 11–15

Task 2: Resolve the error.

1. Click [icon] in the dialog box.
2. Click **Yes** to confirm that you want to accept changes and begin recovering from the failure. The *Design Doctor* dialog box opens, as shown in Figure 11–16.

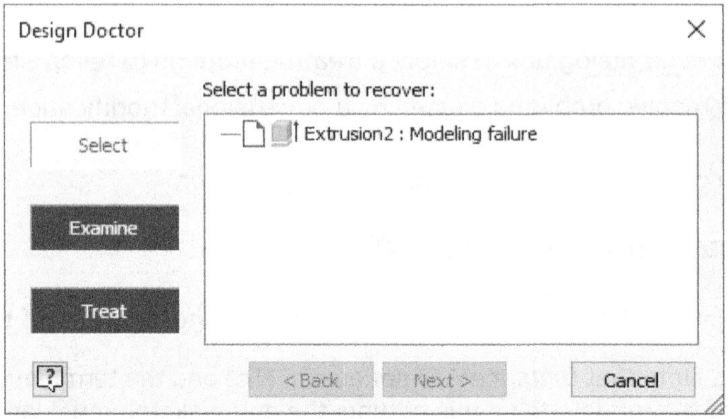

Figure 11–16

3. Click **Cancel** to close the *Design Doctor* dialog box. Note that the **Extrusion2** feature displays [icon] next to its name in the Model browser.
4. The failed feature's geometry is not displayed in the model. Hover the cursor over [icon] **Extrusion2** in the Model browser. The feature is highlighted in its pre-failure state. In large models, being able to highlight failed features in a model is very beneficial.
5. Right-click on **Extrusion2** in the Model browser and select **Recover** to again open the *Design Doctor* dialog box.
6. Select the problem and click **Next** to examine the causes of the error. For the feature to be created, the entire sketch must land on the termination surface when extruded. Now that the hole diameter has been changed, the feature does not entirely terminate on the single surface.
7. Click **Next** to display the treatment options.
8. Select **Edit Extruded Feature** and click **Finish**. The *Properties* panel used to create the feature opens.
9. Select [icon] (Extend face to end feature) to toggle on the option that will extend the termination face. This ensures the larger hole can be created as it will now terminate on the extended face of the model, as shown in Figure 11–17. Alternatively, you can fix the failure by changing the depth extent to **All**. You must also consider your design intent when resolving errors such as these.

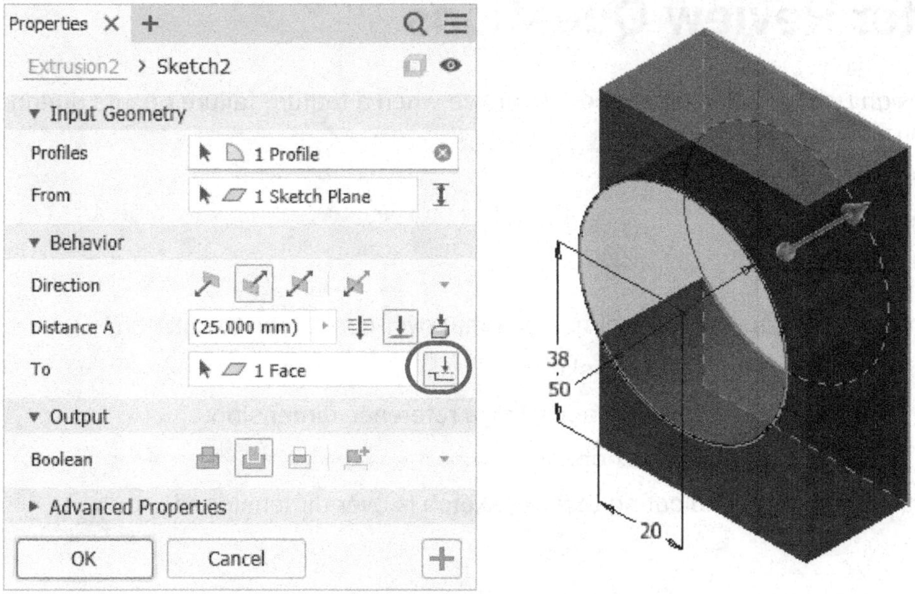

Figure 11–17

10. Click **OK** to close the *Properties* panel. The model displays as shown in Figure 11–18.

Figure 11–18

11. Save the model and close the window.

End of practice

Chapter Review Questions

1. The *Design Doctor* dialog box becomes active when a feature failure occurs during feature creation.
    a. True
    b. False

2. What happens when you add a dimension that over-constrains the sketch?
    a. The dimension is added to the sketch.
    b. The dimension is immediately added as a reference dimension.
    c. The *Sketch Doctor* dialog box opens.
    d. A dialog box opens indicating that the sketch is over-dimensioned.

3. Which actions cause a sketch or feature to fail? (Select all that apply.)
    a. Invalid sketch.
    b. Too many sketch entities in the sketch.
    c. Deleting a feature.
    d. Modifying dimensions.
    e. Deleting sketching references.
    f. Open loop sketch when creating a solid Extrude.
    g. Cut no longer terminated by the termination plane.
    h. Over-constrained sketch.

4. The failed feature can be the modified feature or a feature that references the modified feature.
    a. True
    b. False

5. What does the (red cross) button indicate if it displays in the *Properties* panel, as shown in Figure 11–19, while extruding a sketch?

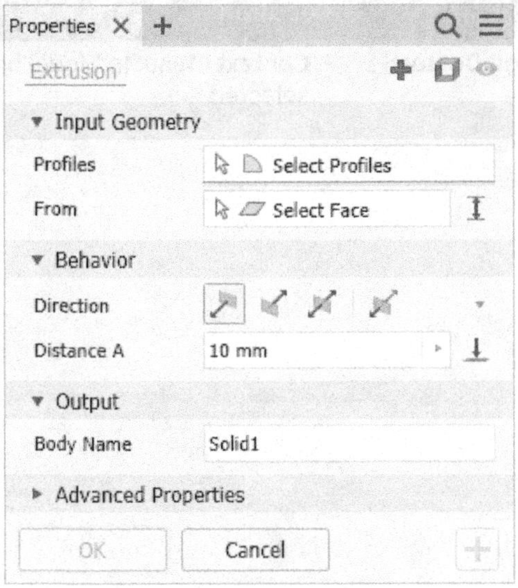

Figure 11–19

a. The sketch might have a problem and the *Sketch Doctor* is available to help fix it.
b. There is applicable information available in the Help files about the **Extrude** command.
c. The sketch selected is not fully constrained.
d. The virtual memory on your computer might be too low for the operation.

6. When adding a dimension that is going to over-constrain the sketch, which options can you perform? (Select all that apply.)
a. Cancel the command.
b. Accept the warning and place a driven dimension.
c. Place the same dimension twice.
d. Replace the conflicting dimension with the new one.

Command Summary

Button	Command	Location
N/A	**Recover (Design Doctor)**	• **Context Menu:** In Model browser with the failed feature selected

Chapter 12

Sweep Features

A sweep feature can be used to create specific geometry that cannot be created using standard extrusions. It enables you to sketch a cross-section and sweep it along a defined path.

Learning Objectives

- Create swept geometry using appropriate path and profile entities.
- Edit a sweep feature.

12.1 Sweep Features

A sweep feature enables you to create geometry that cannot be created using an extrusion or revolve. The geometry is defined by sweeping a profile along a path (as shown in Figure 12–1) and can be used to add or remove material. Sweeps are useful for features that have a uniform shape but an irregular path, such as gaskets and piping.

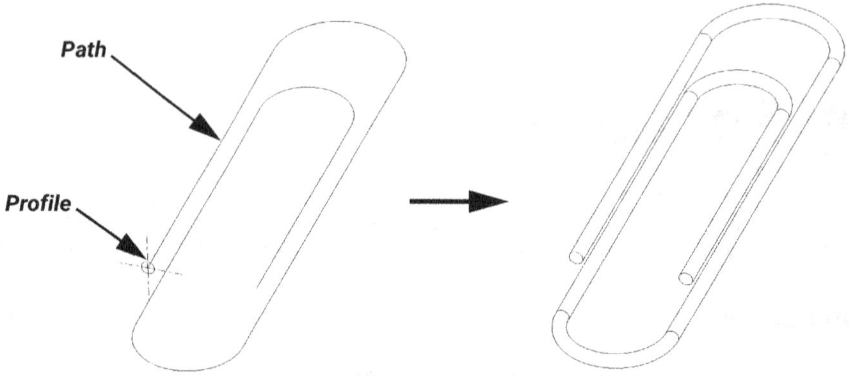

Figure 12–1

Prior to creating a sweep, a sketched profile and a path must be available for selection.

- A sweep's profile must be a closed loop sketch to create a solid sweep, as shown in Figure 12–2. Open profiles can only be used to create a surface sweep.
- A sweep's path can be an open or closed sketch. The sketches and geometry in Figure 12–2 show how both a closed and open path can be used. Alternatively, the path can be an existing model edge.

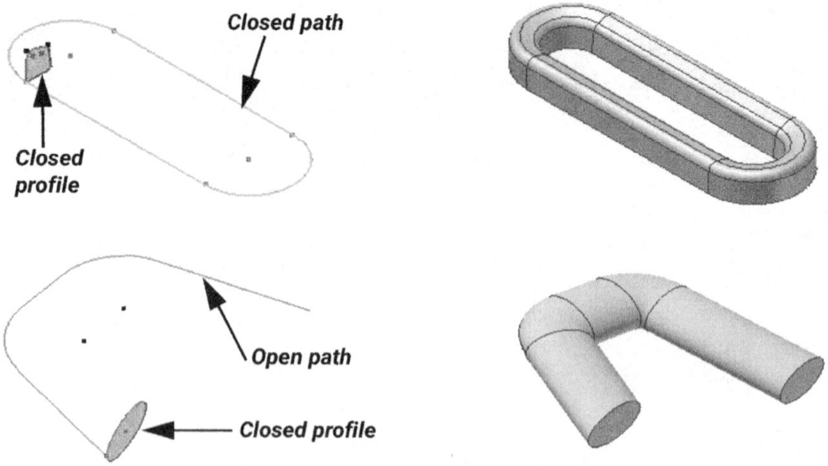

Figure 12–2

- The start point of the sweep is located at the intersection of the profile plane and path. The profile geometry does not need to physically intersect the path.
- The sweep's path can be a 2D or 3D sketch. 3D sketches are created in 3D space without the use of a sketch plane.

Use the following general steps to create a sweep:

1. Start the creation of the sweep.
2. Select the profile and path (Input Geometry).
3. Define the sweep options (Output).
4. Define the type of sweep (Behavior).
5. Complete the feature.

Step 1 - Start the creation of the sweep.

In the *3D Model* tab>*Create* panel, click (Sweep). The *Properties* panel displays, as shown in Figure 12–3.

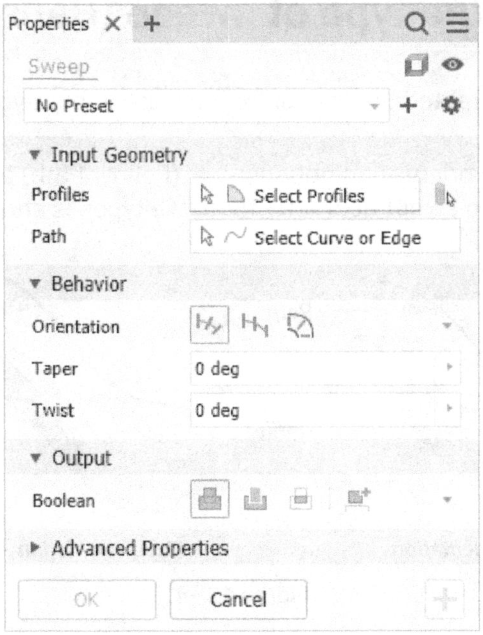

Figure 12–3

Step 2 - Select the profile and path (Input Geometry).

By default, the *Profiles* field is automatically active. If a single closed sketch is visible it will be automatically selected, otherwise, select the profile sketch for the sweep. Multiple profiles can be selected, as required.

Select in the *Path* field to activate it (if it is not already selected) and select the sketched path or an existing solid edge. Once both of these references are selected a preview of the profile being swept along the selected path displays.

> ***Note:*** *Enable* ***Optimize for Single Selection*** *in the Advanced Properties area to automatically advance to the next selector after a single selection is made. Clear this option to be able to select multiple entities for a selection.*

Step 3 - Define the sweep options (Output).

Similar to an extrude, a sweep can add and remove material. Select (Join), (Cut), or (Intersect), as required, to define the sweep.

Step 4 - Define the type of sweep (Behavior).

Three sweep types can be created. In this guide, you learn about two of these orientation types.

- You can select from two orientation options: (Follow Path) and (Fixed). The difference in the resulting swept geometry for these types is shown in Figure 12–4.

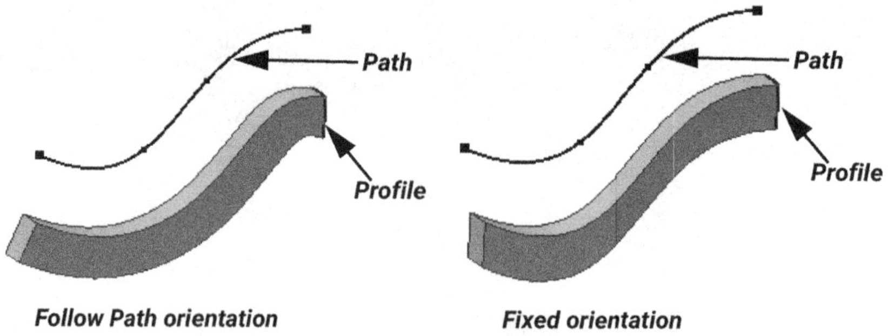

Figure 12–4

> ***Note:*** *(Guide) is the other type of sweep that can be created. This type is not discussed in this guide.*

- Tapering sets the angle of the sweep, as shown at the top of Figure 12–5. To taper a sweep feature, enter an angular value in the *Taper* field of the *Properties* panel. You cannot taper a sweep with a closed path.
- Twisting sets an angular value to control the rotations of the profile along the entire path from the start point of the path to the end, as shown at the bottom of Figure 12–5. To assign twist, enter an angular value in the *Twist* field of the *Properties* panel.

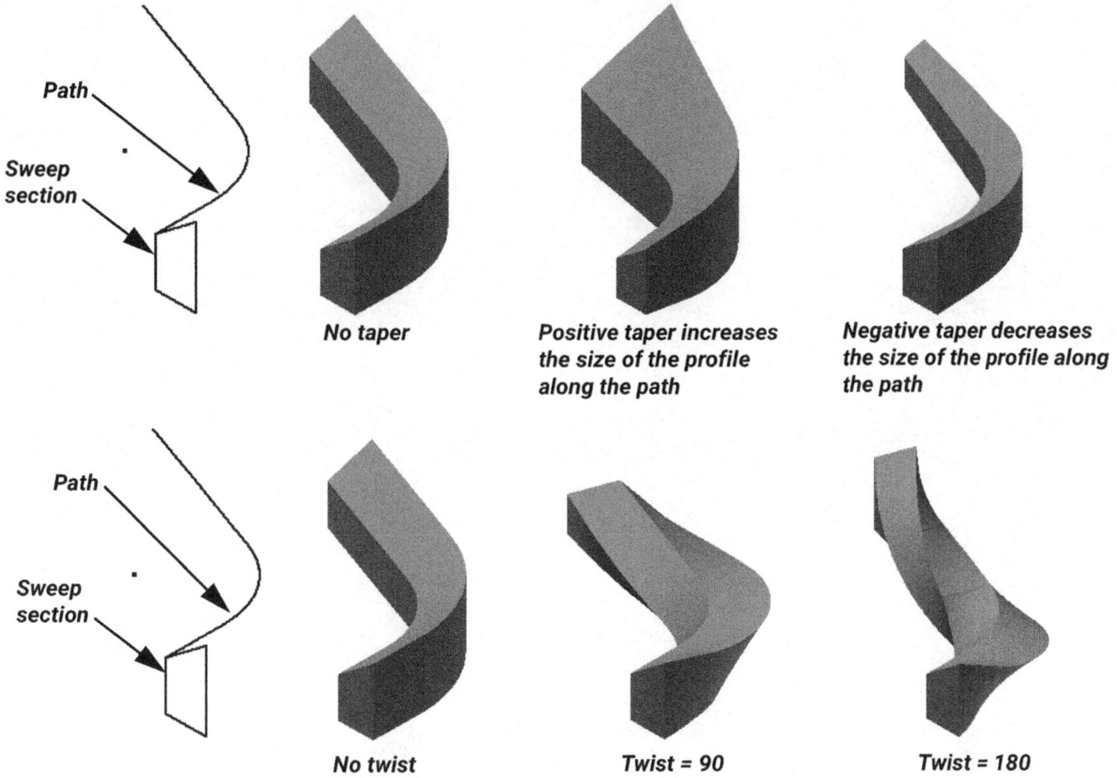

Figure 12–5

> ***Note:*** *The* ***Twist*** *option is only available for the Follow Path orientation sweep.*

Step 5 - Complete the feature.

Once the sweep feature has been defined, click **OK** or right-click and select **OK (Enter)** to complete the sweep feature. Alternatively, you can press <Enter>. To continue creating additional sweep features without closing the panel, click (Apply) and define the references as needed. Once all features have been completed, click **OK**.

> ***Note:*** *When sweeping a profile on a small fillet or bend, geometry overlap might occur. The software does its best to accommodate this if possible; otherwise, a failure occurs.*

Hint: Adding Sweeps Using Multiple Entities in the Same Sketch

If multiple entities exist in a single sketch and each entity is to be used to create a separate sweep, consider enabling the **Keep sketch visible on (+)** option in the (Advanced Settings Menu). You can then use (Apply) to continue selecting entities without the sketch visibility being turned off, as is done when the feature is completed.

Practice 12a
Create Swept Geometry I

Practice Objectives

- Create swept geometry using appropriate path and profile entities.
- Edit a sweep feature.

In this practice, you will create two sweep features. For both of these features, you will sketch their profile entities. However, the path for one will be sketched and the other will be selected. The model will display similar to that shown in Figure 12–6.

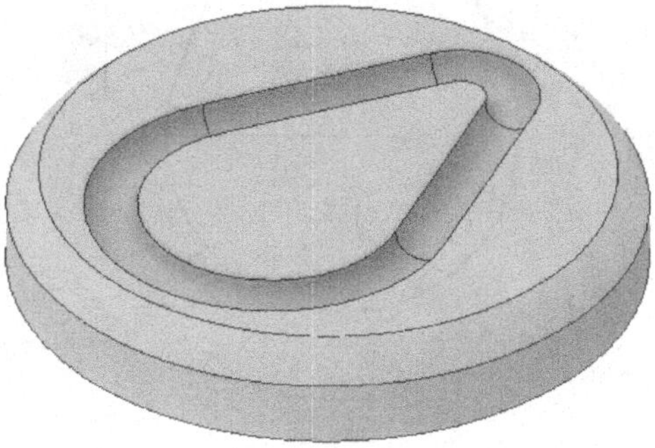

Figure 12–6

Task 1: Open a part file.

1. Open **sweep.ipt**. The model contains a single base feature, as shown in Figure 12–7.

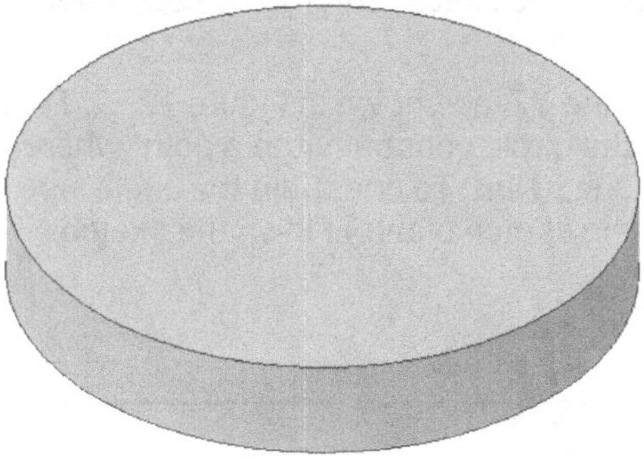

Figure 12–7

Task 2: Create the path and profile for the sweep.

1. Sketch on a flat surface of the cylinder to create the path for the sweep. Draw and constrain the section as shown in Figure 12–8. Finish the sketch.

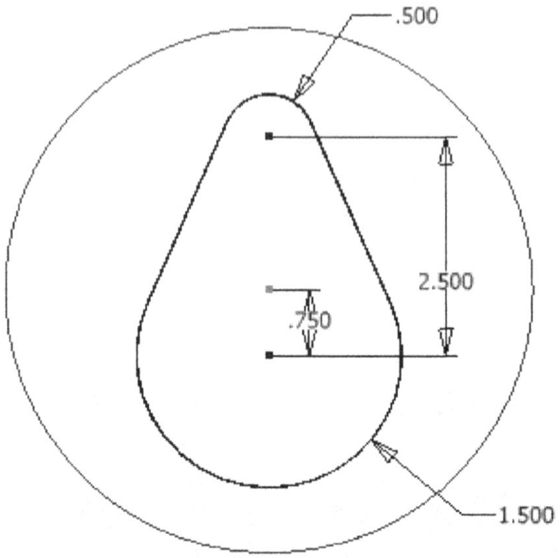

Figure 12–8

Note: To sketch a line tangent to two circles, start the ***Line*** *command and select and hold the cursor over one of the two circles. While continuing to hold, drag it to the next circle and position the cursor so that the Tangent constraint is visible. Release the mouse button. The same procedure can be used for tangent arcs.*

2. In the Model browser, select the sketch and then select it again, and rename the sketch as **Path**.
3. Sketch a circle on workplane YZ, as shown in Figure 12–9. This will be the profile for the sweep. When sketching the circle constrain it to a point where the path previously created intersects the YZ workplane. (**Hint:** To constrain the circle, use Project Geometry to project entities in the path onto the sketch plane.) Finish the sketch.

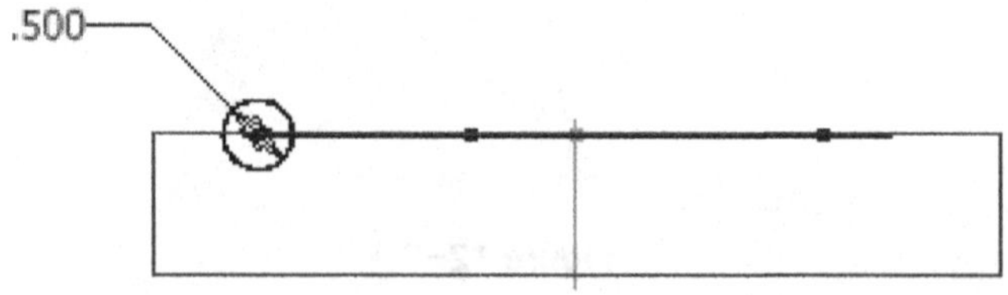

Figure 12–9

4. In the Model browser, select the sketch and then select it again, and rename the sketch as **Profile**.

Task 3: Create the sweep.

1. In the *Create* panel, click (Sweep). The *Properties* panel opens, as shown in Figure 12–10.

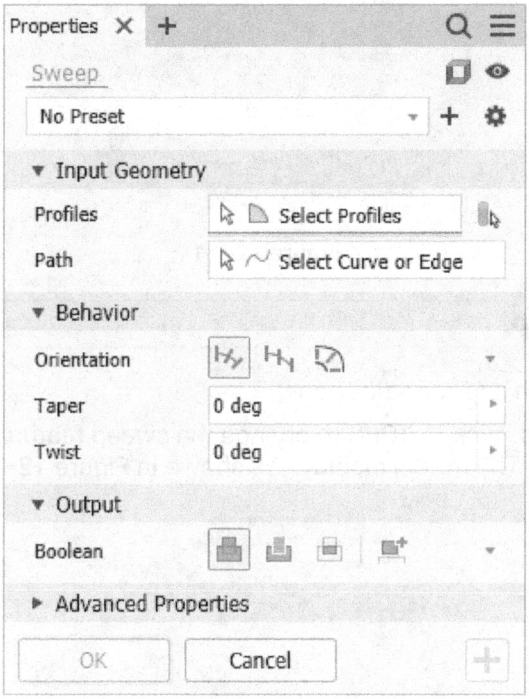

Figure 12–10

2. Expand the *Advanced Properties* area and select the **Optimize for Single Selection** option, if not already selected. This enables you to select a single profile and the feature immediately prompts you for the Path selection.
3. Select the sketch called **Profile** as the profile for the sweep.
4. Select the sketch called **Path** as the path for the sweep.
5. Maintain the default (Follow Path) orientation option.

6. Click **OK** to create the sweep. The model displays as shown in Figure 12–11.

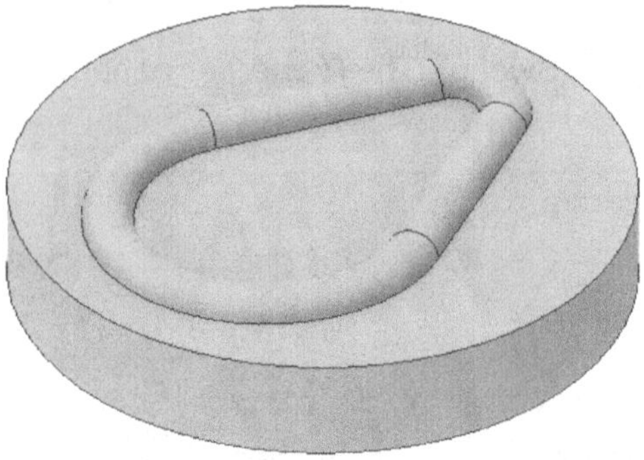

Figure 12–11

Task 4: Edit the sweep.

1. Edit the sweep to open its *Properties* panel.
2. In the *Properties* panel, click (Cut) to change the sweep feature from a join to a cut. Complete the feature. The model displays as shown in Figure 12–12.

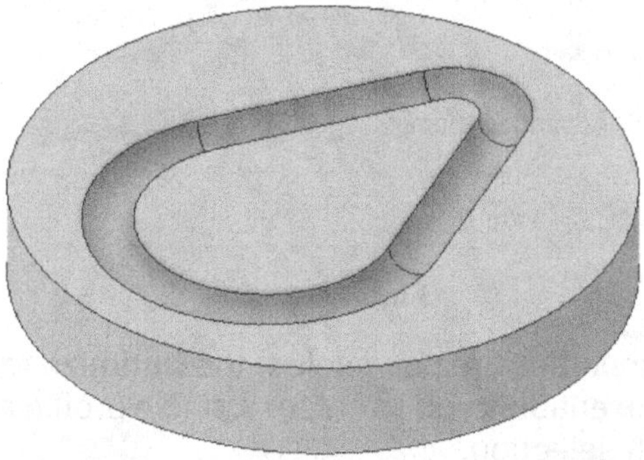

Figure 12–12

Task 5: Create a new sweep feature that references an existing solid edge.

1. Sketch the arc shown in Figure 12–13 on the YZ workplane. This will be the profile for the sweep. When sketching the section, project the outside top and side surfaces to provide a reference edge to which to constrain the arc. Finish the sketch.

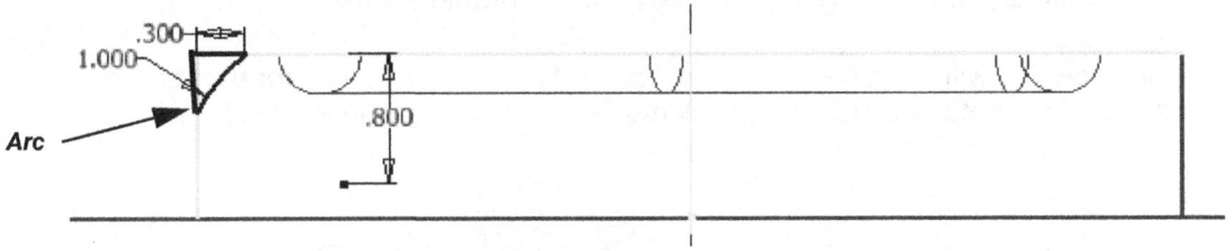

Figure 12–13

2. In the *Create* panel, click (Sweep).
3. The new arc will be selected by default as the profile for the sweep. This is because it is the only sketch in the model.
4. Select the existing outside edge of the cylinder as the path for the sweep.
5. In the *Properties* panel, click (Cut).
6. Maintain the default *Orientation* option.
7. Click **OK** to create the sweep. The model displays similar to that shown in Figure 12–14.

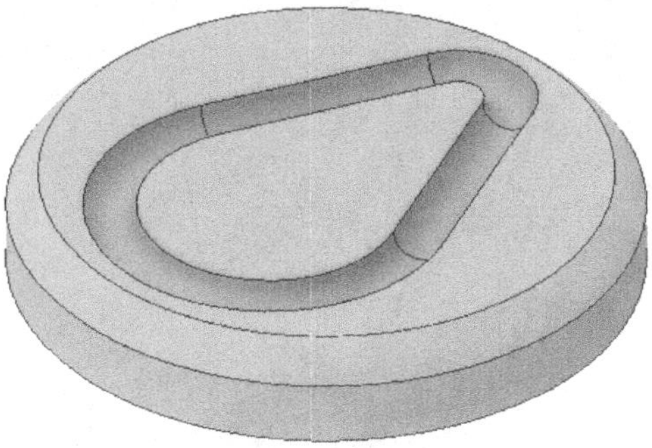

Figure 12–14

8. Save the model and close the window.

End of practice

Practice 12b
Create Swept Geometry II

Practice Objective

- Create swept geometry using appropriate path and profile entities.

In this practice, you will create two sweeps. The first sweep is a handle for the dipstick and the second one is the metal rod on the dipstick model, as shown in Figure 12–15.

Figure 12–15

Task 1: Open a part file.

1. Open **dipstick.ipt**. The model contains two unused sketches and a revolved base feature, as shown in Figure 12–16.

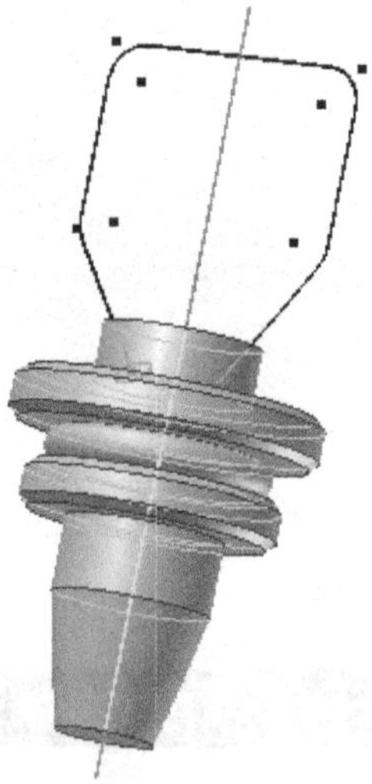

Figure 12–16

Task 2: Create the sweep for the handle.

1. In the *Create* panel, click (Sweep).
2. By default, the circular sketched profile called **Handle Profile** is selected. Select the path called **Handle Path** as the profile to follow.
3. Maintain the default (Follow Path) orientation option.
4. The sweep feature might be created as a cut, rather than as a join. To change the sweep feature to a join, in the *Properties* panel, click (Join).
5. Click **OK** to create the sweep. The model displays as shown in Figure 12–17.

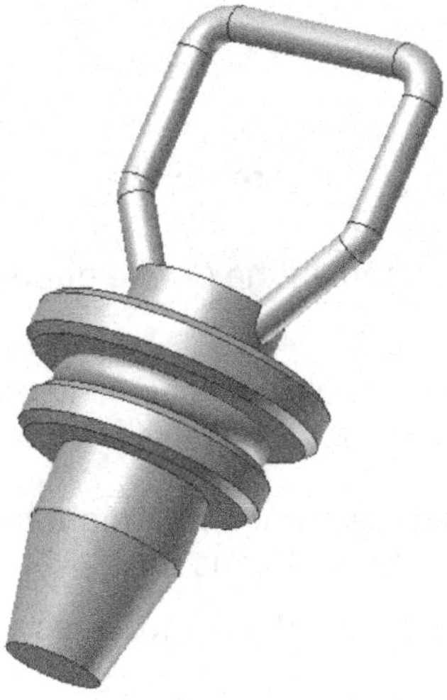

Figure 12–17

Task 3: Create another sweep feature to represent the rod of the dipstick.

1. Sketch the sweep's path similar to that shown in Figure 12–18 on the YZ workplane. Do not worry about the dimensions or its exact shape.

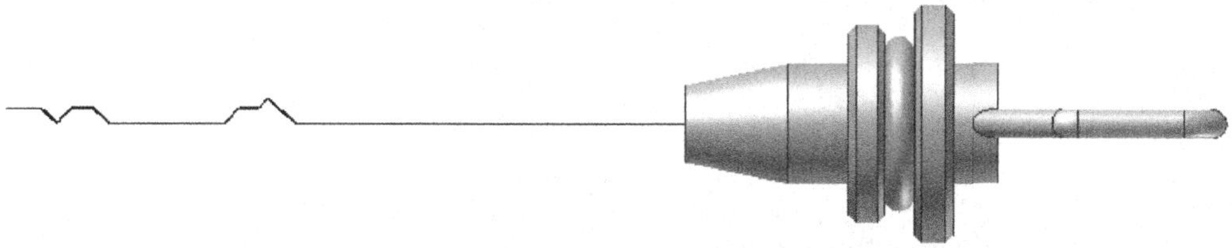

Figure 12–18

2. Sketch the sweep's profile similar to that shown in Figure 12–19 on the bottom face of the revolved feature. Do not worry about the dimensions or its exact shape.

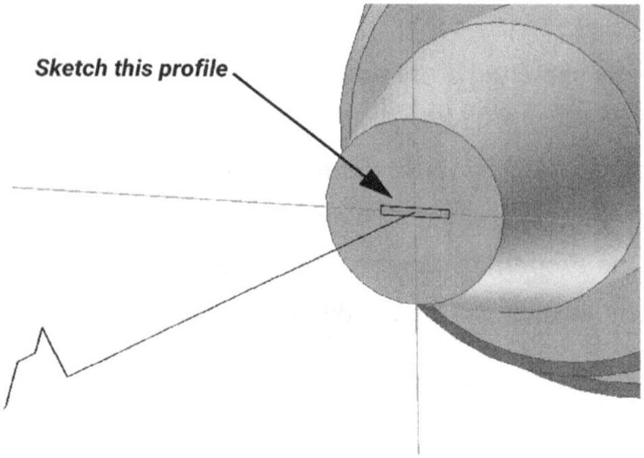

Figure 12–19

3. The profile and path are now defined. In the *Create* panel, click (Sweep).

   Note: In this situation, you could have created the geometry as an extrude. However, the section to extrude would need to be a closed section. Using either method, you can create the same geometry. With more experience, you will establish modeling preferences.

4. Depending on how you sketched the profile, you might be required to select it. If so, select the rectangular profile created in the previous step.
5. Select the path for the profile to follow, if Inventor does not immediately assign it.
6. Maintain the default (Follow Path) orientation option.
7. Click **OK** to create the sweep. The model displays as shown in Figure 12–20.

Figure 12–20

8. Save the model and close the window.

End of practice

Practice 12c
(Optional) Additional Swept Geometry

Practice Objective

- Create swept geometry using appropriate path and profile entities.

In this practice, you are provided some additional geometric shapes that can be created using a Sweep feature. Create each of these using appropriate path and profile geometry.

Task 1: Create new parts using a single feature.

1. Create the parts shown in Figure 12–21 using swept features. Start the models using the standard metric template.

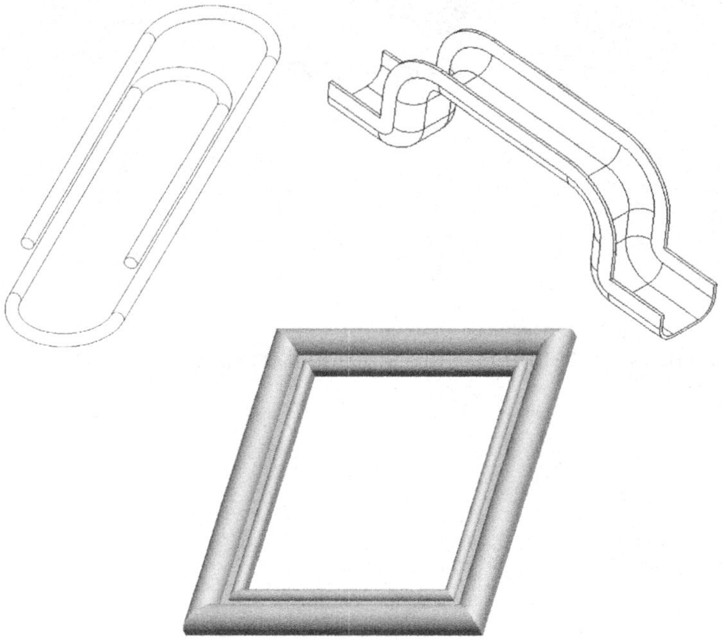

Figure 12–21

End of practice

Chapter Review Questions

1. Which command would you use to create the groove in the model shown in Figure 12–22?

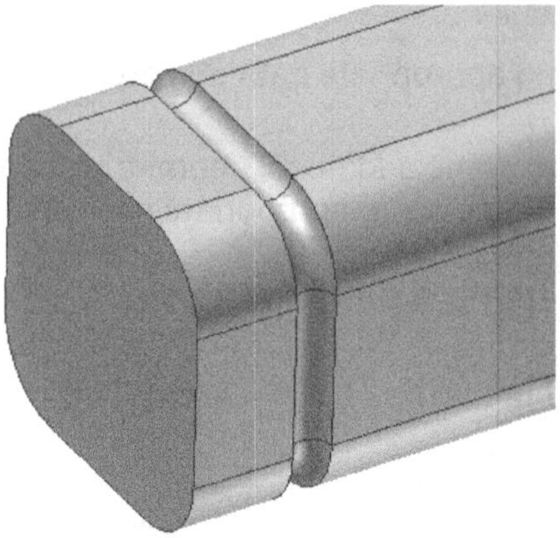

Figure 12–22

   a. Coil
   b. Revolve
   c. Extrude
   d. Sweep

2. Which elements must be defined before starting the creation of a sweep feature? (Select all that apply.)
   a. Profile
   b. Path
   c. Section
   d. Start Point

3. A sweep feature can be used to either add or remove material.
   a. True
   b. False

4. Which of the following statements for sweep features is true?
   a. A sweep creates a single feature whose geometry is blended between multiple profiles.
   b. A sweep creates a single feature whose geometry is swept along a defined path.
   c. A sweep can only be added to the model after the base extrusion has been created.
   d. A sweep path must be sketched geometry.

5. You can taper a sweep with a closed path, but you cannot taper a sweep with an open path.
   a. True
   b. False

6. You can twist the path that defines a sweep by entering a Twist value.
   a. True
   b. False

7. How many unconsumed sketches are required to create the sweep feature shown in Figure 12–23?

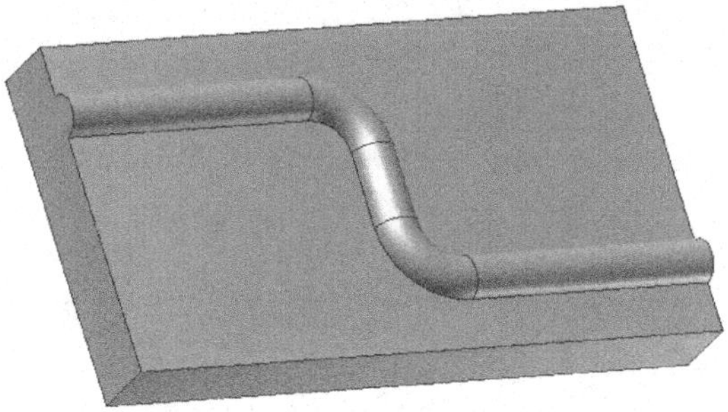

Figure 12–23

   a. 1
   b. 2
   c. 1 for 2D sweep, 2 for 3D sweep.
   d. A sweep is not based on a sketch.

Command Summary

Button	Command	Location
	**Sweep**	• **Ribbon:** *3D Model* tab>*Create* panel

Chapter 13

Loft Features

A loft is a feature that can be used to create complex geometry that blends multiple profiles. Additional control of the resulting shape can be gained by assigning references for the geometry to follow between the profiles.

Learning Objectives

- Create a rail loft feature using appropriate profile and rail entities.
- Create a center line loft feature using appropriate profile and centerline entities.
- Control the shape and weight of how lofted geometry transitions from adjacent solid geometry.
- Control how lofted geometry transitions between sections.

13.1 Creating Rail and Center Line Lofts

A loft feature enables you to create advanced geometry by blending multiple profiles. A loft can either remove or add material in a model. There are three available loft types: **Rail, Center Line**, and **Area**. This section discusses the rail and center line types. When creating a new loft feature, the default type is a rail loft.

Rail lofts enable you to blend between profiles, as shown at the top of Figure 13–1. As an optional reference, you can further define how the geometry is blended between the profiles by selecting rail entities, as shown at the bottom of Figure 13–1.

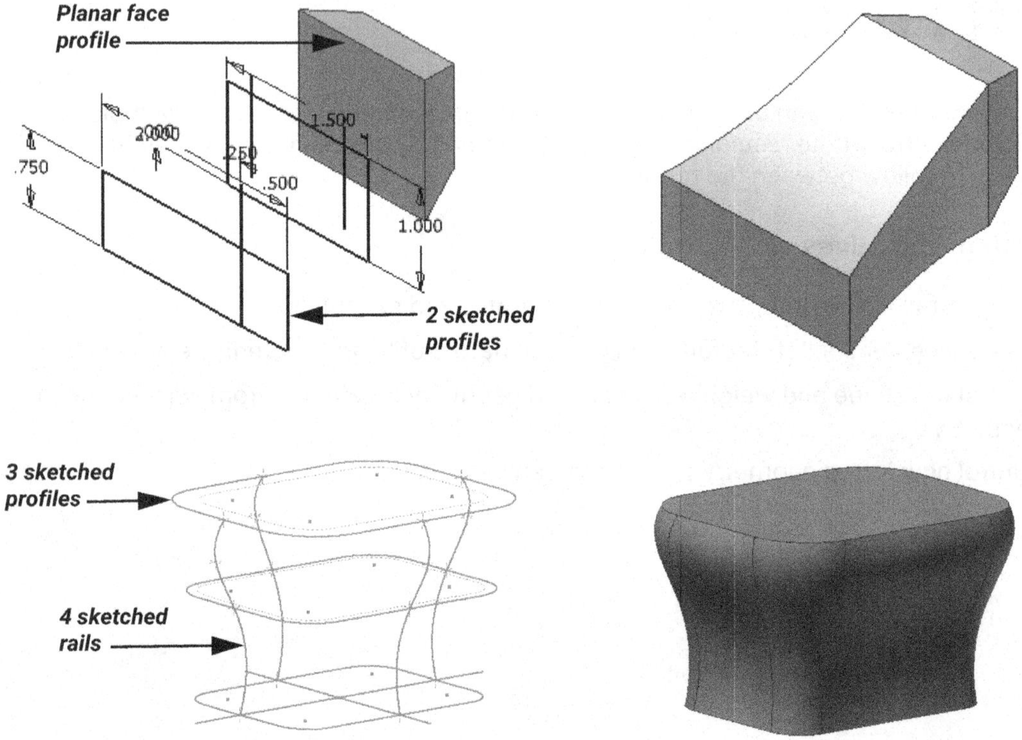

Figure 13–1

Similar to a rail loft, a center line loft blends between selected profiles; however, control of the geometry between profiles is assigned using a single centerline. The centerline sets the profiles so that they remain normal to a centerline reference, as shown in Figure 13–2.

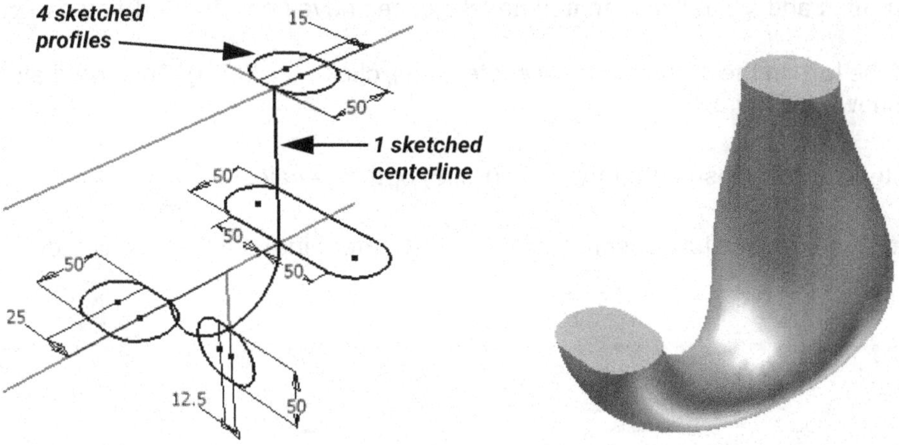

Figure 13–2

Prior to creating either a rail or center line loft, sketched profiles and reference entities must be created so that they are available for selection during feature creation.

- Rail and center line loft profiles must be a closed loop sketch (or existing face) to create a solid loft. Open profiles can only be used to create a surface loft. The profiles (sketched or existing face) should represent cross-sections of the geometry that is required to be blended.
- For a rail loft, you can control the shape of the loft between profiles. Rails are 2D or 3D sketched curves or existing edges and are optional for feature creation. Each sketch or existing edge that is used as a rail must intersect all profiles and be tangent continuous.
- For a center line loft, a centerline is required. It can be a 2D or 3D sketched curve or an existing edge in the model. Only one centerline can be used to create a loft and it does not need to intersect the profiles/sections.

Use the following general steps to create a loft feature:

1. Start the creation of the loft.
2. Define the reference entities.
3. Define the loft options.
4. Complete the feature.

Step 1 - Start the creation of the loft.

Once the profiles and any rail and centerline references have been created, you can start the creation of the loft. In the *3D Model* tab>*Create* panel, click (Loft). The *Loft* dialog box opens, as shown in Figure 13–3.

- To create a rail loft, ensure that the (Rails) option is selected.
- To create a center line loft, ensure that the (Center Line) option is selected.

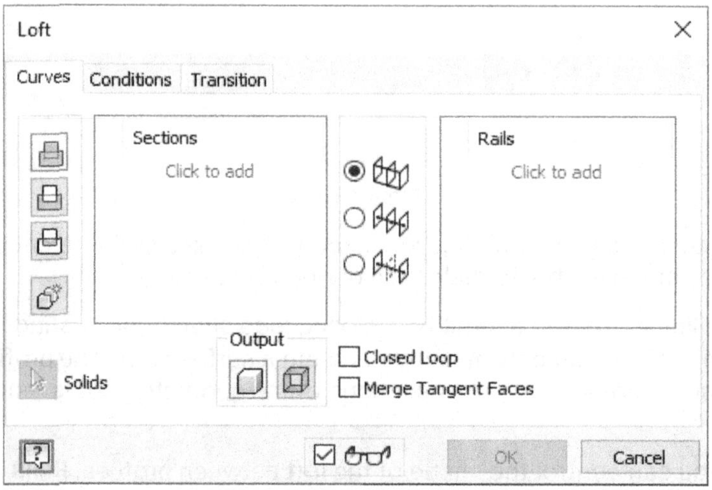

Figure 13–3

Note: *Area lofts are discussed in the Autodesk Inventor: Advanced Part guide.*

Step 2 - Define the reference entities.

By default, on the *Curves* tab, the *Sections* area is automatically active when you start the creation of a loft. Select at least two profiles to be used in creating the geometry.

- The selected profiles can be either sketched sections or a planar face on existing geometry. Planar faces can only be used as start and end sections.
- If you select a sketch with more than one selectable region, you must select the sketch and then select the region to use.
- To reorder profiles, drag and drop their profile names in the *Sections* area, as required.

Depending on whether you are creating a rail or center line loft, the selection of the remaining references vary:

- In the *Rails* area, select **Click to add** and select any reference curves that are to be used to further refine the shape of the geometry between profiles. The selection of a rail reference is optional. As rails are added, the preview updates to display the change.
- In the *Center Line* area, select **Select a Sketch** and select the centerline reference. Once the centerline is selected, a preview displays showing the created geometry. The sections of the loft remain normal to the centerline at all points.

Step 3 - Define the loft options.

By default, a loft is created so that it adds material to the model. To change this behavior, you can use the following options:

- Click  (Join) to add material.
- Click  (Cut) to remove material.
- Click  (Intersect) to intersect material.

Additional options on the *Curves* tab are as follows:

Output options	Enables you to create a solid  or surface  feature. Solids must be created by selecting closed curves or a closed face loop.
Closed Loop	Enables you to create a loft that forms a closed loop by joining the first and last selected profiles. This option is not available when rail curves are specified.
Merge Tangent Faces	Enables you to prevent an edge from being created between tangent faces of the feature.

Step 4 - Complete the feature.

Click **OK** or right-click and select **OK (Enter)** to complete the loft feature. Alternatively, you can press <Enter>.

13.2 Loft Conditions and Transitions

Additional options are available in the *Conditions* and *Transition* tabs in the *Loft* dialog box to better control the shape of the loft. These options are available for all types of loft features.

Conditions Tab

The *Conditions* tab enables you to specify the angle and shape of the lofted geometry when end sections blend into an adjacent solid. Select each item in the list to set its options separately. The conditions that can be set vary depending on the profile geometry and adjacent features. The options are described below. Figure 13–4 shows an example of the options available.

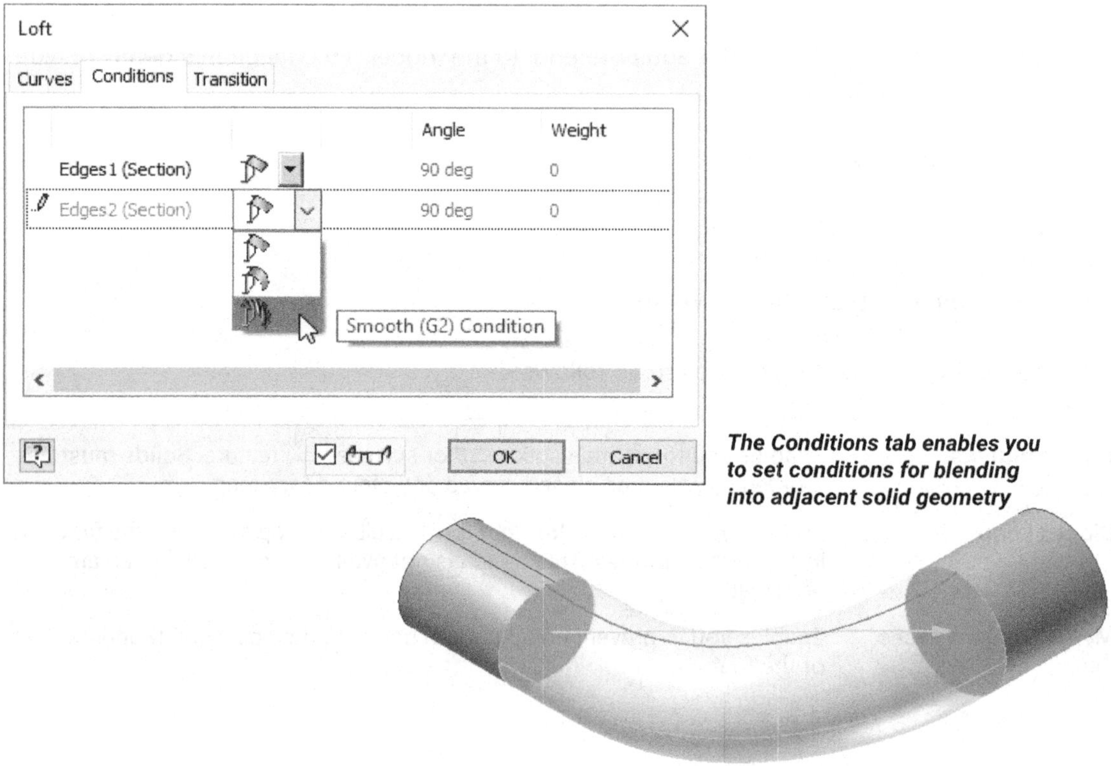

Figure 13–4

Free Condition

The **Free** condition ( ) is applied to the profiles by default, ensuring that no control conditions are set for the loft for its end profiles, as shown on the left in Figure 13–5.

Tangent Condition

The **Tangent** condition ( ) is available when the loft profile is an existing face, or when the profile is adjacent to a lateral surface or body, as shown on the right in Figure 13–5.

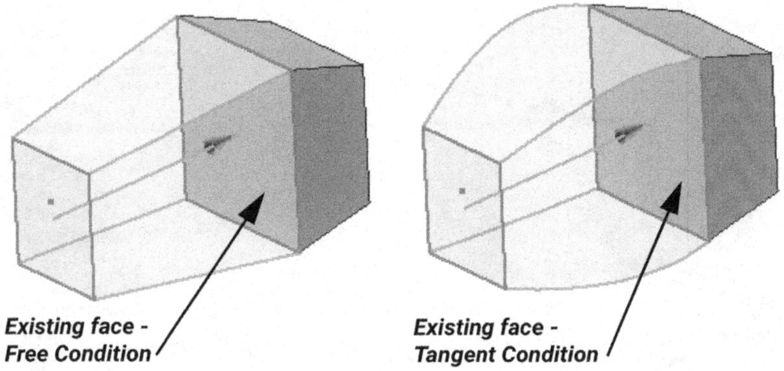

Figure 13–5

- The *Weight* value sets how far the loft follows the starting profile and angle, as shown in Figure 13–6. A large number gives the angle more influence, so the transition near the profile is more gradual. If the *Weight* is 0, the *Angle* is grayed out.

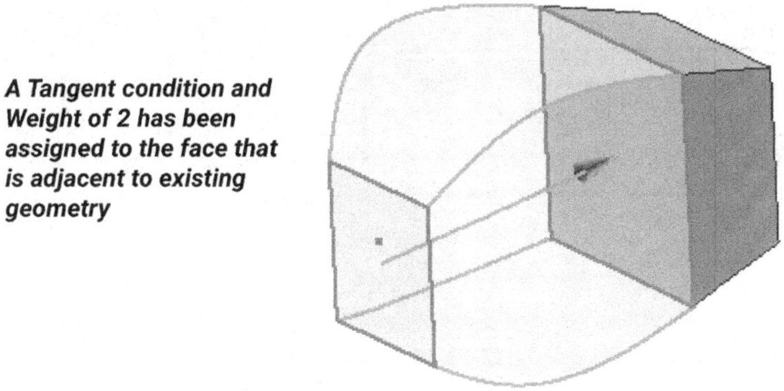

Figure 13–6

Direction Condition

The **Direction** condition ( ) is available when profiles are 2D sketches. This condition measures the angle of the loft body relative to the plane that contains the profile. Once selected, apply angle and weight to the loft body relative to the profile.

- The *Angle* sets the angular value at which the loft should begin from the profile plane, as shown in the example in Figure 13–7. The default angle is 90 degrees, and the range is from 0.0000001 to 179.99999 degrees. Angular values less than 90 create concave geometry between profiles, while values greater than 90 create convex geometry.

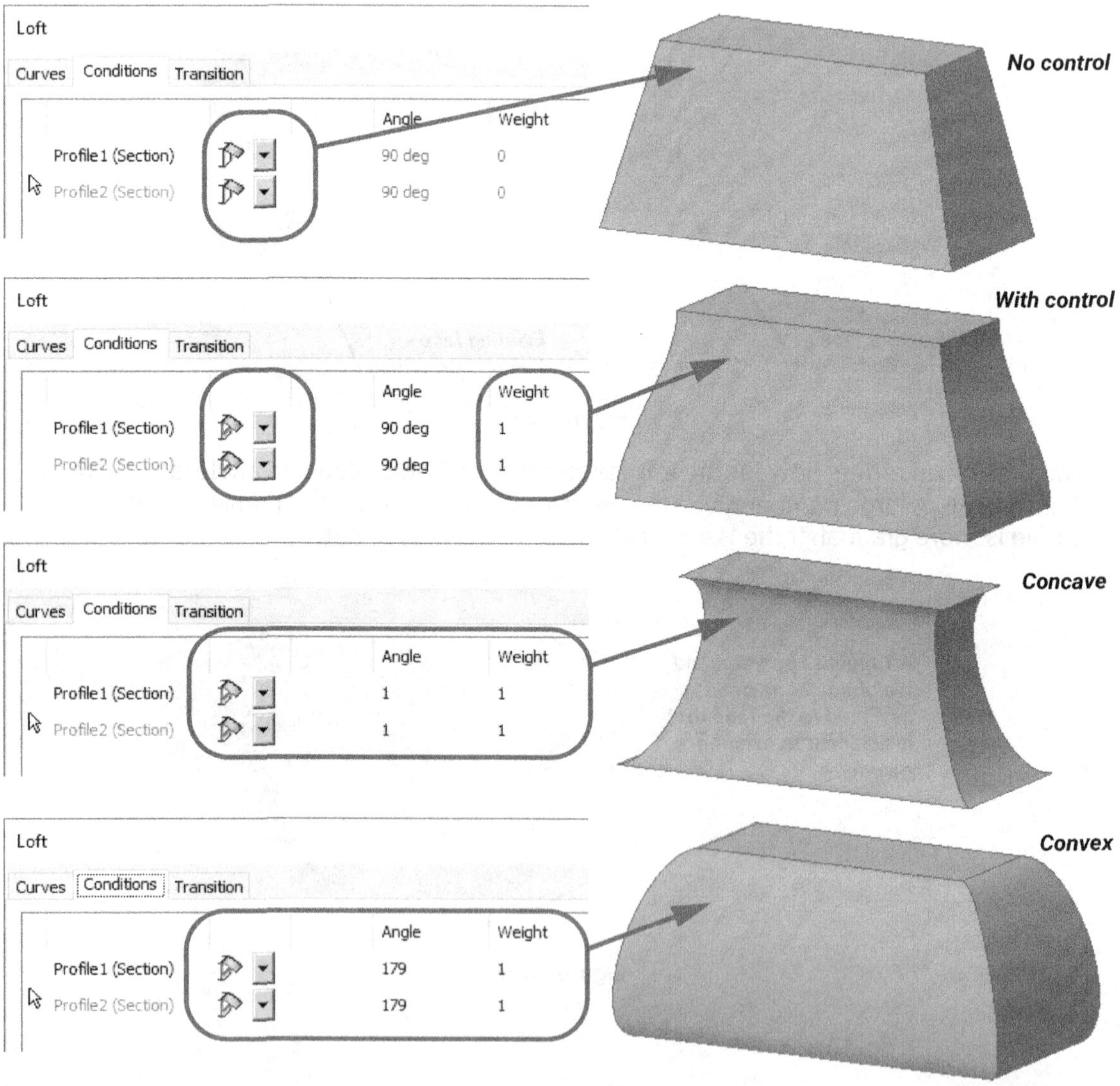

Figure 13–7

- The *Weight* value determines how far the loft follows the starting profile and angle, as shown in Figure 13–8. A large number gives the angle more influence, so that the transition near the profile is more gradual. If the *Weight* is **0**, the *Angle* is grayed out.

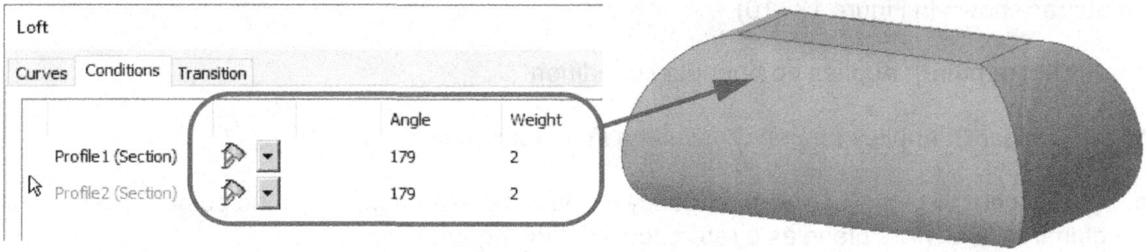

Figure 13–8

Smooth (G2) Condition

The **Smooth (G2)** condition () (shown in Figure 13–9) is available when either:

- The profile is adjacent to a face to which it can be made curvature continuous, or
- A face loop is selected.

Once the Smooth (G2) condition is set, you can control the angle, direction, and weight to the loft body relative to the profile.

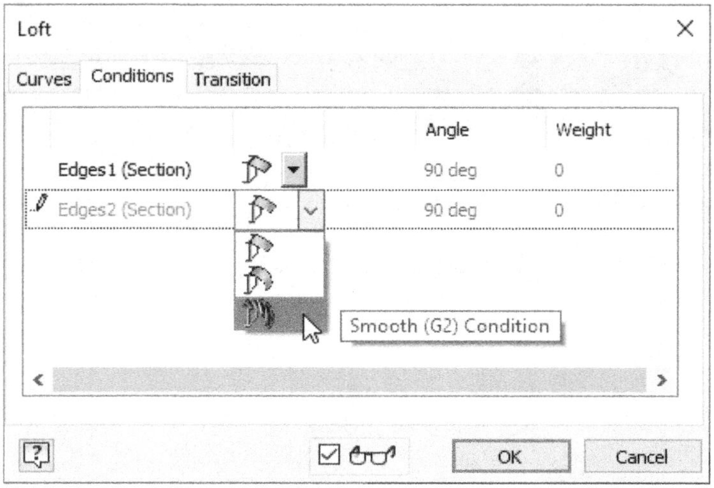

Figure 13–9

Point Conditions

The **Sharp point**, **Tangent**, and **Tangent to plane** conditions for lofts are available when you select a point as the first or last section. The following are the available boundary conditions for points (as shown in Figure 13–10):

- **(Sharp point):** Applies no boundary condition.
- **(Tangent):** Applies tangency, resulting in a round point.
- **(Tangent to plane):** Applies tangency to the point, resulting in a round point. It uses a planar face or work plane as a reference for defining tangency.

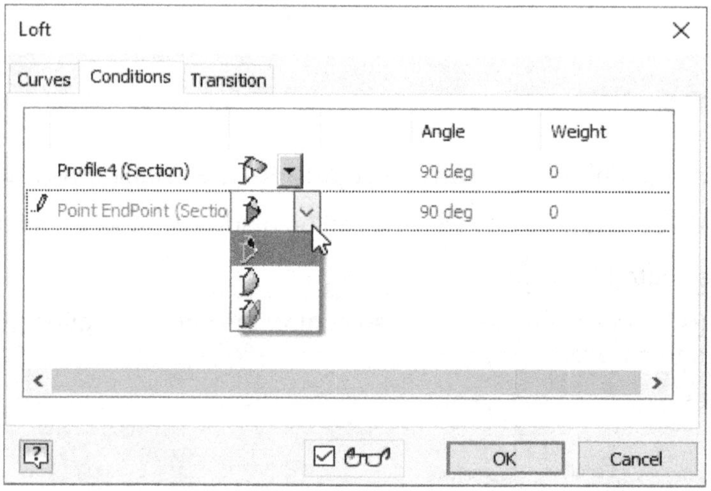

Figure 13–10

Transition Tab

The *Transition* tab defines how the loft transitions from one section to the next. A *Point Set* is a group of points, one on each profile, used to define the edges of the loft. The points in a point set are called *map points,* and the edge of the loft follows the path defined by the point set to determine the twist, as shown in Figure 13–11 (four point sets).

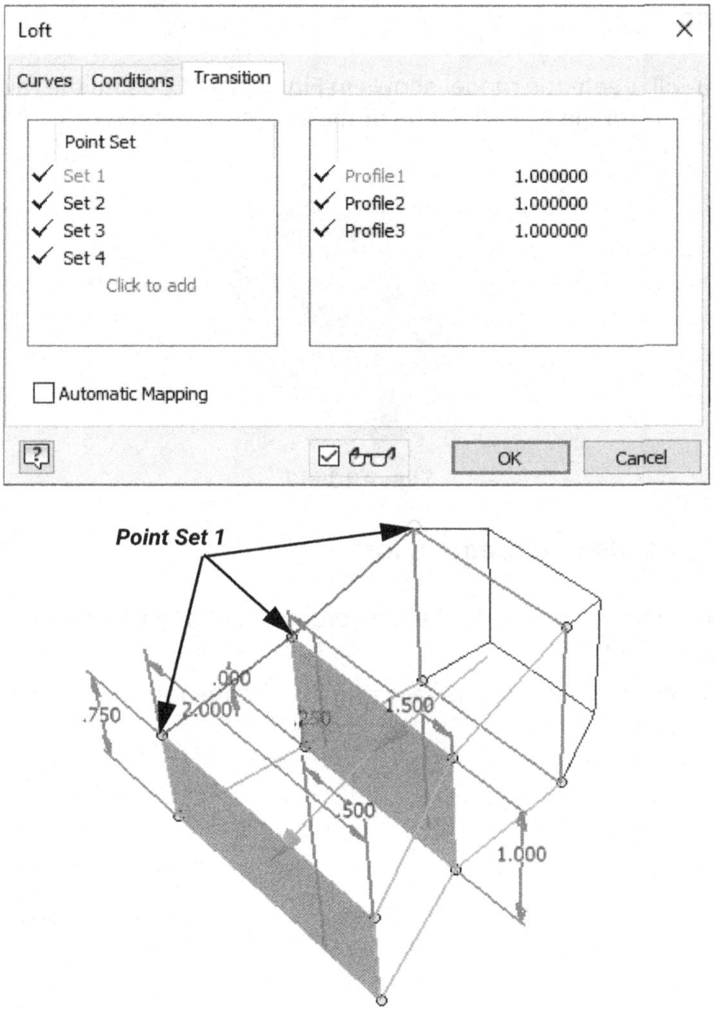

Figure 13–11

By default, the **Automatic Mapping** option is used to calculate this information. You must toggle this option off if you want to manually specify this information. The *Map Point* and *Position* columns list the map points for a point set. You can change the position of a map point by selecting the sketch on which the point lies and select a new location on the sketch. To add a new point set, select **Click to add** in the *Point Set* column.

Practice 13a
Rail Lofts

Practice Objectives

- Create lofted geometry using appropriate profile and rail entities.
- Edit a loft feature.

In this practice, you will create the model shown in Figure 13–12 using the rail loft feature. Rails will be used to help control the overall shape of the sections that are being blended together.

Figure 13–12

Task 1: Open a part file and create a loft.

In this task, you will open an existing model and create a solid loft feature using sections and rails that have been provided.

1. Open **Rail_Loft.ipt**. The sections and rails required for the loft feature are provided, as shown in Figure 13–13.

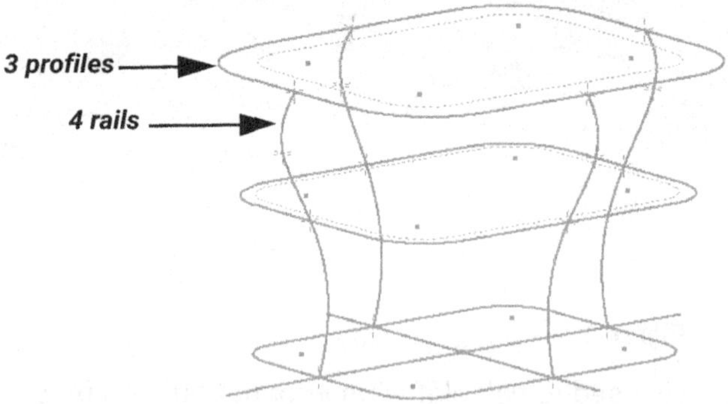

All of the curves and projected entities are shown in blue in the image for improved printing clarity

Figure 13–13

2. In the *Create* panel, click  (Loft). The *Loft* dialog box opens, as shown in Figure 13–14.

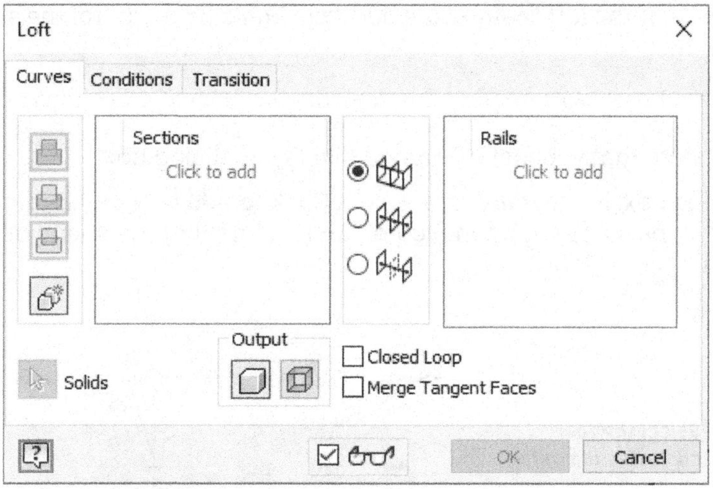

Figure 13–14

3. Ensure that  (Rails) is selected.
4. In the *Sections* area, select **Click to add**.
5. Select **Profile1**, **Profile2**, and **Profile3** in the Model browser. Alternatively, you can select them in the graphics window.
6. Click **OK** to create the loft. The model displays as shown in Figure 13–15. Note that the feature does not follow the shape outlined by the rails, as is the design intent.

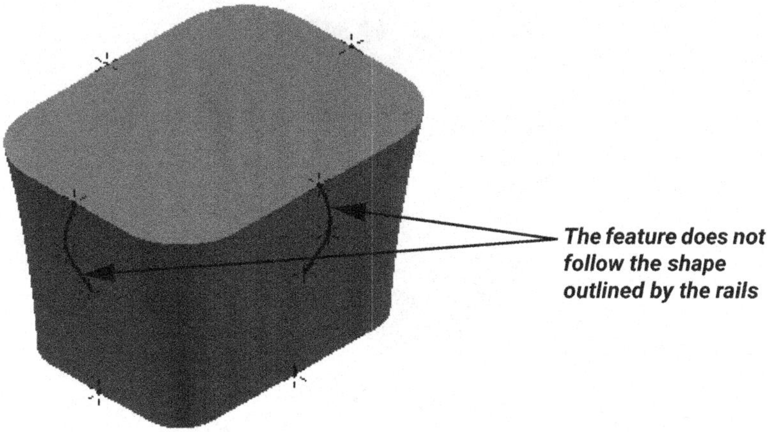

Figure 13–15

Task 2: Add rails to the loft.

In this task, you will edit the loft feature and add rails. Rails help control the shape of the loft between sections.

> ***Note:*** *When creating rails, remember that they must intersect all sections in the loft.*

1. Edit the loft feature that you just created to display its dialog box.
2. In the *Loft* dialog box, in the *Rails* area, select **Click to add** or right-click and select **Select Rails**. Select the four rails shown in Figure 13–16. Note that the shape of the loft updates as you select the rails.

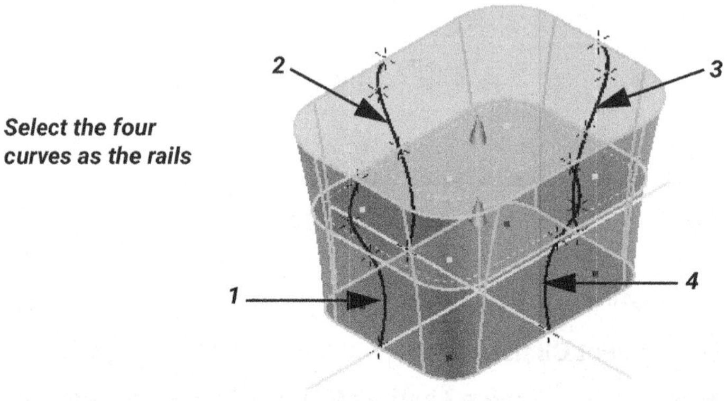

Figure 13–16

3. Click **OK** to update the loft and close the dialog box. The model displays as shown in Figure 13–17.

Figure 13–17

4. Save and close the model.

End of practice

Practice 13b
Center Line Loft

Practice Objective

- Create a center line loft feature using appropriate profile and centerline entities to drive geometry based on a selected centerline.

In this practice, you will create the center line loft shown in Figure 13–18. The geometry is generated by selecting two profiles and a single centerline reference.

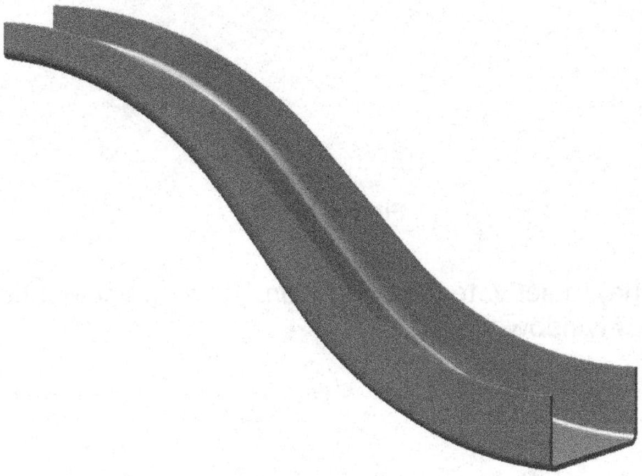

Figure 13–18

Task 1: Open a part file and create a center line loft.

In this task, you will open an existing model and create a center line loft using the sketches provided.

1. Open **CenterLine_loft.ipt**. The loft's centerline and sections have been created for you.
2. In the *Create* panel, click  (Loft). The *Loft* dialog box opens.

3. In the *Sections* area, select **Click to add**, and for the profiles for the loft, select **Profile1** and **Profile2** in the Model browser. The loft is generated by blending between the two profile sketches, as shown in Figure 13–19.

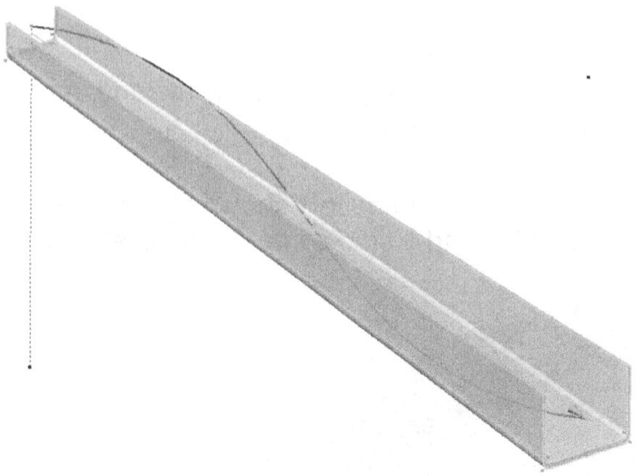

Figure 13–19

4. Click (Center Line) to activate the *Center Line* field and select the **Centerline** sketched spline in the graphics window.

   *Note: Alternatively, you can right-click in the graphics window and select **Select Center Line** to create a center line loft and select the reference centerline sketch.*

5. Click **OK** to complete the loft. The model displays as shown in Figure 13–20.

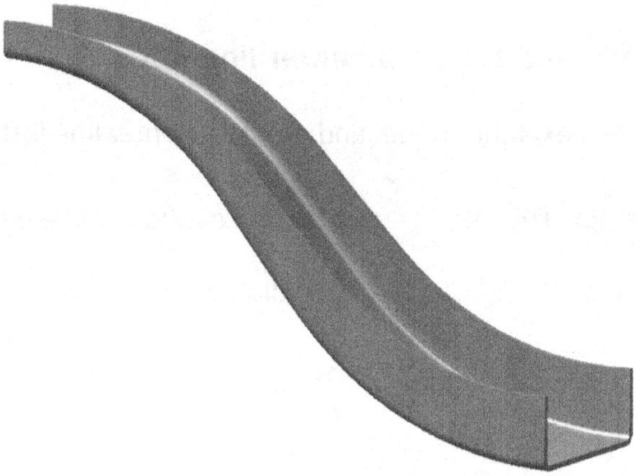

Figure 13–20

6. Save and close the file.

End of practice

Practice 13c
Loft Creation I

Practice Objectives

- Create a loft feature using appropriate reference entities.
- Edit loft features to change their type and reference entities.
- Control the shape and weight of how lofted geometry transitions from adjacent solid geometry.
- Control how lofted geometry transitions between sections.

In this practice, you will create a loft feature between two existing solid features. You will begin by creating a rail loft to compare geometry and then edit this to create a more advanced and customized center line loft feature. The final model is shown in Figure 13–21.

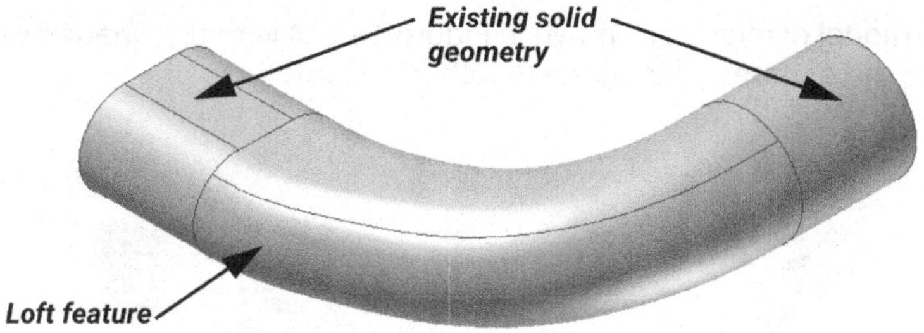

Figure 13–21

Task 1: Open a part file and create a rail loft.

1. Open **loft.ipt**. The model displays as shown in Figure 13–22. The sections and centerline you will use to create the loft in this practice have been created for you.

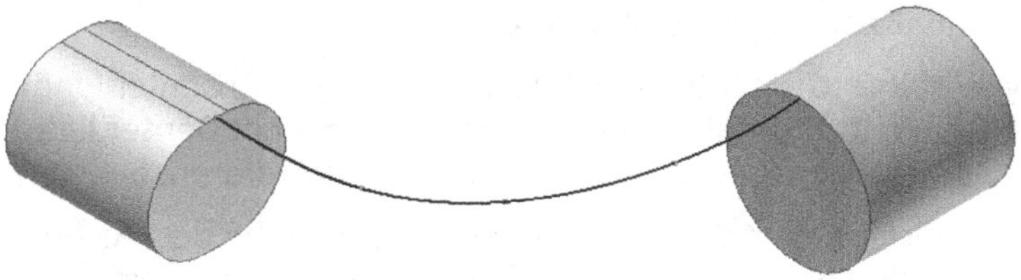

Figure 13–22

2. In the *Create* panel, click (Loft). In the *Loft* dialog box, click (Rails), if not already active.

3. In the *Sections* area, select **Click to add** and select the two sections (existing geometry) shown in Figure 13–23.
4. In the *Rails* area, select **Click to add** and select the curved sketch, as shown in Figure 13–23. Alternatively, you can also right-click in the graphics window and select **Select Rails**.

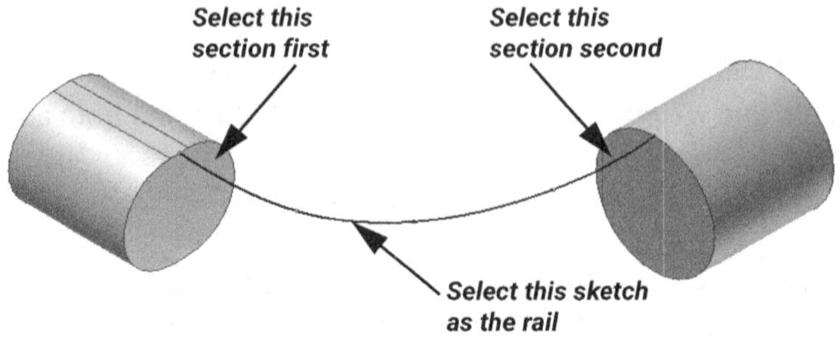

Figure 13–23

5. Click **OK**. The model displays as shown in Figure 13–24 with the **Shaded with Edges** display style set. Note the geometry along the length of the loft.

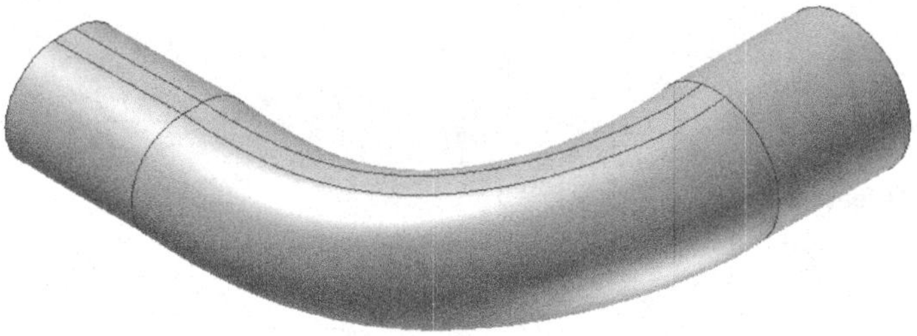

Figure 13–24

Task 2: Create a center line loft feature.

1. Edit the loft feature to display its dialog box.
2. Change the type of loft to a center line loft by selecting (Center Line). Alternatively, you can also right-click in the graphics window and select **Select Center Line**. The sections that were defined for the rail loft remain selected, but the rail reference is removed.
3. In the *Center Line* area, select **Select a Sketch** and select the curved sketch (same as that used for the rail) as the centerline reference. You might need to expand the loft feature and select the curve in the Model browser if it is not displayed in the graphics window.

4. Click **OK**. The model displays as shown in Figure 13–25.

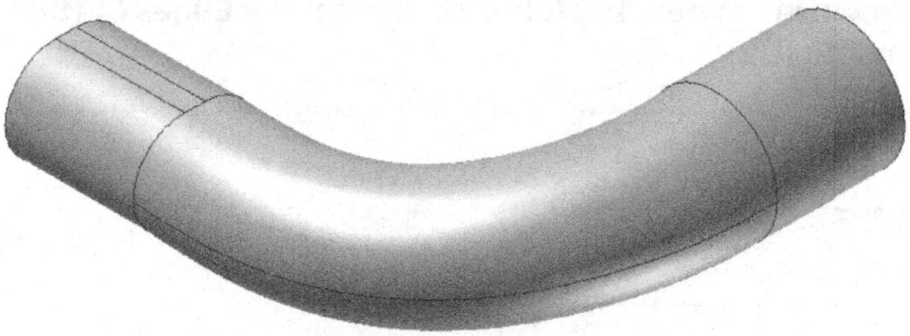

Figure 13–25

Note the subtle difference in the path that the loft geometry takes over the length of the reference curve. This is because with a rail loft, the rail reference defines the exact path of the loft, as shown on the left in Figure 13–26. With a center line loft, the centerline reference is a type of rail to which the loft sections remain normal, as shown on the right. Multiple rail references can be used for a rail loft, but only one centerline reference can be used.

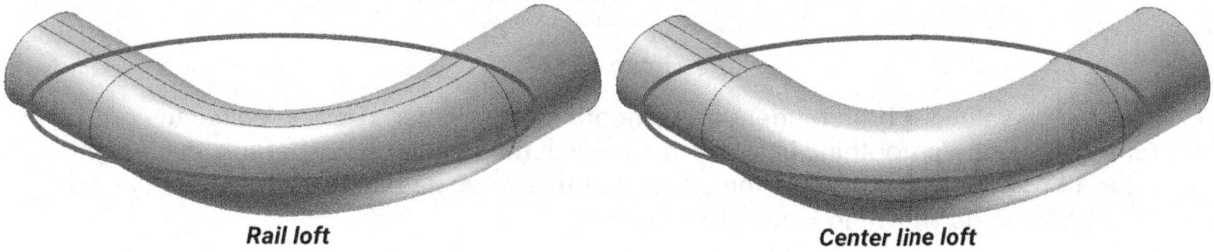

Figure 13–26

Task 3: Customize the end conditions for the center line loft.

1. Edit the loft feature to display its dialog box.
2. Maintain the options in the *Curves* tab. Select the *Conditions* tab. It enables you to control the loft geometry as it transitions from adjacent solid geometry.

3. In the **Edges13 (Section)** row, expand the drop-down list and select (Smooth (G2) Condition), as shown in Figure 13–27. Repeat this for the **Edges14 (Section)** row so that it is also set as Smooth (G2).

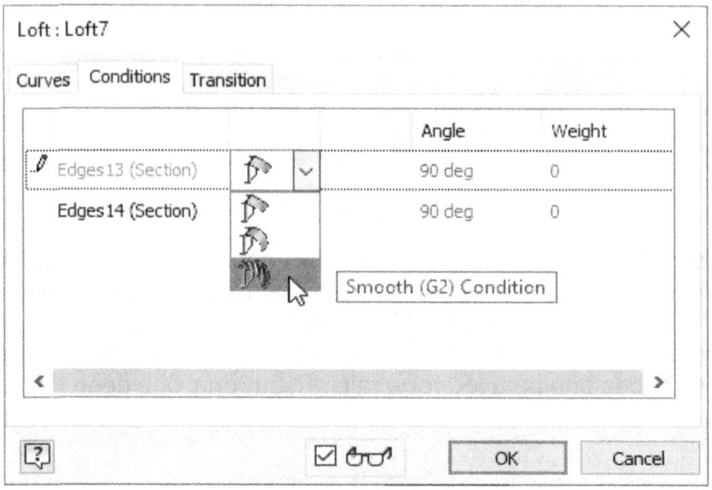

Figure 13–27

4. The *Weight* value for both tangent and smooth end conditions can be edited to control how far the tangency/smoothing is taken to establish the condition. By default, the *Weight* for **Edge 14** (right edge) is **1**. Note the effect that this value has on the loft geometry when changed to **2**, as shown in Figure 13–28.

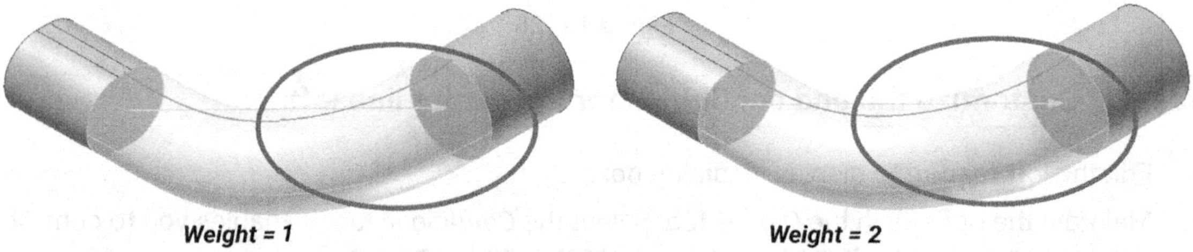

Figure 13–28

5. Return the *Weight* value for both edges to **1**.

6. Click **OK**. The model displays as shown in Figure 13–29.

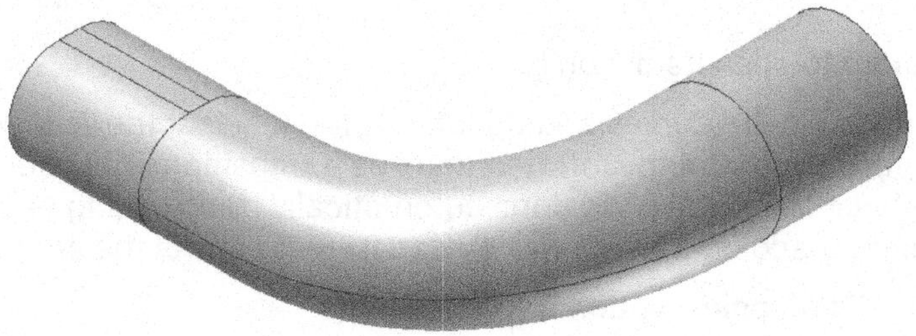

Figure 13–29

Task 4: Edit the dimensions on one of the edges used in the loft.

1. Expand **Extrusion2** in the Model browser, right-click on **Sketch3,** and select **Edit Sketch**.
2. Edit the 4 dimension value and change it to **12**, as shown in Figure 13–30.

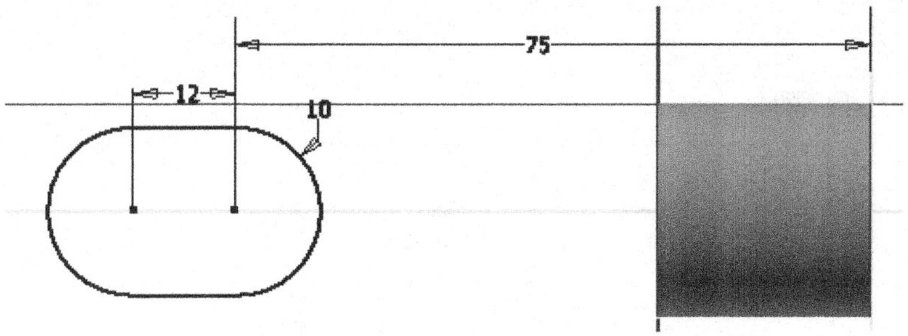

Figure 13–30

3. Finish the sketch. The loft automatically updates, as shown in Figure 13–31.

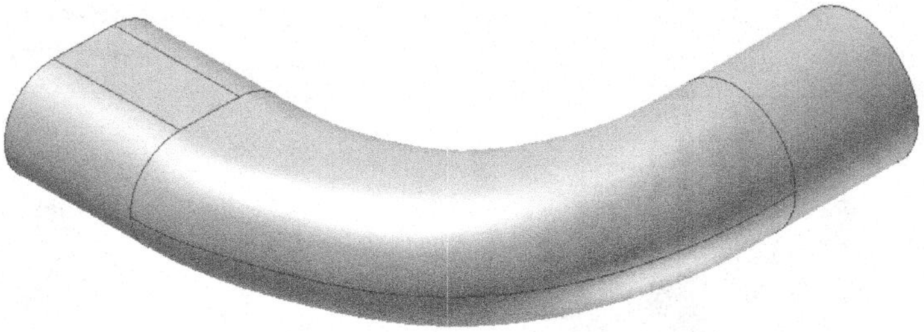

Figure 13–31

Task 5: Create transitions to further customize the loft.

1. Edit the loft feature to open its dialog box.
2. Maintain the options in the *Curves* and *Conditions* tabs. Select the *Transition* tab. This tab enables you to further control the loft geometry as it transitions between the selected sections. By default, transitioning is done automatically by matching points on each section. By manually adding transitions you can further control the shape of the loft.
3. Clear the **Automatic Mapping** option.
4. In the *Point Set* area, if **Set 1** does not already exist, select **Click to add**. The *Loft* dialog box updates to display a *Map Point* for each section in the loft. To define the transition set, select map point locations on the edges of each section. Once selected, you can refine the position by entering a precise value in the *Position* column. Zero indicates one end of a line entity, .5 indicates the middle, and 1 indicates the other end. Any value between 0 and 1 can be used.
5. Select the approximate location on the left and the right sections as shown in Figure 13–32.

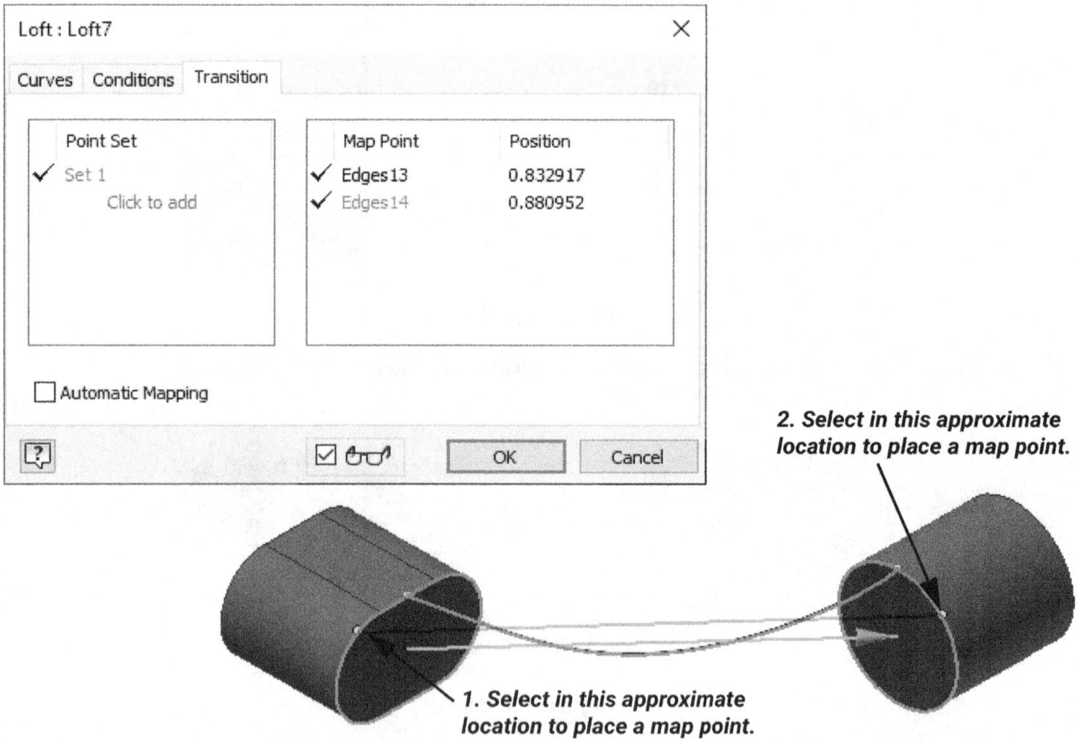

Figure 13–32

Note: *This procedure of defining position values on the sections of a loft can be time-consuming, but is valuable when working with differently shaped sections to obtain the required transitions.*

Editing the values can take some time. For this practice, you will select a location and edit the value as you want. The values depend on the selection point on the line and the entities that make up the section.

6. In the *Point Set* area, select **Click to add** to add a new point set.
7. Select two locations similar to that shown in Figure 13–33.

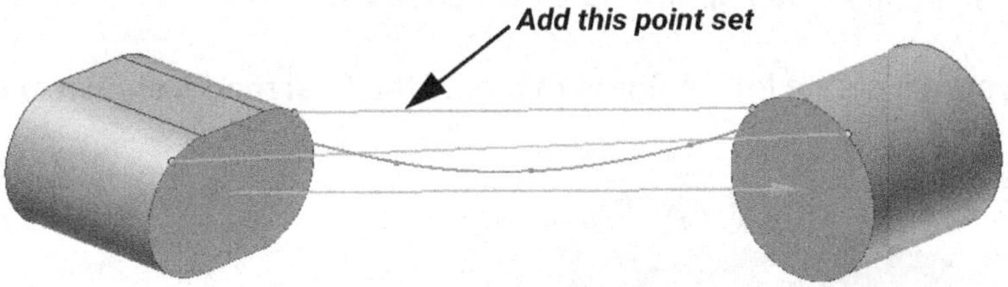

Figure 13–33

8. Continue to add two additional point sets, as shown in Figure 13–34.

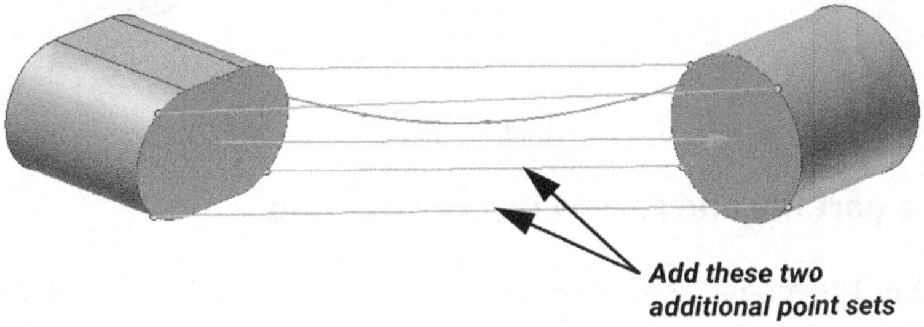

Figure 13–34

9. Click **OK**. The model should display similar to that shown in Figure 13–35.

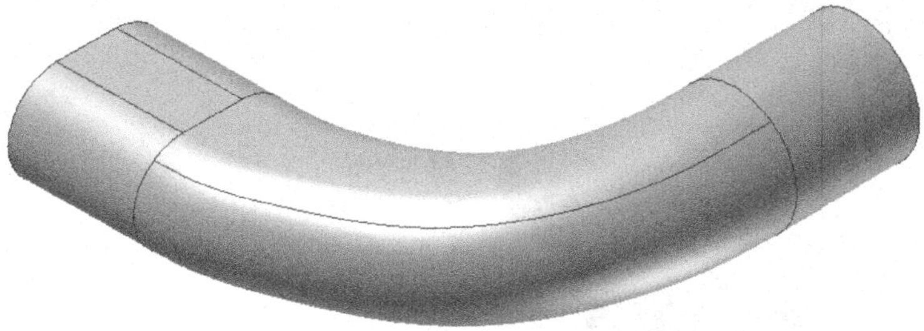

Figure 13–35

10. Save and close the model.

End of practice

Practice 13d
(Optional) Loft Creation II

Practice Objective

- Create lofted geometry using appropriate reference entities.

In this practice, you will create loft features to create the final model shown in Figure 13–36.

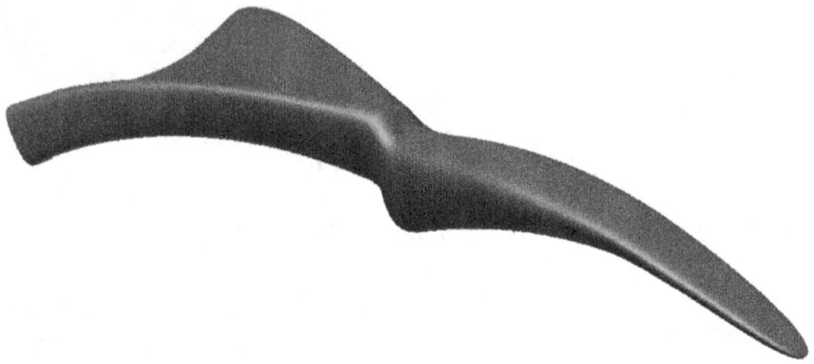

Figure 13–36

Task 1: Open a part file and review its construction.

1. Open **Razor.ipt**. The model displays as shown in Figure 13–37. The sections you will use to create the lofts in this practice have been created for you.

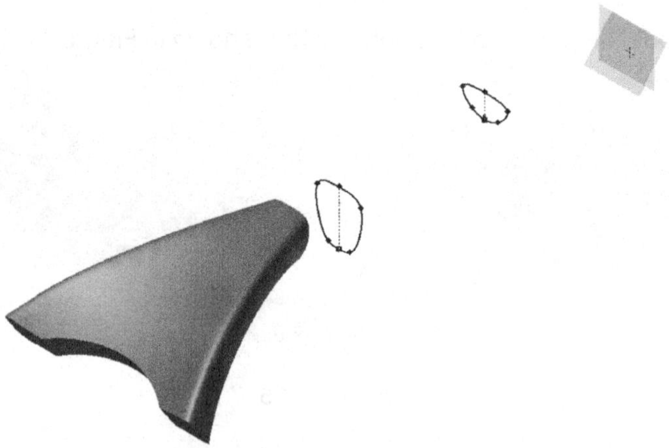

Figure 13–37

Task 2: Create a loft feature to create solid geometry.

1. Create a rail loft.
2. In the *Sections* area, select **Click to add** and then select the existing face of the model, **Profile3**, **Profile4**, and the **EndPoint** point as the sections. The preview of the resulting loft is shown in Figure 13–38. Note that a rail reference is not required for this loft.

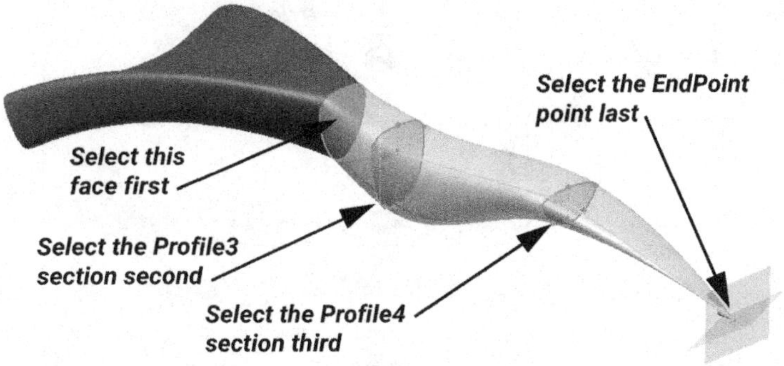

Figure 13–38

3. Select the *Conditions* tab. It enables you to control the loft geometry as it transitions from adjacent solid geometry and the condition at the terminating point.
4. In the **Edges1 (Section)** row, expand the drop-down list and select (Smooth (G2) Condition) to set the end condition, as shown in Figure 13–39.

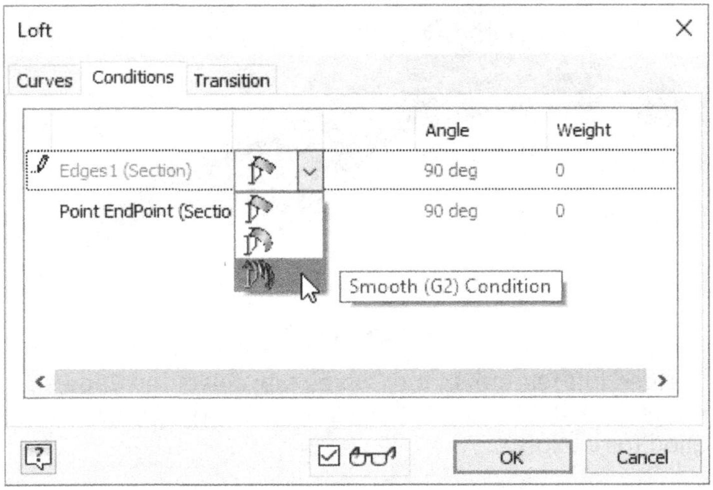

Figure 13–39

5. Edit the *Weight* value for **Edges1 (Section)** to control how far the tangency/smoothing is taken to establish the condition. For the new *Weight* value, enter **2**.

6. In the **Point EndPoint (Section)** row, expand the drop-down list and select (Tangent to Plane) to set the end condition, as shown in Figure 13–40. For the condition reference, select the **EndPoint Tangent Ref** workplane.

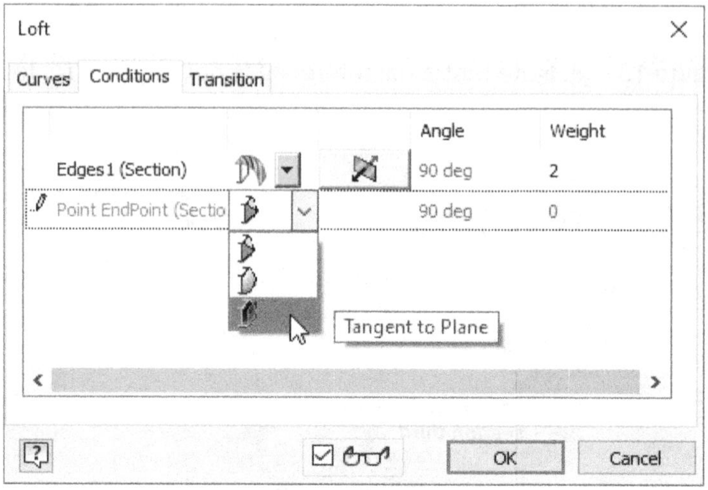

Figure 13–40

7. For **Point EndPoint (Section)**, set the *Weight* value to **5**.
8. Click **OK**. The model displays as shown in Figure 13–41 with the work planes toggled off. Note that the connection between the two solid features is not as smooth as it could be.

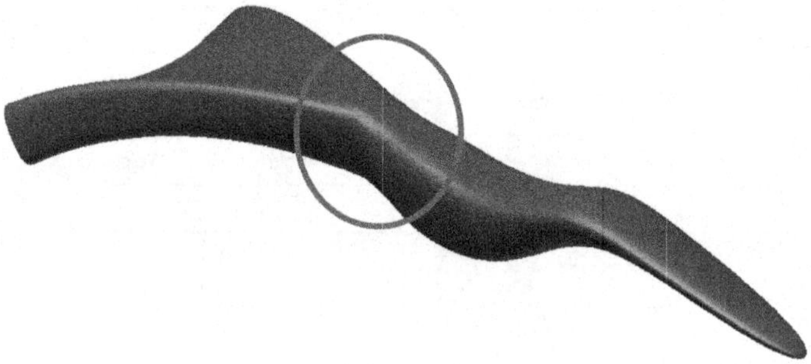

Figure 13–41

9. Edit the newly created loft feature. In the *Curves* tab, select the **Edge** section reference and press <Delete> to remove it from the loft. This is the solid face reference that was selected as a profile section for the loft.
10. Click **OK**.

11. Create a rail loft. Select the two faces shown in Figure 13–42 as the sections for the loft.

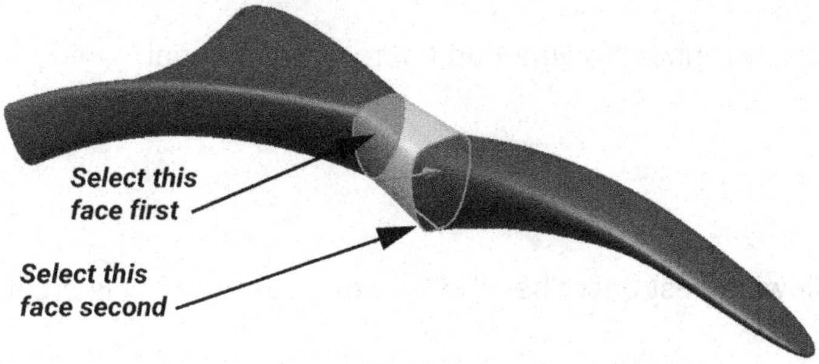

Figure 13–42

12. Select the *Conditions* tab. Expand the drop-down list and select (Smooth (G2) Condition) to set the conditions for both edges. Modify the weight values so that the new loft smoothly blends the two solids. If the values are too large, the geometry will fail and the resulting geometry cannot be calculated. Figure 13–43 shows the completed model using a *Weight* value of **1.25** and **1.5**.

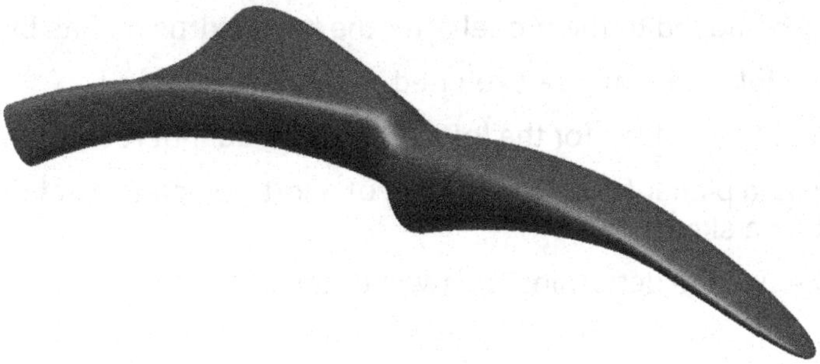

Figure 13–43

13. Save the model and close the window.

End of practice

Chapter Review Questions

1. A loft can be used in a model to either add or remove material.
    a. True
    b. False

2. Which of the following best describes the type of geometry that is created using a loft feature?
    a. A loft creates multiple solid features between each of the profiles.
    b. A loft creates a feature where the geometry is blended between multiple profiles.
    c. A loft creates a feature whose geometry is swept along a defined path.
    d. A loft creates a feature that is rotated around a selected centerline.

3. Which of the following statements are true for loft features? (Select all that apply.)
    a. A loft can only be added to the model after the base extrusion has been created.
    b. The profiles for lofts can only be sketched.
    c. Once you select the profiles for the loft feature, you cannot reorder them.
    d. To use an existing planar face as a section of a loft, you can select the face directly without creating a sketch.
    e. Map points are used to determine the twist of the loft.

4. Which type of loft can be used to create a loft that passes through the three circular sections and is guided along the curve, as shown in Figure 13–44?

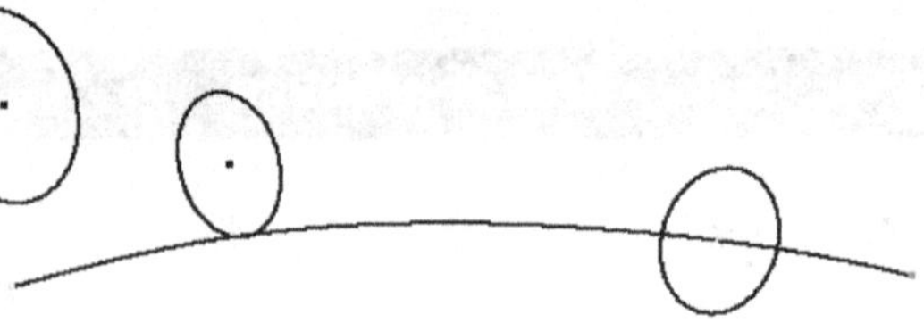

Figure 13–44

    a. Rail
    b. Center Line

5. When referencing existing geometry as the start or end section for a loft, which of the following conditions provides access to the *Weight* settings to control its shape, as shown in Figure 13–45? (Select all that apply.)

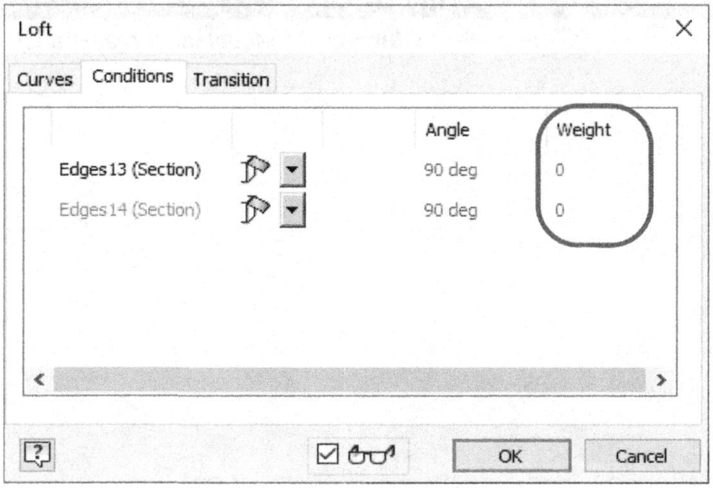

Figure 13–45

a. Free

b. Tangent

c. Smooth (G2)

Command Summary

Button	Command	Location
	**Loft**	• **Ribbon:** *3D Model* tab>*Create* panel

Chapter 14

Feature Duplication Tools

Incorporating the use of duplication techniques when creating similar geometry enables you to efficiently create models. Duplication techniques can include making multiple copies of an entire model, making multiple copies of a feature, or mirroring geometry.

Learning Objectives

- Create a rectangular pattern of features that translate along a first and second direction.
- Create a circular pattern of features that rotate about a selected axis.
- Create a pattern of features that is defined by sketch points in a sketch.
- Mirror a solid to duplicate all of its geometry.
- Mirror select features in a model to create required geometry.
- Suppress individual pattern occurrences in an existing pattern.
- Edit pattern and mirror features to make changes to the original geometry.
- Delete pattern and mirror features from a model.

14.1 Rectangular Feature Patterns

You can create multiple copies of parts or features on a part by creating a pattern. An example of a rectangular feature pattern is shown in Figure 14–1.

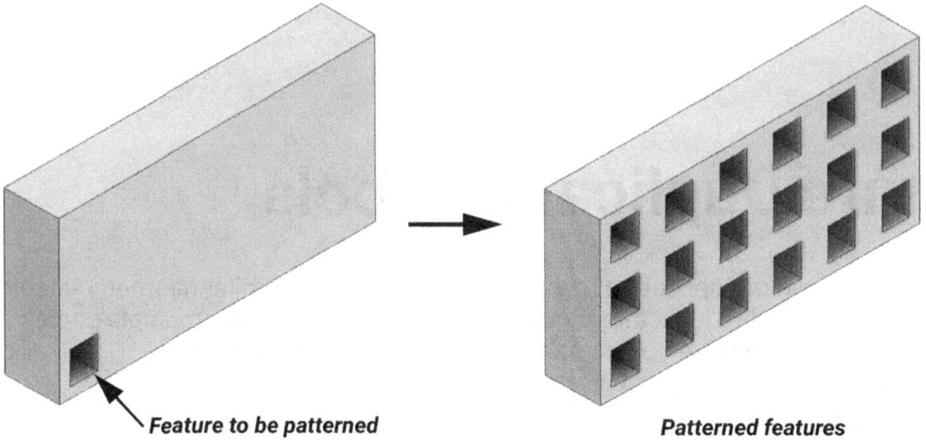

Figure 14–1

Use the following general steps to create a rectangular pattern of features on a part:

1. Start the creation of the pattern.
2. Select the object(s) to pattern.
3. Define the pattern in the first direction.
4. Define the pattern in the second direction, as required.
5. Define the extents, as required.
6. Define the output geometry, as required.
7. Complete the pattern.

Step 1 - Start the creation of the pattern.

In the *3D Model* tab>*Pattern* panel, click (Rectangular Pattern). The *Properties* panel and the tool palette open, as shown in Figure 14–2.

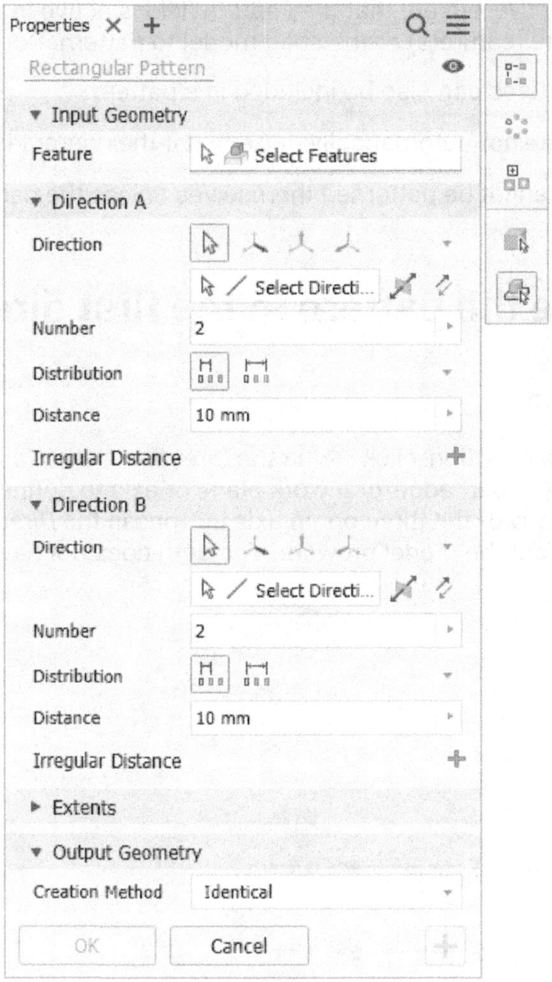

Figure 14–2

Step 2 - Select the object(s) to pattern.

Prior to selecting the object(s) to pattern, use the options in the tool palette to determine the object type that will be selected for patterning:

- Click (Pattern individual features) to create a pattern of individually selected features. This is the default option.
- Click (Pattern a solid) to pattern the entire solid model.

Once the object type is active, ensure that the *Feature* field is active in the *Input Geometry* area and select the appropriate feature(s) or the solid model to pattern. Consider the following:

- Work and surface features can also be included in a pattern.
- Dependent features are not automatically patterned if their parent is selected.
- Dependent features cannot be patterned themselves unless the parent feature is selected.

Step 3 - Define the pattern in the first direction.

Define the Direction

To define the first pattern direction, click in the *Direction A* area (as shown in Figure 14–3) and select a sketch entity, a part edge, or a work plane or axis to define the direction. You can also conveniently select any of the three origin axis buttons in the *Direction* field as an alternative to selecting from the Model browser. The path does not have to be linear, and it can be open or closed.

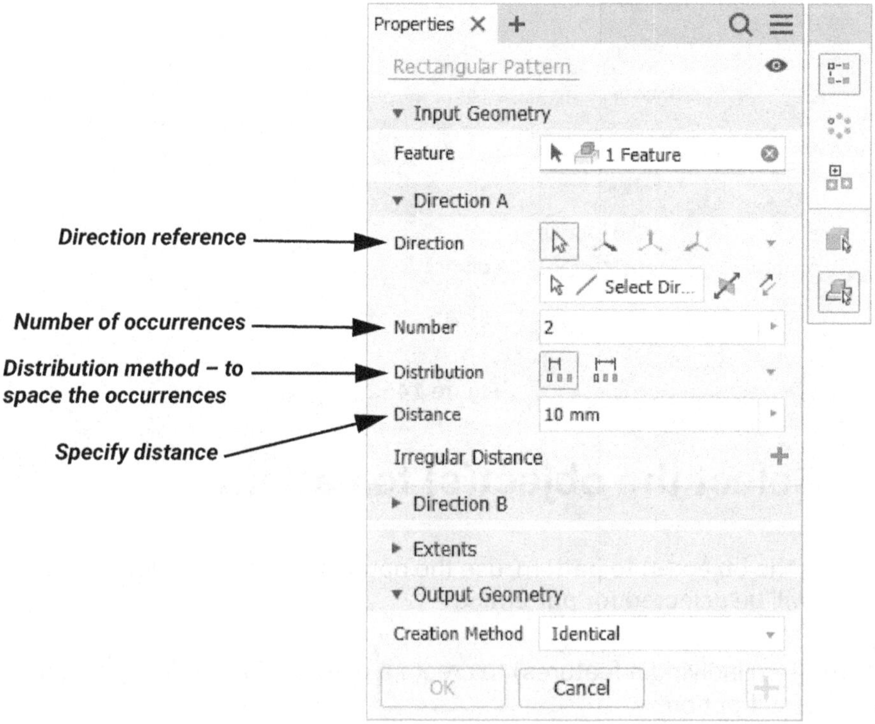

Figure 14–3

Define the Number, Distribution, and Distance of the Pattern

Set the remaining options in the *Direction A* area to define the pattern.

- Enter the number of occurrences (including the selected geometry) in the *Number* field.
- The distance between each occurrence is defined in the *Distance* field. How the value is applied to the model depends on the selected *Distribution* type (**Incremental** or **Fitted**).
    - Use (Incremental) to set the entered spacing value as the distance between individual occurrences, as shown in Figure 14–4.

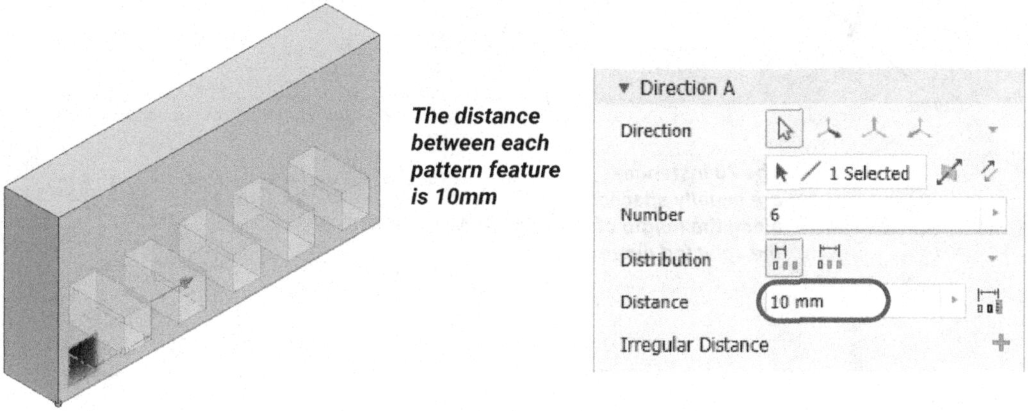

Figure 14–4

- Use (Fitted) to set the entered spacing value as the total distance between the first and last occurrence, as shown in Figure 14–5.

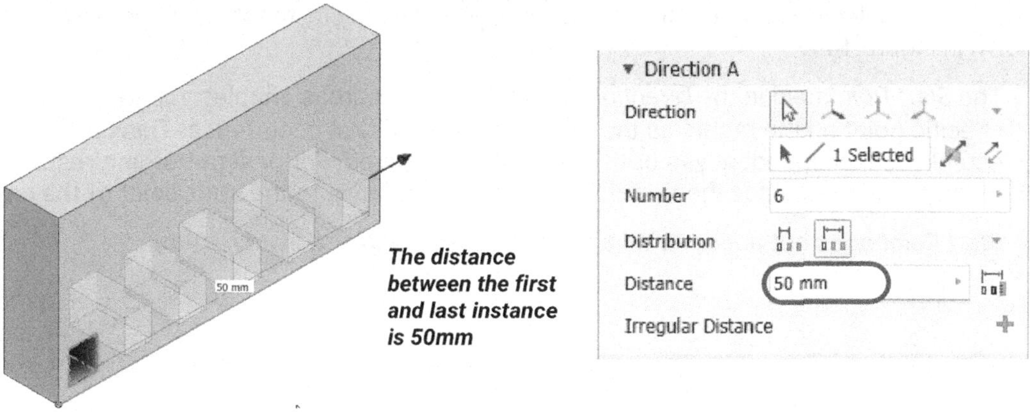

Figure 14–5

- Use (Curve Length) to set the length of the pattern equal to that of a selected curve, as shown in Figure 14–6. The number of occurrences is equally spaced along the curve.

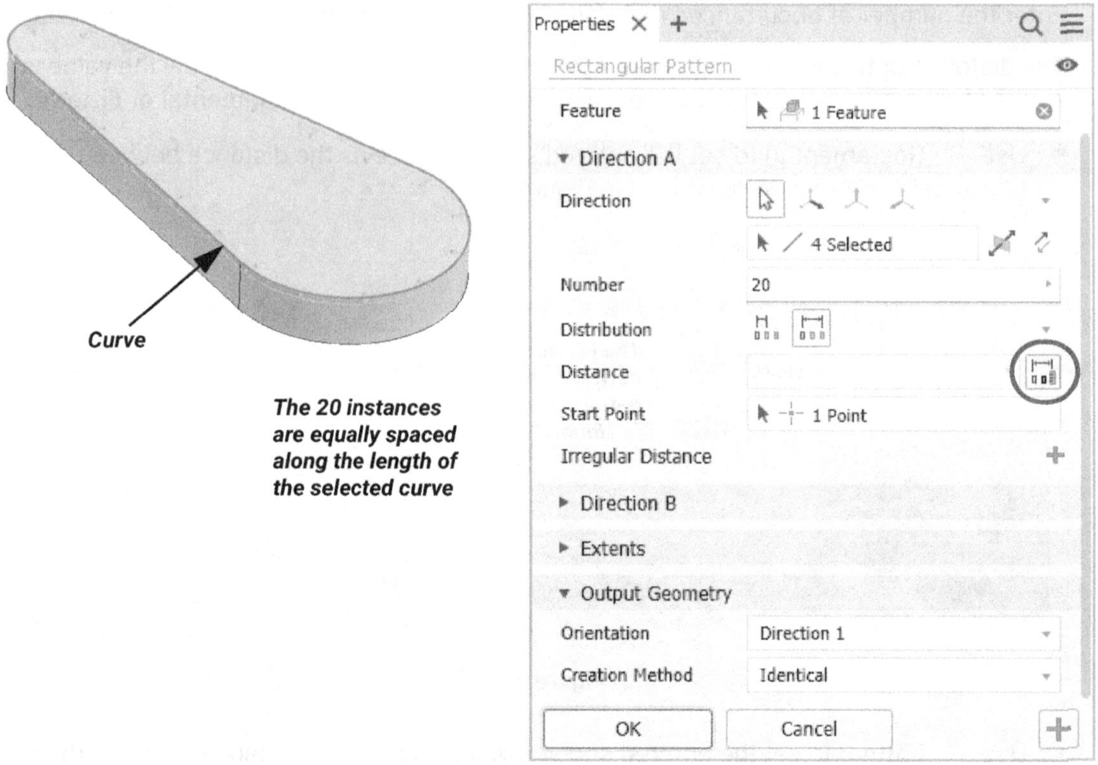

Figure 14–6

When a curve is selected for a rectangular pattern, you can specify the *Start Point* of the pattern, as shown in Figure 14–7.

- The *Start Point* field in the *Direction A* and *Direction B* areas enables you to assign a specific point on the model as the start point for the first occurrence. This can be established independently in both directions, if required. For best patterning results, it is recommended to place the first occurrence on or relative to the start point of the path.
- *Start Point* does not appear until a curve is selected to specify direction.

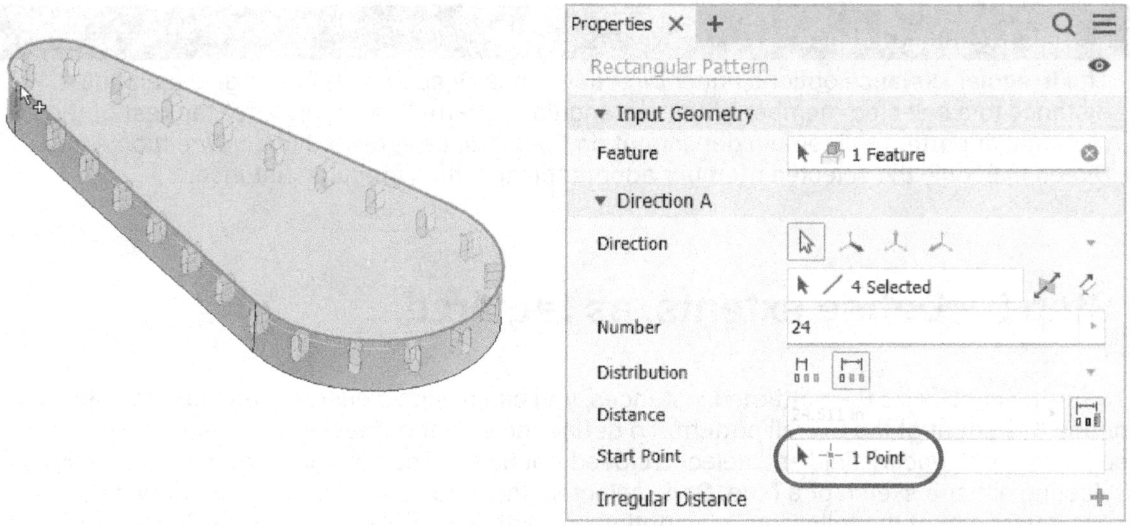

Figure 14–7

Step 4 - Define the pattern in the second direction, as required.

To define the second pattern path, click in the *Direction B* area and select a different direction reference, as shown in Figure 14–8. The second direction does not need to be perpendicular to the first. Similar to the *Direction A* area, set the number of occurrences, distribution type, and distance to define how the pattern is be created in the second direction.

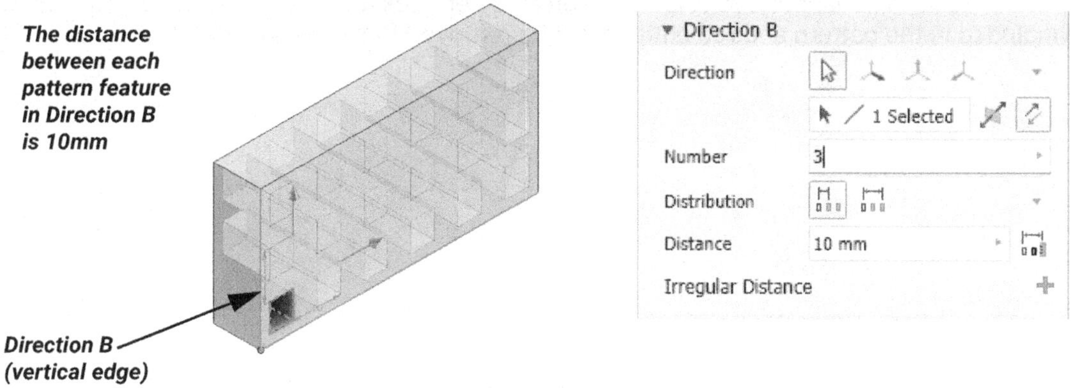

Figure 14–8

Hint: Irregular Distance

The **Irregular Distance** options under *Direction A* and *Direction B* helps to give a unique distance to a selected member of the rectangular pattern. The distance for the rest of the rectangular pattern will remain dependent on the *Distance* specified under *Direction A* and *Direction B*; only the selected member adopts the specified irregular distance.

Step 5 - Define extents, as required.

To further customize the patterned instances, you can assign a customized boundary that will define the extent of the overall pattern. To define the extent of the pattern, in the *Extents* area, select in the *Boundary* field and select a closed boundary. The boundary can be defined by selecting either a sketch or a face. Once selected, the area defined by the boundary displays pink. Select one of the following three options to define whether the patterned instances are included/excluded at the defined boundary. The patterned results using each of these options are shown in Figure 14–9.

- (Include Geometry) includes pattern instances that are fully enclosed by the selected boundary.
- (Include Centroids) includes all pattern instances that have their centroid fully enclosed by the boundary.
- (Include using occurrence base points) includes all pattern instances that have the selected base point fully enclosed by the boundary.

Additionally, an *offset value* can be assigned relative to the selected boundary. It can be flipped to either side of the boundary, as required. Patterned entities that are displayed as solid green are included in the pattern and red entities will be removed from the final pattern.

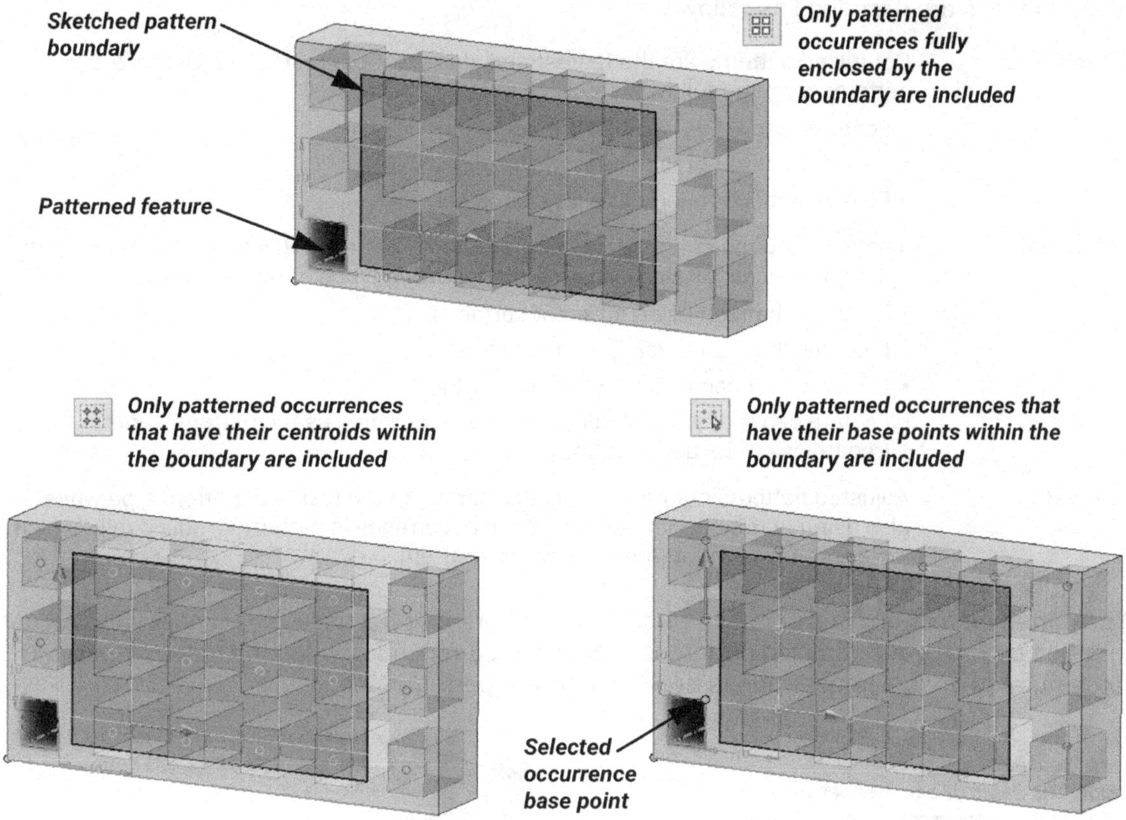

Figure 14–9

Step 6 - Define output geometry, as required.

The *Output Geometry* area, shown in Figure 14–10, enables you to assign a *Creation Method* for the patterned geometry. The available options (**Optimized**, **Identical**, and **Adjust**) enable you to control how the geometry is created to refine the final pattern results.

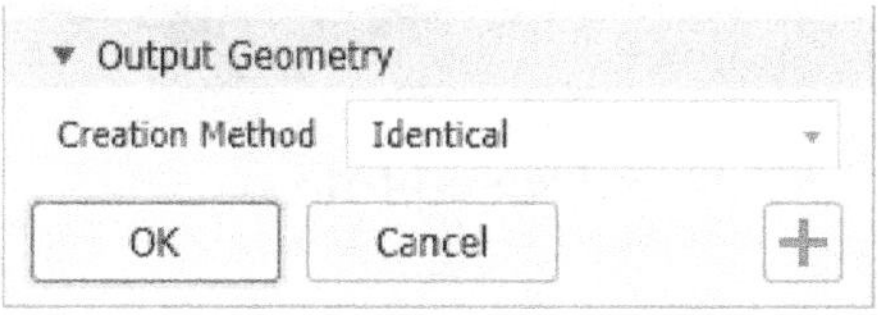

Figure 14–10

These options are described as follows:

Optimized	Optimized patterns are the fastest and also the most restrictive. Optimized patterns have the following restrictions: • Features cannot lie on different surfaces. • Features cannot break edges of the part. • Features cannot intersect with each other.
Identical	Identical patterns create identically patterned features. This is the default pattern option. Identical patterns generate the following types of occurrences: • Features that can lie on different surfaces. • Features that can break the edge of the part. • Features that can intersect with each other. • Feature depth of all occurrences is the same value as the pattern leader (regardless of its depth option).
Adjust	Adjusted patterns create occurrences similar to the Identical pattern type while also using feature depth settings. Each occurrence is patterned individually, which increases the computation time for the pattern.

The patterned features in Figure 14–11 show the differences between the **Identical** and **Adjust** creation options. An **Optimized** pattern is explicitly recommended when the pattern results in a large number of occurrences and is used to optimize performance.

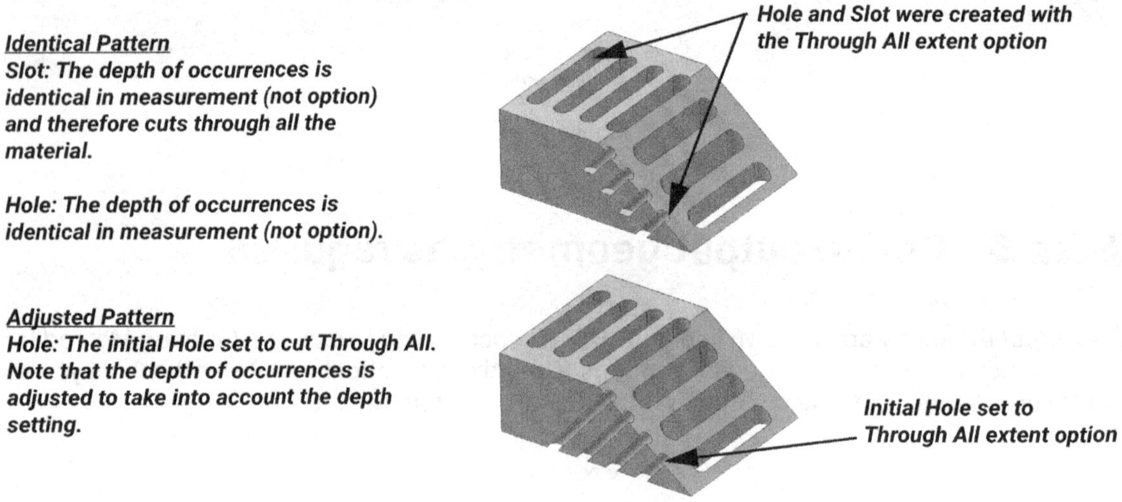

Figure 14–11

When a non-linear curve is selected as a reference for the direction, the *Output Geometry* area updates to include an *Orientation* field, as shown in Figure 14–12.

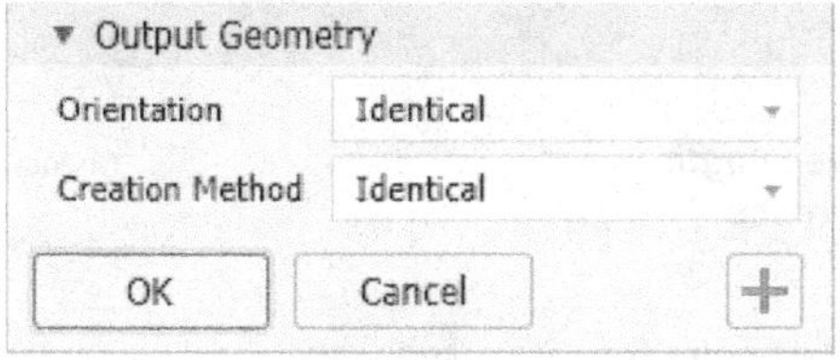

Figure 14–12

The *Orientation* field contains options to define how the patterned features are oriented along the curve, relative to the first selected feature being patterned. The options are as follows:

Identical	Enables you to orient the patterned occurrences such that they are oriented in the same way as the first feature selected for patterning.
Direction 1	Enables you to orient the patterned occurrences such that they are the oriented based on the **Direction 1** (*Direction A*) reference path. Orientation of the occurrences is such that the first feature that was selected for patterning maintains its orientation to the 2D tangent vector of the **Direction 1** (*A*) reference path throughout the pattern.

The pattern shown in Figure 14–13 was created by assigning 23 occurrences in **Direction 1** (*A*) and uses the **Curve Length** measurement type. The **Identical** orientation option was used, which maintains the orientation in the same way as the first occurrence relative as it travels along the curve. The resulting pattern does not produce the required results.

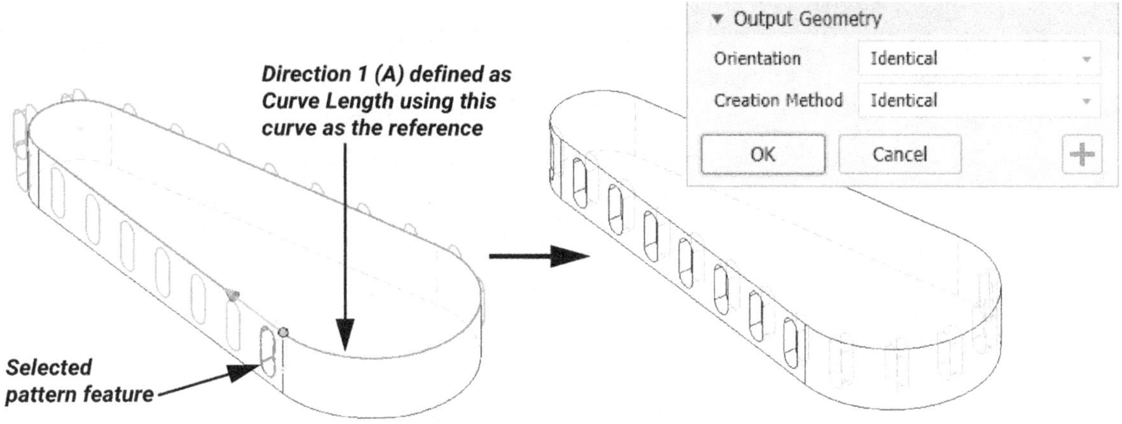

Figure 14–13

The previous pattern was edited. A start point for *Direction A* was defined (as shown in Figure 14–14) and the *Orientation* was set to **Direction 1**. These edits produced the required results.

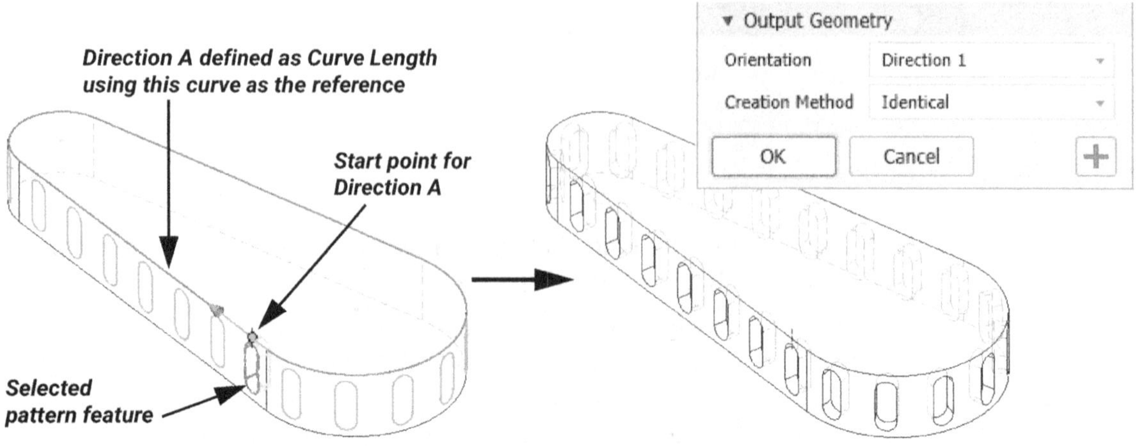

Figure 14–14

Step 7 - Complete the pattern.

Click **OK** to complete the pattern. Alternatively, you can right-click and select **OK (Enter)**.

14.2 Circular Feature Patterns

You can create multiple copies of parts or features on a part by creating a pattern. An example of a circular pattern of holes is shown in Figure 14–15.

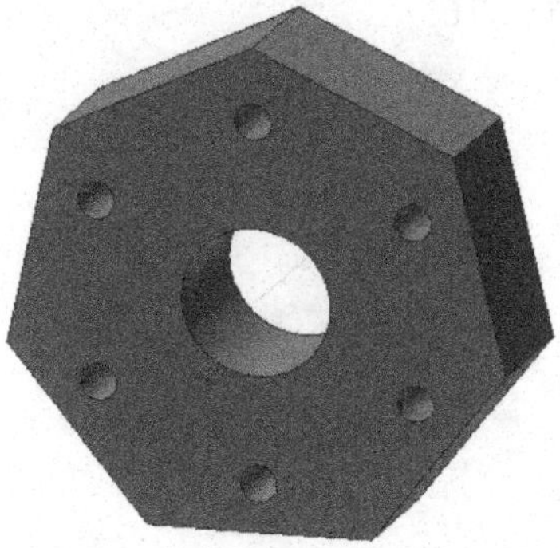

Figure 14–15

Use the following general steps to create a circular pattern:

1. Start the creation of the pattern.
2. Select the object(s) to pattern.
3. Define the orientation options.
4. Define the extents, as required.
5. Define the output geometry, as required.
6. Complete the pattern.

Step 1 - Start the creation of the pattern.

In the *3D Model* tab>*Pattern* panel, click  (Circular Pattern). The *Properties* panel and tool palette open, as shown in Figure 14–16.

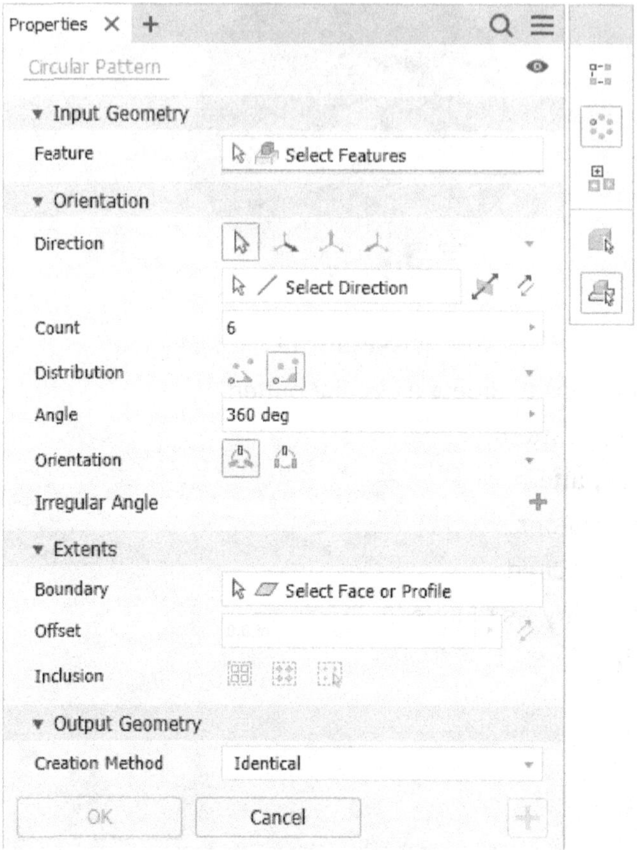

Figure 14–16

Step 2 - Select the object(s) to pattern.

Prior to selecting the object(s) to pattern, use the options in the tool palette to determine the object type that will be selected for patterning:

- Click (Pattern individual features) to create a pattern of individually selected features. This is the default option.
- Click (Pattern a solid) to pattern the entire solid model.

Once the object type is active, ensure that the *Feature* field is active in the *Input Geometry* area and select the appropriate feature(s) or the solid model to pattern. Consider the following:

- Work and surface features can also be included in a pattern.
- Dependent features are not automatically patterned if their parent is selected.
- Dependent features cannot be patterned themselves unless the parent feature is selected.

Step 3 - Define the orientation options.

Define the Direction

To define the reference about which to create the pattern, click (Custom direction) in the *Properties* panel, as shown in Figure 14–17, and select the reference. You can select a cylindrical or conical face or an edge for the pattern axis. You can also conveniently select an axis using the axis options provided in the *Properties* panel as an alternative to selecting from the Model browser. If required, click to reverse the direction of the pattern.

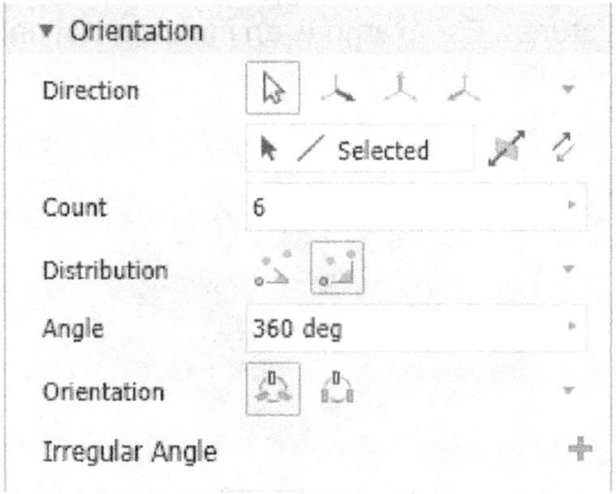

Figure 14–17

Define the Count and Angle of the Pattern

Once objects are selected for patterning and the axis is defined, you can enter values in the *Properties* panel to define the pattern, as shown in Figure 14–18.

- Enter the number of occurrences (including the selected geometry) in the *Count* field.
- Enter the angle between the first and last occurrence in the *Angle* field.

In the example shown in Figure 14–18, a hole is being patterned radially about the larger hole's axis. The values being used are shown in the *Properties* panel.

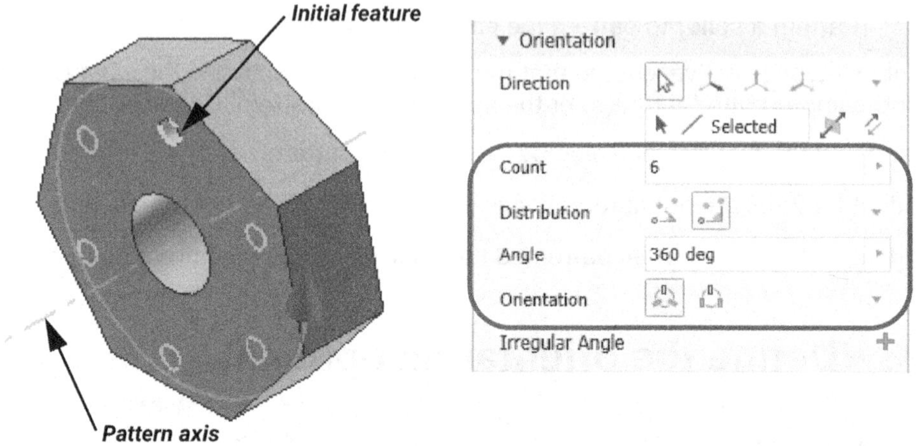

Figure 14–18

Define the Distribution

The *Distribution* option enables you to position the pattered feature in the model. The options are as follows:

-  **(Incremental):** Enables you to use the *Angle* value to incrementally define the spacing between the patterned features. For example, an incremental pattern of 3 occurrences at 90 degrees, as shown in Figure 14–19.

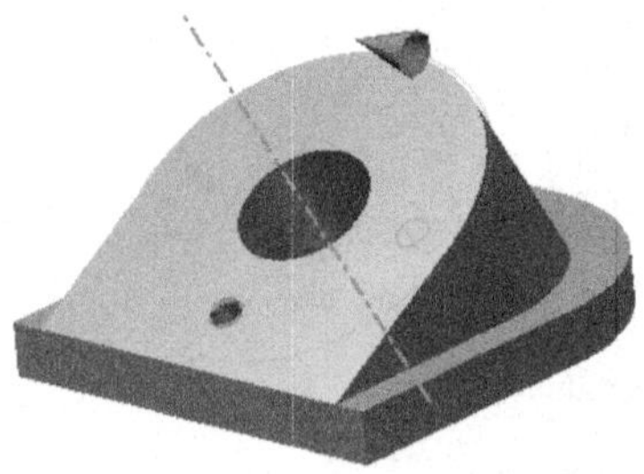

Figure 14–19

- (Fitted): **(Fitted):** Enables you to use the *Angle* value to define the angular range of pattern. The number of occurrences are fit into this value. For example, a fitted pattern of 3 occurrences at 90 degrees, as shown in Figure 14–20.

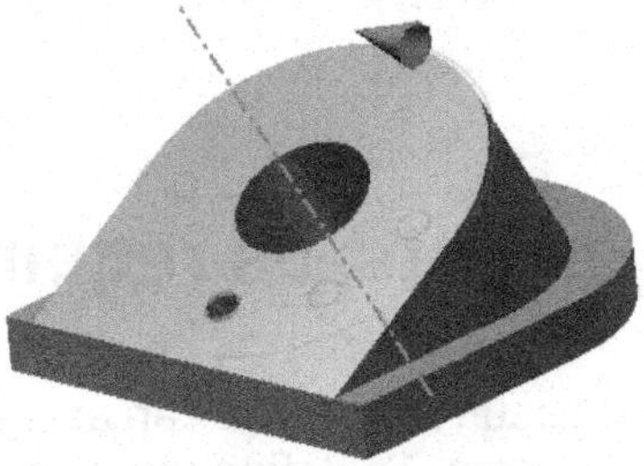

Figure 14–20

Define the Orientation

In the *Orientation* area of the *Properties* panel, select the required pattern orientation.

- Select (Rotational) to ensure that the patterned feature's orientation is rotated, as it extends through the pattern angle.
- Select (Fixed) to ensure that the patterned feature's orientation remains the same as the original feature, as it extends through the pattern angle. When defining a **Fixed** orientation, you can change the default base point, if required.

Figure 14–21 shows examples of both orientation options.

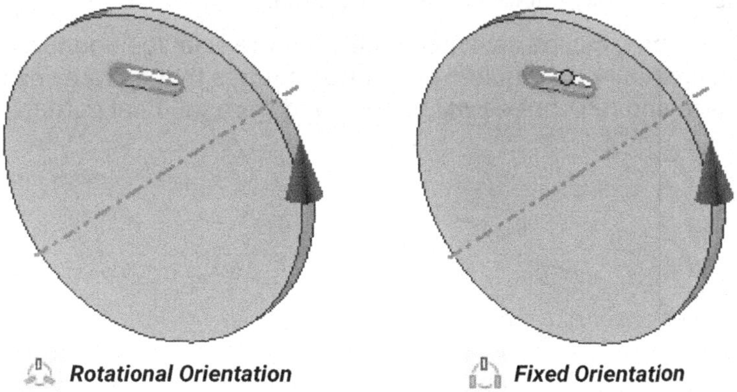

Figure 14–21

Hint: Irregular Angle

The **Irregular Angle** options under *Orientation* helps to give a unique angle to a selected member of the circular pattern. The angle for the rest of the circular pattern will remain dependent on the *Angle* specified under *Orientation*; only the selected member adopts the specified irregular angle.

Step 4 - Define the extents, as required.

To further customize the patterned occurrences, you can assign a customized boundary that will define the extent of the overall pattern. To define the extent of the pattern, in the *Extents* area, select in the *Boundary* field and select a closed boundary. The boundary can be defined by selecting either a sketch or a face. Once selected, the area defined by the boundary displays pink. Select one of the following three options to define whether the patterned instances are included/excluded at the defined boundary. The patterned results using each of these options are shown in Figure 14–22.

- (Include Geometry) includes pattern instances that are fully enclosed by the selected boundary.
- (Include Centroids) includes all pattern instances that have their centroid fully enclosed by the boundary.
- (Include using occurrence base points) includes all pattern instances that have the selected base point fully enclosed by the boundary.

Additionally, an offset value can be assigned relative to the selected boundary. It can be flipped to either side of the boundary, as required. Patterned entities that are previewed in green are included in the pattern and red entities will be removed from the final pattern.

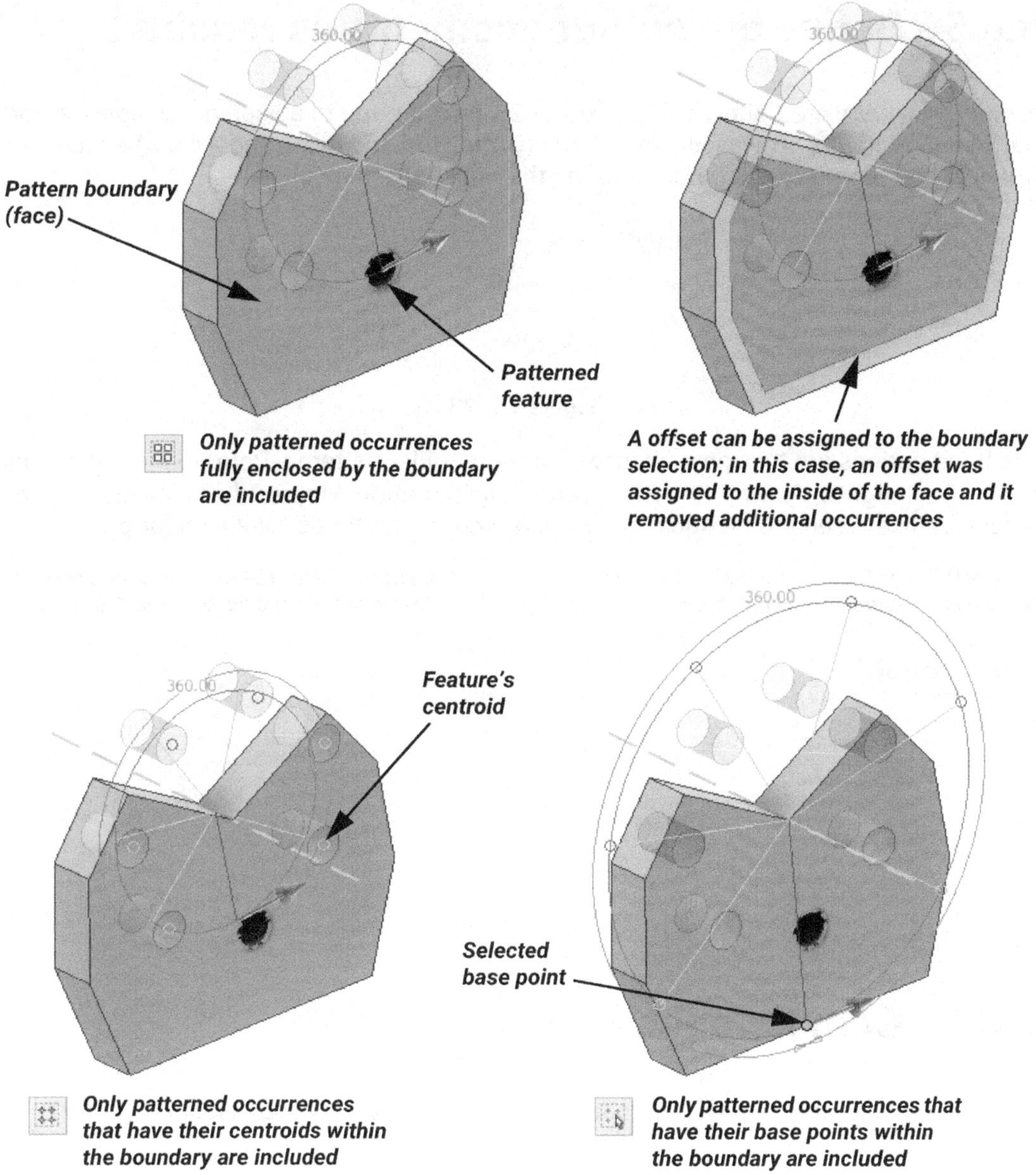
Pattern boundary (face)
Patterned feature
Only patterned occurrences fully enclosed by the boundary are included
A offset can be assigned to the boundary selection; in this case, an offset was assigned to the inside of the face and it removed additional occurrences
Feature's centroid
Selected base point
Only patterned occurrences that have their centroids within the boundary are included
Only patterned occurrences that have their base points within the boundary are included

Figure 14–22

Step 5 - Define the output geometry, as required.

The *Output Geometry* area, shown in Figure 14–23, enables you to assign a *Creation Method* for the patterned geometry. The available options (**Optimized**, **Identical**, and **Adjust**) enable you to control how the geometry is created to refine the final pattern results.

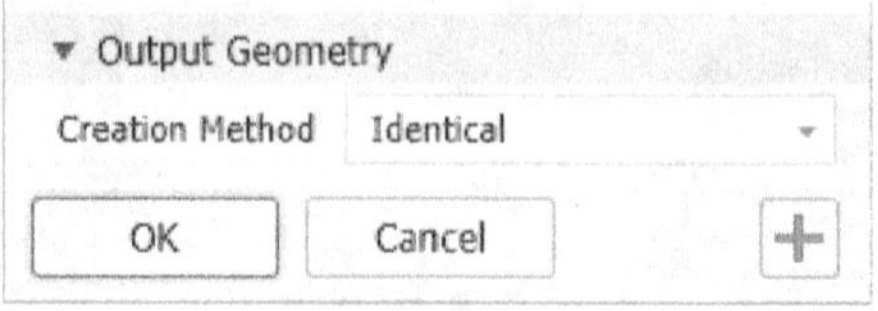

Figure 14–23

- The three options are the same as those for rectangular patterns. Refer to their descriptions in ***14.1 Rectangular Feature Patterns*** for more information. Figure 14–24 illustrates the differences between the **Identical** and **Adjust** creation methods for a circular pattern.

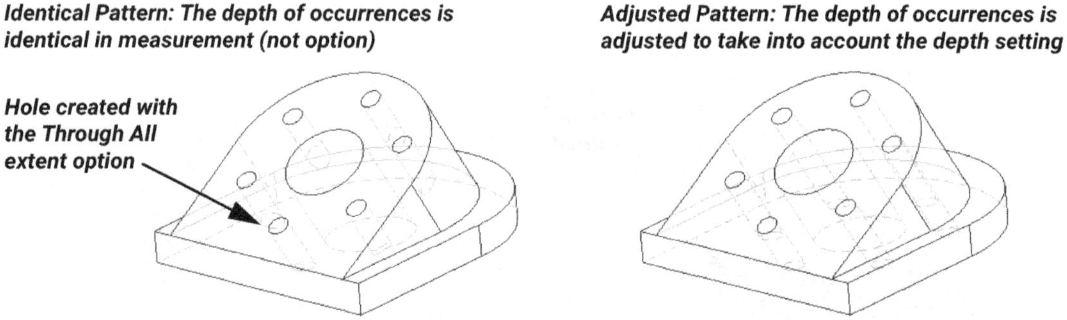

Figure 14–24

Step 6 - Complete the pattern.

Click **OK** to complete the pattern. Alternatively, you can right-click and select **OK (Enter)**.

14.3 Sketch Driven Patterns

You can create multiple copies of parts or features on a part by creating a pattern. Examples of a pattern of slots are shown in Figure 14–25.

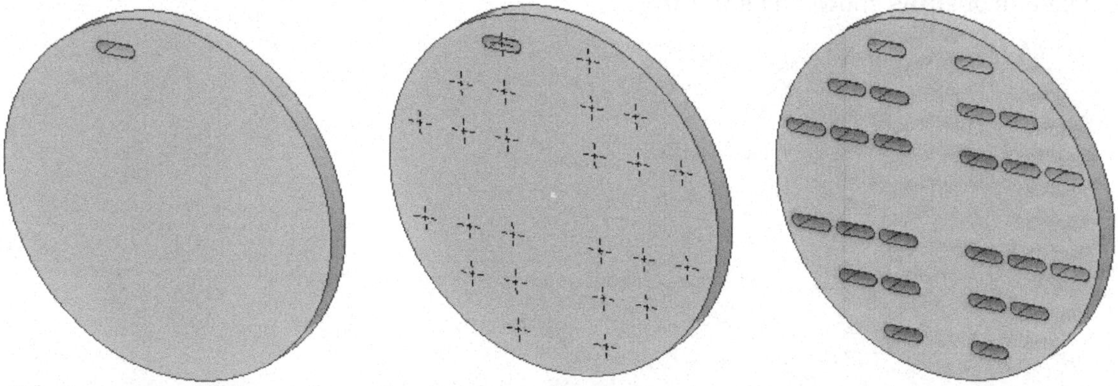

Slot-shaped cut to be patterned on the face of the cylinder

Sketched Points added to a 2D sketch to define pattern placement

Patterned slot-shaped cuts

Figure 14–25

Use the following general steps to create a circular pattern:

1. Start the creation of the pattern.
2. Select the object(s) to pattern.
3. Define the placement.
4. Define the output geometry, as required.
5. Complete the pattern.

Step 1 - Start the creation of the pattern.

In the *3D Model* tab>*Pattern* panel, click (Sketch Driven Pattern). The *Properties* panel and tool palette open, as shown in Figure 14–26.

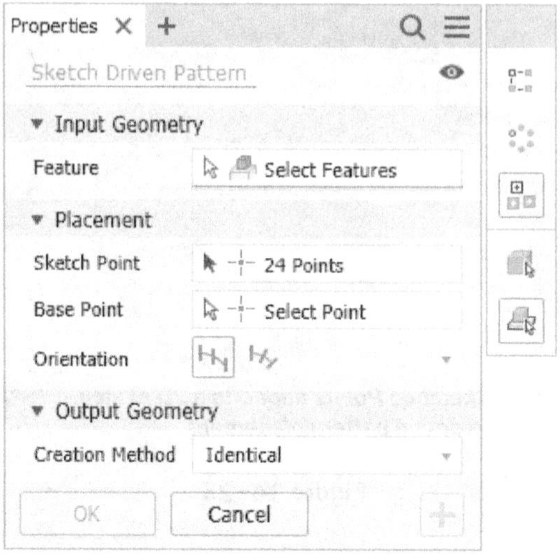

Figure 14–26

Step 2 - Select the object(s) to pattern.

Prior to selecting the object(s) to pattern, use the options in the tool palette to determine the object type that will be selected for patterning:

- Click (Pattern individual features) to create a pattern of individually selected features. This is the default option.
- Click (Pattern a solid) to pattern the entire solid model.

Once the object type is active, ensure that the *Feature* field is active in the *Input Geometry* area and select the appropriate feature(s) or the solid model to pattern. Consider the following:

- Work and surface features can also be included in a pattern.
- Dependent features are not automatically patterned if their parent is selected.
- Dependent features cannot be patterned themselves unless the parent feature is selected.

Step 3 - Define the placement.

Define the Sketch Point

To define the placement of the pattern, you must select sketch points on an existing sketch. The sketch can be a 2D or 3D sketch and must contain sketch points. The sketch points will define the placement of the pattern feature.

> ***Note:*** *If the model has a single displayed sketch, it will automatically be used and the number of points in the sketch will be assigned in the Sketch Point field in the Properties panel.*

Define Base Point

To refine the position of the feature being patterned relative to the sketch points, you can optionally redefine the base point for the pattern. Select in the *Base Point* field in the *Placement* area and select a new point on the feature being patterned. This new point will be used to align the feature with the sketched points for the new pattern.

Define the Orientation

To refine the orientation of the patterned features, you can select from two options: (Fixed) or (Follow Face).

- **Fixed** keeps the pattern occurrence orientation the same as the original feature.
- **Follow Face** enables you to select a reference face on the model to set the occurrence orientation.

Step 4 - Define the output geometry, as required.

The *Output Geometry* area, shown in Figure 14–27, enables you to assign a *Creation Method* for the patterned geometry. The available options (**Optimized**, **Identical**, and **Adjust**) enable you to control how the geometry is created to refine the final pattern results.

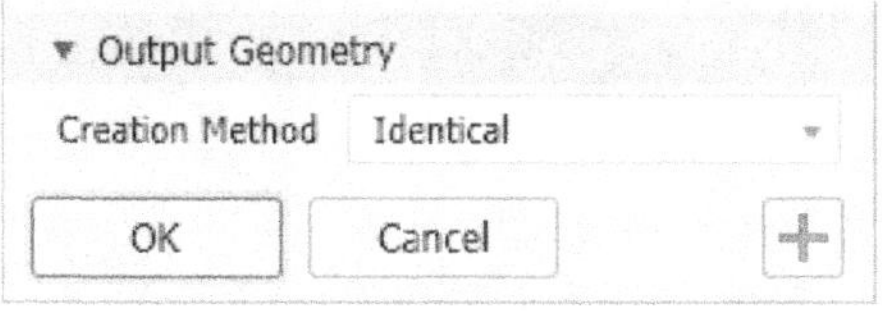

Figure 14–27

These options control how the pattered geometry is calculated and are the same as those for rectangular patterns. Refer to their descriptions in ***14.1 Rectangular Feature Patterns*** for more information.

Step 5 - Complete the pattern.

Click **OK** to complete the pattern. Alternatively, you can right-click and select **OK (Enter)**.

14.4 Mirror Features or Solids

The entire solid model or solid model features can be mirrored about a specified plane. This is useful when designing symmetric parts. The model shown in Figure 14–28 was created by designing one quarter of the model and then mirroring the entire model twice.

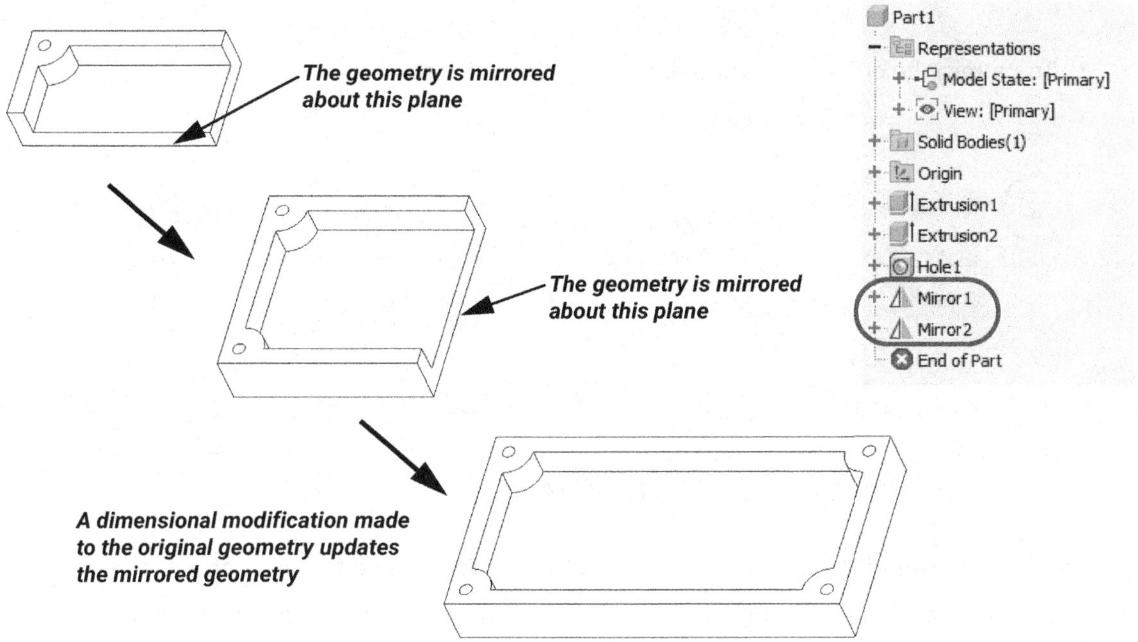

Figure 14–28

How To: Mirror Geometry

1. In the *3D Model* tab>*Pattern* panel, click (Mirror).

2. Define the objects to pattern using the options shown in Figure 14–29. Depending on the option chosen, the dialog box will update as shown.

    - To Mirror individual features in the model, click (Mirror individual features). This is the default option.

    Note: If you mirror a feature that has dependent features, the dependent features are also mirrored.

    - To pattern the entire solid model, click (Mirror a solid).

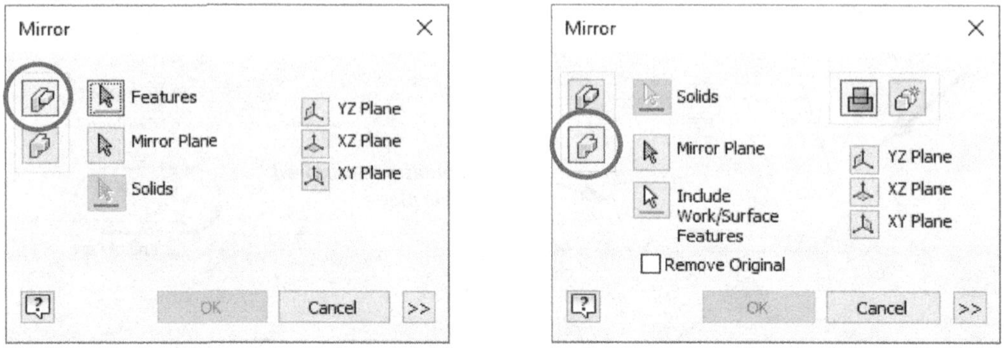

Figure 14–29

3. Click (Mirror Plane) and select a planar face or work plane to mirror about. To select an origin plane, select a plane button (, ,) or select it in the graphics window or Model browser.

    Note: If you had previously renamed the default origin planes in your model, the Mirror dialog box will reflect these names adjacent to the default mirror plane buttons.

4. Depending on whether you are mirroring features or a solid, define the following options:

    - When mirroring a feature in a model that has multiple bodies, activate the **Solids** option and select which body the mirrored feature should be mirrored to.
    - When mirroring a solid, you can select work and surface features to include, and specify if the new mirrored solid will be joined to the existing body () or be created as a new one ().

5. Click **OK** to complete the mirroring process once the mirrored part has been defined. Alternatively, you can right-click and select **OK (Enter)**.

    Note: Fillet features can be mirrored without mirroring their parent feature.

14.5 Manipulating Patterns

Suppress Patterns

To suppress a pattern, right-click on the pattern in the Model browser and select **Suppress Features**. To suppress individual pattern features, expand the pattern feature in the Model browser, right-click on the occurrence you want to suppress, and select **Suppress**, as shown in Figure 14–30.

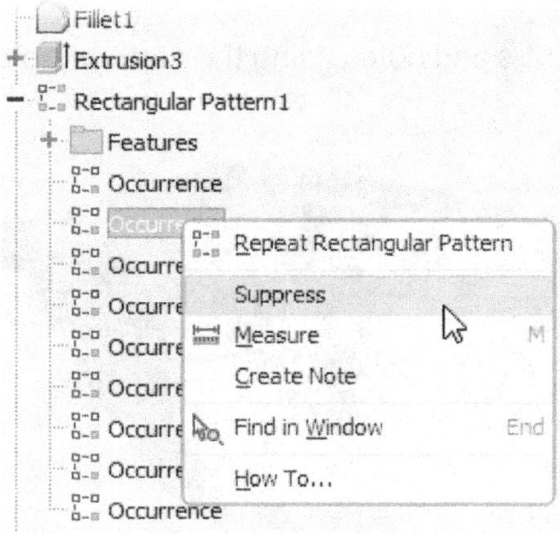

Figure 14–30

- The suppressed occurrence displays in the Model browser with a line across it. To display this occurrence again, right-click on it and select **Suppress** again.
- You cannot suppress the first occurrence (original feature) of the pattern.

*Note: As an alternative to using the **Suppress** option, consider using a boundary during the creation of rectangular and circular feature patterns. This can be used to prevent any unnecessary occurrences from initially being created. For more information on boundaries, refer to **14.1 Rectangular Feature Patterns** and **14.2 Circular Feature Patterns**.*

Edit Pattern

You can edit patterns and mirrored features at any time by right-clicking on the pattern or mirrored feature in the Model browser and selecting **Edit Feature**.

Delete Patterns

You can delete patterns and mirrored features at any time by right-clicking on the pattern or mirrored feature in the Model browser and selecting **Delete**. All occurrences of the pattern or mirrored feature are deleted except for the original occurrence.

Practice 14a
Pattern Features

Practice Objectives

- Create a rectangular pattern of features that translate along a single direction.
- Create a circular pattern of features that rotate about a selected axis.
- Create a rectangular pattern driven by a curve.

In this practice, you will pattern ribs and holes using the pattern tools to create model geometry, as shown in Figure 14–31.

Figure 14–31

Task 1: Open a part file.

1. Open **Air-Box.ipt**. The model displays as shown in Figure 14–32.

Figure 14–32

Task 2: Create a rectangular pattern.

1. In the *Pattern* panel, click (Rectangular Pattern). The *Properties* panel and tool palette open, as shown in Figure 14–33.

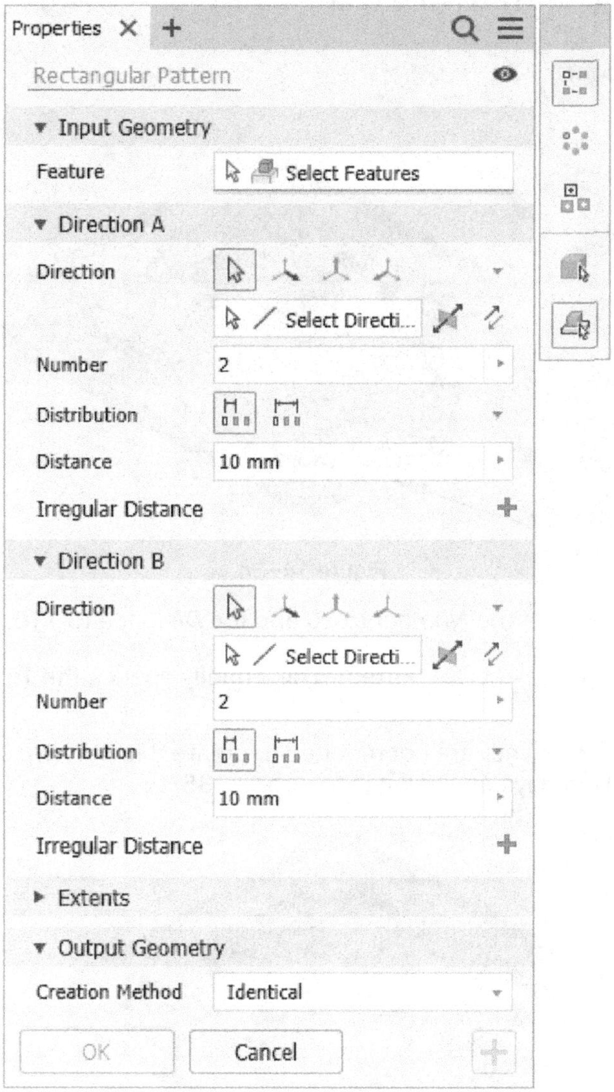

Figure 14–33

2. Verify that (Features) is toggled on in the tool palette. Select **Rib1** and **Fillet4** in the Model browser.

3. In the *Direction A* area, ensure that the (Custom Direction) option is selected and select the **YZ Plane** in the Model browser. The pattern previews as shown in Figure 14–34. If required, change the pattern direction by clicking .

   Note: Alternatively, you can define the pattern direction by selecting an origin axis (for example, (X Axis)) in the Direction field.

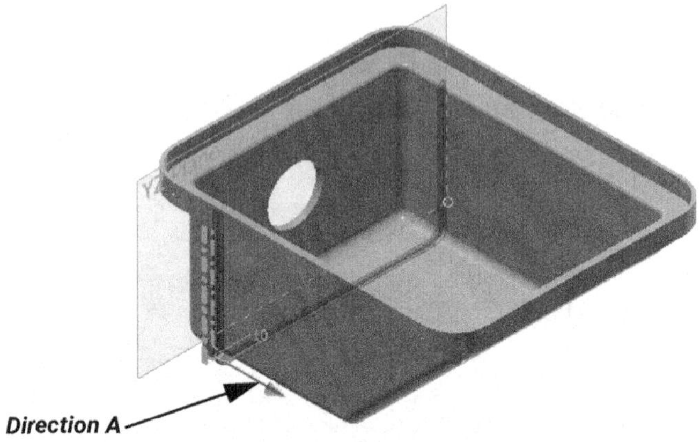

Figure 14–34

4. In the *Direction A* area, set the *Number* to **10** and the *Distance* to **110**.
5. In the *Distribution* field, select (Fitted). This equally spaces the 10 occurrences over the 110 length.
6. A second direction or extents are not required to create this pattern. Click **OK** to apply the pattern. The model displays as shown in Figure 14–35.

Figure 14–35

Task 3: Create a circular pattern.

1. In the *Pattern* panel, click (Circular Pattern). The *Properties* panel opens, as shown in Figure 14–36.

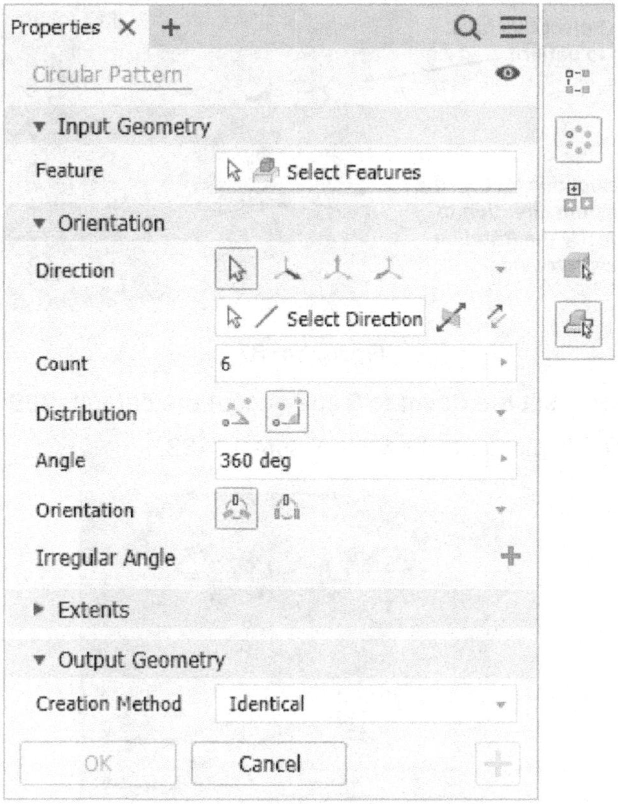

Figure 14–36

2. Verify that (Features) is toggled on in the tool palette. Select the hole shown in Figure 14–37.
3. In the *Direction A* area, ensure that the (Custom Direction) option is selected and select the central hole face for the axis, as shown in Figure 14–37.

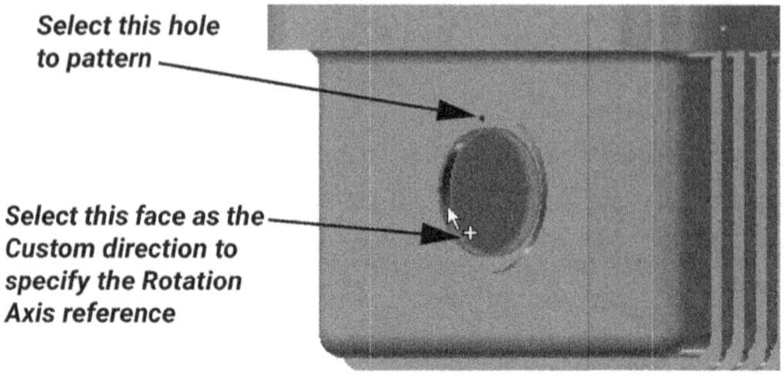

Figure 14–37

4. In the *Direction A* area, set the *Count* to **8** and accept the default (**360deg**) in the *Angle* field.
5. Click **OK**. The model displays as shown in Figure 14–38.

Figure 14–38

Task 4: Create a second rectangular pattern driven by a curve.

In this task, you will create a rectangular pattern along the outside lip of the model, as shown in Figure 14–39. To accomplish this pattern a point and hole have been created for you, but you will create a curve that will be used to drive the path of the patterned hole.

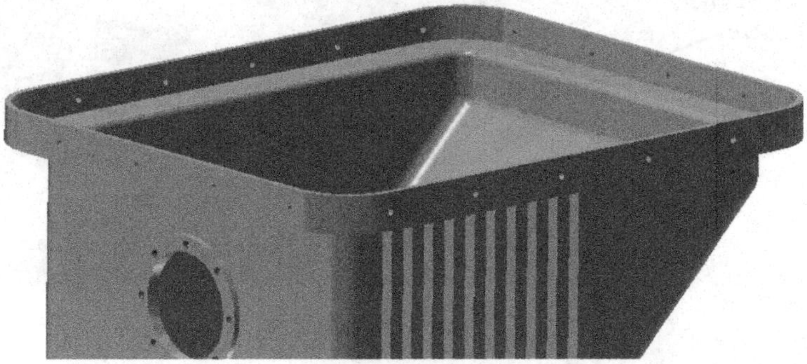

Figure 14–39

1. Create a sketch and select the top edge of the model as the sketch plane, as shown in Figure 14–40. Project the outside edges that intersect this plane onto the sketch plane. Finish the sketch.

Figure 14–40

2. In the *Pattern* panel, click (Rectangular Pattern). The *Properties* panel and tool palette open.

3. Verify that (Features) is toggled on in the tool palette. Select the hole shown in Figure 14–41.

Figure 14–41

4. In the *Direction A* area, click (Custom Direction) and select the outer curve that was created in the sketch. Ensure that the entire curve around the model is selected, not just a single entity.

5. In the *Direction A* area, set the *Number* to **20**. The preview of the holes reveal an incorrect pattern.

6. Select (Fitted) in the *Distribution* field and select (Curve Length) for specifying *Distance*, as shown in Figure 14–42. The preview of the holes still reveals an incorrect pattern. Customization of the additional options is required.

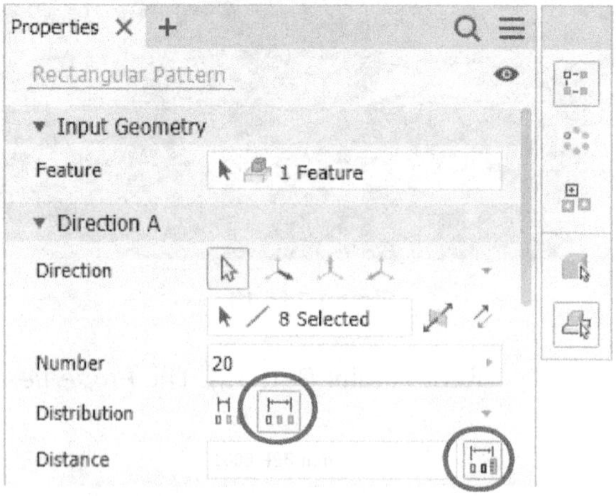

Figure 14–42

7. In the *Direction A* area, select in the *Start Point* field, as shown in Figure 14–43, to define the start point of the path.

   Note: *It is recommended that you place the first occurrence on the start point of the path, as was done.*

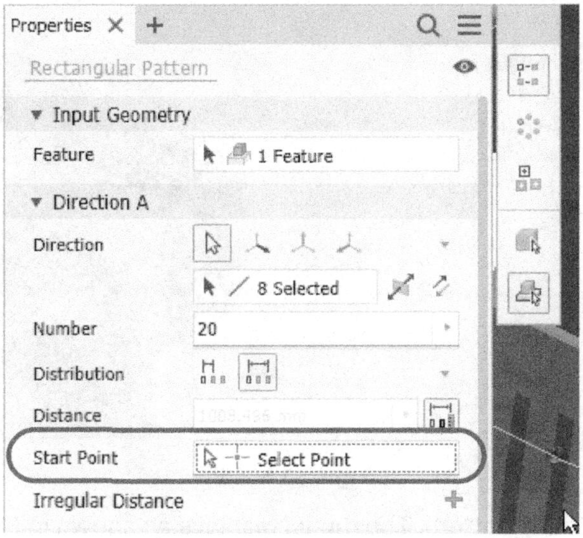

Figure 14–43

8. Select the vertex on the sketched curve, as shown in Figure 14–44, as the reference for the *Start Point*. This sets the start point for the first patterned occurrence.

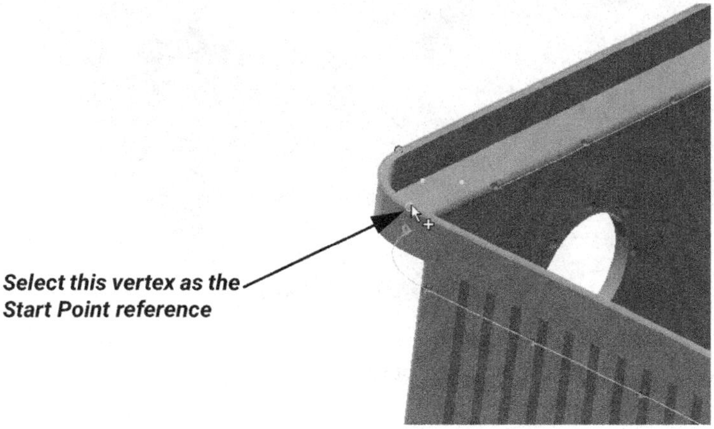

Figure 14–44

9. In the *Output Geometry* area at the bottom of the *Properties* panel, select **Direction 1** for the *Orientation*, as shown in Figure 14–45, to ensure that the orientation of the patterned holes follows the tangent vector of the curve that was selected as the *Direction A* reference.

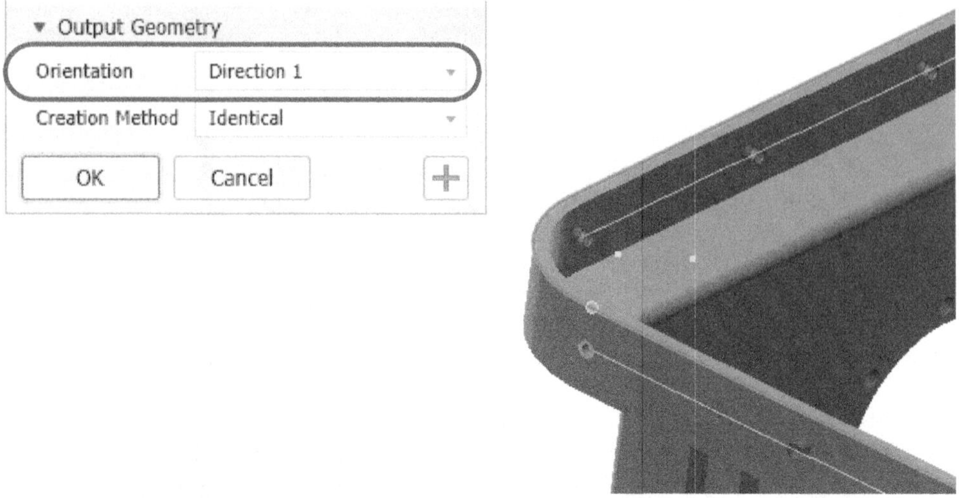

Figure 14–45

10. Click **OK** to complete the pattern. The model displays as shown in Figure 14–46.

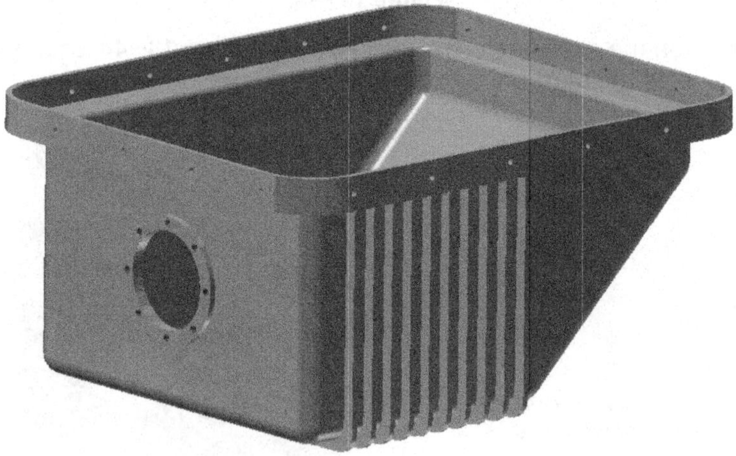

Figure 14–46

Task 5: Remove pattern occurences.

In this task, you will learn to suppress individual occurrences that are created using the Model browser and will also learn how to incorporate a defined boundary when creating a pattern.

1. In the Model browser, expand the **Rectangular Pattern3** node. All 20 occurrences that were created for the pattern are listed.
2. Hover over each feature occurrence in the list and note how the associated patterned hole feature highlights in the model.
3. Locate one of the patterned holes that are located on one of the rounded corners. Right-click on this hole in the Model browser and select **Suppress**. Note how the hole is removed from the model geometry; however, the occurrence remains in the Model browser list and is displayed in gray strikethrough font.
4. Right-click on the suppressed occurrence in the Model browser a second time and select **Suppress** to clear its suppression. The patterned hole is displayed again in the model geometry.

Suppressing individual occurrences is one method to remove patterned instances from the geometry; however, it does require you to scan the list of occurrences and locate and suppress each one individually. Alternatively, you can define a boundary. With a boundary defined, only occurrences that lie within the boundary will be included during pattern creation.

5. Before continuing, ensure that all occurrences of the patterned holes are displayed (not suppressed) by reviewing the occurrence list in the Model browser. There should be 20 holes displayed.
6. In the Model browser, right-click on the **Boundary** sketch and select **Visibility** to display it in the model. The sketched boundary displays as shown in Figure 14–47. This boundary has been sketched for you using the top face of the model geometry as the sketch plane. The design intent is that patterned holes are required if they lie within the closed boundary.

Figure 14–47

7. Edit **Rectangular Pattern3** to open the *Properties* panel.

8. In the *Extents* area of the *Properties* panel, select in the *Boundary* field, as shown in Figure 14–48, and select the boundary sketch in the graphics window. Once selected, the enclosed area displays pink.

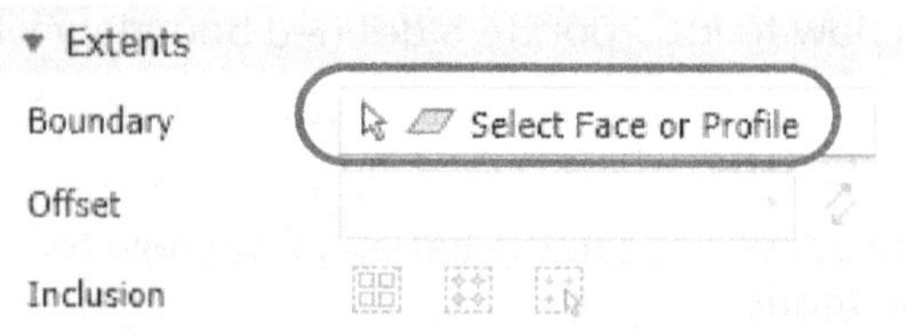

Figure 14–48

9. Review the model geometry and note that holes that lie outside the selected boundary display red, as shown in Figure 14–49. This means that these holes will not be generated by the pattern.

Figure 14–49

10. In the *Properties* panel, click **OK** to complete the change to the pattern.
11. In the Model bowser, expand the **Rectangular Pattern3** node. Note that instead of 20 occurrences, there are now only 17 occurrences listed. Three occurrences were removed because they would have been created outside the boundary.

    Note: *Although a boundary was used, you can still suppress individual occurrences using the Model browser, if necessary. Additionally, if you were to modify the sketched boundary, the pattern will update accordingly if the change removes additional occurrences.*

12. Save the model and close the window.

End of practice

Practice 14b
Mirror a Model

Practice Objectives

- Mirror select features to create required geometry.
- Mirror a solid part to duplicate all of its geometry.

In this practice, you will be provided with the model shown on the left in Figure 14–50. Using mirroring techniques you will create the model shown on the right.

Figure 14–50

Task 1: Open a part file and mirror features.

1. Open **stand.ipt**.
2. In the *Pattern* panel, click (Mirror).
3. In the Model browser, select **Extrusion4** and **Fillet5**.
4. Click (Mirror Plane) and select **Work Plane1** as the mirror plane reference.
5. Click **OK** to mirror the features. The model displays as shown in Figure 14–51.

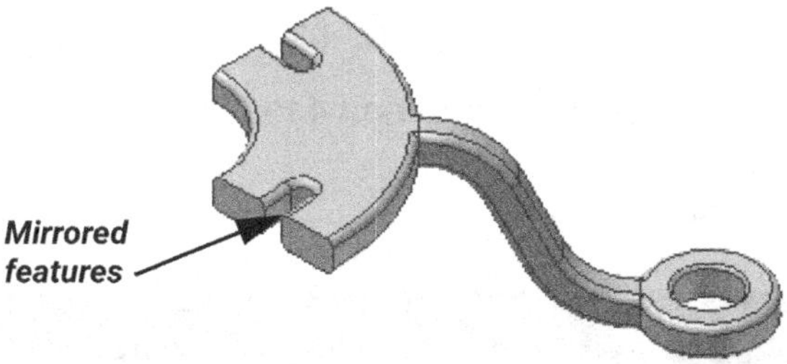

Figure 14–51

Task 2: Mirror the part.

1. In the *Pattern* panel, click (Mirror). The *Mirror* dialog box opens.
2. Click (Mirror solids) to mirror the entire part. The solid model highlights in the graphics window.
3. Click (Mirror Plane) and select the face indicated in Figure 14–52 to mirror the model about.

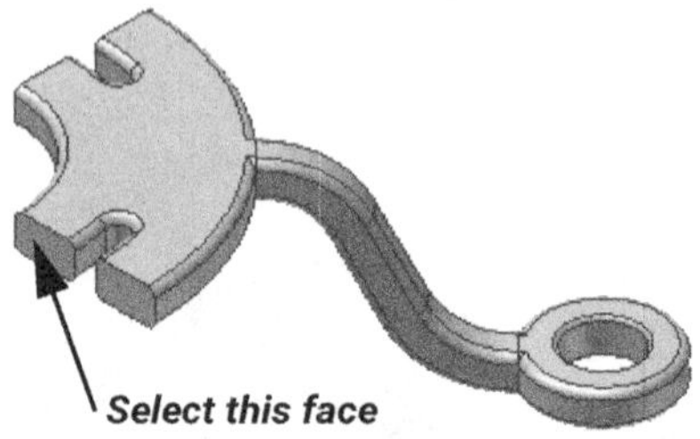

Figure 14–52

4. Click **OK** to mirror the model. The model displayes as shown on the left of Figure 14–53.
5. Complete the part by creating another mirror feature, as shown in Figure 14–53.

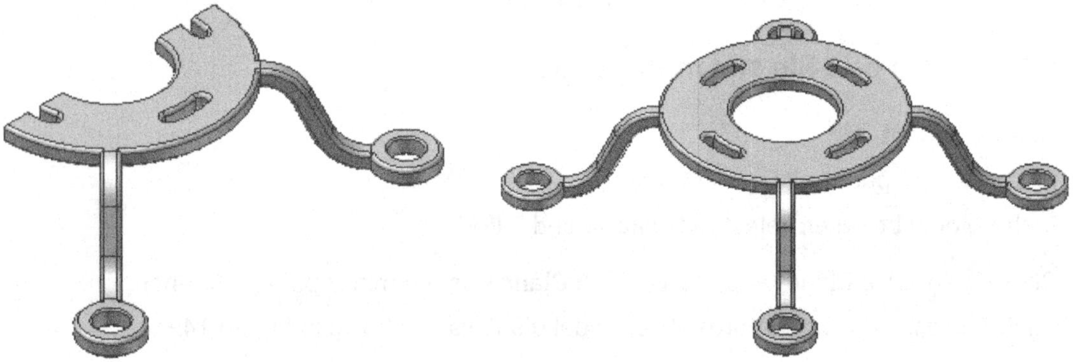

Figure 14–53

6. Modify the *30* diameter dimension in **Extrusion 4** to **60**. Update the model and note that all mirrors features update.
7. Save the part and close the window.

End of practice

Practice 14c
Mirror Features

Practice Objectives

- Mirror features in a model to create the required geometry.
- Edit parent features in the model and ensure that all mirrored geometry updates as expected.

In this practice, you will mirror and edit features in the model shown on the left in Figure 14–54. The completed model displays as shown on the right.

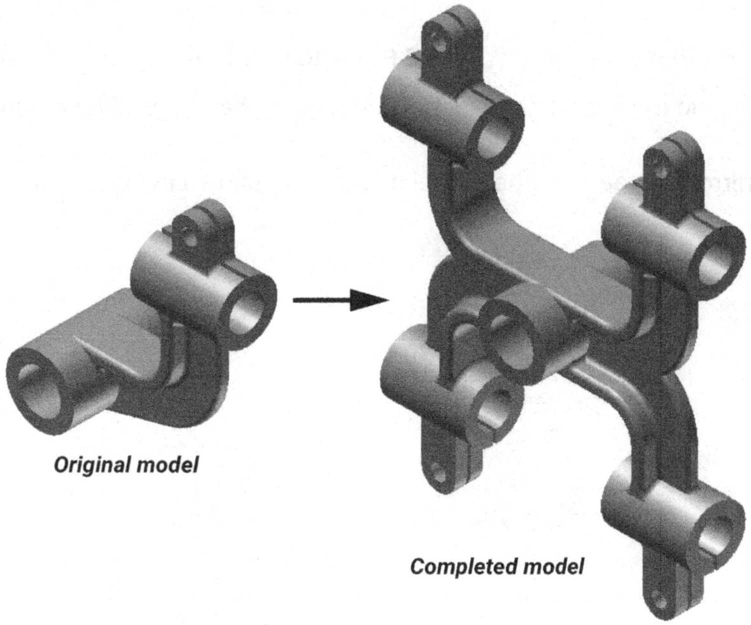

Figure 14–54

Task 1: Open a part file and mirror features.

1. Open **Brace.ipt**.
2. In the *Pattern* panel, click (Mirror). Ensure that you are mirroring individual features and not the solid.

3. Select all of the solid features shown in Figure 14–55 using either the graphics window or the Model browser. Do not include **Extrusion1** in the mirror or the work features.

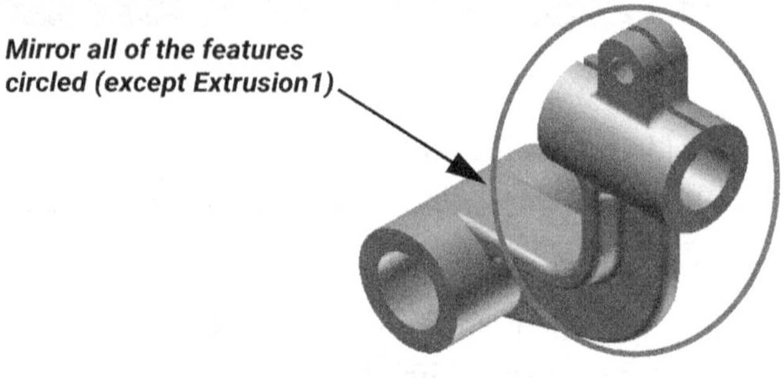

Figure 14–55

4. Click (Mirror Plane) and select the **YZ Plane** to mirror the features about. You can select this plane in the Model browser or by selecting the (YZ Plane) directly in the dialog box.
5. Click **OK** to mirror the feature. The model displays as shown in Figure 14–56.

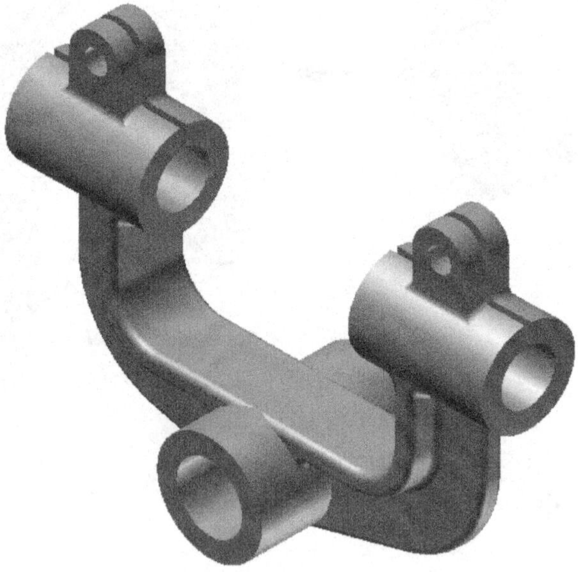

Figure 14–56

6. Mirror the same features and the Mirror instance about the XZ Plane. Note that by selecting the **Mirror** feature as the feature to be mirrored, all parent features are also automatically selected. The mirrored model displays as shown on the left of Figure 14–57.
7. Modify the height dimension on **Extrusion4** from *1.5 in* to **2 in** and update the model. The model displays as shown on the right of Figure 14–57. Both the original feature and its mirrored instances update.

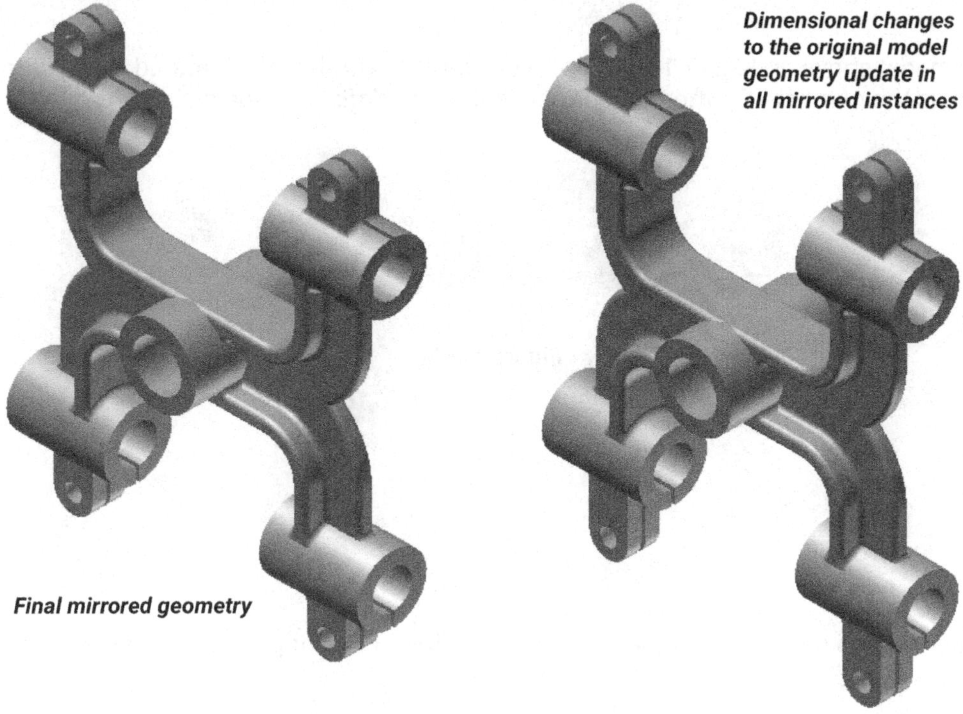

Figure 14–57

8. Save the model and close the window.

End of practice

Chapter Review Questions

1. The direction references selected to create a rectangular feature pattern must be linear.
   a. True
   b. False

2. The model shown in Figure 14–58 has a pattern of extruded cuts created in one direction. What is the number of pattern occurrences that are defined in the dialog box?

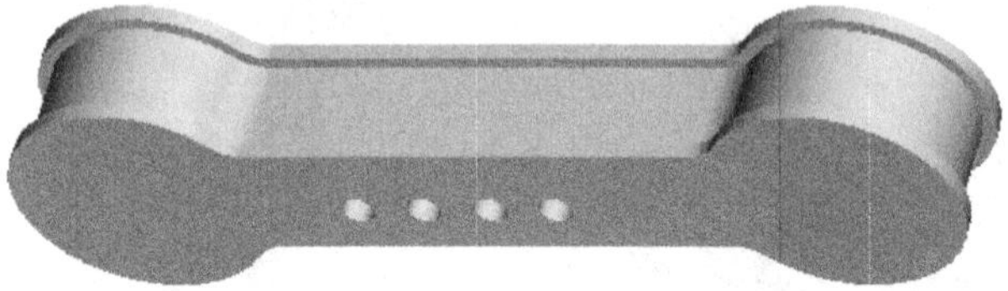

Figure 14–58

   a. 1
   b. 2
   c. 3
   d. 4

3. Which entities can be used as the rotation axis for a circular pattern? (Select all that apply.)
   a. Work plane
   b. Edge
   c. Work axis
   d. Cylindrical face

4. What should you do if the preview of your rectangular pattern is in the wrong direction along a selected path? (Select all that apply.)
   a. Select a new direction reference that is in the correct direction.
   b. Click the **Flip** direction icon in the *Properties* panel to change the direction.
   c. Enter a negative value as the *Distance* value.
   d. Expand the additional options at the bottom of the dialog box and change the *Creation Method*.

5. The sketch that defines the pattern points in a sketch driven pattern must be created after the **Sketch Driven Pattern** command is initiated.

a. True

b. False

6. Which of the following statements is true for suppressing specific occurrences from within a pattern?

a. You can suppress the first occurrence of the pattern (original).

b. You can suppress all but the first occurrence of the pattern.

c. You can select individual occurrences in the pattern for deletion.

d. You can use the **Delete** command to delete the first occurrence in the model.

7. Which of the following are valid characteristics of patterned features when using an **Identical** creation method, as shown in Figure 14–59? (Select all that apply.)

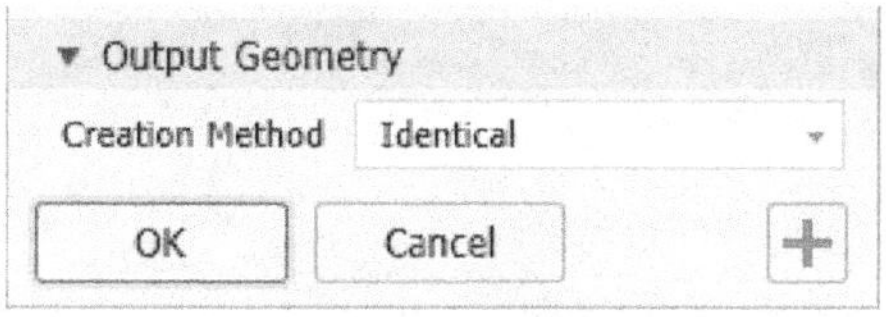

Figure 14–59

a. The created features cannot lie on different surfaces.

b. The created features can break edges of the part.

c. The created features cannot intersect with each other.

d. Feature depth of all occurrences is the same value as the pattern leader (regardless of the depth option set for the feature).

8. Which work feature can be used as a reference for mirroring features?

a. Work plane

b. Work point

c. Work axis

9. You can mirror an entire solid or individual features in a model.

a. True

b. False

Command Summary

Button	Command	Location
	**Circular Pattern (feature)**	• **Ribbon:** *3D Model* tab>*Pattern* panel
N/A	**Delete (entire pattern)**	• **Context Menu**: In Model browser
	**Mirror (feature)**	• **Ribbon:** *3D Model* tab>*Pattern* panel
	**Rectangular Pattern (feature)**	• **Ribbon:** *3D Model* tab>*Pattern* panel
	**Sketch Driven Pattern (feature)**	• **Ribbon:** *3D Model* tab>*Pattern* panel
N/A	**Suppress (pattern instance)**	• **Context Menu:** In Model browser
N/A	**Suppress Feature (pattern)**	• **Context Menu:** In Model browser

Chapter 15

Feature Relationships

Feature relationships are defined as a dependency between features. They are established as you add each additional feature to the model. If the parent feature is modified or deleted, the child features are affected. Learning how to use feature relationships to your advantage and how to make changes to unwanted relationships is a valuable tool in designing models.

Learning Objectives

- Understand the parent/child relationships that are established when creating pick and place features.
- Understand the parent/child relationships that are established when creating sketched features.
- Use the Model browser and *Parameters* dialog box to recognize the possible relationships between features in the model.
- Use editing tools to change an existing parent/child relationship in a model.

15.1 Establishing Feature Relationships

Feature relationships are the result of a dependency between features. The independent feature is referred to as the parent and the dependent feature is called the child. When such a dependency exists, the parent feature is used to place or locate the child feature. Feature relationships can be created when pick and place or sketched features are used.

Pick and Place Features

For pick and place features (e.g., holes, fillets, chamfers) you are only required to select placement references to locate a feature. The placement references establish feature relationships between the new feature and the existing features that were used for placement.

- In Figure 15–1, the hole shown on the right was created by referencing the indicated face and the center of the cylindrical extrusion. A feature relationship has now been established between the hole (child) an the cylindrical extrusion (parent).

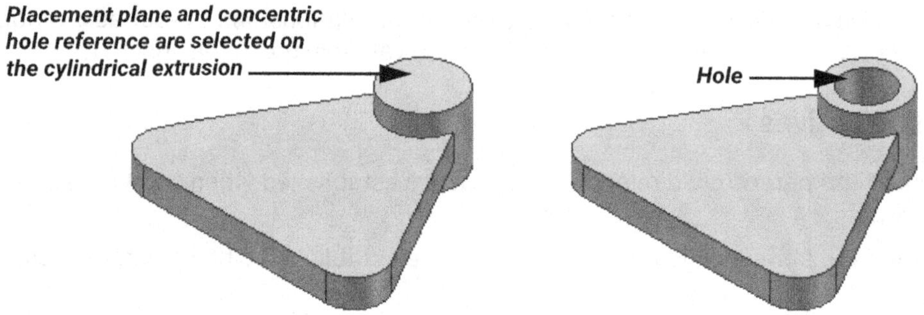

Figure 15–1

- In Figure 15–2, the fillet shown on the right was created by referencing the edge shown. The edge reference establishes a feature relationship with the cylindrical extrusion. A feature relationship has now been established between the fillet (child) an the cylindrical extrusion (parent).

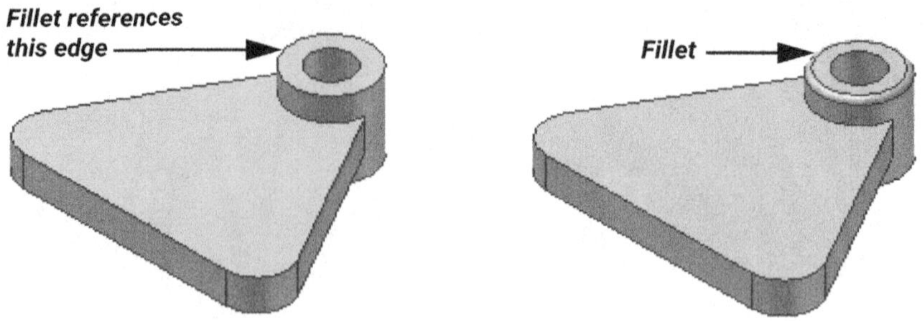

Figure 15–2

- In Figure 15–3, the chamfer shown on the right was created by referencing the edge shown. The edge reference establishes a feature relationship with the cylindrical extrusion. A feature relationship has now been established between the chamfer (child) an the cylindrical extrusion (parent).

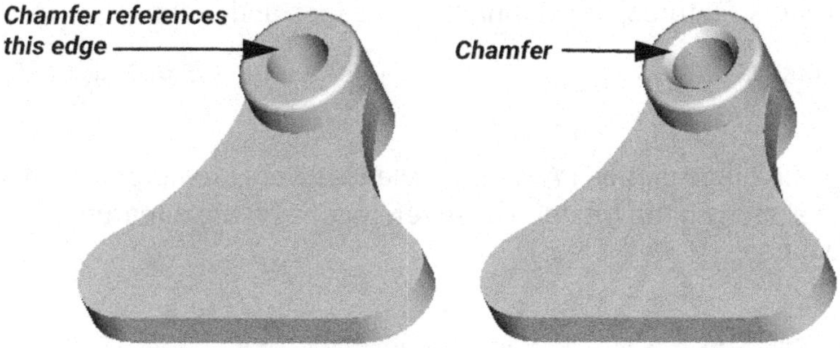

Figure 15–3

Sketched Features

The process of creating a sketched feature results in the creation of feature relationships when the sketch plane and sketch references are selected. Additionally, references might be required for using some of the available depth options.

Sketch Planes

The sketch plane defines a planar reference on which a 2D section is sketched. The sketch plane is then established as a parent of the 2D sketch and any features that are subsequently created from that sketch.

- In Figure 15–4, the sketch plane for a new sketched feature is a face belonging to an extrusion. This makes the new sketch and any feature created from the sketch a child of the extrusion.

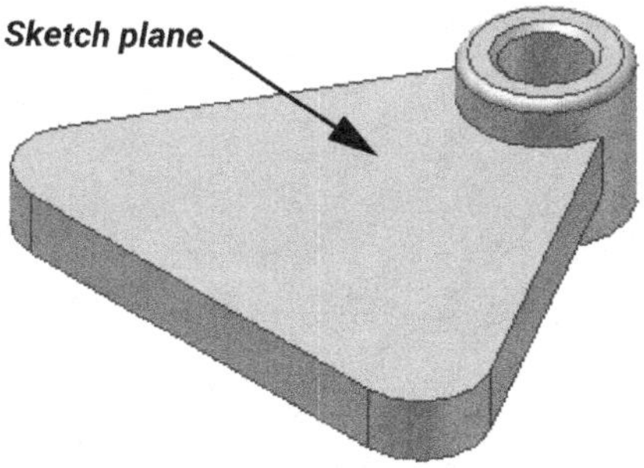

Figure 15–4

Sketching References

Sketching references are used to locate sketched geometry. When you select sketching references, feature relationships are established. The sketched geometry is located with respect to these entities using dimensions and constraints. Sketching references can be projected origin or work features, or existing model edges and faces.

> ***Note:*** *Origin work features provide robust sketching references because they can never be moved or deleted.*

- In Figure 15–5, the origin planes (YZ and XZ Planes) were projected onto the sketch plane for locating the sketch on the model. These references create a feature relationship with the origin plane features.

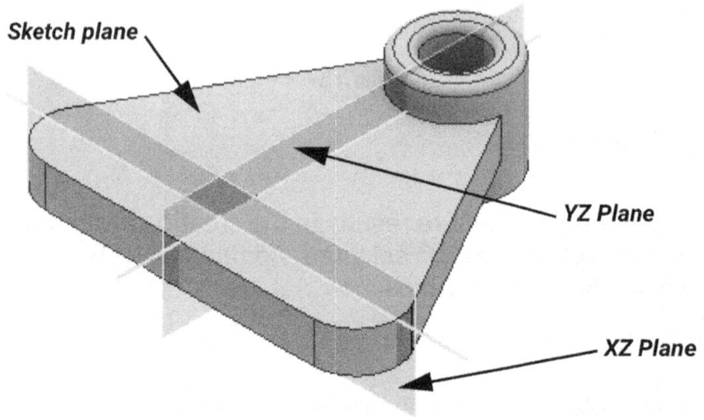

Figure 15–5

- In Figure 15–6, the cut was located relative to the edge of the square extrusion by assigning a dimension and vertical constraint. The cut is a child of the extrusion and remains in alignment. Additionally, the bottom edge of the base feature was also selected to locate the cut so the base feature is also a parent.

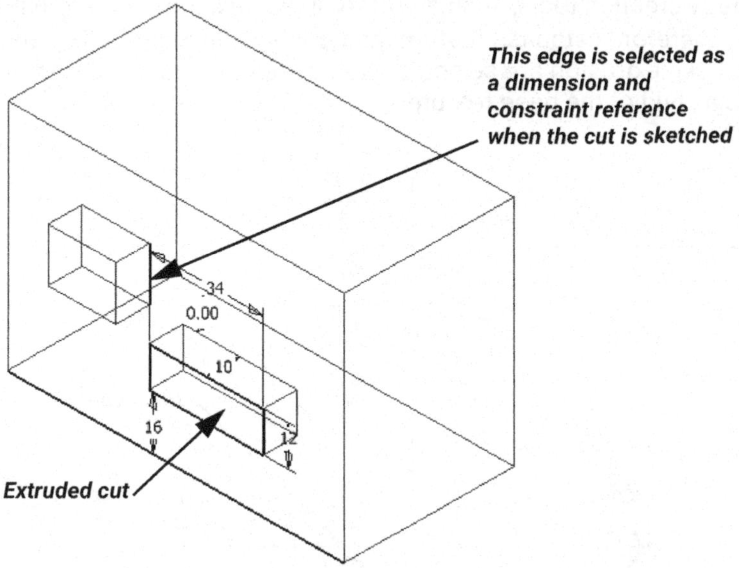

Figure 15–6

- In Figure 15–7, the rectangular sketch was located by dimensioning it to the hole and the chamfer. The features created with this sketch are now a child of both the hole and the chamfer.

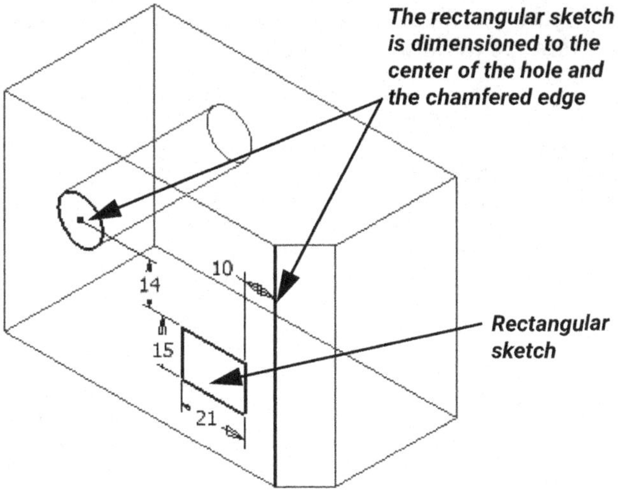

Figure 15–7

Note: *It is not recommended that you dimension a feature to another feature that might change later in the design (e.g., fillets or chamfers). If the reference feature is changed or deleted, the new feature might no longer be positioned correctly, or it might fail because it has lost its reference.*

- Certain geometry creation tools, such as offsetting an existing edge, create an implicit alignment and therefore establish feature relationships. In Figure 15–8, the entities at the bottom of the base extrusion are selected as edge references for offsetting. As a result, the new feature is a child of the base feature.

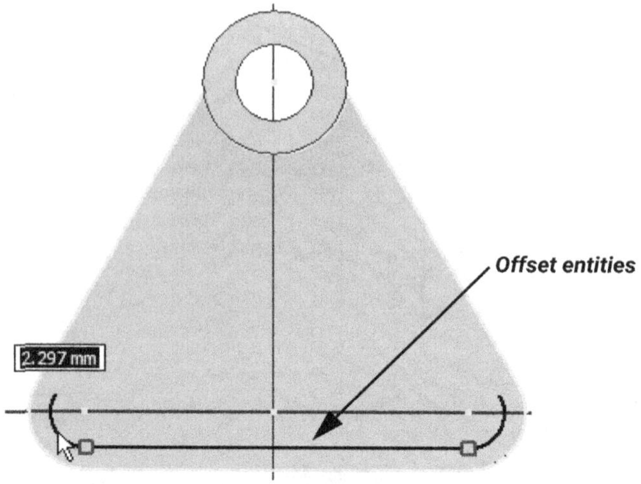

Figure 15–8

Depth Options

Some *From* and *Distance* options establish feature relationships. The (To) and (To Next) options shown in Figure 15–9 establish feature relationships because a plane or face must be selected as a reference to define the depth.

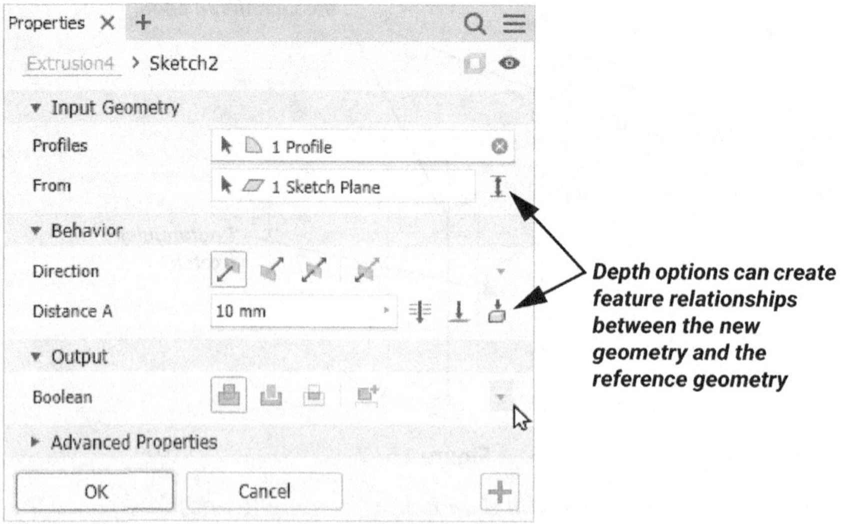

Figure 15–9

15.2 Controlling Feature Relationships

Feature relationships can make models more robust and powerful. Use the following tips to control feature relationships:

- Use the origin features. Since they are never deleted, origin features are useful as sketch planes and sketching references. This establishes the origin feature, rather than a geometry feature, as parents of future features.
- Consider a face carefully before selecting it as a sketch plane. Is it the best selection as a parent for this feature?
- When in the Sketch environment, select references and project from the model in a 3D orientation to ensure that you are selecting the correct references.
- When in the Sketch environment, consider using and offsetting edges, as well as sketching concentric arcs and circles to establish relationships.
- Carefully consider the references before using the **To Next**, **To**, or **Between** depth options. Is this reference the best selection as a parent for this feature?
- Once a pick and place or sketched feature has been created, you can also establish a feature relationship using equations.

15.3 Investigating Feature Relationships

In many cases, you might be required to continue someone else's design or make modifications to a completed model. In such cases, it is important to know how to investigate the model to help understand the existing design and feature relationships. You can use the Model browser and *Parameters* dialog box to accomplish this.

Model Browser

The Model browser displays all of the features in the model. By reviewing the Model browser, you can understand the hierarchy of the model and understand which features can possibly reference others.

To provide a better overview of the relationships between features, you can right-click on a feature name in the Model browser and select **Relationships**. The *Relationships* dialog box displays, similar to that shown in Figure 15–10. This dialog box can quickly reveal the relationships between features and enable you to make changes, if required.

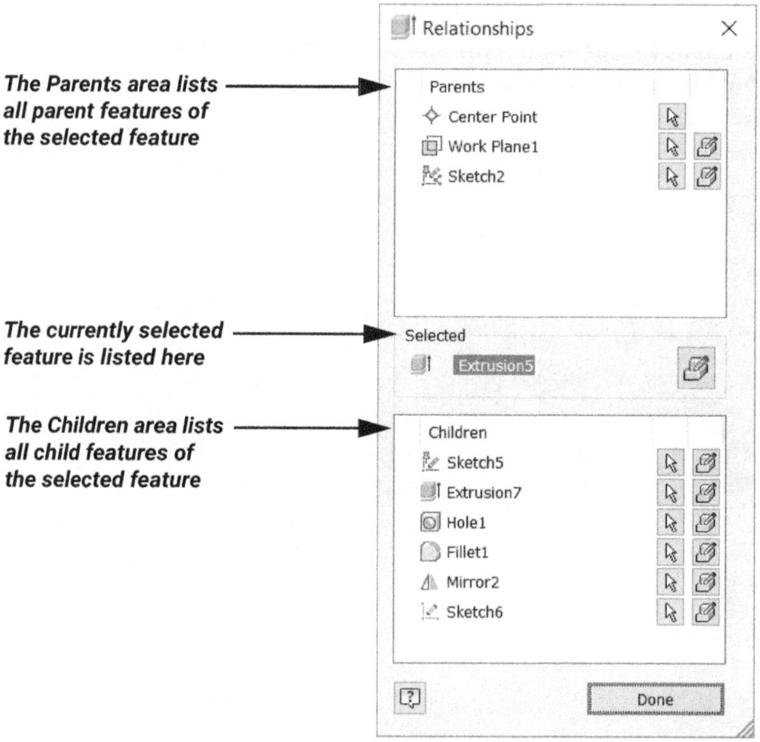

Figure 15–10

Note: *To select features directly in the graphics window, ensure that* ***Select Features*** *is the active option in the selection filter list.*

- **(Make Selected):** Enables you to sets any of the parent or child features as the new selected item.
- **(Edit Feature):** Enables you to access the *Edit Feature* dialog box for any of the parent or child features.

Equations

Equations are used in models to control design intent. In doing so, they establish feature relationships. You can use the *Parameters* dialog box to investigate if equations exist in the model. To open the dialog box, in the *Manage* tab>*Parameters* panel, click f_x (Parameters) or click f_x in the Quick Access Toolbar. Any existing relationships display in the *Equation* column, as shown in Figure 15–11.

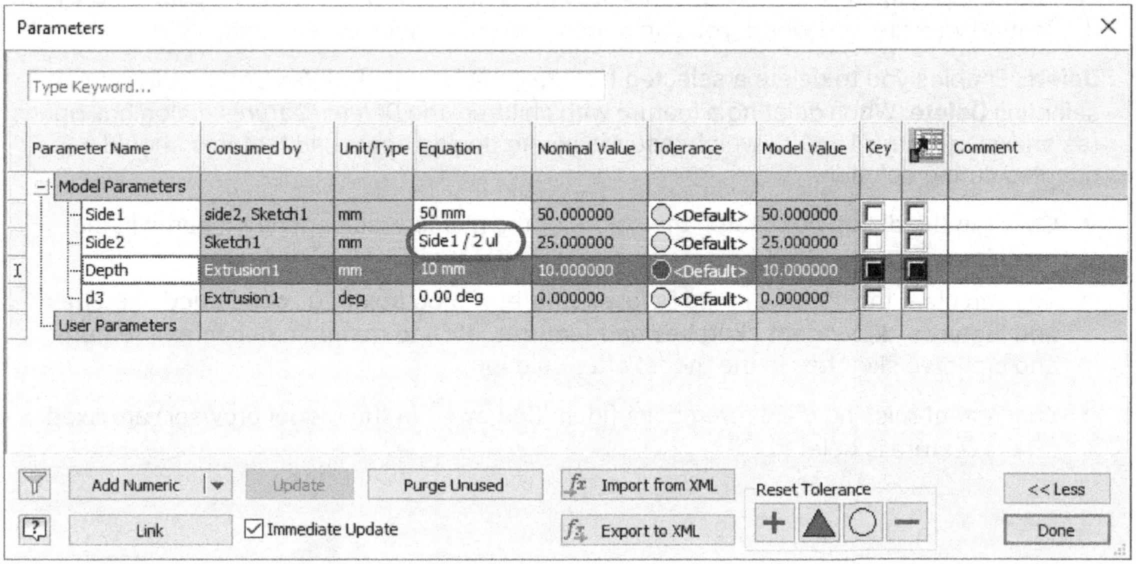

Figure 15–11

Hint: Displaying Equations in a Model

To display equations when dimensions are shown, right-click and select **Dimension Display> Expression**. To display sketch dimensions as an expression, click in the Status Bar and select **Expression**.

15.4 Changing Feature Relationships

When the design intent of the model changes, unwanted relationships might occur as a result of modifying or deleting a parent feature. The goal of making a design change is to ensure that not only the feature being changed is modified, but that any children update as expected. Consider using the following editing tools when changes to parent/child dependency are required: **Edit Sketch**, **Redefine**, **Show Dimensions**, **Dimension Display**, **Edit Feature**, and **Delete**.

- **Edit Sketch:** Enables you to access the Sketch environment to define new references or sketch elements.
- **Redefine:** Enables you to change the sketch plane of an existing sketch.
- **Show Dimensions** and **Dimension Display:** Enable you to display feature dimensions and equation relationships in the graphics window. Double-click on the dimensions to change dimensional values or equations in the *Edit Dimension* dialog box.
- **Edit Feature:** Enables you to access the dialog box or *Properties* panel that was used when the feature was created where you can define new references or elements.
- **Delete:** Enables you to delete a selected feature by pressing <Delete> or right-clicking and selecting **Delete**. When deleting a feature with children, the *Delete Features* dialog box opens (as shown in Figure 15–12), which requires you to decide how child features should be handled during deletion.
    - Colors in the dialog box match the colors of the highlighted dependent items in the graphics window.
    - You can clear the options in the *Delete Features* dialog box (e.g., **consumed sketches and features, dependent sketches and features**, etc.) to maintain dependent features and preserve sketches in the model after deletion.
    - Ensure that missing child references (identified by ⓘ in the Model browser) are fixed after a feature is deleted.

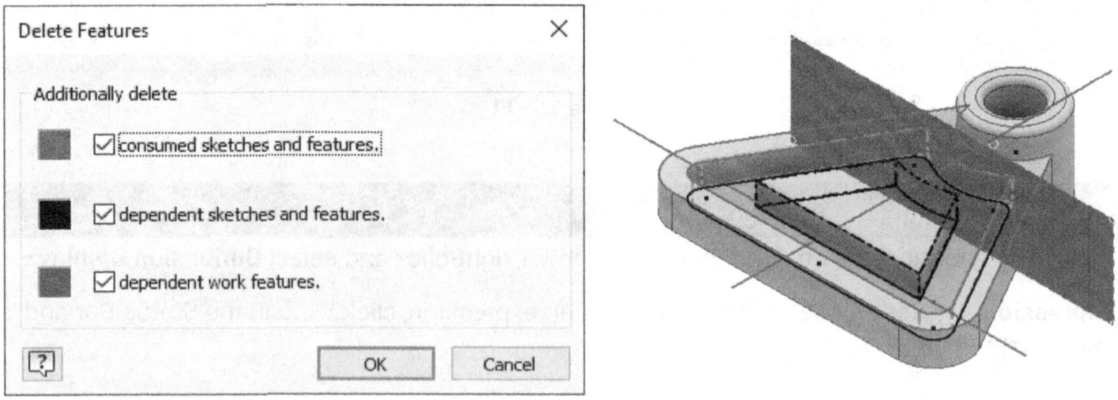

Figure 15–12

Hint: Missing Sketch Planes

When deleting a feature that also removes the sketch plane of another feature, a work plane is automatically created in the model to replace the deleted sketch plane. The new work plane is fixed relative to the coordinate system. It is recommended that you replace the work plane and redefine the sketch plane to a reference that is relative to the model geometry.

Practice 15a
Change Feature Relationships

Practice Objective

- Use editing tools to efficiently change existing parent/child relationships in a model.

In this practice, you will open the model shown on the left in Figure 15–13 and delete the hole and chamfer. In deleting these features, the *Delete Features* dialog box opens, indicating any relationships to these features. You will deal with these relationships to create the model shown on the right.

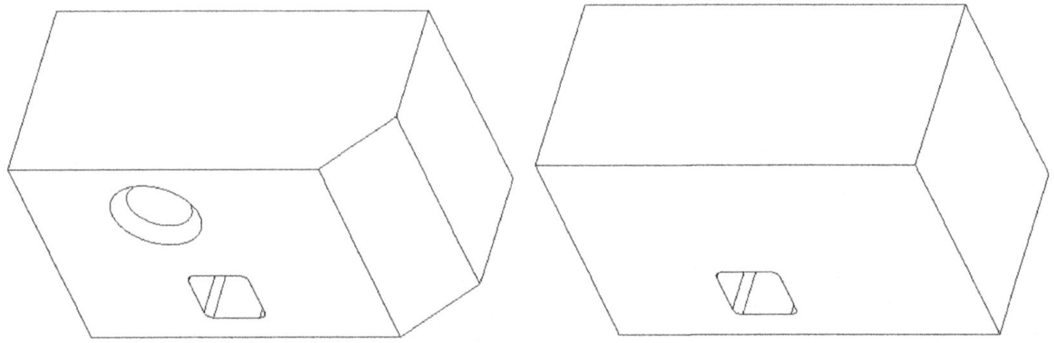

Figure 15–13

Task 1: Open and investigate a part.

1. Open **pc01.ipt**.
2. Review the Model browser to understand the hierarchy of the model and understand which features can reference others.
3. Display the dimensions associated with **Extrusion2** (square cut) to review its dimensioning scheme. The square cut is located with respect to **Hole1** and **Chamfer1** (dimensioned to the center of the hole and the edge of the chamfer).

4. Modify the two **Chamfer1** dimensions to **5.00**. The model before the chamfer dimensions are modified is shown on the left in Figure 15–14, and the model after modifications are finished is shown on the right. The cut has moved to the right as a result of modifying the chamfer. Is this the design intent? Why is it generally not a good idea to dimension the edges created by features, such as fillets and chamfers?

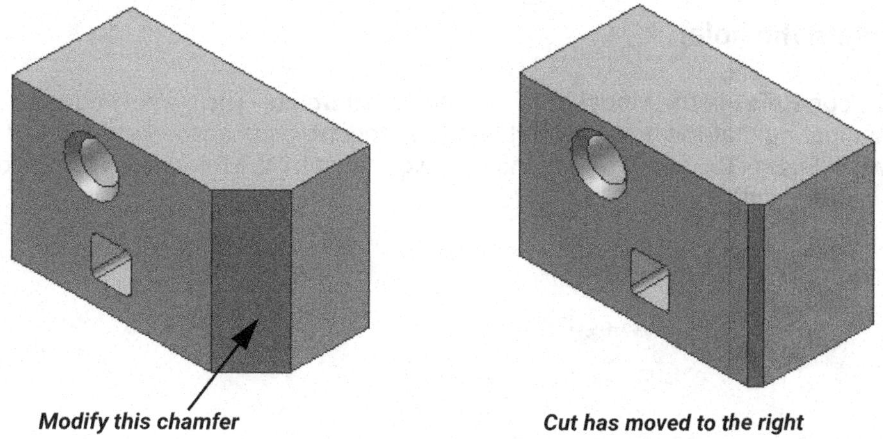

Figure 15–14

Task 2: Redefine the location of the cut.

1. Edit the sketch for **Extrusion2**. You need to re-dimension the cut so that it does not reference the chamfer.
2. Delete the **50** dimension that locates the cut to the chamfer. Additionally, delete the projected edge that was projected from the chamfer.
3. The cut is now under-constrained and needs one dimension added. Add a dimension from the cut to the vertical edge on the left side of the model, as shown in Figure 15–15.

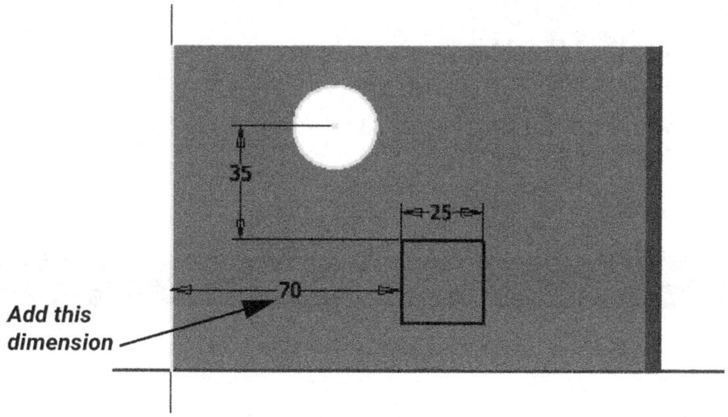

Figure 15–15

4. Finish the sketch.
5. Delete **Chamfer1**. The *Delete Features* dialog box opens, indicating features are dependent on the chamfer. The Model browser indicates that **Hole1** and **Extrusion2** are placed on the face that is affected by a chamfer. This face still exists after the chamfer is deleted so deleting it will not cause a failure. Click **OK**. Are the square cut and the hole affected?

Task 3: Delete the hole.

1. Right-click on **Hole1** in the Model browser and select **Delete**. The *Delete Features* dialog box opens, indicating that the hole has children (dependent/consumed sketches and features), as shown in Figure 15–16. To delete the hole, you must fix the references for the dependent feature (square cut).

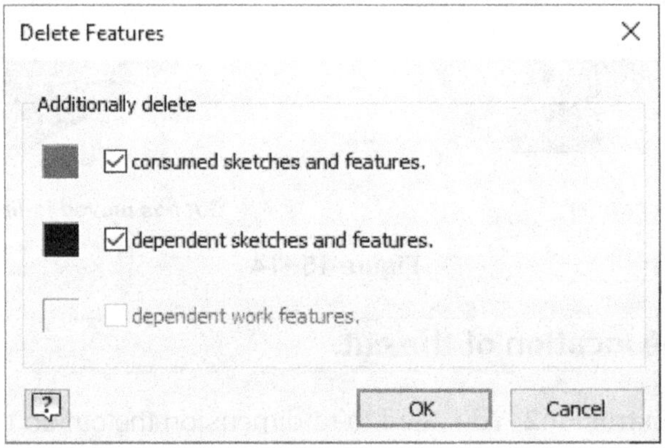

Figure 15–16

2. Click **Cancel** to close the *Delete Features* dialog box and cancel the delete action.
3. Edit the sketch for **Extrusion2**. Re-dimension the cut from the top edge of the base feature instead of from the center of the hole.
4. Finish the sketch.
5. Right-click on **Hole1** in the Model browser and select **Delete**. The *Delete Features* dialog box opens, indicating that the hole has referenced consumed sketches and features.
6. The sketch and chamfer do not need to exist without the hole. Click **OK** to delete both features.
7. Save the part and close the window.

End of practice

Practice 15b
Delete a Sketch Plane

Practice Objective

- Use the *Delete Features* dialog box such that the dependent sketches and features are not deleted with their parent geometry.

In this practice, you will open a model that has been provided for you, delete a feature, and observe how it affects the sketch plane of another feature. The original and final models are shown on the left and right in Figure 15–17 respectively.

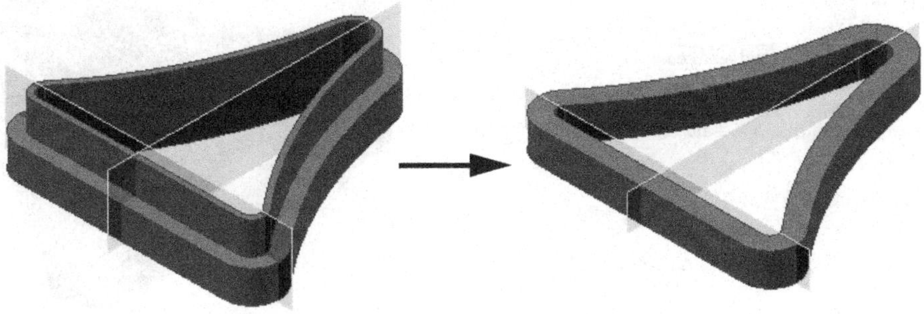

Figure 15–17

Task 1: Open a part file.

1. Open **redefine.ipt**. The model displays as shown in Figure 15–18.

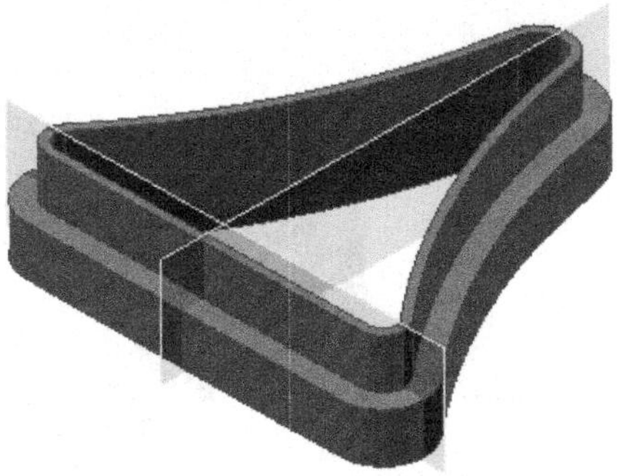

Figure 15–18

2. Edit the sketch for **Extrusion3**. Note that the sketch for the cut is placed on the top face of **Extrusion2**.
3. Finish the sketch. As an alternative, you can also right-click on the sketch associated with Extrusion3 in the Model browser and select **Show Input** to highlight its sketch plane.

Task 2: Delete Extrusion2.

1. Select **Extrusion2** in the Model browser and press <Delete>. The *Delete Features* dialog box opens, as shown in Figure 15–19, indicating that the highlighted features (**Extrusion2, Extrusion3**, and **Sketch3**) will also be deleted. However, the design intent is to maintain the cut.

   Note: *The colors in the dialog box match the highlighted dependent sketches and feature colors in the graphics window.*

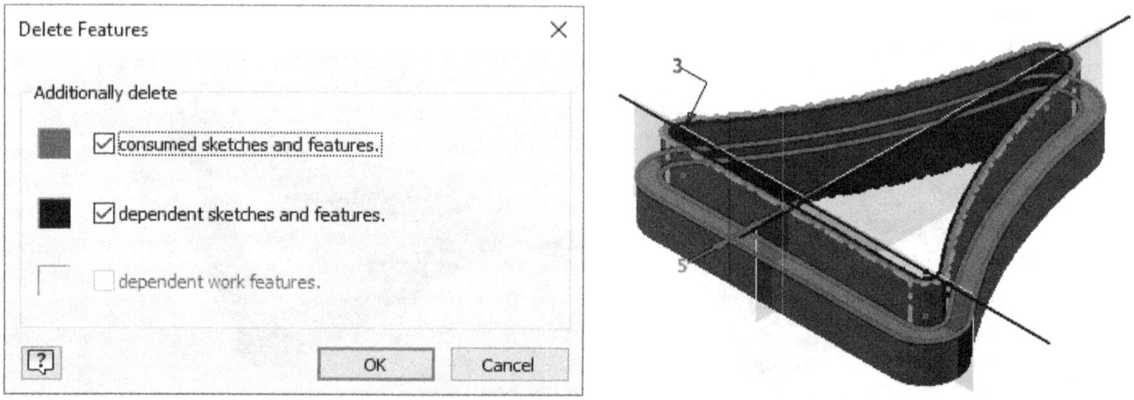

Figure 15–19

2. Clear the **dependent sketches and features** checkbox.
3. Click **OK** to delete the **Extrusion2** sketch. The model displays as shown in Figure 15–20 with **Work Plane1** created automatically in place of the deleted face. The sketch was automatically transferred to **Work Plane1** when the original sketch plane was deleted.

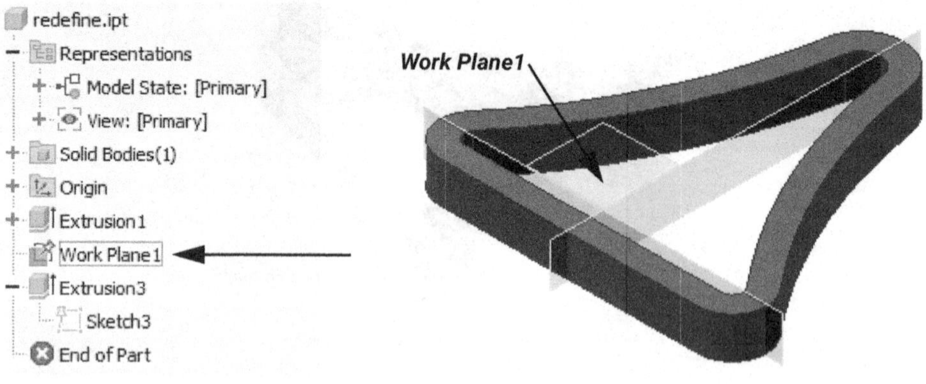

Figure 15–20

4. It is recommended that you redefine the placement plane of the sketch to select a more stable reference that will truly reflect the geometry. Right-click on **Sketch3** and select **Redefine**. Select the face of **Extrusion1** as the new sketch plane.
5. Delete **Work Plane1**.
6. Save the model and close the window.

End of practice

Chapter Review Questions

1. A pick and place feature can be the parent of another pick and place feature.
   a. True
   b. False

2. Which of the following actions create a feature relationship when sketching a feature? (Select all that apply.)
   a. Selecting the sketching plane.
   b. Selecting sketching references.
   c. Creating an offset entity.
   d. Using an existing edge to create a new entity.
   e. Dimensioning the length of a line.
   f. Aligning a new entity with an existing entity.
   g. Extruding to a Blind depth.
   h. Extruding through all surfaces.
   i. Extruding to intersect with a selected face or plane.

3. Which of the following features create a parent/child relationship when created in a model? (Select all that apply.)
   a. Origin Planes
   b. Work Planes
   c. Extrude
   d. Hole
   e. Chamfer
   f. Fillet
   g. Shell

4. Which of the following processes of creating a sketched cut feature result in the creation of feature relationships? (Select all that apply.)
   a. Selecting sketch planes.
   b. Selecting sketching references.
   c. Cutting through all geometry.

5. If a parent feature is deleted, which of the following options can be used to change the references to the child feature? (Select all that apply.)

a. Edit Sketch

b. Share Sketch

c. Redefine

d. Edit Feature

6. The *Delete Features* dialog box opens if you select and delete the hole shown in Figure 15–21. Which of the following best describes why this dialog box becomes available?

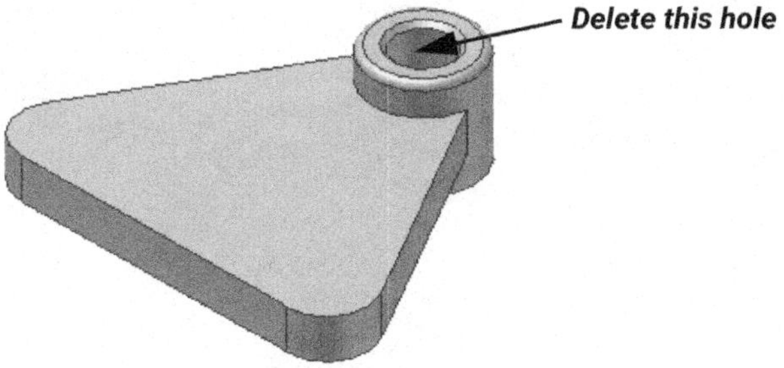

Figure 15–21

a. Because the *Delete Features* dialog box opens when deleting all of the pick and place feature types.

b. Because a chamfer was placed on the edge generated by the creation of the hole.

c. Because there are other pick and place features in the model and you need to select the other ones to delete at the same time.

d. Because the hole was placed as a Coaxial hole and is a child to the extruded cylinder.

7. The  (Make Selected) icon in the *Relationships* dialog box only enables you to change the active feature to a listed parent feature. You cannot use it to activate a child.

a. True

b. False

Appendix

A

Sketching Options

This appendix provides a detailed summary of the options that you can use on the *Sketch* ribbon to create a sketch.

Learning Objective

- Understand the available sketching options.

A.1 Summary of the Sketch Geometry Creation Options

All of the sketch geometry creation options are located in the *Sketch* tab>*Create* panel. Expand the commands to locate all of the options. The following is a summarized list of the available sketch creation options:

(Line)	Creates straight lines or arced segments. Select two points to create a line. Selecting a third point creates a line between the second and third point. To sketch an arc, press and drag an arced entity from the end point of a line. 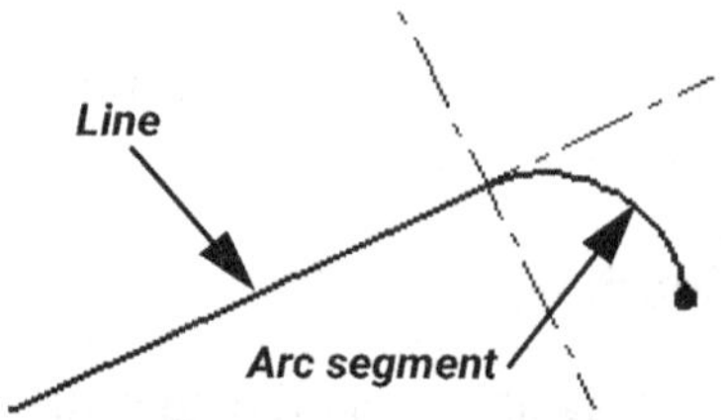
(Line (Midpoint Line))	Enables you to start a line that is symmetrical from the midpoint and then define the end point of the line.
(Spline (Control Vertex))	Enables you to sketch a free-form curve. Select multiple points to create the spline. Each point that is placed defines the vertices of the control frame.
(Spline (Interpolation))	Enables you to sketch a free-form curve. Select multiple points to create the spline. The spline is drawn through each point.
(Equation Curve)	Draws a curve based on the entry of an equation.
(Bridge Curve)	Draws a smooth G2 curve between two selected entities.
(Circle (Center Point))	Creates a circle by selecting its center point and a point on its perimeter.
(Circle (Tangent))	Creates a circle based on three lines that you select. The circle is tangent to all three lines. There might be more than one circle that can be drawn for any three given lines. You can control which circle displays, based on where you select the lines. Select the line near the locations at which the circle should touch.
(Ellipse)	Creates an ellipse based on its center, and one point on each of its major and minor axes.

(Arc (Three Point))	Draws an arc based on three points that you select. First select the two end points, then select a point on the arc. The last point determines the center, radius, and included angle of the arc.
(Arc (Tangent))	Draws an arc tangent to an existing line or an arc. Select the end of the line or arc as the start point. The arc is drawn tangent to the selected object. Complete the arc by selecting a second point. When the first point is selected, the object to which the arc is tangent is highlighted in red, and a green dot displays at its end point.
(Arc (Center Point))	Enables you to select three points to draw the arc. The first point determines the center of the arc and the other two points determine the ends of the arc. You can select the end points in either order. After selecting the first point, move the mouse in the direction in which the arc should be drawn.
(Rectangle (Two Point))	Creates a rectangle with its sides parallel to the X- and Y-axes. Select two opposite corners to create the rectangle.
(Rectangle (Three Point))	Creates a rectangle at any angle. Select three points to create the rectangle. The first two points that you select define one side and the third point locates the opposite side.
(Rectangle (Two Point Center))	Creates a rectangle along the X and Y axis. Select two points to create the rectangle. The first point defines the center of the rectangle and the second point defines the outer corner.
(Rectangle (Three Point Center))	Creates a rectangle at any angle. Select three points to create the rectangle. The first two points define one side and the third point locates the center.
(Slot (Center to Center))	Draws a slot by selecting three points. Select the center points of the two arcs, then select a point to define the slot's thickness.
(Slot (Overall))	Draws a slot by selecting three points. The first two points define the entire length of the slot and the third selection defines the slot's thickness.
(Slot (Center Point))	Draws a slot by selecting three points. Select the center point of the slot, followed by the center point of one arc and finally select a point to define the slot's thickness.
(Slot (Three Point Arc))	Draws a slot by selecting four points. The first three points define the arc length and radius of the slot and the fourth selection defines the slot's thickness.
(Slot (Center Point Arc))	Draws a slot by selecting four points. The first three points define the center point of the arc, its arc length and radius of the slot. The fourth selection defines the slot's thickness.

(Polygon)	Draws regular polygons, where all sides and all angles are the same. Like rectangles, polygons can be drawn with a series of lines, but it is easier to draw using this specialized command. There are two options for drawing polygons: **Inscribed** and **Circumscribed**. **Inscribed** uses a vertex between the two edges to determine the size and orientation of the polygon. **Circumscribed** uses the midpoint of an edge to determine the size and orientation of the polygon. 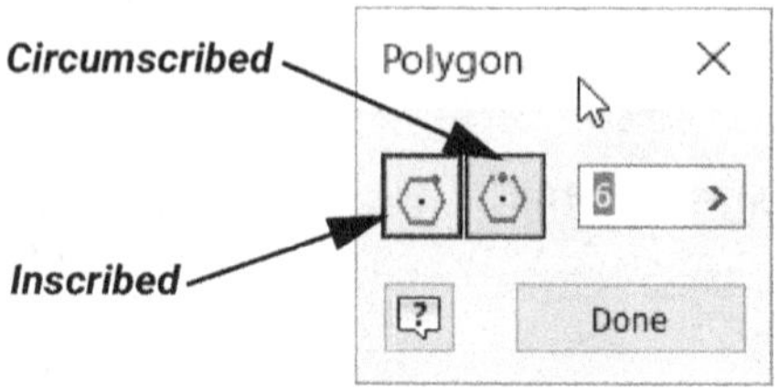
(Chamfer)	Adds an angled corner. The size of the chamfer is determined by distances along each line from their intersection, or by a distance and an angle.
(Fillet)	Adds an arc to create a rounded corner, and dimensions the arc. The *2D Fillet* dialog box enables you to specify the radius of the fillet.
(Point)	Adds points to the sketch.

A.2 Summary of the Sketch Editing Options

All of the sketch editing options are located in the *Sketch* tab>*Modify* and *Pattern* panels. The following is a summarized list of the available options:

(Move)	Moves objects more precisely and enables you to copy sketch entities.
(Trim)	Removes the segment to the nearest intersection in each direction from the point selected. If an intersection only occurs in one direction, the end of an object is removed. If intersections occur in both directions, the center of the object is removed.
(Scale)	Enlarges or reduces the size of sketched entities by entering a scale factor as a multiplier.
(Copy)	Copies source entities to one or more new locations in the sketch. No relationship is established between the newly copied entities and the source.
(Extend)	Continues an object to meet the next object in its path or to close an open sketch.
(Stretch)	Stretches sketched entities. It enables you to stretch constrained geometry while maintaining its constraints. The select-and-drag technique cannot be used to manipulate constrained geometry.
(Rotate)	Rotates objects at a specified angle. You have the option of making a copy of the objects while rotating them.
(Split)	Splits an entity (line, arc, or spline) based on an intersecting entity (entity, work plane, or surface).
(Offset)	Creates parallel shapes with another object tool.
(Rectangular Pattern)	Creates copies of entities in two directions. The directions do not need to be perpendicular to each other.
(Circular Pattern)	Creates copies of entities about an axis.
(Mirror)	Copies entities across a centerline.

A.3 Summary of the Sketch Constraint Options

All of the sketch constraint options are located in the *Sketch* tab>*Constrain* panel. The following is a summarized list of the available constraints:

(Coincident)	Makes two selected points coincident. If the centers of two circles, arcs, or ellipses are selected, the objects become concentric. If a point and an object are selected, the point lies on the object or along the extension of the object.
(Collinear)	Makes selected entities lie on the same line.
(Concentric)	Makes selected arcs, circles, or ellipses have the same center point.
(Fix)	Fixes a selected point or object relative to the default coordinate system (Sketch environment 0,0,0).
(Parallel)	Makes two selected entities parallel to each other. This constraint can be applied between two lines or ellipse axes.
(Perpendicular)	Makes two selected entities perpendicular to each other. This constraint can be applied between two lines or ellipse axes.
(Horizontal)	Makes a line horizontal or aligns two selected points horizontally.
(Vertical)	Makes a line vertical or aligns two selected points vertically.
(Tangent)	Makes the selected items tangent. The objects do not need to touch to be tangent.
(Smooth (G2))	Makes selected entities continuous in curvature.
(Symmetric)	Makes selected lines or points symmetric about a reference line. To apply this constraint, select the first line or point, select the second line or point, and select the line of symmetry.
(Equal)	Makes selected lines the same length or all of the selected circles and arcs the same radius.
(Edit Coordinate System) (*Constrain* panel drop-down list)	Moves or rotates the coordinate system to any location on the sketch plane.

A.4 Dimension Type Options

The following is a summarized list of the dimensioning types that can be used to constrain a sketch:

Linear: Select the entities to dimension. Move the cursor to the required location for the dimension and place the dimension using the left mouse button.

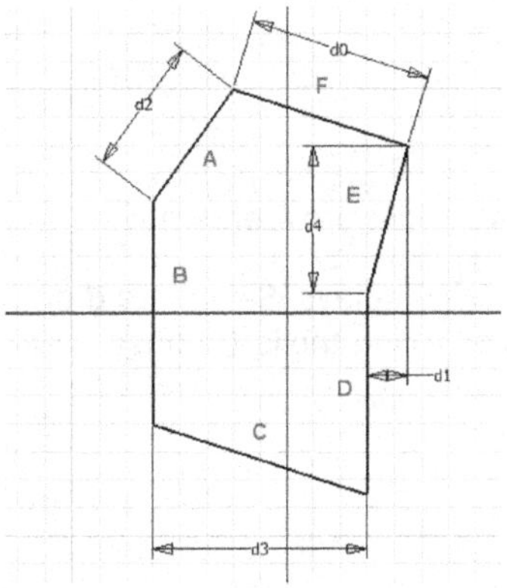

Center: Select two entities. Move the cursor to the required location and place the dimension using the left mouse button. To place an aligned dimension, place the dimension at a point along a line that joins the two entities that are being dimensioned. An

aligned icon ( ) displays. Click the left mouse button, move the cursor to the required location, and click the left mouse button again. An aligned dimension displays. You can also right-click and select the location for the dimension when you are placing it.

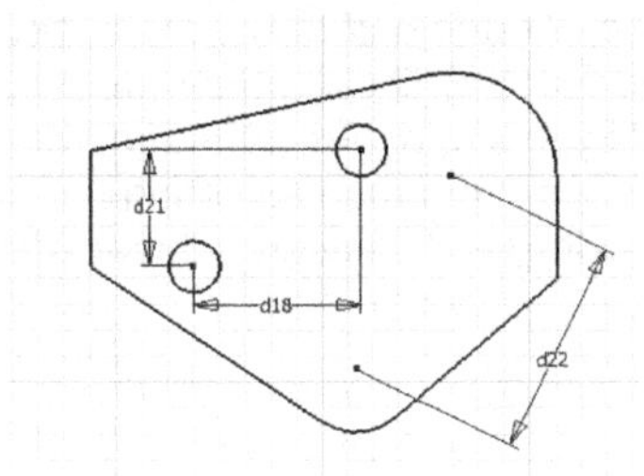

Arc Length: Select the arc, right-click, and select **Dimension Type>Arc Length** and then place the dimension.

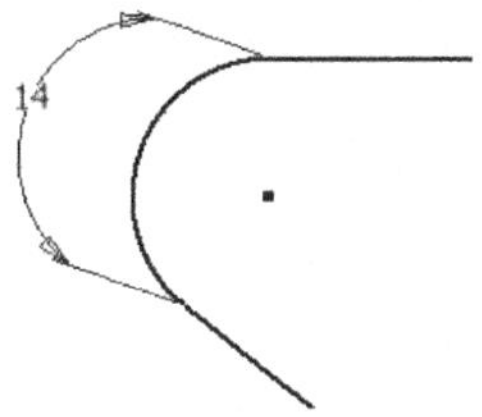

Radius/Diameter: Circles default to a diameter dimension. An arc defaults to a radius dimension.

To dimension a circle with a radial dimension, right-click and select **Radius**. Move the cursor to the required location and place the dimension using the left mouse button.

Use the same technique to dimension an arc with a diameter dimension. Right-click and select **Diameter**.

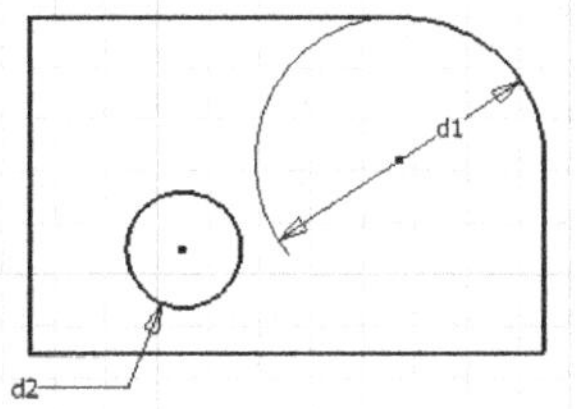

Angular: Select lines **A** and **B** and place the dimension using the left mouse button. The resulting angle depends on the placement location of the dimension.

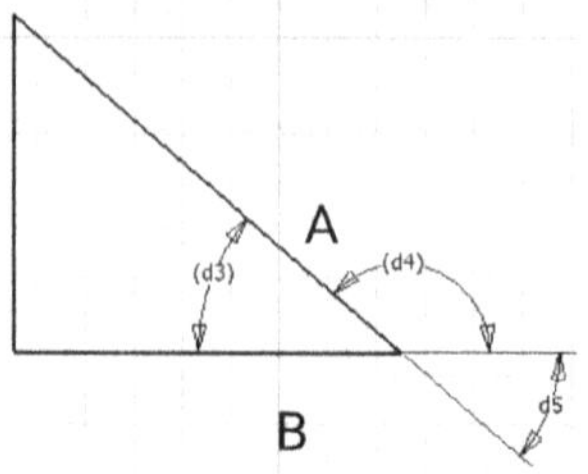

Tangent: Select arc **A** and move the cursor onto arc **B** so that [icon] displays. Select arc **B** and place the dimension using the left mouse button.

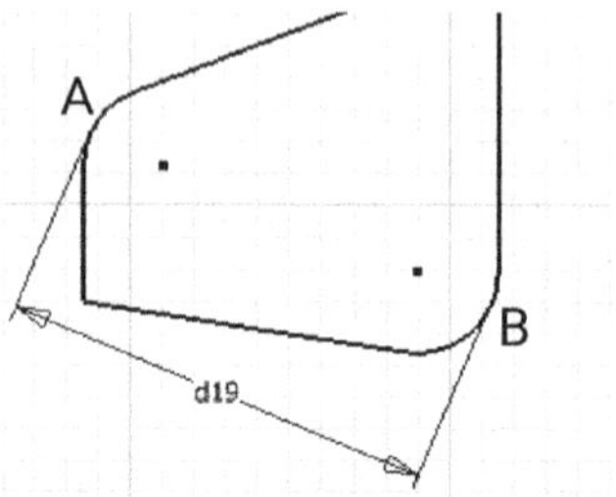

Revolved: Sketch half of the cross-section of a revolved feature. The diameter dimensions are created by selecting the centerline of the revolved cross-section and then selecting the geometry, right-clicking, and selecting **Linear Diameter**.

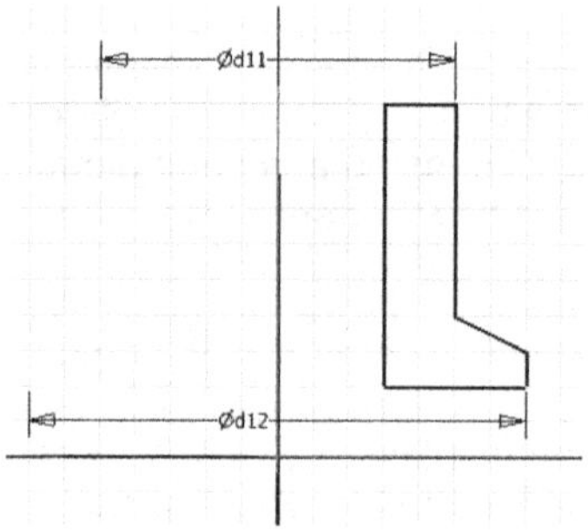

Appendix

B

Primitive Base Features

Base features can be created in two ways. You can use a workflow that creates a sketch using the *Sketch* tab and then use the feature creation options to create solid geometry. Alternatively, you can select from a list of predefined primitive types that refine the workflow process by initiating the sketch entity and feature types for you.

Learning Objective

- Create a base feature using primitive features.

B.1 Primitive Base Features

A set of four primitive features, **Box**, **Cylinder**, **Sphere**, and **Torus**, are provided to enable you to create these standard 3D shapes quickly and easily. They can be used to create geometry as either a base feature or as secondary geometry. These commands bundle together many of the steps that are completed manually when sketching a base feature so that they are done for you. Figure B–1 shows examples of the primitive features.

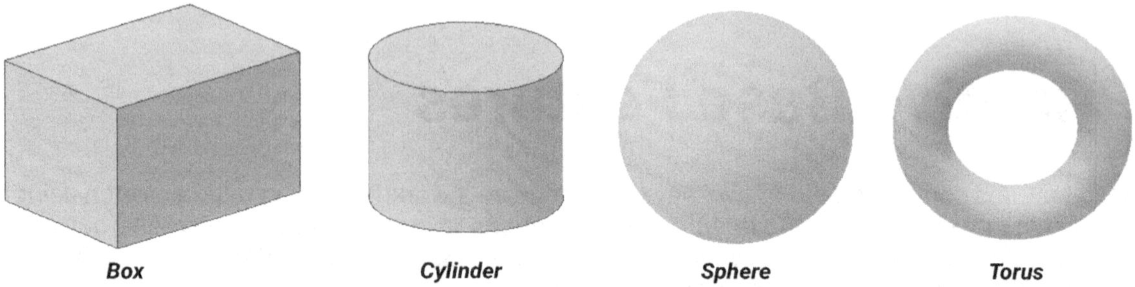

Figure B–1

Use the following steps to create a primitive base feature:

1. Select the primitive type.
2. Define the sketch plane.
3. Sketch the extent of the primitive.
4. Define the depth and direction, if required.
5. Complete the feature.

__Note:__ By default, the Primitives panel is not displayed in the ribbon. Right-click on the ribbon and select __Show Panels>Primitives__ to add the panel.

Step 1 - Select the primitive type.

To create a primitive, select a type in the *3D Model* tab>*Primitives* panel. The available types are (Box), (Cylinder), (Sphere), and (Torus). The *Primitives* panel always displays the last accessed type. If the required type is not displayed in the *Primitives* panel, click under the current option and select the required type in the expanded drop-down list.

Step 2 - Define the sketch plane.

Once the primitive type command has been activated, you can select the sketch plane from the Model browser or from the temporarily displayed origin planes in the graphics window. Similar to a sketched feature, you can select the sketch plane before selecting the primitive type.

Step 3 - Sketch the extent of the primitive.

The model is reoriented into a 2D view and you are prompted to sketch the geometry. The required steps to sketch the geometry are dependent on the type of primitive being created. In all cases, if you fully place the geometry without using the dynamic input fields, the primitive is created without a 2D dimension scheme. To assign a dimension scheme you need to return to the sketch and edit it to add dimensions. The procedure to sketch and include dimensions for each type is as follows:

- **Box:** Click to place the start point of the box. Do not click again to place the opposite corner of the box. Enter a value in the highlighted dynamic input field (do not press <Enter>), press <Tab>, and enter a value in the next dynamic input field to fully define the size of the box. Press <Enter> to complete the box.
- **Cylinder:** Click to place the center point of the cylinder. Do not click again to place the outer extent of the circle. Enter a value in the dynamic input field for the diameter of the circle and press <Enter>.
- **Sphere:** Click to place the center point for the sphere. Do not click again to place the outer extent of the sphere. Enter a value in the dynamic input field for the diameter of the sphere and press <Enter>.
- **Torus:** Click to place the center point of the torus. Do not click again to place the outer extent of the torus. Enter a value in the dynamic input field for the outer diameter of the torus and press <Enter>. Enter another value in the next dynamic input field for the diameter of the torus geometry and press <Enter>.

Step 4 - Define the depth and direction, if required.

Once you have finalized the placement of the sketch, a *Properties* panel and a model preview will display.

- Box and Cylinder primitives are created using the Extrude feature.
- Sphere and Torus primitives are created using the Revolve feature.

The sketch is automatically selected as the profile and, in the case of the Sphere and Torus primitives, it also assumes the reference axis to revolve the geometry. The Box and Cylinder primitives enable you to further define the depth and direction of the feature. Examples of the *Properties* panel and primitives are shown in Figure B–2 through Figure B–4.

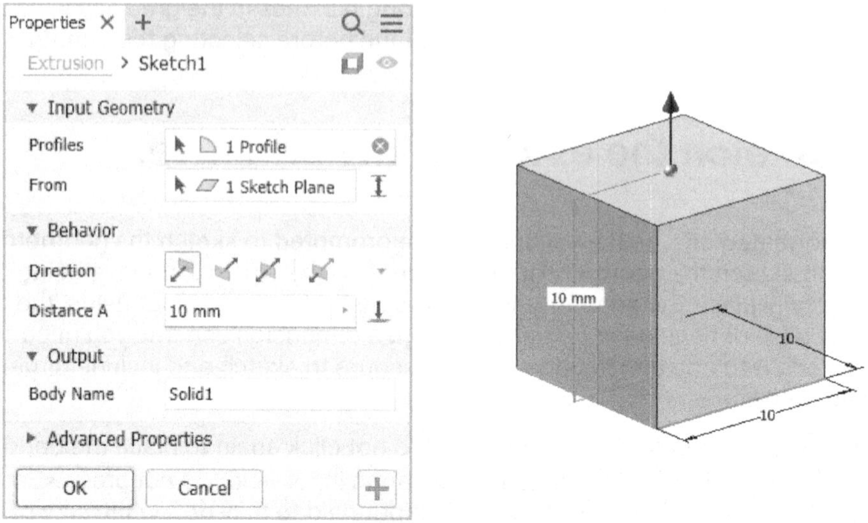

Figure B–2

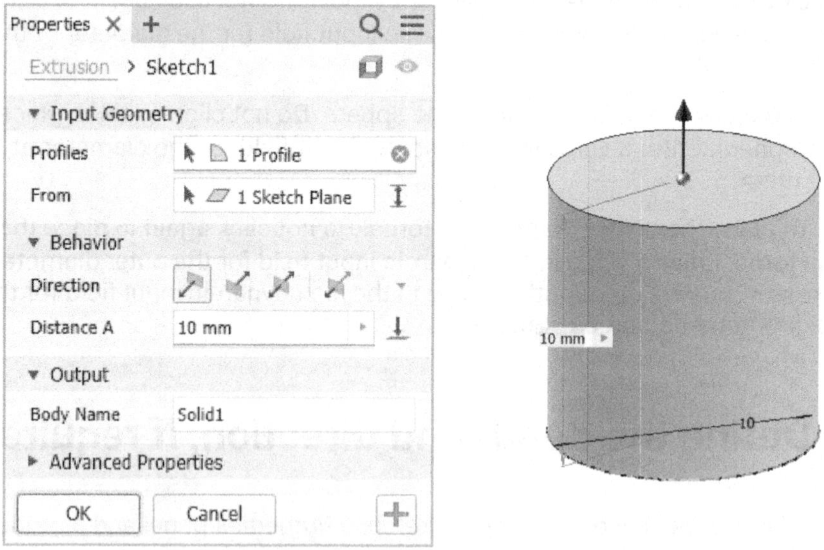

Figure B–3

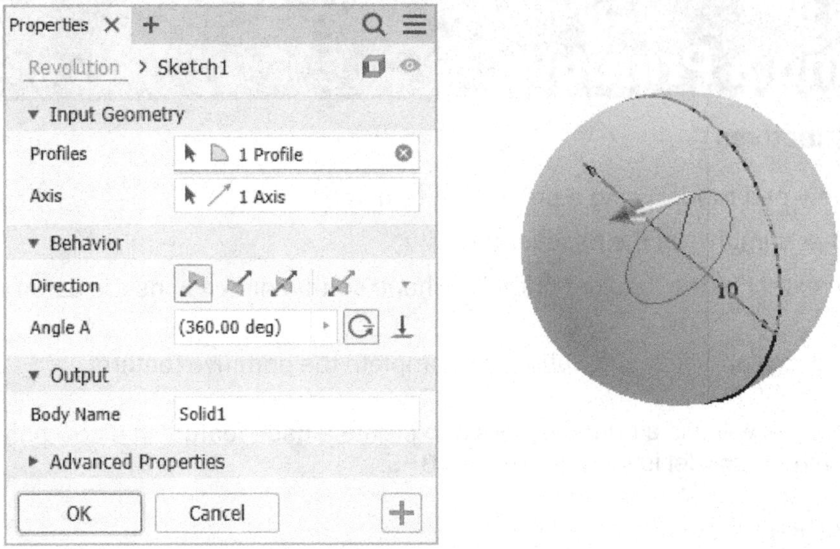

Figure B–4

Step 5 - Complete the feature.

Click **OK** to complete the primitive base feature and close the *Properties* panel. Alternatively, right-click and select **OK (Enter)** or press <Enter>. The Model browser updates to list either the Extrude or Revolve feature.

Hint: Adding Dimensions

If you place the sketch of the primitives without using the dynamic input, the resulting primitive sketch does not contain dimensions. To add dimensions or assign specific constraints, right-click on the feature in the Model browser or in the graphics window and select **Edit Sketch**.

Practice B1
Creating a Primitive

Practice Objectives

- Create a new part model using a predefined template.
- Create a Box primitive as the base feature.
- Sketch the extent of the required primitive shape so that dimensions are automatically assigned.
- Define the depth and direction options to complete the primitive feature.

In this practice, you will use a primitive shape to create a base feature in a new part file. The final geometry in the model is shown in Figure B–5.

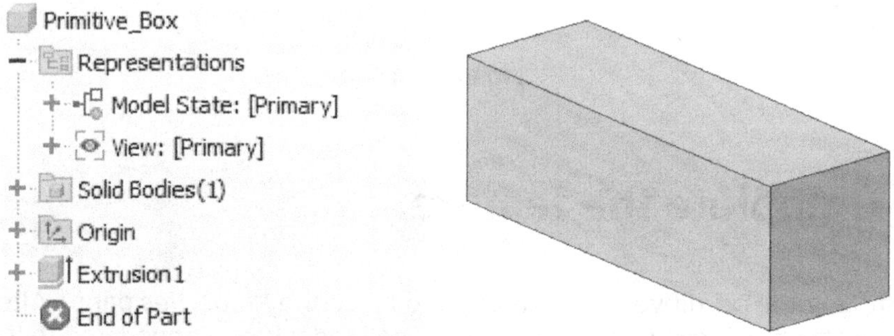

Figure B–5

Task 1: Create a new part model and sketch its geometry.

1. Create a new part file using the standard metric (mm) template.
2. If the *Primitives* panel is not displayed in the ribbon, right-click on the ribbon and select **Show Panels>Primitives**.
3. In the *3D Model* tab>*Primitives* panel, click (Box). The origin planes are temporarily displayed.
4. Select the **XY Plane** in the Model browser or graphics window. The plane is reoriented into a 2D orientation to sketch the geometry. Note that you are still in the *3D Model* tab and not in the *Sketch* tab.

By default, the origin center point is projected onto the XY Plane. However, because you are not in the *Sketch* tab, you cannot project any further reference entities or create any explicit constraints or dimensions.

5. Start the sketch by moving the cursor to the projected center point, as shown in Figure B–6, and click to place the point.
6. Move the cursor to the approximate point shown in Figure B–6 to define the extent of the box, but DO NOT click.

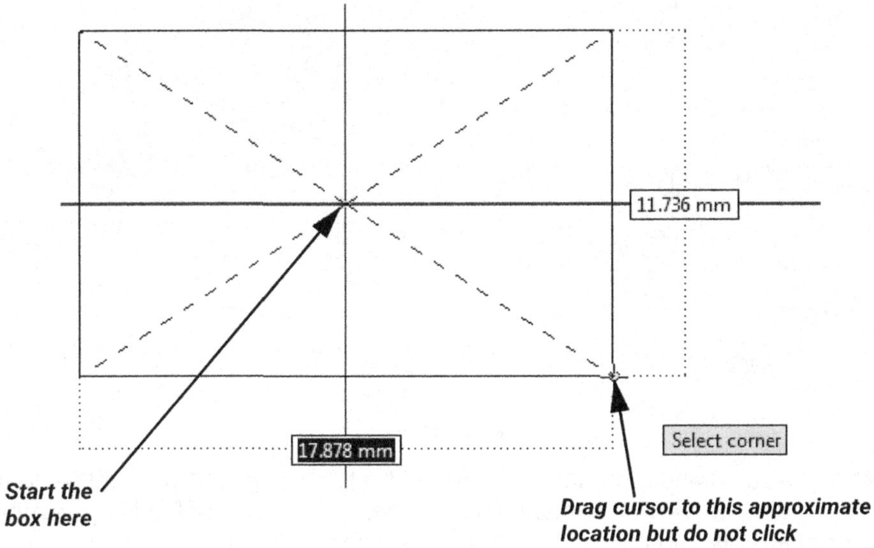

Figure B–6

7. The dynamic entry field for the horizontal dimension is active. Enter **30**. Do not press <Enter>.
8. Press <Tab> to activate the dynamic entry field for the vertical dimension.
9. Enter **10** and press <Enter> to complete the section. The dimensions display on the sketch. The only control over the location of the box is relative to the projected center point.

10. The model is reoriented into its default orientation, and the *Properties* panel and a model preview display similar to that shown in Figure B–7. The section is automatically set as the *Profile* and has been extruded to a default depth.

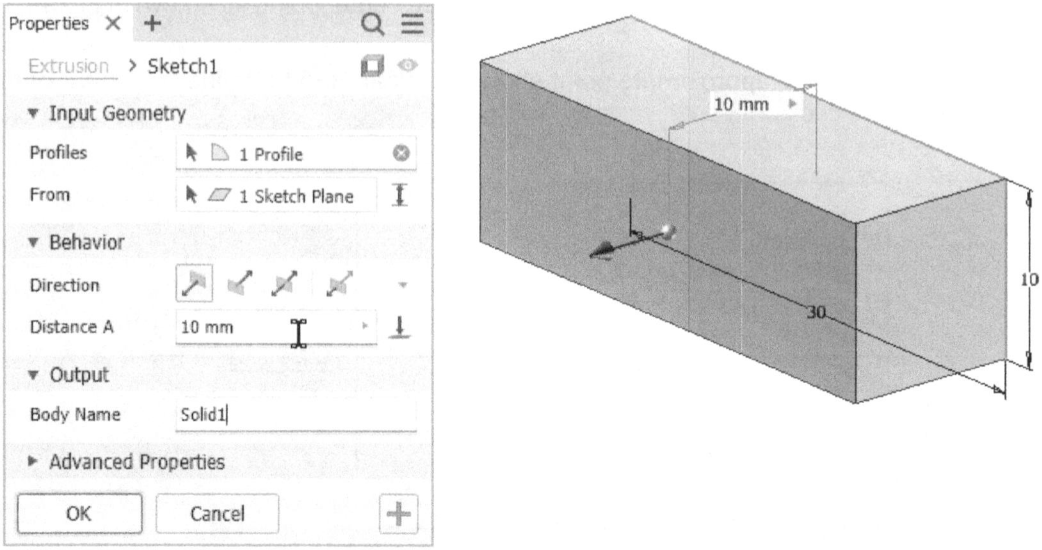

Figure B–7

11. A default depth value and direction is assigned for the Box primitive. Set the depth to **15**. This can be entered in the *Properties* panel or directly on the entry field on the model. Do not press <Enter> after typing the depth value. After typing the value, pause for a few seconds and the model updates with your changes.

12. Once a value has been entered, click **OK** in the *Properties* panel.

13. Hover the cursor over the ViewCube and click (Home) to return to the model to its default 3D orientation. The model displays as shown in Figure B–8. Note that a standard Extrusion and a sketch have been added to the Model browser list.

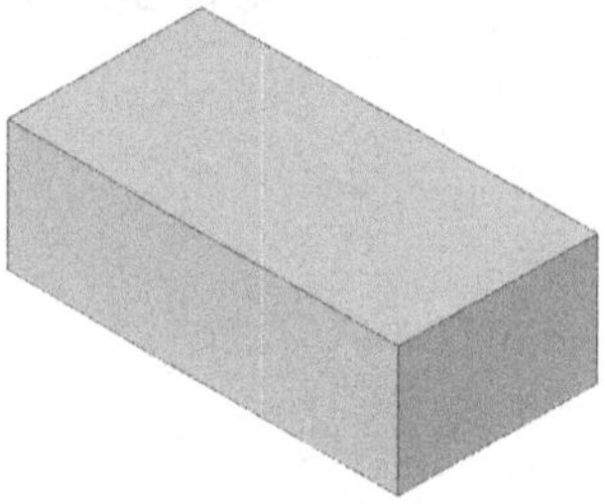

Figure B–8

14. Save the file as **Primitive_Box** and close it.

End of practice

Appendix C

Additional Practices I

This appendix provides additional practices that can be used to review some of the functionality that was previously covered.

Practice C1
Part Creation

Practice Objective

- Use the required features to create the models shown in the provided image.

In this practice, you are provided images of part models that you are to create using the feature creation techniques that you have learned in this guide. Minimal instruction is provided.

Task 1: Create the parts provided.

1. Create the part files shown in Figure C–1 using the standard metric (mm) template.The dimensions of these parts have been omitted to help you understand that the software is a design tool. Once the model has been built, dimensions can be modified as required. Remember the perceived design intent of the model while building the parts.

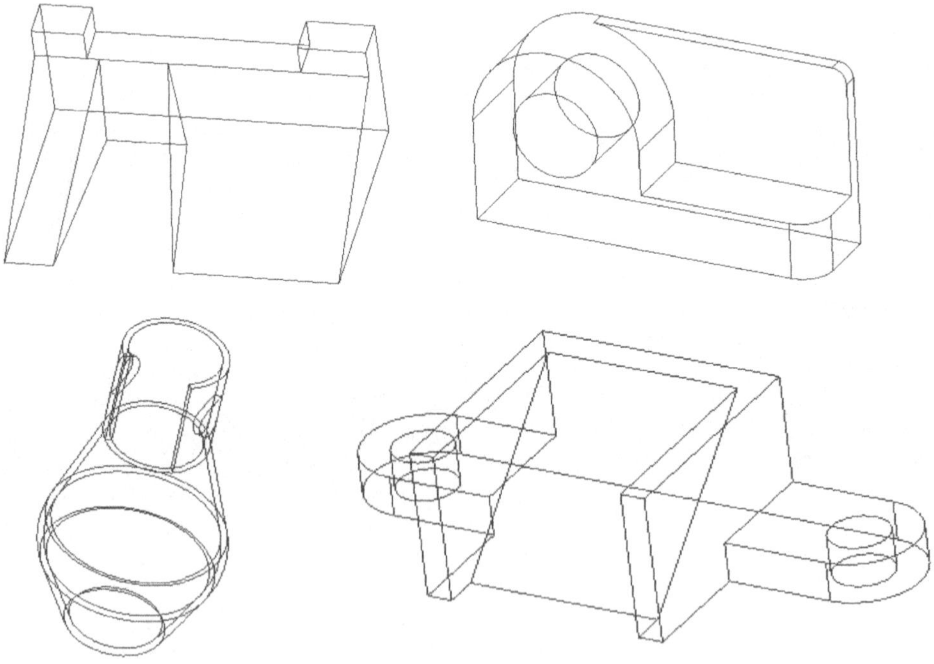

Figure C–1

2. Create the part shown in Figure C–2 using the standard English (in) template.

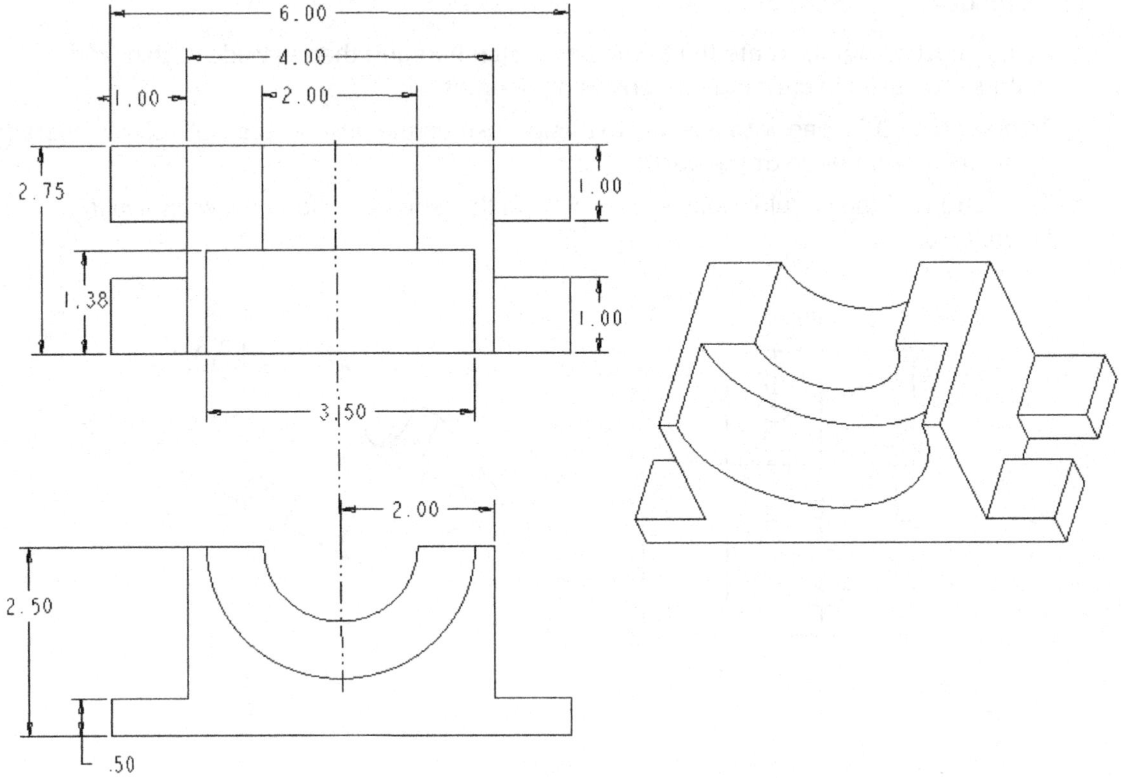

Figure C–2

3. Create the part shown in Figure C–3 using the standard English (in) template. Consider renaming the work features as you work through the practice to help identify their purpose in the model.

- As the starting point, create the triangular sketch first and then extrude it. Use work features to assist in creating the remaining geometry.
- To create the Ø.50 peg with a single extrusion, sketch the profile on a work plane located below the bottom face of the part.
- The bottom of the circular hole is not visible in the isometric Home view shown in Figure C–3.

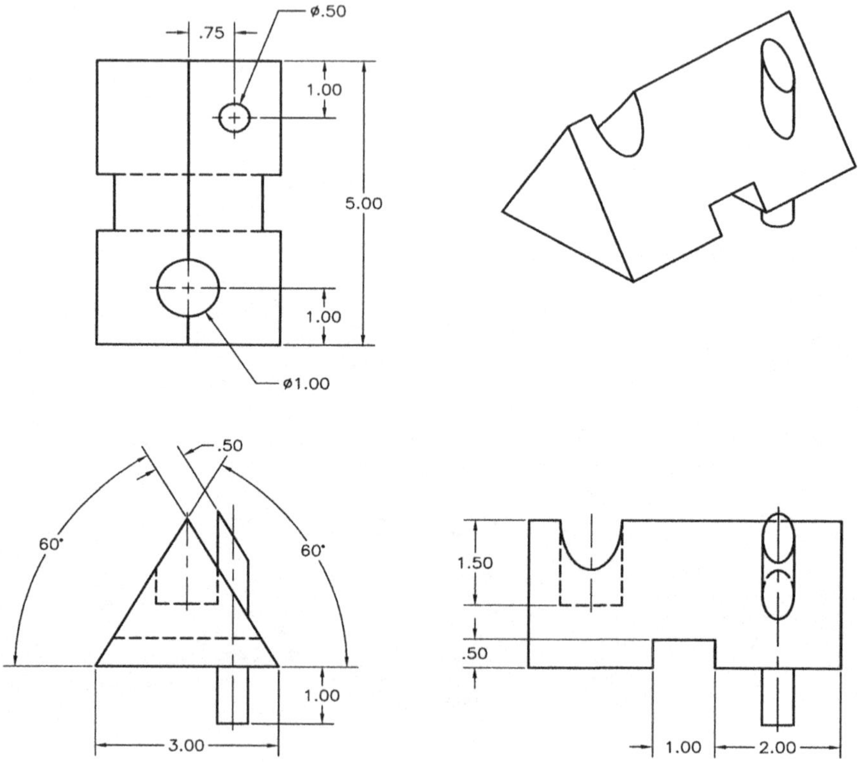

Figure C–3

4. Create the part shown in Figure C–4 using the standard metric (mm) template.

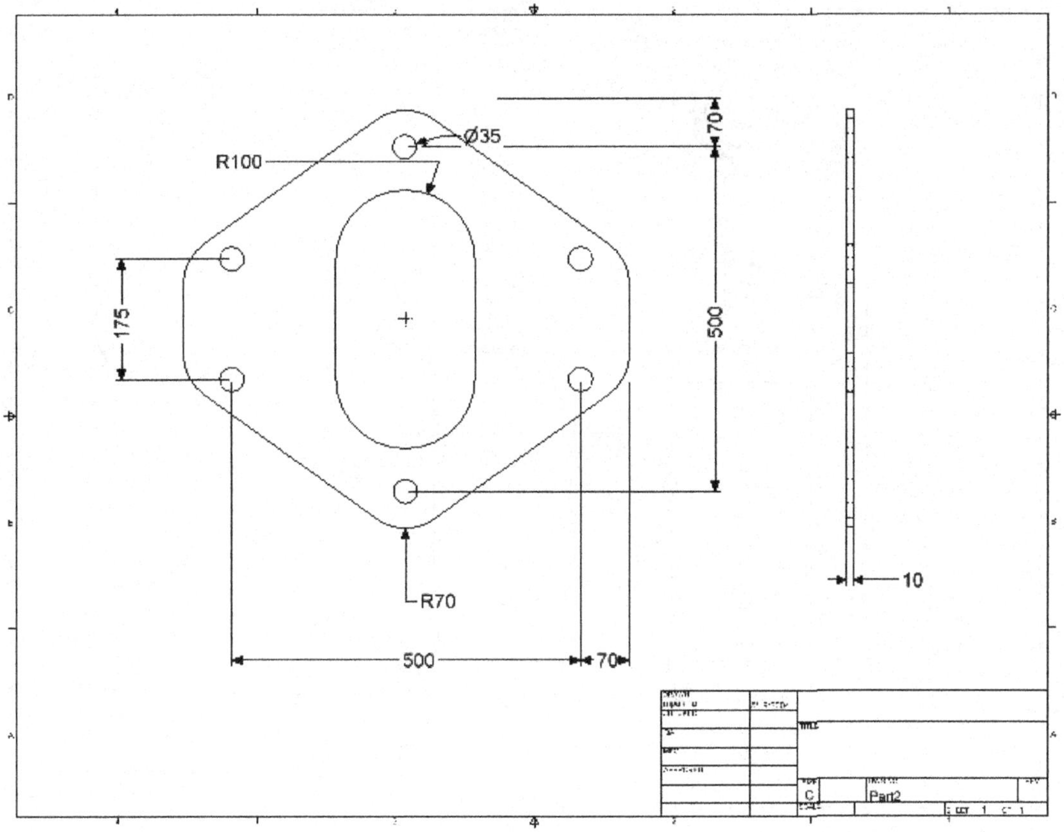

Figure C–4

5. Create the part shown in Figure C–5 using the standard metric (mm) template.

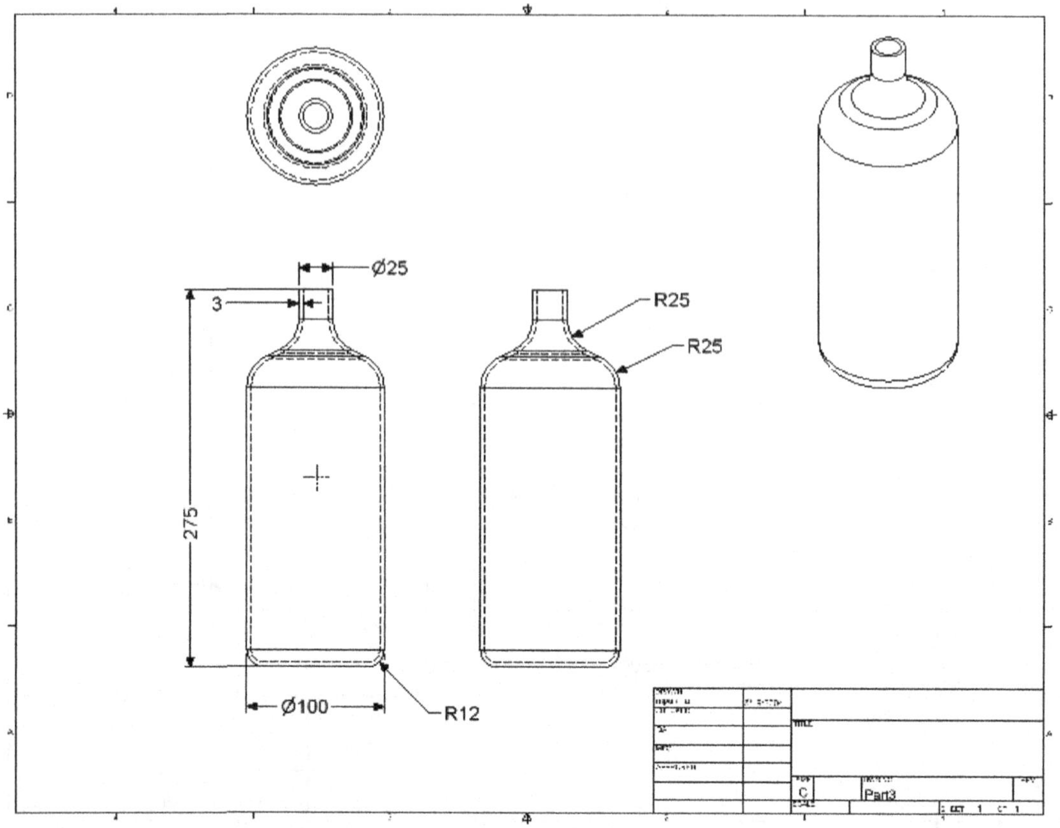

Figure C–5

6. Create the part shown in Figure C–6 using the standard metric (mm) template. Create the extrusion so that it displays in the isometric Home view as shown.

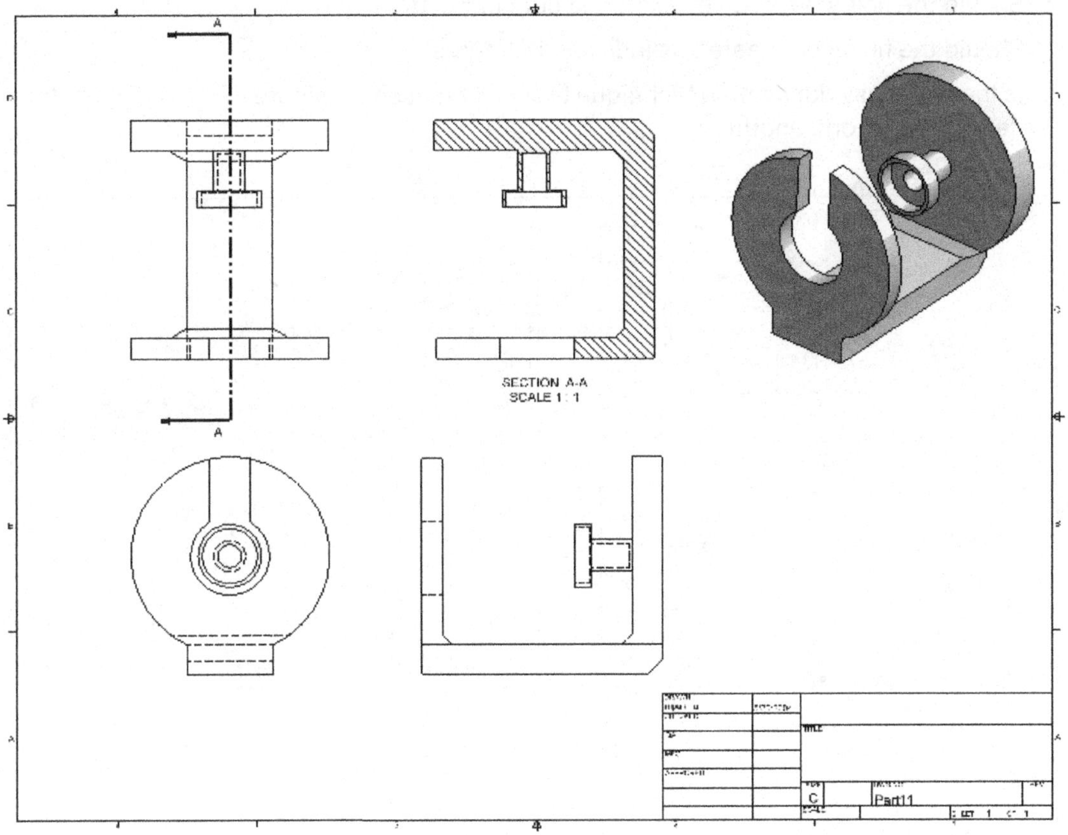

Figure C–6

7. Create the part shown in Figure C–7 using the standard metric (mm) template. Consider the following design intent suggestions when creating feature relationships:
   - Should the holes be revolved sketched cuts or holes?
   - Should the holes be created as individual features?
   - Is there an easy duplication technique that can be used to ensure that all of the holes are dependent on one another?

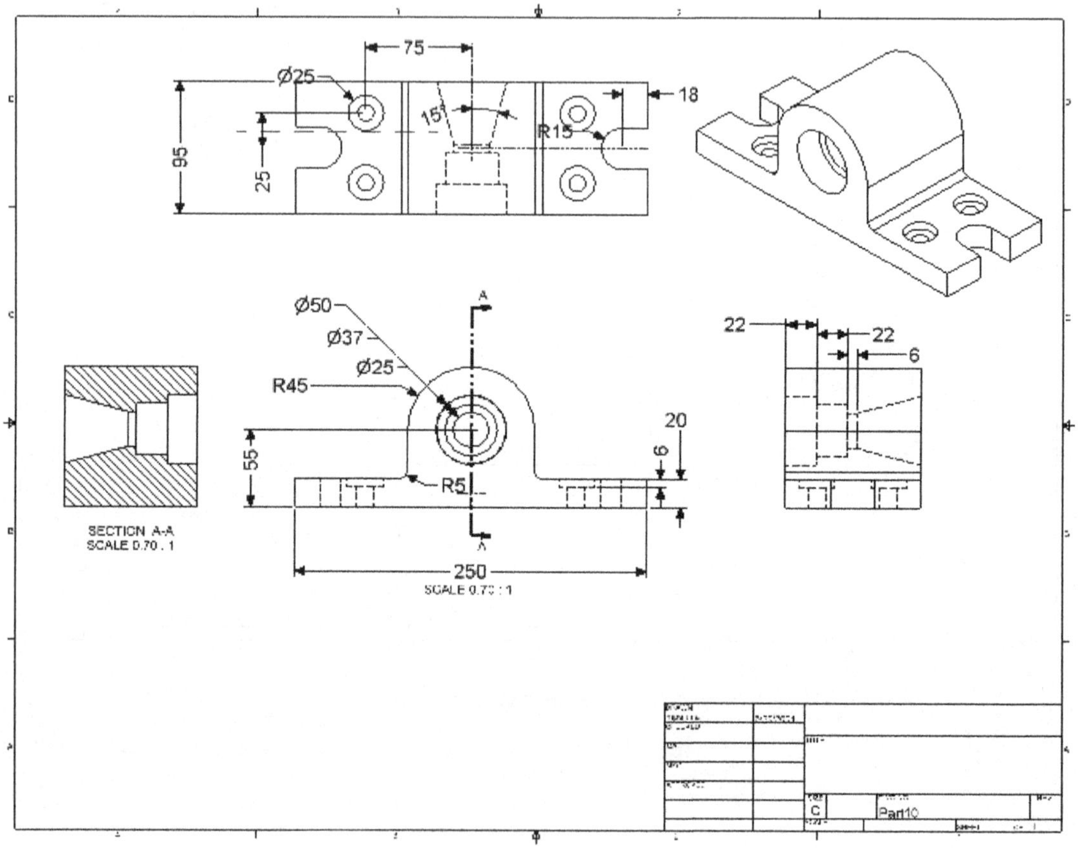

Figure C–7

8. Create the part shown in Figure C–8 using the standard metric (mm) template. Use sweep features as required.

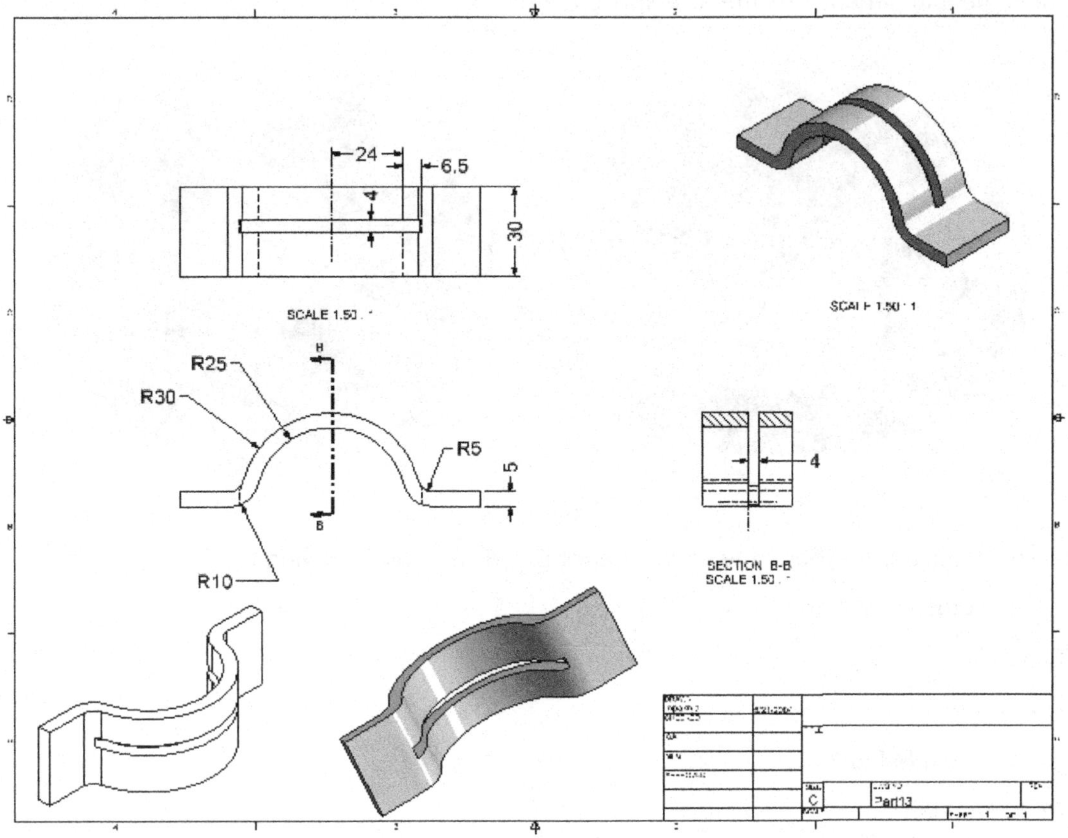

Figure C–8

9. Create a new part using the standard metric part template. Model the geometry so that the completed model displays as shown in Figure C–9. The overall diameter of the model is 60mm and its height is 30mm. To design the remainder of the model, use a dimensioning scheme and dimensions that are appropriate.

Figure C–9

Hint: The small holes around the exterior are tapped with the following thread type:

- ANSI Metric M Profile
- Size 4
- Class 6H
- Designation M4x0.7
- Right Handed

*Note: A complete model (**Housing.ipt**) has been included in your practice files for you to review, if required.*

End of practice

Practice C2
Create a Sweep and Loft

Practice Objective

- Open the provided model and create additional sweep and loft features.

In this practice, you will add sweep and loft geometry to the part shown on the left in Figure C–10. The completed model is shown on the right.

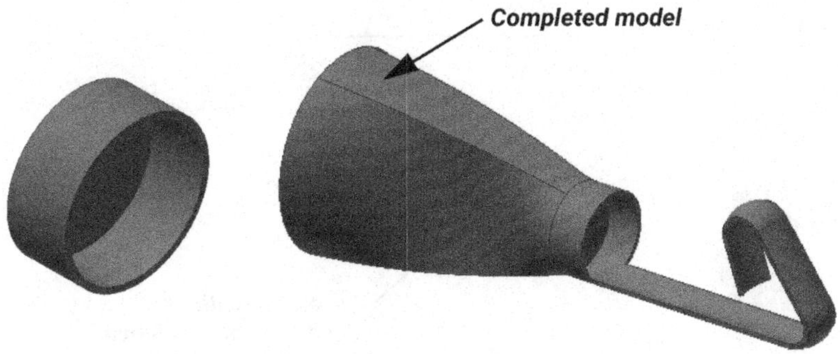

Figure C–10

Task 1: Open a part file and create a sweep.

1. Open **project.ipt**.
2. Right-click on the thin surface of the model shown in Figure C–11 and select **New Sketch**.

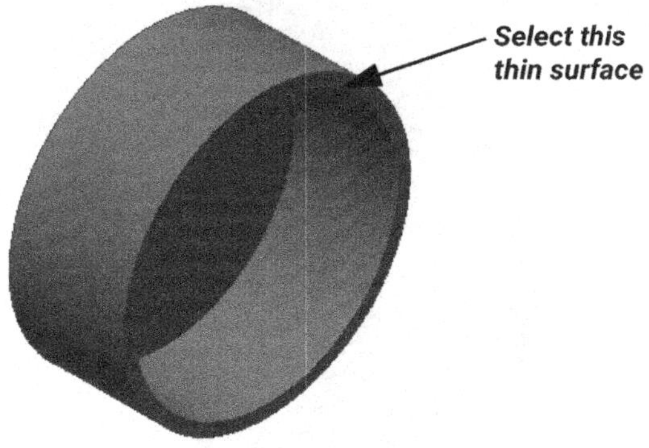

Figure C–11

3. The sketch orients into 2D. Change the visual style to **Wireframe**. Sketch and dimension the section as shown in Figure C–12. Project the edges as required. Ensure that the end points of both sketched lines are coincident with the edges of the sketch plane. Project the XZ Plane and use it to add a Symmetry constraint between the two sketched lines.

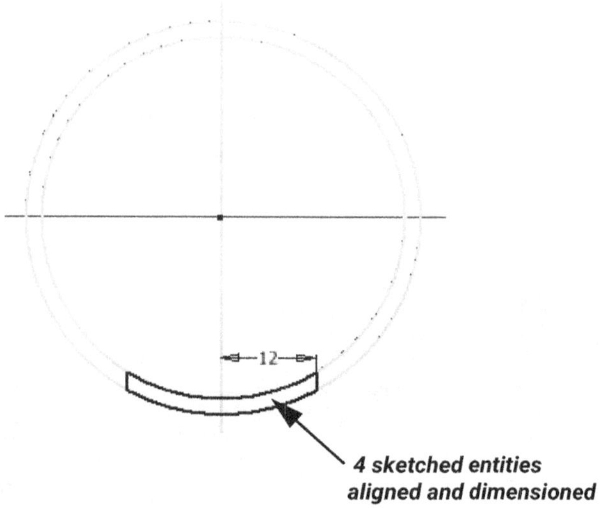

Figure C–12

4. Finish the sketch.
5. Create a work plane through an end point of line shown in Figure C–13 and parallel to an origin work plane. The work plane displays as shown in Figure C–13 with the model displayed in the Shaded visual style.

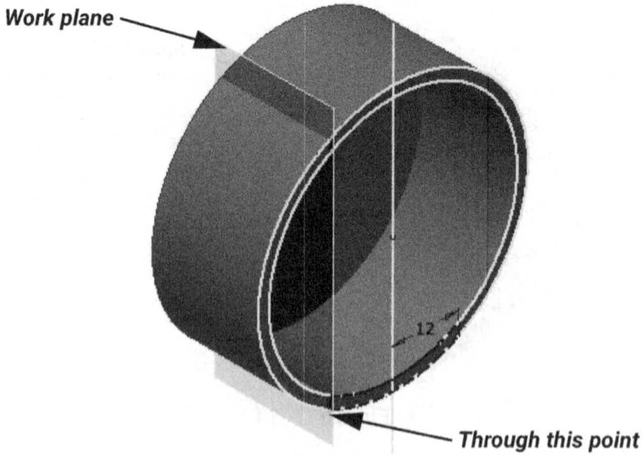

Figure C–13

6. Right-click on the new work plane in the Model browser and select **New Sketch**.

7. Project the end point of the line shown in Figure C–14 onto the sketch plane. Rotate the sketch for clarity in selecting the point.

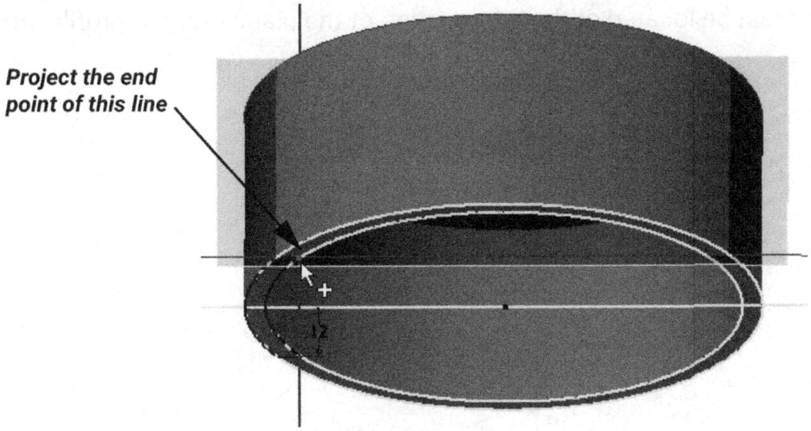

Figure C–14

8. In the Navigation Bar, click (Look At) and select the work plane you created in the Model browser. Enable **Slice Graphics** on the right-click menu for clarity viewing the sketch plane. The sketch displays as shown Figure C–15 (with the work plane's visibility off).

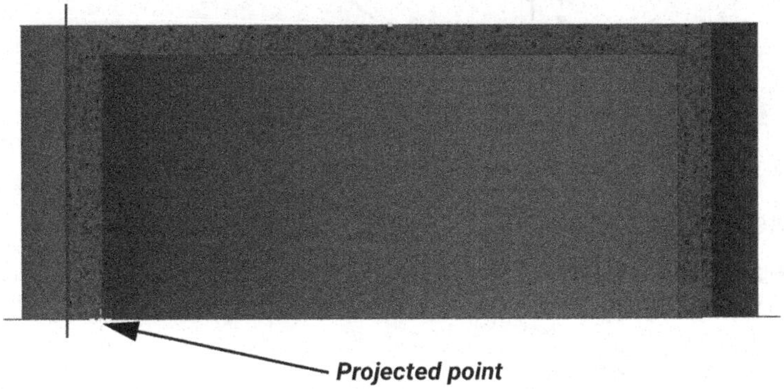

Figure C–15

9. Sketch and dimension the section as shown in Figure C–16. The two arcs have the same radius. Start the geometry from the projected point. Reorient the sketch using the ViewCube if your orientation is different than that shown in Figure C–16. The start point of the sweep must be located at the intersection of the planes for the profile and path.

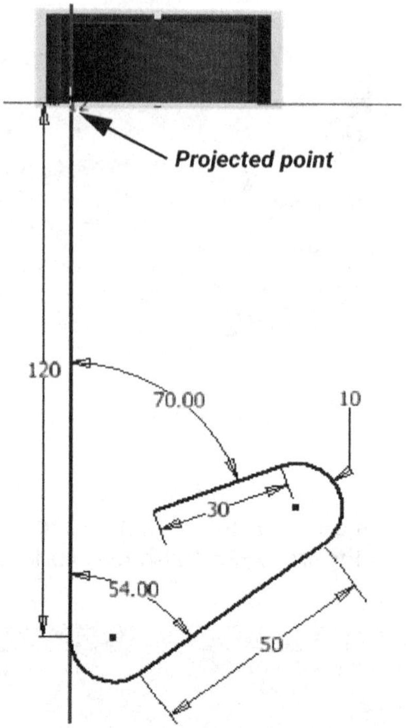

Figure C–16

10. Finish the sketch.
11. Create a **Sweep** feature with the sketched profile and path that you just created. The model displays as shown in Figure C–17.

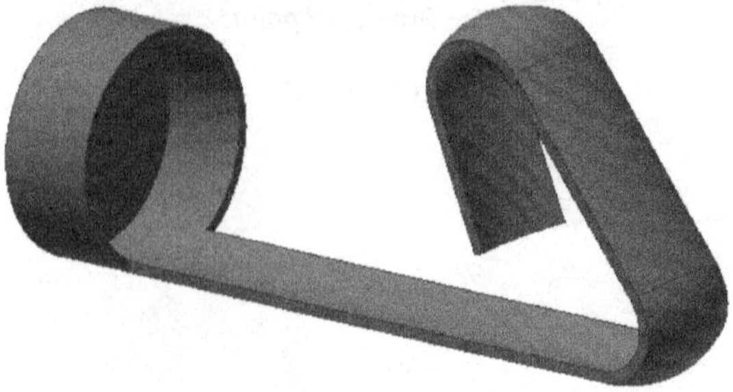

Figure C–17

Task 2: Create a loft feature.

1. Create a work plane parallel to and **55mm** from the bottom face of the first extrusion, as shown in Figure C–18.
2. Create a work plane parallel to and **145mm** from the bottom face of the first extrusion, as shown in Figure C–18.

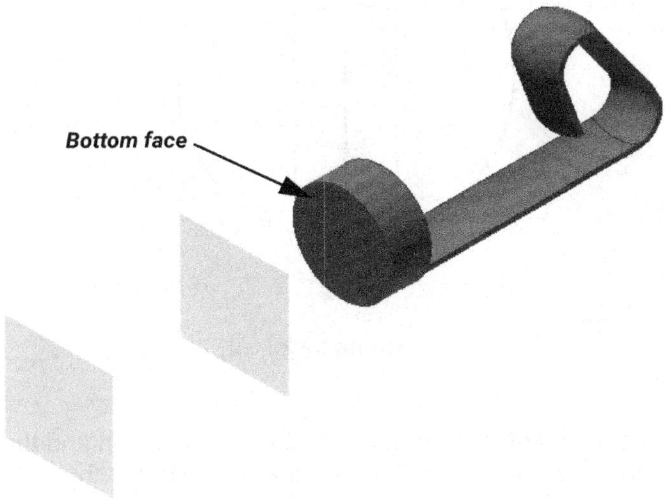

Figure C–18

3. Sketch and dimension the rectangular section on the first work plane, as shown in Figure C–19. Apply the Symmetry constraint about the XY and XZ Planes.

Note: *Project the XY and XZ Planes onto the sketch plane to locate the geometry.*

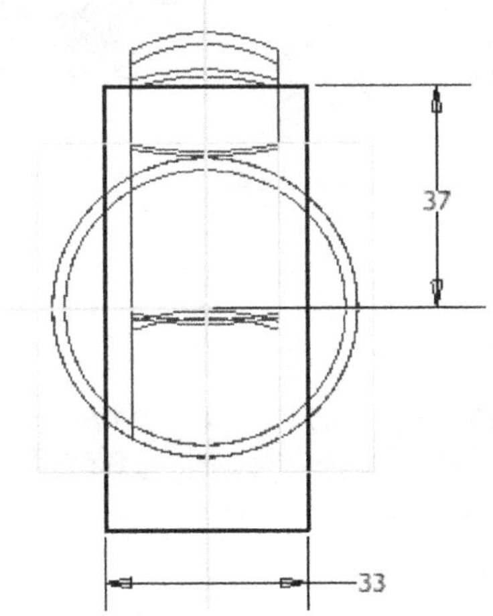

Figure C–19

4. Finish the sketch.
5. Sketch and dimension the circular section with a **110mm** diameter on the second work plane, as shown in Figure C–20.

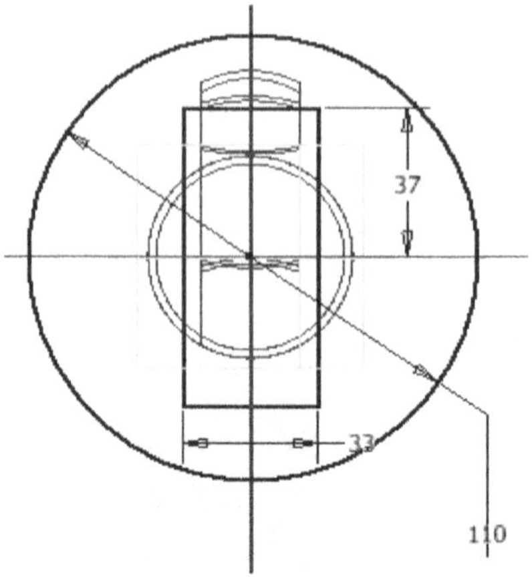

Figure C–20

6. Finish the sketch.
7. Create a loft feature using the bottom face of the first extrusion and the two sketches, as shown on the left in Figure C–21. Use the *Conditions* tab to set the transition between the existing model and the loft geometry to be tangent. The final model displays as shown on the right in Figure C–21 with the work planes visibility turned off.

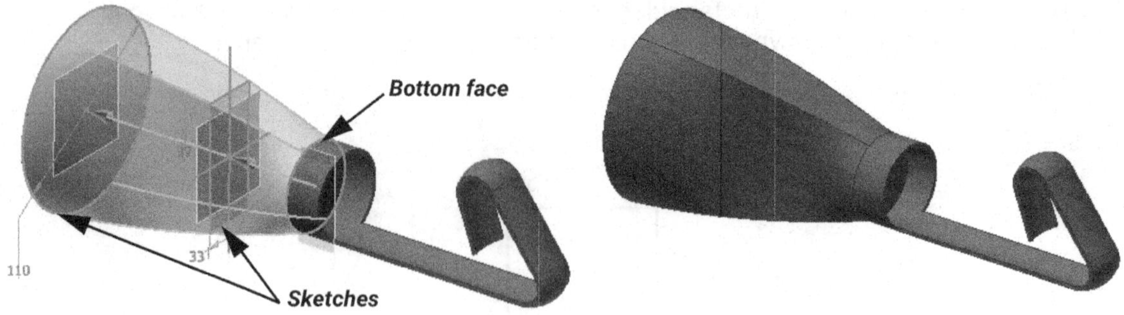

Figure C–21

8. Save the model and close the window.

End of practice

Index

I

J

L

M

N

O

P

Q

R

S

Made in United States
North Haven, CT
05 November 2026

21764895R00359